The Official Guide to the TOEFL® Test
Using the CD-ROM

The test questions on this CD-ROM are from actual TOEFL® tests. However, the screen and delivery formats are not identical to the actual test. When you take the actual TOEFL test, you may notice some variations in how the questions are presented to you on screen.

Installation

On a PC, insert the CD into your computer. If the program does not begin to install automatically, go to the CD-ROM drive and click on the file labeled "Setup." You will be guided through a short series of screens, and at the end of the process, the program will be installed on your computer. On a Mac® computer, the CD-ROM will display its contents. To launch the program, drag the program icon to the Applications folder. For both PCs and Macs, an icon labeled "TOEFL" will appear on your desktop. You can click on that icon to start the program.

Main Menu

When you launch the program, this screen appears:

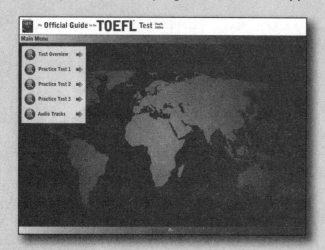

Your choice will depend on how you prefer to practice for the TOEFL iBT® test.

- If you want to take full-length authentic TOEFL iBT practice tests on your computer, choose a test from the Main Menu.

- If you only want to listen to the audio tracks, click on **Audio Tracks**.

Taking TOEFL iBT Practice Tests on Your Computer

On the Main Menu, choose Practice Test 1, 2, or 3. Then click on the test section you wish to take: **Reading, Listening, Speaking,** or **Writing.** Note that you can take each section more than once.

When you open a test section, you will first see the instructions for that section. A timer visible on the screen shows how many minutes and seconds you have left for that section. You can hide the timer if you find it distracting.

If you must take a break during the test, click on the **Menu** button at the bottom and then select **Back to Main Menu**. Your work will not be lost, and when you resume, you will take up exactly where you left off. The timer clock will stop while you are on your break and will restart immediately when you resume the test. Try not to take breaks too often, because on the actual test, the clock keeps running even if you leave the room on a break.

Answering Questions

To answer the questions in the Reading and Listening sections, click on the corresponding answer oval or follow the instructions given. For some questions, you will need to click on more than one answer choice. Once you select an answer(s), the **Next** button is enabled. Click on it to move forward to the next question. For the Reading, section you can move back to review your answer choice by clicking on the **Previous** button.

For the Speaking section, you should record your response to each question into your recording device after you hear the instruction telling you to begin speaking. Stop recording once the response time expires.

For the Writing section, write your response to each question in the space provided in the time allowed.

When all the questions in the section have been answered, click on the **Next** button to complete the section.

Playing Audio Tracks

In the Listening, Speaking, and Writing sections, you will listen to audio tracks. Audio controls are available at the bottom of the screen. At the end of the track, click on **Next** to start answering questions.

Your Performance

On the Main Menu, click on a section of any test you have taken. You will get information on when you completed the section and your score for the Reading and Listening sections only. Select **Review Section**. For each question in the Reading and Listening sections, you will see the correct answer and an explanation of why that is the correct answer. For the Speaking section, you will see the important points for each question, sample responses, and rater comments on the responses. Follow the instructions for listening to the sample responses. Use the important points, sample responses, and rater comments to evaluate your performance on the Speaking section. For the Writing section, you will see the topic notes, sample essays, and rater comments on the essays. Use the topic notes, sample essays, and rate comments to evaluate your performance on the Writing section.

Working Through the Practice Sets and Practice Tests in the Book

On the Main Menu, click on **Audio Tracks**. You will see a window on which you can select the audio Practice Set tracks or the Practice Test tracks. As you work through the Practice Sets and Practice Tests in the book, you will be told when to play each audio track. Each time you need to play a track, you will see the following symbol:

Click on the number of the track as instructed in the book.

The Official Guide to the
TOEFL
Test Fourth Edition

The **Official Guide** to the
TOEFL®
Test   Fourth Edition

New York Chicago San Francisco Lisbon London Madrid Mexico City
Milan New Delhi San Juan Seoul Singapore Sydney Toronto

The McGraw·Hill Companies

Copyright © 2012, 2009 by Educational Testing Service. All rights reserved. Printed in the United States of America. Except as permitted under the United States Copyright Act of 1976, no part of this publication may be reproduced or distributed in any form or by any means, or stored in a database or retrieval system, without the prior written permission of the publisher.

8 9 10 11 12 13 14 15   QVS/QVS   1 9 8 7 6 5

Domestic Edition
ISBN   978-0-07-176658-6 (book and CD set)
MHID   0-07-176658-8

ISBN   978-0-07-176655-5 (book for set)
MHID   0-07-176655-3

e-ISBN 978-0-07-176657-9
e-MHID   0-07-176657-X

Library of Congress Control Number: 2011936597

Copyright © 2012, 2009. Exclusive rights by The McGraw-Hill Companies, Inc., for manufacture and export. This book cannot be re-exported from the country to which it is consigned by McGraw-Hill. The International Edition is not available in North America.

ETS, the ETS logo, TOEFL, and TOEFL iBT are registered trademarks of Educational Testing Service (ETS) in the United States of America and other countries throughout the world.

Interior Designer: Jane Tenenbaum

McGraw-Hill books are available at special quantity discounts to use as premiums and sales promotions or for use in corporate training programs. To contact a representative, please e-mail us at bulksales@mcgraw-hill.com.

This book is printed on acid-free paper.

Contents

1 About the TOEFL iBT® Test   1

2 Reading Section   37

CONTENTS

6   Authentic TOEFL Practice Test 1   231

7   Authentic TOEFL Practice Test 2   343

8   Authentic TOEFL Practice Test 3   459

9 Writer's Handbook for English Language Learners 575

The Official Guide to the
TOEFL
Test
Fourth Edition

1 About the TOEFL iBT® Test

Read this chapter to learn

◥ The main features of the TOEFL iBT test
◥ What kind of questions are on the test
◥ How you can use this book to help you prepare for the test

This *Official Guide* has been created to help English language learners understand the TOEFL® test and prepare for it. By preparing for the test, you will also be building the skills you need to succeed in an academic setting and go anywhere in your career, and in life.

Getting Started

Start your preparation for the TOEFL test by reading the following important information about the test, testing requirements, and your TOEFL scores.

Undergraduate, graduate, and postgraduate programs around the world require students to demonstrate their ability to communicate in English as an entrance requirement.

The TOEFL test gives test takers the opportunity to prove they can communicate ideas effectively by simulating university classroom and student life communication. The language used in the test reflects real-life English language usage in university lectures, classes, and laboratories. It is the same language professors use when they discuss course work or concepts with students. It is the language students use in study groups and everyday university situations, such as buying books at the bookstore. The reading passages are from real textbooks and course materials.

TOEFL Scores Can Help You Go Anywhere

The TOEFL test measures how well test takers *use* English, not just their knowledge of the language. Because it is a valid and reliable test with unbiased, objective scoring, the TOEFL test confirms that a student has the English language skills necessary to succeed in an academic setting.

That's why it is the most highly regarded and widely accepted test in the world. More than 8,500 colleges, universities, and agencies in 130 countries accept TOEFL scores, so test takers have the flexibility to use their TOEFL test scores worldwide. The TOEFL test is also the most accessible English-language test. It is administered at more than 4,500 test centers in 180 countries. More than 27 million people have taken the test since it began in 1964.

Who Creates the TOEFL Test?

ETS (Educational Testing Service) is the nonprofit educational organization that develops and administers the TOEFL test.

Who Is Required to Take the TOEFL Test?

If your first or native language is *not* English, it is likely that the college or university that you wish to attend will require you to take an English-language proficiency test. However, you should check with each institution to which you are applying for admission.

How Is the TOEFL Test Used in the Admissions Process?

Your test scores will be considered together with other information you supply to the institution to determine if you have the appropriate academic and language background to be admitted to a regular or modified program of study. Often, your field of study and whether you are applying as a graduate or undergraduate student will determine what TOEFL scores you need.

Is There a Minimum Acceptable Score?

Each institution that uses TOEFL scores sets its own minimum level of acceptable performance. These minimums vary from one institution to another, depending on factors such as the applicant's field of study, the level of study (undergraduate or graduate), whether the applicant will be a teaching assistant, and whether the institution offers English as a Second Language support for its students.

How to Use This Book/CD Package

This book/CD package gives you instruction, practice, and advice on strategies for performing well on the TOEFL test.

- **Chapter 1** provides an overview of the test, information about test scores, and an introduction to the on-screen appearance of the different parts of the TOEFL iBT test, along with general test-taking suggestions.

- **Chapters 2, 3, 4, and 5** provide in-depth discussions of the kinds of questions that appear in each section of the test. Each chapter also includes practice questions and explanations of correct answers so that you will understand the actual communicative skills that are being tested in each section.

- **Chapters 6–8** provide three full-length actual TOEFL iBT tests that will give you an estimate of how you might perform on the actual test.

- **Chapter 9** is the Writer's Handbook, a guide to help you write essays in English. It covers grammar, usage, mechanics, style, and organization and development. There is also a discussion of different types of essays, tips on how to improve your essay by revising, editing, and proofreading, and a glossary.

- **The CD-ROM** packaged with this book provides on-screen versions of the full-length actual tests from Chapters 6–8. It also includes numbered audio tracks for all of the listening materials that accompany the practice questions in this book. For more information about how to use the CD-ROM, see the instruction page in the front of the book.

You can use this book to familiarize yourself with the appearance, length, and format of the test. For additional practice and to experience the real test, go to TOEFL Practice Online at **www.ets.org/toeflpractice**. TOEFL Practice Online offers:

- a real TOEFL iBT test experience
- a variety of practice tests that help prepare you for test day
- same-day scores and performance feedback on all four tested skills

TOEFL Practice Online can help you become familiar with the way the test is delivered and what it is like to answer the questions under timed conditions. This *Official Guide* will help you understand the language skills you will need to succeed on the test and in the classroom.

Use the practice tests in this book/CD-ROM and from TOEFL Practice Online to determine which of your skills are the weakest. Then follow the advice in each skill chapter to improve those skills. You should use other materials to supplement the practice test questions in this book.

Because the TOEFL test is designed to assess the actual skills you will need to be successful in your studies, the very best way to develop the skills being measured is to study in an English program that focuses on:

- communication using all four skills, especially speaking
- integrated skills (for example, listening/reading/speaking, listening/reading/writing)

However, even students who are not enrolled in an English program should practice the underlying skills that are assessed on the TOEFL test. In other words, the best way to improve performance on the test is to improve your skills. Each chapter of this book gives you explicit advice on how to connect your learning activities to the kinds of questions you will be asked on the test. Perhaps you want to improve your score on the Reading section. The best way to improve reading skills is to read frequently and to read many different types of texts in various subject areas (sciences, social sciences, arts, business, and others). The Internet is one of the best resources for this, but any books, magazines, or journals are very helpful as well. It is best to progress to reading texts that are more academic in style, the kind that would be found in university courses.

In addition, you might try these activities:

- Scan the passages to find and highlight key facts (dates, numbers, terms) and information.
- Increase vocabulary knowledge, perhaps by using flashcards.
- Rather than carefully reading each word and each sentence, practice skimming a passage quickly to get a general impression of the main idea.
- Choose some unfamiliar words in the passage and guess the meanings from the context (surrounding sentences).
- Select all the pronouns (*he, him, they, them,* and others) and identify which nouns each one refers to in the passage.
- Practice making inferences and drawing conclusions based on what is implied in the passage as a whole.

All About the TOEFL iBT Test

The TOEFL iBT test consists of four sections: Reading, Listening, Speaking, and Writing. The entire test is about 4 hours long, and all sections are taken on the same day.

Key Features

- **The TOEFL iBT test measures all four language skills that are important for effective communication: speaking, listening, reading, and writing**, emphasizing the test taker's ability to use English effectively in academic settings.

- **It reflects how language is really used** with integrated tasks that combine more than one skill, just as in real academic settings. The integrated questions ask test takers to:

  ○ read, listen, and then speak in response to a question
  ○ listen and then speak in response to a question
  ○ read, listen, and then write in response to a question

- **It represents the best practices in language learning and teaching.** In the past, English instruction focused on learning *about* the language (especially grammar), and students could receive high scores on tests without being able to communicate. Now teachers and learners understand the importance of using English to communicate, and activities that integrate language skills are popular in many English language programs.

Format

- The TOEFL iBT test is administered via the Internet at a secure network of testing centers around the world.
- Instructions for answering questions are given with each section. There is no computer tutorial.
- The test is not computer-adaptive. Each test taker receives items that cover the full range of ability.
- Test takers can take notes throughout the entire test. At the end of testing, all notes are collected and destroyed at the test center to ensure test security.
- For the Speaking section, test takers wear noise-canceling headphones and speak into a microphone. Responses are recorded digitally and sent to ETS to be scored.
- Human raters, trained and certified by ETS, rate the Speaking responses.
- For the Writing section, test takers type their responses. The typed responses are sent to ETS for scoring.
- Human raters, trained and certified by ETS, rate the Writing responses. In addition to human scoring, automated scoring is used for the Writing tasks.
- Scores are reported both online and by mail.

The following chart shows the possible number of questions and the timing for each section. The time limit for each section varies according to the number of questions. Every test contains additional questions in the Reading or Listening section. These extra questions are being tested by ETS and do not count toward the test taker's score.

Test Format

Test Section	Number of Questions	Timing
Reading	3–4 passages, 12–14 questions each	60–80 minutes
Listening	4–6 lectures, 6 questions each	60–90 minutes
	2–3 conversations, 5 questions each	
BREAK		10 minutes
Speaking	6 tasks: 2 independent and 4 integrated	20 minutes
Writing	1 integrated task	20 minutes
	1 independent task	30 minutes

Toolbar

The on-screen toolbar in each section allows you to navigate through the test with ease. Following are examples of testing tools from the Listening and Reading sections of the test. The section is always listed in the upper left-hand corner of the toolbar.

This is what the toolbar looks like in the Listening section.

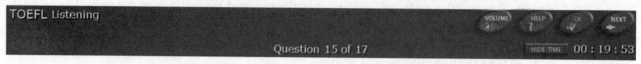

- You will always know what question you are on and how much time is remaining in the section. It is possible to hide the clock at any time by clicking on **Hide Time**.
- **Volume** allows you to adjust the volume as you listen.
- **Help** allows you to get relevant help. When you use the **Help** feature, the clock does not stop.
- **Next** allows you to proceed to the next question.
- Once you click on **Next**, you can confirm your answers by clicking on **OK**. In the Listening section, you cannot see a question again once you click on **OK**.

The toolbar for the Reading section has some important features.

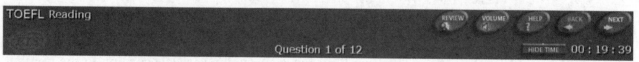

You can view the entire passage when answering questions. For some questions, you need to click on **View Text** to see the entire passage.

You can view all your answers by clicking on **Review**. This allows you to return to any other question and change your answer. You can also see which questions you have skipped and still need to answer.

In the Reading section you can also click on **Back** at any time to return to the previous question.

Reading Section

Academic Reading Skills

The Reading section measures your ability to understand university-level academic texts and passages. In many academic settings around the world, students are expected to read and understand information from textbooks and other academic materials written in English. The following are three purposes for academic reading:

Reading to find information
- effectively scanning text for key facts and important information
- increasing reading fluency and rate

Basic comprehension
- understanding the general topic or main idea, major points, important facts and details, vocabulary in context, and pronoun references[1]
- making inferences[2] about what is implied in a passage

Reading to learn
- recognizing the organization and purpose of a passage
- understanding relationships between ideas
- organizing information into a category chart or a summary in order to recall major points and important details
- inferring how ideas throughout the passage connect

Description

Reading Section Format

Length of Each Passage	Number of Passages and Questions	Timing
Approximately 700 words	3–4 passages 12–14 questions per passage	60–80 minutes

Reading Passages

The TOEFL iBT test uses reading passages from university-level textbooks that introduce a discipline or topic. The excerpts are changed as little as possible so the test can measure how well test takers can read academic material.

The passages cover a variety of subjects. You should not be concerned if you are unfamiliar with a topic. The passage contains all the information needed to answer the questions.

---

1. Pronoun references: The nouns that pronouns refer to in a passage
2. Make an inference: To comprehend an argument or an idea that is strongly suggested but not explicitly stated in a passage

All passages are classified into three basic categories:

- exposition[3]
- argumentation[4]
- historical

Often, passages present information about the topic from more than one perspective or point of view. This is something you should note as you read. Usually, you are asked at least one question that allows you to demonstrate that you understood the general organization of the passage. Common organization types that you should be able to recognize are:

- classification
- compare/contrast
- cause/effect
- problem/solution

You must read through or scroll to the end of each passage before receiving questions on that passage. Once the questions appear, the passage appears on the right side of the computer screen. The questions are on the left. (See the illustration that follows.)

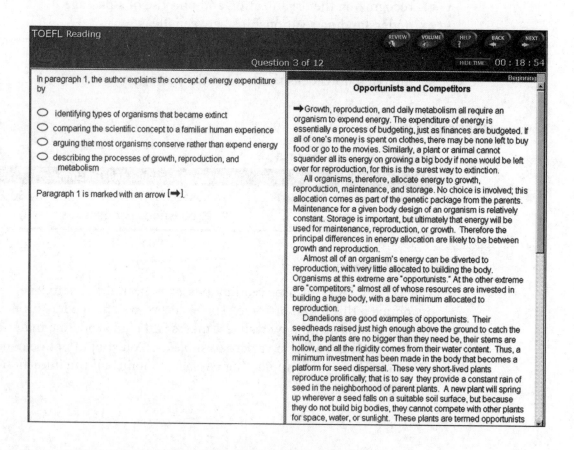

---

3. Exposition: Material that provides an explanation of a topic
4. Argumentation: Material that presents a point of view about a topic and provides evidence to support it

You do *not* need any special background knowledge to answer the questions in the Reading section correctly, but the definition of difficult words or phrases in the passage may be provided. If you click on a hyperlinked word, a definition appears in the lower left part of the screen.

The 60 to 80 minutes allotted for this section include time for reading the passages and answering the questions.

Reading Question Formats

There are three question formats in the Reading section:

- questions with four choices and a single correct answer in traditional multiple-choice format
- questions with four choices and a single answer that ask test takers to "insert a sentence" where it fits best in a passage
- "reading to learn" questions with more than four choices and more than one possible correct answer.

Features

Reading to Learn Questions

These questions test your ability to recognize how the passage is organized and understand the relationships among facts and ideas in different parts of the passage.

You are asked to sort information and place the text options provided into a **category chart** or **summary** (see the examples on page 11). The summary questions are worth up to 2 points each. The chart questions are worth up to 3 points. Partial credit is given in this question format.

Paraphrase Questions

Questions in this category are in multiple-choice format. They test your ability to select the answer choice that most accurately paraphrases a sentence from the passage.

Glossary Feature

You can click on some special-purpose words and phrases in the reading passages to view a definition or explanation of the term. In the example below, test takers can click on the word "shamans" to view its definition.

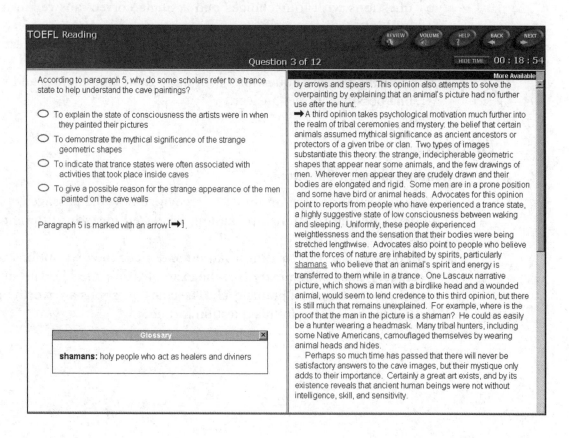

Reading to Learn—Category Chart Question Example

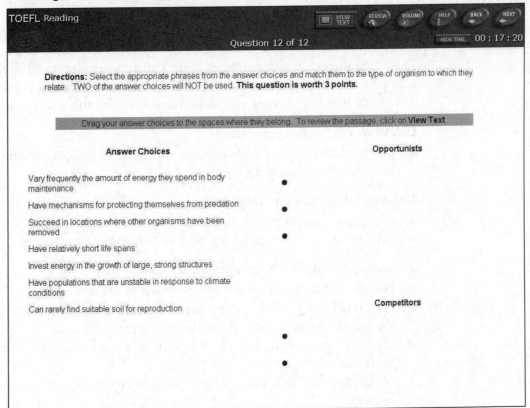

Reading to Learn—Summary Question Example

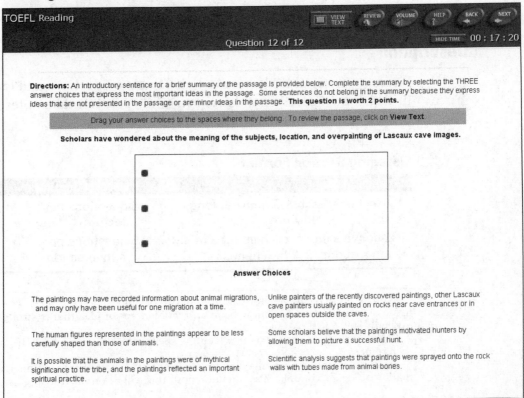

Listening Section

Academic Listening Skills

The Listening section measures your ability to understand spoken English. In academic settings, students must be able to listen to lectures and conversations. Academic listening is typically done for one of the three following purposes:

Listening for basic comprehension

- comprehend the main idea, major points, and important details related to the main idea. (Comprehension of all details is not necessary.)

Listening for pragmatic understanding

- recognize a speaker's attitude and degree of certainty
- recognize the function or purpose of a speaker's statement

Connecting and synthesizing[5] information

- recognize the organization of information presented
- understand the relationships between ideas presented (for example, compare/contrast, cause/effect, or steps in a process)
- make inferences[6] and draw conclusions based on what is implied in the material
- make connections among pieces of information in a conversation or lecture
- recognize topic changes (for example, digressions[7] and aside statements[8]) in lectures and conversations, and recognize introductions and conclusions in lectures

Description

Listening material in the test includes academic lectures and long conversations in which the speech sounds very natural. You can take notes on any listening material throughout the entire test.

Listening Section Format

Listening Material	Number of Questions	Timing
4–6 lectures, each 3–5 minutes long, about 500–800 words	6 questions per lecture	60–90 minutes
2–3 conversations, each about 3 minutes long, about 12–25 exchanges	5 questions per conversation	

---

5. Synthesize: To combine information from two or more sources
6. Make an inference: To comprehend an argument or an idea that is strongly suggested but not explicitly stated in a passage
7. Digressions: Side comments in which the speaker briefly moves away from the main topic and then returns
8. Aside statements: Comments that are relevant to the main theme but interrupt the flow of information or ideas (Example: "Pay attention now; this will be on the test.")

Academic Lectures

The lectures in the TOEFL test reflect the kind of listening and speaking that occurs in the classroom. In some of the lectures, the professor does all or almost all of the talking, with an occasional comment by a student. In other lectures, the professor may engage the students in discussion by asking questions that are answered by the students. The pictures that accompany the lecture help you know whether one or several people will be speaking.

A Lecture Where the Professor Is the Only Speaker

A Lecture Where the Professor and the Students Both Speak

Conversations in an Academic Setting

The conversations on the TOEFL test may take place during an office meeting with a professor or teaching assistant, or during a service encounter with university staff. The contents of the office conversations are generally academic in nature or related to course requirements. Service encounters could involve conversations about a housing payment, registering for a class, or requesting information at the library.

Pictures on the computer screen help you imagine the setting and the roles of the speakers.

Conversation Example

Listening Question Formats

After the listening material is played, you both see and hear each question before you see the answer choices. This encourages you to listen for main ideas.

There are four question formats in the Listening section:
- traditional multiple-choice questions with four answer choices and a single correct answer
- multiple-choice questions with more than one answer (for example, two correct answers out of four choices or three answers out of five choices)
- questions that require you to order events or steps in a process
- questions that require you to match objects or text to categories in a chart

Chart Question Example

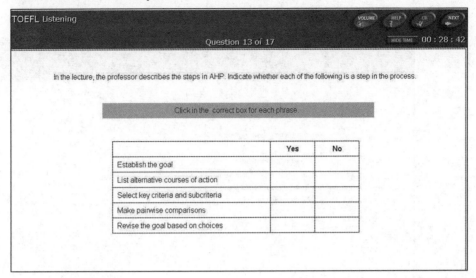

Features

- Note taking is allowed. After testing, notes are collected and destroyed before you leave the test center for test security purposes.
- A multiple-choice question measures understanding of a speaker's attitude, degree of certainty, or purpose. These questions require you to listen for voice tones and other cues and determine how speakers feel about the topic they are discussing.
- In some questions, a portion of the lecture or conversation is replayed. In the replay format, you listen to part of the conversation or lecture again and then answer a question.

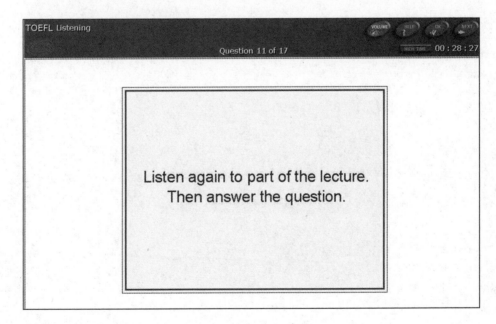

This is an example of a type of question that measures the comprehension of the purpose of a speaker's statement.

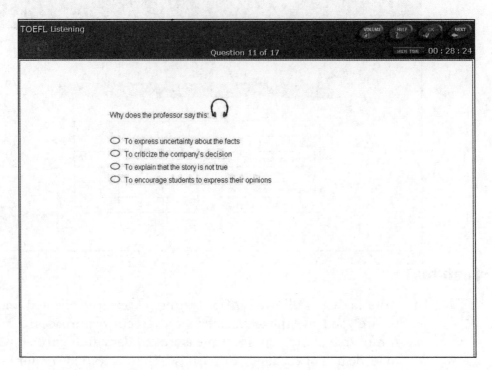

Speaking Section

Academic Speaking Skills

Students should be able to speak English successfully in and outside the classroom. The Speaking section measures your ability to speak effectively in academic settings.

In classrooms, students must:

● respond to questions
● participate in academic discussions with other students
● synthesize[9] and summarize what they have read in their textbooks and heard in class
● express their views on topics under discussion

Outside of the classroom, students must:
● participate in casual conversations
● express their opinions
● communicate with people in such places as the bookstore, the library, and the housing office

Description

The Speaking section is approximately 20 minutes long and includes six tasks.

● The first two tasks are **independent speaking tasks** on topics familiar to you. They ask you to draw upon your own ideas, opinions, and experiences when responding. However, you can respond with any idea, opinion, or experience relevant to completing the task.

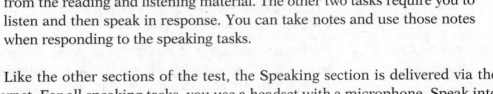

● The remaining four tasks are **integrated tasks** where you must use more than one skill when responding. Two of the tasks require you to read, listen, and then speak in response by relating the information from the reading and listening material. The other two tasks require you to listen and then speak in response. You can take notes and use those notes when responding to the speaking tasks.

Like the other sections of the test, the Speaking section is delivered via the Internet. For all speaking tasks, you use a headset with a microphone. Speak into the microphone to record your responses. Responses are digitally recorded and sent to ETS, where they are scored by certified raters.

---

9. Synthesize: To combine information from two or more sources

Speaking Task Types

Task Type	Task Description	Timing
Independent Tasks		
1. Personal Preference	This question asks the test taker to express and defend a personal choice from a given category—for example, important people, places, events, or activities that the test taker enjoys.	Preparation time: 15 seconds Response time: 45 seconds
2. Choice	This question asks the test taker to make and defend a personal choice between two contrasting behaviors or courses of action.	Preparation time: 15 seconds Response time: 45 seconds
Integrated Tasks		
	Read/Listen/Speak	
3. Campus Situation Topic: Fit and Explain	• A reading passage (75–100 words) presents a campus-related issue. • A listening passage (60–80 seconds; 150–180 words) comments on the issue in the reading passage. • The question asks the test taker to summarize the speaker's opinion within the context of the reading passage.	Preparation time: 30 seconds Response time: 60 seconds
4. Academic Course Topic: General/Specific	• A reading passage (75–100 words) broadly defines a term, process, or idea from an academic subject. • An excerpt from a lecture (60–90 seconds; 150–220 words) provides examples and specific information to illustrate the term, process, or idea from the reading passage. • The question asks the test taker to combine and convey important information from the reading passage and the lecture excerpt.	Preparation time: 30 seconds Response time: 60 seconds
	Listen/Speak	
5. Campus Situation Topic: Problem/Solution	• The listening passage (60–90 seconds; 180–220 words) is a conversation about a student-related problem and two possible solutions. • The question asks the test taker to demonstrate an understanding of the problem and to express an opinion about solving the problem.	Preparation time: 20 seconds Response time: 60 seconds
6. Academic Course Topic: Summary	• The listening passage is an excerpt from a lecture (90–120 seconds; 230–280 words) that explains a term or concept and gives concrete examples to illustrate that term or concept. • The question asks the test taker to summarize the lecture and demonstrate an understanding of the relationship between the examples and the overall topic.	Preparation time: 20 seconds Response time: 60 seconds
TOTAL		**20 minutes**

Writing Section

Academic Writing Skills

In all academic situations where writing in English is required, students must be able to present their ideas in a clear, well-organized manner. The Writing section measures your ability to write English in an academic setting.

- Often, students need to write a paper or an essay response about what they are learning in their classes. This requires combining information they have heard in class lectures with what they have read in textbooks or other materials. This type of writing is referred to as **integrated writing**. In this type of writing, students must:
  - ○ take notes on what they hear and read, and use them to organize information before writing
  - ○ summarize, paraphrase, and cite information from the source material accurately
  - ○ write about the ways the information they heard relates to the information they read

For example, in an academic course, a student might be asked to compare and contrast the points of view expressed by the professor in class with those expressed by an author in the assigned reading material. The student must successfully draw information from each source to explain the contrast.

- Students must also write essays that express and support their opinions. In this type of writing, known as **independent writing**, students express an opinion and support it based on their own knowledge and experience.

For example, students may be asked to write an essay about a controversial issue. The students use past, personal experience to support their position.

In all types of writing, it is helpful for students to:
- identify one main idea and some major points that support it
- plan how to organize the essay (for example, with an outline)
- develop the essay by using reasons, examples, and details
- express information in an organized manner
- use effective linking words (transitional phrases) to connect ideas and help the reader understand the flow of ideas
- use a range of grammar and vocabulary for effective expression
- use grammar and vocabulary accurately; use idiomatic expressions appropriately
- follow the conventions of spelling, punctuation, and layout

Description

The total time for the Writing section is 50 minutes. Test takers write their responses to two writing tasks (see the table below). Responses are typed into the computer and sent to ETS, where they are scored by both certified raters and the automated scoring system.

Writing Task Types

Task Type	Task Description
Task 1 Integrated Writing: Read/Listen/Write	• Test takers read a short text of about 230–300 words (reading time, 3 minutes) on an academic topic. • Test takers may take notes on the reading passage. • The reading passage disappears from the screen during the lecture that follows. It reappears when test takers begin writing so they can refer to it as they work. • Test takers listen to a speaker discuss the same topic from a different perspective. The listening passage is about 230–300 words long (listening time, about 2 minutes). • The listening passage provides additional information that relates to points made in the reading passage. Test takers may take notes on the listening passage. • Test takers write a summary in connected English prose of important points made in the listening passage, and explain how these relate to the key points of the reading passage. Suggested response length is 150–225 words; however, there is no penalty for writing more as long as it is in response to the task presented. • Response time: 20 minutes
Task 2 Independent Writing: Writing from Knowledge and Experience	• Test takers write an essay that states, explains, and supports their opinion on an issue. An effective essay will usually contain a minimum of 300 words; however, test takers may write more if they wish. • Test takers must support their opinions or choices rather than simply list personal preferences or choices. • Typical essay questions begin with statements such as: —Do you agree or disagree with the following statement? Use reasons and specific details to support your answer. —Some people believe X. Other people believe Y. Which of these two positions do you prefer/agree with? Give reasons and specific details. • Response time: 30 minutes

About Test Scores

Score Scales

The TOEFL iBT test provides scores in four skill areas:

Reading	0–30
Listening	0–30
Speaking	0–30
Writing	0–30
Total Score	**0–120**

The total score is the sum of the four skill scores.

Rating of Speaking and Writing Responses

Speaking

Responses to all six Speaking tasks are digitally recorded and sent to ETS. The responses from each test taker are scored by three to six different certified raters. The response for each task is rated on a scale from 0 to 4 according to the rubrics on pages 188–191. The average of all six ratings is converted to a scaled score of 0 to 30.

Raters listen for the following features in test taker responses:

● **Delivery:** How clear was the speech? Good responses are fluid and clear, with good pronunciation, natural pacing, and natural-sounding intonation patterns.

● **Language use:** How effectively does the test taker use grammar and vocabulary to convey ideas? Raters determine the test taker's ability to control both basic and more complex language structures, and use appropriate vocabulary.

● **Topic development:** How fully do test takers answer the question and how coherently do they present their ideas? How well did the test taker synthesize and summarize the information in the integrated tasks? Good responses generally use all or most of the time allotted, and the relationship between ideas and the progression from one idea to the next are clear and easy to follow.

It is important to note that raters do not expect test takers' responses to be perfect. Even high-scoring responses may contain occasional errors and minor problems in any of the three areas described above.

Writing

Responses to all writing tasks also are sent to ETS. The responses are rated by two certified raters and the automated scoring system on a scale of 0 to 5 according to the rubrics on pages 200–201 and 209–210. The average of the scores on the two writing tasks is converted to a scaled score of 0 to 30.

- The response to the integrated writing task is scored on the quality of writing (organization, appropriate and precise use of grammar and vocabulary) and the completeness and accuracy of the content.

- The independent writing essay is scored on the overall quality of the writing: development, organization, and appropriate and precise use of grammar and vocabulary.

It is important to note that the raters recognize that the responses are first drafts. They do not expect test takers to produce a well-researched, comprehensive essay. For that reason, test takers can earn a high score with a response that contains some errors.

Score Reports

TOEFL score reports provide valuable information about a test taker's readiness to participate and succeed in academic studies in an English-speaking environment. Score reports include:

- four skill scores
- total score

Scores are reported online approximately 10 days after the test. Test takers can view their scores online at no charge. Colleges, universities, and agencies receive paper score reports if the test taker has selected them as score recipients. (A paper copy of the score report is mailed to the test taker only upon request.)

Test taker score reports also include performance feedback that indicates whether their performance was high, medium, or low, and describes what test takers in each score range typically know and can do with the English language.

Score Requirements

Each institution sets its own requirements for TOEFL scores. Test takers should consult their target institutions to determine their specific TOEFL score requirements. A list of colleges, universities, and agencies that accept TOEFL scores and a list of institutional score requirements reported to ETS can be obtained at **www.toeflgoanywhere.org**.

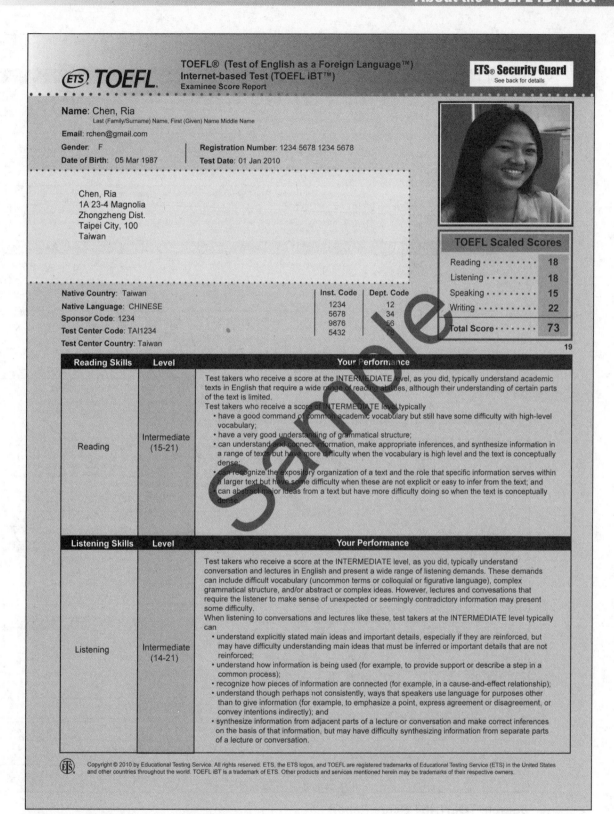

Sample TOEFL iBT Score Report

Speaking Skills	Level	Your Performance
Speaking about Familiar Topics	Limited (1.5-2.0)	Your responses indicate some difficulty speaking in English about everyday experience and opinions. Listeners sometimes have trouble understanding you because of noticeable problems with pronunciation, grammar, and vocabulary. While you are able to respond partially to the questions, you are not able to fully develop your ideas, possibly due to limited vocabulary and grammar.
Speaking about Campus Situations	Limited (1.5-2.0)	Your responses indicate that you have some difficulty speaking in English about information from conversations, newspaper articles, university publications, and so on. While you are able to talk about some of the key information from these sources, limited grammar and vocabulary may prevent you from fully expressing your ideas. Problems with pronunciation make it difficult for listeners to understand you at times.
Speaking about Academic Course Content	Limited (1.5-2.0)	In your response, you are able to use English to talk about the basic ideas from academic reading or lecture materials, but, in general, you include few relevant or accurate details. It is sometimes difficult for listeners to understand your responses because of problems with grammar, vocabulary, and pronunciation. Overall, you are able to respond in a general way to the questions, but the amount of information in your responses is limited and the expression of ideas is often vague and unclear.

Writing Skills	Level	Your Performance
Writing based on Reading and Listening	Good (4.0-5.0)	You responded well to the task, relating the lecture to the reading. Weaknesses, if you have any, might have to do with: • slight imprecision in your summary of some of the main points and/or • use of English that is occasionally ungrammatical or unclear
Writing based on Knowledge and Experience	Fair (2.5-3.5)	You expressed ideas with reasons, examples, and details, but your responses indicate weaknesses such as: • you may not provide enough specific support and development for your main points; • your ideas may be difficult to follow because of how you organize your essay or because of the language you use to connect your ideas; • grammatical mistakes or vague/incorrect uses of words may make the writing difficult to understand.

THIS IS THE ONLY PERSONAL RECORD YOU WILL RECEIVE. PLEASE RETAIN FOR YOUR RECORDS.

This score report provides four section scores and a total score. An analysis of your strengths and weaknesses in English is included. The level pertaining to each skill should not be generalized beyond the performance on this test. Skill levels and their associated descriptions are not intended for use by institutions as part of their admissions criteria and will not be shared unless you grant permission.

Information About Scores: The following scaled scores are reported for TOEFL iBT. A total score is not reported when one or more sections have not been administered. These scores have the following ranges:

Sections	Scaled Scores
Reading	0-30
Listening	0-30
Speaking	0-30
Writing	0-30
Total Score	0-120

Institution Code Numbers: The code numbers on this score report are the ones you selected at the time you registered. If any of the numbers you indicated are not shown, they were incorrect and the TOEFL office was unable to send those score reports. To have additional official score reports sent, follow the directions on the attached Score Report Request Form.

DEPT.	WHERE THE REPORT WAS SENT
00	Admissions office for undergraduate study or an institution or agency that is not a college or university
01, 04-99	Admissions office for graduate study in a field other than management (business) or law according to the codes selected when you registered
02	Admissions office of a graduate school of management (business)
03	Admissions office of a graduate school of law

Additional information about TOEFL iBT scores can be found on the Test Takers section of the TOEFL website at **www.ets.org/toefl**.

Score Legends:

Reading Skills	
Level	Scaled Score Range
High	22-30
Intermediate	15-21
Low	0-14

Speaking Skills		
Level	Task Rating	Scaled Score Range
Good	3.5-4.0	26-30
Fair	2.5-3.0	18-25
Limited	1.5 - 2.0	10-17
Weak	0 - 1.0	0-9

Listening Skills	
Level	Scaled Score Range
High	22-30
Intermediate	14-21
Low	0-13

Writing Skills		
Level	Task Rating	Scaled Score Range
Good	4.0-5.0	24-30
Fair	2.5-3.5	17-23
Limited	1.0-2.0	1-16
Score of Zero	0	0

ETS® Security Guard *text is printed with a special heat sensitive ink for security. To activate this security feature, apply heat to the text, either by rubbing it or blowing on it, and the* **ETS® Security Guard** *text will disappear.*

IMPORTANT NOTE TO INSTITUTIONS: *Scores are valid ONLY if received directly from ETS. Photocopies should never be accepted.* If you received this score report directly from an examinee, please provide your official TOEFL institution code to the examinee so he/she can request that an official score report be sent to you. If you need to contact ETS, use the toll-free number on the back of the official score report. Scores more than two years old cannot be reported or validated.

Sample TOEFL iBT Score Report

General Skill-building Tips

The best way for English language learners to develop the skills measured by the TOEFL test is to enroll in an English language learning program that features:

- reading, speaking, listening, and writing skills, with an emphasis on speaking
- an integrated skills approach (for example, instruction that builds skills in listening/reading/speaking or listening/reading/writing)

In addition to the advice for improvement listed in the Appendix of this book, ETS has created the following tips for test takers, but they also contain information useful to teachers.

Reading Tips

English language learners can improve their reading skills by reading regularly, especially university textbooks or other materials that cover a variety of subject areas (for example, sciences, social sciences, arts, business, and others) and are written in an academic style. A wide variety of academic texts can be found on the Internet as well as in magazines and journals.

Reading to Find Information

- Scan passages to find and highlight key facts (dates, numbers, terms) and information.
- Practice frequently to increase reading rate and fluency.

Reading for Basic Comprehension

- Increase vocabulary. Flash cards can help.
- Practice skimming a passage quickly to get a general impression of the main idea instead of carefully reading each word and each sentence.
- Develop the ability to skim quickly and identify major points.
- After skimming a passage, read it again more carefully and write down the main idea, major points, and important facts.
- Choose some unfamiliar words in the passage and guess the meaning from the context (surrounding sentences). Then, look them up to determine their meaning.
- Underline all pronouns (for example, *he, him, they, them*) and identify the nouns to which they refer in the passage.
- Practice making inferences and drawing conclusions based on what is implied in the passage as a whole.

Practice your reading skills

with TOEFL® Practice Online at **www.ets.org/toeflpractice** and receive same-day scores to confirm you are ready for test day.

Note

The Reading section does not measure summarizing skills, but practicing them builds the skills required for the integrated tasks in the Speaking and Writing sections.

Reading to Learn

- Identify the passage type (for example, cause/effect, compare/contrast, classification, problem/solution, description, narration) and its organization.
- Organize the information in the passage:
  - Create an outline of the passage to distinguish between major and minor points.
  - If the passage categorizes information, create a chart and place the information in appropriate categories.

On the TOEFL test, test takers do not have to create such charts. Instead, a chart with possible answer choices is provided for them, and they are required to fill in the chart with the correct choices. Practicing this skill will help test takers think about categorizing information and be able to do so with ease.

- Create an oral or written summary of the passage using the charts and outlines.
- Paraphrase individual sentences in a passage. Then paraphrase entire paragraphs.

Listening Tips

Listening to the English language frequently and reading a wide variety of academic materials is the best way to improve listening skills.

Watching movies and television and listening to the radio provide excellent opportunities to build listening skills. Audiotapes and CDs of lectures and presentations are equally valuable and are available at libraries and bookstores. Those with transcripts are particularly helpful. The Internet is also a great resource for listening material (for example, **www.npr.org** or **www.bbc.co.uk/radio** or **www.bbc.co.uk/worldservice/learningenglish**).

Listening for Basic Comprehension

- Increase vocabulary.
- Focus on the content and flow of spoken material. Do not be distracted by the speaker's style and delivery.
- Anticipate what a person is going to say as a way to stay focused.
- Stay active by asking yourself questions (for example, What main idea is the professor communicating?).
- Copy the words "main idea," "major points," and "important details" on different lines of paper. Listen carefully, and write these down while listening. Continue listening until all important points and details are written down and then review them.
- Listen to a portion of a lecture or talk and create an outline of important points. Use the outline to write a brief summary. Gradually increase the amount of the presentation you use to write the summary.

Notes

The Reading section measures the ability to recognize paraphrases. The ability to paraphrase is also important for the integrated tasks in the Writing and Speaking sections of the test.

The Listening section does not measure summarizing skills, but practicing summarizing skills is useful for the integrated tasks in the Speaking and Writing sections.

Listening for Pragmatic Understanding[10]

- Think about what each speaker hopes to accomplish: What is the purpose of the speech or conversation? Is the speaker apologizing, complaining, or making suggestions?
- Notice each speaker's style. Is the language formal or casual? How certain does each speaker sound? Is the speaker's voice calm or emotional? What does the speaker's tone of voice tell you?
- Notice the speaker's degree of certainty. How sure is the speaker about the information? Does the speaker's tone of voice indicate something about his/her degree of certainty?
- Listen for changes in topic or digressions[11].
- Watch a recorded TV or movie comedy. Pay careful attention to the way stress and intonation patterns are used to convey meaning.

---

10. Pragmatic understanding: To understand a speaker's purpose, attitude, degree of certainty, etc.
11. Digressions: Side comments in which the speaker briefly moves away from the main topic and then returns

Listening to Connect and Synthesize[12] Ideas

- Think about how the lecture you're hearing is organized. Listen for the signal words that indicate the introduction, major steps or ideas, examples, and the conclusion or summary.
- Identify the relationships between ideas. Possible relationships include: cause/effect, compare/contrast, and steps in a process.
- Listen for words that show connections and relationships between ideas.
- Listen to recorded material and stop the recording at various points. Predict what information or idea will be expressed next.
- Create an outline of the information discussed while listening or after listening.

Practice your listening skills

with TOEFL® Practice Online at **www.ets.org/toeflpractice** and receive same-day scores to confirm you are ready for test day.

Speaking Tips

The best way to practice speaking is with native speakers of English. If you do not live in an English-speaking country, finding native speakers of English might be quite challenging. In some countries, there are English-speaking tutors or assistants who help students with conversation skills and overall communication skills. It is critical to find them and speak with them as often as possible. Another way to practice speaking is by joining an English club whose members converse in English about movies, music, and travel. If a club does not exist in your area, start one and invite native speakers to help you get started.

Independent Speaking Tasks

- Make a list of topics that are familiar, and practice speaking about them.
- Describe a familiar place or recount a personal experience.
- Later, state an opinion or a preference and present clear, detailed reasons for it.
- Make a recommendation and explain why it is the best way to proceed.
- Practice giving one-minute responses to topics.

---

12. Synthesize: To combine information from two or more sources

Integrated Speaking Tasks

- Find a textbook that includes questions about the material at the end of chapters, and practice answering the questions orally.

- Read a short article (100–200 words). Make an outline that includes only the major points of the article. Use the outline to orally summarize the information.

- Find listening and reading material on the same topic covered by the article. The material can contain similar or different views. (The Internet and the library are good places to find information.) Take notes or create outlines on the listening and reading material:[13]

  - Orally summarize the information in both the written and spoken materials. Be sure to paraphrase using different words and grammatical structures.
  - Orally synthesize the material by combining the information from the reading and listening materials and explain how they relate.
  - State an opinion about the ideas and information presented in the reading and listening material and explain how they relate.
  - If the reading and/or listening material describes a problem, suggest and explain a solution to the problem.

- Recognize the attitude of the speaker or the writer of the original material through intonation, stress, and word choice. This helps you to understand their point of view and plan an appropriate response.

All Speaking Tasks

- Increase vocabulary and learn to use idiomatic speech appropriately.

- Learn grammatical structures and use them naturally when speaking.

- Work on pronunciation, including word stress, intonation patterns, and pauses. (There are a number of products and websites that can help you develop pronunciation skills.)

- When practicing for the TOEFL test using the tips above, take 15 seconds to think about what you are going to say before you speak. Write down a few key words and ideas, but do not attempt to write down exactly what you are going to say. (Raters will be able to detect responses that are read and give them a lower score.)

- Use signal words and expressions to introduce new information or ideas, to connect ideas, and to mark important words or ideas. This will help the listener easily follow what you are saying. (For example, "on the one hand...," "but on the other hand...," "what that means is...," "The first reason is...," "another difference is...")

---

13. Taking notes on the reading and listening material in the integrated Speaking tasks is allowed. Since the reading and listening material is very brief, taking notes on the material may not be necessary. However, the activity described above will help test takers prepare for entering the academic setting. If test takers can do this well, they will most likely succeed on the integrated Speaking tasks on the TOEFL test.

- Make recordings of the preceding activities and evaluate your effort by asking yourself these questions:
    - Did I complete the task?
    - Did I speak clearly?
    - Did I make grammatical errors?
    - Did I use words correctly?
    - Did I organize my ideas clearly and appropriately?
    - Did I use the time effectively?
    - Did I speak too fast or too slowly?
    - Did I pause too often?

- Monitor your progress and ask an English teacher or tutor to evaluate your speech using the appropriate Speaking rubrics. (See pages 188–191 for the rubrics.)

Practice your speaking skills

with TOEFL® Practice Online at **www.ets.org/toeflpractice** and receive same-day scores to confirm that you are ready for test day.

Writing Tips

Integrated Writing Tasks

- Find a textbook that includes questions about the material at the end of chapters, and practice writing answers to the questions.

- Read an article that is about 300–400 words long. Make an outline that includes the major points and important details of the article. Use the outline to write a summary of the information and ideas. Summaries should be brief and clearly communicate only the major points and important details. Be sure to paraphrase using different words and grammatical structures.

- Find listening and reading material on a single topic on the Internet or in the library. The material can provide similar or different views. Take notes on the written and spoken portions, and do the following:
    - Summarize the information and ideas in both the written and spoken portions.
    - Synthesize the information and discuss how the reading and listening materials relate. Explain how the ideas expressed are similar, how one idea expands upon another, or how the ideas are different or contradict each other.

Paraphrasing

Paraphrasing involves restating something from the source material in one's own words. On the TOEFL test, test takers receive a score of zero if all they do is copy words from the reading passage. Practice paraphrasing words, phrases, sentences, and entire paragraphs frequently using the following tips:

- Learn to find synonyms with ease. Pick 10 to 15 words or phrases in a reading passage and quickly think of synonyms without looking them up in a dictionary or thesaurus.

- Write a paraphrase of a reading passage using only your notes. If you have not taken notes, write the paraphrase without looking at the original text. Then check the paraphrase with the original passage to make sure that it is factually accurate and that you have used different words and grammatical structures.

Independent Writing Tasks

- Make a list of familiar topics and practice writing about them.
- For each topic, state an opinion or a preference and then support it with evidence.
- Practice planning and writing at least one essay for each topic. Be sure to take 30 minutes to plan, write, and revise each essay.
- Think about and list all ideas related to a topic or task before writing. This is also called "prewriting."
- Identify one main idea and some major points to support that idea, and plan how to communicate them (by creating, for example, an outline to organize ideas).
- Create a focused thesis statement and use it to develop the ideas presented in the essay.
- Develop the essay by using appropriate explanation and detail.

All Writing Tasks

- Increase vocabulary and knowledge of idiomatic speech so you can use it appropriately.
- Learn grammatical structures so well that you can use them naturally when writing.
- Learn the conventions of spelling, punctuation, and layout (for example, paragraph creation).
- Express information in an organized manner, displaying unity of thought and coherence.
- Use signal words and phrases, such as "on the one hand" or "in conclusion," to create a clear structure for your response.

- As you practice, ask yourself these questions:
    - ○ Did I complete the task?
    - ○ Did I write clearly?
    - ○ Did I make grammatical errors?
    - ○ Did I use words correctly?
    - ○ Did I organize my ideas clearly and coherently?
    - ○ Did I use the time effectively?
- Monitor your own progress and ask an English teacher or tutor to evaluate the writing by using the appropriate Writing rubrics. (See pages 200–201 and 209–210 for the rubrics.)

Practice your writing skills

with TOEFL® Practice Online at **www.ets.org/toeflpractice** and receive same-day scores to confirm that you are ready for test day.

Note

Teachers: It is a good idea for English programs to use the TOEFL Speaking and Writing rubrics (pages 188–191, 200–201, and 209–210) to measure students' abilities and evaluate their progress. This helps test takers build their skills for the TOEFL test.

Test Preparation Tips from ETS

Once you have built your skills and practiced, you will be ready for the TOEFL test. Here are some good test-taking strategies recommended by ETS:

- **Carefully follow the directions** in each section to avoid wasting time.

- **Click on Help** to review the directions **only when absolutely necessary** because the test clock will not stop when the Help function is being used.

- **Do not panic.** Concentrate on the current question only, and do not think about how you answered other questions. This is a habit that can be learned through practice.

- **Avoid spending too much time on any one question**. If you have given the question some thought and you still do not know the answer, eliminate as many answer choices as possible and then select the best remaining choice. You can review your responses in the Reading section by clicking on **Review**. However, it is best to do this only after all the questions have been answered so you stay focused and save time.

- **Pace yourself** so you have enough time to answer every question. Be aware of the time limit for every section/task, and budget enough time for each question/task so you do not have to rush at the end. You can hide the time clock if you wish, but it is a good idea to check the clock periodically to monitor progress. The clock will automatically alert you when 5 minutes remain in the Listening and Reading sections, as well as in the independent and integrated tasks in the Writing section.

Questions Frequently Asked by Test Takers

Test Benefits

Why should I take the TOEFL test?

No matter where in the world you want to study, the TOEFL test can help you get there. You will be eligible for admission to virtually any institution in the world, including the top colleges and universities in the United States, Canada, the United Kingdom, Australia, and New Zealand. See the Destinations Directory at **www.ets.org/toefl**.

The TOEFL test gives you more flexibility on when, where, and how often you take the test, and more practice tools and feedback, than any other English language test in the world.

Test takers who are well prepared for the TOEFL test can feel confident that they are also well prepared for academic success.

What makes the TOEFL test better than other English language tests?

The TOEFL test assesses a test taker's ability to integrate English skills and to communicate about what he or she reads and hears. These are the skills you will actually use in an academic classroom.

The test also measures speaking more fairly than other tests. Each Speaking response is evaluated by three to six raters, which is more objective and reliable than other tests that use only one interviewer from a local test site.

Who else benefits from the test?

Admissions officials and faculty at colleges and universities, as well as administrators of certification and licensing agencies, receive better information on an applicant's English communication skills.

Registration

How and when do I register for the test?

Online registration is the easiest method. You can also register by mail or by phone. See **www.ets.org/toefl** for details. Registration is available 3–4 months before the test date. Register early, as seats can fill up quickly.

Where and when can I take the TOEFL test?

The test is given on fixed dates, 30–40 times a year, via the Internet at secure test centers. The ETS testing network, with more than 4,500 test centers in 180 countries, is the largest in the world. Go to **www.ets.org/toefl** for a list of locations and dates.

How much does the TOEFL test cost?

The price of the test varies by country. Please check the TOEFL website at **www.ets.org/toefl** for the test fees in your country.

Test Preparation

Are sample questions available?

Yes, test takers who register for the TOEFL iBT test receive a link to the TOEFL iBT Sampler, a one-time-use set of actual TOEFL questions. The Sampler includes questions from all four sections of the test. The Reading and Listening sections are interactive, and sample responses are provided for the Speaking and Writing questions.

Can I take a practice test and get a score?

Yes. Practice tests can be purchased at TOEFL Practice Online, at **www.ets.org/toeflpractice**. This site features practice tests that include *exclusive* TOEFL iBT practice questions covering all four skills: Reading, Listening, Speaking, and Writing, with scoring provided by certified ETS raters.

Scores and Score Reports

How do I get my scores?

Scores are posted online approximately 10 days after the test date, then mailed to the institutions you selected.

Included with your registration fees are:

- 1 online score report for you and 1 printed score report if requested
- up to 4 official score reports that ETS will send directly to the institutions or agencies that you select before you take the test

Can I order additional score reports?

Yes. For a small fee, you can send score reports to as many institutions as you choose. See **www.ets.org/toefl** for details.

How long are scores valid?

ETS will report scores for 2 years after the test date.

Will institutions accept scores from previous tests?

Check with each institution or agency directly.

Test Delivery

What skills are tested on the TOEFL iBT Test?

The test is given in English, has four sections on reading, listening, speaking, and writing, and takes about 4 hours.

Section	Time Limit	Number of Questions
Reading	60–80 minutes	36–56
Listening	60–90 minutes	34–51
Break	10 minutes	
Speaking	20 minutes	6 tasks
Writing	50 minutes	2 tasks

Can I take only one section of the test?

No. The entire test must be taken to receive a score.

Which computer keyboard is used?

QWERTY, the most common English-language keyboard, is used. It takes its name from the first six letters at the top of the keyboard. Test takers should practice on a QWERTY keyboard before taking the TOEFL iBT test.

2 Reading Section

Read this chapter to learn	➥ The 10 types of TOEFL Reading questions
	➥ How to recognize each Reading question type
	➥ Tips for answering each Reading question type
	➥ Strategies for preparing for the Reading section

The TOEFL iBT Reading section includes three or four reading passages, each approximately 700 words long. There are 12 to 14 questions per passage. You have from 60 to 80 minutes to answer all questions in the section.

Reading Passages

TOEFL iBT reading passages are excerpts from college-level textbooks that would be used in introductions to a discipline or topic. The excerpts are changed as little as possible because the goal of the test is to assess how well test takers can read the kind of writing that is used in an academic environment.

The passages will cover a variety of subjects. Do not worry if you are unfamiliar with the topic of a passage. All the information needed to answer the questions will be in the passage. All TOEFL reading passages are classified into three basic categories based on author purpose: (1) Exposition, (2) Argumentation, and (3) Historical.

Often, passages will present information about the topic from more than one perspective or point of view. This is something you should note as you read because usually you will be asked at least one question that allows you to show that you have understood the general organization of the passage. Common types of organization you should be able to recognize are:

- classification
- comparison/contrast
- cause/effect
- problem/solution

TOEFL reading passages are approximately 700 words long, but the passages used may vary somewhat in length. Some passages may be slightly longer than 700 words, and some may be slightly shorter.

Reading Questions

Reading questions cover Basic Information skills, Inferencing skills, and Reading to Learn skills. There are 10 question types. The following chart summarizes the categories and types of TOEFL iBT Reading questions.

TOEFL Reading Question Types

Basic Information and Inferencing questions (12 to 14 questions per set)
1. Factual Information questions (3 to 6 questions per set)
2. Negative Factual Information questions (0 to 2 questions per set)
3. Inference questions (1 to 3 questions per set)
4. Rhetorical Purpose questions (1 to 2 questions per set)
5. Vocabulary questions (3 to 5 questions per set)
6. Reference questions (0 to 2 questions per set)
7. Sentence Simplification questions (0 or 1 question per set)
8. Insert Text question (1 question per set)

Reading to Learn questions (1 per set)
9. Prose Summary
10. Fill in a Table

The following sections will explain each of these question types. You will find out how to recognize each type and see examples of each type with explanations. You will also find tips that can help you answer each Reading question type.

Basic Information and Inferencing Questions

Type 1: Factual Information Questions

These questions ask you to identify factual information that is explicitly stated in the passage. Factual Information questions can focus on facts, details, definitions, or other information presented by the author. They ask you to identify specific information that is typically mentioned only in part of the passage. They generally do not ask about general themes that the passage as a whole discusses. Often, the relevant information is in one or two sentences.

How to Recognize Factual Information Questions

Factual Information questions are often phrased in one of these ways:

- According to the paragraph, which of the following is true of X?
- The author's description of X mentions which of the following?
- According to the paragraph, X occurred because . . .
- According to the paragraph, X did Y because . . .
- According to the paragraph, why did X do Y?
- The author's description of X mentions which of the following?

Tips for Factual Information Questions
- You may need to refer back to the passage in order to know what exactly is said about the subject of the question. Since the question may be about a detail, you may not recall the detail from your first reading of the passage.
- Eliminate choices that present information that is contradicted in the passage.
- Do not select an answer just because it is mentioned in the passage. Your choice should answer the specific question that was asked.

Example

PASSAGE EXCERPT: ". . . Sculptures must, for example, be stable, which requires an understanding of the properties of mass, weight distribution, and stress. Paintings must have rigid stretchers so that the canvas will be taut, and the paint must not deteriorate, crack, or discolor. These are problems that must be overcome by the artist because they tend to intrude upon his or her conception of the work. For example, in the early Italian Renaissance, bronze statues of horses with a raised foreleg usually had a cannonball under that hoof. This was done because the cannonball was needed to support the weight of the leg. In other words, the demands of the laws of physics, not the sculptor's aesthetic intentions, placed the ball there. That this device was a necessary structural compromise is clear from the fact that the cannonball quickly disappeared when sculptors learned how to strengthen the internal structure of a statue with iron braces (iron being much stronger than bronze) . . . "

According to paragraph 2, sculptors in the Italian Renaissance stopped using cannonballs in bronze statues of horses because

- ◯ they began using a material that made the statues weigh less
- ◯ they found a way to strengthen the statues internally
- ◯ the aesthetic tastes of the public had changed over time
- ◯ the cannonballs added too much weight to the statues

Explanation

The question tells you to look for the answer in the excerpted paragraph, which in this case is paragraph 2. You do not need to skim the entire passage to find the relevant information.

Choice 1 says that sculptors stopped putting cannonballs under the raised legs of horses in statues because they learned how to make the statue weigh less and not require support for the leg. The passage does not mention making the statues weigh less; it says that sculptors learned a better way to support the weight. Choice 3 says that the change occurred only because people's taste changed, meaning that the cannonballs were never structurally necessary. That directly contradicts the passage. Choice 4 says that the cannonballs weakened the structure of the statues. This choice also contradicts the passage. Choice 2 correctly identifies the reason the passage gives for the change: sculptors developed a way to strengthen the statue from the inside, making the cannonballs physically unnecessary.

Type 2: Negative Factual Information Questions

These questions ask you to verify what information is true and what information is NOT true or not included in the passage based on information that is explicitly stated in the passage. To answer this kind of question, first locate the relevant information in the passage. Then verify that three of the four answer choices are true and that the remaining choice is false. Remember, for this type of question, the correct answer is the one that is NOT true.

How to Recognize Negative Factual Information Questions

You can recognize negative fact questions because the word "NOT" or "EXCEPT" appears in the question in capital letters.

- According to the passage, which of the following is NOT true of X?
- The author's description of X mentions all of the following EXCEPT . . .

Tips for Negative Factual Information Questions

- Usually a Negative Factual Information question requires you to check more of the passage than a Factual Information question. The three choices that are mentioned in the passage may be spread across a paragraph or several paragraphs.
- In Negative Factual Information questions, the correct answer either directly contradicts one or more statements in the passage or is not mentioned in the passage at all.
- After you finish a Negative Factual Information question, check your answer to make sure you have accurately understood the task.

Example

PASSAGE EXCERPT: "The United States in the 1800s was full of practical, hardworking people who did not consider the arts—from theater to painting—useful occupations. In addition, the public's attitude that European art was better than American art both discouraged and infuriated American artists. In the early 1900s there was a strong feeling among artists that the United States was long overdue in developing art that did not reproduce European traditions. Everybody agreed that the heart and soul of the new country should be reflected in its art. But opinions differed about what this art would be like and how it would develop."

According to paragraph 1, all of the following were true of American art in the late 1800s and early 1900s EXCEPT:

- ○ Most Americans thought art was unimportant.
- ○ American art generally copied European styles and traditions.
- ○ Most Americans considered American art inferior to European art.
- ○ American art was very popular with European audiences.

Explanation

Sometimes in Negative Factual Information questions, it is necessary to check the entire passage in order to make sure that your choice is not mentioned. However, in this example, the question is limited to one paragraph, so your answer should be based just on the information in that paragraph. Choice 1 is a restatement of the first sentence in the paragraph: since most Americans did not think that the arts were useful occupations, they considered them unimportant. Choice

2 makes the same point as the third sentence: ". . . the United States was long overdue in developing art that did not reproduce European traditions" means that up to this point in history, American art did reproduce European traditions. Choice 3 is a restatement of the second sentence in the paragraph: American artists were frustrated because of "the public's attitude that European art was better than American art. . . ." Choice 4 is not mentioned anywhere in the paragraph. Because you are asked to identify the choice that is NOT mentioned in the passage or that contradicts the passage, the correct answer is choice 4.

Type 3: Inference Questions

These questions measure your ability to comprehend an argument or an idea that is strongly implied but not explicitly stated in the text. For example, if an effect is cited in the passage, an Inference question might ask about its cause. If a comparison is made, an Inference question might ask for the basis of the comparison. You should think about not only the explicit meaning of the author's words but also the logical implications of those words.

How to Recognize Inference Questions

Inference questions will usually include the word *infer*, *suggest*, or *imply*.

- Which of the following can be inferred about X?
- The author of the passage implies that X . . .
- Which of the following can be inferred from paragraph 1 about X?

Tips for Inference Questions
- Make sure your answer does not contradict the main idea of the passage.
- Do not choose an answer just because it seems important or true. The correct answer must be inferable from the passage.
- You should be able to defend your choice by pointing to explicitly stated information in the passage that leads to the inference you have selected.

Example

PASSAGE EXCERPT: ". . . The nineteenth century brought with it a burst of new discoveries and inventions that revolutionized the candle industry and made lighting available to all. In the early-to-mid-nineteenth century, a process was developed to refine tallow (fat from animals) with alkali and sulfuric acid. The result was a product called stearin. Stearin is harder and burns longer than unrefined tallow. This breakthrough meant that it was possible to make tallow candles that would not produce the usual smoke and rancid odor. Stearins were also derived from palm oils, so vegetable waxes as well as animal fats could be used to make candles . . . "

Which of the following can be inferred from paragraph 1 about candles before the nineteenth century?

○ They did not smoke when they were burned.
○ They produced a pleasant odor as they burned.
○ They were not available to all.
○ They contained sulfuric acid.

Explanation

In the first sentence from the excerpt the author says that "new discoveries and inventions" made "lighting available to all." The only kind of lighting discussed in the passage is candles. If the new discoveries were important because they made candles available to all, we can infer that before the discoveries, candles were not available to everyone. Therefore choice 3 is an inference about candles we can make from the passage. Choices 1 and 2 can be eliminated because they explicitly contradict the passage ("the usual smoke" and "rancid odor"). Choice 4 can be eliminated because sulfuric acid was first used to make stearin in the nineteenth century, not before the nineteenth century.

Type 4: Rhetorical Purpose Questions

Rhetoric is the art of speaking or writing effectively. In Factual Information questions you are asked *what* information an author has presented. In Rhetorical Purpose questions you are asked *why* the author has presented a particular piece of information in a particular place or manner. Rhetorical Purpose questions ask you to show that you understand the rhetorical function of a statement or paragraph as it relates to the rest of the passage.

Sometimes you will be asked to identify how one paragraph relates to another. For instance, the second paragraph may give examples to support a statement in the first paragraph. The answer choices may be expressed in general terms (for example, "a theory is explained and then illustrated") or in terms that are specific to the passage. ("The author explains the categories of adaptation to deserts by mammals and then gives an example.")

A Rhetorical Purpose question may also ask why the author quotes a certain person or why the author mentions a particular piece of information (*Example:* Why does the author mention "the ability to grasp a pencil"? *Correct answer:* It is an example of a motor skill developed by children at 10 to 11 months of age.)

How to Recognize Rhetorical Purpose Questions

These are examples of the way Rhetorical Purpose questions are typically worded:

- The author discusses X in paragraph 2 in order to . . .
- Why does the author mention X?
- The author uses X as an example of . . .

Tips for Rhetorical Purpose Questions

- Know the definitions of these words or phrases, which are often used to describe different kinds of rhetorical purposes: "definition," "example," "to illustrate," "to explain," "to contrast," "to refute," "to note," "to criticize," "function of."
- Rhetorical Purpose questions usually do not ask about the overall organization of the reading passage. Instead, they typically focus on the logical links between sentences and paragraphs.

Example   **PASSAGE EXCERPT:** ". . . Sensitivity to physical laws is thus an important consideration for the maker of applied-art objects. It is often taken for granted that this is also true for the maker of fine-art objects. This assumption misses a significant difference between the two disciplines. Fine-art objects are not constrained by the laws of physics in the same way that applied-art objects are. Because their primary purpose is not functional, they are only limited in terms of the materials used to make them. Sculptures must, for example, be stable, which requires an understanding of the properties of mass, weight distribution, and stress. Paintings must have rigid stretchers so that the canvas will be taut, and the paint must not deteriorate, crack, or discolor. These are problems that must be overcome by the artist because they tend to intrude upon his or her conception of the work. For example, in the early Italian Renaissance, bronze statues of horses with a raised foreleg usually had a cannonball under that hoof. This was done because the cannonball was needed to support the weight of the leg . . . "

Why does the author discuss the "bronze statues of horses" created by artists in the early Italian Renaissance?

- ✗ To provide an example of a problem related to the laws of physics that a fine artist must overcome
- ○ To argue that fine artists are unconcerned with the laws of physics
- ○ To contrast the relative sophistication of modern artists in solving problems related to the laws of physics
- ○ To note an exceptional piece of art constructed without the aid of technology

Explanation

You should note that the sentence that first mentions "bronze statues of horses" begins "For example . . ." The author is giving an example of something he has introduced earlier in the paragraph. The paragraph overall contrasts how the constraints of physical laws affect the fine arts differently from applied arts or crafts. The fine artist is not concerned with making an object that is useful, so he or she is less constrained than the applied artist. However, because even a fine-arts object is made of some material, the artist must take into account the physical properties of the material. In the passage, the author uses the example of the bronze statues of horses to discuss how artists had to include some support for the raised foreleg of the horse because of the physical properties of the bronze. So the correct answer is choice 1.

Type 5: Vocabulary Questions

These questions ask you to identify the meanings of individual words and phrases as they are used in the reading passage (a word might have more than one meaning, but *in the reading passage,* only one of those meanings is relevant.) Vocabulary that is tested actually occurs in the passage; there is no "list of words" that must be tested. Usually a word or phrase is chosen to be tested as a vocabulary question because understanding that word or phrase is important to understanding a large or important part of the passage. On the TOEFL test, some words in the passage that are unusual, are technical, or have special meanings in the context of the topic are defined for you. If you click on the hyperlinked word in the passage, a definition will appear in a box. In this book, words of this type are defined at the end of the passage. Naturally, words that are tested as vocabulary questions are not defined for you.

How to Recognize Vocabulary Questions

Vocabulary questions are usually easy to identify. You will see one word or phrase highlighted in the passage. You are then asked a question like any of the following:

- The word "X" in the passage is closest in meaning to . . .
- The phrase "X" in the passage is closest in meaning to . . .
- In stating X, the author means that . . .

> **Tips for Vocabulary Questions**
> - Remember that the question is not just asking the meaning of a word; it is asking for the meaning *as it is used in the passage*. Do not choose an answer just because it can be a correct meaning of the word; understand which meaning the author is using in the passage.
> - Reread the sentence in the passage, substituting the word or phrase you have chosen. Confirm that the sentence still makes sense in the context of the whole passage.

Examples

PASSAGE EXCERPT: "In the animal world the task of moving about is fulfilled in many ways. For some animals locomotion is accomplished by changes in body shape . . ."

The word "locomotion" in the passage is closest in meaning to

○ evolution
○ movement
○ survival
○ escape

Explanation

Locomotion means "the ability to move from place to place." In this example, it is a way of restating the phrase "the task of moving" in the preceding sentence. So the correct answer is choice 2.

PASSAGE EXCERPT: "Some poisonous snake bites need to be treated immediately or the victim will suffer paralysis . . ."

In stating that the victim will "suffer paralysis" the author means that the victim will

○ lose the ability to move
○ become unconscious
○ undergo shock
○ feel great pain

Explanation

In this example, both the words tested from the passage and the possible answers are phrases. *Paralysis* means "the inability to move," so if the poison from a snake bite causes someone to "suffer paralysis," that person will "lose the ability to move." The correct answer is choice 1.

Type 6: Reference Questions

These questions ask you to identify referential relationships between the words in the passage. Often, the relationship is between a pronoun and its antecedent (the word to which the pronoun refers). Sometimes other kinds of grammatical reference are tested (like *which* or *this*).

How to Recognize Reference Questions

Reference questions look similar to vocabulary questions. In the passage, one word or phrase is highlighted. Usually the word is a pronoun. Then you are asked:

● The word "X" in the passage refers to . . .

The four answer choices will be words or phrases from the passage. The highlighted word or phrase refers to only one of the choices.

> ### Tips for Reference Questions
> ● If the Reference question is about a pronoun, make sure your answer is the same number (singular or plural) and case (first person, second person, third person) as the highlighted pronoun.
> ● Substitute your choice for the highlighted word or words in the sentence. Does it violate any grammar rules? Does it make sense?

Examples

PASSAGE EXCERPT: ". . . These laws are universal in their application, regardless of cultural beliefs, geography, or climate. If pots have no bottoms or have large openings in their sides, they could hardly be considered containers in any traditional sense. Since the laws of physics, not some arbitrary decision, have determined the general form of applied-art objects, they follow basic patterns, so much so that functional forms can vary only within certain limits . . . "

The word "they" in the passage refers to

- ⊗ applied-art objects
- ⊘ the laws of physics
- ○ containers
- ○ the sides of pots

Explanation

This is an example of a simple pronoun-referent question. The highlighted word *they* refers to the phrase "applied-art objects," which immediately precedes it, so choice 1 is the correct answer.

Often, the grammatical referent for a pronoun will be separated from the pronoun. It may be located in a preceding clause or even in the preceding sentence.

PASSAGE EXCERPT: ". . . The first weekly newspaper in the colonies was the Boston Gazette, established in 1719, the same year that marked the appearance of Philadelphia's first newspaper, the *American Mercury,* where the young Benjamin Franklin worked. By 1760 Boston had 4 newspapers and 5 other printing establishments; Philadelphia, 2 newspapers and 3 other presses; and New York, 3 newspapers. The distribution, if not the sale, of newspapers was assisted by the establishment of a postal service in 1710, which had a network of some 65 offices by 1770, serving all 13 colonies . . ."

The word "which" in the passage refers to

- ○ distribution
- ○ sale
- ○ newspaper
- ○ postal service

Explanation

In this example, the highlighted word is a relative pronoun, the grammatical subject of the relative clause "which had a network of some 65 offices . . ." The relative clause is describing the postal service, so choice 4 is the correct answer.

PASSAGE EXCERPT: ". . . Roots anchor the plant in one of two ways or sometimes by a combination of the two. The first is by occupying a large volume of shallow soil around the plant's base with a *fibrous root* system, one consisting of many thin, profusely branched roots. Since these kinds of roots grow relatively close to the soil surface, they effectively control soil erosion. Grass roots are especially well suited to this purpose. Fibrous roots capture water as it begins to percolate into the ground and so must draw their mineral supplies from the surface soil before the nutrients are leached to lower levels . . ."

The phrase "this purpose" in the passage refers to

- ○ combining two root systems
- ○ feeding the plant
- ○ preventing soil erosion
- ○ leaching nutrients

Explanation

In the example, the highlighted words are a phrase containing a demonstrative adjective (*this*) and a noun (*purpose*). Because a fibrous root system can keep soil in place, it can be used to stop erosion, and grass roots are a fibrous root system. The sentence could be reworded as "Grass roots are especially well suited to preventing soil erosion," so choice 3 is the correct answer.

Type 7: Sentence Simplification Questions

In this type of question you are asked to choose a sentence that has the same essential meaning as a sentence that occurs in the passage. Not every reading set includes a Sentence Simplification question. There is never more than one in a set.

How to Recognize Sentence Simplification Questions

Sentence Simplification questions always look the same. A single sentence in the passage is highlighted. You are then asked:

● Which of the following best expresses the essential information in the highlighted sentence? Incorrect answer choices change the meaning in important ways or leave out essential information.

Tips for Sentence Simplification Questions

● Make sure you understand both ways a choice can be incorrect:

○ It contradicts something in the highlighted sentence.
○ It leaves out something important from the highlighted sentence.

● Make sure your answer does not contradict the main argument of the paragraph in which the sentence occurs, or the passage as a whole.

Example   **PASSAGE EXCERPT:** ". . . Although we now tend to refer to the various crafts according to the materials used to construct them—clay, glass, wood, fiber, and metal—it was once common to think of crafts in terms of function, which led to their being known as the "applied arts." Approaching crafts from the point of view of function, we can divide them into simple categories: containers, shelters, and supports. There is no way around the fact that containers, shelters, and supports must be functional. The applied arts are thus bound by the laws of physics, which pertain to both the materials used in their making and the substances and things to be contained, supported, and sheltered. These laws are universal in their application, regardless of cultural beliefs, geography, or climate. If a pot has no bottom or has large openings in its sides, it could hardly be considered a container in any traditional sense. Since the laws of physics, not some arbitrary decision, have determined the general form of applied-art objects, they follow basic patterns, so much so that functional forms can vary only within certain limits. Buildings without roofs, for example, are unusual because they depart from the norm. However, not all functional objects are exactly alike; that is why we recognize a Shang Dynasty vase as being different from an Inca vase. What varies is not the basic form but the incidental details that do not obstruct the object's primary function . . ."

Which of the following best expresses the essential information in the highlighted sentence? Incorrect answer choices change the meaning in important ways or leave out essential information.

⊗ Functional applied-art objects cannot vary much from the basic patterns determined by the laws of physics.

○ The function of applied-art objects is determined by basic patterns in the laws of physics.

⊗ Since functional applied-art objects vary only within certain limits, arbitrary decisions cannot have determined their general form.

○ The general form of applied-art objects is limited by some arbitrary decision that is not determined by the laws of physics.

Explanation

It is important to note that the question says that *incorrect* answers change the original meaning of the sentence or leave out essential information. In this example, choice 4 changes the meaning of the sentence to its opposite; it says that the form of functional objects is arbitrary, when the highlighted sentence says that the forms of functional objects are *never* arbitrary. Choice 2 also changes the meaning. It says that the functions of applied-art objects are determined by physical laws. The highlighted sentence says that the *form of the object* is determined by physical laws but the function is determined by people. Choice 3 leaves out an important idea from the highlighted sentence. Like the highlighted sentence, it says that the form of functional objects is not arbitrary, but it does not say that it is physical laws that determine basic form. Only choice 1 makes the same point as the highlighted sentence and includes all the essential meaning.

Type 8: Insert Text Questions

In this type of question, you are given a new sentence and are asked where in the passage it would best fit. You need to understand the logic of the passage as well as the grammatical connections (like pronoun references) between sentences. Every set includes an Insert Text question. There is never more than one in a set.

How to Recognize Insert Text Questions

In the passage you will see four black squares. The squares are located at the beginnings or ends of sentences. Sometimes all four squares appear in one paragraph. Sometimes they are spread across the end of one paragraph and the beginning of another. You are then asked this question:

Look at the four squares [■] that indicate where the following sentence could be added to the passage.

> **[You will see a sentence in bold.]**

Where would the sentence best fit?

Your job is to click on one of the squares and insert the sentence in the text.

Tips for Insert Text Questions

- Try the sentence in each of the places indicated by the squares. You can place and replace the sentence as many times as you want.

- Look at the structure of the sentence you are inserting. Pay special attention to connecting words; they can provide important information about where the sentence should be placed.

- Frequently used connecting words:

On the other hand	Further, or Furthermore	Similarly
For example	Therefore	In contrast
On the contrary	In other words	Finally
As a result		

- Make sure that the inserted sentence connects logically to both the sentence before it and the sentence after it, and that any pronouns agree with the nouns they refer to.

Example

PASSAGE EXCERPT WITH EXAMPLE SQUARES: "Scholars offer three related but different opinions about this puzzle. ■ One opinion is that the paintings were a record of the seasonal migrations made by herds. ■ Because some paintings were made directly over others, obliterating them, it is probable that a painting's value ended with the migration it pictured. ■ Unfortunately, this explanation fails to explain the hidden locations, unless the migrations were celebrated with secret ceremonies. ■ "

Look at the four squares [■] that indicate where the following sentence could be added to the passage.

> **All three of them have strengths and weaknesses, but none adequately answers all of the questions the paintings present.**

Where would the sentence best fit?

○ Scholars offer three related but different opinions about this puzzle. **All three of them have strengths and weaknesses, but none adequately answers all of the questions the paintings present.** One opinion is that the paintings were a record of the seasonal migrations made by herds. ■ Because some paintings were made directly over others, obliterating them, it is probable that a painting's value ended with the migration it pictured. ■ Unfortunately, this explanation fails to explain the hidden locations, unless the migrations were celebrated with secret ceremonies. ■

○ Scholars offer three related but different opinions about this puzzle. ■ One opinion is that the paintings were a record of the seasonal migrations made by herds. **All three of them have strengths and weaknesses, but none adequately answers all of the questions the paintings present.** Because some paintings were made directly over others, obliterating them, it is probable that a painting's value ended with the migration it pictured. ■ Unfortunately, this explanation fails to explain the hidden locations, unless the migrations were celebrated with secret ceremonies. ■

○ Scholars offer three related but different opinions about this puzzle. ■ One opinion is that the paintings were a record of the seasonal migrations made by herds. ■ Because some paintings were made directly over others, obliterating them, it is probable that a painting's value ended with the migration it pictured. **All three of them have strengths and weaknesses, but none adequately answers all of the questions the paintings present.** Unfortunately, this explanation fails to explain the hidden locations, unless the migrations were celebrated with secret ceremonies. ■

○ Scholars offer three related but different opinions about this puzzle. ■ One opinion is that the paintings were a record of the seasonal migrations made by herds. ■ Because some paintings were made directly over others, obliterating them, it is probable that a painting's value ended with the migration it pictured. ■ Unfortunately, this explanation fails to explain the hidden locations, unless the migrations were celebrated with secret ceremonies. **All three of them have strengths and weaknesses, but none adequately answers all of the questions the paintings present.**

Explanation

In this example, choice 1 is the correct answer. The new sentence makes sense only if it occurs in the first position, after the first sentence. In that place, "All three of them" refers back to "three related but different opinions." The information in the sentence is a commentary on all three of the "opinions"; the opinions are related, but none is a complete explanation. Logically, this evaluation of all three opinions must come either as an introduction to the three opinions, or as a conclusion about all three. Only the introductory position is available, because the paragraph does not include all three opinions.

Reading to Learn Questions

There are two types of Reading to Learn questions: "Prose Summary" and "Fill in a Table." Reading to Learn questions require you to do more than the Basic Information questions. As you have seen, the Basic Information questions focus on your ability to understand or locate specific points in a passage at the sentence level. The Reading to Learn questions also involve:

- recognizing the organization and purpose of the passage
- organizing the information in the passage into a mental framework
- distinguishing major from minor ideas and essential from nonessential information
- understanding rhetorical functions such as cause-effect relationships, compare-contrast relationships, arguments, and the like

In other words, these questions require you to demonstrate an understanding of the passage as a whole, not just specific information within it.

Reading to Learn questions require you to show that you are able not only to comprehend individual points, but also to place the major ideas and supporting information from the passage into an organizational framework or structure such as a prose summary or a table. By answering correctly, you will demonstrate that you can recognize the major points of a text, how and why the text has been organized, and the nature of the relationships within the text. Having an organized mental representation of a text is critical to learning because it allows you to remember important information from the text and apply it in new situations. If you have such a mental framework, you should be able to reconstruct the major ideas and supporting information from the text. By doing so, you will demonstrate a global understanding of the text as a whole. On the TOEFL test, each reading passage will have one Reading to Learn question. It will be either a Prose Summary or a Fill in a Table question, never both.

Type 9: Prose Summary Questions

These questions measure your ability to understand and recognize the major ideas and the relative importance of information in a passage. You will be asked to select the major ideas in the passage by distinguishing them from minor ideas or ideas that are not in the passage. The correct answer choice will synthesize major ideas in the passage. Because the correct answer represents a synthesis of ideas, it will not match any particular sentence from the passage. To select the correct answer, you will need to create a mental framework to organize and remember major ideas and other important information. Understanding the relative importance of information in a passage is critical to this ability.

In a Prose Summary question, you will be given six answer choices and asked to pick the three that express the most important ideas in the passage. Unlike the Basic Information questions, each of which is worth just 1 point, a Prose Summary question is worth 2 points. You can earn 0 to 2 points depending on how many correct answers you choose. If you choose no correct answers or just one correct answer, you will earn no points. If you choose two correct answers, you will earn 1 point. If you choose all three correct answers, you will earn 2 points. The order in which you choose your answers does not matter for scoring purposes.

Example

Because the Prose Summary question asks you to show an understanding of the different parts of the passage, it is necessary to read the entire passage. Parts of the following passage have already been used to illustrate other question types.

APPLIED ARTS AND FINE ARTS

Although we now tend to refer to the various crafts according to the materials used to construct them—clay, glass, wood, fiber, and metal—it was once common to think of crafts in terms of function, which led to their being known as the "applied arts." Approaching crafts from the point of view of function, we can divide them into simple categories: containers, shelters, and supports. There is no way around the fact that containers, shelters, and supports must be functional. The applied arts are thus bound by the laws of physics, which pertain to both the materials used in their making and the substances and things to be contained, supported, and sheltered. These laws are universal in their application, regardless of cultural beliefs, geography, or climate. If a pot has no bottom or has large openings in its sides, it could hardly be considered a container in any traditional sense. Since the laws of physics, not some arbitrary decision, have determined the general form of applied-art objects, they follow basic patterns, so much so that functional forms can vary only within certain limits. Buildings without roofs, for example, are unusual because they depart from the norm. *standard* However, not all functional objects are exactly alike; that is why we recognize a Shang Dynasty vase as being different from an Inca vase. What varies is not the basic form but the incidental details that do not obstruct the object's primary function.

Sensitivity to physical laws is thus an important consideration for the maker of applied-art objects. It is often taken for granted that this is also true for the maker of fine-art objects. This assumption misses a significant difference between the two disciplines. Fine-art objects are not constrained by the laws of physics in the same way that applied-art objects are. Because their primary purpose is not functional, they are only limited in terms of the materials used to make them. Sculptures must, for example, be stable, which requires an understanding of the properties of mass, weight distribution, and stress. Paintings must have rigid stretchers so that the canvas will be taut, and the paint must not deteriorate, crack, or discolor. These are problems that must be overcome by the artist because they tend to intrude upon his or her conception of the work. For example, in the early Italian Renaissance, bronze statues of horses with a raised foreleg usually had a cannonball under that hoof. This was done because the cannonball was needed to support the weight of the leg. In other words, the demands of the laws of physics, not the sculptor's aesthetic intentions, placed the ball there. That this device was a necessary structural compromise is clear from the fact that the cannonball quickly disappeared when sculptors learned how to strengthen the internal structure of a statue with iron braces (iron being much stronger than bronze).

Even though the fine arts in the twentieth century often treat materials in new ways, the basic difference in attitude of artists in relation to their materials in the fine arts and the applied arts remains relatively constant. It would therefore not be too great an exaggeration to say that practitioners of the fine arts work to overcome the limitations of their materials, whereas those engaged in the applied arts work in concert with their materials.

An introductory sentence for a brief summary of the passage is provided below. Complete the summary by selecting the THREE answer choices that express the most important ideas in the passage. Some sentences do not belong in the summary because they express ideas that are not presented in the passage or are minor ideas in the passage. **This question is worth 2 points.**

> **This passage discusses fundamental differences between applied-art objects and fine-art objects.**

-
-
-

Answer Choices

1. Applied-art objects fulfill functions, such as containing or sheltering, and objects with the same function have similar characteristics because they are constrained by their purpose.

2. It is easy to recognize that Shang Dynasty vases are different from Inca vases.

3. Fine-art objects are not functional, so they are limited only by the properties of the materials used.

4. Renaissance sculptors learned to use iron braces to strengthen the internal structures of bronze statues.

5. In the twentieth century, fine artists and applied artists became more similar to one another in their attitudes toward their materials.

6. In all periods, fine artists tend to challenge the physical limitations of their materials while applied artists tend to cooperate with the physical properties of their materials.

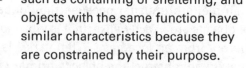
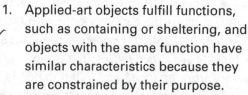

Explanation

Correct Choices

Choice 1: Applied-art objects fulfill functions, such as containing or sheltering, and objects with the same function have similar characteristics because they are constrained by their purpose.

Explanation: As the introductory sentence states, the passage is mainly a contrast of applied-art objects and fine-art objects. The main point of contrast is functionality: applied-art objects are functional, whereas fine-art objects are not. The first part of the passage explains the consequences of functionality for the materials and "basic forms" of applied-art objects. The second part of the passage explains the consequences of not being functional to the materials and forms of fine-art objects. A good summary of the passage must include the definition of "applied-art objects" and the major consequence (objects with the same function will follow similar patterns), so Choice 1 should be included.

Choice 3: Fine-art objects are not functional, so they are limited only by the properties of the materials used.

Explanation: Because the passage contrasts applied-art objects and fine-art objects, a good summary should include the basic difference. Including Choice 3 in the summary provides the basic contrast discussed in the passage: applied art objects are functional; fine-art objects are not. Fine-art objects are not as constrained as applied-art objects because they do not have to perform a function.

Choice 6: In all periods, fine artists tend to challenge the physical limitations of their materials, while applied artists tend to cooperate with the physical properties of their materials.

Explanation: The last paragraph of the passage presents a further consequence of the basic contrast between applied-art objects and fine-art objects. This is the difference between the attitude of fine artists toward their materials and the attitude of applied artists toward their materials. A good summary will include this last contrast.

Incorrect Choices

Choice 2: It is easy to recognize that Shang Dynasty vases are different from Inca vases.

Explanation: Although this statement is true, it is not the main point of the first paragraph or of the passage. In fact, it contrasts with the main point of the paragraph: objects that have the same function are all similar. The last sentence of the first paragraph says that the Shang Dynasty vase and the Inca vase are different in "incidental details," but the "basic form" is the same. Including Choice 2 in the summary misrepresents the passage.

Choice 4: Renaissance sculptors learned to use iron braces to strengthen the internal structures of bronze statues.

Explanation: Choice 4 summarizes the information in sentences 9, 10, and 11 of paragraph 2. Within the context of the passage, this information helps you understand the meaning of the limitations that materials can impose on fine artists. However, remember that the directions say to choose the statements that express *the most important ideas in the passage*. The example is less important than the general statements of difference. If Choice 4 is included, then Choice 1 or 3 or 6 would be left out and the summary would be missing an essential point of contrast between fine arts and applied arts.

Choice 5: In the twentieth century, fine artists and applied artists became more similar to one another in their attitudes toward their materials.

Explanation: This choice should be excluded because it is not supported by the passage. It is a misreading of paragraph 3, which says that the difference in attitude between fine artists and applied artists has not changed. Obviously, a choice that contradicts the information or argument in the passage should not be part of your summary.

Type 10: Fill in a Table Questions

In this kind of question, you will be given a partially completed table based on information in the passage. Your job is to complete the table by clicking on correct answer choices and dragging them to their correct locations in the table.

Fill in a Table questions measure your ability to conceptualize and organize major ideas and other important information from across the passage and then to place them in appropriate categories. This means that you must first recognize and identify the major points from the passage, and then place those points in their proper context.

Just as for Prose Summary questions, the able reader will create a mental framework to organize and remember major ideas and other important information.

Doing so requires the ability to understand rhetorical functions such as cause-effect relationships, compare-contrast relationships, arguments, and the like.

When building your mental framework, keep in mind that the major ideas in the passage are the ones you would include if you were making a fairly high-level outline of the passage. The correct answer choices are usually ideas that would be included in a slightly more detailed outline. Minor details and examples are generally not included in such an outline because they are used only to support the more important, higher-level themes. The distinction between major ideas/important information and less important information can also be thought of as a distinction between essential and nonessential information.

Passages used with Fill in a Table questions have more than one focus of development in that they include more than one point of view or perspective. Typical passages have the following types of organization: compare/contrast, problem/solution, cause/effect, alternative arguments (such as theories, hypotheses), and the like.

Correct answers represent major ideas and important supporting information in the passage. Generally these answers will not match specific phrases in the passage. They are more likely to be abstract concepts based on passage information or paraphrases of passage information. Correct answers will be easy to confirm by able readers who can remember or easily locate relevant text information.

Incorrect answers may include information about the topic that is not mentioned in the passage or that is not directly relevant to the classification categories in the table. They may also be obviously incorrect generalizations or conclusions based on what is stated in the passage. Be aware that incorrect answers may include words and phrases that match or resemble words or phrases in the passage.

Table Rules

Tables can have two or three columns/rows containing bullets representing five correct answer choices.

There will always be more answer choices than there are correct answers. Some answer choices will not be used.

An answer choice can be used only once in the table. If an answer choice applies to more than one answer category, or to no category in a table, a row or column labeled "both" or "neither" will be available in the table for placement of that answer choice.

Scoring

To earn points, you must not only select correct answer choices, but also organize them correctly in the table. You may receive partial credit, depending on how many correct answers you choose.

You can earn up to a total of 3 points, depending on how many correct answers you select and correctly place. For zero, one, or two correct answers you will receive no points. For three correct answers you will receive 1 point; for four correct answers you will receive 2 points; and for all five correct answers you will receive the entire 3 points.

Example

Note: The passage used for this example is the same one that was used above for the Prose Summary example question. In an actual test, you will not receive both a Prose Summary question and a Fill in a Table question about the same passage.

Directions: Complete the table below to summarize information about the two types of art discussed in the passage. Match the appropriate statements to the types of art with which they are associated. **This question is worth 3 points.**

TYPES OF ART	STATEMENTS
The Applied Arts	**Select 3** ● ● ●
The Fine Arts	**Select 2** ● ●

Statements

An object's purpose is primarily aesthetic.

Objects serve a functional purpose.

The incidental details of objects do not vary.

Artists work to overcome the limitations of their materials.

The basic form of objects varies little across cultures.

Artists work in concert with their materials.

An object's place of origin is difficult to determine.

Drag your answer choices to the spaces where they belong. (This question type fills the computer screen. To see the passage, click on **View Text**.)

Correctly Completed Table

Directions: Complete the table below to summarize information about the two types of art discussed in the passage. Match the appropriate statements to the types of art with which they are associated. **This question is worth 3 points.**

TYPES OF ART	STATEMENTS
The Applied Arts	**Select 3** ● Objects serve a functional purpose. ● The basic form of objects varies little across cultures. ● Artists work in concert with their materials.
The Fine Arts	**Select 2** ● An object's purpose is primarily aesthetic. ● Artists work to overcome the limitations of their materials.

Explanation

Correct Choices

Choice 1: An object's purpose is primarily aesthetic. (Fine Arts)

Explanation: This is an example of a correct answer that requires you to identify an abstract concept based on text information and paraphrases of text information. In paragraph 2, sentence 5, the passage states that the primary purpose of Fine Arts is not function. Then, in paragraph 2, sentence 11, the passage mentions a situation in which a sculptor had to sacrifice an aesthetic purpose due to the laws of physics. Putting these statements together, the reader can infer that fine artists, such as sculptors, are primarily concerned with aesthetics.

Choice 2: Objects serve a functional purpose. (Applied Arts)

Explanation: This is stated more directly than the previous correct answer. In paragraph 1, sentences 1, 2, and 3 make it clear how important function is in the applied arts. At the same time, paragraph 2 states that Fine Arts are not concerned with function, so the only correct place for this statement is in the Applied Arts category.

Choice 4: Artists work to overcome the limitations of their materials. (Fine Arts)

Explanation: This is stated explicitly in the last paragraph of the passage. In that paragraph, it is made clear that this applies only to practitioners of the fine arts.

Choice 5: The basic form of objects varies little across cultures. (Applied Arts)

Explanation: In paragraph 1, sentence 5, the passage states that certain laws of physics are universal. Then in sentence 7, that idea is further developed with the statement that functional forms can vary only within limits. From these two sentences, you can conclude that because of the laws of physics and the need for functionality, the basic forms of applied-art objects will vary little across cultures.

Choice 6: Artists work in concert with their materials. (Applied Arts)

Explanation: This is stated explicitly in the last paragraph of the passage. In that paragraph, it is made clear that this applies only to practitioners of the applied arts.

Incorrect Choices

Choice 3: The incidental details of objects do not vary.

Explanation: This idea is explicitly refuted by the last sentence of paragraph 1 in reference to the applied arts. That sentence (referring only to applied arts) states that the incidental details of such objects do vary, so this answer cannot be placed in the Applied Arts category. This subject is not discussed at all in reference to fine-art objects, so it cannot be correctly placed in that category either.

Choice 7: An object's place of origin is difficult to determine.

Explanation: This answer choice is implicitly refuted in reference to applied arts in the next-to-last sentence of paragraph 1. That sentence notes that both Shang Dynasty and Inca vases are identifiable as such based upon differences in detail. By inference, then, it seems that it is not difficult to determine an applied-art object's place of origin. Like the previous incorrect answer, this idea is not discussed at all in reference to fine-art objects, so it cannot be correctly placed in that category either.

Strategies for Preparing for the Reading Section

Now that you are familiar with the 10 question types that are used in the TOEFL Reading section, you are ready to sharpen your skills by working on whole reading sets. In the following pages, you can practice on six reading sets created by ETS for the TOEFL iBT test. The question types are not labeled, but you should be able to identify them and understand what you need to do to answer each correctly. After each passage and question set you will find answers and explanations for each question.

In addition to practicing on these sets, here are some other suggestions for improving the skills that will help you perform well on the Reading section:

The best way to improve reading skills is to read frequently and to read many different types of texts in various subject areas (sciences, social sciences, arts, business, and others). The Internet is one of the best resources for this, and of course books, magazines, and journals are very helpful as well. Make sure to regularly read texts that are academic in style, the kind that are used in university courses.

Here are some suggestions for ways to build skills for the three reading purposes covered by the TOEFL iBT test.

1. Reading to find information

- Scan passages to find and highlight key facts (dates, numbers, terms) and information.
- Practice this frequently to increase reading rate and fluency.

2. Reading for basic comprehension

- Increase your vocabulary knowledge, perhaps by using flashcards.
- Rather than carefully reading each word and each sentence, practice skimming a passage quickly to get a general impression of the main idea.
- Build up your ability to skim quickly and to identify the major points.
- After skimming a passage, read it again more carefully and write down the main idea, major points, and important facts.
- Choose some unfamiliar words in a passage and guess the meaning from the context (surrounding sentences).
- Select all the pronouns (*he, him, they, them*, and others) and identify which nouns they refer to in a passage.
- Practice making inferences and drawing conclusions based on what is implied in the passage as a whole.

3. Reading to learn

- Identify the passage type (classification, cause/effect, compare/contrast, problem/solution, description, narration, and so on).
- Do the following to organize the information in the passage:
  - ○ Create an outline of the passage to distinguish between major and minor points.
  - ○ If the passage categorizes information, create a chart and place the information in appropriate categories. (Remember: on the test, you do not have to create such a chart. Instead, a chart with possible answer choices is provided for you, and you must fill in the chart with the correct choices.) Practicing this skill will help you think about categorizing information and be able to do so with ease.
  - ○ If the passage describes the steps in a process, create an outline of the steps in their correct order.
- Create a summary of the passage using the charts and outlines.
- Paraphrase individual sentences in a passage, and then progress to paraphrasing an entire paragraph. Note: the TOEFL iBT Reading section measures the ability to recognize paraphrases. The ability to paraphrase is also important for the integrated tasks in the Writing and Speaking sections of the test.

Reading Practice Sets

PRACTICE SET 1

THE ORIGINS OF CETACEANS

It should be obvious that cetaceans—whales, porpoises, and dolphins—are mammals. They breathe through lungs, not through gills, and give birth to live young. Their streamlined bodies, the absence of hind legs, and the presence of a fluke[1] and blowhole[2] cannot disguise their affinities with land-dwelling mammals. However, unlike the cases of sea otters and pinnipeds (seals, sea lions, and walruses, whose limbs are functional both on land and at sea), it is not easy to envision what the first whales looked like. Extinct but already fully marine cetaceans are known from the fossil record. How was the gap between a walking mammal and a swimming whale bridged? Missing until recently were fossils clearly intermediate, or transitional, between land mammals and cetaceans.

Very exciting discoveries have finally allowed scientists to reconstruct the most likely origins of cetaceans. In 1979, a team looking for fossils in northern Pakistan found what proved to be the oldest fossil whale. The fossil was officially named *Pakicetus* in honor of the country where the discovery was made. *Pakicetus* was found embedded in rocks formed from river deposits that were 52 million years old. The river that formed these deposits was actually not far from an ancient ocean known as the Tethys Sea.

The fossil consists of a complete skull of an archaeocyte, an extinct group of ancestors of modern cetaceans. Although limited to a skull, the *Pakicetus* fossil provides precious details on the origins of cetaceans. The skull is cetacean-like but its jawbones lack the enlarged space that is filled with fat or oil and used for receiving underwater sound in modern whales. *Pakicetus* probably detected sound through the ear opening as in land mammals. The skull also lacks a blowhole, another cetacean adaptation for diving. Other features, however, show experts that *Pakicetus* is a transitional form between a group of extinct flesh-eating mammals, the mesonychids, and cetaceans. It has been suggested that *Pakicetus* fed on fish in shallow water and was not yet adapted for life in the open ocean. It probably bred and gave birth on land.

Another major discovery was made in Egypt in 1989. Several skeletons of another early whale, *Basilosaurus*, were found in sediments left by the Tethys Sea and now exposed in the Sahara desert. This whale lived around 40 million years ago, 12 million years after *Pakicetus*. Many incomplete skeletons were found but they included, for the first time in an archaeocyte, a complete hind leg that features a foot with three tiny toes. Such legs would have been far too small to have supported the 50-foot-long *Basilosaurus* on land. *Basilosaurus* was undoubtedly a fully marine whale with possibly nonfunctional, or vestigial, hind legs.

An even more exciting find was reported in 1994, also from Pakistan. The now extinct whale *Ambulocetus natans* ("the walking whale that swam") lived in the Tethys Sea 49 million years ago. It lived around 3 million years after *Pakicetus* but 9 million years before *Basilosaurus*. The fossil luckily includes a good portion of the hind legs. The legs were strong and ended in long feet very much like those of a modern pinniped. The legs were certainly functional both on land and at sea. The whale retained a tail and lacked a fluke, the major means of locomotion in modern cetaceans. The structure of the backbone shows, however, that *Ambulocetus* swam like modern whales by moving the rear portion of its body up and down, even though a fluke was missing. The large hind legs were used for propulsion in water. On land, where it probably bred and gave birth, *Ambulocetus* may have moved around very much like a modern sea lion. It was undoubtedly a whale that linked life on land with life at sea.

1. Fluke: The two parts that constitute the large triangular tail of a whale
2. Blowhole: A hole in the top of the head used for breathing

PARAGRAPH 1

It should be obvious that cetaceans—whales, porpoises, and dolphins—are mammals. They breathe through lungs, not through gills, and give birth to live young. Their streamlined bodies, the absence of hind legs, and the presence of a fluke[1] and blowhole[2] cannot disguise their affinities with land-dwelling mammals. However, unlike the cases of sea otters and pinnipeds (seals, sea lions, and walruses, whose limbs are functional both on land and at sea), it is not easy to envision what the first whales looked like. Extinct but already fully marine cetaceans are known from the fossil record. How was the gap between a walking mammal and a swimming whale bridged? Missing until recently were fossils clearly intermediate, or transitional, between land mammals and cetaceans.

1. Fluke: The two parts that constitute the large triangular tail of a whale
2. Blowhole: A hole in the top of the head used for breathing

Directions: Mark your answer by filling in the oval next to your choice.

factual Q

1. In paragraph 1, what does the author say about the presence of a blowhole in cetaceans?

   ○ It clearly indicates that cetaceans are mammals.

   ⊗ It cannot conceal the fact that cetaceans are mammals.

   ⊘ It is the main difference between cetaceans and land-dwelling mammals.

   ○ It cannot yield clues about the origins of cetaceans.

inference Q

2. Which of the following can be inferred from paragraph 1 about early sea otters?

   ⊗ It is not difficult to imagine what they looked like.

   ○ There were great numbers of them.

   ○ They lived in the sea only.

   ⊘ They did not leave many fossil remains.

The fossil consists of a complete skull of an archaeocyte, an extinct group of ancestors of modern cetaceans. Although limited to a skull, the *Pakicetus* fossil provides precious details on the origins of cetaceans. The skull is cetacean-like but its jawbones lack the enlarged space that is filled with fat or oil and used for receiving underwater sound in modern whales. *Pakicetus* probably detected sound through the ear opening as in land mammals. The skull also lacks a blowhole, another cetacean adaptation for diving. Other features, however, show experts that *Pakicetus* is a transitional form between a group of extinct flesh-eating mammals, the mesonychids, and cetaceans. It has been suggested that *Pakicetus* fed on fish in shallow water and was not yet adapted for life in the open ocean. It probably bred and gave birth on land.

3. The word "precious" in the passage is closest in meaning to

   ○ exact
   ○ scarce
   ○ valuable
   ○ initial

4. *Pakicetus* and modern cetaceans have similar

   ○ hearing structures
   ○ adaptations for diving
   ○ skull shapes
   ○ breeding locations

5. The word "It" in the passage refers to

   ○ *Pakicetus*
   ○ fish
   ○ life
   ○ ocean

Another major discovery was made in Egypt in 1989. Several skeletons of another early whale, *Basilosaurus*, were found in sediments left by the Tethys Sea and now exposed in the Sahara desert. This whale lived around 40 million years ago, 12 million years after *Pakicetus*. Many incomplete skeletons were found but they included, for the first time in an archaeocyte, a complete hind leg that features a foot with three tiny toes. Such legs would have been far too small to have supported the 50-foot-long *Basilosaurus* on land. *Basilosaurus* was undoubtedly a fully marine whale with possibly nonfunctional, or vestigial, hind legs.

6. The word "exposed" in the passage is closest in meaning to

   ○ explained
   ○ visible
   ○ identified
   ○ located

7. The hind leg of *Basilosaurus* was a significant find because it showed that *Basilosaurus*

   ○ lived later than *Ambulocetus natans*
   ○ lived at the same time as *Pakicetus*
   ○ was able to swim well
   ○ could not have walked on land

8. It can be inferred that *Basilosaurus* bred and gave birth in which of the following locations?

   ○ On land
   ○ Both on land and at sea
   ○ In shallow water
   ○ In a marine environment

PARAGRAPH 5

An even more exciting find was reported in 1994, also from Pakistan. The now extinct whale *Ambulocetus natans* ("the walking whale that swam") lived in the Tethys Sea 49 million years ago. It lived around 3 million years after *Pakicetus* but 9 million years before *Basilosaurus*. The fossil luckily includes a good portion of the hind legs. The legs were strong and ended in long feet very much like those of a modern pinniped. The legs were certainly functional both on land and at sea. The whale retained a tail and lacked a fluke, the major means of locomotion in modern cetaceans. The structure of the backbone shows, however, that *Ambulocetus* swam like modern whales by moving the rear portion of its body up and down, even though a fluke was missing. The large hind legs were used for propulsion in water. On land, where it probably bred and gave birth, *Ambulocetus* may have moved around very much like a modern sea lion. It was undoubtedly a whale that linked life on land with life at sea.

9. Why does the author use the word "luckily" in mentioning that the *Ambulocetus natans* fossil included hind legs?

- ⊘ Fossil legs of early whales are a rare find.
- ⊘ The legs provided important information about the evolution of cetaceans.
- ○ The discovery allowed scientists to reconstruct a complete skeleton of the whale.
- ○ Until that time, only the front legs of early whales had been discovered.

10. Which of the sentences below best expresses the essential information in the highlighted sentence in the passage? Incorrect choices change the meaning in important ways or leave out essential information.

- ○ Even though *Ambulocetus* swam by moving its body up and down, it did not have a backbone.
- ○ The backbone of *Ambulocetus*, which allowed it to swim, provides evidence of its missing fluke.
- ⊘ Although *Ambulocetus* had no fluke, its backbone structure shows that it swam like modern whales. ✔
- ○ By moving the rear parts of their bodies up and down, modern whales swim in a different way from the way *Ambulocetus* swam.

11. The word "propulsion" in the passage is closest in meaning to

- ⊘ staying afloat
- ⊘ changing direction
- ○ decreasing weight
- ⊘ moving forward

Extinct but already fully marine cetaceans are known from the fossil record. ■ How was the gap between a walking mammal and a swimming whale bridged? ■ Missing until recently were fossils clearly intermediate, or transitional, between land mammals and cetaceans.

■ Very exciting discoveries have finally allowed scientists to reconstruct the most likely origins of cetaceans. ■ In 1979, a team looking for fossils in northern Pakistan found what proved to be the oldest fossil whale.

12. Look at the four squares [■] that indicate where the following sentence can be added to the passage.

This is a question that has puzzled scientists for ages.

Where would the sentence best fit?

○ Extinct but already fully marine cetaceans are known from the fossil record. **This is a question that has puzzled scientists for ages.** How was the gap between a walking mammal and a swimming whale bridged? ■ Missing until recently were fossils clearly intermediate, or transitional, between land mammals and cetaceans.

■ Very exciting discoveries have finally allowed scientists to reconstruct the most likely origins of cetaceans. ■ In 1979, a team looking for fossils in northern Pakistan found what proved to be the oldest fossil whale.

Extinct but already fully marine cetaceans are known from the fossil record. ■ How was the gap between a walking mammal and a swimming whale bridged? **This is a question that has puzzled scientists for ages.** Missing until recently were fossils clearly intermediate, or transitional, between land mammals and cetaceans.

■ Very exciting discoveries have finally allowed scientists to reconstruct the most likely origins of cetaceans. ■ In 1979, a team looking for fossils in northern Pakistan found what proved to be the oldest fossil whale.

Extinct but already fully marine cetaceans are known from the fossil record. ■ How was the gap between a walking mammal and a swimming whale bridged? ■ Missing until recently were fossils clearly intermediate, or transitional, between land mammals and cetaceans.

This is a question that has puzzled scientists for ages. Very exciting discoveries have finally allowed scientists to reconstruct the most likely origins of cetaceans. ■ In 1979, a team looking for fossils in northern Pakistan found what proved to be the oldest fossil whale.

○ Extinct but already fully marine cetaceans are known from the fossil record. ■ How was the gap between a walking mammal and a swimming whale bridged? ■ Missing until recently were fossils clearly intermediate, or transitional, between land mammals and cetaceans.

■ Very exciting discoveries have finally allowed scientists to reconstruct the most likely origins of cetaceans. **This is a question that has puzzled scientists for ages.** In 1979, a team looking for fossils in northern Pakistan found what proved to be the oldest fossil whale.

13. **Directions:** An introductory sentence for a brief summary of the passage is provided below. Complete the summary by selecting the THREE answer choices that express the most important ideas in the passage. Some answer choices do not belong in the summary because they express ideas that are not presented in the passage or are minor ideas in the passage. **This question is worth 2 points.**

This passage discusses fossils that help to explain the likely origins of cetaceans—whales, porpoises, and dolphins.

-
-
-

Answer Choices

1. Recent discoveries of fossils have helped to show the link between land mammals and cetaceans.

2. The discovery of *Ambulocetus natans* provided evidence for a whale that lived both on land and at sea.

3. The skeleton of *Basilosaurus* was found in what had been the Tethys Sea, an area rich in fossil evidence.

4. *Pakicetus* is the oldest fossil whale yet to be found.

5. Fossils thought to be transitional forms between walking mammals and swimming whales were found.

6. *Ambulocetus*'s hind legs were used for propulsion in the water.

PRACTICE SET 1 ANSWERS AND EXPLANATIONS

1. ❷ This is a Factual Information question asking for specific information that can be found in paragraph 1. Choice 2 is the correct answer. It is essentially a rephrasing of the statement in paragraph 1 that blowholes cannot disguise cetaceans' affinities with other mammals. The other three choices are refuted, either directly or indirectly, by that paragraph.

2. ❶ This is an Inference question asking for information that can be inferred from paragraph 1. Choice 1 is the correct answer because paragraph 1 says that sea otters are unlike early mammals whose appearances are *not* easy to imagine. By inference, then, the early appearance of sea otters must be easy (or not difficult) to imagine.

3. ❸ This is a Vocabulary question. The word being tested is *precious*. It is highlighted in the passage. The correct answer is choice 3, "valuable." Anything that is precious is very important and therefore valuable.

4. ❸ This is a Factual Information question asking for specific information that can be found in the passage. Choice 3 is the correct answer. Paragraph 3 describes the differences and similarities between *Pakicetus* and modern ceta-

ceans. Sentence 3 of that paragraph states that their skulls are similar. The other three choices describe differences, not similarities.

5. ❶ This is a Reference question. The word being tested is *It*. That word is highlighted in the passage. This is a simple pronoun-referent item. Choice 1, "*Pakicetus*," is the correct answer. The word *It* here refers to a creature that probably bred and gave birth on land. *Pakicetus* is the only one of the choices to which this could apply.

6. ❷ This is a Vocabulary question. The word being tested is *exposed*. It is highlighted in the passage. The correct answer is choice 2, "visible." *Exposed* means "uncovered." A skeleton that is uncovered can be seen. *Visible* means "can be seen."

7. ❹ This is a Factual Information question asking for specific information that can be found in the passage. Choice 4 is the correct answer because it is the only detail about the skeleton of *Basilosaurus* mentioned in paragraph 4, meaning that it is significant. Choice 1 is true, but it is not discussed in the detail that choice 4 is, and does not represent the significance of the discovery. Choice 3 is not mentioned, and choice 2 is not true.

8. ❹ This is an Inference question asking for a conclusion that can be drawn from the entire passage. Choice 4 is the correct answer based on the last sentence of paragraph 4, which describes *Basilosaurus* as a fully marine whale. That implies that everything it did, including breeding and giving birth, could have been done only in a marine environment.

9. ❷ This is an Inference question asking for a conclusion that can be drawn from the passage. Paragraph 5 explains that this discovery provided important information to scientists that they might not have been able to obtain without it. Therefore you can infer that the discovery was a "lucky" one. The passage offers no support for the other choices. Therefore choice 2 is the correct answer.

10. ❸ This is a Sentence Simplification question. As with all of these questions, a single sentence in the passage is highlighted:

> The structure of the backbone shows, however, that *Ambulocetus* swam like modern whales by moving the rear portion of its body up and down, even though a fluke was missing.

Choice 3 is the correct answer because it contains all of the essential information in the highlighted sentence. Choice 1 is not true because *Ambulocetus* did have a backbone. Choice 2 is not true because the sentence says that the backbone showed how the *Ambulocetus* swam, not that it was missing a fluke. Choice 4 is untrue because the sentence states that *Ambulocetus* and modern whales swam in the same way.

11. ❹ This is a Vocabulary question. The word being tested is *propulsion*. It is highlighted in the passage. Choice 4, "moving forward," is the correct answer because it means "the action of propelling." The whale in the sentence used its hind legs to push itself forward in the water.

12. ❷ This is an Insert Text question. You can see the four black squares in paragraphs 1 and 2 that represent the possible answer choices here.

Extinct but already fully marine cetaceans are known from the fossil record. ■ How was the gap between a walking mammal and a swimming whale bridged? ■ Missing until recently were fossils clearly intermediate, or transitional, between land mammals and cetaceans. ■ Very exciting discoveries have finally allowed scientists to reconstruct the most likely origins of cetaceans. ■ In 1979, a team looking for fossils in northern Pakistan found what proved to be the oldest fossil whale.

The sentence provided is "This is a question that has puzzled scientists for ages." The correct place to insert it is at square 2.

The sentence that precedes square 2 is in the form of a rhetorical question, and the inserted sentence explicitly provides a response to it. None of the other sentences preceding squares is a question, so the inserted sentence cannot logically follow any one of them.

13. ❶ ❷ ❺ This is a Prose Summary question. It is completed correctly below. The correct choices are 1, 2, and 5. Choices 3, 4, and 6 are therefore incorrect.

Directions: An introductory sentence for a brief summary of the passage is provided below. Complete the summary by selecting the THREE answer choices that express the most important ideas in the passage. Some answer choices do not belong in the summary because they express ideas that are not presented in the passage or are minor ideas in the passage. **This question is worth 2 points.**

This passage discusses fossils that help to explain the likely origins of cetaceans—whales, porpoises, and dolphins.

- Recent discoveries of fossils have helped to show the link between land mammals and cetaceans.
- The discovery of *Ambulocetus natans* provided evidence for a whale that lived both on land and at sea.
- Fossils thought to be transitional forms between walking mammals and swimming whales were found.

Answer Choices

1. Recent discoveries of fossils have helped to show the link between land mammals and cetaceans.

2. The discovery of *Ambulocetus natans* provided evidence for a whale that lived both on land and at sea.

3. The skeleton of *Basilosaurus* was found in what had been the Tethys Sea, an area rich in fossil evidence.

4. *Pakicetus* is the oldest fossil whale yet to be found.

5. Fossils thought to be transitional forms between walking mammals and swimming whales were found.

6. *Ambulocetus*'s hind legs were used for propulsion in the water.

Correct Choices

Choice 1, "Recent discoveries of fossils have helped to show the link between land mammals and cetaceans," is correct because it represents the major idea of the entire passage. The bulk of the passage consists of a discussion of the major discoveries (*Pakicetus*, *Basilosaurus*, and *Ambulocetus*) that show this link.

Choice 2, "The discovery of *Ambulocetus natans* provided evidence for a whale that lived both on land and at sea," is correct because it is one of the major discoveries cited in the passage in support of the passage's main point, that land mammals and cetaceans are related.

Choice 5, "Fossils thought to be transitional forms between walking mammals and swimming whales were found," is correct because like choice 1, this is a statement of the passage's major theme as stated in paragraph 1: these fossils were "clearly intermediate, or transitional, between land mammals and cetaceans." The remainder of the passage discusses these discoveries.

Incorrect Choices

Choice 3, "The skeleton of *Basilosaurus* was found in what had been the Tethys Sea, an area rich in fossil evidence," is true, but it is a minor detail and therefore incorrect.

Choice 4, "*Pakicetus* is the oldest fossil whale yet to be found," is true, but it is a minor detail and therefore incorrect.

Choice 6, "*Ambulocetus*'s hind legs were used for propulsion in the water," is true, but it is a minor detail and therefore incorrect.

DESERT FORMATION

The deserts, which already occupy approximately a fourth of the Earth's land surface, have in recent decades been increasing at an alarming pace. The expansion of desertlike conditions into areas where they did not previously exist is called **desertification**. It has been estimated that an additional one-fourth of the Earth's land surface is threatened by this process.

Desertification is accomplished primarily through the loss of stabilizing natural vegetation and the subsequent accelerated erosion of the soil by wind and water. In some cases the loose soil is blown completely away, leaving a stony surface. In other cases, the finer particles may be removed, while the sand-sized particles are accumulated to form mobile hills or ridges of sand.

Even in the areas that retain a soil cover, the reduction of vegetation typically results in the loss of the soil's ability to absorb substantial quantities of water. The impact of raindrops on the loose soil tends to transfer fine clay particles into the tiniest soil spaces, sealing them and producing a surface that allows very little water penetration. Water absorption is greatly reduced, consequently runoff is increased, resulting in accelerated erosion rates. The gradual drying of the soil caused by its diminished ability to absorb water results in the further loss of vegetation, so that a cycle of progressive surface deterioration is established.

In some regions, the increase in desert areas is occurring largely as the result of a trend toward drier climatic conditions. Continued gradual global warming has produced an increase in aridity for some areas over the past few thousand years. The process may be accelerated in subsequent decades if global warming resulting from air pollution seriously increases.

There is little doubt, however, that desertification in most areas results primarily from human activities rather than natural processes. The semiarid lands bordering the deserts exist in a delicate ecological balance and are limited in their potential to adjust to increased environmental pressures. Expanding populations are subjecting the land to increasing pressures to provide them with food and fuel. In wet periods, the land may be able to respond to these stresses. During the dry periods that are common phenomena along the desert margins, though, the pressure on the land is often far in excess of its diminished capacity, and desertification results.

Four specific activities have been identified as major contributors to the desertification process: overcultivation, overgrazing, firewood gathering, and overirrigation. The cultivation of crops has expanded into progressively drier regions as population densities have grown. These regions are especially likely to have periods of severe dryness, so that crop failures are common. Since the raising of most crops necessitates the prior removal of the natural vegetation, crop failures leave extensive tracts of land devoid of a plant cover and susceptible to wind and water erosion.

The raising of livestock is a major economic activity in semiarid lands, where grasses are generally the dominant type of natural vegetation. The consequences of an excessive number of livestock grazing in an area are the reduction of the vegetation cover and the trampling and pulverization of the soil. This is usually followed by the drying of the soil and accelerated erosion.

Firewood is the chief fuel used for cooking and heating in many countries. The increased pressures of expanding populations have led to the removal of woody plants so that many cities and towns are surrounded by large areas completely lacking in trees and shrubs. The increasing use of dried animal waste as a substitute fuel has also hurt the soil because this valuable soil conditioner and source of plant nutrients is no longer being returned to the land.

The final major human cause of desertification is soil salinization resulting from overirrigation. Excess water from irrigation sinks down into the water table. If no drainage system exists, the water table rises, bringing dissolved salts to the surface. The water evaporates and the salts are left behind, creating a white crustal layer that prevents air and water from reaching the underlying soil.

The extreme seriousness of desertification results from the vast areas of land and the tremendous numbers of people affected, as well as from the great difficulty of reversing or even slowing the process. Once the soil has been removed by erosion, only the passage of centuries or millennia will enable new soil to form. In areas where considerable soil still remains, though, a rigorously enforced program of land protection and cover-crop planting may make it possible to reverse the present deterioration of the surface.

PARAGRAPH 1

The deserts, which already occupy approximately a fourth of the Earth's land surface, have in recent decades been increasing at an alarming pace. The expansion of desertlike conditions into areas where they did not previously exist is called **desertification**. It has been estimated that an additional one-fourth of the Earth's land surface is threatened by this process.

Directions: *Mark your answer by filling in the oval next to your choice.*

1. The word "threatened" in the passage is closest in meaning to

   ○ restricted
   ⊘ endangered
   ○ prevented
   ○ rejected

PARAGRAPH 3

Even in the areas that retain a soil cover, the reduction of vegetation typically results in the loss of the soil's ability to absorb substantial quantities of water. The impact of raindrops on the loose soil tends to transfer fine clay particles into the tiniest soil spaces, sealing them and producing a surface that allows very little water penetration. Water absorption is greatly reduced, consequently runoff is increased, resulting in accelerated erosion rates. The gradual drying of the soil caused by its diminished ability to absorb water results in the further loss of vegetation, so that a cycle of progressive surface deterioration is established.

2. According to paragraph 3, the loss of natural vegetation has which of the following consequences for soil?

   ○ Increased stony content
   ⊘ Reduced water absorption
   ○ Increased numbers of spaces in the soil
   ○ Reduced water runoff

PARAGRAPH 5

There is little doubt, however, that desertification in most areas results primarily from human activities rather than natural processes. The semiarid lands bordering the deserts exist in a delicate ecological balance and are limited in their potential to adjust to increased environmental pressures. Expanding populations are subjecting the land to increasing pressures to provide them with food and fuel. In wet periods, the land may be able to respond to these stresses. During the dry periods that are common phenomena along the desert margins, though, the pressure on the land is often far in excess of its diminished capacity, and desertification results.

3. The word "delicate" in the passage is closest in meaning to

⊗ fragile
○ predictable
○ complex
○ valuable

4. According to paragraph 5, in dry periods, border areas have difficulty

○ adjusting to stresses created by settlement
○ retaining their fertility after desertification
○ providing water for irrigating crops
○ attracting populations in search of food and fuel

PARAGRAPH 6

Four specific activities have been identified as major contributors to the desertification process: overcultivation, overgrazing, firewood gathering, and overirrigation. The cultivation of crops has expanded into progressively drier regions as population densities have grown. These regions are especially likely to have periods of severe dryness, so that crop failures are common. Since the raising of most crops necessitates the prior removal of the natural vegetation, crop failures leave extensive tracts of land devoid of a plant cover and susceptible to wind and water erosion.

5. The word "progressively" in the passage is closest in meaning to

○ openly
○ impressively
○ objectively
○ increasingly

6. According to paragraph 6, which of the following is often associated with raising crops?

○ Lack of proper irrigation techniques
○ Failure to plant crops suited to the particular area
○ Removal of the original vegetation
○ Excessive use of dried animal waste

7. The phrase "devoid of" in the passage is closest in meaning to

○ consisting of
○ hidden by
○ except for
⊗ lacking in

PARAGRAPH 9

The final major human cause of desertification is soil salinization resulting from over-irrigation. Excess water from irrigation sinks down into the water table. If no drainage system exists, the water table rises, bringing dissolved salts to the surface. The water evaporates and the salts are left behind, creating a white crustal layer that prevents air and water from reaching the underlying soil.

8. According to paragraph 9, the ground's absorption of excess water is a factor in desertification because it can

   ○ interfere with the irrigation of land
   ○ limit the evaporation of water
   ○ require more absorption of air by the soil
   ○ bring salts to the surface

9. All of the following are mentioned in the passage as contributing to desertification EXCEPT

   ○ soil erosion
   ○ global warming
   ⊗ insufficient irrigation
   ○ the raising of livestock

PARAGRAPH 10

The extreme seriousness of desertification results from the vast areas of land and the tremendous numbers of people affected, as well as from the great difficulty of reversing or even slowing the process. Once the soil has been removed by erosion, only the passage of centuries or millennia will enable new soil to form. In areas where considerable soil still remains, though, a rigorously enforced program of land protection and cover-crop planting may make it possible to reverse the present deterioration of the surface.

10. Which of the sentences below best expresses the essential information in the highlighted sentence in the passage? Incorrect choices change the meaning in important ways or leave out essential information.

    ○ Desertification is a significant problem because it is so hard to reverse and affects large areas of land and great numbers of people.
    ○ Slowing down the process of desertification is difficult because of population growth that has spread over large areas of land.
    ○ The spread of deserts is considered a very serious problem that can be solved only if large numbers of people in various countries are involved in the effort.
    ○ Desertification is extremely hard to reverse unless the population is reduced in the vast areas affected.

11. It can be inferred from the passage that the author most likely believes which of the following about the future of desertification?

    ○ Governments will act quickly to control further desertification.
    ○ The factors influencing desertification occur in cycles and will change in the future.
    ○ Desertification will continue to increase.
    ○ Desertification will soon occur in all areas of the world.

**P
A
R
A
G
R
A
P
H

7**

■ The raising of livestock is a major economic activity in semiarid lands, where grasses are generally the dominant type of natural vegetation. ■ The consequences of an excessive number of livestock grazing in an area are the reduction of the vegetation cover and the trampling and pulverization of the soil. ■ This is usually followed by the drying of the soil and accelerated erosion. ■

12. Look at the four squares [■] that indicate where the following sentence can be added to the passage.

This economic reliance on livestock in certain regions makes large tracts of land susceptible to overgrazing.

Where would the sentence best fit?

○ **This economic reliance on livestock in certain regions makes large tracts of land susceptible to overgrazing.** The raising of livestock is a major economic activity in semiarid lands, where grasses are generally the dominant type of natural vegetation. ■ The consequences of an excessive number of livestock grazing in an area are the reduction of the vegetation cover and the trampling and pulverization of the soil. ■ This is usually followed by the drying of the soil and accelerated erosion. ■

○ ■ The raising of livestock is a major economic activity in semiarid lands, where grasses are generally the dominant type of natural vegetation. **This economic reliance on livestock in certain regions makes large tracts of land susceptible to overgrazing.** The consequences of an excessive number of livestock grazing in an area are the reduction of the vegetation cover and the trampling and pulverization of the soil. ■ This is usually followed by the drying of the soil and accelerated erosion. ■

○ ■ The raising of livestock is a major economic activity in semiarid lands, where grasses are generally the dominant type of natural vegetation. ■ The consequences of an excessive number of livestock grazing in an area are the reduction of the vegetation cover and the trampling and pulverization of the soil. **This economic reliance on livestock in certain regions makes large tracts of land susceptible to overgrazing.** This is usually followed by the drying of the soil and accelerated erosion. ■

○ ■ The raising of livestock is a major economic activity in semiarid lands, where grasses are generally the dominant type of natural vegetation. ■ The consequences of an excessive number of livestock grazing in an area are the reduction of the vegetation cover and the trampling and pulverization of the soil. ■ This is usually followed by the drying of the soil and accelerated erosion. **This economic reliance on livestock in certain regions makes large tracts of land susceptible to overgrazing.**

13. **Directions:** An introductory sentence for a brief summary of the passage is provided below. Complete the summary by selecting the THREE answer choices that express the most important ideas in the passage. Some answer choices do not belong in the summary because they express ideas that are not presented in the passage or are minor ideas in the passage. **This question is worth 2 points.**

Many factors have contributed to the great increase in desertification in recent decades.

-
-
-

Answer Choices

1. Growing human populations and the agricultural demands that come with such growth have upset the ecological balance in some areas and led to the spread of deserts.

2. As periods of severe dryness have become more common, failures of a number of different crops have increased.

3. Excessive numbers of cattle and the need for firewood for fuel have reduced grasses and trees, leaving the land unprotected and vulnerable.

4. Extensive irrigation with poor drainage brings salt to the surface of the soil, a process that reduces water and air absorption.

5. Animal dung enriches the soil by providing nutrients for plant growth.

6. Grasses are generally the dominant type of natural vegetation in semi-arid lands.

PRACTICE SET 2 ANSWERS AND EXPLANATIONS

1. ❷ This is a Vocabulary question. The word being tested is *threatened*. It is highlighted in the passage. To threaten is to speak or act as if you will cause harm to someone or something. The object of the threat is in danger of being hurt, so the correct answer is choice 2, "endangered."

2. ❷ This is a Factual Information question asking for specific information that can be found in paragraph 3. The correct answer is choice 2, "reduced water absorption." The paragraph explicitly states that the reduction of vegetation greatly reduces water absorption. Choice 4, "reduced water runoff," explicitly contradicts the paragraph, so it is incorrect. The "spaces in the soil" are mentioned in another context: the paragraph does not say that they increase, so choice 3 is incorrect. The paragraph does not mention choice 1.

3. ❶ This is a Vocabulary question. The word being tested is *delicate*. It is highlighted in the passage. The correct answer is choice 1, "fragile," meaning "easily broken." *Delicate* has the same meaning as *fragile*.

4. ❶ This is a Factual Information question asking for specific information that can be found in paragraph 5. The correct answer is choice 1: border areas have difficulty "adjusting to stresses created by settlement." The paragraph says that "expanding populations," or settlement, subject border areas to "pressures," or stress, that the land may not "be able to respond to." Choice 2 is incorrect because the paragraph does not discuss "fertility" after desertification. Choice 3 is also incorrect because "irrigation" is not mentioned here. The paragraph mentions "increasing populations" but not the difficulty of "attracting populations," so choice 4 is incorrect.

5. ❹ This is a Vocabulary question. The word being tested is *progressively*. It is highlighted in the passage. The correct answer is choice 4, "increasingly." *Progressively* as it is used here means "more," and "more" of something means that it is increasing.

6. ❸ This is a Factual Information question asking for specific information that can be found in paragraph 6. The correct answer is choice 3, "removal of the original vegetation." Sentence 4 of this paragraph says that "the raising of most crops necessitates the prior removal of the natural vegetation," an explicit statement of answer choice 3. Choice 1, "lack of proper irrigation techniques," is incorrect because the paragraph mentions only "overirrigation" as a cause of desertification. No irrigation "techniques" are discussed. Choices 2 and 4, failure to plant suitable crops and use of animal waste, are not discussed.

7. ❹ This is a Vocabulary question. A phrase is being tested here, and all of the answer choices are phrases. The phrase is "devoid of." It is highlighted in the passage. "Devoid of" means "without," so the correct answer is choice 4, "lacking in." If you lack something, that means you are without that thing.

8. ❹ This is a Factual Information question asking for specific information that can be found in paragraph 9. The correct answer is choice 4, "bring salts to the surface." The paragraph says that the final human cause of desertification is salinization resulting from overirrigation. The paragraph goes on to say that the overirrigation causes the water table to rise, bringing salts to the surface. There is no mention of the process as "interfering" with or "limiting" irrigation, or of the "amount of air" the soil is required to absorb, so choices 1, 2, and 3 are all incorrect.

9. ❸ This is a Negative Factual Information question asking for specific information that can be found in the passage. Choice 3, "insufficient irrigation," is the correct answer. Choice 1, "soil erosion," is explicitly mentioned in paragraph 2 as one of the primary causes of desertification, so it is not the correct answer. Choice 2, "global warming," is mentioned as a cause of desertification in paragraph 4, so it is incorrect. Choice 4, "the raising of livestock," is described in paragraph 7 as another cause of desertification, so it is incorrect. The passage includes excessive irrigation as a cause of desertification, but not its opposite, insufficient irrigation, so that is the correct answer.

10. ❶ This is a Sentence Simplification question. As with all of these questions, a single sentence in the passage is highlighted:

> The extreme seriousness of desertification results from the vast areas of land and the tremendous numbers of people affected, as well as from the great difficulty of reversing or even slowing the process.

The correct answer is choice 1. That choice contains all of the essential information in the highlighted sentence and does not change its meaning. The only substantive difference between choice 1 and the tested sentence is the order in which the information is presented. Two clauses in the highlighted sentence, "the great difficulty of reversing . . . the process" and "the tremendous numbers of people affected," have simply been reversed; no meaning has been changed, and no information has been removed. Choices 2, 3, and 4 are all incorrect because they change the meaning of the highlighted sentence.

11. ❸ This is an Inference question asking for an inference that can be supported by the passage. The correct answer is choice 3; the passage suggests that the author believes "Desertification will continue to increase." The last paragraph of the passage says that slowing or reversing the erosion process will be very difficult, but that it *may* occur in those areas that are not too affected already if rigorously enforced anti-erosion processes are implemented. Taken together, this suggests that the author is not confident this will happen; therefore it can be inferred that the author thinks erosion will continue. The passage provides no basis for inferring choices 1, 2, or 4.

12. ❷ This is an Insert Text question. You can see the four black squares in paragraph 7 that represent the possible answer choices here:

■ The raising of livestock is a major economic activity in semiarid lands, where grasses are generally the dominant type of natural vegetation. ■ The consequences of an excessive number of livestock grazing in an area are the reduction of the vegetation cover and the trampling and pulverization of the soil. ■ This is usually followed by the drying of the soil and accelerated erosion. ■

The sentence provided, "This economic reliance on livestock in certain regions makes large tracts of land susceptible to overgrazing," is best inserted at Square 2. The inserted sentence refers explicitly to relying on "livestock in certain regions." Those regions are the ones described in the sentence preceding square 2, which states that raising livestock is "a major economic activity in semiarid lands." The inserted sentence then explains that this reliance "makes large tracts of land susceptible to overgrazing." The sentence that follows square 2 goes on to say that "The consequences of an excessive number of livestock grazing in an area are . . ." Thus the inserted sentence contains references to both the sentence before square 2 and the sentence after square 2. This is not true of any of the other possible insert points, so square 2 is correct.

13. ❶ ❸ ❹ This is a Prose Summary question. It is completed correctly below. The correct choices are 1, 3, and 4. Choices 2, 5, and 6 are therefore incorrect.

Directions: An introductory sentence for a brief summary of the passage is provided below. Complete the summary by selecting the THREE answer choices that express the most important ideas in the passage. Some answer choices do not belong in the summary because they express ideas that are not presented in the passage or are minor ideas in the passage. **This question is worth 2 points.**

Many factors have contributed to the great increase in desertification in recent decades.

- Growing human populations and the agricultural demands that come with such growth have upset the ecological balance in some areas and led to the spread of deserts.
- Excessive numbers of cattle and the need for firewood for fuel have reduced grasses and trees, leaving the land unprotected and vulnerable.
- Extensive irrigation with poor drainage brings salt to the surface of the soil, a process that reduces water and air absorption.

Answer Choices

1. Growing human populations and the agricultural demands that come with such growth have upset the ecological balance in some areas and led to the spread of deserts.

2 As periods of severe dryness have become more common, failures of a number of different crops have increased.

3. Excessive numbers of cattle and the need for firewood for fuel have reduced grasses and trees, leaving the land unprotected and vulnerable.

4. Extensive irrigation with poor drainage brings salt to the surface of the soil, a process that reduces water and air absorption.

5. Animal dung enriches the soil by providing nutrients for plant growth.

6. Grasses are generally the dominant type of natural vegetation in semi-arid lands.

Correct Choices

Choice 1, "Growing human populations and the agricultural demands that come with such growth have upset the ecological balance in some areas and led to the spread of deserts," is correct because it is a recurring theme in the passage, one of the main ideas. Paragraphs 5, 6, 7, and 9 all provide details in support of this statement.

Choice 3, "Excessive numbers of cattle and the need for firewood for fuel have reduced grasses and trees, leaving the land unprotected and vulnerable," is correct because these are two of the human activities that are major causes of desertification. The causes of desertification is the main theme of the passage. Paragraphs 6, 7, and 8 are devoted to describing how these activities contribute to desertification.

Choice 4, "Extensive irrigation with poor drainage brings salt to the surface of the soil, a process that reduces water and air absorption," is correct because it is another of the human activities that are a major cause of desertification, the main theme of the passage. Paragraph 6 mentions this first, then all of paragraph 9 is devoted to describing how this activity contributes to desertification.

Incorrect Choices

Choice 2, "As periods of severe dryness have become more common, failures of a number of different crops have increased," is incorrect because it is a supporting detail, not a main idea of the passage.

Choice 5, "Animal dung enriches the soil by providing nutrients for plant growth," is incorrect because it is contradicted by paragraph 8 of the passage.

Choice 6, "Grasses are generally the dominant type of natural vegetation in semi-arid lands," is incorrect because it is a minor detail, mentioned once in passing in paragraph 7.

PRACTICE SET 3

EARLY CINEMA

The cinema did not emerge as a form of mass consumption until its technology evolved from the initial "peepshow" format to the point where images were projected on a screen in a darkened theater. In the peepshow format, a film was viewed through a small opening in a machine that was created for that purpose. Thomas Edison's peepshow device, the Kinetoscope, was introduced to the public in 1894. It was designed for use in Kinetoscope parlors, or arcades, which contained only a few individual machines and permitted only one customer to view a short, 50-foot film at any one time. The first Kinetoscope parlors contained five machines. For the price of 25 cents (or 5 cents per machine), customers moved from machine to machine to watch five different films (or, in the case of famous prizefights, successive rounds of a single fight).

These Kinetoscope arcades were modeled on phonograph parlors, which had proven successful for Edison several years earlier. In the phonograph parlors, customers listened to recordings through individual ear tubes, moving from one machine to the next to hear different recorded speeches or pieces of music. The Kinetoscope parlors functioned in a similar way. Edison was more interested in the sale of Kinetoscopes (for roughly $1,000 apiece) to these parlors than in the films that would be run in them (which cost approximately $10 to $15 each). He refused to develop projection technology, reasoning that if he made and sold projectors, then exhibitors would purchase only one machine—a projector—from him instead of several.

Exhibitors, however, wanted to maximize their profits, which they could do more readily by projecting a handful of films to hundreds of customers at a time (rather than one at a time) and by charging 25 to 50 cents admission. About a year after the opening of the first Kinetoscope parlor in 1894, showmen such as Louis and Auguste Lumière, Thomas Armat and Charles Francis Jenkins, and Orville and Woodville Latham (with the assistance of Edison's former assistant, William Dickson) perfected projection devices. These early projection devices were used in vaudeville theaters, legitimate theaters, local town halls, makeshift storefront theaters, fairgrounds, and amusement parks to show films to a mass audience.

With the advent of projection in 1895–1896, motion pictures became the ultimate form of mass consumption. Previously, large audiences had viewed spectacles at the theater, where vaudeville, popular dramas, musical and minstrel shows, classical plays, lectures, and slide-and-lantern shows had been presented to several hundred spectators at a time. But the movies differed significantly from these other forms of entertainment, which depended on either live performance or (in the case of the slide-and-lantern shows) the active involvement of a master of ceremonies who assembled the final program.

Although early exhibitors regularly accompanied movies with live acts, the substance of the movies themselves is mass-produced, prerecorded material that can easily be reproduced by theaters with little or no active participation by the exhibitor. Even though early exhibitors shaped their film programs by mixing films and other entertainments together in whichever way they thought would be most attractive to audiences or by accompanying them with lectures, their creative control remained limited. What audiences came to see was the technological marvel of the movies; the lifelike reproduction of the commonplace motion of trains, of waves striking the shore, and of people walking in the street; and the magic made possible by trick photography and the manipulation of the camera.

With the advent of projection, the viewer's relationship with the image was no longer private, as it had been with earlier peepshow devices such as the Kinetoscope and the Mutoscope, which was a similar machine that reproduced motion by means of successive images on individual photographic cards instead of on strips of celluloid. It suddenly became public—an experience that the viewer shared with dozens, scores, and even hundreds of others. At the same time, the image that the spectator looked at expanded from the minuscule peepshow dimensions of 1 or 2 inches (in height) to the life-size proportions of 6 or 9 feet.

PARAGRAPH 1

The cinema did not emerge as a form of mass consumption until its technology evolved from the initial "peepshow" format to the point where images were projected on a screen in a darkened theater. In the peepshow format, a film was viewed through a small opening in a machine that was created for that purpose. Thomas Edison's peepshow device, the Kinetoscope, was introduced to the public in 1894. It was designed for use in Kinetoscope parlors, or arcades, which contained only a few individual machines and permitted only one customer to view a short, 50-foot film at any one time. The first Kinetoscope parlors contained five machines. For the price of 25 cents (or 5 cents per machine), customers moved from machine to machine to watch five different films (or, in the case of famous prizefights, successive rounds of a single fight).

Directions: Mark your answer by filling in the oval next to your choice.

1. According to paragraph 1, all of the following were true of viewing films in Kinetoscope parlors EXCEPT:

   ○ One individual at a time viewed a film.
   ○ Customers could view one film after another.
   ○ Prizefights were the most popular subjects for films.
   ○ Each film was short.

PARAGRAPH 2

These Kinetoscope arcades were modeled on phonograph parlors, which had proven successful for Edison several years earlier. In the phonograph parlors, customers listened to recordings through individual ear tubes, moving from one machine to the next to hear different recorded speeches or pieces of music. The Kinetoscope parlors functioned in a similar way. Edison was more interested in the sale of Kinetoscopes (for roughly $1,000 apiece) to these parlors than in the films that would be run in them (which cost approximately $10 to $15 each). He refused to develop projection technology, reasoning that if he made and sold projectors, then exhibitors would purchase only one machine—a projector—from him instead of several.

2. The author discusses phonograph parlors in paragraph 2 in order to

- ⊘ explain Edison's financial success
- ⊘ describe the model used to design Kinetoscope parlors
- ○ contrast their popularity to that of Kinetoscope parlors
- ○ illustrate how much more techno-logically advanced Kinetoscope parlors were

3. Which of the sentences below best expresses the essential information in the highlighted sentence in the passage? Incorrect answer choices change the meaning in impor-tant ways or leave out essential information.

- ○ Edison was more interested in devel-oping a variety of machines than in developing a technology based on only one.
- ○ Edison refused to work on projection technology because he did not think exhibitors would replace their pro-jectors with newer machines.
- ○ Edison did not want to develop pro-jection technology because it limited the number of machines he could sell.
- ○ Edison would not develop projection technology unless exhibitors agreed to purchase more than one projector from him.

PARAGRAPH 3

Exhibitors, however, wanted to maximize their profits, which they could do more readily by projecting a handful of films to hundreds of customers at a time (rather than one at a time) and by charging 25 to 50 cents admission. About a year after the opening of the first Kinetoscope parlor in 1894, showmen such as Louis and Auguste Lumière, Thomas Armat and Charles Francis Jenkins, and Orville and Woodville Latham (with the assistance of Edison's former assistant, William Dickson) perfected projection devices. These early projection devices were used in vaudeville theaters, legitimate theaters, local town halls, makeshift storefront theaters, fairgrounds, and amusement parks to show films to a mass audience.

4. The word "readily" in the passage is closest in meaning to

○ frequently
⊘ easily
○ intelligently
○ obviously

5. The word "assistance" in the passage is closest in meaning to

○ criticism
○ leadership
○ help
○ approval

PARAGRAPH 4

With the advent of projection in 1895–1896, motion pictures became the ultimate form of mass consumption. Previously, large audiences had viewed spectacles at the theater, where vaudeville, popular dramas, musical and minstrel shows, classical plays, lectures, and slide-and-lantern shows had been presented to several hundred spectators at a time. But the movies differed significantly from these other forms of entertainment, which depended on either live performance or (in the case of the slide-and-lantern shows) the active involvement of a master of ceremonies who assembled the final program.

6. According to paragraph 4, how did the early movies differ from previous spectacles that were presented to large audiences?

○ They were a more expensive form of entertainment.
○ They were viewed by larger audiences.
○ They were more educational.
○ They did not require live entertainers.

PARAGRAPH 5

Although early exhibitors regularly accompanied movies with live acts, the substance of the movies themselves is mass-produced, prerecorded material that can easily be reproduced by theaters with little or no active participation by the exhibitor. Even though early exhibitors shaped their film programs by mixing films and other entertainments together in whichever way they thought would be most attractive to audiences or by accompanying them with lectures, their creative control remained limited. What audiences came to see was the technological marvel of the movies; the lifelike reproduction of the commonplace motion of trains, of waves striking the shore, and of people walking in the street; and the magic made possible by trick photography and the manipulation of the camera.

7. According to paragraph 5, what role did early exhibitors play in the presentation of movies in theaters?

○ They decided how to combine various components of the film program.
○ They advised filmmakers on appropriate movie content.
○ They often took part in the live-action performances.
○ They produced and prerecorded the material that was shown in the theaters.

PARAGRAPH 6

With the advent of projection, the viewer's relationship with the image was no longer private, as it had been with earlier peepshow devices such as the Kinetoscope and the Mutoscope, which was a similar machine that reproduced motion by means of successive images on individual photographic cards instead of on strips of celluloid. It suddenly became public—an experience that the viewer shared with dozens, scores, and even hundreds of others. At the same time, the image that the spectator looked at expanded from the minuscule peepshow dimensions of 1 or 2 inches (in height) to the life-size proportions of 6 or 9 feet.

8. Which of the following is mentioned in paragraph 6 as one of the ways the Mutoscope differed from the Kinetoscope?

○ Sound and motion were simultaneously produced in the Mutoscope.
○ More than one person could view the images at the same time with the Mutoscope.
○ The Mutoscope was a less sophisticated earlier prototype of the Kinetoscope.
○ A different type of material was used to produce the images used in the Mutoscope.

9. The word "It" in the passage refers to

○ the advent of projection
○ the viewer's relationship with the image
○ a similar machine
○ celluloid

10. According to paragraph 6, the images seen by viewers in the earlier peepshows, compared with the images projected on the screen, were relatively

○ small in size
○ inexpensive to create
○ unfocused
○ limited in subject matter

11. The word "expanded" in the passage is closest in meaning to

○ was enlarged
○ was improved
○ was varied
○ was rejected

83

PARAGRAPH 3

■ Exhibitors, however, wanted to maximize their profits, which they could do more readily by projecting a handful of films to hundreds of customers at a time (rather than one at a time) and by charging 25 to 50 cents admission. ■ About a year after the opening of the first Kinetoscope parlor in 1894, showmen such as Louis and Auguste Lumière, Thomas Armat and Charles Francis Jenkins, and Orville and Woodville Latham (with the assistance of Edison's former assistant, William Dickson) perfected projection devices. ■ These early projection devices were used in vaudeville theaters, legitimate theaters, local town halls, makeshift storefront theaters, fairgrounds, and amusement parks to show films to a mass audience. ■

12. Look at the four squares [■] that indicate where the following sentence can be added to the passage.

When this widespread use of projection technology began to hurt his Kinetoscope business, Edison acquired a projector developed by Armat and introduced it as "Edison's latest marvel, the Vitascope."

Where would the sentence best fit?

○ **When this widespread use of projection technology began to hurt his Kinetoscope business, Edison acquired a projector developed by Armat and introduced it as "Edison's latest marvel, the Vitascope."** Exhibitors, however, wanted to maximize their profits, which they could do more readily by projecting a handful of films to hundreds of customers at a time (rather than one at a time) and by charging 25 to 50 cents admission. ■ About a year after the opening of the first Kinetoscope parlor in 1894, showmen such as Louis and Auguste Lumière, Thomas Armat and Charles Francis Jenkins, and Orville and Woodville Latham (with the assistance of Edison's former assistant, William Dickson) perfected projection devices. ■ These early projection devices were used in vaudeville theaters, legitimate theaters, local town halls, makeshift storefront theaters, fairgrounds, and amusement parks to show films to a mass audience. ■

○ ■ Exhibitors, however, wanted to maximize their profits, which they could do more readily by projecting a handful of films to hundreds of customers at a time (rather than one at a time) and by charging 25 to 50 cents admission. **When this widespread use of projection technology began to hurt his Kinetoscope business, Edison acquired a projector developed by Armat and introduced it as "Edison's latest marvel, the Vitascope."** About a year after the opening of the first Kinetoscope parlor in 1894, showmen such as Louis and Auguste Lumière, Thomas Armat and Charles Francis Jenkins, and Orville and Woodville Latham (with the assistance of Edison's former assistant, William Dickson) perfected projection devices. ■ These early projection devices were used in vaudeville theaters, legitimate theaters, local town halls, makeshift storefront theaters, fairgrounds, and amusement parks to show films to a mass audience. ■

○ ■ Exhibitors, however, wanted to maximize their profits, which they could do more readily by projecting a handful of films to hundreds of customers at a time (rather than one at a time) and by charging 25 to 50 cents admission. ■ About a year after the opening of the first Kinetoscope parlor in 1894, showmen such as Louis and Auguste Lumière, Thomas Armat and Charles Francis Jenkins, and Orville and Woodville Latham (with the assistance of Edison's former assistant, William Dickson) perfected projection devices. **When this widespread use of projection technology began to hurt his Kinetoscope business, Edison acquired a projector developed by Armat and introduced it as "Edison's latest marvel, the Vitascope."** These early projection devices were used in vaudeville theaters, legitimate theaters, local town halls, makeshift storefront theaters, fairgrounds, and amusement parks to show films to a mass audience. ■

■ Exhibitors, however, wanted to maximize their profits, which they could do more readily by projecting a handful of films to hundreds of customers at a time (rather than one at a time) and by charging 25 to 50 cents admission. ■ About a year after the opening of the first Kinetoscope parlor in 1894, showmen such as Louis and Auguste Lumière, Thomas Armat and Charles Francis Jenkins, and Orville and Woodville Latham (with the assistance of Edison's former assistant, William Dickson) perfected projection devices. ■ These early projection devices were used in vaudeville theaters, legitimate theaters, local town halls, makeshift storefront theaters, fairgrounds, and amusement parks to show films to a mass audience. **When this widespread use of projection technology began to hurt his Kinetoscope business, Edison acquired a projector developed by Armat and introduced it as "Edison's latest marvel, the Vitascope."**

13. **Directions:** An introductory sentence for a brief summary of the passage is provided below. Complete the summary by selecting the THREE answer choices that express the most important ideas in the passage. Some answer choices do not belong in the summary because they express ideas that are not presented in the passage or are minor ideas in the passage. **This question is worth 2 points.**

The technology for modern cinema evolved at the end of the nineteenth century.

-
-
-

Answer Choices

1. Kinetoscope parlors for viewing films were modeled on phonograph parlors.

2. Thomas Edison's design of the Kinetoscope inspired the development of large-screen projection.

3. Early cinema allowed individuals to use special machines to view films privately.

4. Slide-and-lantern shows had been presented to audiences of hundreds of spectators.

5. The development of projection technology made it possible to project images on a large screen.

6. Once film images could be projected, the cinema became a form of mass consumption.

PRACTICE SET 3 ANSWERS AND EXPLANATIONS

1. ❸ This is a Negative Factual Information question asking for specific information that can be found in paragraph 1. Choice 3 is the correct answer. The paragraph does mention that one viewer at a time could view the films (choice 1), that films could be viewed one after another (choice 2), and that films were short (choice 4). Prizefights are mentioned as one subject of these short films, but not necessarily the most popular one.

2. ❷ This is a Rhetorical Purpose question. It asks why the author mentions "phonograph parlors" in paragraph 2. The correct answer is choice 2. The author is explaining why Edison designed his arcades like phonograph parlors; that design had been successful for him in the past. The paragraph does not mention the phonograph parlors to explain Edison's financial success, so choice 1 is incorrect. The paragraph does not directly discuss the situations described in choices 3 and 4, so those answers too are incorrect.

3. ❸ This is a Sentence Simplification question. As with all of these questions, a single sentence in the passage is highlighted:

> He refused to develop projection technology, reasoning that if he made and sold projectors, then exhibitors would purchase only one machine—a projector—from him, instead of several.

   The correct answer is choice 3. That choice contains all of the essential ideas in the highlighted sentence. It is also the only choice that does not change the meaning of the sentence. Choice 1 says that Edison was more interested in developing a variety of machines, which is not true. Choice 2 says that the reason Edison refused to work on projection technology was that exhibitors would never replace the projectors. That also is not true; the highlighted sentence implies that he refused to do this because he wanted exhibitors to buy several Kinetoscope machines at a time instead of a single projector. Choice 4 says that Edison refused to develop projection technology unless exhibitors agreed to purchase more than one projector from him. The highlighted sentence actually says that Edison had already reasoned or concluded that exhibitors would not buy more than one, so choice 4 is a change in essential meaning.

4. ❷ This is a Vocabulary question. The word being tested is *readily*. It is highlighted in the passage. *Readily* means "easily," so choice 2 is the correct answer. The other choices do not fit in the context of the sentence.

5. ❸ This is a Vocabulary question. The word being tested is *assistance*. It is highlighted in the passage. An assistant is a person who helps a leader, so choice 3, "help," is the correct answer.

6. ❹ This is a Factual Information question asking for specific information that can be found in paragraph 4. The correct answer is choice 4. Early movies were different from previous spectacles because they did not require live actors. The paragraph states (emphasis added):

"But the movies differed significantly from these other forms of entertainment, which depended on either *live performance* or (in the case of the slide-and-lantern shows) the active involvement of a master of ceremonies who assembled the final program."

So the fact that previous spectacles depended on live performances is explicitly stated as one of the ways (but not the only way) that those earlier entertainments differed from movies. The other answer choices are not mentioned in the paragraph.

7. ❶ This is a Factual Information question asking for specific information that can be found in paragraph 5. The correct answer is choice 1, "They decided how to combine various components of the film program," because that idea is stated explicitly in the paragraph:

"Early exhibitors shaped their film programs by mixing films and other entertainments together."

The other choices, while possibly true, are not explicitly mentioned in the paragraph as being among the exhibitors' roles.

8. ❹ This is a Factual Information question asking for specific information that can be found in paragraph 6. The correct answer is choice 4, "A different type of material was used to produce the images used in the Mutoscope." The paragraph says that these machines were very similar but that they differed in one particular way:

". . . the Mutoscope, which was a similar machine that reproduced motion by means of successive images on individual photographic cards instead of on strips of celluloid."

9. ❷ This is a Reference question. The word being tested is *It*. That word is highlighted in the passage. Choice 2, "the viewer's relationship with the image," is the correct answer. This is a simple pronoun-referent item. The sentence says that "It" suddenly became "public," which implies that whatever "It" is, it was formerly private. The paragraph says that "the viewer's relationship with the image was no longer private," so that relationship is the "It" referred to here.

10. ❶ This is a Factual Information question asking for specific information that can be found in paragraph 6. The correct answer is choice 1. The paragraph says that the images expanded from an inch or two to life-size proportions, so "small in size" must be correct. The paragraph does not mention the other choices.

11. ❶ This is a Vocabulary question. The word being tested is *expanded*. It is highlighted in the passage. Choice 1, "was enlarged," is the correct answer. If something *expanded*, it grew or got bigger. *Enlarged* also means "grew or got bigger."

12. ❹ This is an Insert Text question. You can see the four black squares in paragraph 3 that represent the possible answer choices here.

■ Exhibitors, however, wanted to maximize their profits, which they could do more readily by projecting a handful of films to hundreds of customers at a time (rather than one at a time) and by charging 25 to 50 cents admission. ■ About a year after the opening of the first Kinetoscope parlor in 1894, showmen such as Louis and Auguste Lumière, Thomas Armat and Charles Francis Jenkins, and Orville and Woodville Latham (with the assistance of Edison's former assistant, William Dickson) perfected projection devices. ■ These early projection devices were used in vaudeville theaters, legitimate theaters, local town halls, makeshift storefront theaters, fairgrounds, and amusement parks to show films to a mass audience. ■

The inserted sentence fits best at square 4 because it represents the final result of the general use of projectors. After projectors became popular, Edison lost money, and although he had previously refused to develop projection technology, now he was forced to do so. To place the sentence anyplace else would interrupt the logical narrative sequence of the events described. None of the sentences in this paragraph can logically follow the inserted sentence, so squares 1, 2, and 3 are all incorrect.

13. ❸ ❺ ❻ This is a Prose Summary question. It is completed correctly below. The correct choices are 3, 5, and 6. Choices 1, 2, and 4 are therefore incorrect.

Directions: An introductory sentence for a brief summary of the passage is provided below. Complete the summary by selecting the THREE answer choices that express the most important ideas in the passage. Some answer choices do not belong in the summary because they express ideas that are not presented in the passage or are minor ideas in the passage. **This question is worth 2 points.**

The technology for modern cinema evolved at the end of the nineteenth century.

- Early cinema allowed individuals to use special machines to view films privately.
- The development of projection technology made it possible to project images on a large screen.
- Once film images could be projected, the cinema became a form of mass consumption.

Answer Choices

1. Kinetoscope parlors for viewing films were modeled on phonograph parlors.

2. Thomas Edison's design of the Kinetoscope inspired the development of large-screen projection.

3. Early cinema allowed individuals to use special machines to view films privately.

4. Slide-and-lantern shows had been presented to audiences of hundreds of spectators.

5. The development of projection technology made it possible to project images on a large screen.

6. Once film images could be projected, the cinema became a form of mass consumption.

Correct Choices

Choice 3, "Early cinema allowed individuals to use special machines to view films privately," is correct because it represents one of the chief differences between Kinetoscope and projection viewing. This idea is discussed at several places in the passage. It is mentioned in paragraphs 1, 3, 4, and 6. Thus it is a basic, recurring theme of the passage and, as such, a "major idea."

Choice 5, "The development of projection technology made it possible to project images on a large screen," is correct because this is a major idea that is treated in paragraphs 3, 4, 5, and 6. This development was essentially the reason that the cinema did "emerge as a form of mass consumption."

Choice 6, "Once film images could be projected, the cinema became a form of mass consumption," is correct because it represents the primary theme of the passage. It is explicitly stated in the passage's opening sentence; then the remainder of the passage describes that evolution.

Incorrect Choices

Choice 1, "Kinetoscope parlors for viewing films were modeled on phonograph parlors," is incorrect because, while true, it is a minor detail. The Kinetoscope parlors are described in paragraph 2, but the fact that they were modeled on phonograph parlors is not central to the "evolution" of cinema.

Choice 2, "Thomas Edison's design of the Kinetoscope inspired the development of large-screen projection," is incorrect because it is not clear that it is true, based on the passage. While it may be inferred from paragraph 3 that the Kinetoscope inspired the development of large-screen projection, it seems more likely that the pursuit of greater profits is what really inspired large-screen-projection development. Since this answer is not clearly supported in the passage, it cannot be considered a "main idea" and is incorrect.

Choice 4, "Slide-and-lantern shows had been presented to audiences of hundreds of spectators," is incorrect because it is a minor detail, mentioned only once in paragraph 4 as part of a larger list of theatrical spectacles.

AGGRESSION

When one animal attacks another, it engages in the most obvious example of aggressive behavior. Psychologists have adopted several approaches to understanding aggressive behavior in people.

The Biological Approach. Numerous biological structures and chemicals appear to be involved in aggression. One is the hypothalamus, a region of the brain. In response to certain stimuli, many animals show instinctive aggressive reactions. The hypothalamus appears to be involved in this inborn reaction pattern: electrical stimulation of part of the hypothalamus triggers stereotypical aggressive behaviors in many animals. In people, however, whose brains are more complex, other brain structures apparently moderate possible instincts.

An offshoot of the biological approach called *sociobiology* suggests that aggression is natural and even desirable for people. Sociobiology views much social behavior, including aggressive behavior, as genetically determined. Consider Darwin's theory of evolution. Darwin held that many more individuals are produced than can find food and survive into adulthood. A struggle for survival follows. Those individuals who possess characteristics that provide them with an advantage in the struggle for existence are more likely to survive and contribute their genes to the next generation. In many species, such characteristics include aggressiveness. Because aggressive individuals are more likely to survive and reproduce, whatever genes are linked to aggressive behavior are more likely to be transmitted to subsequent generations.

The sociobiological view has been attacked on numerous grounds. One is that people's capacity to outwit other species, not their aggressiveness, appears to be the dominant factor in human survival. Another is that there is too much variation among people to believe that they are dominated by, or at the mercy of, aggressive impulses.

The Psychodynamic Approach. Theorists adopting the psychodynamic approach hold that inner conflicts are crucial for understanding human behavior, including aggression. Sigmund Freud, for example, believed that aggressive impulses are inevitable reactions to the frustrations of daily life. Children normally desire to vent aggressive impulses on other people, including their parents, because even the most attentive parents cannot gratify all of their demands immediately. Yet children, also fearing their parents' punishment and the loss of parental love, come to repress most aggressive impulses. The Freudian perspective, in a sense, sees us as "steam engines." By holding in rather than venting "steam," we set the stage for future explosions. Pent-up aggressive impulses demand outlets. They may be expressed toward parents in indirect ways such as destroying furniture, or they may be expressed toward strangers later in life.

According to psychodynamic theory, the best ways to prevent harmful aggression may be to encourage less harmful aggression. In the steam-engine analogy, verbal aggression may vent some of the aggressive steam. So might cheering on one's favorite sports team. Psychoanalysts, therapists adopting a psychodynamic approach, refer to the venting of aggressive impulses as "catharsis."[1] Catharsis is theorized to be a safety valve. But research findings on the usefulness of catharsis are mixed. Some studies suggest that catharsis leads to reductions in tension and a lowered likelihood of future aggression. Other studies, however, suggest that letting some steam escape actually encourages more aggression later on.

The Cognitive Approach. Cognitive psychologists assert that our behavior is influenced by our values, by the ways in which we interpret our situations, and by choice. For example, people who believe that aggression is necessary and justified—as during wartime—are likely to act aggressively, whereas people who believe that a particular war or act of aggression is unjust, or who think that aggression is never justified, are less likely to behave aggressively.

One cognitive theory suggests that aggravating and painful events trigger unpleasant feelings. These feelings, in turn, can lead to aggressive action, but *not* automatically. Cognitive factors intervene. People *decide* whether they will act aggressively or not on the basis of factors such as their experiences with aggression and their interpretation of other people's motives. Supporting evidence comes from research showing that aggressive people often distort other people's motives. For example, they assume that other people mean them harm when they do not.

1. Catharsis: In psychodynamic theory, the purging of strong emotions or the relieving of tensions

PARAGRAPH 2

The Biological Approach. Numerous biological structures and chemicals appear to be involved in aggression. One is the hypothalamus, a region of the brain. In response to certain stimuli, many animals show instinctive aggressive reactions. The hypothalamus appears to be involved in this inborn reaction pattern: electrical stimulation of part of the hypothalamus triggers stereotypical aggressive behaviors in many animals. In people, however, whose brains are more complex, other brain structures apparently moderate possible instincts.

Directions: Mark your answer by filling in the oval next to your choice.

1. According to paragraph 2, what evidence indicates that aggression in animals is related to the hypothalamus?

   ○ Some aggressive animal species have a highly developed hypothalamus.
   ○ Electrical stimulation of the hypothalamus delays animals' inborn reaction patterns.
   ○ Animals behaving aggressively show increased activity in the hypothalamus.
   ○ Animals who lack a hypothalamus display few aggressive tendencies.

PARAGRAPH 3

An offshoot of the biological approach called *sociobiology* suggests that aggression is natural and even desirable for people. Sociobiology views much social behavior, including aggressive behavior, as genetically determined. Consider Darwin's theory of evolution. Darwin held that many more individuals are produced than can find food and survive into adulthood. A struggle for survival follows. Those individuals who possess characteristics that provide them with an advantage in the struggle for existence are more likely to survive and contribute their genes to the next generation. In many species, such characteristics include aggressiveness. Because aggressive individuals are more likely to survive and reproduce, whatever genes are linked to aggressive behavior are more likely to be transmitted to subsequent generations.

2. According to Darwin's theory of evolution, members of a species are forced to struggle for survival because

○ not all individuals are skilled in finding food
○ individuals try to defend their young against attackers
○ many more individuals are born than can survive until the age of reproduction
○ individuals with certain genes are more likely to reach adulthood

PARAGRAPH 5

The Psychodynamic Approach. Theorists adopting the psychodynamic approach hold that inner conflicts are crucial for understanding human behavior, including aggression. Sigmund Freud, for example, believed that aggressive impulses are inevitable reactions to the frustrations of daily life. Children normally desire to vent aggressive impulses on other people, including their parents, because even the most attentive parents cannot gratify all of their demands immediately. Yet children, also fearing their parents' punishment and the loss of parental love, come to repress most aggressive impulses. The Freudian perspective, in a sense, sees us as "steam engines." By holding in rather than venting "steam," we set the stage for future explosions. Pent-up aggressive impulses demand outlets. They may be expressed toward parents in indirect ways such as destroying furniture, or they may be expressed toward strangers later in life.

3. The word "inevitable" in the passage is closest in meaning to

○ unavoidable
○ regrettable
○ controllable
○ unsuitable

4. The word "gratify" in the passage is closest in meaning to

○ identify
○ modify
○ satisfy
○ simplify

5. The word "they" in the passage refers to

○ future explosions
○ pent-up aggressive impulses
○ outlets
○ indirect ways

6. According to paragraph 5, Freud believed that children experience conflict between a desire to vent aggression on their parents and

○ a frustration that their parents do not give them everything they want
○ a fear that their parents will punish them and stop loving them
○ a desire to take care of their parents
○ a desire to vent aggression on other family members

7. Freud describes people as "steam engines" in order to make the point that people

○ deliberately build up their aggression to make themselves stronger
○ usually release aggression in explosive ways
○ must vent their aggression to prevent it from building up
○ typically lose their aggression if they do not express it

PARAGRAPH 7

The Cognitive Approach. Cognitive psychologists assert that our behavior is influenced by our values, by the ways in which we interpret our situations, and by choice. For example, people who believe that aggression is necessary and justified—as during wartime—are likely to act aggressively, whereas people who believe that a particular war or act of aggression is unjust, or who think that aggression is never justified, are less likely to behave aggressively.

PARAGRAPH 8

One cognitive theory suggests that aggravating and painful events trigger unpleasant feelings. These feelings, in turn, can lead to aggressive action, but *not* automatically. Cognitive factors intervene. People *decide* whether they will act aggressively or not on the basis of factors such as their experiences with aggression and their interpretation of other people's motives. Supporting evidence comes from research showing that aggressive people often distort other people's motives. For example, they assume that other people mean them harm when they do not.

8. Which of the sentences below best expresses the essential information in the highlighted sentence in the passage? Incorrect answer choices change the meaning in important ways or leave out essential information.

○ People who believe that they are fighting a just war act aggressively while those who believe that they are fighting an unjust war do not.

○ People who believe that aggression is necessary and justified are more likely to act aggressively than those who believe differently.

○ People who normally do not believe that aggression is necessary and justified may act aggressively during wartime.

○ People who believe that aggression is necessary and justified do not necessarily act aggressively during wartime.

9. According to the cognitive approach described in paragraphs 7 and 8, all of the following may influence the decision whether to act aggressively EXCEPT a person's

○ moral values
○ previous experiences with aggression
○ instinct to avoid aggression
○ beliefs about other people's intentions

10. The word "distort" in the passage is closest in meaning to

○ mistrust
○ misinterpret
○ criticize
○ resent

PARAGRAPH 5

The Psychodynamic Approach. Theorists adopting the psychodynamic approach hold that inner conflicts are crucial for understanding human behavior, including aggression. Sigmund Freud, for example, believed that aggressive impulses are inevitable reactions to the frustrations of daily life. Children normally desire to vent aggressive impulses on other people, including their parents, because even the most attentive parents cannot gratify all of their demands immediately. ■ Yet children, also fearing their parents' punishment and the loss of parental love, come to repress most aggressive impulses. ■ The Freudian perspective, in a sense, sees us as "steam engines." ■ By holding in rather than venting "steam," we set the stage for future explosions. ■ Pent-up aggressive impulses demand outlets. They may be expressed toward parents in indirect ways such as destroying furniture, or they may be expressed toward strangers later in life.

11. Look at the four squares [■] that indicate where the following sentence can be added to the passage.

    According to Freud, however, impulses that have been repressed continue to exist and demand expression.

    Where would the sentence best fit?

○ **The Psychodynamic Approach.** Theorists adopting the psychodynamic approach hold that inner conflicts are crucial for understanding human behavior, including aggression. Sigmund Freud, for example, believed that aggressive impulses are inevitable reactions to the frustrations of daily life. Children normally desire to vent aggressive impulses on other people, including their parents, because even the most attentive parents cannot gratify all of their demands immediately. **According to Freud, however, impulses that have been repressed continue to exist and demand expression.** Yet children, also fearing their parents' punishment and the loss of parental love, come to repress most aggressive impulses. ■ The Freudian perspective, in a sense, sees us as "steam engines." ■ By holding in rather than venting "steam," we set the stage for future explosions. ■ Pent-up aggressive impulses demand outlets. They may be expressed toward parents in indirect ways such as destroying furniture, or they may be expressed toward strangers later in life.

○ **The Psychodynamic Approach.** Theorists adopting the psychodynamic approach hold that inner conflicts are crucial for understanding human behavior, including aggression. Sigmund Freud, for example, believed that aggressive impulses are inevitable reactions to the frustrations of daily life. Children normally desire to vent aggressive impulses on other people, including their parents, because even the most attentive parents cannot gratify all of their demands immediately. ■ Yet children, also fearing their parents' punishment and the loss of parental love, come to repress most aggressive impulses. **According to Freud, however, impulses that have been repressed continue to exist and demand expression.** The Freudian perspective, in a sense, sees us as "steam engines." ■ By holding in rather than venting "steam," we set the stage for future explosions. ■ Pent-up aggressive impulses demand outlets. They may be expressed toward parents in indirect ways such as destroying furniture, or they may be expressed toward strangers later in life.

○ **The Psychodynamic Approach.** Theorists adopting the psychodynamic approach hold that inner conflicts are crucial for understanding human behavior, including aggression. Sigmund Freud, for example, believed that aggressive impulses are inevitable reactions to the frustrations of daily life. Children normally desire to vent aggressive impulses on other people, including their parents, because even the most attentive parents cannot gratify all of their demands immediately. ■ Yet children, also fearing their parents' punishment and the loss of parental love, come to repress most aggressive impulses. ■ The Freudian perspective, in a sense, sees us as "steam engines." **According to Freud, however, impulses that have been repressed continue to exist and demand expression.** By holding in rather than venting "steam," we set the stage for future explosions. ■ Pent-up aggressive impulses demand outlets. They may be expressed toward parents in indirect ways such as destroying furniture, or they may be expressed toward strangers later in life.

○ **The Psychodynamic Approach.** Theorists adopting the psychodynamic approach hold that inner conflicts are crucial for understanding human behavior, including aggression. Sigmund Freud, for example, believed that aggressive impulses are inevitable reactions to the frustrations of daily life. Children normally desire to vent aggressive impulses on other people, including their parents, because even the most attentive parents cannot gratify all of their demands immediately. ■ Yet children, also fearing their parents' punishment and the loss of parental love, come to repress most aggressive impulses. ■ The Freudian perspective, in a sense, sees us as "steam engines." ■ By holding in rather than venting "steam," we set the stage for future explosions. **According to Freud, however, impulses that have been repressed continue to exist and demand expression.** Pent-up aggressive impulses demand outlets. They may be expressed toward parents in indirect ways such as destroying furniture, or they may be expressed toward strangers later in life.

12. **Directions:** Complete the table below by matching five of the six answer choices with the approach to aggression that they exemplify. **This question is worth 3 points.**

Approach to Understanding Aggression	Associated Claims
Biological Approach	● _____ 2 _____
Psychodynamic Approach	● _____ 1 _____
	● _____ 6 _____
Cognitive Approach	● _____ 3 _____
	● _____ 5 _____

Answer Choices

1. Aggressive impulses toward people are sometimes expressed in indirect ways.

2. Aggressiveness is often useful for individuals in the struggle for survival.

3. Aggressive behavior may involve a misunderstanding of other people's intentions.

4. The need to express aggressive impulses declines with age.

5. Acting aggressively is the result of a choice influenced by a person's values and beliefs.

6. Repressing aggressive impulses can result in aggressive behavior.

PRACTICE SET 4 ANSWERS AND EXPLANATIONS

1. ❸ This is a Factual Information question asking for specific information that can be found in paragraph 2. The correct answer is choice 3. The question asks specifically for evidence that "indicates that aggression in animals is related to the hypothalamus." Answer choice 1 is not supported by the passage. It does not discuss more and less aggressive species or relative development of the hypothalamus. Answer choice 2 contradicts the passage. Electrical stimulation of the hypothalamus causes the instinctive reaction of aggression; it does not delay it. Answer choice 4 is incorrect because the passage does not cite as evidence, or even mention, the removal of the hypothalamus.

2. ❸ This is a Factual Information question asking for specific information that can be found in the passage. The correct answer is choice 3, "many more individuals are born than can survive until the age of reproduction." This answer choice is essentially a paraphrase of paragraph 3, sentence 4: "Darwin held that many more individuals are produced than can find food and survive into adulthood." Choices 1 and 2 are not mentioned at all. Choice 4 may be true, but it is not stated in the passage as a fact; an inference is needed to support it.

3. ❶ This is a Vocabulary question. The word being tested is *inevitable*. It is highlighted in the passage. The correct answer is choice 1, "unavoidable." If something is *inevitable*, that means that it will occur no matter what; in other words, it is unavoidable.

4. ❸ This is a Vocabulary question. The word being tested is *gratify*. It is highlighted in the passage. The correct answer is choice 3, "satisfy." If a person's desires are gratified, those desires are fulfilled. Thus the person is satisfied.

5. ❷ This is a Reference question. The word being tested is *they*. It is highlighted in the passage. The correct answer is choice 2, "pent-up aggressive impulses." This is a simple pronoun-referent item. The word *they* here refers to something that "may be expressed toward strangers later in life." This is the "outlet" toward which the "aggressive impulses" mentioned may be directed.

6. ❷ This is a Factual Information question asking for specific information that can be found in paragraph 5. The correct answer is choice 2, "a fear that their parents will punish them and stop loving them." The question asks what causes the conflict between the desire to vent aggression and children's fears. The answer is found in paragraph 5 in the sentence that reads, "Yet children, also fearing their parents' punishment and the loss of parental love, come to repress most aggressive impulses." Answer choice 2 is the only choice that correctly identifies the cause of the conflict created by repressing aggression in children.

7. ❸ This is a Rhetorical Purpose question. It asks you why the author mentions that Freud described people as "steam engines" in the passage. The phrase being tested is highlighted in the passage. The correct answer is choice 3, "must vent their aggression to prevent it from building up." Steam engines will explode if their steam builds up indefinitely. The same is true of people, as choice 3 indicates. The other choices are not necessarily true of both people and steam engines, so they are incorrect.

8. ❷ This is a Sentence Simplification question. As with all of these questions, a single sentence in the passage is highlighted:

> For example, people who believe that aggression is necessary and justified—as during wartime—are likely to act aggressively, whereas people who believe that a particular war or act of aggression is unjust, or who think that aggression is never justified, are less likely to behave aggressively.

The correct answer is choice 2. It contains all of the essential information in the highlighted sentence. The highlighted sentence compares people who believe particular acts of aggression are necessary and those who do not, in terms of their relative likelihood to act aggressively under certain conditions. This is precisely what choice 2 says: "People who believe that aggression is necessary and justified are more likely to act aggressively than those who believe differently." It compares the behavior of one type of person with that of another type of person. Nothing essential has been left out, and the meaning has not been changed.

Choice 1 changes the meaning of the sentence; it says categorically that "those [people] who believe that they are fighting an unjust war do not [act aggressively]." The highlighted sentence merely says that such people are "less likely" to act aggressively, not that they never will; this changes the meaning.

Choice 3 says, "People who normally do not believe that aggression is necessary and justified may act aggressively during wartime." This is incorrect because it leaves out critical information: it does not mention people who do believe aggression is necessary. This choice does not make the same comparison as the highlighted sentence.

Choice 4, "People who believe that aggression is necessary and justified do not necessarily act aggressively during wartime," also changes the meaning of the sentence by leaving out essential information. In this choice, no mention is made of people who do not believe aggression is necessary. This choice does not make the same comparison as the highlighted sentence.

9. ❸ This is a Negative Factual Information question asking for specific information that can be found in paragraphs 7 and 8. Choice 3 is the correct answer.

Choice 1, "moral values," is explicitly mentioned as one of the influences on aggressive behavior, so it is incorrect. Choices 2 ("previous experiences") and 4 ("beliefs about other people") are both explicitly mentioned in this context. The sentence in paragraph 8 says, "People decide whether they will act aggressively or not on the basis of factors such as their experiences with aggression and their interpretation of other people's motives." Choice 3, the "instinct to avoid aggression," is not mentioned, so it is the correct answer here.

10. ❷ This is a Vocabulary question. The word being tested is *distort*. It is highlighted in the passage. The correct answer is choice 2, "misinterpret." To distort other people's motives is to twist them, or view them incorrectly and thereby not understand them properly. Something that is not understood properly is misinterpreted.

11. ❷ This is an Insert Text question. You can see the four black squares in paragraph 5 that represent the possible answer choices here.

The Psychodynamic Approach. Theorists adopting the psychodynamic approach hold that inner conflicts are crucial for understanding human behavior, including aggression. Sigmund Freud, for example, believed that aggressive impulses are inevitable reactions to the frustrations of daily life. Children normally desire to vent aggressive impulses on other people, including their parents, because even the most attentive parents cannot gratify all of their demands immediately. ■ Yet children, also fearing their parents' punishment and the loss of parental love, come to repress most aggressive impulses. ■ The Freudian perspective, in a sense, sees us as "steam engines." ■ By holding in rather than venting "steam," we set the stage for future explosions. ■

Pent-up aggressive impulses demand outlets. They may be expressed toward parents in indirect ways such as destroying furniture, or they may be expressed toward strangers later in life.

The sentence provided, "According to Freud, however, impulses that have been repressed continue to exist and demand expression," is best inserted at square 2.

Square 2 is correct because the sentence being inserted is a connective sentence, connecting the idea of childhood repression in the preceding sentence to the "Freudian perspective" in the sentence that follows. The use of the word *however* in this sentence indicates that an idea already introduced (the repression of children's aggressive impulses) is being modified. Here, the inserted sentence tells us that Freud thought that even though these impulses are repressed, they continue to exist. This serves as a connection to the next sentence and the "Freudian perspective." Inserting the sentence at square 1 would place the modification ("however, impulses . . . continue to exist") before the idea that it modifies (repression of impulses). This makes no logical sense. Inserting the sentence at square 3 would move the modifying sentence away from its logical position immediately following the idea that it modifies (repression of impulses). Placing the insert sentence at square 4 moves the sentence farther from its logical antecedent and with no connection to the sentence that follows it.

12. This is a Fill in a Table question. It is completed correctly below. Choice 2 is the correct answer for the "Biological Approach" row. Choices 1 and 6 are the correct answers for the "Psychodynamic Approach" row. Choices 3 and 5 are the correct answers for the "Cognitive Approach" row. Choice 4 should not be used in any row.

Directions: Complete the table below by matching five of the six answer choices with the approach to aggression that they exemplify. **This question is worth 3 points.**

Approach to Understanding Aggression	Associated Claims
Biological Approach	● Aggressiveness is often useful for individuals in the struggle for survival.
Psychodynamic Approach	● Aggressive impulses toward people are sometimes expressed in indirect ways. ● Repressing aggressive impulses can result in aggressive behavior.
Cognitive Approach	● Aggressive behavior may involve a misunderstanding of other people's intentions. ● Acting aggressively is the result of a choice influenced by a person's values and beliefs.

Answer Choices

1. Aggressive impulses toward people are sometimes expressed in indirect ways.

2. Aggressiveness is often useful for individuals in the struggle for survival.

3. Aggressive behavior may involve a misunderstanding of other people's intentions.

4. The need to express aggressive impulses declines with age.

5. Acting aggressively is the result of a choice influenced by a person's values and beliefs.

6. Repressing aggressive impulses can result in aggressive behavior.

Correct Choices

Choice 1: "Aggressive impulses toward people are sometimes expressed in indirect ways" belongs in the "Psychodynamic Approach" row based on paragraph 5. That paragraph, in explaining the psychodynamic approach, states, "Pent-up aggressive impulses demand outlets. They may be expressed toward parents in indirect ways such as destroying furniture . . ."

Choice 2: "Aggressiveness is often useful for individuals in the struggle for survival" belongs in the "Biological Approach" row because, as stated in paragraph 3, "An offshoot of the biological approach called *sociobiology* suggests that aggression is natural and even desirable for people." The remainder of that paragraph explains the ways in which aggressive behavior can be useful in the struggle for survival. Neither of the other approaches discusses this idea, so this answer choice belongs here.

Choice 3: "Aggressive behavior may involve a misunderstanding of other people's intentions" belongs in the "Cognitive Approach" row based on paragraph 8. The theme of that paragraph is that people decide to be aggressive (or not) largely based upon their interpretations of other people's motives. It goes on to say that these interpretations may be "distorted," or misunderstood. Accordingly, this answer choice belongs in this row.

Choice 5: "Acting aggressively is the result of a choice influenced by a person's values and beliefs" belongs in the "Cognitive Approach" row based on paragraph 7, which states, "Cognitive psychologists assert that our behavior is influenced by our values, by the ways in which we interpret our situations, and by choice." Thus this is an important aspect of the cognitive approach.

Choice 6: "Repressing aggressive impulses can result in aggressive behavior" belongs in the "Psychodynamic Approach" row based on paragraphs 5 and 6. Both of those paragraphs explicitly make this point in the section of the passage on the psychodynamic approach.

Incorrect Choice

Choice 4: "The need to express aggressive impulses declines with age" is not mentioned in connection with any of the approaches to aggression discussed in the passage, so it should not be used.

ARTISANS AND INDUSTRIALIZATION

Before 1815 manufacturing in the United States had been done in homes or shops by skilled artisans. As master craftworkers, they imparted the knowledge of their trades to apprentices and journeymen. In addition, women often worked in their homes part-time, making finished articles from raw material supplied by merchant capitalists. After 1815 this older form of manufacturing began to give way to factories with machinery tended by unskilled or semiskilled laborers. Cheap transportation networks, the rise of cities, and the availability of capital and credit all stimulated the shift to factory production.

The creation of a labor force that was accustomed to working in factories did not occur easily. Before the rise of the factory, artisans had worked within the home. Apprentices were considered part of the family, and masters were responsible not only for teaching their apprentices a trade but also for providing them some education and for supervising their moral behavior. Journeymen knew that if they perfected their skill, they could become respected master artisans with their own shops. Also, skilled artisans did not work by the clock, at a steady pace, but rather in bursts of intense labor alternating with more leisurely time.

The factory changed that. Goods produced by factories were not as finished or elegant as those done by hand, and pride in craftsmanship gave way to the pressure to increase rates of productivity. The new methods of doing business involved a new and stricter sense of time. Factory life necessitated a more regimented schedule, where work began at the sound of a bell and workers kept machines going at a constant pace. At the same time, workers were required to discard old habits, for industrialism demanded a worker who was alert, dependable, and self-disciplined. Absenteeism and lateness hurt productivity and, since work was specialized, disrupted the regular factory routine. Industrialization not only produced a fundamental change in the way work was organized; it transformed the very nature of work.

The first generation to experience these changes did not adopt the new attitudes easily. The factory clock became the symbol of the new work rules. One mill worker who finally quit complained revealingly about "obedience to the ding-dong of the bell—just as though we are so many living machines." With the loss of personal freedom also came the loss of standing in the community. Unlike artisan workshops in which apprentices worked closely with the masters supervising them, factories sharply separated workers from management. Few workers rose through the ranks to supervisory positions, and even fewer could achieve the artisan's dream of setting up one's own business. Even well-paid workers sensed their decline in status.

In this newly emerging economic order, workers sometimes organized to protect their rights and traditional ways of life. Craftworkers such as carpenters, printers, and tailors formed unions, and in 1834 individual unions came together in the National Trades' Union. The labor movement gathered some momentum in the decade before the Panic of 1837, but in the depression that followed, labor's strength collapsed. During hard times, few workers were willing to strike[1] or engage in collective action. And skilled craftworkers, who spearheaded the union movement, did not feel a particularly strong bond with semiskilled factory workers and unskilled laborers. More than a decade of agitation did finally bring a workday shortened to 10 hours to most industries by the 1850s, and the courts also recognized workers' right to strike, but these gains had little immediate impact.

Workers were united in resenting the industrial system and their loss of status, but they were divided by ethnic and racial antagonisms, gender, conflicting religious perspectives, occupational differences, political party loyalties, and disagreements over tactics. For them, the factory and industrialism were not agents of opportunity but reminders of their loss of independence and a measure of control over their lives. As United States society became more specialized and differentiated, greater extremes of wealth began to appear. And as the new markets created fortunes for the few, the factory system lowered the wages of workers by dividing labor into smaller, less skilled tasks.

1. Strike: A stopping of work that is organized by workers

PARAGRAPH 1

Before 1815 manufacturing in the United States had been done in homes or shops by skilled artisans. As master craftworkers, they imparted the knowledge of their trades to apprentices and journeymen. In addition, women often worked in their homes part-time, making finished articles from raw material supplied by merchant capitalists. After 1815 this older form of manufacturing began to give way to factories with machinery tended by unskilled or semiskilled laborers. Cheap transportation networks, the rise of cities, and the availability of capital and credit all stimulated the shift to factory production.

Directions: Mark your answer by filling in the oval next to your choice.

1. Which of the following can be inferred from the passage about articles manufactured before 1815?

   ○ They were primarily produced by women.
   ○ They were generally produced in shops rather than in homes.
   ⊘ They were produced with more concern for quality than for speed of production.
   ○ They were produced mostly in large cities with extensive transportation networks.

PARAGRAPH 2

The creation of a labor force that was accustomed to working in factories did not occur easily. Before the rise of the factory, artisans had worked within the home. Apprentices were considered part of the family, and masters were responsible not only for teaching their apprentices a trade but also for providing them some education and for supervising their moral behavior. Journeymen knew that if they perfected their skill, they could become respected master artisans with their own shops. Also, skilled artisans did not work by the clock, at a steady pace, but rather in bursts of intense labor alternating with more leisurely time.

2. Which of the sentences below best expresses the essential information in the highlighted sentence in the passage? Incorrect answer choices change the meaning in important ways or leave out essential information.

   ○ Masters demanded moral behavior from apprentices but often treated them irresponsibly.

   ○ The responsibilities of the master to the apprentice went beyond the teaching of a trade.

   ○ Masters preferred to maintain the trade within the family by supervising and educating the younger family members.

   ○ Masters who trained members of their own family as apprentices demanded excellence from them.

PARAGRAPH 3

The factory changed that. Goods produced by factories were not as finished or elegant as those done by hand, and pride in craftsmanship gave way to the pressure to increase rates of productivity. The new methods of doing business involved a new and stricter sense of time. Factory life necessitated a more regimented schedule, where work began at the sound of a bell and workers kept machines going at a constant pace. At the same time, workers were required to discard old habits, for industrialism demanded a worker who was alert, dependable, and self-disciplined. Absenteeism and lateness hurt productivity and, since work was specialized, disrupted the regular factory routine. Industrialization not only produced a fundamental change in the way work was organized; it transformed the very nature of work.

3. The word "disrupted" in the passage is closest in meaning to
   ○ prolonged
   ○ established
   ○ followed
   ○ upset

PARAGRAPH 4

The first generation to experience these changes did not adopt the new attitudes easily. The factory clock became the symbol of the new work rules. One mill worker who finally quit complained revealingly about "obedience to the ding-dong of the bell— just as though we are so many living machines." With the loss of personal freedom also came the loss of standing in the community. Unlike artisan workshops in which apprentices worked closely with the masters supervising them, factories sharply separated workers from management. Few workers rose through the ranks to supervisory positions, and even fewer could achieve the artisan's dream of setting up one's own business. Even well-paid workers sensed their decline in status.

4. In paragraph 4, the author includes the quotation from a mill worker in order to

○ support the idea that it was difficult for workers to adjust to working in factories

○ show that workers sometimes quit because of the loud noise made by factory machinery

○ argue that clocks did not have a useful function in factories

○ emphasize that factories were most successful when workers revealed their complaints

5. All of the following are mentioned in paragraph 4 as consequences of the new system for workers EXCEPT a loss of

○ freedom

○ status in the community

○ opportunities for advancement

○ contact among workers who were not managers

PARAGRAPH 5

In this newly emerging economic order, workers sometimes organized to protect their rights and traditional ways of life. Craftworkers such as carpenters, printers, and tailors formed unions, and in 1834 individual unions came together in the National Trades' Union. The labor movement gathered some momentum in the decade before the Panic of 1837, but in the depression that followed, labor's strength collapsed. During hard times, few workers were willing to strike or engage in collective action. And skilled craftworkers, who spearheaded the union movement, did not feel a particularly strong bond with semiskilled factory workers and unskilled laborers. More than a decade of agitation did finally bring a workday shortened to 10 hours to most industries by the 1850s, and the courts also recognized workers' right to strike, but these gains had little immediate impact.

6. The phrase "gathered some momentum" in the passage is closest in meaning to

○ made progress

○ became active

○ caused changes

○ combined forces

7. The word "spearheaded" in the passage is closest in meaning to

○ led

○ accepted

○ changed

○ resisted

8. Which of the following statements about the labor movement of the 1800s is supported by paragraph 5?

○ It was successful during times of economic crisis.
○ Its primary purpose was to benefit unskilled laborers
○ It was slow to improve conditions for workers.
○ It helped workers of all skill levels form a strong bond with each other.

PARAGRAPH 6

Workers were united in resenting the industrial system and their loss of status, but they were divided by ethnic and racial antagonisms, gender, conflicting religious perspectives, occupational differences, political party loyalties, and disagreements over tactics. For them, the factory and industrialism were not agents of opportunity but reminders of their loss of independence and a measure of control over their lives. As United States society became more specialized and differentiated, greater extremes of wealth began to appear. And as the new markets created fortunes for the few, the factory system lowered the wages of workers by dividing labor into smaller, less skilled tasks.

9. The author identifies "political party loyalties" and "disagreements over tactics" as two of several factors that

○ encouraged workers to demand higher wages
○ created divisions among workers
○ caused work to become more specialized
○ increased workers' resentment of the industrial system

10. The word "them" in the passage refers to

○ workers
○ political party loyalties
○ disagreements over tactics
○ agents of opportunity

PARAGRAPH 1

Before 1815 manufacturing in the United States had been done in homes or shops by skilled artisans. ■ As master craftworkers, they imparted the knowledge of their trades to apprentices and journeymen. ■ In addition, women often worked in their homes part-time, making finished articles from raw material supplied by merchant capitalists. ■ After 1815 this older form of manufacturing began to give way to factories with machinery tended by unskilled or semiskilled laborers. ■ Cheap transportation networks, the rise of cities, and the availability of capital and credit all stimulated the shift to factory production.

11. Look at the four squares [■] that indicate where the following sentence can be added to the passage.

This new form of manufacturing depended on the movement of goods to distant locations and a centralized source of laborers.

Where would the sentence best fit?

○ Before 1815 manufacturing in the United States had been done in homes or shops by skilled artisans. **This new form of manufacturing depended on the movement of goods to distant locations and a centralized source of laborers.** As master craftworkers, they imparted the knowledge of their trades to apprentices and journeymen. ■ In addition, women often worked in their homes part-time, making finished articles from raw material supplied by merchant capitalists. ■ After 1815 this older form of manufacturing began to give way to factories with machinery tended by unskilled or semiskilled laborers. ■ Cheap transportation networks, the rise of cities, and the availability of capital and credit all stimulated the shift to factory production.

○ Before 1815 manufacturing in the United States had been done in homes or shops by skilled artisans. ■ As master craftworkers, they imparted the knowledge of their trades to apprentices and journeymen. **This new form of manufacturing depended on the movement of goods to distant locations and a centralized source of laborers.** In addition, women often worked in their homes part-time, making finished articles from raw material supplied by merchant capitalists. ■ After 1815 this older form of manufacturing began to give way to factories with machinery tended by unskilled or semiskilled laborers. ■ Cheap transportation networks, the rise of cities, and the availability of capital and credit all stimulated the shift to factory production.

○ Before 1815 manufacturing in the United States had been done in homes or shops by skilled artisans. ■ As master craftworkers, they imparted the knowledge of their trades to apprentices and journeymen. ■ In addition, women often worked in their homes part-time, making finished articles from raw material supplied by merchant capitalists. **This new form of manufacturing depended on the movement of goods to distant locations and a centralized source of laborers.** After 1815 this older form of manufacturing began to give way to factories with machinery tended by unskilled or semiskilled laborers. ■ Cheap transportation networks, the rise of cities, and the availability of capital and credit all stimulated the shift to factory production.

○ Before 1815 manufacturing in the United States had been done in homes or shops by skilled artisans. ■ As master craftworkers, they imparted the knowledge of their trades to apprentices and journeymen. ■ In addition, women often worked in their homes part-time, making finished articles from raw material supplied by merchant capitalists. ■ After 1815 this older form of manufacturing began to give way to factories with machinery tended by unskilled or semiskilled laborers. **This new form of manufacturing depended on the movement of goods to distant locations and a centralized source of laborers.** Cheap transportation networks, the rise of cities, and the availability of capital and credit all stimulated the shift to factory production.

12. **Directions:** Complete the table below by indicating which of the answer choices describe characteristics of the period before 1815 and which describe characteristics of the 1815–1850 period. **This question is worth 3 points.**

Before 1815	1815–1850
•	•
•	•
	•

Answer Choices

1. A united, highly successful labor movement took shape.

2. Workers took pride in their workmanship.

3. The income gap between the rich and the poor increased greatly.

4. Transportation networks began to decline.

5. Emphasis was placed on following schedules.

6. Workers went through an extensive period of training.

7. Few workers expected to own their own businesses.

PRACTICE SET 5 ANSWERS AND EXPLANATIONS

1. ❸ This is an Inference question asking for an inference that can be supported by the passage. The correct answer is choice 3, "They were produced with more concern for quality than for speed of production."

    A number of statements throughout the passage support choice 3. Paragraph 1 states, "Before 1815 manufacturing in the United States had been done in homes or shops by skilled artisans . . . After 1815 this older form of manufacturing began to give way to factories with machinery tended by unskilled or semiskilled laborers."

    Paragraph 2 states, "Before the rise of the factory . . . skilled artisans did not work by the clock, at a steady pace, but rather in bursts of intense labor alternating with more leisurely time."

    Paragraph 3 states, "The factory changed that. Goods produced by factories were not as finished or elegant as those done by hand, and pride in craftsmanship gave way to the pressure to increase rates of productivity."

    Taken together, these three statements, about production rates, the rise of factories after 1815, and the decline of craftsmanship after 1815, support the inference that before 1815, the emphasis had been on quality rather than on speed of production. Answer choices 1, 2, and 4 are all contradicted by the passage.

2. ❷ This is a Sentence Simplification question. As with all of these questions, a single sentence in the passage is highlighted:

> Apprentices were considered part of the family, and masters were responsible not only for teaching their apprentices a trade but also for providing them some education and for supervising their moral behavior.

The correct answer is choice 2. Choice 2 contains all of the essential information in the highlighted sentence. The highlighted sentence explains why (part of the family) and how (education, moral behavior) a master's responsibility went beyond teaching a trade. The essential information is the fact that the master's responsibility went beyond teaching a trade. Therefore choice 2 contains all that is essential without changing the meaning of the highlighted sentence.

Choice 1 changes the meaning of the highlighted sentence by stating that masters often treated apprentices irresponsibly.

Choice 3 contradicts the essential meaning of the highlighted sentence. The fact that "Apprentices were considered part of the family" suggests that they were not actual family members.

Choice 4, like choice 3, changes the meaning of the highlighted sentence by discussing family members as apprentices.

3. ❹ This is a Vocabulary question. The word being tested is *disrupted*. It is highlighted in the passage. The correct answer is choice 4, "upset." The word *upset* here is used in the context of "hurting productivity." When something is hurt or damaged, it is "upset."

4. ❶ This is a Factual Information question asking for specific information that can be found in paragraph 4. The correct answer is choice 1, "support the idea that it was difficult for workers to adjust to working in factories." The paragraph begins by stating that workers did not adopt new attitudes toward work easily and that the clock symbolized the new work rules. The author provides the quotation as evidence of that difficulty. There is no indication in the paragraph that workers quit due to loud noise, so choice 2 is incorrect. Choice 3 (usefulness of clocks) is contradicted by the paragraph. The factory clock was "useful," but workers hated it. Choice 4 (workers' complaints as a cause of a factory's success) is not discussed in this paragraph.

5. ❹ This is a Negative Factual Information question asking for specific information that can be found in paragraph 4. Choice 4, "contact among workers who were not managers," is the correct answer. The paragraph explicitly contradicts this by stating that "factories sharply separated workers from management." The paragraph explicitly states that workers lost choice 1 (freedom), choice 2 (status in the community), and choice 3 (opportunities for advancement) in the new system, so those choices are all incorrect.

6. ❶ This is a Vocabulary question. The phrase being tested is *gathered some momentum*. It is highlighted in the passage. The correct answer is choice 1, "made progress." To *gather momentum* is to advance with increasing speed.

7. ❶ This is a Vocabulary question. The word being tested is *spearheaded*. It is highlighted in the passage. The correct answer is choice 1, "led." The head of a spear leads the rest of the spear, so the craftsworkers who "spearheaded" this movement led it.

8. ❸ This is a Factual Information question asking for specific information that can be found in paragraph 5. The correct answer is choice 3, "It was slow to improve conditions for workers." The paragraph states, "More than a decade of agitation did finally bring a workday shortened to 10 hours to most industries by the 1850s, and the courts also recognized workers' right to strike, but these gains had little immediate impact." This statement explicitly supports choice 3. All three other choices are contradicted by the paragraph.

9. ❷ This is a Factual Information question asking for specific information about a particular phrase in the passage. The phrase in question is highlighted in the passage. The correct answer is choice 2, "created divisions among workers." The paragraph states, "they (workers) were divided by ethnic and racial antagonisms, gender, conflicting religious perspectives, occupational differences, political party loyalties, and disagreements over tactics." So "political party loyalties" and "disagreements over tactics" are explicitly stated as two causes of division among workers. The other choices are not stated and are incorrect.

10. ❶ This is a Reference question. The word being tested is *them*. It is highlighted in the passage. This is a simple pronoun-referent item. The word *them* in this sentence refers to those people to whom "the factory and industrialism were not agents of opportunity but reminders of their loss of independence and a measure of control over their lives." Choice 1, "workers," is the only choice that refers to this type of person, so it is the correct answer.

11. ❹ This is an Insert Text question. You can see the four black squares in paragraph 1 that represent the possible answer choices here.

Before 1815 manufacturing in the United States had been done in homes or shops by skilled artisans. ■ As master craftworkers, they imparted the knowledge of their trades to apprentices and journeymen. ■ In addition, women often worked in their homes part-time, making finished articles from raw material supplied by merchant capitalists. ■ After 1815 this older form of manufacturing began to give way to factories with machinery tended by unskilled or semiskilled laborers. ■ Cheap transportation networks, the rise of cities, and the availability of capital and credit all stimulated the shift to factory production.

The sentence provided, "This new form of manufacturing depended on the movement of goods to distant locations and a centralized source of laborers," is best inserted at square 4. The inserted sentence refers explicitly to a "new form of manufacturing." This "new form of manufacturing" is the one mentioned in the sentence preceding square 4, "factories with machinery tended by unskilled or semiskilled laborers." The inserted sentence then explains that this new system "depended on the movement of goods to distant locations and a centralized source of laborers." The sentence that follows square 4 goes on to say, "Cheap transportation networks, the rise of cities, and the availability of capital and credit all stimulated the shift to factory production." Thus the inserted sentence contains references to both the sentence before square 4 and the sentence after square 4. This is not true of any of the other possible insert points, so square 4 is the correct answer.

12. This is a Fill in a Table question. It is completed correctly below. The correct choices for the "Before 1815" column are 2 and 6. Choices 3, 5, and 7 belong in the "1815–1850" column. Choices 1 and 4 should not be used in either column.

Directions: Complete the table below by indicating which of the answer choices describe characteristics of the period before 1815 and which describe characteristics of the 1815–1850 period. **This question is worth 3 points.**

Before 1815	1815–1850
● Workers took pride in their workmanship. ● Workers went through an extensive period of training.	● The income gap between the rich and the poor increased greatly. ● Emphasis was placed on following schedules. ● Few workers expected to own their own businesses.

Answer Choices

1. A united, highly successful labor movement took shape.

2. Workers took pride in their workmanship.

3. The income gap between the rich and the poor increased greatly.

4. Transportation networks began to decline.

5. Emphasis was placed on following schedules.

6. Workers went through an extensive period of training.

7. Few workers expected to own their own businesses.

Correct Choices

Choice 2: "Workers took pride in their workmanship" belongs in the "Before 1815" column because it is mentioned in the passage as one of the characteristics of labor before 1815.

Choice 3: "The income gap between the rich and the poor increased greatly" belongs in the "1815–1850" column because it is mentioned in the passage as one of the characteristics of society that emerged in the period between 1815 and 1850.

Choice 5: "Emphasis was placed on following schedules" belongs in the "1815–1850" column because it is mentioned in the passage as one of the characteristics of labor in the factory system that emerged between 1815 and 1850.

Choice 6: "Workers went through an extensive period of training" belongs in the "Before 1815" column because it is mentioned in the passage as one of the characteristics of labor before 1815.

Choice 7: "Few workers expected to own their own businesses" belongs in the "1815–1850" column because it is mentioned in the passage as one of the characteristics of society that emerged in the period between 1815 and 1850.

Incorrect Choices

Choice 1: "A united, highly successful labor movement took shape" does not belong in the table because it contradicts the passage.

Choice 4: "Transportation networks began to decline" does not belong in the table because it is not mentioned in the passage in connection with either the period before 1815 or the period between 1815 and 1850.

PRACTICE SET 6

SWIMMING MACHINES

Tunas, mackerels, and billfishes (marlins, sailfishes, and swordfish) swim continuously. Feeding, courtship, reproduction, and even "rest" are carried out while in constant motion. As a result, practically every aspect of the body form and function of these swimming "machines" is adapted to enhance their ability to swim.

Many of the adaptations of these fishes serve to reduce water resistance (drag). Interestingly enough, several of these hydrodynamic adaptations resemble features designed to improve the aerodynamics of high-speed aircraft. Though human engineers are new to the game, tunas and their relatives evolved their "high-tech" designs long ago.

Tunas, mackerels, and billfishes have made streamlining into an art form. Their bodies are sleek and compact. The body shapes of tunas, in fact, are nearly ideal from an engineering point of view. Most species lack scales over most of the body, making it smooth and slippery. The eyes lie flush with the body and do not protrude at all. They are also covered with a slick, transparent lid that reduces drag. The fins are stiff, smooth, and narrow, qualities that also help cut drag. When not in use, the fins are tucked into special grooves or depressions so that they lie flush with the body and do not break up its smooth contours. Airplanes retract their landing gear while in flight for the same reason.

Tunas, mackerels, and billfishes have even more sophisticated adaptations than these to improve their hydrodynamics. The long bill of marlins, sailfishes, and swordfish probably helps them slip through the water. Many supersonic aircraft have a similar needle at the nose.

Most tunas and billfishes have a series of keels and finlets near the tail. Although most of their scales have been lost, tunas and mackerels retain a patch of coarse scales near the head called the corselet. The keels, finlets, and corselet help direct the flow of water over the body surface in such a way as to reduce resistance (see the figure). Again, supersonic jets have similar features.

Because they are always swimming, tunas simply have to open their mouths and water is forced in and over their gills. Accordingly, they have lost most of the muscles that other fishes use to suck in water and push it past the gills. In fact, tunas must swim to breathe. They must also keep swimming to keep from sinking, since most have largely or completely lost the swim bladder, the gas-filled sac that helps most other fish remain buoyant.

One potential problem is that opening the mouth to breathe detracts from the streamlining of these fishes and tends to slow them down. Some species of tuna have specialized grooves in their tongue. It is thought that these grooves help to channel water through the mouth and out the gill slits, thereby reducing water resistance.

There are adaptations that increase the amount of forward thrust as well as those that reduce drag. Again, these fishes are the envy of engineers. Their high, narrow tails with swept-back tips are almost perfectly adapted to provide propulsion with the least possible effort. Perhaps most important of all to these and other fast swimmers is their ability to sense and make use of swirls and eddies (circular currents) in the water. They can glide past eddies that would slow them down and then gain extra thrust by "pushing off" the eddies. Scientists and engineers are beginning to study this ability of fishes in the hope of designing more efficient propulsion systems for ships.

The muscles of these fishes and the mechanism that maintains a warm body temperature are also highly efficient. A bluefin tuna in water of 7°C (45°F) can maintain a core temperature of over 25°C (77°F). This warm body temperature may help not only the muscles to work better, but also the brain and the eyes. The billfishes have gone one step further. They have evolved special "heaters" of modified muscle tissue that warm the eyes and brain, maintaining peak performance of these critical organs.

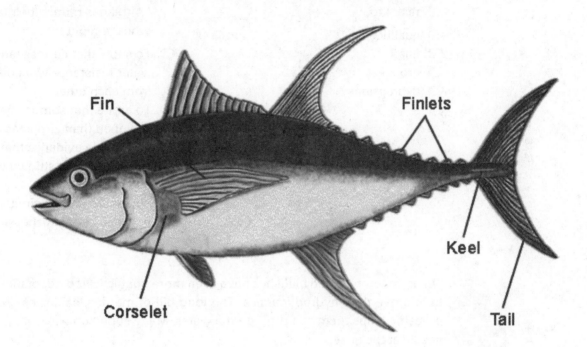

PARAGRAPH 1

Tunas, mackerels, and billfishes (marlins, sailfishes, and swordfish) swim continuously. Feeding, courtship, reproduction, and even "rest" are carried out while in constant motion. As a result, practically every aspect of the body form and function of these swimming "machines" is adapted to enhance their ability to swim.

Directions: Mark your answer by filling in the oval next to your choice.

1.   The word "enhance" in the passage is closest in meaning to
   ○ use
   ○ improve
   ○ counteract
   ○ balance

PARAGRAPH 3

Tunas, mackerels, and billfishes have made streamlining into an art form. Their bodies are sleek and compact. The body shapes of tunas, in fact, are nearly ideal from an engineering point of view. Most species lack scales over most of the body, making it smooth and slippery. The eyes lie flush with the body and do not protrude at all. They are also covered with a slick, transparent lid that reduces drag. The fins are stiff, smooth, and narrow, qualities that also help cut drag. When not in use, the fins are tucked into special grooves or depressions so that they lie flush with the body and do not break up its smooth contours. Airplanes retract their landing gear while in flight for the same reason.

2. The word "they" in the passage refers to

○ qualities
○ fins
○ grooves
○ depressions

3. Why does the author mention that "Airplanes retract their landing gear while in flight"?

○ To show that air resistance and water resistance work differently from each other
○ To argue that some fishes are better designed than airplanes are
○ To provide evidence that airplane engineers have studied the design of fish bodies
○ To demonstrate a similarity in design between certain fishes and airplanes

PARAGRAPH 4

Tunas, mackerels, and billfishes have even more sophisticated adaptations than these to improve their hydrodynamics. The long bill of marlins, sailfishes, and swordfish probably helps them slip through the water. Many supersonic aircraft have a similar needle at the nose.

4. The word "sophisticated" in the passage is closest in meaning to

○ complex
○ amazing
○ creative
○ practical

5. According to paragraph 4, the long bills of marlins, sailfish, and swordfish probably help these fishes by

○ increasing their ability to defend themselves
○ allowing them to change direction easily
○ increasing their ability to detect odors
○ reducing water resistance as they swim

PARAGRAPH 6

Because they are always swimming, tunas simply have to open their mouths and water is forced in and over their gills. Accordingly, they have lost most of the muscles that other fishes use to suck in water and push it past the gills. In fact, tunas must swim to breathe. They must also keep swimming to keep from sinking, since most have largely or completely lost the swim bladder, the gas-filled sac that helps most other fish remain buoyant.

6. According to the passage, which of the following is one of the reasons that tunas are in constant motion?

○ They lack a swim bladder.
○ They need to suck in more water than other fishes do.
○ They have large muscles for breathing.
○ They cannot open their mouths unless they are in motion.

PARAGRAPH 7

One potential problem is that opening the mouth to breathe detracts from the stream-lining of these fishes and tends to slow them down. Some species of tuna have specialized grooves in their tongue. It is thought that these grooves help to channel water through the mouth and out the gill slits, thereby reducing water resistance.

7. Which of the sentences below best expresses the essential information in the highlighted sentence in the passage? Incorrect answer choices change the meaning in important ways or leave out essential information.

○ These fishes often have a problem opening their mouths while swimming.
○ The streamlining of these fishes prevents them from slowing down.
○ The streamlining of these fishes tends to slow down their breathing.
○ Opening the mouth to breathe can reduce the speed of these fishes.

8. The word "channel" in the passage is closest in meaning to

○ reduce
○ remove
○ direct
○ provide

PARAGRAPH 8

There are adaptations that increase the amount of forward thrust as well as those that reduce drag. Again, these fishes are the envy of engineers. Their high, narrow tails with swept-back tips are almost perfectly adapted to provide propulsion with the least possible effort. Perhaps most important of all to these and other fast swimmers is their ability to sense and make use of swirls and eddies (circular currents) in the water. They can glide past eddies that would slow them down and then gain extra thrust by "pushing off" the eddies. Scientists and engineers are beginning to study this ability of fishes in the hope of designing more efficient propulsion systems for ships.

9. According to the passage, one of the adaptations of fast-swimming fishes that might be used to improve the performance of ships is these fishes' ability to

○ swim directly through eddies
○ make efficient use of water currents
○ cover great distances without stopping
○ gain speed by forcing water past their gills

PARAGRAPH 9

The muscles of these fishes and the mechanism that maintains a warm body temperature are also highly efficient. A bluefin tuna in water of 7°C (45°F) can maintain a core temperature of over 25°C (77°F). This warm body temperature may help not only the muscles to work better, but also the brain and the eyes. The billfishes have gone one step further. They have evolved special "heaters" of modified muscle tissue that warm the eyes and brain, maintaining peak performance of these critical organs.

10. According to paragraph 9, which of the following is true of bluefin tunas?

○ Their eyes and brain are more efficient than those of any other fish.
○ Their body temperature can change greatly depending on the water temperature.
○ They can swim in waters that are much colder than their own bodies.
○ They have special muscle tissue that warms their eyes and brain.

Again, supersonic jets have similar features.

■ Because they are always swimming, tunas simply have to open their mouths and water is forced in and over their gills. ■ Accordingly, they have lost most of the muscles that other fishes use to suck in water and push it past the gills. ■ In fact, tunas must swim to breathe. ■ They must also keep swimming to keep from sinking, since most have largely or completely lost the swim bladder, the gas-filled sac that helps most other fish remain buoyant.

11. Look at the four squares [■] that indicate where the following sentence can be added to the passage.

Consequently, tunas do not need to suck in water.

Where would the sentence best fit?

○ Again, supersonic jets have similar features.

 Consequently, tunas do not need to suck in water. Because they are always swimming, tunas simply have to open their mouths and water is forced in and over their gills. ■ Accordingly, they have lost most of the muscles that other fishes use to suck in water and push it past the gills. ■ In fact, tunas must swim to breathe. ■ They must also keep swimming to keep from sinking, since most have largely or completely lost the swim bladder, the gas-filled sac that helps most other fish remain buoyant.

○ Again, supersonic jets have similar features.

 ■ Because they are always swimming, tunas simply have to open their mouths and water is forced in and over their gills. **Consequently, tunas do not need to suck in water.** Accordingly, they have lost most of the muscles that other fishes use to suck in water and push it past the gills. ■ In fact, tunas must swim to breathe. ■ They must also keep swimming to keep from sinking, since most have largely or completely lost the swim bladder, the gas-filled sac that helps most other fish remain buoyant.

○ Again, supersonic jets have similar features.

 ■ Because they are always swimming, tunas simply have to open their mouths and water is forced in and over their gills. ■ Accordingly, they have lost most of the muscles that other fishes use to suck in water and push it past the gills. **Consequently, tunas do not need to suck in water.** In fact, tunas must swim to breathe. ■ They must also keep swimming to keep from sinking, since most have largely or completely lost the swim bladder, the gas-filled sac that helps most other fish remain buoyant.

○ Again, supersonic jets have similar features.

 ■ Because they are always swimming, tunas simply have to open their mouths and water is forced in and over their gills. ■ Accordingly, they have lost most of the muscles that other fishes use to suck in water and push it past the gills. ■ In fact, tunas must swim to breathe. **Consequently, tunas do not need to suck in water.** They must also keep swimming to keep from sinking, since most have largely or completely lost the swim bladder, the gas-filled sac that helps most other fish remain buoyant.

12. **Directions:** Complete the table below by indicating which features of fishes are associated in the passage with reducing water resistance and which are associated with increasing thrust. **This question is worth 3 points.**

Reducing Water Resistance	Increasing Thrust
•	•
•	•
•	

Answer Choices

1. The absence of scales from most of the body

2. The ability to take advantage of eddies

3. The ability to feed and reproduce while swimming

4. Eyes that do not protrude

5. Fins that are stiff, narrow, and smooth

6. The habit of swimming with the mouth open

7. A high, narrow tail with swept-back tips

PRACTICE SET 6 ANSWERS AND EXPLANATIONS

1. **2** This is a Vocabulary question. The word being tested is *enhance*. It is highlighted in the passage. The correct answer is choice 2, "improve." To *enhance* something means to "make it better." If something has been "improved," it has been made better.

2. **2** This is a Reference question. The word being tested is *they*. It is highlighted in the passage. Choice 2, "fins," is the correct answer. This is a simple pronoun-referent item. The word *they* refers to something that lies flush with the body when not in use. This is true only of "fins."

3. **4** This is a Rhetorical Purpose question. It asks why the author mentions that "Airplanes retract their landing gear while in flight." The phrase being tested is highlighted in the passage. The correct answer is choice 4, "To demonstrate a similarity in design between certain fishes and airplanes." The paragraph in which the highlighted phrase appears describes how certain fish use their fins. The highlighted phrase is used to provide a more familiar example (airplanes) of the principle involved to help the reader visualize how fins work. The paragraph does not discuss airplanes in any other context, so choices 2 and 3 are incorrect. Air and water resistance are not mentioned in this paragraph, so choice 1 is incorrect.

4. **1** This is a Vocabulary question. The word being tested is *sophisticated*. It is highlighted in the passage. The correct answer is choice 1, "complex." If something is *sophisticated*, it is "not simple," so it must be "complex."

5. ❹ This is a Factual Information question asking for specific information that can be found in paragraph 4. The correct answer is choice 4, "reducing water resistance as they swim." The overall theme of the passage is how certain fish swim so efficiently. Paragraphs 1 and 2 make the general statement that "practically every aspect of the body form and function of these swimming 'machines' is adapted to enhance their ability to swim. Many of the adaptations of these fishes serve to reduce water resistance (drag)."

Paragraph 4 explicitly states (emphasis added), "Tunas, mackerels, and billfishes have even more sophisticated *adaptations than these to improve their hydrodynamics. The long bill* of marlins, sailfishes, and swordfish probably helps them slip through the water." This is a specific example of one adaptation that these fish have made to increase their swimming efficiency. None of the other choices is mentioned in the paragraph.

6. ❶ This is a Factual Information question asking for specific information that can be found in the passage. The correct answer is choice 1, "They lack a swim bladder."

Paragraph 6 explicitly states, "tunas must swim to breathe. They must also keep swimming to keep from sinking, since most have largely or completely lost the swim bladder." The other choices are not supported by the passage.

7. ❹ This is a Sentence Simplification question. As with all of these questions, a single sentence in the passage is highlighted:

One potential problem is that opening the mouth to breathe detracts from the streamlining of these fishes and tends to slow them down.

The correct answer is choice 4. That choice contains all of the essential ideas in the highlighted sentence. It is also the only choice that does not change the meaning of the sentence. It omits the fact that this is a "problem" and also that it "detracts from the streamlining" because that information is not essential to the meaning.

Choice 1 says that these fish have trouble opening their mouths while swimming, which is not true. Choice 2, that streamlining prevents fish from slowing down, may be true, but it is not mentioned in this sentence. The fish are slowed down when they open their mouths, which reduces streamlining. Choice 3, that streamlining slows the fishes' breathing, is also not mentioned.

8. ❸ This is a Vocabulary question. The word being tested is *channel*. It is highlighted in the passage. The correct answer is choice 3, "direct." *Channel* here is used as a verb, meaning "move" or "push."

9. ❷ This is a Factual Information question asking for specific information that can be found in the passage. The correct answer is choice 2, "make efficient use of water currents." Paragraph 8 explicitly states, "Perhaps most important of all to these and other fast swimmers is their ability to sense and make use of swirls and eddies (circular currents) in the water. They can glide past eddies that would slow them down and then gain extra thrust by 'pushing off'

the eddies. Scientists and engineers are beginning to study this ability of fishes in the hope of designing more efficient propulsion systems for ships." The other choices are not mentioned in connection with the performance of ships.

10. ❸ This is a Factual Information question asking for specific information that can be found in paragraph 9. The correct answer is choice 3, "They can swim in waters that are much colder than their own bodies." That paragraph says, "A bluefin tuna in water of 7°C (45°F) can maintain a core temperature of over 25°C (77°F)." So it is clear that choice 3 is correct. Choice 1 is not stated in the paragraph. Choice 2 is contradicted by the paragraph. Choice 4 is true of billfish, not bluefin tuna.

11. ❷ This is an Insert Text question. You can see the four black squares in paragraph 6 that represent the possible answer choices here. The last sentence of paragraph 5 is also reproduced below.

Again, supersonic jets have similar features. ■ Because they are always swimming, tunas simply have to open their mouths and water is forced in and over their gills. ■ Accordingly, they have lost most of the muscles that other fishes use to suck in water and push it past the gills. ■ In fact, tunas must swim to breathe. ■ They must also keep swimming to keep from sinking, since most have largely or completely lost the swim bladder, the gas-filled sac that helps most other fish remain buoyant.

The sentence provided, "Consequently, tunas do not need to suck in water," is best inserted at square 2. The sentence offers an explanation for the muscle loss described in the sentence that follows square 2 and is a result of the fact described in the preceding sentence, which says that because the fish are always swimming, they only have to open their mouths to suck in water. Thus if the provided sentence is inserted at square 2, it offers a logical bridge between cause and effect. The sentence makes no logical sense anywhere else.

12. This is a Fill in a Table question. It is completed correctly below. The correct choices for the "Reducing Water Resistance" column are 1, 4, and 5. Choices 2 and 7 belong in the "Increasing Thrust" column. Choices 3 and 6 should not be used in either column.

Directions: Complete the table below by indicating which features of fishes are associated in the passage with reducing water resistance and which are associated with increasing thrust. **This question is worth 3 points.**

Reducing Water Resistance	Increasing Thrust
● The absence of scales from most of the body	● The ability to take advantage of eddies
● Eyes that do not protrude	● A high, narrow tail with swept-back tips
● Fins that are stiff, narrow, and smooth	

Answer Choices

1. The absence of scales from most of the body

2. The ability to take advantage of eddies

3. The ability to feed and reproduce while swimming

4. Eyes that do not protrude

5. Fins that are stiff, narrow, and smooth

6. The habit of swimming with the mouth open

7. A high, narrow tail with swept-back tips

Correct Choices

Choice 1: "The absence of scales from most of the body" belongs in the "Reducing Water Resistance" column because it is mentioned in paragraphs 3 and 5 as a factor that reduces water resistance.

Choice 2: "The ability to take advantage of eddies" belongs in the "Increasing Thrust" column because it is mentioned in paragraph 8 as a characteristic that helps increase thrust.

Choice 4: "Eyes that do not protrude" belongs in the "Reducing Water Resistance" column because it is mentioned in paragraph 3 as a factor that reduces water resistance.

Choice 5: "Fins that are stiff, narrow, and smooth" belongs in the "Reducing Water Resistance" column because it is mentioned in paragraph 3 as a factor that reduces water resistance.

Choice 7: "A high, narrow tail with swept-back tips" belongs in the "Increasing Thrust" column because it is mentioned in paragraph 8 as a characteristic that helps increase thrust.

Incorrect Choices

Choice 3: "The ability to feed and reproduce while swimming" does not belong in the table because it is not mentioned in the passage in connection with either reducing water resistance or increasing thrust.

Choice 6: "The habit of swimming with the mouth open" does not belong in the table because it is not mentioned in the passage in connection with either reducing water resistance or increasing thrust.

3 Listening Section

Read this chapter to learn

- The 8 types of TOEFL iBT Listening questions
- How to recognize each Listening question type
- Tips for answering each Listening question type
- Strategies for preparing for the Listening section

In the TOEFL iBT Listening section you will listen to four to six lectures and two to three conversations. There will be six questions per lecture and five questions per conversation. You will have a total of 60 to 90 minutes to answer all of the Listening questions.

Listening Materials

There are two types of Listening materials on the TOEFL iBT test, conversations and lectures. Both are based on the actual speech that is used in North American colleges and universities.

Each lecture or conversation is 3–6 minutes long and, as far as possible, represents authentic academic language. For example, a professor giving a lecture may digress somewhat from the main topic, interactions between students and the professor can be extensive, and explanations of content can be elaborate. Features of oral language such as false starts, misspeaks with self-corrections, and repetitions are included. The speakers who record the texts are encouraged to use their own speech patterns (for example, with pauses and hesitations), as long as they preserve the content of the text. You should take notes during the lectures and conversations. This material is not meant to test your memory.

Conversations

There are two types of conversations in the Listening section:

- office hours
- service encounters

These conversations are typical of those that occur on North American university campuses. Office hours conversations are interactions that take place in a professor's office. The content may be academic or related to course requirements. For example, in an office conversation a student could request an extension on a due date (nonacademic content), or a student could ask for clarification about the content of a lecture (academic content). Service encounters are interactions that take place on a university campus and have nonacademic content. Examples include inquiring about a payment for housing and registering for class. Each conversation is followed by five questions.

Lectures

Lectures in the Listening section represent the kind of language used when professors teach in a classroom. The lecture excerpt may include just a professor speaking, a student asking the professor a question, or the professor asking the students a question and calling on one student for a response. Each lecture is approximately 5 minutes in length and is followed by six questions.

The content of the lectures reflects the content that is presented in introductory-level academic settings. Lecture topics cover a broad range of subjects. You will not be expected to have any prior knowledge of the subject matter. All the information you need to answer the questions will be contained in the lecture. The lists below are provided to give you an idea of the topics that typically appear in the Listening section. In general these topics are divided into four major categories:

- Arts
- Life Science
- Physical Science
- Social Science

Arts lectures may be on topics such as:

- Architecture
- Industrial design/art
- City planning
- Crafts (weaving, knitting, fabrics, furniture, carving, mosaics, ceramics, folk and tribal art)
- Cave/rock art
- Music and music history
- Photography
- Literature and authors
- Books, newspapers, magazines, journals

Life Science lectures may be on topics such as:

- Extinction of or conservation efforts for animals and plants
- Fish and other aquatic organisms
- Bacteria and other one-celled organisms
- Viruses
- Medical techniques
- Public health
- Physiology of sensory organs
- Biochemistry
- Animal behavior (migration, food foraging, defenses)

- Habitats and the adaptation of animals and plants to them
- Nutrition and its impact on the body
- Animal communication

Physical Science lectures may be on topics such as:

- Weather and atmosphere
- Oceanography
- Glaciers, glacial landforms, ice ages
- Deserts and other extreme environments
- Pollution, alternative energy, environmental policy
- Other planets' atmospheres
- Astronomy and cosmology
- Properties of light, optics
- Properties of sound
- Electromagnetic radiation
- Particle physics
- Technology of TV, radio, radar
- Chemistry of inorganic things
- Computer science
- Seismology (plate structure, earthquakes, tectonics, continental drift, structure of volcanoes)

Social Science lectures may be on topics such as:

- Anthropology of nonindustrialized civilizations
- Early writing systems
- Historical linguistics
- Business, management, marketing, accounting
- TV/radio as mass communication
- Social behavior of groups, community dynamics, communal behavior
- Child development
- Education
- Modern history (including the history of urbanization and industrialization and their economic and social effects)

Listening Questions

Most of the Listening questions that follow the lectures and conversations are traditional multiple-choice questions with four answer choices and a single correct answer. There are, however, some other types of questions:

- multiple-choice questions with more than one correct answer (for example, two answers out of four choices or three answers out of five choices)
- questions that require you to put in order events or steps in a process
- questions that require you to match objects or text to categories in a table

Some questions replay a part of the lecture or conversation. You will then be asked a multiple-choice question about what you have just heard.

There are eight types of questions in the Listening section. These types are divided into three categories as follows:

TOEFL Listening Question Types

Basic Comprehension questions
1. Gist-content
2. Gist-purpose
3. Detail

Pragmatic Understanding questions
4. Understanding the Function of What Is Said
5. Understanding the Speaker's Attitude

Connecting Information questions
6. Understanding Organization
7. Connecting Content
8. Making Inferences

The following sections will explain each of these question types. You will find out how to recognize each type and see examples of each type with explanations. You will also find tips that can help you answer each Listening question type.

Basic Comprehension Questions

Basic comprehension of the lecture or conversation is tested in three ways: with Gist-content, Gist-purpose, and Detail questions.

Type 1: Gist-content Questions

Understanding the *gist* of a lecture or conversation means understanding the general topic or main idea. The gist of the lecture or conversation may be expressed explicitly or implicitly. Questions that test understanding the gist of a lecture or converation may require you to generalize or synthesize information from what you hear.

How to Recognize Gist-content Questions

Gist-content questions are typically phrased as follows:

- What problem does the man have?
- What are the speakers mainly discussing?
- What is the main topic of the lecture?
- What is the lecture mainly about?
- What aspect of X does the professor mainly discuss?

Tips for Gist-content Questions

- Gist-content questions ask about the *overall* content of the lecture or converation. Eliminate choices that refer to only small portions of what you just listened to.

- Use your notes. Decide what overall theme ties the details in your notes together. Choose the answer that comes closest to describing this overall theme.

Example　Excerpt from a lecture:

Professor

. . . So the Earth's surface is made up of these huge segments, these tectonic plates. And these plates move, right? But how can, uh, motion of plates, do you think, influence climate on the Earth? Again, all of you probably read this section in the book, I hope, but, uh, uh, how—how can just motion of the plates impact the climate?

. . . when a plate moves, if there's landmass on the plate, then the landmass moves too, okay? That's why continents shift their positions, because the plates they're on move. So as a landmass moves away from the equator, its climate would get colder. So, right now we have a continent—the landmass Antarctica—that's on a pole.

So that's dramatically influencing the climate in Antarctica. Um, there was a time when most of the landmasses were closer to a pole; they weren't so close to the equator. Uh, maybe 200 million years ago Antarctica was attached to the South American continent; oh, and Africa was attached too, and the three of them began moving away from the equator together.

. . . in the Himalayas. That was where two continental plates collided. Two continents on separate plates. Um, when this, uh, Indian, uh, uh, plate collided with the Asian plate, it wasn't until then that we created the Himalayas. When we did that, then we started creating the type of cold climate that we see there now. Wasn't there until this area was uplifted.

So again, that's something else that plate tectonics plays a critical role in. Now, these processes are relatively slow; the, uh, Himalayas are still rising, but on the order of millimeters per year. So they're not dramatically influencing climate on your—the time scale of your lifetime. But over the last few thousands of—tens of thousands of years, uh—hundreds of thousands of years—yes, they've dramatically influenced it.

Uh, another important thing—number three—on how plate tectonics have influenced climate is how they've influenced—we talked about how changing landmasses can affect atmospheric circulation patterns, but if you alter where the landmasses are connected, it can impact oceanic, uh, uh, uh, circulation patterns.

. . . Um, so, uh, these other processes, if, if we were to disconnect North and South America right through the middle—say, through Panama—that would dramatically influence climate in North and South America—probably the whole globe. So suddenly now as the two continents gradually move apart, you can have different circulation patterns in the ocean between the two. So, uh, that might cause a dramatic change in climate if that were to happen, just as we've had happen here in Antarctica to separate, uh, from South America.

What is the main topic of the lecture?

○ The differences in climate that occur in different countries
○ How movement of the Earth's plates can affect climate
○ Why the ocean has less effect on climate than previously thought
○ The history of the climate of the region where the university is located

Explanation

Choice 2 is the answer that best represents the main topic of the lecture. The professor uses Antarctica and the Himalayas as examples to make the general point that climate is affected by plate tectonics, the movement of Earth's plates.

Note that for Gist-content questions the correct answer and the incorrect choices can sometimes be worded more abstractly.

The following Gist-content question refers to the same lecture:

What is the main topic of the lecture?

○ A climate experiment and its results
○ A geologic process and its effect
○ How a theory was disproved
○ How land movement is measured

Explanation

Once again, the correct answer is choice 2. Even though the wording is very different, it basically says the same thing as choice 2 in the previous example: a geologic process (movement of Earth's plates) has an effect (changes in climate).

Type 2: Gist-purpose Questions

Some gist questions focus on the purpose of the conversation or lecture rather than on the content. This type of question will more likely occur with conversations, but Gist-purpose questions may also occasionally be asked about lectures.

How to Recognize Gist-purpose Questions

Gist-purpose questions are typically phrased as follows:

- Why does the student visit the professor?
- Why does the student visit the registrar's office?
- Why did the professor ask to see the student?
- Why does the professor explain X?

Tips for Gist-purpose Questions

- Students visit professors during office hours for various reasons, including cases in which a professor invites a student in to discuss the student's performance on an assignment. To answer a Gist-purpose question, look in your notes for information that identifies the reason that the student visited the professor in the first place.

- The purpose of a conversation is not always related to the conversation's main topic. For example, a student might visit her professor for the purpose of asking a question about the professor's grading policy. After answering her question, the professor might spontaneously ask how the student is progressing on a research project, and the rest of the conversation is about that project.

- In service encounter conversations, the student is often trying to solve a problem. Understanding what the student's problem is and how it will be solved will help you answer the Gist-purpose question.

Example

Narrator

Listen to a conversation between a professor and a student.

Student

I was hoping you could look over my note cards for my presentation . . . just to see what you think of it.

Professor

Okay, so refresh my memory: what's your presentation about?

Student

Two models of decision making . . .

Professor

Oh, yes—the classical and the administrative model.

Student

Yeah, that's it.

Professor

And what's the point of your talk?

Student

I'm gonna talk about the advantages and disadvantages of both models.

Professor

But what's the point of your talk? Are you going to say that one's better than the other?

Student

Well, I think the administrative model's definitely more realistic. But I don't think it's complete. It's kind of a tool . . . a tool to see what can go wrong.

Professor

Okay, so what's the point of your talk? What are you trying to convince me to believe?

Student

Well, uh, the classical model—you shouldn't use it by itself. A lot of companies just try to follow the classical model, but they should really use both models together.

Professor

Okay, good. So let me take a look at your notes here . . . Oh, typed notes, . . . Wow you've got a lot packed in here. Are you sure you're going to be able to follow this during your talk?

Student

Oh, sure; that's why I typed them, because otherwise . . . well, my handwriting's not very clear.

Why does the student visit the professor?

- ○ To get some note cards for his presentation
- ○ To show her some examples of common errors in research
- ○ To review the notes for his presentation with her
- ○ To ask for help in finding a topic for his presentation

Explanation

While much of the conversation is concerned with the content of the man's presentation, the correct answer to the question "Why does the man visit the professor?" is choice 3: "To review the notes for his presentation with her."

Type 3: Detail Questions

Detail questions require you to understand and remember explicit details or facts from a lecture or conversation. These details are typically related, directly or indirectly, to the gist of the conversation or lecture, by providing elaboration, examples, or other support. In some cases where there is a long digression that is not clearly related to the main idea, you may be asked about some details of the digression.

How to Recognize Detail Questions

Detail questions are typically phrased as follows:

- According to the professor, what is one way that X can affect Y?
- What is X?
- What resulted from the invention of the X?
- According to the professor, what is the main problem with the X theory?

> ### *Tips for Detail Questions*
>
> - Refer to your notes as you answer. You will not be asked about minor points. Your notes should contain the major details from the conversation or lecture.
>
> - Do not choose an answer only because it contains some of the words that were used in the conversation or lecture. Incorrect responses will often contain words and phrases from the lecture or conversation.
>
> - If you are unsure of the correct response, decide which one of the choices is most consistent with the main idea of the conversation or lecture.

Examples | ### Professor

Uh, other things that glaciers can do is, uh, as they retreat, instead of depositing some till, uh, scraped-up soil, in the area, they might leave a big ice block, and it breaks off, and as the ice block melts, it leaves a depression, which can become a lake. These are called kettle lakes. These are very critical ecosystems in this region, um, because, uh, uh, they support some unique biological diversity, these kettle lakes do.

The Great Lakes are like this; they were left over from the Pleist—from the Pleistocene glaciers. Uh, the Great Lakes used to be a lot bigger as the glaciers were retreating; some of the lakes were as much as a hundred feet higher in elevation. The beach of a former higher stage of Lake Erie was about 50 miles away from where the beach—the current beach of Lake Erie—is right now. So I just wanted to tell you a little bit more about glaciers and some *positive* things, uh, that we get from climate change, like the ecosystems that develop in these kettle lakes, and how we can look at them in an environmental perspective . . .

What are kettle lakes?

○ Lakes that form in the center of a volcano
○ Lakes that have been damaged by the greenhouse effect
○ Lakes formed by unusually large amounts of precipitation
○ Lakes formed when pieces of glaciers melt

How did the glaciers affect the Great Lakes?

○ They made the Great Lakes smaller.
○ They made the Great Lakes deeper.
○ They reduced the biodiversity of the Great Lakes.
○ They widened the beaches around the Great Lakes.

Explanation

The answer to the first question is found in the beginning of the lecture when the professor explains what a kettle lake is. Remember that new terminology is often tested in Detail questions. The answer to the second question is found later in the lecture where the professor says, "the Great Lakes used to be a lot bigger as the glaciers were retreating."

Pragmatic Understanding Questions

Pragmatic Understanding questions test understanding of certain features of spoken English that go beyond basic comprehension. In general, these types of questions test how well you understand the *function* of an utterance or the *stance*, or attitude, that the speaker expresses. In most instances, Pragmatic Understanding questions will test parts of the conversation or lecture where a speaker's purpose or attitude is not expressed directly. In these cases, what is directly stated—the surface expression—will not be an exact match of the statement's function or purpose.

What people say is often intended to be understood on a level that lies beyond or beneath the surface expression. To use an often-cited example, the sentence "It sure is cold in here" can be understood literally as a statement of fact about the temperature of a room. But suppose the speaker is, say, a guest in your home, who is also shivering and glancing at an open window. In that case, what your guest may really mean is that he wants you to close the open window. In this example, the *function* of the speaker's statement—getting you to close the window—lies beneath the surface expression. Functions that often lie beneath the surface expression include directing, recommending, complaining, accepting, agreeing, narrating, questioning, and others.

Understanding meaning within the context of an entire lecture or conversation is critical in instances where the speaker's *stance* is involved. Is a given statement intended to be taken as fact or opinion? How certain is the speaker of the information she is reporting? Is the speaker conveying certain feelings or attitudes about some person or thing or event? As above, these feelings or attitudes may lie beneath the surface expression. Thus they can easily go unrecognized or be misunderstood by nonnative speakers.

Some Pragmatic Understanding questions involve a replay of part of the lecture or conversation in order to focus your attention on the relevant portion. There are two types of Pragmatic Understanding questions: Understanding the Function of What Is Said questions and Understanding the Speaker's Attitude questions.

Type 4: Understanding the Function of What Is Said Questions

The first type of Pragmatic Understanding question tests whether you can understand the *function* of what is said. This question type often involves listening again to a portion of the lecture or conversation.

How to Recognize Understanding the Function of What Is Said Questions

Understanding the Function of What Is Said questions are typically phrased as follows:

- What does the professor imply when he says this? *(replay)*
- Why does the student say this? *(replay)*
- What does the professor mean when she says this? *(replay)*

Example   Excerpt from a conversation between a male student and a female administrative assistant. They are discussing his dorm fees.

Narrator

Listen again to a part of the conversation. Then answer the question.

Student

Okay. I'll just pay with a credit card. *[pause]* And where do I do that at?

Administrative Assistant

At, um, the housing office.

Student

Housing office, all right.

Administrative Assistant

Do you know where they are?

Narrator

What is the woman trying to find out from the man?

- ○ Where the housing office is
- ○ Approximately how far away the housing office is
- ○ Whether she needs to tell him where the housing office is
- ○ Whether he has been to the housing office already

Explanation

The pragmatic function of the woman's question is to ask the man whether or not he needs to be told the location of the housing office. The best answer for this question is choice 3.

Type 5: Understanding the Speaker's Attitude Questions

The second type of Pragmatic Understanding question tests whether you understand a speaker's attitude or opinion. You may be asked a question about the speaker's feelings, likes and dislikes, or reason for anxiety or amusement. Also included in this category are questions about a speaker's degree of certainty: Is the speaker referencing a source or giving a personal opinion? Are the facts presented generally accepted or are they disputed? Occasionally, a question will test your ability to detect and understand irony. A speaker is being ironic when the intended meaning is the opposite of what he or she is actually saying. For example, the utterance "That's just great" can be delivered with an intonation that gives the utterance the meaning "That's not good at all." Speakers use irony for a variety of purposes, including emphasizing a point being made, bringing humor to a situation in order to win audience sympathy, or expressing disapproval in an indirect way. Listeners must infer the ironic statement's real meaning both from clues provided in the context and from the speaker's intonation.

How to Recognize Understanding the Speaker's Attitude Questions

Understanding the Speaker's Attitude questions are typically phrased as follows:

- What can be inferred about the student?
- What is the professor's attitude toward X?
- What is the professor's opinion of X?
- What can be inferred about the student when she says this? *(replay)*
- What does the woman mean when she says this? *(replay)*

Tip for Understanding the Speaker's Attitude Questions

- Learn to pay attention to the speaker's tone of voice. Does the speaker sound apologetic? Confused? Enthusiastic? The speaker's tone can help you answer this kind of question.

Example

Excerpt from a conversation between a male student and his female advisor. In this part of a longer conversation, they are discussing the student's job.

Advisor

Well, good. So, bookstore isn't working out?

Student

Oh, bookstore's working out fine. I just, I—this pays almost double what the bookstore does.

Advisor

Oh, wow!

Student

Yeah. Plus credit.

Advisor

Plus credit.

Student

And it's more hours, which . . . The bookstore's—I mean it's a decent job 'n' all. Everybody I work with . . . that part's great; it's just . . . I mean I'm shelving books and kind of hanging out and not doing much else . . . if it weren't for the people, it'd be totally boring.

Narrator

What is the student's attitude toward the people he currently works with?

○ He finds them boring.
○ He likes them.
○ He is annoyed by them.
○ He does not have much in common with them.

Explanation

In this example it may be easy to confuse the student's attitude toward his job with his attitude toward the people he works with. The correct answer is choice 2. The student is bored with the job, not the people he works with.

Connecting Information Questions

Connecting Information questions require you to make connections between or among pieces of information in the lecture or conversation. Your ability to integrate information from different parts of the lecture or conversation, to make inferences, to draw conclusions, to form generalizations, and to make predictions is tested. To choose the right answer, you will need to be able to identify and explain relationships among ideas and details in a lecture or conversation. These relationships may be explicit or implicit.

There are three types of Connecting Information questions.

Type 6: Understanding Organization Questions

In Understanding Organization questions you may be asked about the overall organization of the lecture, or you may be asked about the relationship between two portions of what you heard. Here are two examples:

1. How does the professor organize the information that she presents to the class?

   ○ In the order in which the events occurred

2. How does the professor clarify the points he makes about Mexico?

   ○ By comparing Mexico to a neighboring country

The first of these questions asks about the overall organization of information, testing understanding of connections throughout the whole lecture. The second asks about a portion of the lecture, testing understanding of the relationship between two different ideas.

Some Understanding Organization questions may ask you to identify or recognize how one statement functions with respect to surrounding statements. Functions may include indicating or signaling a topic shift, connecting a main topic to a subtopic, providing an introduction or a conclusion, giving an example, starting a digression, or even making a joke.

Example

Narrator

Listen again to a statement made by the professor. Then answer the question.

Professor

There's this committee I'm on . . . Th-the name of the thing, and it's probably, well, you don't have to take notes about this, um, the name of the thing is academic standards."

Narrator

Why does the professor tell the students that they do not have to take notes?

○ The information is in their books.
○ The information may not be accurate.
○ She is going to tell a personal story.
○ They already know what she is going to talk about.

The statement preceding the replayed statement is about how bureaucracies work. What follows the replayed statement is a personal story about bureaucracies. The key lies in recognizing that the portion of the lecture following the replayed statement is a personal story. The correct answer is choice 3. With the replayed statement the professor indicates to the class that what she is about to say does not have the same status as what she was talking about previously.

How to Recognize Understanding Organization Questions

Understanding Organization questions are typically phrased as follows:

- How does the professor organize the information about X?
- How is the discussion organized?
- Why does the professor discuss X?
- Why does the professor mention X?

Tips for Understanding Organization Questions

- Questions that ask about overall organization are more likely to be found after lectures than after conversations. Refer to your notes to answer these questions. It may not have been apparent from the start that the professor organized the information (for example) chronologically, or from least to most complex, or in some other way.

- Pay attention to comparisons made by the professor. In the following example the professor is discussing the structure of plants. He uses steel and the steel girders in a new building to make a point. When the professor mentions something that is seemingly off-topic, you should ask yourself what point the professor is making.

Examples

Professor

So we have reproductive parts—the seeds, the fruit walls—we have leaf parts, but the great majority of plant fibers come from vasculature within the stem . . . fibers that occur in stem material. And what we do is consider these fibers *[false start]*—basically they're what are called *bast* fibers. Bast fibers. Now, basically bast fibers are parts of the plant that the plant uses to maintain vertical structure.

Think about it this way: what's the first thing you see when you see a building being built . . . uh, what's the first thing they put up? Besides the foundation, of course? The metalwork, right? They put all those steel girders up there, the framework. OK, well, think of *[false start]*—bast fibers basically constitute the structural framework to support the stem of the plant. OK? So as the plant grows, it basically builds a girder system within that plant, like steel, so to speak.

So suppose you cut across the stem of one of these plants . . . take a look at how the bast fibers are arranged, so you're looking at a cross section . . . you'll see that the fibers run vertically side by side. Up and down next to each other, forming a kind of tube, which is significant . . . 'cause, which is physically stronger: a solid rod or a tube? The tube—physics tells you that. What's essentially happening—well, the plant is forming a structural ring of these bast fibers all around the stem, and that shape allows for structural rigidity, but also allows for bending and motion.

Why does the professor talk about steel?

○ To identify the substance that has replaced fiber products.
○ To explain a method for separating fibers from a plant.
○ To compare the chemical structure of fibers to metals.
○ To illustrate the function of fibers in a plant's stem.

Why does the professor mention a tube?

○ To explain how some fibers are arranged in a plant.
○ To show how plants carry water to growing fibers.
○ To describe an experiment involving plant fibers.
○ To explain why some plant stems cannot bend.

Explanation

The lecture is about plants and plant fibers, not steel girders. The professor mentions steel girders only to compare them to the structural framework of fibers in a plant. The correct answer to the first question is choice 4. Likewise, the second question also concerns the professor's attempts to help the students visualize a plant's structure. The correct answer to the second question is choice 1.

Type 7: Connecting Content Questions

Connecting Content questions measure your understanding of the relationships among ideas in a lecture. These relationships may be explicitly stated, or you may have to infer them from the words you hear.

The questions may ask you to organize information in a different way from the way it was presented in the lecture. You might be asked to identify comparisons, cause and effect, or contradiction and agreement. You may also be asked to classify items in categories, identify a sequence of events or steps in a process, or specify relationships among objects along some dimension.

| **Example** | **Narrator** |

What type of symmetry do these animals have? Place a check mark in the correct box.

	Asymmetry	Radial Symmetry	Bilateral Symmetry
Earthworm			✓
Human			✓
Sponge	✓		
Sea Anemone	✓	✓	

In this question you are asked to present information in a different format from that in which it was presented in a lecture.

Other Connecting Content questions will require you to make inferences about the relationships among things mentioned in the lecture. You may have to predict an outcome, draw a logical conclusion, extrapolate some additional information, infer a cause-and-effect relationship, or specify some particular sequence of events.

How to Recognize Connecting Content Questions

Connecting Content questions are typically phrased as follows:

- What is the likely outcome of doing procedure X before procedure Y?
- What can be inferred about X?
- What does the professor imply about X?

Tip for Connecting Content Questions

- Questions that require you to fill in a chart or table or put events in order fall into this category. As you listen to the lectures accompanying this study guide, pay attention to the way you format your notes. Clearly identifying terms and their definitions as well as steps in a process will help you answer questions of this type.

| **Example** | **Professor** |

OK, Neptune and its moons. Neptune has several moons, but there's only . . . we'll probably only worry about two of them, the two fairly interesting ones. The first one's Triton. So you have this little struggle with the word *Titan*, which is the big moon of Saturn, and the name *Triton*, which is the big moon of *Neptune*. Triton: it's, it's the only *large moon* in the solar system to go backwards, to go around its—what we call its parent planet—in this case Neptune, the wrong way. OK? Every other large moon orbits the *parent planet* in the same counterclockwise direction . . . same as most of the other bodies in the solar system. But this moon . . . the reverse direction, which is perfectly OK as far as the laws of gravity are concerned. But it indicates some sort of peculiar event in the early solar system that gave this moon a motion in contrast to the general spin of the raw material that it was formed from.

The other moon orbiting Neptune that I want to talk about is Nereid [NEER-ee-ihd]. Nereid is, Nereid has the most eccentric orbit, the most lopsided, elliptical-type orbit for a large moon in the solar system. The others tend more like circular orbits.

. . . Does it mean that Pluto and Neptune might have been related somehow in the past and then drifted slowly into their present orbits? If Pluto . . . did Pluto ever belong to the Neptune system? Do Neptune's moons represent Pluto-type bodies that have been captured by Neptune? Was some sort of . . . was Pluto the object that disrupted the Neptune system at some point in the past?

It's really hard to prove any of those things. But now we're starting to appreciate that there's quite a few junior Plutos out there: not big enough to really call a planet, but large enough that they're significant in history of the early solar system. So we'll come back to those when we talk about comets and other small bodies in the fringes of the outer solar system.

What does the professor imply about the orbits of Triton and Nereid?

○ They used to be closer together.
○ They might provide evidence of an undiscovered planet.
○ They might reverse directions in the future.
○ They might have been changed by some unusual event.

Explanation

In Connecting Content questions you will have to use information from more than one place in the lecture. In this example, the professor describes the orbits of Triton and Nereid. In both cases he refers to events in the early solar system that might have changed or disrupted their orbits. The correct answer for this question is choice 4, "They might have been changed by some unusual event."

Type 8: Making Inferences Questions

The final type of Connecting Information question is Making Inferences questions. In this kind of question you usually have to reach a conclusion based on facts presented in the lecture or conversation.

How to Recognize Making Inferences Questions

Making Inferences questions are typically phrased as follows:

- What does the professor imply about X?
- What will the student probably do next?
- What can be inferred about X?
- What does the professor imply when he says this? *(replay)*

> *Tip for Making Inferences Questions*
> • In some cases, answering this kind of question correctly means adding up details from the lecture or conversation to reach a conclusion. In other cases, the professor may imply something without directly stating it. In most cases the answer you choose will use vocabulary not found in the lecture or conversation.

Example **Professor**

Dada is often considered under the broader category of Fantasy. It's one of the early directions in the Fantasy style. The term "Dada" itself is a nonsense word—it has no meaning . . . and where the word originated isn't known. The "philosophy" behind the "Dada" movement was to create works that conveyed the concept of *absurdity*—the artwork was meant to shock the public by presenting the ridiculous, absurd concepts. Dada artists rejected reason—or rational thought. They did not believe that rational thought would help solve social problems . . .

. . . When he turned to Dada, he quit painting and devoted himself to making a type of sculpture he referred to as a "ready-made" . . . probably because they were constructed of readily available objects . . . At the time, many people reacted to Dadaism by saying that the works were not art at all . . . and in fact, that's exactly how Duchamp and others conceived of it—as a form of "non-art" . . . or anti-art.

Duchamp also took a reproduction of da Vinci's famous painting the *Mona Lisa*, and he drew a mustache and goatee on the subject's face. Treating this masterpiece with such disrespect was another way Duchamp was challenging the established cultural standards of his day.

What does the professor imply about the philosophy of the Dada movement?

○ It was not taken seriously by most artists.
○ It varied from one country to another.
○ It challenged people's concept of what art is.
○ It was based on a realistic style of art.

Explanation

Note the highlighted portions of the lecture. You can see that Dadaism was meant to challenge the public's conception of what art was meant to be. The correct answer to the question is choice 3.

Strategies for Preparing for the Listening Section

- Take notes while you listen. Only the major points will be tested, so do not try to write down every detail. After testing, notes are collected and shredded before you leave the test center.

- When listening to a lecture, pay attention to the new words or concepts introduced by the professor. These words may be written on a chalkboard and will often be tested.

- When listening to a lecture, pay attention to the way the lecture is organized and the way the ideas in the lecture are connected.

- Choose the best answer. The computer will ask you to confirm your choice. After clicking on **OK**, you automatically go on to the next question.

- Listening questions must be answered in order. Once you click on **OK**, you cannot go back to a previous question.

How to Sharpen Your Listening Skills

Listening is one of the most important skills necessary for success on the TOEFL test and in academics in general. The ability to listen and understand is tested in three out of four sections of the TOEFL iBT test.

The best way to improve your listening skills is to listen frequently to many different types of material in various subject areas (sciences, social sciences, arts, business, and others). Of course, watching movies and TV and listening to the radio are excellent ways to practice listening. Audiotapes and CDs of talks are available in libraries and bookstores; those with transcripts of the listening material are particularly helpful. The Internet is also a great resource for listening material.

Here are some ways you can strengthen skills for the three listening purposes tested on the TOEFL iBT test.

1. Listening for basic comprehension

- Increase your vocabulary knowledge, perhaps by using flash cards.

- Focus on the content and flow of material. Do not be distracted by the speaker's style and delivery.

- Anticipate what the speaker is going to say as a way to stay focused, and adjust your predictions when you receive additional information.

- Stay active by asking yourself questions (for example, What main idea is the professor communicating?).

- Copy the words "main idea," "major points," and "important details" on different lines of paper. Listen carefully and write these things down while listening. Listen again until all important points and details are written down.

- Listen to a portion of a lecture or talk and write a brief summary of important points. Gradually increase the amount you listen to and summarize. Note: summarizing skills are not tested in the Listening section, but they are useful for the integrated tasks in the Writing and Speaking sections.

2. Listening for pragmatic understanding

- Think about what each speaker hopes to accomplish; that is, what is the purpose of the speech or conversation? Is the speaker apologizing, complaining, making suggestions?

- Notice the way each speaker talks. Is the language formal or casual? How certain does each speaker sound? Is the speaker's voice calm or emotional? What does the speaker's tone of voice tell you?

- Notice the degree of certainty of the speaker. How sure is the speaker about the information? Does the speaker's tone of voice indicate something about his or her degree of certainty?

- Listen for changes in topic or side comments in which the speaker briefly moves away from the main topic and then returns (digressions).

- Watch television or movie comedies and pay attention to stress and intonation patterns used to convey meaning.

3. Listening to connect ideas

- Think about how the lecture is organized. Listen for the signal words that indicate the introduction, major steps or ideas, examples, and the conclusion or summary.

- Identify the relationships between ideas in the information being discussed. Possible relationships include cause/effect, compare/contrast, and steps in a process.

- Listen for words that show connections and relationships between ideas.

- When you listen to recorded material, stop the recording at various points and try to predict what information or idea will be expressed next.

- Create an outline of the information discussed while listening or after listening.

Listening Practice Sets

PRACTICE SET 1

Now listen to Track 1 on the CD.

Questions

Directions: Mark your answer by filling in the oval next to your choice.

1. Why does the man go to see his professor?

    ◯ To borrow some charts and graphs from her
    ◯ To ask her to explain some statistical procedures
    ◯ To talk about a report he is writing
    ◯ To discuss a grade he got on a paper

2. *Listen again to part of the conversation by playing Track 2.*
    Then answer the question.

    Why does the professor say this?

    ◯ To question the length of the paper
    ◯ To offer encouragement
    ◯ To dispute the data sources
    ◯ To explain a theory

3. What information will the man include in his report?

For each phrase below, place a check mark in the "Include" column or the "Not Include" column.

	Include in Report	Not Include in Report
Climate charts		
Interviews with meteorologists		
Journal notes		
Statistical tests		

4. Why does the professor tell the man about the appointment at the doctor's office?

- ◯ To demonstrate a way of remembering things
- ◯ To explain why she needs to leave soon
- ◯ To illustrate a point that appears in his report
- ◯ To emphasize the importance of good health

5. What does the professor offer to do for the man?

- ◯ Help him collect more data in other areas of the state
- ◯ Submit his research findings for publication
- ◯ Give him the doctor's telephone number
- ◯ Review the first version of his report

PRACTICE SET 1 SCRIPT AND ANSWERS

Track 1 Listening Script

Narrator

Listen to a conversation between a student and a professor.

Student

Uh, excuse me, Professor Thompson. I know your office hours are tomorrow, but I was wondering if you had a few minutes free now to discuss something.

Professor

Sure, John. What did you wanna talk about?

Student

Well, I have some quick questions about how to write up the research project I did this semester—about climate variations.

Professor

Oh, yes. You were looking at variations in climate in the Grant City area, right? How far along have you gotten?

Student

I've got all my data, so I'm starting to summarize it now, preparing graphs and stuff. But I'm just . . . I'm looking at it and I'm afraid that it's not enough, but I'm not sure what else to put in the report.

Professor

I hear the same thing from every student. You know, you have to remember now that you're the expert on what you've done. So think about what you'd need to include if you were going to explain your research project to someone with general or casual knowledge about the subject, like . . . like your parents. That's usually my rule of thumb: would my parents understand this?

Student

OK. I get it.

Professor

I hope you can recognize by my saying that how much you do know about the subject.

Student

Right. I understand. I was wondering if I should also include the notes from the research journal you suggested I keep?

Professor

Yes, definitely. You should use them to indicate what your evolution in thought was through time. So just set up, you know, what was the purpose of what you were doing—to try to understand the climate variability of this area—and what you did, and what your approach was.

Student

OK. So, for example, I studied meteorological records; I looked at climate charts; I used different methods for analyzing the data, like certain statistical tests; and then I discuss the results. Is that what you mean?

Professor

Yes, that's right. You should include all of that. The statistical tests are especially important. And also be sure you include a good reference section where all your published and unpublished data came from, 'cause you have a lot of unpublished climate data.

Student

Hmm . . . something just came into my mind and went out the other side.

Professor

That happens to me a lot, so I've come up with a pretty good memory management tool. I carry a little pad with me all the time and jot down questions or ideas that I don't wanna forget. For example, I went to the doctor with my daughter and her baby son last week, and we knew we wouldn't remember everything we wanted to ask the doctor, so we actually made a list of five things we wanted answers to.

Student

A notepad is a good idea. Since I'm so busy now at the end of the semester, I'm getting pretty forgetful these days. OK. I just remembered what I was trying to say before.

Professor

Good. I was hoping you'd come up with it.

Student

Yes. It ends up that I have data on more than just the immediate Grant City area, so I also included some regional data in the report. With everything else it should be a pretty good indicator of the climate in this part of the state.

Professor

Sounds good. I'd be happy to look over a draft version before you hand in the final copy, if you wish.

Student

Great. I'll plan to get you a draft of the paper by next Friday. Thanks very much. Well, see ya.

Professor

OK.

Answers and Explanations

1. ❸ This is a Gist-purpose question. The man says, "I have some quick questions about how to write up the research project I did this semester." He is going to write a report about his project and is unsure of what to include. Choice 3 is the correct answer.

2. ❷ This is an Understanding the Function of What Is Said question. The question asks you to listen again to this part of the conversation:

Professor

You know, you have to remember now that you're the expert on what you've done. So think about what you'd need to include if you were going to explain your research project to someone with general or casual knowledge about the subject, like . . . like your parents. That's usually my rule of thumb: would my parents understand this?

Student

OK. I get it.

Professor

I hope you can recognize by my saying that how much you do know about the subject.

Then you are asked specifically about this sentence:

Narrator

Why does the professor say this:

Professor

I hope you can recognize by my saying that how much you do know about the subject.

The student is unsure of how to present the information in his report. The professor is trying to give the student confidence in his own judgment. Therefore the correct answer is choice 2, "To offer encouragement."

3. This question is easy to recognize as a Connecting Content question. The student and the professor discuss several sources of information that the student used to investigate climate variation. They do not discuss interviewing meteorologists, even though they mention other kinds of conversations, like the professor's discussion with her child's doctor. The chart correctly filled out looks like this:

For each phrase below, place a check mark in the "Include" column or the "Not Include" column.

	Include in Report	Not Include in Report
Climate charts	✓	
Interviews with meteorologists		✓
Journal notes	✓	
Statistical tests	✓	

4. ❶ This is an Understanding the Function of What Is Said question. The correct answer is choice 1. The professor's purpose in mentioning the doctor's office is to show the man how writing down questions as they occur can be useful. The man has forgotten a question he wanted to ask the professor. The professor, when she spoke to the doctor, wrote down her questions beforehand, so she would not forget. She mentions the doctor's office in order to demonstrate a strategy for remembering.

5. ❹ This is a Detail question. The discussion ends with the professor offering to "look over a draft version" of the man's paper.

Now listen to Track 3 on the CD.

Questions

Directions: Mark your answer by filling in the oval next to your choice.

1. What is the main purpose of the lecture?

○ To illustrate the importance of extrinsic values
○ To explain Aristotle's views about the importance of teaching
○ To explain why people change what they value
○ To discuss Aristotle's views about human happiness

2. The professor gives examples of things that have value for her. Indicate for each example what type of value it has for her.

Place a check mark in the correct box. **This question is worth 2 points.**

	Only Extrinsic Value	Only Intrinsic Value	Both Extrinsic and Intrinsic Value
Teaching		\	
Exercise	\		
Health			\
Playing a musical instrument		\	

3. Why is happiness central to Aristotle's theory?

○ Because it is so difficult for people to attain
○ Because it is valued for its own sake by all people
○ Because it is a means to a productive life
○ Because most people agree about what happiness is

4. According to the professor, why does Aristotle think that fame cannot provide true happiness?

○ Fame cannot be obtained without help from other people.
○ Fame cannot be obtained by all people.
○ Fame does not last forever.
○ People cannot share their fame with other people.

5. *Listen again to part of the lecture by playing Track 4. Then answer the question.*

What does the professor mean when she says this?

○ Teaching is not a highly valued profession in society.
○ She may change professions in order to earn more money.
○ The reason she is a teacher has little to do with her salary.
○ More people would become teachers if the salary were higher.

PRACTICE SET 2 SCRIPT AND ANSWERS

Track 3 Listening Script

Narrator

Listen to part of a lecture in a philosophy class.

Professor

OK. Another ancient Greek philosopher we need to discuss is Aristotle—Aristotle's ethical theory. What Aristotle's ethical theory is all about is this: he's trying to show you how to be happy—what true happiness is.

Now, why is he interested in human happiness? It's not just because it's something that all people want or aim for. It's more than that. But to get there, we need to first make a very important distinction. Let me introduce a couple of technical terms: extrinsic value and intrinsic value.

To understand Aristotle's interest in happiness, you need to understand this distinction.

Some things we aim for and value, not for themselves, but for what they bring about in addition to themselves. If I value something as a means to something else, then it has what we will call "extrinsic value." Other things we desire and hold to be valuable for themselves alone. If we value something not as a means to something else, but for its own sake, let us say that it has "intrinsic value."

Exercise. There may be some people who value exercise for itself, but I don't. I value exercise because if I exercise, I tend to stay healthier than I would if I didn't. So I desire to engage in exercise, and I value exercise extrinsically . . . not for its own sake, but as a means to something beyond it. It brings me good health.

Health. Why do I value good health? Well, here it gets a little more complicated for me. Um, health is important for me because I can't . . . do other things I wanna do—play music, teach philosophy—if I'm ill. So health is important to me—has value to me—as a means to a productive life. But health is also important to me because I just kind of like to be healthy—it feels good. It's pleasant to be healthy, unpleasant not to be. So to some degree I value health both for itself and as a means to something else: productivity. It's got extrinsic and intrinsic value for me.

Then there's some things that are just valued for themselves. I'm a musician, not a professional musician; I just play a musical instrument for fun. Why do I value playing music? Well, like most amateur musicians, I only play because, well, I just enjoy it. It's something that's an end in itself.

Now, something else I value is teaching. Why? Well, it brings in a modest income, but I could make more money doing other things. I'd do it even if they didn't pay me. I just enjoy teaching. In that sense it's an end to itself.

But teaching's not something that has intrinsic value for all people—and that's true generally. Most things that are enjoyed in and of themselves vary from person to person. Some people value teaching intrinsically, but others don't.

So how does all this relate to human happiness? Well, Aristotle asks: is there something that all human beings value . . . and value only intrinsically, for its own sake and only for its own sake? If you could find such a thing, that would be the universal final good, or truly the ultimate purpose or goal for all human beings. Aristotle thought the answer was yes. What is it? Happiness. Everyone will agree, he argues, that happiness is the ultimate end to be valued for itself and really only for itself. For what other purpose is there in being happy? What does it yield? The attainment of happiness becomes the ultimate or highest good for Aristotle.

The next question that Aristotle raises is: what is happiness? We all want it; we all desire it; we all seek it. It's the goal we have in life. But what is it? How do we find it? Here he notes, with some frustration, people disagree.

But he does give us a couple of criteria, or features, to keep in mind as we look for what true human happiness is. True human happiness should be, as he puts it, complete. Complete in that it's all we require. Well, true human happiness . . . if you had that, what else do you need? Nothing.

And, second, true happiness should be something that I can obtain on my own. I shouldn't have to rely on other people for it. Many people value fame and seek fame. Fame for them becomes the goal. But, according to Aristotle, this won't work either, because fame depends altogether too much on other people. I can't get it on my own, without help from other people.

In the end, Aristotle says that true happiness is the exercise of reason—a life of intellectual contemplation . . . of thinking. So let's see how he comes to that.

Answers and Explanations

1. **④** This is a Gist-purpose question. The professor discusses the difference between extrinsic and intrinsic value, but what is her purpose in doing this? "To understand Aristotle's interest in happiness, you need to understand this distinction [extrinsic and intrinsic]." The professor's purpose is choice 4: "To discuss Aristotle's views about human happiness."

2. This question is easy to recognize as a Connecting Content question. The professor gives examples of some activities and discusses whether they have intrinsic value, extrinsic value, or both. Her explanations of why she values exercise, health, and playing a musical instrument are fairly clear and explicit. For teaching, it is clear that for her it has intrinsic value, but she admits this may be different for others. The question is about "what type of value it has for her." The chart correctly filled out looks like this:

	Only Extrinsic Value	Only Intrinsic Value	Both Extrinsic and Intrinsic Value
Teaching		✓	
Exercise	✓		
Health			✓
Playing a musical instrument		✓	

3. **②** This is a Detail question. The question is answered by the professor when she says, "Everyone will agree, he [Aristotle] argues, that happiness is the ultimate end to be valued for itself and really only for itself." The correct answer for this question is choice 2. Note that this Detail question is directly related to the main idea or gist of the passage.

4. **①** This is another Detail question. It is not as closely related to the gist as the previous question. At the end of the passage the professor compares happiness and fame. She says, "according to Aristotle, this won't work either, because fame depends altogether too much on other people. I can't get it on my own." The correct answer is choice 1.

5. **③** This is an Understanding the Function of What Is Said question. The professor discusses teaching to stress its intrinsic value for her. Therefore the correct answer is choice 3. The reason she is a teacher has little to do with money. Salary would be an extrinsic value, but she does not value teaching because of the salary.

PRACTICE SET 3

Now listen to Track 5 on the CD.

Questions

Directions: Mark your answer by filling in the oval next to your choice.

1. What is the professor mainly discussing?

    ○ The development of motor skills in children
    ○ How psychologists measure muscle activity in the throat
    ○ A theory about the relationship between muscle activity and thinking
    ○ A study on deaf people's problem-solving techniques

2. *Listen again to part of the lecture by playing Track 6.*
    Then answer the question.

    Why does the professor say this?

    ○ To give an example of a laryngeal habit
    ○ To explain the meaning of a term
    ○ To explain why he is discussing laryngeal habits
    ○ To remind students of a point he had discussed previously

3. What does the professor say about people who use sign language?

    ○ It is not possible to study their thinking habits.
    ○ They exhibit laryngeal habits.
    ○ The muscles in their hands move when they solve problems.
    ○ They do not exhibit ideomotor action.

4. What point does the professor make when he refers to the university library?

○ A study on problem solving took place there.
○ Students should go there to read more about behaviorism.
○ Students' eyes will turn toward it if they think about it.
○ He learned about William James's concept of thinking there.

5. The professor describes a magic trick to the class. What does the magic trick demonstrate?

○ An action people make that they are not aware of
○ That behaviorists are not really scientists
○ How psychologists study children
○ A method for remembering locations

6. What is the professor's opinion of the motor theory of thinking?

○ Most of the evidence he has collected contradicts it.
○ It explains adult behavior better than it explains child behavior.
○ It is the most valid theory of thinking at the present time.
○ It cannot be completely proved or disproved.

PRACTICE SET 3 SCRIPT AND ANSWERS

Track 5 Listening Script

Narrator

Listen to part of a psychology lecture. The professor is discussing behaviorism.

Professor

Now, many people consider John Watson to be the founder of behaviorism. And like other behaviorists, he believed that psychologists should study only the behaviors they can observe and measure. They're not interested in mental processes. While a person could describe his thoughts, no one else can see or hear them to verify the accuracy of his report. But one thing you can observe is muscular habits. What Watson did was to observe muscular habits because he viewed them as a manifestation of thinking. One kind of habit that he studied are laryngeal habits.

Watson thought laryngeal habits—you know, from *larynx*; in other words, related to the voice box—he thought those habits were an expression of thinking. He argued that for very young children, thinking is really talking out loud to oneself because they talk out loud even if they're not trying to communicate with someone in particular. As the individual matures, that overt talking to oneself becomes covert talking to oneself, but thinking still shows up as a laryngeal habit. One of the bits of evidence that supports this is that when people are trying to solve a problem, they, um, typically have increased muscular activity in the throat region. That is, if you put electrodes on the throat and measure muscle potential—muscle activity—you discover that when people are thinking, like if they're diligently trying to solve a problem, that there is muscular activity in the throat region.

So Watson made the argument that problem solving, or thinking, can be defined as a set of behaviors—a set of responses—and in this case the response he observed was the throat activity. That's what he means when he calls it a laryngeal habit. Now, as I am thinking about what I am going to be saying, my muscles in my throat are responding. So thinking can be measured as muscle activity. Now, the motor theory . . . yes?

Student

Professor Blake, um, did he happen to look at people who sign? I mean deaf people?

Professor

Uh, he did indeed, um, and to jump ahead, what one finds in deaf individuals who use sign language when they're given problems of various kinds, they have muscular changes in their hands when they are trying to solve a problem . . . muscle changes in the hand, just like the muscular changes going on in the throat region for speaking individuals.

So, for Watson, thinking is identical with the activity of muscles. A related concept of thinking was developed by William James. It's called ideomotor action.

Ideomotor action is an activity that occurs without our noticing it, without our being aware of it. I'll give you one simple example. If you think of locations, there tends to be eye movement that occurs with your thinking about that location. In particular, from where we're sitting, imagine that you're asked to think of our university library. Well, if you close your eyes and think of the library, and if you're sitting directly facing me, then according to this notion, your eyeballs will move slightly to the left, to your left, 'cause the library's in that general direction.

James and others said that this is an idea leading to a motor action, and that's why it's called "ideomotor action"—an idea leads to motor activity. If you wish to impress your friends and relatives, you can change this simple process into a magic trick. Ask people to do something such as I've just described: think of something on their left; think of something on their right. You get them to think about two things on either side with their eyes closed, and you watch their eyes very carefully. And if you do that, you'll discover that you can see rather clearly the eye movement—that is, you can see the movement of the eyeballs. Now, then you say, "Think of either one and I'll tell which you're thinking of."

OK. Well, Watson makes the assumption that muscular activity is equivalent to thinking. But given everything we've been talking about here, one has to ask: are there alternatives to this motor theory—this claim that muscular activities are equivalent to thinking? Is there anything else that might account for this change in muscular activity, other than saying that it is thinking? And the answer is clearly yes. Is there any way to answer the question definitively? I think the answer is no.

Answers and Explanations

1. ❸ This is a Gist-content question. The professor discusses two types of muscular activities: laryngeal habits and ideomotor activity, and how they are related to thinking. The correct answer is choice 3, "A theory about the relationship between muscle activity and thinking." The other choices are mentioned by the professor, but they are not the main topic of the discussion.

2. ❷ This is an Understanding the Function of What Is Said question. The professor introduces an unusual term, "laryngeal habits." He then says, "you know, from *larynx*; in other words, related to the voice box." His brief explanation is meant to help the students understand the term "laryngeal habits." Choice 2 is the correct answer to this question.

3. ❸ This is a Detail question. The professor responds to a student who asks a question about people who use sign language. He says that "they have muscular changes in their hands . . . just like the muscular changes going on in the throat region for speaking individuals." The correct answer is choice 3. This Detail question is related to the main idea of the passage, as both are concerned with the relationship between muscular changes and thinking.

4. ❸ This is an Understanding Organization question. The professor talks about muscular activity in the eyes that will occur if the students think about the location of the library. The question asks for the conclusion of that example. The correct answer is choice 3, "Students' eyes will turn toward it if they think about it."

5. ❶ This is a Connecting Content question. Answering the question correctly requires you to understand that the magic trick the professor is describing is an "ideomotor activity" and that this type of activity "occurs without our noticing it, without our being aware of it." The correct answer to this question is choice 1.

6. ❹ Questions like this one that ask for the professor's opinion are Understanding the Speaker's Attitude questions. The professor's opinion can be found at the end of the lecture. He says that there may be alternative theories, but there is no way to answer the question definitively. The correct answer to this question is choice 4, "It cannot be completely proved or disproved."

PRACTICE SET 4

Now listen to Track 7 on the CD. Play Audio

Questions

Directions: Mark your answer by filling in the oval or square next to your choice.

1. What is Bode's Law?

○ A law of gravitation
○ An estimate of the distance between Mars and Jupiter
○ A prediction of how many asteroids there are
◐ A pattern in the spacing of planets

2. Why does the professor explain Bode's Law to the class?

○ To describe the size of the asteroids
◐ To explain how the asteroid belt was discovered
○ To explain how gravitational forces influence the planets
○ To describe the impact of telescopes on astronomy

3. How does the professor introduce Bode's Law?

   ○ By demonstrating how it is derived mathematically
   ○ By describing the discovery of Uranus
   ○ By drawing attention to the inaccuracy of a certain pattern
   ○ By telling the names of several of the asteroids

4. *Listen again to part of the lecture by playing Track 8. Then answer the question.*

   Why does the professor say this?

   ○ To introduce an alternative application of Bode's Law
   ○ To give an example of what Bode's Law cannot explain
   ○ To describe the limitations of gravitational theory
   ○ To contrast Bode's Law with a real scientific law

5. According to the professor, what two factors contributed to the discovery of the asteroid Ceres?

   Choose 2 answers.

   ☒ Improved telescopes
   ☐ Advances in mathematics
   ☐ The discovery of a new star
   ☒ The position of Uranus in a pattern

6. What does the professor imply about the asteroid belt?

   ○ It is farther from the Sun than Uranus.
   ○ Bode believed it was made up of small stars.
   ○ It is located where people expected to find a planet.
   ○ Ceres is the only one of the asteroids that can be seen without a telescope.

PRACTICE SET 4 SCRIPT AND ANSWERS

Track 7 Listening Script

Narrator

Listen to part of a lecture in an astronomy class. You will not need to remember the numbers the professor mentions.

Professor

OK. Let's get going. Today I'm going to talk about how the asteroid belt was discovered. And . . . I'm going to start by writing some numbers on the board. Here they are: we'll start with zero, then 3, . . . 6, . . . 12. Uh, tell me what I'm doing.

Female Student

Multiplying by 2?

Professor

Right. I'm doubling the numbers, so 2 times 12 is 24, and the next one I'm going to write after 24 would be . . .

Female Student

48.

Professor

48. Then 96. We'll stop there for now. Uh, now I'll write another row of numbers under that. Tell me what I'm doing: 4, 7, 10 . . . How am I getting this second row?

Male Student

Adding 4 to the numbers in the first row.

Professor

I'm adding 4 to each number in the first row to give you a second row. So the last two will be 52, 100, and now tell me what I'm doing.

Female Student

Putting in a decimal?

Professor

Yes, I divided all those numbers by 10 by putting in a decimal point. Now I'm going to write the names of the planets under the numbers. Mercury . . . Venus . . . Earth . . . Mars.

So, what do the numbers mean? Do you remember from the reading?

Male Student

Is it the distance of the planets from the Sun?

Professor

Right. In astronomical units—not perfect, but tantalizingly close. The value for Mars is off by . . . 6 or 7 percent or so. It's . . . but it's within 10 percent of the average distance to Mars from the Sun. But I kind of have to skip the one after Mars for now. Then Jupiter's right there at 5-point something, and then Saturn is about 10 astronomical units from the Sun. Um, well, this pattern is known as Bode's Law.

Um, it isn't really a scientific law, not in the sense of predicting gravitation mathematically or something, but it's attempting a pattern in the spacing of the planets, and it was noticed by Bode hundreds of years ago. Well, you can imagine that there was some interest in why the 2.8 spot in the pattern was skipped, and um . . . but there wasn't anything obvious there, in the early telescopes. Then what happened in the late 1700s? The discovery of . . . ?

Female Student

Another planet?

Professor

The next planet out, Uranus—after Saturn.

And look, Uranus fits in the next spot in the pattern pretty nicely, um, not perfectly, but close. And so then people got really excited about the validity of this thing and finding the missing object between Mars and Jupiter. And telescopes, remember, were getting better. So people went to work on finding objects that would be at that missing distance from the Sun, and then in 1801, the object Ceres was discovered.

And Ceres was in the right place—the missing spot. Uh, but it was way too faint to be a planet. It looked like a little star. Uh, and because of its starlike appearance, um, it was called an "asteroid." OK? *Aster* is Greek for "star," as in *astronomy*. Um, and so, Ceres was the first and is the largest of what became many objects discovered at that same distance. Not just one thing, but all the objects found at that distance form the asteroid belt. So the asteroid belt is the most famous success of this Bode's Law. That's how the asteroid belt was discovered.

Answers and Explanations

1. ❹ This is a Detail question. Although the entire passage is concerned with answering "What is Bode's Law?" the professor specifically answers the question when he says, "it's attempting a pattern in the spacing of the planets." The correct answer to this question is choice 4.

2. ❷ This is a Gist-purpose question. Gist questions are not usually answered very explicitly in the passage, but in this case the professor addresses the purpose of the discussion twice. At one point he says, "Today I'm going to talk about how the asteroid belt was discovered," and later he states, "That's how the asteroid belt was discovered." The correct answer to this question is choice 2.

3. ❶ This is an Understanding Organization question. The professor first demonstrates the pattern of numbers before explaining Bode's Law and what the pattern means. The correct answer to this question is choice 1.

4. ❹ This is an Understanding the Function of What Is Said replay question. The pattern the professor describes is called Bode's Law. The professor is pointing out how Bode's Law differs from other scientific laws. The correct answer to this question is choice 4.

5. ❶ ❹ This is a Detail question. Note that for this question there are two correct answers. The professor explains that "Uranus fits in the next spot in the pattern pretty nicely" and telescopes "were getting better . . . and then in 1801, the object Ceres was discovered." Choices 1 and 4 are the correct answers. Advances in mathematics and the discovery of a new star are not mentioned by the professor.

6. ❸ This is a Making Inferences question. Starting at the point in the passage where the professor says, "there was some interest in why the 2.8 spot in the pattern was skipped . . . there wasn't anything obvious there," it's clear that what the astronomers were looking for was a planet. He later says, "Ceres was in the right place . . . but it was way too faint to be a planet." The clear implication is that astronomers were expecting to find a planet. The correct answer to the question is choice 3.

Now listen to Track 9 on the CD. Play Audio

Questions

Directions: Mark your answer by filling in the oval or square next to your choice.

1. What aspect of Manila hemp fibers does the professor mainly describe in the lecture?

   ○ Similarities between cotton fibers and Manila hemp fibers
   ○ Various types of Manila hemp fibers
   ○ The economic importance of Manila hemp fibers
   ○ A use of Manila hemp fibers

2. *Listen again to part of the lecture by playing Track 10.* Play Audio
   Then answer the question.

   Why does the professor mention going away for the weekend?

   ○ To tell the class a joke
   ○ To apologize for not completing some work
   ○ To introduce the topic of the lecture
   ○ To encourage students to ask about her trip

3. What does the professor imply about the name "Manila hemp"?

   ○ It is a commercial brand name.
   ○ Part of the name is inappropriate.
   ○ The name has recently changed.
   ○ The name was first used in the 1940s.

4. Why does the professor mention the Golden Gate Bridge?

   ○ To demonstrate a disadvantage of steel cables
   ○ To give an example of the creative use of color
   ○ To show that steel cables are able to resist salt water
   ○ To give an example of a use of Manila hemp

5. According to the professor, what was the main reason that many ships used Manila hemp ropes instead of steel cables?

   ○ Manila hemp was cheaper.
   ○ Manila hemp was easier to produce.
   ○ Manila hemp is more resistant to salt water.
   ○ Manila hemp is lighter in weight.

6. According to the lecture, what are two ways to increase the strength of rope made from Manila hemp fibers?
   Choose 2 answers.

   ☐ Coat the fibers with zinc-based paint
   ☐ Combine the fibers into bundles
   ☐ Soak bundles of fibers in salt water
   ☐ Twist bundles of fibers

PRACTICE SET 5 SCRIPT AND ANSWERS

Track 9 Listening Script

Narrator

Listen to part of a lecture from a botany class.

Professor

Hi, everyone. Good to see you all today. Actually, I expected the population to be a lot lower today. It typically runs between 50 and 60 percent on the day the research paper is due. Um, I was hoping to have your exams back today, but, uh, the situation was that I went away for the weekend, and I was supposed to get in yesterday at five, and I expected to fully complete all the exams by midnight or so, which is the time that I usually go to bed, but my flight was delayed, and I ended up not getting in until one o'clock in the morning. Anyway, I'll do my best to have them finished by the next time we meet.

OK. In the last class, we started talking about useful plant fibers. In particular, we talked about cotton fibers, which we said were very useful, not only in the textile industry, but also in the chemical industry, and in the production of many products, such as plastics, paper, explosives, and so on. Today we'll continue talking about useful fibers, and we'll begin with a fiber that's commonly known as "Manila hemp."

Now, for some strange reason, many people believe that Manila hemp is a hemp plant. But Manila hemp is not really hemp. It's actually a member of the banana family—it even bears little banana-shaped fruits. The "Manila" part of the name makes sense, because Manila hemp is produced chiefly in the Philippine Islands, and, of course, the capital city of the Philippines is Manila.

Now, as fibers go, Manila hemp fibers are very long. They can easily be several feet in length and they're also very strong, very flexible. They have one more characteristic that's very important, and that is that they are exceptionally resistant to salt water. And this combination of characteristics—long, strong, flexible, resistant to salt water—makes Manila hemp a great material for ropes, especially for ropes that are gonna be used on oceangoing ships. In fact, by the early 1940s, even though steel cables were available, most ships in the United States Navy were not moored with steel cables; they were moored with Manila hemp ropes.

Now, why was that? Well, the main reason was that steel cables degrade very, very quickly in contact with salt water. If you've ever been to San Francisco, you know that the Golden Gate Bridge is red. And it's red because of the zinc paint that goes on those stainless steel cables. That, if they start at one end of the bridge and they work to the other end, by the time they finish, it's already time to go back and start painting the beginning of the bridge again, because the bridge was built with steel cables, and steel cables can't take the salt air unless they're treated repeatedly with a zinc-based paint.

On the other hand, plant products like Manila hemp, you can drag through the ocean for weeks on end. If you wanna tie your anchor to it and drop it right into the ocean, that's no problem, because plant fibers can stand up for months, even years, in direct contact with salt water. OK. So how do you take plant fibers that individually you could break with your hands and turn them into a rope that's strong enough to moor a ship that weighs thousands of tons? Well, what you do is extract these long fibers from the Manila hemp plant, and then you take several of these fibers, and you group them into a bundle, because by grouping the fibers, you greatly increase their breaking strength—that bundle of fibers is much stronger than any of the individual fibers that compose it. And then you take that bundle of fibers and you twist it a little bit, because by twisting it, you increase its breaking strength even more. And then you take several of these little bundles, and you group and twist them into bigger bundles, which you then group and twist into even bigger bundles, and so on, until eventually, you end up with a very, very strong rope.

Answers and Explanations

1. ❹ Questions like this one that ask about what the professor mainly discusses are Gist-content questions. This question asks what aspect of Manila hemp fibers are mainly discussed, so it has a narrower focus than other Gist-content questions. The professor mainly discusses characteristics of Manila hemp and how these characteristics make Manila hemp useful to the shipping industry. The correct answer to this question is choice 4.

2. ❷ This is an Understanding the Function of What Is Said replay question. The professor mentions that she went away for the weekend and because a flight was delayed, she was late returning. She tells this story in order to apologize for not completing marking exams. The correct answer to this question is choice 2.

3. ❷ This is a Making Inferences question. The professor explains that Manila hemp is produced chiefly in the area near Manila, so the word *Manila* in the name is appropriate. However, Manila hemp is not a type of hemp plant, so the word *hemp* in the name is not appropriate. The correct answer to this question is choice 2.

4. ❶ This is an Understanding Organization question. The professor mentions the Golden Gate Bridge in order to make a comparison between the steel cables of the bridge and Manila hemp ropes. The fact that the steel cables must be constantly repainted is a disadvantage. The correct answer to the question is choice 1.

5. ❸ This is a Detail question. It is related to the professor's main point about Manila hemp. The professor says that Manila hemp is "exceptionally resistant to salt water." Much of the lecture deals with the professor's reinforcing and exemplifying this point. The correct answer to this question is choice 3.

6. ❷ ❹ Near the end of the lecture, the professor describes how Manila hemp ropes are made. The answer to this Detail question can be found there. The professor talks about grouping fibers into bundles and then twisting the bundles to make them stronger. Note that this question requires two answers. The correct answers to this question are choices 2 and 4.

Speaking Section

- The format of the 6 TOEFL iBT Speaking questions
- How your spoken responses are evaluated
- Tips for answering each Speaking question type
- Strategies for preparing for the Speaking section

The Speaking Section

The TOEFL iBT Speaking section is designed to evaluate the English speaking proficiency of students whose native language is not English but who want to pursue undergraduate or graduate study in an English-speaking context. Like all the other sections of the TOEFL iBT test, the Speaking section is delivered via the Internet.

In the Speaking section you will be asked to speak on a variety of topics that draw on personal experience, campus-based situations, and academic-type content material. There are six questions. The first two questions are called Independent Speaking tasks because they require you to draw entirely on your own ideas, opinions, and experiences when responding. The other four questions are Integrated Speaking tasks. In these tasks you will listen to a conversation or to an excerpt from a lecture, or read a passage and then listen to a brief discussion or lecture excerpt, before you are asked the question. These questions are called Integrated tasks because they require that you integrate your English-language skills—listening and speaking, or reading, listening, and speaking. In responding to these questions, you will be asked to base your spoken response on the information in the discussion or lecture, or on both the discussion or lecture and the reading passage together.

Tip

For each question, you are given 45 or 60 seconds to respond. So when practicing, time your speech accordingly.

The Speaking section takes approximately 20 minutes. Response time allowed for each question is 45 or 60 seconds. For Speaking questions that involve listening, you will hear short lectures or conversations on headphones. For Speaking questions that involve reading, you will read short written passages on your computer screen. You can take notes throughout the Speaking section and use your notes when responding to the Speaking questions. For each of the six questions, you will be given a short time to prepare a response. You will answer each of the questions by speaking into a microphone. Your responses will be recorded and sent to a scoring center, and they will be scored by experienced raters.

Tip

Familiarize yourself with the scoring rubric. It will help you understand how responses are evaluated.

Your responses will be scored holistically. This means that the rater will listen for various features in your response and assign a single score based on the overall skill you display in your answer. Although scoring criteria vary somewhat depending on the question, the raters will generally be listening for the following features in your answer:

- **Delivery:** How clear your speech is. Good responses are those in which the speech is fluid and clear, with good pronunciation, natural pacing, and natural-sounding intonation patterns.
- **Language Use:** How effectively you use grammar and vocabulary to convey your ideas. Raters will be listening for how well you can control both basic and more complex language structures and use appropriate vocabulary.
- **Topic Development:** How fully you answer the question and how coherently you present your ideas. Good responses generally use all or most of the time allotted, and the relationship between ideas and the progression from one idea to the next is clear and easy to follow.

It is important to note that raters do not expect your response to be perfect, and high-scoring responses may contain occasional errors and minor lapses in any of the three areas described above.

Use the sample Independent and Integrated Speaking rubrics on pages 188 to 191 to see how responses are scored.

Speaking Question Types

Independent: Questions 1 and 2

Question 1

For this task, you will be asked to speak about a person, place, object, or event that is familiar to you. You will be given 45 seconds to speak your response. The topics for this question will vary, but you will always be asked to base your response on personal experience or a familiar topic. You might, for example, be asked about a place you like to visit, an important event in your life, a person who influenced you, or an activity that you enjoy.

Make a list of familiar topics, and practice speaking about them. You may want to begin by describing a familiar place or recounting a personal experience.

This question will always ask you both to *describe* something (for example, an important event, a favorite activity, an influential person) and to *give reasons*—to explain why the event was important, why the activity is one of your favorites, how the person influenced you, and so on. Be sure to respond to all parts of the question. Your response should include specific details and/or examples because they will make your description informative and your reasons comprehensible.

Tip

When giving descriptions, try to avoid presenting long lists, since this will reduce the time you have available to elaborate on the rest of your response.

After you are presented with the question, you will have 15 seconds to prepare an answer. You may want to jot down a few brief notes about what you will want to say, but you should not try to write out a full and complete answer. There will not be enough time for you to do that, and raters want to know how well you can *speak* in response to a question, not how well you can *read aloud* from something you have written. If you do jot down notes during the preparation time, you should not rely on them too much in giving your answer.

The question will be read aloud by a narrator and will remain on the screen throughout the time you are giving your response.

Example   The following example shows how a question of this type will appear on your computer screen.

---

1. Choose a teacher you admire and explain why you admire him or her. Please include specific examples and details in your explanation.

| **Preparation Time: 15 Seconds** |
| **Response Time: 45 Seconds** |

You will be told when to begin to prepare your response and when to begin speaking. After the question is read, a "Preparation Time" clock will appear below the question and begin to count down from 15 seconds (00:00:15). At the end of 15 seconds you will hear a short beep. After the beep, the clock will change to read "Response Time" and will begin to count down from 45 seconds (00:00:45). When the response time has ended, recording will stop and a new screen will appear alerting you that the response time has ended.

> **Tip**
>
> *Do not memorize responses before the test, especially ones that you get from the Internet, or from test preparation instructors who say this is a good idea. It is not a good idea and it will lower your score. Raters will know it is a memorized response because the rhythm, intonation, and even the content of the response will be very different from a spontaneous response. They are easy to identify.*

To answer a question like the one preceding, you would probably begin by briefly identifying the teacher you are going to speak about—not necessarily by name, of course, but by giving just enough relevant information so that someone listening to your response can make sense of your explanation. For example, what subject did the teacher teach? How old were you when you had him or her as a teacher? After briefly describing the teacher in whatever way is useful, you could then proceed to explain what it was about the teacher that made you admire him or her. Perhaps it was something specific that he or she did. If so, you should describe what the teacher did and provide details that illustrate why the action was admirable. Maybe the teacher displayed a special personal quality or had a special character trait. If so, you would want to describe it and give details that provide evidence of it—occasions when you noticed it, the effect it had on you, and so forth. There are many, many ways to answer this question, and of course there is no "right" or "wrong" answer. The important thing, if you were to receive this particular question, is that you communicate enough information about the person to help the rater understand why you find that person admirable.

Question 2

In this second Independent Speaking task, you will be presented with two possible actions, situations, or opinions. Then you will be asked to say which of the actions or situations you think is preferable or which opinion you think is more justified and then explain your choice by providing reasons and details. As with question 1, you will have 45 seconds to give your response.

Topics for this question include everyday issues of general interest to a student. You may be asked, for example, whether you think it is better to study at home or at the library, or whether you think students should take courses from a wide variety of fields or focus on a single subject area, or whether first-year college students should be required to live in the dormitory or be allowed to live off campus in apartments of their own. You could also be presented with two opposing opinions about a familiar topic—for example, about whether television has been a benefit to humanity—and you would then be asked which of the opinions you agree with.

This question will always ask you to state what your choice or preference or opinion is and to explain why—in other words, to support your answer with reasons, explanations, details, and/or examples. It is important that you respond to all parts of the question, and that you are clear about what your opinion is and give reasons that will communicate why you have made the choice you did. It does not matter which of the actions, situations, or opinions you choose, and, as with question 1, there is no "right" or "wrong" answer. Your response will be rated not on which of the alternatives you choose, but rather on how well you explain your choice by supporting it with reasons and details.

Tip

One good exercise would be to state an opinion or a preference and then present supporting reasons clearly and with detail.

Like question 1, this question will appear on your computer screen and be read aloud at the same time by the narrator, and you will be given 15 seconds to prepare an answer. You should use this time to think about what you want to say, organize your thoughts, and jot down some notes if you feel this will be helpful. But remember, you should not try to write out a full answer—just a few words or phrases that may help remind you of the direction you want to take in giving your response.

Tip

Study and practice words and expressions commonly used to express opinions, such as:

> *In my opinion . . .*
> *I believe . . .*

Example   The following example shows how a question of this type will appear on your computer screen.

---

2. Some students study for classes individually. Others study in groups. Which method of studying do you think is better for students and why?

Preparation Time: 15 Seconds
Response Time: 45 Seconds

After you hear the question, you will be told when to begin to prepare your response and when to begin speaking. As with question 1, a "Preparation Time" clock will appear below the question and begin to count down from 15 seconds (00:00:15). At the end of 15 seconds you will hear a short beep. After the beep, the clock will change to read "Response Time" and will begin to count down from 45 seconds (00:00:45). When the response time has ended, recording will stop and a new screen will appear alerting you that the response time has ended.

In answering a question like this one, it is important that you begin by clearly stating what your opinion is: do you think it is better for students to study for classes individually, or do you think it is better for them to study in groups? If you do not begin by stating your opinion, it may be difficult for someone listening to your response to understand your reasons for holding that opinion. As for the reasons you give in support of your opinion, they can vary widely and may be based on your own experience and observations. For example, if the position you take is that it is better for students to study alone, you might say that when students meet to study in groups, they often waste time discussing matters that have nothing to do with their class work. You might continue this explanation by contrasting the inefficiency of studying in a group with the kind of productivity a student can achieve when studying alone. If you have personal experiences that help illustrate your point, you might want to include them in your explanation. If so, you should be clear about how they illustrate your point. Or perhaps you want to take the opposite position, that it is better for students to study in groups. In that case, you would explain the advantages of group study and the disadvantages of studying alone. Perhaps you think that the more capable students can help the less capable students when students study together. Or perhaps you have found that students who study in groups often share each other's lecture notes, and this way they can make sure everyone understands all the material that has been covered in a course. There are many good reasons for either choice. In fact, it may be your opinion that in some cases it is better to study in groups and in other cases it is better to study alone. If that is the opinion you would like to express, you should explain—with reasons, examples, and/or specific details—why group study is better in some cases and individual study is better in others. Here again, there is no "right" or "wrong" answer to a question like this. The important thing is to clearly communicate to the person who will be listening to your response what your opinion is and explain the reasons you have for holding it.

Tip

Practice making a recommendation and explaining why it is your preferred course of action.

Integrated Reading/Listening/Speaking: Questions 3 and 4

Question 3

Question 3 is the first of the four Integrated Tasks in the Speaking section. For this question, you will read a short passage on your computer screen about a topic of campus-related interest. You will then listen to two people discussing that topic and expressing an opinion about the topic from the reading. Then you will be asked a question based on what you have read and what you have heard. You will have 60 seconds to speak your response. The general areas from which these topics are typically drawn include university policies, rules, or procedures; university plans; campus facilities; and quality of life on campus. The topics are designed to be accessible to all test takers and will be presented to you in a way that does not require that you have prior firsthand experience of college or university life in North America.

The reading passage could take various forms. For example, it could be a bulletin from the administration of a university regarding a new parking rule, or a letter to the editor of a campus newspaper responding to a new university policy restricting the use of radios in dormitory rooms, or an article from the campus newspaper discussing a proposal to build a new football stadium. In addition to describing the proposal, the reading passage will usually present two reasons either for or against the proposal. The reading passage is brief, usually between 75 and 100 words long. You will be given sufficient time to read the passage.

In the dialogue that will be played after you have read the reading passage, you will hear two students discussing the same article (or letter or announcement) that you have just read. One of the speakers will have a strong opinion about the proposed change—either in favor of it or against it—and will give reasons to support that opinion. The discussion is brief and typically lasts between 60 and 80 seconds.

After you have read the passage and then listened to the discussion, you will be asked a question about what you have read and heard. For example, there may be a reading passage that describes plans to make a new university rule and a conversation in which a professor and a student are discussing the rule. If in the conversation the student thinks the new rule is a bad idea, you would be asked to state what the student's opinion is and to explain the reasons the student gives for holding that opinion, using information from both the reading and the discussion.

This task tests your ability to integrate information from two sources—what you read and what you heard—and to summarize some aspect of it. The reading passage provides the context that allows you to understand what the speakers are talking about. The speakers will generally refer to the reading passage only indirectly. Therefore as you read the reading passage, you should pay attention to a number of things: the description of the proposal (*what* has been proposed, planned, or changed), and the reasons that are given for the proposal. This will help you understand what it is that the two speakers are discussing as you listen to their conversation.

In some cases, a speaker will object to the position taken in the reading and will give information that challenges the reasons offered in the reading for that position. In other cases, a speaker will agree with the position from the reading and will give information that supports those reasons. It is therefore important, as you listen to the discussion, to determine the speaker's opinion toward the proposal and to understand the relationship between what the speakers say and what you have learned from the reading passage.

To answer question 3, it is important to understand not only what the question asks you to do, but also what the question does *not* ask you to do. This type of Integrated Speaking task does not ask for your own opinion; rather, it asks you to state the opinion of one of the speakers and to summarize the speaker's reasons for having that opinion.

You will be given 45 or 50 seconds to read the passage, depending on its length, after which you will listen to the discussion. Then you will be given 30 seconds to prepare your answer and 60 seconds to respond. As with all the other questions, you may take notes while reading, listening, and preparing your answer, and you may refer to your notes while answering the question.

Tip

Remember that taking notes on the reading and listening material in the Integrated Speaking tasks on the TOEFL iBT test is allowed.

Example The following sample question consists of an announcement of a university's decision to increase tuition and a discussion between students about whether the increase is justified. This example shows how a question of this type will be presented to you on your computer.

You will hear:

Narrator

In this question, you will read a short passage about a campus situation and then listen to a conversation on the same topic. You will then answer a question using information from both the reading passage and the conversation. After you hear the question, you will have 30 seconds to prepare your response and 60 seconds to speak.

Then you will hear this:

Narrator

City University is planning to increase tuition and fees. Read the announcement about the increase from the president of City University.

You will have 45 seconds to read the announcement. Begin reading now.

Announcement from the President

The university has decided to increase tuition and fees for all students by approximately 8% next semester. For the past 5 years, the tuition and fees have remained the same, but it is necessary to increase them now for several reasons. The university has many more students than we had 5 years ago, and we must hire additional professors to teach these students. We have also made a new commitment to research and technology and will be renovating and upgrading our laboratory facilities to better meet our students' needs.

The reading passage will appear on the screen.

When the passage appears, a clock at the top of your computer screen will begin counting down the time you have to read. When reading time has ended, the passage will disappear from the screen and will be replaced by a picture of two students engaged in conversation.

You will then hear:

Narrator

Now listen to two students as they discuss the announcement.

Then the dialogue will begin.

Man

Oh, great, now we have to come up with more money for next semester.

Woman

Yeah, I know, but I can see why. When I first started here, classes were so much smaller than they are now. With this many students, it's hard to get the personal attention you need . . .

Man

Yeah, I guess you're right. You know, in some classes I can't even get a seat. And I couldn't take the math course I wanted to because it was already full when I signed up.

Woman

And the other thing is, well, I am kind of worried about not being able to get a job after I graduate.

Man

Why? I mean you're doing really well in your classes, aren't you?

Woman

I'm doing OK, but the facilities here are so limited. There are some great new experiments in microbiology that we can't even do here . . . there isn't enough equipment in the laboratories, and the equipment they have is out of date. How am I going to compete for jobs with people who have practical research experience? I think the extra tuition will be a good investment.

When the dialogue has ended, the picture of the students will be replaced by the following:

Now get ready to answer the question.

The question will then appear on your computer screen and will also be read aloud by the narrator.

3. The woman expresses her opinion of the announcement by the university president. State her opinion and explain the reasons she gives for holding that opinion.

Preparation Time: 30 Seconds
Response Time: 60 Seconds

After you hear the question, you will be told when to begin to prepare your response and when to begin speaking. A "Preparation Time" clock will appear below the question and begin to count down from 30 seconds (00:00:30). At the end of 30 seconds you will hear a short beep. After the beep, the clock will change to read "Response Time" and will begin counting down from 60 seconds (00:01:00). When the response time has ended, recording will stop and a new screen will appear alerting you that the response time has ended.

Tip

Try to recognize the attitude of the speaker by listening for intonation, stress, and word choice. This helps you understand his or her point of view and plan an appropriate response.

In giving your response to this question, you should state what the woman's opinion about the tuition increase is, and then explain her reasons for holding that opinion. You will probably have noticed as you listened to the conversation that the woman's reasons are essentially the same as those of the university president but are drawn from her own experience as a student, so in your answer you would probably want to connect information from the two sources. You could perhaps begin by saying that the woman agrees with the announcement and thinks that the university is right to increase its fees. In describing her reasons, you might say that she thinks the tuition increase is necessary because the university can then hire more teachers. She feels that classes are getting too crowded and more teachers are needed. You might also want to mention that she has found it hard to get personal attention from her professors. You could also point out that she agrees that the money should be spent to improve laboratory facilities because they are out of date, and that this has made it hard for her to get the practical laboratory experience she feels she needs to get a good job. Your response should be complete enough that someone listening to your response who has not read the announcement or heard the conversation would understand what the new policy is, what the woman's opinion about it is, and the reasons she has for her opinion. There is a great deal of information in the reading passage and the conversation, and you are not expected to summarize all of the information in giving your response.

Question 4

Question 4 is the second of the Integrated Speaking tasks. For this task you will read a short passage about an academic subject and listen to a professor give a brief excerpt from a lecture on that subject. You will then be asked a question, which you will answer based on what you have read and heard. You will have 60 seconds in which to give your spoken response.

Tip

Find listening and reading material on a topic that you like. The reading material and the listening material can provide similar or different views. Take notes on what you listen to and read, and create outlines. Use your notes and outlines to orally summarize the information and ideas from the listening and reading materials. Try to paraphrase what you have heard and read by using different words and grammatical structures.

The topics for this question are drawn from a variety of fields: life science, social science, physical science, and the humanities. Although the topics are academic in nature, none of the written passages, lectures, or questions themselves requires prior knowledge of any academic field in particular. The language and concepts used are designed to be accessible to you no matter what your academic specialization may be.

The reading passage is usually between 75 and 100 words in length. It provides background or context to help you understand the lecture that will follow. The reading passage will usually treat the topic in somewhat general and abstract terms, and the lecture will treat the topic more specifically and concretely, often by providing an extended example, counterexample, or application of the concept presented in the reading. To answer the question that follows the lecture, you will need to draw on the reading as well as the lecture, and integrate and convey key information from both sources.

For example, some tasks will contain a reading passage that gives the definition of a general principle or process and a lecture that discusses a specific instance and/or counterexample of the principle or process. For a pairing like this, you might be asked to explain the principle or process using the specific information from the listening. Or another pairing might include a reading passage that describes a problem and a lecture that presents the success, failure, or unintended consequences of an attempt to solve the problem, together with a question that asks you to explain the attempt to solve the problem and account for its results.

The sample question 4 task presented below is a typical example. It begins with a reading passage discussing a general concept—the domestication of animal species—by describing two characteristics that make an animal species suitable for domestication. This passage is coupled with a lecture in which the professor talks about the behavior of two species of animals—a familiar domesticated animal that has both of the characteristics and a common, undomesticated species that lacks these characteristics. The question asks you to apply the more general information you have learned in the reading to the examples discussed in the lecture and explain how the behavior of the two species of animals is related to their suitability for domestication.

Example   The following example shows how a question of this type will be presented to you on your computer. Question 4 will be presented visually in the same way as question 3.

First you will hear the narrator say this:

Narrator

In this question, you will read a short passage on an academic subject and then listen to a talk on the same topic. You will then answer a question using information from both the reading passage and the talk. After you hear the question, you will have 30 seconds to prepare your response and 60 seconds to speak.

Then you will hear this:

Narrator

Now read the passage about animal domestication. You have 45 seconds to read the passage. Begin reading now.

The reading passage will then appear on the screen.

Animal Domestication

For thousands of years, humans have been able to domesticate, or tame, many large mammals that in the wild live together in herds. Once tamed, these mammals are used for agricultural work and transportation. Yet some herd mammals are not easily domesticated.

A good indicator of an animal's suitability for domestication is how protective the animal is of its territory. Nonterritorial animals are more easily domesticated than territorial animals because they can live close together with animals from other herds. A second indicator is that animals with a hierarchical social structure, in which herd members follow a leader, are easy to domesticate, since a human can function as the "leader."

A clock at the top of your computer screen will count down the time you have to read. When reading time has ended, a picture of a professor in front of a class will appear on the screen:

And you will hear this:

Narrator

Now listen to a lecture on this topic in an ecology class.

Then you will hear the lecture.

Professor

So we've been discussing the suitability of animals for domestication . . . particularly animals that live together in herds. Now, if we take horses, for example . . . in the wild, horses live in herds that consist of one male and several females and their young. When a herd moves, the dominant male leads, with the dominant female and her young immediately behind him. The dominant female and her young are then followed immediately by the second most important female and her young, and so on. This is why domesticated horses can be harnessed one after the other in a row.

They're "programmed" to follow the lead of another horse. On top of that, you often find different herds of horses in the wild occupying overlapping areas—they don't fight off other herds that enter the same territory.

But it's exactly the opposite with an animal like the, uh, the antelope . . . which . . . well, antelopes are herd animals too. But unlike horses, a male antelope will fight fiercely to prevent another male from entering its territory during the breeding season; OK—very different from the behavior of horses. Try keeping a couple of male antelopes together in a small space and see what happens. Also, antelopes don't have a social hierarchy—they don't instinctively follow any leader. That makes it harder for humans to control their behavior.

When the lecture has ended, the picture of the professor will be replaced by a screen instructing you to get ready to answer the question. Then the question will appear on the screen and will be read aloud by a narrator as well.

---

4. The professor describes the behavior of horses and antelope in herds. Explain how their behavior is related to their suitability for domestication.

Preparation Time: 30 Seconds
Response Time: 60 Seconds

After you hear the question, you will be told when to begin to prepare your response and when to begin speaking. A "Preparation Time" clock will appear below the question and begin to count down from 30 seconds (00:00:30). At the end of 30 seconds you will hear a short beep. After the beep, the clock will change to read "Response Time" and will begin to count down from 60 seconds (00:01:00). When the response time has ended, recording will stop and a new screen will appear alerting you that the response time has ended.

Tip

Read a short article. Make an outline that includes only the major points of the article. Use the outline to orally summarize the information. Then add detail to the outline and orally summarize it again.

To answer this question, you would use information from both the reading passage and the lecture, linking the specific information the professor provides in the lecture with the more general concepts introduced in the reading. For example, you could begin your response by saying that herd animals can be easily domesticated if they have a hierarchical social structure and are not territorial, and that this is why it is easier to domesticate horses than antelopes. You would want to provide some details about the behavior of horses, pointing out that their hierarchical social structure makes them willing to follow one another and thus allows a human being to act as their leader. You could also say that because horses are not territorial, they can be harnessed together without fighting. You would probably want to contrast horses' behavior with that of antelopes, which are territorial. You could explain that unlike horses, male antelopes fight if they are together, and that because antelopes do not have a social hierarchy, humans cannot control them by acting as their leader. Notice that you are not asked to summarize all the information in the reading and in the lecture. But you should provide enough information so that even a listener who had not read the passage or listened to the lecture would be able to understand your explanation.

Another example of a question 4 task is a reading passage about malaria that discusses, in general terms, what is now known about the causes of this disease, how it is spread, and how it can be prevented, coupled with a lecture about the history of malaria research that describes the work of one particular doctor in the 1800s. The question that follows this lecture asks you to describe the doctor's beliefs about the cause of malaria and the recommendations he made to prevent its spread, and then to explain why his recommendations were effective. To answer this question, you would tell how the doctor's recommendations were in line with what is now known to be true about the disease. Here, as in all speaking questions that are based on academic content, you are provided with all the facts necessary to give your response, and no outside knowledge is required.

Integrated Listening/Speaking: Questions 5 and 6

Question 5

The Integrated Listening/Speaking tasks in questions 5 and 6 do not have a reading passage associated with them. For question 5, you will listen to a short conversation about a campus-related situation and respond to a question based on what you have heard. In the conversation, two people will typically discuss a problem and two possible solutions. The problem is one that concerns one of them or both of them directly. After you listen to the conversation, you will be asked to briefly describe the situation that was discussed in the conversation and to give your own opinion about solutions to the problem. You will have 60 seconds in which to give your spoken response. The topics for this task are based on common, everyday situations or problems that might arise at a college or university.

Typically, the speakers in the conversation will be students, or a student and a professor, or a student and a university staff member (for example, a teaching assistant, librarian, or administrator). The problems may involve such issues as scheduling conflicts, unavoidable absences, unavailable resources, student elections, financial difficulties, and so forth. In some cases, the problem is one that affects both speakers equally, and they must decide on a single, common solution. In other cases, the problem may involve only one of the speakers, and in this situation that speaker will present his or her problem, and the other speaker (or both of them) will propose the two possible solutions. The conversations are usually between 60 and 90 seconds long.

The question you are asked when the conversation has ended has several parts: you are asked first to describe the problem that the speakers are discussing, then to state which *one* of the solutions you prefer (note that you do not need to talk about *both* solutions), and finally to explain why you prefer that solution. The reasons you give for your preference can include information provided by the speakers in their discussion as well as your own experiences. For example, if your own experience with a similar or related problem is relevant to your choice of one solution over the other, you may draw on that experience when explaining your reasons. Here, as in other Speaking tasks in which you are asked to choose between two alternatives and give reasons for your choice, it does not matter which of the proposed solutions you choose, and there is no "right" solution or "wrong" solution. Your response will be rated not on which solution you choose, but rather on how well you describe the problem, state the solution you prefer, and explain the reasons for your preference.

Tip

It is very important to practice your conversational speaking skills as often as possible. One way of doing this might be by joining an English language conversation club. If such clubs do not exist in your area, you may want to start your own and, if possible, invite native speakers to join in.

The types of problems discussed by the speakers in these conversations will vary. The problem could be that one of the speakers needs to arrange transportation for a class field trip and does not know whom to ask. Or the problem could be that a student has a doctor's appointment scheduled at the same time as a meeting with job recruiters. Another could be about a student who is not getting along with other members of his or her study group. In the following sample question, the speakers are discussing a problem that you may find very familiar: too much schoolwork and not enough time to do it.

Example   The following example shows how you would hear and see this task on your computer:

You will hear:

Narrator

In this question, you will listen to a conversation. You will then be asked to talk about the information in the conversation and to give your opinion about the ideas presented. After you hear the question, you will have 20 seconds to prepare your response and 60 seconds to speak.

Then a picture of two students will appear on the screen.

Then you will hear the conversation.

Man

Hey, Lisa, how's it going?

Woman

Hi, Mark. Uh, I'm OK, I guess, but my schoolwork is really stressing me out.

Man

[sympathetically] Yeah? What's wrong?

Woman

Well, I've got a paper to write and two exams to study for. And a bunch of math problems to finish. It's just so much that I can't concentrate on any of it. I start concentrating on studying for one of my exams, and then I'm like, how long's it gonna take to finish that problem set?

Man

Wow. Sounds like you've got a lot more work than you can handle right now. *[not wanting to sound too pushy]* Look, have you talked to some of your professors . . . I mean, you know, try to explain the problem. Look, you could probably get an extension on your paper, or on the math assignment . . .

Woman

You think? It would give me a little more time to prepare for my exams right now.

Man

Well, I mean another thing that you might do . . . I mean have you tried making yourself a schedule? I mean that's what I do when I'm feeling overwhelmed.

Woman

What does that do for you?

Man

Well, I mean it helps you to focus your energies. You know, you make yourself a chart that shows the next few days and the time till your stuff is due and . . .

Woman

Uh-huh . . . *[meaning "I'm listening"]*

Man

I mean think about what you need to do and when you have to do it by. You know, then start filling in your schedule—like, all right, 9:00 [nine] to 11:30 [eleven thirty] A.M., study for exam; 12:00 [twelve] to 3:00 [three], work on problem set. But I mean don't make the time periods too long. Like, don't put in eight hours of studying—you know, you'll get tired, or start worrying about your other work again. But if you keep to your schedule, you know, you'll just have to worry about one thing at a time.

Woman

[somewhat noncommittally] Yeah, that might work.

When the conversation has ended, the picture of the two students will be replaced by a screen instructing you to get ready to answer the question. Then the question will appear on the screen and will be read aloud by the narrator.

5. The students discuss two possible solutions to the woman's problem. Describe the problem. Then state which of the two solutions you prefer and explain why.

Preparation Time: 20 Seconds
Response Time: 60 Seconds

After you hear the question, you will be told when to begin to prepare your response and when to begin speaking. A "Preparation Time" clock will appear below the question and begin to count down from 20 seconds (00:00:20). At the end of 20 seconds you will hear a short beep. After the beep, the clock will change to read "Response Time" and will begin to count down from 60 seconds (00:01:00). When the response time has ended, recording will stop and a new screen will appear alerting you that the response time has ended.

To answer this question, you should begin by briefly describing the woman's problem, giving just enough details so that someone listening to your response but who has not heard the conversation would know what you are talking about. Then you would state which solution you prefer and explain why. If you believe the second solution is preferable, you would probably begin by saying that you think it would be better if the woman prepared a schedule, and then you would proceed to explain why. There are many possible reasons you can give: you might say, for example, that the problem of too much work to do is something that the woman is going to confront in the future as well, and that if she learns how to organize a schedule now, this will help her throughout her academic career. You could also speak about the disadvantages of the other solution: for example, even though her professors might be willing to give her an extension, they might somehow penalize her for it by grading her assignments more severely. If your own personal experiences are relevant to your reasons for choosing one solution over the other, you may wish to mention those experiences, but you should keep in mind that the focus of the question is the problem faced by the speaker or speakers, not your own situation. Remember, too, a question like this can be answered in many different ways, and there is no "right" or "wrong" choice.

Question 6

This Integrated task, the last of the six Speaking tasks, is based on academic content. For this task you will first listen to a professor present a brief excerpt from a lecture on an academic subject, and then you will be asked a question about what you have heard. You will have 60 seconds in which to give your spoken response.

As with question 4 (the other Speaking task that is based on academic content), the topics for this question are drawn from a variety of fields within the life sciences, social sciences, physical sciences, and humanities. Here too, no prior knowledge of any academic field in particular is required for you to understand the lecture or answer the question.

The lecture excerpt is between 60 and 90 seconds long and focuses on a single topic. Usually the professor will begin the lecture by defining a concept, by highlighting an issue, or by introducing a phenomenon, and will then go on to discuss important aspects of it or perspectives relating to it. The lecture will contain illustrative examples that help explain or clarify the main concept or issue. The question you are asked after you have heard the lecture will typically ask that you explain the main concept or issue of the lecture, using points and examples that were given in the lecture.

The lectures can be about processes, methods, theories, ideas, or phenomena of any type—natural, social, psychological, and others. If a lecture is about a process, the professor might explain the process by describing some of its functions. In a lecture about a theory, the professor might explain the theory by describing its applications. In a lecture about a phenomenon, the professor might explain it through examples that illustrate its causes or its effects.

Tip

Find a textbook that includes questions about the material at the end of chapters. Practice answering the questions orally.

In the sample question 6 given below, the lecture is about a social phenomenon—the emergence of a national culture in the United States in the early twentieth century. The professor illustrates this phenomenon by describing two of its causes—radio and the automobile—and how they contributed to it. After you hear the lecture, you are asked to use information from the lecture to explain how the causes contributed to the formation of a national culture.

Example

The following example shows how a question of this type will be presented to you on your computer.

First you will hear the narrator say this:

Narrator

In this question, you will listen to part of a lecture. You will then be asked to summarize important information from the lecture. After you hear the question, you will have 20 seconds to prepare your response and 60 seconds to speak.

Then a picture of a professor standing in front of a class will appear on your screen.

You will hear:

Narrator

Now listen to part of a talk in a United States history class.

The professor will then begin the lecture.

Professor

Because the United States is such a large country, it took time for a common national culture to emerge. One hundred years ago there was very little communication among the different regions of the United States. One result of this lack of communication was that people around the United States had very little in common with one another. People in different parts of the country spoke differently, dressed differently, and behaved differently. But connections among Americans began to increase thanks to two technological innovations: the automobile and the radio.

Automobiles began to be mass-produced in the 1920s, which meant they became less expensive and more widely available. Americans in small towns and rural communities now had the ability to travel with ease to nearby cities. They could even take vacations to other parts of the country. The increased mobility provided by automobiles changed people's attitudes and created links that had not existed before. For example, people in small towns began to adopt behaviors, clothes, and speech that were popular in big cities or in other parts of the country.

As more Americans were purchasing cars, radio ownership was also increasing dramatically. Americans in different regions of the country began to listen to the same popular radio programs and musical artists. People repeated things they heard on the radio—some phrases and speech patterns heard in songs and radio programs began to be used by people all over the United States. People also listened to news reports on the radio. They heard the same news throughout the country, whereas in newspapers much news tended to be local. Radio brought Americans together by offering them shared experiences and information about events around the country.

When the lecture has ended, the picture of the professor will be replaced by a screen instructing you to get ready to answer the question. Then the question will appear on the screen and be read aloud at the same time by the narrator.

---

6. Using points and examples from the talk, explain how the automobile and the radio contributed to a common culture in the United States.

Preparation Time: 20 Seconds
Response Time: 60 Seconds

After you hear the question, you will be told when to begin preparing your response and when to begin speaking. A "Preparation Time" clock will appear below the question and begin to count down from 20 seconds (00:00:20). At the end of 20 seconds you will hear a short beep. After the beep, the clock will change to read "Response Time" and will begin to count down from 60 seconds (00:01:00). When the response time has ended, recording will stop and a new screen will appear alerting you that the response time has ended.

To answer this question, you might begin with a little background and mention that the United States did not have a common culture 100 years ago because people in different regions of the country did not communicate much with each other. Then you could say that the automobile and the radio changed this situation, and go on to summarize the information from the lecture that explains how they caused this change. For example, you could say that when automobiles became inexpensive, people from small towns could travel easily to cities or to other parts of the country, and that when they began to do this, they started acting like people from those other regions and started to dress and speak in the same way. As for the role that radio played in the emergence of a national culture, you could point out that when radio became popular, people from different parts of the country began listening to the same programs and the same news reports and began to speak alike and have similar experiences and ideas. If you have time, you could conclude by saying that these similar ways of speaking and dressing and thinking became the national culture of the United States. Remember that you do not need to repeat all of the details provided in the lecture. There is simply too much information in the lecture for you to do that. You should, however, convey enough information so that someone who has not heard the lecture would be able to form a clear idea of what the professor was explaining to the class.

Other lectures for question 6 could include topics such as how people learn, and the central concept might be that learning occurs when two events are associated in the brain. The professor would illustrate that concept by describing two different ways that events can be associated in the brain, and you would be asked to use points and examples from the lecture to explain how these ways of associating events result in learning. Or in a lecture about money, the professor might provide two different definitions of the concept and illustrate them with examples, and you would be asked in your response to explain the definitions, using the examples. The question that follows a lecture like this would typically ask you to use points and examples that you heard in the lecture to explain how people learn or what the definitions of money are.

Speaking Scoring Rubric

Independent Tasks (Questions 1 and 2)

Score	General Description	Delivery	Language Use	Topic Development
4	The response fulfills the demands of the task, with at most minor lapses in completeness. It is highly intelligible and exhibits sustained, coherent discourse. A response at this level is characterized by all of the following:	Generally well-paced flow (fluid expression). Speech is clear. It may include minor lapses, or minor difficulties with pronunciation or intonation patterns, which do not affect intelligibility.	The response demonstrates effective use of grammar and vocabulary. It exhibits a fairly high degree of automaticity with good control of basic and complex structures (as appropriate). Some minor (or systematic) errors are noticeable but do not obscure meaning.	Response is sustained and sufficient to the task. It is generally well developed and coherent; relationships between ideas are clear (or there is a clear progression of ideas).
3	The response addresses the task appropriately, but may fall short of being fully developed. It is generally intelligible and coherent, with some fluidity of expression, though it exhibits some noticeable lapses in the expression of ideas. A response at this level is characterized by at least two of the following:	Speech is generally clear, with some fluidity of expression, though minor difficulties with pronunciation, intonation, or pacing are noticeable and may require listener effort at times (though overall intelligibility is not significantly affected).	The response demonstrates fairly automatic and effective use of grammar and vocabulary and fairly coherent expression of relevant ideas. Response may exhibit some imprecise or inaccurate use of vocabulary or grammatical structures. This may affect overall fluency, but it does not seriously interfere with the communication of the message.	Response is mostly coherent and sustained and conveys relevant ideas/ information. Overall development is somewhat limited, usually lacking elaboration or specificity. Relationships between ideas may at times not be immediately clear.

Speaking Scoring Rubric

Independent Tasks (Questions 1 and 2)

Score	General Description	Delivery	Language Use	Topic Development
2	The response addresses the task, but development of the topic is limited. It contains intelligible speech, although problems with delivery and/or overall coherence occur; meaning may be obscured in places. A response at this level is characterized by at least two of the following:	Speech is basically intelligible, though listener effort is needed because of unclear articulation, awkward intonation, or choppy rhythm/pace; meaning may be obscured in places.	The response demonstrates limited range and control of grammar and vocabulary. These limitations often prevent full expression of ideas. For the most part, only basic sentence structures are used successfully and spoken with fluidity. Structures and vocabulary may express mainly simple (short) and/or general propositions, with simple or unclear connections made among them (serial listing, conjunction, juxtaposition).	The response is connected to the task, though the number of ideas presented or the development of ideas is limited. Mostly basic ideas are expressed, with limited elaboration (details and support). At times relevant substance may be vaguely expressed or repetitious. Connections of ideas may be unclear.
1	The response is very limited in content and/or coherence or is only minimally connected to the task, or speech is largely unintelligible. A response at this level is characterized by at least two of the following:	Consistent pronunciation, stress, and intonation difficulties cause considerable listener effort; delivery is choppy, fragmented, or telegraphic; frequent pauses and hesitations.	Range and control of grammar and vocabulary severely limit (or prevent) expression of ideas and connections among ideas. Some low-level responses may rely heavily on practiced or formulaic expressions.	Limited relevant content expressed. The response generally lacks substance beyond expression of very basic ideas. Speaker may be unable to sustain speech to complete the task and may rely heavily on repetition of the prompt.
0	Speaker makes no attempt to respond OR response is unrelated to the topic.			

Speaking Scoring Rubric

Integrated Tasks (Questions 3, 4, 5, and 6)

Score	General Description	Delivery	Language Use	Topic Development
4	The response fulfills the demands of the task, with at most minor lapses in completeness. It is highly intelligible and exhibits sustained, coherent discourse. A response at this level is characterized by all of the following:	Speech is generally clear, fluid, and sustained. It may include minor lapses or minor difficulties with pronunciation or intonation. Pace may vary at times as speaker attempts to recall information. Overall intelligibility remains high.	The response demonstrates good control of basic and complex grammatical structures that allow for coherent, efficient (automatic) expression of relevant ideas. Contains generally effective word choice. Though some minor (or systematic) errors or imprecise use may be noticeable, they do not require listener effort (or obscure meaning).	The response presents a clear progression of ideas and conveys the relevant information required by the task. It includes appropriate detail, though it may have minor errors or minor omissions.
3	The response addresses the task appropriately, but may fall short of being fully developed. It is generally intelligible and coherent, with some fluidity of expression, though it exhibits some noticeable lapses in the expression of ideas. A response at this level is characterized by at least two of the following:	Speech is generally clear, with some fluidity of expression, but it exhibits minor difficulties with pronunciation, intonation, or pacing and may require some listener effort at times. Overall intelligibility remains good, however.	The response demonstrates fairly automatic and effective use of grammar and vocabulary and fairly coherent expression of relevant ideas. Response may exhibit some imprecise or inaccurate use of vocabulary or grammatical structures or be somewhat limited in the range of structures used. Such limitations do not seriously interfere with the communication of the message.	The response is sustained and conveys relevant information required by the task. However, it exhibits some incompleteness, inaccuracy, lack of specificity with respect to content, or choppiness in the progression of ideas.

Speaking Scoring Rubric

Integrated Tasks (Questions 3, 4, 5, and 6)

Score	General Description	Delivery	Language Use	Topic Development
2	The response is connected to the task, though it may be missing some relevant information or contain inaccuracies. It contains some intelligible speech, but at times problems with intelligibility and/or overall coherence may obscure meaning. A response at this level is characterized by at least two of the following:	Speech is clear at times, though it exhibits problems with pronunciation, intonation, or pacing and so may require significant listener effort. Speech may not be sustained at a consistent level throughout. Problems with intelligibility may obscure meaning in places (but not throughout).	The response is limited in the range and control of vocabulary and grammar demonstrated (some complex structures may be used, but typically contain errors). This results in limited or inaccurate connections. Automaticity of expression may be evident only at the phrasal level.	The response conveys some relevant information but is clearly incomplete or inaccurate. It is incomplete if it omits key ideas, makes vague reference to key ideas, or demonstrates limited development of important information. An inaccurate response demonstrates misunderstanding of key ideas from the stimulus. Typically, ideas expressed may not be well connected or cohesive, so that familiarity with the stimulus is necessary in order to follow what is being discussed.
1	The response is very limited in content or coherence or is only minimally connected to the task. Speech may be largely unintelligible. A response at this level is characterized by at least two of the following:	Consistent pronunciation and intonation problems cause considerable listener effort and frequently obscure meaning. Delivery is choppy, fragmented, or telegraphic. Speech contains frequent pauses and hesitations.	Range and control of grammar and vocabulary severely limit (or prevent) expression of ideas and connections among ideas. Some very low-level responses may rely on isolated words or short utterances to communicate ideas.	The response fails to provide much relevant content. Ideas that are expressed are often inaccurate, or limited to vague utterances or repetitions (including repetition of prompt).
0	Speaker makes no attempt to respond OR response is unrelated to the topic.			

Strategies for Preparing for the Speaking Section

- When you address the practice TOEFL Speaking sections in the practice tests in this book, listen carefully to each of your recorded responses. Create a set of guiding questions to help you evaluate your performance. Here are some examples of the kind of questions you may want to include:

  ○ Did I complete the task?
  ○ Did I speak clearly?
  ○ Did I avoid grammatical errors?
  ○ Did I use words correctly?
  ○ Did I organize my ideas clearly and appropriately?
  ○ Did I provide a complete response?
  ○ Did I use the time effectively?

  Once you have completed your evaluation, decide what changes you want to make to your response. Then try again, making a new recording. Compare the recordings and determine if any further revisions are necessary.

- Try to periodically analyze your strengths and weaknesses. Try to understand what you are and are not able to do well and why.

- When you monitor your speaking practice, try to evaluate the pace of your speech. After each practice, ask yourself the following questions:

  ○ Did I speak too fast?
  ○ Did I speak too slowly?
  ○ Did I pause too often?

- You may want to monitor your own progress by keeping an audio journal, which entails keeping samples of your speaking activities or practices. You can also ask for feedback from one or more friends, tutors, or teachers.

Tips for the Day of the Test

- Remember that taking notes on the reading and listening material in the Integrated Speaking tasks on the TOEFL iBT test is allowed.
- Listen to the item directions carefully to understand exactly what you are being asked to do.
- Use your preparation time as effectively as possible. Plan your response by thinking about the important ideas you want to convey in a simple, organized way.
- Do not begin speaking until you are told to do so.
- Answer each question as completely as possible in the time allowed.
- Make sure to adjust your microphone and volume carefully.
- Speak into the microphone at an appropriate volume. Do not put your mouth directly onto the microphone. If you touch your mouth to the microphone, scorers may find it difficult to understand what you are saying.
- Avoid whispering. If you whisper, scorers may find it difficult to understand what you are saying.

Frequently Asked Questions About the TOEFL Speaking Section

1. Why does the TOEFL iBT test include a Speaking section?

The focus of the test is on communicative competence and encompasses your ability to use English to communicate effectively in an academic setting. Speaking is a key communication skill, along with listening, reading, and writing.

2. Why are some of the questions in the Speaking section based on reading passages and/or dialogues or lectures?

Speaking tasks that combine reading passages and/or dialogues or lectures with speaking are called integrated tasks. They are included in the TOEFL iBT test in recognition of the fact that to succeed academically in English-speaking colleges and universities, students need to be able to combine all their English language skills—in reading, listening, and speaking, as well as writing—inside and outside the classroom.

3. How much reading and listening will I have to do for the Speaking section?

The reading and listening materials that are associated with the integrated tasks vary in length but are all quite brief. Reading passages range from approximately 75 to 100 words, and the dialogues or lectures are generally between 60 and 90 seconds long. In addition to being short, the reading passages, dialogues, and lectures are not intended to be difficult. They are designed to provide you with clear and accessible information to use in answering the questions.

4. May I take notes at all times during the Speaking section?

Yes. You may take notes at any time during the Speaking section—while reading the written passages, listening to the spoken dialogues or lectures, and preparing your responses. While you listen to the dialogues or lectures and take notes, you should not try to write down word for word everything you hear. If you try to do this, you will probably miss hearing important information. Similarly, while preparing your spoken response, do not try to write out an answer that you will then try to speak. You will not have enough time to write out a full response, and raters will be rating you on your ability to speak, not on your ability to read aloud from a text that you have written. Instead, you should use your preparation time to review whatever notes you have taken and to organize your ideas.

5. How will my responses be rated?

Each of the six tasks in the Speaking section is rated by human scorers who will assign ratings ranging from 0 to 4 for each response. The scorers will evaluate your responses for topic development, delivery, and language use, and assign an overall score for each response, based on these factors.

6. How will the total Speaking section score be determined?

The scores on your individual speaking tasks are added up, with each individual task score carrying the same weight. The sum of these individual scores is converted into a scaled score of 0 to 30, and that is the Speaking section score that will be reported to the institutions you request.

7. How will mistakes affect my score?

Raters will not focus on the number of errors you make. They will score the response based on the overall performance. A response that contains minor or occasional errors may still be scored at the highest level.

8. What happens if I do not have time to finish my answer?

You may find that for some tasks, you are not able to include in your answer all the information you would like to. The time allotted for each speaking response is considered sufficient for you to give a complete answer, and you should try to give as thorough an answer as possible. However, the raters who evaluate your responses recognize that it may not always be possible for you to anticipate precisely how much of what you want to say will fit into the amount of time provided. Keep in mind that how clearly and coherently you convey information is as important as how much information you convey. Therefore you should avoid speaking at an unnaturally rapid pace if you see that time is going to run out before you say everything you have planned to say. You may find it useful to time yourself when practicing the speaking tasks. This will help you get an idea of how much can be said in the allotted time.

9. What happens if I finish my response before time runs out?

If you finish your answer before time runs out, you may want to consider what additional information you could add that would make your answer more complete. If you have extra time, it may not be a good idea for you to merely repeat what you have already said. Rather, ask yourself what else you could say to clarify, elaborate on, or otherwise develop your response more fully. Timing yourself when practicing the speaking tasks should help you get accustomed to the time allowances.

10. May I go back and change an answer?

No. Each of your spoken responses is recorded, and it is not possible to go back and rerecord what you have said. For each question, you will be given some time to prepare your answer, and this should help you plan ahead of time what you want to say. You should also remember that your speaking responses are not expected to be perfect. If in the course of giving your spoken response, you realize that you should have said something differently, you should feel free to correct your mistake if you wish, just as you would if you had made a mistake while speaking in your native language and wanted to correct it. Otherwise you may want to simply ignore an error and continue with your response, making sure that the remainder of what you say is as intelligible, coherent, and accurate as possible.

11. How will my accent and pronunciation affect my score?

All TOEFL iBT test takers speak with an accent to some degree or another, and your score will not be affected by your accent, unless your accent interferes with the intelligibility of your response. Minor and/or occasional pronunciation mistakes are also expected, even among the most proficient test takers, and, here again, as long as pronunciation mistakes do not interfere with the intelligibility of your response, they will not count against your score.

5 Writing Section

The Writing Section

There are two tasks in the Writing section of the TOEFL iBT test: an Integrated Writing task and an Independent Writing task.

The Integrated Writing task comes first because it requires some listening, and when you are taking the real TOEFL iBT test, you will be wearing headphones. When you finish the Integrated Writing task, which takes about 20 minutes, you may take the headphones off to work on the Independent Writing task. You will then have 30 minutes to complete the Independent Writing task.

This chapter discusses each of the writing tasks in detail and the scoring criteria that raters will use to evaluate your writing. It includes samples of each task, sample responses to each task, and specific advice on how to approach writing your own response.

For both writing tasks, the raters evaluating your writing recognize that your response is a first draft. You are not expected to produce a well-researched, comprehensive essay about a highly specific, specialized topic. You can receive a high score with an essay that contains some errors.

The Integrated Writing Task

You will read a passage about an academic topic for 3 minutes, and then you will hear a short lecture related to the topic. Then you will be asked to summarize the points in the lecture and explain how they relate to specific points in the reading passage.

This task gives you the opportunity to show that you can communicate in writing about academic information you have read and listened to.

Example   A reading passage like the following will appear on your computer screen. You will have 3 minutes to read the passage.

> In many organizations, perhaps the best way to approach certain new projects is to assemble a group of people into a team. Having a team of people attack a project offers several advantages. First of all, a group of people has a wider range of knowledge, expertise, and skills than any single individual is likely to possess. Also, because of the number of people involved and the greater resources they possess, a group can work more quickly in response to the task assigned to it and can come up with highly creative solutions to problems and issues. Sometimes these creative solutions come about because a group is more likely to make risky decisions that an individual might not undertake. This is because the group spreads responsibility for a decision to all the members and thus no single individual can be held accountable if the decision turns out to be wrong.
>
> Taking part in a group process can be very rewarding for members of the team. Team members who have a voice in making a decision will no doubt feel better about carrying out the work that is entailed by that decision than they might doing work that is imposed on them by others. Also, the individual team member has a much better chance to "shine," to get his or her contributions and ideas not only recognized but recognized as highly significant, because a team's overall results can be more far-reaching and have greater impact than what might have otherwise been possible for the person to accomplish or contribute working alone.

Then you will hear:

Narrator

Now listen to part of a lecture on the topic you just read about.

Professor

Now I want to tell you about what one company found when it decided that it would turn over some of its new projects to teams of people and make the team responsible for planning the projects and getting the work done. After about six months, the company took a look at how well the teams performed.

On virtually every team, some members got almost a "free ride" . . . they didn't contribute much at all, but if their team did a good job, they nevertheless benefited from the recognition the team got. And what about group members who worked especially well and who provided a lot of insight on problems and issues? Well . . . the recognition for a job well done went to the group as a whole; no names were named. So it won't surprise you to learn that when the real contributors were asked how they felt about the group process, their attitude was just the opposite of what the reading predicts.

Another finding was that some projects just didn't move very quickly. Why? Because it took so long to reach consensus; it took many, many meetings to build the agreement among group members about how they would move the project along.

On the other hand, there were other instances where one or two people managed to become very influential over what their group did. Sometimes when those influencers said, "That will never work" about an idea the group was developing, the idea was quickly dropped instead of being further discussed. And then there was another occasion when a couple influencers convinced the group that a plan of theirs was "highly creative." And even though some members tried to warn the rest of the group that the project was moving in directions that might not work, they were basically ignored by other group members. Can you guess the ending to this story? When the project failed, the blame was placed on all the members of the group.

The reading passage will then reappear on your computer screen, along with the following directions and writing task:

> You have **20 minutes** to plan and write your response. Your response will be judged on the basis of the quality of your writing and on how well your response presents the points in the lecture and their relationship to the reading passage. Typically, an effective response will be 150 to 225 words.

Summarize the points made in the lecture you just heard, explaining how they cast doubt on the points made in the reading passage.

The writing clock will then start a countdown for 20 minutes of writing time.

How the Task Is Phrased

If the lecture challenges the information in the reading passage, the writing task will usually be phrased in one of the following ways:

- Summarize the points made in the lecture, being sure to explain how they cast doubt on specific points made in the reading passage.

- Summarize the points made in the lecture, being sure to explain how they challenge specific claims/arguments made in the reading passage.

- Summarize the points made in the lecture, being sure to specifically explain how they answer the problems raised in the reading passage.

If the lecture supports or strengthens the information in the reading passage, the writing task will usually be phrased in one of the following ways:

- Summarize the points made in the lecture, being sure to specifically explain how they support the explanations in the reading passage.

- Summarize the points made in the lecture, being sure to specifically explain how they strengthen specific points made in the reading passage.

Strategies for Preparing for the Integrated Writing Task

As you read:

- Take notes on your scratch paper.

- Look for the main idea of the reading passage. The main idea often has to do with some policy or practice or some position on an issue. Or it may have to do with proposing some overall hypothesis about the way some process or procedure works or should work or how some natural phenomenon is believed to work.

- See how this main idea is evaluated or developed. Usually it will be developed in one of the following ways:

  1. Arguments or explanations are presented that support the main position; for example, why there are good reasons to believe that some policy or practice will be beneficial or prove useful or advisable or perhaps why it has been a good thing in the past.

  2. Arguments or explanations or problems are brought up concerning why some policy or practice or position or hypothesis will not or does not work or will not be useful or advisable.

- You do not need to memorize the reading passage. It will reappear on your computer screen when it is time to write.

- Note points in the passage that either support the main idea or provide reasons to doubt the main idea. Typically, the main idea will be developed with three points.

As you listen:

- Take notes on your scratch paper.

- Listen for information, examples, or explanations that make points in the reading passage seem wrong or less convincing or even untrue. For instance, in the example just given, the reading passage says that working in teams is a good thing because it gives individuals a chance to stand out. But the lecture says that often everyone gets equal credit for the work of a team, even if some people do not do any work at all. The reading says that work proceeds quickly on a team because there are more people involved, and each person brings his or her expertise. But the lecture completely contradicts this claim by stating that it may take a long time for the group to reach consensus. The lecture brings up the idea that the whole team can be blamed for a failure when the fault lies with only a few team members. This casts doubt on the claim in the reading passage that teams can take risks and be creative because no one individual is held accountable.

As you write your response:

- You may take off your headset if you wish. You will not need your headset for the remainder of the test.

- Before you start writing, briefly reread the passage, consult your notes, and make a very brief outline of the points you wish to make. You can write this outline on your scratch paper or draw lines between the notes you took on the reading passage and the notes you took on the lecture. You can even type your outline and notes right into the answer area and then replace these with sentences and paragraphs as you compose your response.

- Remember that you are *not* being asked for your opinion. You *are* being asked to explain how the points in the lecture relate to points in the reading passage.

- Write in full English sentences. You can write either one long paragraph or a series of short paragraphs listing the points of opposition between the reading passage and the lecture. Occasional language errors will not count against you as long as they do not cause you to misrepresent the meaning of points from the reading passage and the lecture.

- Remember that your job is to select the important information from the lecture and coherently and accurately present this information in relation to the relevant information from the reading passage. Your response should contain the following:

  1. The specific ideas, explanations, and arguments in the lecture that oppose or challenge points in the reading passage.

  2. Coherent and accurate presentation of each point that you make; that is, the language you use should make sense and should accurately reflect the ideas presented in the lecture and the reading passage.

  3. A clear, coherent structure that enables the reader to understand what points in the lecture relate to what points in the reading passage.

- Suggested length is between 150 and 225 words. You will not be penalized if you write more, so long as what you write answers the question.

- CAUTION: You will receive a score of 0 if all you do is copy words from the reading passage. You will receive a score of 1 if you write *only* about the reading passage. *To respond successfully, you must do your best to write about the ways the points in the lecture are related to specific points in the reading passage.*

Integrated Writing Scoring Rubric

Here is the official scoring guide used by raters when they read Integrated Writing Task responses.

Score	Task Description
5	A response at this level successfully selects the important information from the lecture and coherently and accurately presents this information in relation to the relevant information presented in the reading. The response is well organized, and occasional language errors that are present do not result in inaccurate or imprecise presentation of content or connections.
4	A response at this level is generally good in selecting the important information from the lecture and in coherently and accurately presenting this information in relation to the relevant information in the reading, but it may have minor omission, inaccuracy, vagueness, or imprecision of some content from the lecture or in connection to points made in the reading. A response is also scored at this level if it has more frequent or noticeable minor language errors, as long as such usage and grammatical structures do not result in anything more than an occasional lapse of clarity or in the connection of ideas.
3	A response at this level contains some important information from the lecture and conveys some relevant connection to the reading, but it is marked by one or more of the following:

- Although the overall response is definitely oriented to the task, it conveys only vague, global, unclear, or somewhat imprecise connection of the points made in the lecture to points made in the reading.

- The response may omit one major key point made in the lecture.

- Some key points made in the lecture or the reading, or connections between the two, may be incomplete, inaccurate, or imprecise.

- Errors of usage and/or grammar may be more frequent or may result in noticeably vague expressions or obscured meanings in conveying ideas and connections.

Score	Task Description

2   A response at this level contains some relevant information from the lecture, but is marked by significant language difficulties or by significant omission or inaccuracy of important ideas from the lecture or in the connections between the lecture and the reading; a response at this level is marked by one or more of the following:

- The response significantly misrepresents or completely omits the overall connection between the lecture and the reading.

- The response significantly omits or significantly misrepresents important points made in the lecture.

- The response contains language errors or expressions that largely obscure connections or meaning at key junctures, or that would likely obscure understanding of key ideas for a reader not already familiar with the reading and the lecture.

1   A response at this level is marked by one or more of the following:

- The response provides little or no meaningful or relevant coherent content from the lecture.

- The language level of the response is so low that it is difficult to derive meaning.

0   A response at this level merely copies sentences from the reading, rejects the topic or is otherwise not connected to the topic, is written in a foreign language, consists of keystroke characters, or is blank.

Sample Scored Responses for the Integrated Writing Task

The following were written in response to the task "Working in Teams" on pages 196 to 197.

Score 5 Response

The lecturer talks about research conducted by a firm that used the group system to handle their work. He says that the theory stated in the passage was very different and somewhat inaccurate when compared to what happened for real.

First, some members got free rides. That is, some didn't work hard but gotrecognition for the success nontheless. This also indicates that people who worked hard was not given recognition they should have got. In other words, they weren't given the oppotunity to "shine." This derectly contradicts what the passage indicates.

Second, groups were slow in progress. The passage says that groups are nore responsive than individuals because of the number of people involved and their aggregated resources. However, the speaker talks about how the firm found out that groups were slower than individuals in dicision making. Groups needed more time for meetings, which are neccesary procceedures in decision making. This was another part where experience contradicted theory.

Third, influetial people might emerge, and lead the group towards glory or failure. If the influent people are going in the right direction there would be no problem. But in cases where they go in the wrong direction, there is nobody that has enough influence to counter the decision made. In other words, the group might turn into a dictatorship, with the influential party as the leader, and might be less flexible in thinking. They might become one-sided, and thus fail to succeed.

Rater Comments

There are several errors of spelling, word formation, and subject-verb agreement in this response; however, most of these errors seem to be the result of typing errors common to first drafts. This writer does an excellent job of presenting the lecturer's points that contradict the arguments made in the reading passage. The writer is very specific and has organized his points so that they are parallel with one another: in each of the supporting paragraphs, the lecturer's observation of what really happened is given first, then explicitly connected to a theoretical point from the reading. The final paragraph contains one noticeable error ("influent"), which is then used correctly two sentences later ("influential"). Overall, this is a successful response and earns a score of 5.

Score 4 Response

> The lecture that followed the paragraph on the team work in organizations, gave some negative views of the team work itself. Firstly, though it was said in the paragraph that the whole team idea would probably be faster than the individual work, it was said in the lecture just the opposite: it could actually be a lot slower. That is because team members would sometimes take more time than needed just to reach the same conclusions, or just even to simply decide where to go from certain point to the next on.
>
> Secondly, paragraph suggests that by doing work as a team might give you an "edge," the lecture suggests that that might also be a negative thing as well. The people who made themselves leaders in the group may just be wrong in certain decisions, or just simple thing something is so creative, when in reality it is not and it would not work, but the rest of the people would nevertheless still follow them, and end up not doing well at all.
>
> And lastly, paragraph says that everyone feels responsible for their own part, and all together they are all more effective as a team. The lecture suggests quite the opposite in this case as well. It suggests that some team members are there only for the "free ride," and they don't do much of anything to contribute, but still get the credit as a whole.

Rater Comments

The writer of this response is clearly attempting to interweave the points from the passage and lecture and does a good job of discussing what the lecturer says about group decision-making and the issue of some group members failing to contribute. The writer's second point, however, is not as clearly stated as the first and third points. The key sentence in this paragraph ("The people who made themselves leaders in the group may just be wrong in certain decisions, or just simple thing something is so creative, when in reality it is not and it would not work, but the rest of the people would nevertheless still follow them, and end up not doing well at all.") is difficult to follow. This is what the Scoring Guide calls "an occasional lapse of clarity" in a response that earns a score of 4. Overall, this is still a very strong response that directly addresses the task and generally presents the relevant information from the lecture.

Score 3 Response

The lecturer provide the opposite opinion concerning what the article offered. The team work often bring negative effet. As we all know superficially, team work and team spirits are quite popular in today's business world and also the fashionable terms.

However, the lecturer find deeper and hiding results.

Firstly, the working results of team members can't be fully valued. For example, if a team member does nothing in the process of team discussion, decision making and final pratice, his or her work deliquency will not be recognized because we only emphasize team work. Also, the real excellent and creative member's work might be obliterated for the same reason.

Secondly, the team work might lose its value when team members are leading by several influential people in the group. One of the essential merits of team is to avoid the individule wrong. But one or two influential or persuasive people will make the team useless.

Thirdly, team work oftem become the excuse of taking responsibillity. All in charge, nobody care.

All in all, what we should do is the fully distinguish the advantages and disadvantages of a concept or widely used method. That is to keep the common sense.

Rater Comments

This response frames the issue well. The first point is clearly stated and accurately conveys the lecturer's comments about team members who contribute very little and team members who contribute a great deal. However, the writer discusses the second point about influencers in somewhat error-prone or vague and non-idiomatic language ("hiding results," "working results," and "when team members are leading by . . . influential people"). The point about influencers drops off at making the team "useless" and does not fully explain the reason these influencers create problems. The final point, beginning with the word "Thirdly," is not fully related to the passage and lecture, and the meaning of it is unclear. This response illustrates many of the typical features that can cause a response to receive a score of 3.

Score 2 Response

In a company's experement, some new projects were planed and acomplished by different teams. Some teams got very good results while some teams didn't. That is to say it's not nessesary for teams to achieve more than individuals do because some team members may only contribute a little in a team for they may relying on the others to do the majority.

Another thing is the recognition for the achievement by the team is for the whole team, for everyone in the team. It's not only the dicision makers in the team feel good after successfully finishing the project, but also every member in the team.

It is also showed in the lecture that in a team with one or two leaders, sometimes good ideas from some team member are dropped and ignored while sometimes they may be highly creative. In some teams decisions were made without collecting ideas from all team members. Then it would be hard to achieve creative solutions.

For those failed projects, blames are always given to the whole team even though it's the leader or someone in the team who caught the unexpected result.

Rater Comments

Although it has the appearance of a stronger response, on close reading, this example suffers from significant problems with connecting ideas and misrepresenting points. For instance, the third sentence of paragraph 1 seems to be getting at a point from the lecture ("some team members may only contribute a little . . ."). However, it is couched in a way that makes it very unclear how it relates to the point of the task ("That is to say it's not necessary for teams to achieve more than individuals do because some team members may only contribute . . ."). In addition, it is not clear where the information in paragraph 2 is coming from and what point the writer is trying to make. In paragraph 3 the writer tries to make a point about influencers, but again, it is not clear what information relates to what. For all these reasons, this response earns a score of 2.

Score 1 Response

In this lecture, the example shows only one of the group succeed the project. Why the group will succeed on this project it is because of few factor.

First of all, a group of people has a wider range of knowledge, expertise, and skills than any single individual is like to prossess, and easier to gather the information and resources to make the work effectively and the group will willingly to trey somethihg is risky decision to make the project for interesting and suceessful it is because all the member of the group carries the differnt responsibility for a decision, so once the decision turn wrong, no a any individual one will be blame for the whole responsiblity.

On the other way, the groups which are fail the project is because they are lay on some more influence people in the group, so even the idea is come out. Once the inflenced people say that is no good, then the process of the idea will be drop down immediately instead taking more further discussion! So the idea will not be easy to settle down for a group.

The form of the group is very important, and each of the member should be respect another and try out all the idea others had suggested, then it will develop a huge idea and the cooperate work environment for each other for effectively work!

Rater Comments

The level of language used in this response is fairly low, and it is lowest in the second paragraph, which is the only reference to the lecture. Because the reader has difficulty gleaning meaning from that paragraph, the response contributes little coherent information and therefore earns a score of 1.

The Independent Writing Task

The second task in the Writing section is the Independent Writing task. You are presented with a question, and you have 30 minutes to write an essay in response. The question asks you to give your opinion on an issue. Here is how the question is typically phrased:

Do you agree or disagree with the following statement?

[A sentence or sentences presenting an issue will appear here.]

Use specific reasons and examples to support your answer.

An effective response is typically about 300 words long. If you write fewer than 300 words, you may still receive a top score, but experience has shown that shorter responses typically do not demonstrate the development of ideas needed to earn a score of 5. There is no maximum word limit. You may write as much as you wish in the time allotted. But do not write just to be writing; write to respond to the topic. The number of ideas you express is important, but it is the quality of your ideas and the effectiveness with which you express them that will be most valued by the raters.

Example   Do you agree or disagree with the following statement?

Always telling the truth is the most important consideration in any relationship.

Use specific reasons and examples to support your answer.

> *Essay-writing Tips*
>
> - Think before you write. Make a brief outline or some notes on scratch paper to help you organize your thoughts. You can even type your outline and notes right in the answer area on the computer and then replace your outline with sentences and paragraphs.
>
> - Keep track of your time. Try to finish writing your essay by the time the clock counts down to 4 or 5 minutes. Use the remaining time to check your work and make final changes. At the end of 30 minutes your essay will be automatically saved.

How Essays Are Scored

Raters will judge the quality of your writing. They will consider how well you develop your ideas, how well you organize your essay, and how well you use language to express your ideas.

Development is the amount and kinds of support (examples, details, reasons) for your ideas that you present in your essay. To get a top score, your essay should be, according to the rater guidelines, "well developed, using clearly appropriate explanations, exemplifications, and/or details." The raters will judge whether you have addressed the topic and how well your details, examples, and reasons support your ideas.

Do not "memorize" long introductory and concluding paragraphs just to add words to your essay. Raters will not look favorably on wordy introductory and concluding paragraphs such as the following:

The importance of the issue raised by the posed statement, namely creating a new holiday for people, cannot be underestimated, as it concerns the very fabric of society. As it stands, the issue of creating a new holiday raises profound implications for the future. However, although the subject matter in general cannot be dismissed light-heartedly, the perspective of the issue as presented by the statement raises certain qualms regarding practical application.

In conclusion, although I have to accept that it is imperative that something be done about creating a new holiday for people and find the underlying thrust of the implied proposal utterly convincing, I cannot help but feel wary of taking such irrevocable steps and personally feel that a more measured approach would be more rewarding.

Likewise, raters will not look favorably on paragraphs like the following one, which uses a lot of words but fails to develop any real ideas:

At the heart of any discussion regarding an issue pertaining to creating a new holiday, it has to be borne in mind that a delicate line has to be trod when dealing with such matters. The human resources involved in such matters cannot be guaranteed regardless of all the good intentions that may be lavished. While it is true that creating a new holiday might be a viable and laudable remedy, it is transparently clear that applied wrongly such a course of action could be calamitous and compound the problem rather than provide a solution.

In your writing, make sure you develop some solid ideas about the given topic. Do not just use a lot of words saying that a certain issue exists. Your essay may be 300 or even 400 words long, but if it consists largely of the sorts of empty or content-free paragraphs shown above, you will probably earn a score of just 1 or 2.

Organization is something that raters notice—when you fail to organize. If an essay is organized, a reader will be able to read it from the beginning to the end without becoming confused. Writing in paragraphs and marking transitions from one idea to another in various ways usually helps the reader to follow your ideas. But be aware that just using transition words such as *first* or *second* does not guarantee that your essay is organized. The points you make must all relate to the topic of the essay and to the main idea you are presenting in response. In other words, your essay should be unified. The scoring guide mentions "unity" as well as "progression" and "coherence"—these are terms that all have to do with how well your essay is organized and how easy it is for the reader to follow your ideas. To earn a top score, you need to avoid redundancy (repetition of ideas), digression (points that are not related to your main point, that take away from the "unity" of your ideas), and unclear connections (places where it is hard for the reader to understand how two ideas or parts of your writing are related).

Language use is the third criterion on which your essay will be judged. To get a top score, an essay must display "consistent facility in the use of language." There should be a variety of sentence structures, and word choice should be appropriate. If your essay includes a few minor lexical or grammatical errors, you can still get a high score. However, if you make a lot of grammatical errors and if those errors make it hard to understand your meaning, you will get a lower score. Raters will also judge your essay based on the complexity of sentence structures and on the quality and complexity of your vocabulary. If you use very simple sentences and very basic vocabulary, you will probably not be able to express very complex ideas. If your language is hard to follow, your sentences are overly simple, and your vocabulary is limited, you may score no higher than a 3 no matter how impressive your ideas may be.

Independent Writing Scoring Rubric

| Score | Task Description |

5 An essay at this level largely accomplishes all of the following:

- Effectively addresses the topic and task

- Is well organized and well developed, using clearly appropriate explanations, exemplifications, and/or details

- Displays unity, progression, and coherence

- Displays consistent facility in the use of language, demonstrating syntactic variety, appropriate word choice, and idiomaticity, though it may have minor lexical or grammatical errors

4 An essay at this level largely accomplishes all of the following:

- Addresses the topic and task well, though some points may not be fully elaborated

- Is generally well organized and well developed, using appropriate and sufficient explanations, exemplifications, and/or details

- Displays unity, progression, and coherence, though it may contain occasional redundancy, digression, or unclear connections

- Displays facility in the use of language, demonstrating syntactic variety and range of vocabulary, though it will probably have occasional noticeable minor errors in structure, word form, or use of idiomatic language that do not interfere with meaning

3 An essay at this level is marked by one or more of the following:

- Addresses the topic and task using somewhat developed explanations, exemplifications, and/or details

- Displays unity, progression, and coherence, though connection of ideas may be occasionally obscured

- May demonstrate inconsistent facility in sentence formation and word choice that may result in lack of clarity and occasionally obscure meaning

- May display accurate but limited range of syntactic structures and vocabulary

Score	Task Description

2   An essay at this level may reveal one or more of the following weaknesses:

- Limited development in response to the topic and task

- Inadequate organization or connection of ideas

- Inappropriate or insufficient exemplifications, explanations, or details to support or illustrate generalizations in response to the task

- A noticeably inappropriate choice of words or word forms

- An accumulation of errors in sentence structure and/or usage

1   An essay at this level is seriously flawed by one or more of the following weaknesses:

- Serious disorganization or underdevelopment

- Little or no detail, or irrelevant specifics, or questionable responsiveness to the task

- Serious and frequent errors in sentence structure or usage

0   An essay at this level merely copies words from the topic, rejects the topic or is otherwise not connected to the topic, is written in a foreign language, consists of keystroke characters, or is blank.

Sample Scored Responses for the Independent Writing Task

The following essays are responses to this Independent Writing task:

Do you agree or disagree with the following statement?

Always telling the truth is the most important consideration in any relationship.

Use specific reasons and examples to support your answer.

This topic supports a variety of approaches. Some writers disagree with the statement and describe instances where to them it is appropriate to lie; typically these include white lies, lies to avoid hurting others, and lies in a business context (which often have more to do with not disclosing proprietary information than with outright lying). Others take the position that lies beget more lies and undermine trust. These writers present examples that support the statement. Still others look at both sides of the issue, often delineating or classifying situations where they consider lying appropriate and others where they consider lying inappropriate or more consequential. The telling of stories—real and hypothetical— is not inappropriate; it is reasonable to illustrate one's ideas on this topic with examples.

Score 5 Essay

DISHONESTY KILLS RELIABILITY

There are certain considerations or factors that everyone takes into account in a relationship. People may look for honesty, altruism, understanding, loyalty, being thoughtful etc! Everyone would more or less wish that the person s/he is dealing with, has some of these virtues above. Putting them in an order according to their importance, however can be very subjective and relative.

When someone asks him/herself the question "What do I consider to be the most important thing in my relationship?" the answer depends on a lot of factors such as how his/her earlier relationships were.

After stating that everyone's opinion can be different about this, for me honesty, in other words, always telling the truth is the most important consideration in a relationship. Opposite of this is inarguably lying and if someone needs to lie, either s/he is hiding something or is afraid of telling me something.

In any relationship of mine, I would wish that first of all, the person I'm dealing with is honest. Even though s/he thinks that s/he did something wrong that I wouldn't like, s/he'd better tell me the truth and not lie about it. Later on if I find out about a lie or hear the truth from someone else, that'd be much more unpleasant. In that case how can I ever believe or trust that person again? How can I ever believe that this person has enough confidence in me to forgive him/her and carry on with the relationship from there. So if I cannot trust a person anymore, if the person doesn't think I can handle the truth, there's no point to continuing that relationship.

Although I would like to see altruistic, understanding, thoughtful and loyal

altruistic

behavior from people, an instance of the opposite of these behaviors would not upset me as much as dishonesty would. Among all the possible behaviors, dishonesty is the only one for me that terminates how I feel about a person's reliability. Therefore honesty would be my first concern and the most important consideration in a relationship.

Rater Comments

In this response the writer first approaches the topic by underscoring that a number of character traits are important to a relationship. The writer then effectively develops an argument that, unlike other negative behaviors, dishonesty or unwillingness to fully disclose some bad action cannot be forgiven and can be the most important factor in destroying a relationship. The writer's language is fluent, accurate, and varied enough to effectively support the progression and connection of ideas. There is a variety of sentence structures, including rhetorical questions. The essay is not mechanically perfect, but as long as such errors are occasional, are minor, and do not interfere with the reader's understanding, an essay like this one can still earn a top score.

Score 4 Essay

Always telling the truth in any relationship is really the most important consideration for many reasons. I could say that when you lie to someone, this person will not trust you anymore and what is a relationship based on? Trust, confidence, so the sense of relationship is being lost. Another point is that if the true is ommited once, it will surely appear sometime, somewhere and probably in the most unexpected way, causing lots of problems for the ones involved. So, the truth is the basis for everything.

First, confidence is the most important aspect of a friendship or a marriage, or anything like that, so, once it is lost, the whole thing goes down in a way that no one can bear it. To avoid losing confidence, there is only one way, telling the truth, lying will just help throwing it away. For example, a couple decided to go out on the weekend, but the man has a party to go with his friends to where he can not take his girlfriend and then he lies to her saying that he is sick and can not go to the date. She undertands him and they do not see each other in that weekend, but he goes to the party and has much fun. Suppose on monday, the girl talks to a friend that saw him at the party and asked why did not she go with him. She found out the true and all confidence was lost, the basis for their relation is now gone and what happens next is that they break up or if they do not, he will persist on lyes and someday it will end.

What happened to this couple is very common around here and many relationships, even friends and marriages end because of something like that. Some may argue that lying once or another will not interfere anything and it is part of a relation, but I strongly disagree, the most important thing is the true, even if it is to determine the end of a relation, it must be told. There are more chances to end something lying than saying what really happened

Rater Comments

This essay earned a score of 4. It clearly develops reasons why lying is a bad thing, with a first paragraph that introduces the writer's position ("truth is the basis for everything"), a hypothetical story in paragraph 2, and a final paragraph that entertains and quickly dismisses a possible counterargument. All this amounts to solid development of the idea. The response displays facility in language use through a variety of sentence structures and the use of clear transitions between sentences. However, sometimes the writer's sentences include noticeable errors in word form ("if the true is ommited," "lying will just help throwing it away," "persist on lyes," "lying once or another"), and in some places the writer extends, or "runs on," a sentence to include many steps in the argument when using two or more sentences would make the relationships between ideas clearer. For example, "Some may argue that lying once or another will not interfere anything and it is part of a relation, but I strongly disagree, the most important thing is the true, even if it is to determine the end of a relation, it must be told."

Score 3 Essay

Some people believe that it is one of the most important value in many relationships to tell the truth all the time. However, it cannot be always the best choice to tell the truth in many situatioins. Sometimes white lies are indispensible to keep relationships more lively and dilightly. There are some examples to support this idea.

Firstly, in the relationships between lovers, it is often essential to compliment their lovers on their appearance and their behavior. Even though they do not think that their boyfriend or girlfriend looks good on their new shoes and new clothes, it will probably diss them by telling the truth. On the other hand, little compliments will make them confident and happy making their relationship more tight.

Secondly, parents need to encourage their children by telling lies. Even if they are doing bad work on studying or exercising, telling the truth will hurt their hearts. What they need is a little encouraging words instead of truthful words.

Thirdly, for some patients telling them their current state of their desease will probably desperate them. It is accepted publically not to let the patients know the truth. They may be able to have hope to overcome their desease without knowing the truth.

In conclusion, it is not always better to tell the truth than lies. Some lies are acceptable in terms of making people's life more profusely. Not everybody has to know the truth, and it will lead them more happier not knowing it. In these cases, white lies are worth to be regarded as a virtue of people's relationships

Rater Comments

This essay focuses on explaining why "white lies" are sometimes appropriate. The explanations here are somewhat developed. Each example does support the main point; however, at critical junctures in the writer's attempt to explain why the positive effect of the white lie outweighs any negative effect, inconsistent facility with language hinders the writer's effort. So, with errors in both structure and vocabulary that obscure meaning ("keep relationships . . . dilightly," "will probably desperate them," "making people's life more profusely," "it will lead them more happier not knowing it"), this essay earns a score of 3.

Score 2 Essay

Recently, there is a big debate on the issue that telling the truth or not is the most important consideration in the relationship between people. For my experience, I think telling a truth is the most important consideration in people's relationship. In the following, I will illustrate my opinion by two reasons.

First of all, honest make the trust stronger between friends or colleages. As we know, if people tell a lie to others he will not be trusted. When he tell a truth, others will believe that he tells a lie. For example, a person who is honest to others, can get real help and get trust of others.

Secondly, telling a lie always makes things worse not only in work but also in family life. When somebody do something wrong in his job he should annouce his mistake to his manager. If he don't do that others may continue their jobs base on the mistake. Consequently, the work will be worse and worse.

On the contrary, sometimes it is better to tell a lie to others, such as telling a lie to a patient. As we know, the sick become worse when a cancer patient know his illness. A good way to protect their life is to tell a lie. So that many doctors will not tell the truth to a dying patient.

To sum up, people should tell the truth to maintain their relationship with other people, although sometimes people have to tell a lie. People can get trust when they are honest to others.

Rater Comments

This essay is quite long, but even though it uses several examples, each idea is only partly developed, and the connections among ideas are weak or contradictory. For instance, in paragraph 2 the first sentence says, "honest make the trust stronger." The next two sentences present a contrast: "if people tell a lie to others he will not be trusted"; then "when he tell a truth, others will believe that he tells a lie." Then the last sentence in the paragraph says, "For example, a person who is honest to others, can get real help and get trust of others." But that is not an example of the previous sentence and only confuses the reader. This last sentence does not advance the progression of ideas much beyond the first sentence and certainly is not an example of the point made by the second and third sentences. Thus connections throughout this paragraph are tenuous. Paragraph 3 begins by saying that telling a lie makes things worse at work and at home, but it does not follow through at all on the latter. The "On the contrary" paragraph comes as a surprise to the reader, since paragraph 1 said that the writer was going to give two reasons why telling the truth was the most important consideration in human relationships. Because of all these weaknesses, this essay earns a score of 2.

Score 1 Essay

Nowadays, many people think that the people who always telling the true is the most inportant consideration in any relationship between human. but another think that is necessary to tell some lies. It is seldom to reach the same issue.I agree with the first thinking because of the following reasons.

First fo all, we all live in the realized world , people can respect you unless you want to use correct method to communicate with other people. It is very important, especially in business , if you want to recieve the good resulit ,you must tell the ture about your own so that gain the considement.

Secondly, if you are honest man/woman, many people may be want to make friend with you. You can have more chance to communate with other people . you may be gain more information from them.

However,sometimes we must speak some lie.for examlpe, when our relatives have heavy illness such as cancer,we couldn't telling them the ture. because that not good for their health,and may be affect their life.

In conclusion,tellingthe ture is the people good behavire .we must require most of people to tell the ture.thus,we can see the better world in our life unless we always tell the ture.

Rater Comments

This essay contains serious and frequent errors in sentence structure and usage. Paragraph 2, beginning "First fo all," is nearly incomprehensible and contains vocabulary that is either vague at best or nonstandard English ("realized world," "considement"). Paragraph 3 is completely vague, and paragraph 4 (actually one sentence), though it mentions a familiar example, is poorly expressed and certainly underdeveloped. For all these reasons, this essay earns a score of 1.

Independent Writing Topics

The following is a list of actual Independent Writing topics that were used in former versions of the TOEFL test. You will see topics very similar to these on the TOEFL iBT test. Whatever the topic, you will be asked to give your opinion and to support your opinion with specific reasons and examples.

It does not matter whether you agree or disagree with the topic; the raters are trained to accept all varieties of opinions. What matters are the skills discussed in the previous section: your ability to respond directly to the question, to take a clear position, and to write an essay characterized by good organization, proper use of supporting examples, sentence variety, correct sentence structures, and appropriate vocabulary.

None of the topics requires specialized knowledge. Most topics are general and are based on the common experience of people in general and students in particular.

What should you do with this list of topics? To prepare for the test, choose topics from the list and practice writing essays in response. Make sure you time yourself, taking 30 minutes to read the question, plan your work, and write your essay. After completing the essay, read it over and compare it with the scoring guide. Or better yet, have a friend or teacher evaluate the essay against the scoring criteria and give you feedback.

3 points for each,

Topic List

- People attend college or university for many different reasons (for example, new experiences, career preparation, increased knowledge). Why do you think people attend college or university? Use specific reasons and examples to support your answer.

- Do you agree or disagree with the following statement? Parents are the best teachers. Use specific reasons and examples to support your answer.

- Nowadays, food has become easier to prepare. Has this change improved the way people live? Use specific reasons and examples to support your answer.

- It has been said, "Not everything that is learned is contained in books." Compare and contrast knowledge gained from experience with knowledge gained from books. In your opinion, which source is more important? Why? Use specific reasons and examples to support your answer.

- A company has announced that it wishes to build a large factory near your community. Discuss the advantages and disadvantages of this new influence on your community. Do you support or oppose the factory? Explain your position.

- If you could change one important thing about your hometown, what would you change? Use reasons and specific examples to support your answer.

- How do movies or television influence people's behavior? Use reasons and specific examples to support your answer.

- Do you agree or disagree with the following statement? Television has destroyed communication among friends and family. Use specific reasons and examples to support your opinion.

- Some people prefer to live in a small town. Others prefer to live in a big city. Which place would you prefer to live in? Use specific reasons and details to support your answer.

- "When people succeed, it is because of hard work. Luck has nothing to do with success." Do you agree or disagree with the quotation above? Use specific reasons and examples to explain your position.

- Do you agree or disagree with the following statement? Universities should give the same amount of money to their students' sports activities as they give to their university libraries. Use specific reasons and examples to support your opinion.

- Many people visit museums when they travel to new places. Why do you think people visit museums? Use specific reasons and examples to support your answer.

- Some people prefer to eat at food stands or restaurants. Other people prefer to prepare and eat food at home. Which do you prefer? Use specific reasons and examples to support your answer.

- Some people believe that university students should be required to attend classes. Others believe that going to classes should be optional for students. Which point of view do you agree with? Use specific reasons and details to explain your answer.

- Neighbors are the people who live near us. In your opinion, what are the qualities of a good neighbor? Use specific details and examples in your answer.

- It has recently been announced that a new restaurant may be built in your neighborhood. Do you support or oppose this plan? Why? Use specific reasons and details to support your answer.

- Some people think that they can learn better by themselves than with a teacher. Others think that it is always better to have a teacher. Which do you prefer? Use specific reasons to develop your essay.

- What are some important qualities of a good supervisor (boss)? Use specific details and examples to explain why these qualities are important.

- Should governments spend more money on improving roads and highways, or should governments spend more money on improving public transportation (buses, trains, subways)? Why? Use specific reasons and details to develop your essay.

- It is better for children to grow up in the countryside than in a big city. Do you agree or disagree? Use specific reasons and examples to develop your essay.

- In general, people are living longer now. Discuss the causes of this phenomenon. Use specific reasons and details to develop your essay.

- We all work or will work in our jobs with many different kinds of people. In your opinion, what are some important characteristics of a coworker (someone you work closely with)? Use reasons and specific examples to explain why these characteristics are important.

- In some countries, teenagers have jobs while they are still students. Do you think this is a good idea? Support your opinion by using specific reasons and details.

- A person you know is planning to move to your town or city. What do you think this person would like and dislike about living in your town or city? Why? Use specific reasons and details to develop your essay.

- *new building* It has recently been announced that a large shopping center may be built in your neighborhood. Do you support or oppose this plan? Why? Use specific reasons and details to support your answer.

- It has recently been announced that a new movie theater may be built in your neighborhood. Do you support or oppose this plan? Why? Use specific reasons and details to support your answer.

- *work.* Do you agree or disagree with the following statement? People should sometimes do things that they do **not** enjoy doing. Use specific reasons and examples to support your answer.

- *medias.* Do you agree or disagree with the following statement? Television, newspapers, magazines, and other media pay too much attention to the personal lives of famous people such as public figures and celebrities. Use specific reasons and details to explain your opinion.

- *human and earth* Some people believe that the Earth is being harmed (damaged) by human activity. Others feel that human activity makes the Earth a better place to live. What is your opinion? Use specific reasons and examples to support your answer.

- It has recently been announced that a new high school may be built in your community. Do you support or oppose this plan? Why? Use specific reasons and details in your answer.

- *moving vs staying* Some people spend their entire lives in one place. Others move a number of times throughout their lives, looking for a better job, house, community, or even climate. Which do you prefer: staying in one place or moving in search of another place? Use reasons and specific examples to support your opinion.

- *spending vs. saving* Is it better to enjoy your money when you earn it or is it better to save your money for some time in the future? Use specific reasons and examples to support your opinion.

- *jewelry or tickets* You have received a gift of money. The money is enough to buy either a piece of jewelry you like or tickets to a concert you want to attend. Which would you buy? Use specific reasons and details to support your answer.

- *employees* Businesses should hire employees for their entire lives. Do you agree or disagree? Use specific reasons and examples to support your answer.

TV or live show   (ai) live

- Do you agree or disagree with the following statement? Attending a live performance (for example, a play, concert, or sporting event) is more enjoyable than watching the same event on television. Use specific reasons and examples to support your opinion.

- Choose **one** of the following transportation vehicles and explain why you think it has changed people's lives.
  - automobiles   cars
  - bicycles
  - airplanes

  Use specific reasons and examples to support your answer.

Language
- Do you agree or disagree that progress is always good? Use specific reasons and examples to support your answer.

past vs present — History

- Learning about the past has no value for those of us living in the present. Do you agree or disagree? Use specific reasons and examples to support your answer.

technology for learning

- Do you agree or disagree with the following statement? With the help of technology, students nowadays can learn more information and learn it more quickly. Use specific reasons and examples to support your answer.

- The expression "Never, never give up" means to keep trying and never stop working for your goals. Do you agree or disagree with this statement? Use specific reasons and examples to support your answer.

- Some people think that human needs for farmland, housing, and industry are more important than saving land for endangered animals. Do you agree or disagree with this point of view? Why or why not? Use specific reasons and examples to support your answer.

- What is a very important skill a person should learn in order to be successful in the world today? Choose **one** skill and use specific reasons and examples to support your choice.

fearless courage challenge

- Why do you think some people are attracted to dangerous sports or other dangerous activities? Use specific reasons and examples to support your answer.

- Some people like to travel with a companion. Other people prefer to travel alone. Which do you prefer? Use specific reasons and examples to support your choice.

- Some people prefer to get up early in the morning and start the day's work. Others prefer to get up later in the day and work until late at night. Which do you prefer? Use specific reasons and examples to support your choice.

- What are the important qualities of a good son or daughter? Have these qualities changed or remained the same over time in your culture? Use specific reasons and examples to support your answer.

- Some people prefer to work for a large company. Others prefer to work for a small company. Which would you prefer? Use specific reasons and details to support your choice.

- People work because they need money to live. What are some **other** reasons that people work? Discuss one or more of these reasons. Use specific examples and details to support your answer.

- Do you agree or disagree with the following statement? Face-to-face communication is better than other types of communication, such as letters, email, or telephone calls. Use specific reasons and details to support your answer.

- Some people like to do only what they already do well. Other people prefer to try new things and take risks. Which do you prefer? Use specific reasons and examples to support your choice.

- Some people believe that success in life comes from taking risks or chances. Others believe that success results from careful planning. In your opinion, what does success come from? Use specific reasons and examples to support your answer.

- What change would make your hometown more appealing to people your age? Use specific reasons and examples to support your opinion.

- Do you agree or disagree with the following statement? The most important aspect of a job is the money a person earns. Use specific reasons and examples to support your answer.

- Do you agree or disagree with the following statement? One should never judge a person by external appearances. Use specific reasons and details to support your answer.

- Do you agree or disagree with the following statement? A person should never make an important decision alone. Use specific reasons and examples to support your answer.

- A company is going to give some money either to support the arts or to protect the environment. Which do you think the company should choose? Use specific reasons and examples to support your answer.

- Some movies are serious, designed to make the audience think. Other movies are designed primarily to amuse and entertain. Which type of movie do you prefer? Use specific reasons and examples to support your answer.

- Do you agree or disagree with the following statement? Businesses should do anything they can to make a profit. Use specific reasons and examples to support your position.

- Some people are always in a hurry to go places and get things done. Other people prefer to take their time and live life at a slower pace. Which do you prefer? Use specific reasons and examples to support your answer.

- Do you agree or disagree with the following statement? Games are as important for adults as they are for children. Use specific reasons and examples to support your answer.

- Do you agree or disagree with the following statement? Parents or other adult relatives should make important decisions for their older (15- to 18-year-old) teenage children. Use specific reasons and examples to support your opinion.

- What do you want **most** in a friend—someone who is intelligent, someone who has a sense of humor, or someone who is reliable? Which **one** of these characteristics is most important to you? Use reasons and specific examples to explain your choice.

- Do you agree or disagree with the following statement? Most experiences in our lives that seemed difficult at the time become valuable lessons for the future. Use reasons and specific examples to support your answer.

- Some people prefer to work for themselves or own a business. Others prefer to work for an employer. Would you rather be self-employed, work for someone else, or own a business? Use specific reasons to explain your choice.

- Should a city try to preserve its old, historic buildings or destroy them and replace them with modern buildings? Use specific reasons and examples to support your opinion.

- Do you agree or disagree with the following statement? Classmates are a more important influence than parents on a child's success in school. Use specific reasons and examples to support your answer.

- If you were an employer, which kind of worker would you prefer to hire: an inexperienced worker at a lower salary or an experienced worker at a higher salary? Use specific reasons and details to support your answer.

- Many teachers assign homework to students every day. Do you think that daily homework is necessary for students? Use specific reasons and details to support your answer.

- If you could study a subject that you have never had the opportunity to study, what would you choose? Explain your choice, using specific reasons and details.

- Some people think that the automobile has improved modern life. Others think that the automobile has caused serious problems. What is your opinion? Use specific reasons and examples to support your answer.

- Which would you choose: a high-paying job with long hours that would give you little time with family and friends **or** a lower-paying job with shorter hours that would give you more time with family and friends? Explain your choice, using specific reasons and details.

- Do you agree or disagree with the following statement? Grades (marks) encourage students to learn. Use specific reasons and examples to support your opinion.

- Some people say that computers have made life easier and more convenient. Other people say that computers have made life more complex and stressful. What is your opinion? Use specific reasons and examples to support your answer.

- Do you agree or disagree with the following statement? The best way to travel is in a group led by a tour guide. Use specific reasons and examples to support your answer.

- Some universities require students to take classes in many subjects. Other universities require students to specialize in one subject. Which is better? Use specific reasons and examples to support your answer.

- Do you agree or disagree with the following statement? Children should begin learning a foreign language as soon as they start school. Use specific reasons and examples to support your position.

- Do you agree or disagree with the following statement? Boys and girls should attend separate schools. Use specific reasons and examples to support your answer.

real world

teamwork

- Is it more important to be able to work with a group of people on a team or to work independently? Use reasons and specific examples to support your answer.

Cui Jian
Rock.
liberal

- Your city has decided to build a statue or monument to honor a famous person in your country. Whom would you choose? Use reasons and specific examples to support your choice.

share food.

- Describe a custom from your country that you would like people from other countries to adopt. Explain your choice, using specific reasons and examples.

- Do you agree or disagree with the following statement? Technology has made the world a better place to live. Use specific reasons and examples to support your opinion.

- Do you agree or disagree with the following statement? Advertising can tell you a lot about a country. Use specific reasons and examples to support your answer.

fast food

- Do you agree or disagree with the following statement? Modern technology is creating a single world culture. Use specific reasons and examples to support your opinion.

Internet

- Some people say that the Internet provides people with a lot of valuable information. Others think access to so much information creates problems. Which view do you agree with? Use specific reasons and examples to support your opinion.

My hometown

- A foreign visitor has only one day to spend in your country. Where should this visitor go on that day? Why? Use specific reasons and details to support your choice.

grandpa
and sears

- If you could go back to some time and place in the past, when and where would you go? Why? Use specific reasons and details to support your choice.

the truth Culture
revolution
of Mao

- What discovery in the last 100 years has been most beneficial for people in your country? Use specific reasons and examples to support your choice.

- Do you agree or disagree with the following statement? Telephones and email have made communication between people less personal. Use specific reasons and examples to support your opinion.

Mao

- If you could travel back in time to meet a famous person from history, what person would you like to meet? Use specific reasons and examples to support your choice.

- If you could meet a famous entertainer or athlete, who would that be, and why? Use specific reasons and examples to support your choice.

- If you could ask a famous person one question, what would you ask? Why? Use specific reasons and details to support your answer.

- Some people prefer to live in places that have the same weather or climate all year long. Others like to live in areas where the weather changes several times a year. Which do you prefer? Use specific reasons and examples to support your choice.

- Many students have to live with roommates while going to school or university. What are some of the important qualities of a good roommate? Use specific reasons and examples to explain why these qualities are important.

- Do you agree or disagree with the following statement? Dancing plays an important role in a culture. Use specific reasons and examples to support your answer.

- Some people think governments should spend as much money as possible exploring outer space (for example, traveling to the moon and to other planets). Other people disagree and think governments should spend this money on our basic needs on Earth. Which of these two opinions do you agree with? Use specific reasons and details to support your answer.

- People have different ways of escaping the stress and difficulties of modern life. Some read; some exercise; others work in their gardens. What do you think are the best ways of reducing stress? Use specific details and examples in your answer.

- Do you agree or disagree with the following statement? Teachers should be paid according to how much their students learn. Give specific reasons and examples to support your opinion.

- If you were asked to send one thing representing your country to an international exhibition, what would you choose? Why? Use specific reasons and details to explain your choice.

- You have been told that dormitory rooms at your university must be shared by two students. Would you rather have the university assign a student to share a room with you, or would you rather choose your own roommate? Use specific reasons and details to explain your answer.

- Some people think that governments should spend as much money as possible on developing or buying computer technology. Other people disagree and think that this money should be spent on more basic needs. Which one of these opinions do you agree with? Use specific reasons and details to support your answer.

- Some people like doing work by hand. Others prefer using machines. Which do you prefer? Use specific reasons and examples to support your answer.

- Schools should ask students to evaluate their teachers. Do you agree or disagree? Use specific reasons and examples to support your answer.

intelligence • In your opinion, what is the most important characteristic (for example, honesty, intelligence, a sense of humor) that a person can have to be successful in life? Use specific reasons and examples from your experience to explain your answer.

• It is generally agreed that society benefits from the work of its members. Compare the contributions of artists to society with the contributions of scientists to society. Which type of contribution do you think is valued more by your society? Give specific reasons to support your answer.

• Students at universities often have a choice of places to live. They may choose to live in university dormitories, or they may choose to live in apartments in the community. Compare the advantages of living in university housing with the advantages of living in an apartment in the community. Where would you prefer to live? Give reasons for your preference.

automobile • You need to travel from your home to a place 40 miles (64 kilometers) away. Compare the different kinds of transportation you could use. Tell which method of travel you would choose. Give specific reasons for your choice.

• Some people believe that a college or university education should be available to all students. Others believe that higher education should be available only to good students. Discuss these views. Which view do you agree with? Explain why.

• Some people believe that the best way of learning about life is by listening to the advice of family and friends. Other people believe that the best way of learning about life is through personal experience. Compare the advantages of these two different ways of learning about life. Which do you think is preferable? Use specific examples to support your preference.

adapt to • When people move to another country, some of them decide to follow the customs of the new country. Others prefer to keep their own customs. Compare these two choices. Which one do you prefer? Support your answer with specific details.

• Some people prefer to spend most of their time alone. Others like to be with friends most of the time. Do you prefer to spend your time alone or with friends? Use specific reasons to support your answer.

• Some people prefer to spend time with one or two close friends. Others choose to spend time with a large number of friends. Compare the advantages of each choice. Which of these two ways of spending time do you prefer? Use specific reasons to support your answer.

• Some people think that children should begin their formal education at a very early age and should spend most of their time on school studies. Others believe that young children should spend most of their time playing. Compare these two views. Which view do you agree with? Why?

resources • The government has announced that it plans to build a new university. Some *price* people think that your community would be a good place to locate the univer- *traffic* sity. Compare the advantages and disadvantages of establishing a new university in your community. Use specific details in your discussion.

- Some people think that the family is the most important influence on young adults. Other people think that friends are the most important influence on young adults. Which view do you agree with? Use examples to support your position.

- Some people prefer to plan activities for their free time very carefully. Others choose not to make any plans at all for their free time. Compare the benefits of planning free-time activities with the benefits of not making plans. Which do you prefer—planning or not planning for your leisure time? Use specific reasons and examples to explain your choice.

- People learn in different ways. Some people learn by doing things; other people learn by reading about things; others learn by listening to people talk about things. Which of these methods of learning is best for you? Use specific examples to support your choice.

- Some people choose friends who are different from themselves. Others choose friends who are similar to themselves. Compare the advantages of having friends who are different from you with the advantages of having friends who are similar to you. Which kind of friend do you prefer for yourself? Why?

- Some people enjoy change, and they look forward to new experiences. Others like their lives to stay the same, and they do not change their usual habits. Compare these two approaches to life. Which approach do you prefer? Explain why.

- Do you agree or disagree with the following statement? People behave differently when they wear different clothes. Do you agree that different clothes influence the way people behave? Use specific examples to support your answer.

- Decisions can be made quickly, or they can be made after careful thought. Do you agree or disagree with the following statement? The decisions that people make quickly are always wrong. Use reasons and specific examples to support your opinion.

- Some people trust their first impressions about a person's character because they believe these judgments are generally correct. Other people do not judge a person's character quickly because they believe first impressions are often wrong. Compare these two attitudes. Which attitude do you agree with? Support your choice with specific examples.

- Do you agree or disagree with the following statement? People are never satisfied with what they have; they always want something more or something different. Use specific reasons to support your answer.

- Do you agree or disagree with the following statement? People should read only those books that are about real events, real people, and established facts. Use specific reasons and details to support your opinion.

- Do you agree or disagree with the following statement? It is more important for students to study history and literature than it is for them to study science and mathematics. Use specific reasons and examples to support your opinion.

- Do you agree or disagree with the following statement? All students should be required to study art and music in secondary school. Use specific reasons to support your answer.

- Do you agree or disagree with the following statement? There is nothing that young people can teach older people. Use specific reasons and examples to support your position.

- Do you agree or disagree with the following statement? Reading fiction (such as novels and short stories) is more enjoyable than watching movies. Use specific reasons and examples to explain your position.

- Some people say that physical exercise should be a required part of every school day. Other people believe that students should spend the whole school day on academic studies. Which opinion do you agree with? Use specific reasons and details to support your answer.

- A university plans to develop a new research center in your country. Some people want a center for business research. Other people want a center for research in agriculture (farming). Which of these two kinds of research centers do you recommend for your country? Use specific reasons in your recommendation.

- Some young children spend a great amount of their time participating in sports. Discuss the advantages and disadvantages of this. Use specific reasons and examples to support your answer.

- Do you agree or disagree with the following statement? Only people who earn a lot of money are successful. Use specific reasons and examples to support your answer.

- If you could invent something new, what product would you develop? Use specific details to explain why this invention is needed.

- Do you agree or disagree with the following statement? A person's childhood years (the time from birth to 12 years of age) are the most important years of a person's life. Use specific reasons and examples to support your answer.

- Do you agree or disagree with the following statement? Children should be required to help with household tasks as soon as they are able to do so. Use specific reasons and examples to support your answer.

- Some high schools require all students to wear school uniforms. Other high schools permit students to decide what to wear to school. Which of these two school policies do you think is better? Use specific reasons and examples to support your opinion.

- Do you agree or disagree with the following statement? Playing a game is fun only when you win. Use specific reasons and examples to support your answer.

- Do you agree or disagree with the following statement? High schools should allow students to study the courses that students want to study. Use specific reasons and examples to support your opinion.

- Do you agree or disagree with the following statement? It is better to be a member of a group than to be the leader of a group. Use specific reasons and examples to support your answer.

- What do you consider to be the most important room in a house? Why is this room more important to you than any other room? Use specific reasons and examples to support your opinion.

- Some items (such as clothes or furniture) can be made by hand or by machine. Which do you prefer—items made by hand or items made by machine? Use reasons and specific examples to explain your choice.

- If you could make one important change in a school that you attended, what change would you make? Use reasons and specific examples to support your answer.

- A gift (such as a camera, a soccer ball, or an animal) can contribute to a child's development. What gift would you give to help a child develop? Why? Use reasons and specific examples to support your choice.

- Some people believe that students should be given one long vacation each year. Others believe that students should have several short vacations throughout the year. Which viewpoint do you agree with? Use specific reasons and examples to support your choice.

- Would you prefer to live in a traditional house or in a modern apartment building? Use specific reasons and details to support your choice.

- Some people say that advertising encourages us to buy things we really do not need. Others say that advertisements tell us about new products that may improve our lives. Which viewpoint do you agree with? Use specific reasons and examples to support your answer.

- Some people prefer to spend their free time outdoors. Other people prefer to spend their leisure time indoors. Would you prefer to be outside, or would you prefer to be inside for your leisure activities? Use specific reasons and examples to explain your choice.

- Your school has received a gift of money. What do you think is the best way for your school to spend this money? Use specific reasons and details to support your choice.

- Do you agree or disagree with the following statement? Playing games teaches us about life. Use specific reasons and examples to support your answer.

- Imagine that you have received some land to use as you wish. How would you use this land? Use specific details to explain your answer.

- Do you agree or disagree with the following statement? Watching television is bad for children. Use specific details and examples to support your answer.

- What is the most important animal in your country? Why is the animal important? Use reasons and specific details to explain your answer.

- Many parts of the world are losing important natural resources, such as forests, animals, or clean water. Choose one resource that is disappearing and explain why it needs to be saved. Use specific reasons and examples to support your opinion.

- Do you agree or disagree with the following statement? A zoo has no useful purpose. Use specific reasons and examples to explain your answer.

- In some countries, people are no longer allowed to smoke in many public places and office buildings. Do you think this is a good rule or a bad rule? Use specific reasons and details to support your position.

- Plants can provide food, shelter, clothing, or medicine. What is one kind of plant that is important to you or the people in your country? Use specific reasons and details to explain your choice.

- You have the opportunity to visit a foreign country for two weeks. Which country would you like to visit? Use specific reasons and details to explain your choice.

- In the future, students may have the choice of studying at home by using technology such as computers or television or of studying at traditional schools. Which would you prefer? Use reasons and specific details to explain your choice.

- When famous people such as actors, athletes, and rock stars give their opinions, many people listen. Do you think we should pay attention to these opinions? Use specific reasons and examples to support your answer.

- The 20th century saw great change. In your opinion, what is one change that should be remembered about the 20th century? Use specific reasons and details to explain your choice.

- When people need to complain about a product or poor service, some prefer to complain in writing and others prefer to complain in person. Which way do you prefer? Use specific reasons and examples to support your answer.

- People remember special gifts or presents that they have received. Why? Use specific reasons and examples to support your answer.

- Some famous athletes and entertainers earn millions of dollars every year. Do you think these people deserve such high salaries? Use specific reasons and examples to support your opinion.

- Is the ability to read and write more important today than in the past? Why or why not? Use specific reasons and examples to support your answer.

- People do many different things to stay healthy. What do you do for good health? Use specific reasons and examples to support your answer.

- You have decided to give several hours of your time each month to improve the community where you live. What is one thing you will do to improve your community? Why? Use specific reasons and details to explain your choice.

- People recognize a difference between children and adults. What events (experiences or ceremonies) make a person an adult? Use specific reasons and examples to explain your answer.

- Your school has enough money to purchase either computers for students or books for the library. Which should your school choose to buy—computers or books? Use specific reasons and examples to support your recommendation.

- Many students choose to attend schools or universities outside their home countries. Why do some students study abroad? Use specific reasons and details to explain your answer.

- People listen to music for different reasons and at different times. Why is music important to many people? Use specific reasons and examples to support your choice.

- Groups or organizations are an important part of some people's lives. Why are groups or organizations important to people? Use specific reasons and examples to explain your answer.

- Imagine that you are preparing for a trip. You plan to be away from your home for a year. In addition to clothing and personal care items, you can take one additional thing. What would you take and why? Use specific reasons and details to support your choice.

- When students move to a new school, they sometimes face problems. How can schools help these students with their problems? Use specific reasons and examples to explain your answer.

- It is sometimes said that borrowing money from a friend can harm or damage the friendship. Do you agree? Why or why not? Use reasons and specific examples to explain your answer.

- Every generation of people is different in important ways. How is your generation different from your parents' generation? Use specific reasons and examples to explain your answer.

- Some students like classes where teachers lecture (do all of the talking) in class. Other students prefer classes where the students do some of the talking. Which type of class do you prefer? Give specific reasons and details to support your choice.

- Holidays honor people or events. If you could create a new holiday, what person or event would it honor and how would you want people to celebrate it? Use specific reasons and details to support your answer.

- A friend of yours has received some money and plans to use all of it either to go on vacation or to buy a car. Your friend has asked you for advice. Compare your friend's two choices and explain which one you think your friend should choose. Use specific reasons and details to support your choice.

- The 21st century has begun. What changes do you think this new century will bring? Use examples and details in your answer.

- What are some of the qualities of a good parent? Use specific details and examples to explain your answer.

- Movies are popular all over the world. Explain why movies are so popular. Use reasons and specific examples to support your answer.

- In your country, is there more need for land to be left in its natural condition or is there more need for land to be developed for housing and industry? Use specific reasons and examples to support your answer.

- Many people have a close relationship with their pets. These people treat their birds, cats, or other animals like members of their family. In your opinion, are such relationships good? Why or why not? Use specific reasons and examples to support your answer.

- Films can tell us a lot about the country in which they were made. What have you learned about a country from watching its movies? Use specific examples and details to support your response.

- Some students prefer to study alone. Others prefer to study with a group of students. Which do you prefer? Use specific reasons and examples to support your answer.

- You have enough money to purchase either a house or a business. Which would you choose to buy? Give specific reasons to explain your choice.

6 Authentic TOEFL iBT Practice Test 1

In this chapter you will find the first of three authentic TOEFL iBT Practice Tests. You can take the test in two different ways:

- **In the book:** You can read through the test questions in the following pages, marking your answers in the spaces provided. To hear the listening portions of the test, follow instructions to play the numbered audio tracks on the CD-ROM that accompanies this book.

- **On the CD:** For a test-taking experience that more closely resembles the actual TOEFL iBT test, you can take this same test on your computer using the accompanying CD-ROM. Reading passages and questions will appear on-screen, and you can enter your answers by clicking on the spaces provided. Follow instructions to hear the listening portions of the test.

Following this test, you will find answer keys and scoring information. You will also find scripts for the listening portions. Complete answer explanations, as well as sample test taker spoken responses and essays, are also provided.

TOEFL iBT Practice Test 1
READING

Directions: This section measures your ability to understand academic passages in English.

The Reading section is divided into separately timed parts.

Most questions are worth 1 point, but the last question for each passage is worth more than 1 point. The directions for the last question indicate how many points you may receive.

You will now begin the Reading section. There are three passages in the section. You should allow **20 minutes** to read each passage and answer the questions about it. You should allow **60 minutes** to complete the entire section.

At the end of this Practice Test, you will find an answer key, information to help you determine your score, and explanations of the answers.

NINETEENTH-CENTURY POLITICS IN THE UNITED STATES

The development of the modern presidency in the United States began with Andrew Jackson, who swept to power in 1829 at the head of the Democratic Party and served until 1837. During his administration he immeasurably enlarged the power of the presidency. "The President is the direct representative of the American people," he lectured the Senate when it opposed him. "He was elected by the people, and is responsible to them." With this declaration, Jackson redefined the character of the presidential office and its relationship to the people.

During Jackson's second term, his opponents had gradually come together to form the Whig Party. Whigs and Democrats held different attitudes toward the changes brought about by the market, banks, and commerce. The Democrats tended to view society as a continuing conflict between "the people"—farmers, planters, and workers—and a set of greedy aristocrats. This "paper money aristocracy" of bankers and investors manipulated the banking system for their own profit, Democrats claimed, and sapped the nation's virtue by encouraging speculation and the desire for sudden, unearned wealth. The Democrats wanted the rewards of the market without sacrificing the features of a simple agrarian republic. They wanted the wealth that the market offered without the competitive, changing society; the complex dealing; the dominance of urban centers; and the loss of independence that came with it.

Whigs, on the other hand, were more comfortable with the market. For them, commerce and economic development were agents of civilization. Nor did the Whigs envision any conflict in society between farmers and workers on the one hand and businesspeople and bankers on the other. Economic growth would benefit everyone by raising national income and expanding opportunity. The government's responsibility was to provide a well-regulated economy that guaranteed opportunity for citizens of ability.

Whigs and Democrats differed not only in their attitudes toward the market but also about how active the central government should be in people's lives. Despite Andrew Jackson's inclination to be a strong President, Democrats as a rule believed in limited government. Government's role in the economy was to promote competition by destroying monopolies[1] and special privileges. In keeping with this philosophy of limited government, Democrats also rejected the idea that moral beliefs were the proper sphere of government action. Religion and politics, they believed, should be kept clearly separate, and they generally opposed humanitarian legislation.

The Whigs, in contrast, viewed government power positively. They believed that it should be used to protect individual rights and public liberty, and that it had a special role where individual effort was ineffective. By regulating the economy and competition, the government could ensure equal opportunity. Indeed, for Whigs the concept of government promoting the general welfare went beyond the economy. In particular, Whigs in the northern sections of the United States also believed that government power should be used to foster the moral welfare of the country. They were much more likely to favor social-reform legislation and aid to education.

In some ways the social makeup of the two parties was similar. To be competitive in winning votes, Whigs and Democrats both had to have significant support among farmers, the largest group in society, and workers. Neither party could win an election by appealing exclusively to the rich or the poor. The Whigs, however, enjoyed disproportionate strength among the business and commercial classes. Whigs appealed to planters who needed credit to finance their cotton and rice trade in the world market, to farmers who were eager to sell their surpluses, and to workers who wished to improve themselves. Democrats attracted farmers isolated from the market or uncomfortable with it, workers alienated from the emerging industrial system, and rising entrepreneurs who wanted to break monopolies and open the economy to newcomers like themselves. The Whigs were strongest in the towns, cities, and those rural areas that were fully integrated into the market economy, whereas Democrats dominated areas of semisubsistence farming that were more isolated and languishing economically.

1. Monopolies: Companies or individuals that exclusively own or control commercial enterprises with no competitors

PARAGRAPH 1

The development of the modern presidency in the United States began with Andrew Jackson, who swept to power in 1829 at the head of the Democratic Party and served until 1837. During his administration he immeasurably enlarged the power of the presidency. "The President is the direct representative of the American people," he lectured the Senate when it opposed him. "He was elected by the people, and is responsible to them." With this declaration, Jackson redefined the character of the presidential office and its relationship to the people.

Directions: Mark your answer by filling in the oval next to your choice.

1. The word "immeasurably" in the passage is closest in meaning to
   ○ frequently
   ◐ greatly
   ○ rapidly
   ○ reportedly

2. According to paragraph 1, the presidency of Andrew Jackson was especially significant for which of the following reasons?
   ○ The President granted a portion of his power to the Senate.
   ○ The President began to address the Senate on a regular basis.
   ◐ It was the beginning of the modern presidency in the United States.
   ○ It was the first time that the Senate had been known to oppose the President.

PARAGRAPH 2

During Jackson's second term, his opponents had gradually come together to form the Whig Party. Whigs and Democrats held different attitudes toward the changes brought about by the market, banks, and commerce. The Democrats tended to view society as a continuing conflict between "the people"—farmers, planters, and workers—and a set of greedy aristocrats. This "paper money aristocracy" of bankers and investors manipulated the banking system for their own profit, Democrats claimed, and sapped the nation's virtue by encouraging speculation and the desire for sudden, unearned wealth. The Democrats wanted the rewards of the market without sacrificing the features of a simple agrarian republic. They wanted the wealth that the market offered without the competitive, changing society; the complex dealing; the dominance of urban centers; and the loss of independence that came with it.

3. The author mentions "bankers and investors" in the passage as an example of which of the following?
   ○ The Democratic Party's main source of support
   ◐ The people that Democrats claimed were unfairly becoming rich
   ○ The people most interested in a return to a simple agrarian republic
   ○ One of the groups in favor of Andrew Jackson's presidency

GO ON TO THE NEXT PAGE ↘

PARAGRAPH 3

Whigs, on the other hand, were more comfortable with the market. For them, commerce and economic development were agents of civilization. Nor did the Whigs envision any conflict in society between farmers and workers on the one hand and businesspeople and bankers on the other. Economic growth would benefit everyone by raising national income and expanding opportunity. The government's responsibility was to provide a well-regulated economy that guaranteed opportunity for citizens of ability.

4. According to paragraph 3, Whigs believed that commerce and economic development would have which of the following effects on society?

- ⊘ They would promote the advancement of society as a whole.
- ◯ They would cause disagreements between Whigs and Democrats.
- ◯ They would supply new positions for Whig Party members.
- ◯ They would prevent conflict between farmers and workers.

5. According to paragraph 3, which of the following describes the Whig Party's view of the role of government?

- ◯ To regulate the continuing conflict between farmers and businesspeople
- ◯ To restrict the changes brought about by the market
- ⊘ To maintain an economy that allowed all capable citizens to benefit
- ◯ To reduce the emphasis on economic development

PARAGRAPH 4

Whigs and Democrats differed not only in their attitudes toward the market but also about how active the central government should be in people's lives. Despite Andrew Jackson's inclination to be a strong President, Democrats as a rule believed in limited government. Government's role in the economy was to promote competition by destroying monopolies[1] and special privileges. In keeping with this philosophy of limited government, Democrats also rejected the idea that moral beliefs were the proper sphere of government action. Religion and politics, they believed, should be kept clearly separate, and they generally opposed humanitarian legislation.

1. Monopolies: Companies or individuals that exclusively own or control commercial enterprises with no competitors

6. The word "inclination" in the passage is closest in meaning to

- ◯ argument
- ⊘ tendency
- ◯ example
- ◯ warning

7. According to paragraph 4, a Democrat would be most likely to support government action in which of the following areas?

- ◯ Creating a state religion
- ◯ Supporting humanitarian legislation
- ⊘ Destroying monopolies
- ◯ Recommending particular moral beliefs

PARAGRAPH 5

The Whigs, in contrast, viewed government power positively. They believed that it should be used to protect individual rights and public liberty, and that it had a special role where individual effort was ineffective. By regulating the economy and competition, the government could ensure equal opportunity. Indeed, for Whigs the concept of government promoting the general welfare went beyond the economy. In particular, Whigs in the northern sections of the United States also believed that government power should be used to foster the moral welfare of the country. They were much more likely to favor social-reform legislation and aid to education.

8. The word "concept" in the passage is closest in meaning to

○ power
○ reality
○ difficulty
◎ idea

9. Which of the following can be inferred from paragraph 5 about variations in political beliefs within the Whig Party?

○ They were focused on issues of public liberty.
○ They caused some members to leave the Whig Party.
○ They were unimportant to most Whigs.
◎ They reflected regional interests.

GO ON TO THE NEXT PAGE ↘

PARAGRAPH 6

In some ways the social makeup of the two parties was similar. To be competitive in winning votes, Whigs and Democrats both had to have significant support among farmers, the largest group in society, and workers. Neither party could win an election by appealing exclusively to the rich or the poor. The Whigs, however, enjoyed disproportionate strength among the business and commercial classes. Whigs appealed to planters who needed credit to finance their cotton and rice trade in the world market, to farmers who were eager to sell their surpluses, and to workers who wished to improve themselves. Democrats attracted farmers isolated from the market or uncomfortable with it, workers alienated from the emerging industrial system, and rising entrepreneurs who wanted to break monopolies and open the economy to newcomers like themselves. The Whigs were strongest in the towns, cities, and those rural areas that were fully integrated into the market economy, whereas Democrats dominated areas of semisubsistence farming that were more isolated and languishing economically.

10. According to paragraph 6, the Democrats were supported by all of the following groups EXCEPT

○ workers unhappy with the new industrial system
⊘ planters involved in international trade
○ rising entrepreneurs
○ individuals seeking to open the economy to newcomers

11. Which of the sentences below best expresses the essential information in the highlighted sentence in the passage? Incorrect choices change the meaning in important ways or leave out essential information.

○ Whigs were able to attract support only in the wealthiest parts of the economy because Democrats dominated in other areas.
○ Whig and Democratic areas of influence were naturally split between urban and rural areas, respectively.
○ The semisubsistence farming areas dominated by Democrats became increasingly isolated by the Whigs' control of the market economy.
○ The Democrats' power was greatest in poorer areas, while the Whigs were strongest in those areas where the market was already fully operating.

PARAGRAPH 2

During Jackson's second term, his opponents had gradually come together to form the Whig Party. ■ Whigs and Democrats held different attitudes toward the changes brought about by the market, banks, and commerce. ■ The Democrats tended to view society as a continuing conflict between "the people"—farmers, planters, and workers—and a set of greedy aristocrats. ■ This "paper money aristocracy" of bankers and investors manipulated the banking system for their own profit, Democrats claimed, and sapped the nation's virtue by encouraging speculation and the desire for sudden, unearned wealth. ■ The Democrats wanted the rewards of the market without sacrificing the features of a simple agrarian republic. They wanted the wealth that the market offered without the competitive, changing society; the complex dealing; the dominance of urban centers; and the loss of independence that came with it.

12. Look at the four squares [■] that indicate where the following sentence can be added to the passage.

   This new party argued against the policies of Jackson and his party in a number of important areas, beginning with the economy.

   Where would the sentence best fit?

○ During Jackson's second term, his opponents had gradually come together to form the Whig Party. **This new party argued against the policies of Jackson and his party in a number of important areas, beginning with the economy.** Whigs and Democrats held different attitudes toward the changes brought about by the market, banks, and commerce. ■ The Democrats tended to view society as a continuing conflict between "the people"—farmers, planters, and workers—and a set of greedy aristocrats. ■ This "paper money aristocracy" of bankers and investors manipulated the banking system for their own profit, Democrats claimed, and sapped the nation's virtue by encouraging speculation and the desire for sudden, unearned wealth. ■ The Democrats wanted the rewards of the market without sacrificing the features of a simple agrarian republic. They wanted the wealth that the market offered without the competitive, changing society; the complex dealing; the dominance of urban centers; and the loss of independence that came with it.

○ During Jackson's second term, his opponents had gradually come together to form the Whig Party. ■ Whigs and Democrats held different attitudes toward the changes brought about by the market, banks, and commerce. **This new party argued against the policies of Jackson and his party in a number of important areas, beginning with the economy.** The Democrats tended to view society as a continuing conflict between "the people"—farmers, planters, and workers—and a set of greedy aristocrats. ■ This "paper money aristocracy" of bankers and investors manipulated the banking system for their own profit, Democrats claimed, and sapped the nation's virtue by encouraging speculation and the desire for sudden, unearned wealth. ■ The Democrats wanted the rewards of the market

GO ON TO THE NEXT PAGE ↘

without sacrificing the features of a simple agrarian republic. They wanted the wealth that the market offered without the competitive, changing society; the complex dealing; the dominance of urban centers; and the loss of independence that came with it.

○ During Jackson's second term, his opponents had gradually come together to form the Whig Party. ■ Whigs and Democrats held different attitudes toward the changes brought about by the market, banks, and commerce. ■ The Democrats tended to view society as a continuing conflict between "the people"—farmers, planters, and workers—and a set of greedy aristocrats. **This new party argued against the policies of Jackson and his party in a number of important areas, beginning with the economy.** This "paper money aristocracy" of bankers and investors manipulated the banking system for their own profit, Democrats claimed, and sapped the nation's virtue by encouraging speculation and the desire for sudden, unearned wealth. ■ The Democrats wanted the rewards of the market without sacrificing the features of a simple agrarian republic. They wanted the wealth that the market offered without the competitive, changing society; the complex dealing; the dominance of urban centers; and the loss of independence that came with it.

○ During Jackson's second term, his opponents had gradually come together to form the Whig Party. ■ Whigs and Democrats held different attitudes toward the changes brought about by the market, banks, and commerce. ■ The Democrats tended to view society as a continuing conflict between "the people"—farmers, planters, and workers—and a set of greedy aristocrats. ■ This "paper money aristocracy" of bankers and investors manipulated the banking system for their own profit, Democrats claimed, and sapped the nation's virtue by encouraging speculation and the desire for sudden, unearned wealth. **This new party argued against the policies of Jackson and his party in a number of important areas, beginning with the economy.** The Democrats wanted the rewards of the market without sacrificing the features of a simple agrarian republic. They wanted the wealth that the market offered without the competitive, changing society; the complex dealing; the dominance of urban centers; and the loss of independence that came with it.

13. **Directions:** An introductory sentence for a brief summary of the passage is provided below. Complete the summary by selecting the THREE answer choices that express the most important ideas in the passage. Some answer choices do not belong in the summary because they express ideas that are not presented in the passage or are minor ideas in the passage. **This question is worth 2 points.**

The political system of the United States in the mid-nineteenth century was strongly influenced by the social and economic circumstances of the time.

-
-
-

Answer Choices

1. The Democratic and Whig Parties developed in response to the needs of competing economic and political constituencies.

2. During Andrew Jackson's two terms as President, he served as leader of both the Democratic and Whig Parties.

3. The Democratic Party primarily represented the interests of the market, banks, and commerce.

4. In contrast to the Democrats, the Whigs favored government aid for education.

5. A fundamental difference between Whigs and Democrats involved the importance of the market in society.

6. The role of government in the lives of the people was an important political distinction between the two parties.

GO ON TO THE NEXT PAGE ◥

THE EXPRESSION OF EMOTIONS

Joy and sadness are experienced by people in all cultures around the world, but how can we tell when other people are happy or despondent? It turns out that the expression of many emotions may be universal. Smiling is apparently a universal sign of friendliness and approval. Baring the teeth in a hostile way, as noted by Charles Darwin in the nineteenth century, may be a universal sign of anger. As the originator of the theory of evolution, Darwin believed that the universal recognition of facial expressions would have survival value. For example, facial expressions could signal the approach of enemies (or friends) in the absence of language.

Most investigators concur that certain facial expressions suggest the same emotions in all people. Moreover, people in diverse cultures recognize the emotions manifested by the facial expressions. In classic research Paul Ekman took photographs of people exhibiting the emotions of anger, disgust, fear, happiness, and sadness. He then asked people around the world to indicate what emotions were being depicted in them. Those queried ranged from European college students to members of the Fore, a tribe that dwells in the New Guinea highlands. All groups, including the Fore, who had almost no contact with Western culture, agreed on the portrayed emotions. The Fore also displayed familiar facial expressions when asked how they would respond if they were the characters in stories that called for basic emotional responses. Ekman and his colleagues more recently obtained similar results in a study of ten cultures in which participants were permitted to report that multiple emotions were shown by facial expressions. The participants generally agreed on which two emotions were being shown and which emotion was more intense.

Psychological researchers generally recognize that facial expressions reflect emotional states. In fact, various emotional states give rise to certain patterns of electrical activity in the facial muscles and in the brain. The facial-feedback hypothesis argues, however, that the causal relationship between emotions and facial expressions can also work in the opposite direction. According to this hypothesis, signals from the facial muscles ("feedback") are sent back to emotion centers of the brain, and so a person's facial expression can influence that person's emotional state. Consider Darwin's words: "The free expression by outward signs of an emotion intensifies it. On the other hand, the repression, as far as possible, of all outward signs softens our emotions." Can smiling give rise to feelings of goodwill, for example, and frowning to anger?

Psychological research has given rise to some interesting findings concerning the facial-feedback hypothesis. Causing participants in experiments to smile, for example, leads them to report more positive feelings and to rate cartoons (humorous drawings of people or situations) as being more humorous. When they are caused to frown, they rate cartoons as being more aggressive.

What are the possible links between facial expressions and emotion? One link is arousal, which is the level of activity or preparedness for activity in an organism. Intense contraction of facial muscles, such as those used in signifying fear, heightens arousal. Self-perception of heightened arousal then leads to heightened emotional activity. Other links may involve changes in brain temperature and the release of neurotransmitters (substances that transmit nerve impulses). The contraction of facial muscles both influences the internal emotional state and reflects it. Ekman has found that the so-called Duchenne smile, which is characterized by "crow's-feet" wrinkles around the eyes and a subtle drop in the eye cover fold so that the skin above the eye moves down slightly toward the eyeball, can lead to pleasant feelings.

Ekman's observation may be relevant to the British expression "keep a stiff upper lip"[1] as a recommendation for handling stress. It might be that a "stiff" lip suppresses emotional response—as long as the lip is not quivering with fear or tension. But when the emotion that leads to stiffening the lip is more intense, and involves strong muscle tension, facial feedback may heighten emotional response.

1. "Keep a stiff upper lip": Avoid showing emotions in difficult situations

PARAGRAPH 1

Joy and sadness are experienced by people in all cultures around the world, but how can we tell when other people are happy or despondent? It turns out that the expression of many emotions may be universal. Smiling is apparently a universal sign of friendliness and approval. Baring the teeth in a hostile way, as noted by Charles Darwin in the nineteenth century, may be a universal sign of anger. As the originator of the theory of evolution, Darwin believed that the universal recognition of facial expressions would have survival value. For example, facial expressions could signal the approach of enemies (or friends) in the absence of language.

Directions: Mark your answer by filling in the oval next to your choice.

1. The word "despondent" in the passage is closest in meaning to
   - ○ curious
   - ○ unhappy
   - ○ thoughtful
   - ○ uncertain

2. The author mentions "Baring the teeth in a hostile way" in order to
   - ○ differentiate one possible meaning of a particular facial expression from other meanings of it
   - ○ support Darwin's theory of evolution
   - ○ provide an example of a facial expression whose meaning is widely understood
   - ○ contrast a facial expression that is easily understood with other facial expressions

GO ON TO THE NEXT PAGE ➤

**P
A
R
A
G
R
A
P
H
2**

Most investigators concur that certain facial expressions suggest the same emotions in all people. Moreover, people in diverse cultures recognize the emotions manifested by the facial expressions. In classic research Paul Ekman took photographs of people exhibiting the emotions of anger, disgust, fear, happiness, and sadness. He then asked people around the world to indicate what emotions were being depicted in them. Those queried ranged from European college students to members of the Fore, a tribe that dwells in the New Guinea highlands. All groups, including the Fore, who had almost no contact with Western culture, agreed on the portrayed emotions. The Fore also displayed familiar facial expressions when asked how they would respond if they were the characters in stories that called for basic emotional responses. Ekman and his colleagues more recently obtained similar results in a study of ten cultures in which participants were permitted to report that multiple emotions were shown by facial expressions. The participants generally agreed on which two emotions were being shown and which emotion was more intense.

3. The word "concur" in the passage is closest in meaning to
   ○ estimate
   ○ agree
   ○ expect
   ○ understand

4. The word "them" in the passage refers to
   ○ emotions
   ○ people
   ○ photographs
   ○ cultures

5. According to paragraph 2, which of the following was true of the Fore people of New Guinea?
   ○ They did not want to be shown photographs.
   ○ They were famous for their storytelling skills.
   ○ They knew very little about Western culture.
   ○ They did not encourage the expression of emotions.

6. Which of the sentences below best expresses the essential information in the highlighted sentence in the passage? Incorrect choices change the meaning in important ways or leave out essential information.
   ○ The Fore's facial expressions indicated their unwillingness to pretend to be story characters.
   ○ The Fore were asked to display familiar facial expressions when they told their stories.
   ○ The Fore exhibited the same relationship of facial expressions and basic emotions that is seen in Western culture when they acted out stories.
   ○ The Fore were familiar with the facial expressions and basic emotions of characters in stories.

PARAGRAPH 3

Psychological researchers generally recognize that facial expressions reflect emotional states. In fact, various emotional states give rise to certain patterns of electrical activity in the facial muscles and in the brain. The facial-feedback hypothesis argues, however, that the causal relationship between emotions and facial expressions can also work in the opposite direction. According to this hypothesis, signals from the facial muscles ("feedback") are sent back to emotion centers of the brain, and so a person's facial expression can influence that person's emotional state. Consider Darwin's words: "The free expression by outward signs of an emotion intensifies it. On the other hand, the repression, as far as possible, of all outward signs softens our emotions." Can smiling give rise to feelings of goodwill, for example, and frowning to anger?

7. According to the passage, what did Darwin believe would happen to human emotions that were not expressed?

○ They would become less intense.
○ They would last longer than usual.
○ They would cause problems later.
○ They would become more negative.

PARAGRAPH 4

Psychological research has given rise to some interesting findings concerning the facial-feedback hypothesis. Causing participants in experiments to smile, for example, leads them to report more positive feelings and to rate cartoons (humorous drawings of people or situations) as being more humorous. When they are caused to frown, they rate cartoons as being more aggressive.

8. According to the passage, research involving which of the following supported the "facial-feedback hypothesis"?

○ The reactions of people in experiments to cartoons
○ The tendency of people in experiments to cooperate
○ The release of neurotransmitters by people during experiments
○ The long-term effects of repressing emotions

9. The word "rate" in the passage is closest in meaning to

○ judge
○ reject
○ draw
○ want

GO ON TO THE NEXT PAGE ↘

PARAGRAPH 6

Ekman's observation may be relevant to the British expression "keep a stiff upper lip" as a recommendation for handling stress. It might be that a "stiff" lip suppresses emotional response—as long as the lip is not quivering with fear or tension. But when the emotion that leads to stiffening the lip is more intense, and involves strong muscle tension, facial feedback may heighten emotional response.

10. The word "relevant" in the passage is closest in meaning to

○ contradictory
○ confusing
○ dependent
○ applicable

11. According to the passage, stiffening the upper lip may have which of the following effects?

○ It first suppresses stress, then intensifies it.
○ It may cause fear and tension in those who see it.
○ It can damage the lip muscles.
○ It may either heighten or reduce emotional response.

PARAGRAPH 2

■ Most investigators concur that certain facial expressions suggest the same emotions in all people. ■ Moreover, people in diverse cultures recognize the emotions manifested by the facial expressions. ■ In classic research Paul Ekman took photographs of people exhibiting the emotions of anger, disgust, fear, happiness, and sadness. ■ He then asked people around the world to indicate what emotions were being depicted in them. Those queried ranged from European college students to members of the Fore, a tribe that dwells in the New Guinea highlands. All groups, including the Fore, who had almost no contact with Western culture, agreed on the portrayed emotions. The Fore also displayed familiar facial expressions when asked how they would respond if they were the characters in stories that called for basic emotional responses. Ekman and his colleagues more recently obtained similar results in a study of ten cultures in which participants were permitted to report that multiple emotions were shown by facial expressions. The participants generally agreed on which two emotions were being shown and which emotion was more intense.

12. Look at the four squares [■] that indicate where the following sentence could be added to the passage.

This universality in the recognition of emotions was demonstrated by using rather simple methods.

Where would the sentence best fit?

○ **This universality in the recognition of emotions was demonstrated by using rather simple methods.** Most investigators concur that certain facial expressions suggest the same emotions in all people. ■ Moreover, people in diverse cultures recognize the emotions manifested by the facial expressions. ■ In classic research Paul Ekman took photographs of people exhibiting the emotions of anger, disgust, fear, happiness, and sadness. ■ He then asked people around the world to indicate what emotions were being depicted in them. Those queried ranged from European college students to members of the Fore, a tribe that dwells in the New Guinea highlands. All groups, including the Fore, who had almost no contact with Western culture, agreed on the portrayed emotions. The Fore also displayed familiar facial expressions when asked how they would respond if they were the characters in stories that called for basic emotional responses. Ekman and his colleagues more recently obtained similar results in a study of ten cultures in which participants were permitted to report that multiple emotions were shown by facial expressions. The participants generally agreed on which two emotions were being shown and which emotion was more intense.

○ ■ Most investigators concur that certain facial expressions suggest the same emotions in all people. **This universality in the recognition of emotions was demonstrated by using rather simple methods.** Moreover, people in diverse cultures recognize the emotions manifested by the facial expressions. ■ In classic research Paul Ekman took photographs of people exhibiting the emotions of anger, disgust, fear, happiness, and sadness. ■ He then asked people around the world to indicate what emotions were being depicted in them. Those queried ranged from European college students to members of the Fore, a tribe that dwells in the New Guinea highlands. All groups, including the Fore, who had almost no contact with Western culture, agreed on the portrayed emotions. The Fore also displayed familiar facial expressions when asked how they would respond if they were the characters in stories that called for basic emotional responses. Ekman and his colleagues more recently obtained similar results in a study of ten cultures in which participants were permitted to report that multiple emotions were shown by facial expressions. The participants generally agreed on which two emotions were being shown and which emotion was more intense.

○ ■ Most investigators concur that certain facial expressions suggest the same emotions in all people. ■ Moreover, people in diverse cultures recognize the emotions manifested by the facial expressions. **This universality in the recognition of emotions was demonstrated by using rather simple methods.** In classic research Paul Ekman took photographs of people exhibiting the emotions of anger, disgust, fear, happiness, and sadness. ■ He then asked people around the world to indicate what emotions were being depicted in them. Those queried ranged from European college students to members of the Fore, a tribe that dwells in the New Guinea highlands. All groups, including the Fore, who had almost no contact with Western culture, agreed on the portrayed emotions. The Fore also displayed familiar facial expressions when asked how they would respond if they were the characters in stories that called for basic emotional responses. Ekman and his colleagues more recently obtained similar results in a study of ten cultures in which participants were permitted to report that multiple

GO ON TO THE NEXT PAGE ◥

emotions were shown by facial expressions. The participants generally agreed on which two emotions were being shown and which emotion was more intense.

○ ■ Most investigators concur that certain facial expressions suggest the same emotions in all people. ■ Moreover, people in diverse cultures recognize the emotions manifested by the facial expressions. ■ In classic research Paul Ekman took photographs of people exhibiting the emotions of anger, disgust, fear, happiness, and sadness. **This universality in the recognition of emotions was demonstrated by using rather simple methods.** He then asked people around the world to indicate what emotions were being depicted in them. Those queried ranged from European college students to members of the Fore, a tribe that dwells in the New Guinea highlands. All groups, including the Fore, who had almost no contact with Western culture, agreed on the portrayed emotions. The Fore also displayed familiar facial expressions when asked how they would respond if they were the characters in stories that called for basic emotional responses. Ekman and his colleagues more recently obtained similar results in a study of ten cultures in which participants were permitted to report that multiple emotions were shown by facial expressions. The participants generally agreed on which two emotions were being shown and which emotion was more intense.

13. **Directions:** An introductory sentence for a brief summary of the passage is provided below. Complete the summary by selecting the THREE answer choices that express the most important ideas in the passage. Some sentences do not belong in the summary because they express ideas that are not presented in the passage or are minor ideas in the passage. **This question is worth 2 points.**

Psychological research seems to confirm that people associate particular facial expressions with the same emotions across cultures.

-
-
-

Answer Choices

1. Artificially producing the Duchenne smile can cause a person to have pleasant feelings.

2. Facial expressions and emotional states interact with each other through a variety of feedback mechanisms.

3. People commonly believe that they can control their facial expressions so that their true emotions remain hidden.

4. A person's facial expression may reflect the person's emotional state.

5. Ekman argued that the ability to accurately recognize the emotional content of facial expressions was valuable for human beings.

6. Facial expressions that occur as a result of an individual's emotional state may themselves feed back information that influences the person's emotions.

GO ON TO THE NEXT PAGE ↘

GEOLOGY AND LANDSCAPE

Most people consider the landscape to be unchanging, but Earth is a dynamic body, and its surface is continually altering—slowly on the human time scale, but relatively rapidly when compared to the great age of Earth (about 4.5 billion years). There are two principal influences that shape the terrain: constructive processes such as uplift, which create new landscape features, and destructive forces such as erosion, which gradually wear away exposed landforms.

Hills and mountains are often regarded as the epitome of permanence, successfully resisting the destructive forces of nature, but in fact they tend to be relatively short-lived in geological terms. As a general rule, the higher a mountain is, the more recently it was formed; for example, the high mountains of the Himalayas are only about 50 million years old. Lower mountains tend to be older, and are often the eroded relics of much higher mountain chains. About 400 million years ago, when the present-day continents of North America and Europe were joined, the Caledonian mountain chain was the same size as the modern Himalayas. Today, however, the relics of the Caledonian orogeny (mountain-building period) exist as the comparatively low mountains of Greenland, the northern Appalachians in the United States, the Scottish Highlands, and the Norwegian coastal plateau.

The Earth's crust is thought to be divided into huge, movable segments, called plates, which float on a soft plastic layer of rock. Some mountains were formed as a result of these plates crashing into each other and forcing up the rock at the plate margins. In this process, sedimentary rocks that originally formed on the seabed may be folded upwards to altitudes of more than 26,000 feet. Other mountains may be raised by earthquakes, which fracture the Earth's crust and can displace enough rock to produce block mountains. A third type of mountain may be formed as a result of volcanic activity which occurs in regions of active fold mountain belts, such as in the Cascade Range of western North America. The Cascades are made up of lavas and volcanic materials. Many of the peaks are extinct volcanoes.

Whatever the reason for mountain formation, as soon as land rises above sea level it is subjected to destructive forces. The exposed rocks are attacked by the various weather processes and gradually broken down into fragments, which are then carried away and later deposited as sediments. Thus, any landscape represents only a temporary stage in the continuous battle between the forces of uplift and those of erosion.

The weather, in its many forms, is the main agent of erosion. Rain washes away loose soil and penetrates cracks in the rocks. Carbon dioxide in the air reacts with the rainwater, forming a weak acid (carbonic acid) that may chemically attack the rocks. The rain seeps underground and the water may reappear later as springs. These springs are the sources of streams and rivers, which cut through the rocks and carry away debris from the mountains to the lowlands.

Under very cold conditions, rocks can be shattered by ice and frost. Glaciers may form in permanently cold areas, and these slowly moving masses of ice cut out valleys, carrying with them huge quantities of eroded rock debris. In dry areas the wind is the principal agent of erosion. It carries fine particles of sand, which bombard exposed rock surfaces, thereby wearing them into yet more sand. Even living things contribute to the formation of landscapes. Tree roots force their way into cracks in rocks and, in so doing, speed their splitting. In contrast, the roots of grasses and other small plants may help to hold loose soil fragments together, thereby helping to prevent erosion by the wind.

Most people consider the landscape to be unchanging, but Earth is a dynamic body, and its surface is continually altering—slowly on the human time scale, but relatively rapidly when compared to the great age of Earth (about 4.5 billion years). There are two principal influences that shape the terrain: constructive processes such as uplift, which create new landscape features, and destructive forces such as erosion, which gradually wear away exposed landforms.

Directions: Mark your answer by filling in the oval next to your choice.

1. According to paragraph 1, which of the following statements is true of changes in Earth's landscape?
   ◯ They occur more often by uplift than by erosion.
   ◯ They occur only at special times.
   ◯ They occur less frequently now than they once did.
   ◯ They occur quickly in geological terms.

2. The word "relatively" in the passage is closest in meaning to
   ◯ unusually
   ◯ comparatively
   ◯ occasionally
   ◯ naturally

**P
A
R
A
G
R
A
P
H

2**

Hills and mountains are often regarded as the epitome of permanence, success-fully resisting the destructive forces of nature, but in fact they tend to be relatively short-lived in geological terms. As a general rule, the higher a mountain is, the more recently it was formed; for example, the high mountains of the Himalayas are only about 50 million years old. Lower mountains tend to be older, and are often the eroded relics of much higher mountain chains. About 400 million years ago, when the present-day continents of North America and Europe were joined, the Caledonian mountain chain was the same size as the modern Himalayas. Today, however, the relics of the Caledonian orogeny (mountain-building period) exist as the compara-tively low mountains of Greenland, the northern Appalachians in the United States, the Scottish Highlands, and the Norwegian coastal plateau.

3. Which of the sentences below best expresses the essential information in the highlighted sentence in the passage? Incorrect choices change the meaning in important ways or leave out essential information.

○ When they are relatively young, hills and mountains successfully resist the destructive forces of nature.

○ Although they seem permanent, hills and mountains exist for a relatively short period of geological time.

○ Hills and mountains successfully resist the destructive forces of nature, but only for a short time.

○ Hills and mountains resist the destructive forces of nature better than other types of landforms.

4. Which of the following can be inferred from paragraph 2 about the mountains of the Himalayas?

○ Their current height is not an indication of their age.

○ At present, they are much higher than the mountains of the Caledonian range.

○ They were a uniform height about 400 million years ago.

○ They are not as high as the Caledonian mountains were 400 million years ago.

5. The word "relics" in the passage is closest in meaning to

○ resemblances

○ regions

○ remains

○ restorations

PARAGRAPH 3

The Earth's crust is thought to be divided into huge, movable segments, called plates, which float on a soft plastic layer of rock. Some mountains were formed as a result of these plates crashing into each other and forcing up the rock at the plate margins. In this process, sedimentary rocks that originally formed on the seabed may be folded upwards to altitudes of more than 26,000 feet. Other mountains may be raised by earthquakes, which fracture the Earth's crust and can displace enough rock to produce block mountains. A third type of mountain may be formed as a result of volcanic activity which occurs in regions of active fold mountain belts, such as in the Cascade Range of western North America. The Cascades are made up of lavas and volcanic materials. Many of the peaks are extinct volcanoes.

6. According to paragraph 3, one cause of mountain formation is the

○ effect of climatic change on sea level
○ slowing down of volcanic activity
○ force of Earth's crustal plates hitting each other
○ replacement of sedimentary rock with volcanic rock

PARAGRAPH 5

The weather, in its many forms, is the main agent of erosion. Rain washes away loose soil and penetrates cracks in the rocks. Carbon dioxide in the air reacts with the rainwater, forming a weak acid (carbonic acid) that may chemically attack the rocks. The rain seeps underground and the water may reappear later as springs. These springs are the sources of streams and rivers, which cut through the rocks and carry away debris from the mountains to the lowlands.

7. Why does the author mention "Carbon dioxide" in the passage?

○ To explain the origin of a chemical that can erode rocks
○ To contrast carbon dioxide with carbonic acid
○ To give an example of how rainwater penetrates soil
○ To argue for the desirability of preventing erosion

8. The word "seeps" in the passage is closest in meaning to

○ dries gradually
○ flows slowly
○ freezes quickly
○ warms slightly

GO ON TO THE NEXT PAGE ➘

PARAGRAPH 6

Under very cold conditions, rocks can be shattered by ice and frost. Glaciers may form in permanently cold areas, and these slowly moving masses of ice cut out valleys, carrying with them huge quantities of eroded rock debris. In dry areas the wind is the principal agent of erosion. It carries fine particles of sand, which bombard exposed rock surfaces, thereby wearing them into yet more sand. Even living things contribute to the formation of landscapes. Tree roots force their way into cracks in rocks and, in so doing, speed their splitting. In contrast, the roots of grasses and other small plants may help to hold loose soil fragments together, thereby helping to prevent erosion by the wind.

9. The word "them" in the passage refers to

○ cold areas
○ masses of ice
○ valleys
○ rock debris

10. According to paragraph 6, which of the following is both a cause and result of erosion?

○ Glacial activity
○ Rock debris
○ Tree roots
○ Sand

PARAGRAPH 6

Under very cold conditions, rocks can be shattered by ice and frost. Glaciers may form in permanently cold areas, and these slowly moving masses of ice cut out valleys, carrying with them huge quantities of eroded rock debris. ■ In dry areas the wind is the principal agent of erosion. ■ It carries fine particles of sand, which bombard exposed rock surfaces, thereby wearing them into yet more sand. ■ Even living things contribute to the formation of landscapes. ■ Tree roots force their way into cracks in rocks and, in so doing, speed their splitting. In contrast, the roots of grasses and other small plants may help to hold loose soil fragments together, thereby helping to prevent erosion by the wind.

11. Look at the four squares [■] that indicate where the following sentence could be added to the passage.

   Under different climatic conditions, another type of destructive force contributes to erosion.

   Where would the sentence best fit?

○ Under very cold conditions, rocks can be shattered by ice and frost. Glaciers may form in permanently cold areas, and these slowly moving masses of ice cut out valleys, carrying with them huge quantities of eroded rock debris. **Under differ-**

ent climatic conditions, another type of destructive force contributes to erosion. In dry areas the wind is the principal agent of erosion. ■ It carries fine particles of sand, which bombard exposed rock surfaces, thereby wearing them into yet more sand. ■ Even living things contribute to the formation of landscapes. ■ Tree roots force their way into cracks in rocks and, in so doing, speed their splitting. In contrast, the roots of grasses and other small plants may help to hold loose soil fragments together, thereby helping to prevent erosion by the wind.

○ Under very cold conditions, rocks can be shattered by ice and frost. Glaciers may form in permanently cold areas, and these slowly moving masses of ice cut out valleys, carrying with them huge quantities of eroded rock debris. ■ In dry areas the wind is the principal agent of erosion. **Under different climatic conditions, another type of destructive force contributes to erosion.** It carries fine particles of sand, which bombard exposed rock surfaces, thereby wearing them into yet more sand. ■ Even living things contribute to the formation of landscapes. ■ Tree roots force their way into cracks in rocks and, in so doing, speed their splitting. In contrast, the roots of grasses and other small plants may help to hold loose soil fragments together, thereby helping to prevent erosion by the wind.

○ Under very cold conditions, rocks can be shattered by ice and frost. Glaciers may form in permanently cold areas, and these slowly moving masses of ice cut out valleys, carrying with them huge quantities of eroded rock debris. ■ In dry areas the wind is the principal agent of erosion. ■ It carries fine particles of sand, which bombard exposed rock surfaces, thereby wearing them into yet more sand. **Under different climatic conditions, another type of destructive force contributes to erosion.** Even living things contribute to the formation of landscapes. ■ Tree roots force their way into cracks in rocks and, in so doing, speed their splitting. In contrast, the roots of grasses and other small plants may help to hold loose soil fragments together, thereby helping to prevent erosion by the wind.

○ Under very cold conditions, rocks can be shattered by ice and frost. Glaciers may form in permanently cold areas, and these slowly moving masses of ice cut out valleys, carrying with them huge quantities of eroded rock debris. ■ In dry areas the wind is the principal agent of erosion. ■ It carries fine particles of sand, which bombard exposed rock surfaces, thereby wearing them into yet more sand. ■ Even living things contribute to the formation of landscapes. **Under different climatic conditions, another type of destructive force contributes to erosion.** Tree roots force their way into cracks in rocks and, in so doing, speed their splitting. In contrast, the roots of grasses and other small plants may help to hold loose soil fragments together, thereby helping to prevent erosion by the wind.

GO ON TO THE NEXT PAGE ↘

12. **Directions:** Three of the answer choices below are used in the passage to illustrate constructive processes, and two are used to illustrate destructive processes. Complete the table by matching appropriate answer choices to the processes they are used to illustrate. **This question is worth 3 points.**

Constructive Processes	Destructive Processes
•	•
•	•
•	

Answer Choices

1. Collision of Earth's crustal plates
2. Separation of continents
3. Wind-driven sand
4. Formation of grass roots in soil

5. Earthquakes
6. Volcanic activity
7. Weather processes

STOP. This is the end of the Reading section of TOEFL iBT Practice Test 1.

LISTENING

Directions: This section measures your ability to understand conversations and lectures in English.

You should listen to each conversation and lecture only **once**.

After each conversation or lecture, you will answer some questions about it. The questions typically ask about the main idea and supporting details. Some questions ask about the purpose of a speaker's statement or a speaker's attitude. Answer the questions based on what is stated or implied by the speakers.

You may take notes while you listen. You may use your notes to help you answer the questions. Your notes will **not** be scored.

In some questions, you will see this icon: 🎧 **Play Audio** This means that you will hear, but not see, part of the question.

Most questions are worth 1 point. If a question is worth more than 1 point, it will have special directions that indicate how many points you can receive.

It will take about **60 minutes** to listen to the conversations and lectures and to answer the questions. You will have **35 minutes** to respond to the questions. You should answer each question, even if you must guess the answer.

At the end of this Practice Test you will find an answer key, information to help you determine your score, scripts for the audio tracks, and explanations of the answers.

Turn the page to begin the Listening section.

Listen to Track 11 on the CD.

Questions

Directions: Mark your answer by filling in the oval or square next to your choice.

1. Why does the student go to see the professor?
   ○ To prepare for her graduate school interview
   ○ To get advice about her graduate school application
   ○ To give the professor her graduate school application
   ○ To find out if she was accepted into graduate school

2. According to the professor, what information should the student include in her statement of purpose?
   Choose 2 answers.
   ☐ Her academic motivation
   ☐ Her background in medicine
   ☐ Some personal information
   ☐ The ways her teachers have influenced her

3. What does the professor consider unusual about the student's background?
   ○ Her work experience
   ○ Her creative writing experience
   ○ Her athletic achievements
   ○ Her music training

4. Why does the professor tell a story about his friend who went to medical school?

○ To warn the student about how difficult graduate school can be

○ To illustrate a point he is making

○ To help the student relax

○ To change the subject

5. What does the professor imply about the people who admit students to graduate school?

○ They often lack expertise in the fields of the applicants.

○ They do not usually read the statement of purpose.

○ They are influenced by the appearance of an application.

○ They remember most of the applications they receive.

GO ON TO THE NEXT PAGE ➘

Listen to Track 12 on the CD.

Questions

6. What are the students mainly discussing?

○ Drugs that are harmful to the human body

○ Bacteria that produce antibiotics

○ DNA that is related to athletic performance

○ Genes that protect bacteria from antibiotics

7. *Listen to Track 13 to answer the question.*

Why does the woman say this?

○ To find out if the man has done his assignment

○ To ask the man to find out if the library is open

○ To let the man know that she cannot study much longer

○ To ask if the man has ever met her roommate

8. According to the conversation, why are transposons sometimes called "jumping genes"?

○ They are able to move from one bacteria cell to another.

○ They are found in people with exceptional jumping ability.

○ They occur in every other generation of bacteria.

○ Their movements are rapid and unpredictable.

9. According to the conversation, what are two ways in which bacteria cells get resistance genes?
   Choose 2 answers.

   ☐ The resistance genes are carried from nearby cells.

   ☐ The resistance genes are carried by white blood cells.

   ☐ The resistance genes are inherited from the parent cell.

   ☐ The resistance genes are carried by antibiotics.

10. What can be inferred about the resistance genes discussed in the conversation?

    ○ They are found in all bacteria cells.

    ○ They are not able to resist antibiotics.

    ○ They make the treatment of bacterial diseases more difficult.

    ○ They are essential to the body's defenses against bacteria.

GO ON TO THE NEXT PAGE ↘

Listen to Track 14 on the CD.

Questions

11. What is the talk mainly about?

○ A common method of managing water supplies

○ The formation of underground water systems

○ Natural processes that renew water supplies

○ Maintaining the purity of underground water systems

12. What is the professor's point of view concerning the method of "safe yield"?

○ It has helped to preserve the environment.

○ It should be researched in states other than Arizona.

○ It is not an effective resource policy.

○ It ignores the different ways people use water.

13. According to the professor, what are two problems associated with removing water from an underground system?
Choose 2 answers.

☐ Pollutants can enter the water more quickly.

☐ The surface area can dry and crack.

☐ The amount of water stored in the system can drop.

☐ Dependent streams and springs can dry up.

14. *Listen to Track 15 to answer the question.* **Play Audio**

Why does the professor say this?

○ To find out whether the students are familiar with the issue

○ To introduce a new problem for discussion

○ To respond to a student's question

○ To encourage the students to care about the topic

15. What is a key feature of a sustainable water system?

○ It is able to satisfy short-term and long-term needs.

○ It is not affected by changing environmental conditions.

○ It usually originates in lakes, springs, or streams.

○ It is not used to supply human needs.

16. What does the professor imply about water systems managed by the "safe-yield" method?

○ They recharge at a rapid rate.

○ They are not sustainable.

○ They must have large storage areas.

○ They provide a poor quality of water.

GO ON TO THE NEXT PAGE ➥

 Listen to Track 16 on the CD.

Questions

17. Why does the professor talk about Plato's description of society?

○ To explain why societies face certain problems

○ To point out problems with Plato's ethical theory

○ To introduce students to the political structure of ancient Greece

○ To help explain Plato's view about the nature of the human soul

18. *Listen again to part of the lecture by playing Track 17.* *Then answer the question.*

What does the professor imply about Plato's ethical theory?

○ It may be familiar to some of the students.

○ It will be discussed in more detail in a later class.

○ It is not an interesting theory.

○ It is not a very complicated theory.

19. *Listen again to part of the lecture by playing Track 18.* *Then answer the question.*

Why does the professor ask this?

○ To find out if students have understood what she just said

○ To suggest an answer to a question that she just asked

○ To express disagreement with a point made by Plato

○ To explain why harmony is difficult for a society to achieve

20. What are two points that reflect Plato's views about education?
    Choose 2 answers.

    ☐ All people can be trained to become leaders.

    ☐ All people should learn to use their intellect.

    ☐ Leaders should be responsible for the education of workers and soldiers.

    ☐ All people should learn about the nature of the human soul.

21. Based on information in the lecture, indicate whether the statements below about human emotion reflect beliefs held by Plato.

    For each sentence, put a check mark in the YES or NO column.

	YES	NO
Emotion is usually controlled by the faculty of desire.		
Emotion ought to be controlled by the faculty of intellect.		
Emotion is what motivates soldiers.		

22. According to Plato, what is the main characteristic of a good or just person?

    ○ The parts of the person's soul exist in harmony.

    ○ The person does not try to control other people.

    ○ The person's relationships with other people are harmonious.

    ○ The person does not act in an emotional manner.

GO ON TO THE NEXT PAGE ↘

 Listen to Track 19 on the CD.

Questions

23. What is the main topic of the lecture?

○ The size of root systems

○ Various types of root systems

○ The nutrients required by rye plants

○ Improving two types of plant species

24. According to the professor, why did one scientist grow a rye plant in water?

○ To expose the roots to sunlight

○ To be able to fertilize it with gas

○ To be able to see its entire root system

○ To see how minerals penetrate its roots

25. *Listen again to part of the lecture by playing Track 20.*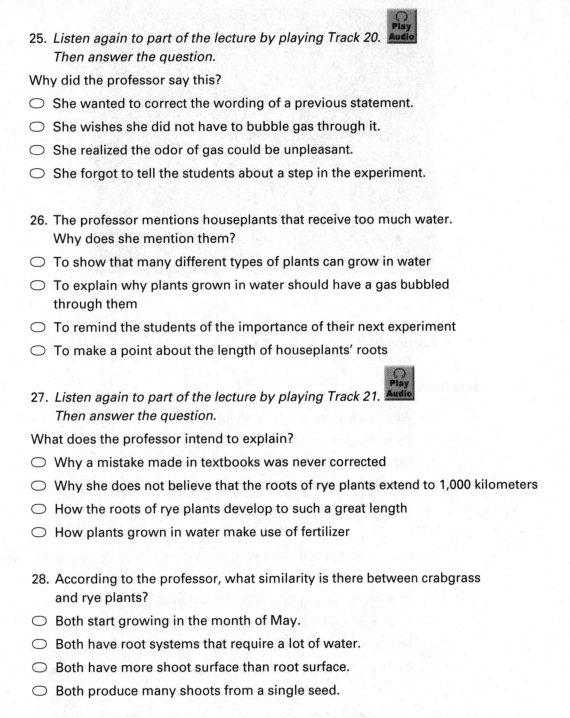
    Then answer the question.

Why did the professor say this?

○ She wanted to correct the wording of a previous statement.

○ She wishes she did not have to bubble gas through it.

○ She realized the odor of gas could be unpleasant.

○ She forgot to tell the students about a step in the experiment.

26. The professor mentions houseplants that receive too much water. Why does she mention them?

○ To show that many different types of plants can grow in water

○ To explain why plants grown in water should have a gas bubbled through them

○ To remind the students of the importance of their next experiment

○ To make a point about the length of houseplants' roots

27. *Listen again to part of the lecture by playing Track 21.*
    Then answer the question.

What does the professor intend to explain?

○ Why a mistake made in textbooks was never corrected

○ Why she does not believe that the roots of rye plants extend to 1,000 kilometers

○ How the roots of rye plants develop to such a great length

○ How plants grown in water make use of fertilizer

28. According to the professor, what similarity is there between crabgrass and rye plants?

○ Both start growing in the month of May.

○ Both have root systems that require a lot of water.

○ Both have more shoot surface than root surface.

○ Both produce many shoots from a single seed.

GO ON TO THE NEXT PAGE ↘

Listen to Track 22 on the CD. **Play Audio**

Questions

29. What is the lecture mainly about?

○ Technological innovations in the automobile industry

○ The organizational structure of companies

○ Ways to improve efficiency in an engineering department

○ Methods of resolving conflicts in organizations

30. Why does the professor talk about a construction company that has work in different cities?

○ To give an example of functional organization

○ To give an example of organization around projects

○ To illustrate problems with functional organization

○ To illustrate the types of conflict that can arise in companies

31. *Listen again to part of the lecture by playing Track 23.* **Play Audio** *Then answer the question.*

Why does the professor say this?

○ He does not understand why the student is talking about engineers.

○ He wants to know how the engineers will communicate with their coworkers.

○ The student has not provided a complete answer to his question.

○ He wants the student to do more research on the topic.

32. What is an example of a violation of the "unity of command" principle?

○ More than one person supervises the same employee.

○ A company decides not to standardize its products.

○ Several project managers are responsible for designing a new product.

○ An employee does not follow a supervisor's instructions.

33. According to the professor, where might there be a conflict in an organizational structure based on both projects and function?

○ Between architects and finance experts

○ Between the need to specialize and the need to standardize

○ Between two engineers who work on the same project

○ Between the needs of projects in different cities

34. Indicate whether each sentence below describes functional organization or project organization. Place a check mark in the correct box.

	Functional Organization	Project Organization
It encourages people with similar expertise to work closely together.		
It helps the company to adapt quickly and meet changing needs.		
It helps to achieve uniformity in projects.		

STOP. This is the end of the Listening section of TOEFL iBT Practice Test 1.

SPEAKING

Directions: The following Speaking section of the test will last approximately **20 minutes**. To complete it, you will need a CD player, as well as a recording device that you can play back to listen to your response.

During the test, you will answer six speaking questions. Two of the questions ask about familiar topics. Four questions ask about short conversations, lectures, and reading passages. You may take notes as you listen to the conversations and lectures. The questions and the reading passages are printed here. The time you will have to prepare your response and to speak is printed below each question. You should answer all of the questions as completely as possible in the time allowed. The preparation time begins immediately after you hear the question. When you take the actual test, you will be told when to begin to prepare and when to begin speaking.

Play the audio tracks listed in the test instructions. Record each of your responses.

At the end of this Practice Test you will find scripts for the audio tracks, important points for each question, directions for listening to sample spoken responses, and comments on those responses by official raters.

Questions

1. You will now be asked a question about a familiar topic. After you hear the question, you will have 15 seconds to prepare your response and 45 seconds to speak.

Now play Track 24 on the CD to hear Question 1.

Choose a place you go to often that is important to you and explain why it is important. Please include specific details in your explanation.

> **Preparation Time: 15 Seconds**
> **Response Time: 45 Seconds**

2. You will now be asked to give your opinion about a familiar topic. After you hear the question, you will have 15 seconds to prepare your response and 45 seconds to speak.

Now play Track 25 on the CD to hear Question 2.

Some college students choose to take courses in a variety of subject areas in order to get a broad education. Others choose to focus on a single subject area in order to have a deeper understanding of that area. Which approach to course selection do you think is better for students and why?

> **Preparation Time: 15 Seconds**
> **Response Time: 45 Seconds**

3. You will now read a short passage and then listen to a conversation on the same topic. You will then be asked a question about them. After you hear the question, you will have 30 seconds to prepare your response and 60 seconds to speak.

Now play Track 26 on the CD to hear Question 3.

Reading Time: 45 Seconds

Bus Service Elimination Planned

The university has decided to discontinue its free bus service for students. The reason given for this decision is that few students ride the buses and the buses are expensive to operate. Currently, the buses run from the center of campus past university buildings and through some of the neighborhoods surrounding the campus. The money saved by eliminating the bus service will be used to expand the overcrowded student parking lots.

The man expresses his opinion of the university's plan to eliminate the bus service. State his opinion and explain the reasons he gives for holding that opinion.

Preparation Time: 30 Seconds
Response Time: 60 Seconds

GO ON TO THE NEXT PAGE ↘

4. You will now read a short passage and then listen to a talk on the same academic topic. You will then be asked a question about them. After you hear the question, you will have 30 seconds to prepare your response and 60 seconds to speak.

Now play Track 27 on the CD to hear Question 4.

Reading Time: 45 Seconds

Social Interaction

People deal with each other every day. This interaction is at the heart of social life. The study of social interaction is concerned with the influence people have over one another's behavior. People take each other into account in their daily behavior and in fact, the very presence of others can affect behavior. For example, one principle of social interaction, audience effects, suggests that individuals' work is affected by their knowledge that they are visible to others, that the presence of others tends to alter the way people behave or perform an activity.

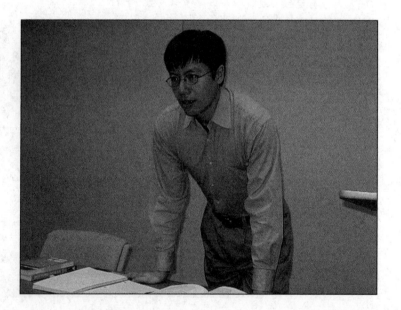

Explain how the examples of tying shoes and learning to type demonstrate the principle of audience effects.

Preparation Time: 30 Seconds
Response Time: 60 Seconds

5. You will now listen to a conversation. You will then be asked a question about it. After you hear the question, you will have 20 seconds to prepare your response and 60 seconds to speak.

Now play Track 28 on the CD to hear Question 5.

The speakers discuss two possible solutions to the woman's problem. Describe the problem and the two solutions. Then explain what you think the woman should do and why.

Preparation Time: 20 Seconds
Response Time: 60 Seconds

GO ON TO THE NEXT PAGE ↘

6. You will now listen to part of a lecture. You will then be asked a question about it. After you hear the question, you will have 20 seconds to prepare your response and 60 seconds to speak.

Now play Track 29 on the CD to hear Question 6.

Using points and examples from the talk, explain the two definitions of money presented by the professor.

Preparation Time: 20 Seconds
Response Time: 60 Seconds

STOP. This is the end of the Speaking section of TOEFL iBT Practice Test 1.

WRITING

Directions: This section measures your ability to use writing to communicate in an academic environment. There will be two writing tasks.

For the first writing task, you will read a passage and listen to a lecture and then answer a question based on what you have read and heard. For the second task, you will answer a question based on your own knowledge and experience.

At the end of this Practice Test you will find a script for the audio track, topic notes, sample test taker essays, and comments on those essays by official raters.

Turn the page to see the directions for the first writing task.

Writing Based on Reading and Listening

Directions: For this task, you will read a passage about an academic topic and you will listen to a lecture about the same topic. You may take notes while you read and listen.

Then you will write a response to a question that asks you about the relationship between the lecture you heard and the reading passage. Try to answer the question as completely as possible using information from the reading passage and the lecture. The question does not ask you to express your personal opinion. You may refer to the reading passage again when you write. You may use your notes to help you answer the question.

Typically, an effective response will be 150 to 225 words. Your response will be judged on the quality of your writing and on the completeness and accuracy of the content.

You should allow **3 minutes** to read the passage. Then listen to the lecture. Then allow **20 minutes** to plan and write your response.

Write your response in the space provided.

Altruism is a type of behavior in which an animal sacrifices its own interest for that of another animal or group of animals. Altruism is the opposite of selfishness; individuals performing altruistic acts gain nothing for themselves.

Examples of altruism abound, both among humans and among other mammals. Unselfish acts among humans range from the sharing of food with strangers to the donation of body organs to family members, and even to strangers. Such acts are altruistic in that they benefit another, yet provide little reward to the one performing the act.

In fact, many species of animals appear willing to sacrifice food, or even their life, to assist other members of their group. The meerkat, which is a mammal that dwells in burrows in grassland areas of Africa, is often cited as an example. In groups of meerkats, an individual acts as a sentinel, standing guard and looking out for predators while the others hunt for food or eat food they have obtained. If the sentinel meerkat sees a predator such as a hawk approaching the group, it gives an alarm cry alerting the other meerkats to run and seek shelter. By standing guard, the sentinel meerkat gains nothing—it goes without food while the others eat, and it places itself in grave danger. After it issues an alarm, it has to flee alone, which might make it more at risk to a predator, since animals in groups are often able to work together to fend off a predator. So the altruistic sentinel behavior helps ensure the survival of other members of the meerkat's group.

Now play Track 30 on the CD.

Question

Summarize the points made in the lecture, being sure to explain how they oppose specific points made in the reading passage.

You must finish your answer in 20 minutes.

_____

_____

_____

_____

_____

_____

_____

_____

_____

_____

_____

_____

_____

_____

_____

GO ON TO THE NEXT PAGE

Writing Based on Knowledge and Experience

Directions: For this task, you will write an essay in response to a question that asks you to state, explain, and support your opinion on an issue.

Typically, an effective essay will contain a minimum of 300 words. Your essay will be judged on the quality of your writing. This includes the development of your ideas, the organization of your essay, and the quality and accuracy of the language you use to express your ideas.

You have **30 minutes** to plan and complete your essay.

Write your essay in the space provided.

Question

Some young adults want independence from their parents as soon as possible. Other young adults prefer to live with their families for a longer time. Which of these situations do you think is better? Use specific reasons and examples to support your opinion.

_____

_____

_____

_____

_____

_____

_____

_____

_____

_____

_____

_____

GO ON TO THE NEXT PAGE ↘

STOP. This is the end of the Writing section of TOEFL iBT Practice Test 1.

Answers, Explanations, and Listening Scripts

Reading

Answer Key and Self-scoring Chart

Directions: Check your answers against the answer key below. Write the number 1 on the line to the right of each question if you picked the correct answer. For questions worth more than one point, follow the directions given. Total your points at the bottom of the chart.

Question Number	Correct Answer	Your Raw Points
Nineteenth-Century Politics in the United States		
1.	2	_____
2.	3	_____
3.	2	_____
4.	1	_____
5.	3	_____
6.	2	_____
7.	3	_____
8.	4	_____
9.	4	_____
10.	2	_____
11.	4	_____
12.	1	_____

For question 13, write 2 if you picked all three correct answers. Write 1 if you picked two correct answers.

13.	1,5,6	_____

Question Number	Correct Answer	Your Raw Points
The Expression of Emotions		
1.	2	_____
2.	3	_____
3.	2	_____
4.	3	_____
5.	3	_____
6.	3	_____
7.	1	_____
8.	1	_____
9.	1	_____
10.	4	_____
11.	4	_____
12.	3	_____

For question 13, write 2 if you picked all three correct answers. Write 1 if you picked two correct answers.

13.	2,4,6	_____

Question Number	Correct Answer	Your Raw Points
Geology and Landscape		
1.	4	_____
2.	2	_____
3.	2	_____
4.	2	_____
5.	3	_____
6.	3	_____
7.	1	_____
8.	2	_____
9.	2	_____
10.	4	_____
11.	1	_____

For question 12, write 3 if you placed five answer choices correctly. Write 2 if you placed four choices correctly. Write 1 if you placed three choices correctly.

12. Constructive:	1,5,6	
Destructive:	3,7	_____
TOTAL:		_____

On the next page is a table that converts your Reading practice section answers into a TOEFL iBT Reading scaled score. Take the total of raw points from your answer key and find that number in the left-hand column of the table. The right-hand column of the table gives a range of TOEFL iBT Reading scores for each number of raw points. For example, if the total points from your answer key is 26, the table shows a scaled score of 19 to 21. Your scaled score is given as a range instead of a single number for the following reasons:

- The estimates of scores are based on the performance of students who participated in a field study for these Reading Comprehension questions. Those students took the test on computer; you used a book. Although the two experiences are comparable, the differences make exact comparisons impossible.

- The students who participated in the field study were volunteers and may have differed in average ability from the actual TOEFL test-taking population.

- The conversion of scores from the field study in which these questions were administered to the current TOEFL iBT scale involved two scale conversions. Converting from one scale to another always involves some statistical error.

You should use your score estimate as a general guide only. Your actual score on the TOEFL iBT test may be higher or lower than your score on the practice version.

Reading

Raw Point Total	Scaled Score
42–41	30
40–39	27–30
38	28
37–36	26–28
35–33	25–27
32	23–25
31–30	22–24
29	20–22
28–27	19–22
26	19–21
25–24	18–21
23	16–18
22–21	15–18
20	14–16
19–17	12–16
16–15	9–15
14	9–13
13–12	5–13
11	3–13
10–9	0–13
8	0–11
7–1	0–4

Answer Explanations

Nineteenth-century Politics in the United States

1. ❷ This is a Vocabulary question. The word being tested is *immeasurably*. It is highlighted in the passage. *Immeasurably* means "in a manner too big to be measured." So if Jackson enlarged the President's powers so much that the results cannot be measured, he enlarged them "greatly."

2. ❸ This is a Factual Information question asking for specific information that can be found in paragraph 1. The correct answer is choice 3 because the first sentence of the paragraph explicitly states that this was when the development of the modern presidency began. The remainder of the paragraph is devoted to explaining the significant changes in government that this development involved. The result, as stated in sentence 5, was that the nature of the presidency itself was redefined. Choice 1 is contradicted by the paragraph; Jackson did not give presidential power away, but rather he increased it. Choice 2 is not mentioned in the paragraph: it says Jackson addressed the Senate, but not that this was the beginning of regular addresses. Choice 4, which says that this was the first time the Senate opposed the President, is not stated in the passage.

3. ❷ This is a Rhetorical Purpose question. It is asking you why the author mentions "bankers and investors" in the passage. The phrase being tested is highlighted in the passage. The correct answer is choice 2. The author is using bankers and investors as examples of people that the Democrats claimed "manipulated" the banking system for their own profit. That means that they were unfairly becoming rich. Choices 1, 3, and 4 are all incorrect because, based upon the passage, they seem unlikely to be true. Therefore the author would not use them as examples.

4. ❶ This is a Factual Information question asking for specific information that can be found in paragraph 3. Choice 1 is the correct answer. The paragraph says that Whigs believed commerce and economic development "would benefit everyone." That means essentially the same thing as choice 1, which says that Whigs believed economic growth "would promote the advancement of society as a whole." "Society as a whole" is another way of saying "everyone." Choices 2 and 3 are not mentioned in the paragraph. Choice 4, about conflict between groups, is mentioned but in a different context, so it is not a belief held by Whigs.

5. ❸ This is a Factual Information question asking for specific information that can be found in paragraph 3. The correct answer is choice 3: the Whigs viewed government as responsible for maintaining an economy that allowed all capable citizens to benefit. This is a restatement of paragraph 3, sentence 5. The paragraph states that Whigs did not envision continuing conflict between farmers and businesspeople, so choice 1 is wrong. Whigs favored changes

brought about by the market, so choice 2 is wrong. Whigs were in favor of increased emphasis on economic development, so choice 4 is incorrect.

6. ❷ This is a Vocabulary question. The word being tested is *inclination*. It is highlighted in the passage. The fact that Jackson had an *inclination* to be a strong President means that he preferred being strong to having limited powers. In other words, his "tendency" was to favor a strong presidency, so choice 2 is the correct answer.

7. ❸ This is a Factual Information question asking for specific information that can be found in paragraph 4. The correct answer is choice 3, which is explicitly stated in sentence 3 of the paragraph. Sentences 4 and 5 explicitly refute the other choices.

8. ❹ This is a Vocabulary question. The word being tested is *concept*. It is highlighted in the passage. The passage says, "for Whigs the concept of government . . ." In other words, "the way Whigs thought about government . . ." That process of thinking represents ideas, so choice 4 is the correct answer here.

9. ❹ This is an Inference question asking for an inference that can be supported by paragraph 5. The correct answer is choice 4: variations in Whigs' political beliefs reflected regional differences. This is supported by sentence 5 of the paragraph, which says that certain beliefs "In particular" reflected the views of northern Whigs. That suggests that Whigs in other regions of the country had beliefs that varied from this view and implies that such differences were regional. The other three choices are not mentioned in the passage in connection with "variations" in Whig beliefs, so there is no basis for inferring any of them.

10. ❷ This is a Negative Factual Information question asking for specific information that can be found in paragraph 6. Choice 2 is the correct answer. Sentence 5 says that it was Whigs, not Democrats, who had the support of planters involved in international trade. The next sentence, sentence 6, says that in contrast, Democrats had the support of the groups mentioned in choices 1, 3, and 4 ("workers," "entrepreneurs," and certain other "individuals"). Therefore all of the groups described in the answer choices, except the planters of choice 2, did support the Democrats.

11. ❹ This is a Sentence Simplification question. As with all of these questions, a single sentence in the passage is highlighted:

> The Whigs were strongest in the towns, cities, and those rural areas that were fully integrated into the market economy, whereas Democrats dominated areas of semi-subsistence farming that were more isolated and languishing economically.

The correct answer is choice 4. Choice 4 contains all of the essential information in the tested sentence, but the order in which it is presented is reversed. The highlighted sentence describes areas of Whig strength first, and then the areas where Democrats were strong. The correct answer, choice 4, describes Democrat strongholds first, and then Whig areas. No meaning has been changed, and no information has been left out.

Choice 1 is incorrect because it states that Whigs were able to attract support only in the wealthiest areas. The highlighted sentence does not say that; it says their support came from places integrated into the market, which can include areas of all economic levels.

Choice 2 is incorrect because it says that the two parties were split between rural and urban areas. However, the highlighted sentence says that Whigs were strong in rural areas that were integrated into the market economy. In other words, the split between the parties was based on the degree to which an area was integrated into the market, not whether it was urban or rural.

Choice 3 is incorrect because the highlighted sentence makes no mention of how (or if) the Whigs' control of the market economy affected the areas dominated by the Democrats.

12. ❶ This is an Insert Text question. You can see the four black squares in paragraph 2 that represent the possible answer choices here.

During Jackson's second term, his opponents had gradually come together to form the Whig Party. ■ Whigs and Democrats held different attitudes toward the changes brought about by the market, banks, and commerce. ■ The Democrats tended to view society as a continuing conflict between "the people"—farmers, planters, and workers—and a set of greedy aristocrats. ■ This "paper money aristocracy" of bankers and investors manipulated the banking system for their own profit, Democrats claimed, and sapped the nation's virtue by encouraging speculation and the desire for sudden, unearned wealth. ■ The Democrats wanted the rewards of the market without sacrificing the features of a simple agrarian republic. They wanted the wealth that the market offered without the competitive, changing society; the complex dealing; the dominance of urban centers; and the loss of independence that came with it.

The sentence provided, "This new party argued against the policies of Jackson and his party in a number of important areas, beginning with the economy," is best inserted at square 1.

Square 1 is correct because the phrase "This new party" refers directly and only to the Whigs, who are first mentioned (as a recently formed party) in sentence 1 of this paragraph.

Square 2 is incorrect because the sentence before is not limited to the new Whig Party. It discusses both Whigs and Democrats.

Squares 3 and 4 are both incorrect because the sentences preceding them refer to the Democrats (the old party), not the Whigs.

13. **①** **⑤** **⑥** This is a Prose Summary question. It is completed correctly below. The correct choices are 1, 5, and 6. Choices 2, 3, and 4 are therefore incorrect.

Directions: An introductory sentence for a brief summary of the passage is provided below. Complete the summary by selecting the THREE answer choices that express the most important ideas in the passage. Some answer choices do not belong in the summary because they express ideas that are not presented in the passage or are minor ideas in the passage. **This question is worth 2 points.**

The political system of the United States in the mid-nineteenth century was strongly influenced by the social and economic circumstances of the time.

- The Democratic and Whig Parties developed in response to the needs of competing economic and political constituencies.
- A fundamental difference between Whigs and Democrats involved the importance of the market in society.
- The role of government in the lives of the people was an important political distinction between the two parties.

Answer Choices

1. The Democratic and Whig Parties developed in response to the needs of competing economic and political constituencies.

2. During Andrew Jackson's two terms as President, he served as leader of both the Democratic and Whig Parties.

3. The Democratic Party primarily represented the interests of the market, banks, and commerce.

4. In contrast to the Democrats, the Whigs favored government aid for education.

5. A fundamental difference between Whigs and Democrats involved the importance of the market in society.

6. The role of government in the lives of the people was an important political distinction between the two parties.

Correct Choices

Choice 1, "The Democratic and Whig Parties developed in response to the needs of competing economic and political constituencies," is correct because it is a recurring theme throughout the entire passage. It is a general statement about the development of the Whigs and Democrats. Paragraphs 2, 3, 4, 5, and 6 all provide support for this statement with examples of the nature of the competing constituencies in the United States at that time and the ways in which these two parties responded to them.

Choice 5, "A fundamental difference between Whigs and Democrats involved the importance of the market in society," is correct because it is a general statement about the differences between the Whigs and Democrats. Paragraphs 2, 3, 4, and 6 all provide support for this statement with examples of the differences in the ways that the two parties viewed the market and society.

Choice 6, "The role of government in the lives of the people was an important political distinction between the two parties," is correct because it is another general statement about the differences between the Whigs and Democrats. Paragraphs 2, 3, 4, and 5 all explicitly explore this distinction between Whigs and Democrats.

Incorrect Choices

Choice 2, "During Andrew Jackson's two terms as President, he served as leader of both the Democratic and Whig Parties," is incorrect because it contradicts the passage. Jackson was head of the Democratic Party.

Choice 3, "The Democratic Party primarily represented the interests of the market, banks, and commerce," is incorrect because it is not true. The Whigs primarily represented these groups, as stated in paragraphs 3 and 6.

Choice 4, "In contrast to the Democrats, the Whigs favored government aid for education," is incorrect because the passage states only that Whigs in the North were likely to favor aid to education. It is not clearly stated how other Whigs or Democrats felt on this issue.

The Expression of Emotions

1. ❷ This is a Vocabulary question. The word being tested is *despondent*. It is highlighted in the passage. The correct answer is choice 2, "unhappy." The sentence in which the highlighted word appears uses *despondent* as a contrast to *happy*. Since *unhappy* is the opposite of *happy*, it provides the fullest possible contrast and is equivalent to the contrast between *Joy* and *sadness* at the beginning of the sentence.

2. ❸ This is a Rhetorical Purpose question. It is asking you why the author mentions "Baring the teeth in a hostile way" in the passage. This phrase is highlighted in the passage. The correct answer is choice 3; baring the teeth is "an example of a facial expression whose meaning is widely understood." The central theme of paragraph 1 of the passage is facial expressions that are universal. The author provides various examples of such expressions, and baring the teeth is mentioned as a universal sign of anger. The other choices are all mentioned in the passage, but not in conjunction with baring the teeth, so they are all incorrect.

3. ❷ This is a Vocabulary question. The word being tested is *concur*. It is highlighted in the passage. The correct answer is choice 2, "agree." *Concur* means "agree," so if investigators concur about the meaning of certain facial expressions, they agree on their meaning.

4. ❸ This is a Reference question. The word being tested is *them*, and it is highlighted in the passage. This is a simple pronoun-referent question. The word *them* refers to the photographs that Paul Ekman showed to people from diverse cultures, so the correct answer is choice 3, "photographs."

5. ❸ This is a Factual Information question asking for specific information that can be found in paragraph 2. The correct answer is choice 3, which states that the Fore people of New Guinea "knew very little about Western culture." The paragraph explicitly says that the Fore had almost no contact with Western culture. None of the other three choices is mentioned in connection with the Fore, so none of them is correct.

6. ❸ This is a Sentence Simplification question. As with all of these questions, a single sentence in the passage is highlighted:

> The Fore also displayed familiar facial expressions when asked how they would respond if they were the characters in stories that called for basic emotional responses.

The correct answer is choice 3. It contains all of the essential ideas in the highlighted sentence without changing the meaning. This choice says that the Fore "exhibited the same relationship of facial expression and basic emotions that is seen in Western culture when they acted out stories." The sentence that precedes the highlighted sentence states that in a survey, the Fore agreed with Westerners on how various emotions are portrayed. Then the highlighted sentence says that in a different situation (storytelling) the Fore's expressions were also familiar; that is, these expressions were the same as those exhibited by Westerners in this situation.

Choices 1 and 2 are incorrect because each one changes the highlighted sentence into a statement that is not true.

Choice 4 is incorrect because it says that the Fore were familiar with the facial expressions of characters in stories. The highlighted sentence says that it was the investigators who were familiar with the Fore's expressions. This is a change in meaning, so it is incorrect.

7. ❶ This is a Factual Information question asking for specific information that can be found in the passage. The correct answer is choice 1: emotions that are not expressed become less intense. This is correct based on the direct quotation of Darwin in paragraph 3. In that quotation, Darwin says that emotions that are freely expressed become more intense, while "On the other hand" those that are not freely expressed are softened, meaning that they become less intense. Choices 2, 3, and 4 are all incorrect because there is nothing in the passage that indicates Darwin ever believed these things about expressing emotions. Some or all of them may actually be true, but there is nothing in this passage that supports them.

8. ❶ This is a Factual Information question asking for specific information that can be found in the passage. You can see that the phrase "facial-feedback hypothesis" is highlighted where it first appears in the passage in paragraph 3. The correct answer is choice 1: research supporting this hypothesis came from studying experiments of the reactions of people to cartoons. This idea is found in paragraph 4, which uses these experiments as an example of how facial feedback works.

Choice 3, the release of neurotransmitters, is mentioned in paragraph 5, but not in connection with the facial-feedback hypothesis, so it is incorrect.

Choices 2 and 4 are not explicitly mentioned at all in the passage.

9. **❶** This is a Vocabulary question. The word being tested is *rate*, and it is highlighted in the passage. The correct answer is choice 1, "judge." *Rate* in this context means "judge."

10. **❹** This is a Vocabulary question. The word being tested is *relevant*, and it is highlighted in the passage. The correct answer is choice 4, "applicable." *Relevant* means that Ekman's observation applies ("is applicable") to an expression.

11. **❹** This is a Factual Information question asking for specific information that can be found in the passage. The correct answer is choice 4: stiffening the upper lip "may either heighten or reduce emotional response." This is stated explicitly in paragraph 6 of the passage as a possible paradox in the relationship between facial expressions and emotions.

Choice 1 is incorrect because paragraph 6 contradicts it.

Choice 2 is incorrect because the passage mentions only the fear and tension of a person trying to keep a stiff upper lip, not any fear or tension that the expression may cause in others.

Choice 3 is incorrect because there is no suggestion anywhere in the passage that stiffening the upper lip may damage lip muscles.

12. **❸** This is an Insert Text question. You can see the four black squares in paragraph 2 that represent the possible answer choices here.

■ Most investigators concur that certain facial expressions suggest the same emotions in all people. ■ Moreover, people in diverse cultures recognize the emotions manifested by the facial expressions. ■ In classic research Paul Ekman took photographs of people exhibiting the emotions of anger, disgust, fear, happiness, and sadness. ■ He then asked people around the world to indicate what emotions were being depicted in them. Those queried ranged from European college students to members of the Fore, a tribe that dwells in the New Guinea highlands. All groups, including the Fore, who had almost no contact with Western culture, agreed on the portrayed emotions. The Fore also displayed familiar facial expressions when asked how they would respond if they were the characters in stories that called for basic emotional responses. Ekman and his colleagues more recently obtained similar results in a study of ten cultures in which participants were permitted to report that multiple emotions were shown by facial expressions. The participants generally agreed on which two emotions were being shown and which emotion was more intense.

The sentence provided, "This universality in the recognition of emotions was demonstrated by using rather simple methods," is best inserted at square 3.

Square 3 is correct because the inserted sentence begins with the phrase "This universality." The universality being referred to is the fact, stated in the second sentence, that "people in diverse cultures recognize the emotions manifested by the facial expressions."

None of the other answer choices follows a sentence that contains a universal statement. Sentence 1 mentions that "Most investigators concur," which means that some do not. Therefore this is not a universal statement.

Squares 2 and 4 are incorrect because there is nothing in either sentence to which "This universality" could refer.

13. **②④⑥** This is a Prose Summary question. It is completed correctly below. The correct choices are 2, 4, and 6. Choices 1, 3, and 5 are therefore incorrect.

Directions: An introductory sentence for a brief summary of the passage is provided below. Complete the summary by selecting the THREE answer choices that express the most important ideas in the passage. Some answer choices do not belong in the summary because they express ideas that are not presented in the passage or are minor ideas in the passage. **This question is worth 2 points.**

Psychological research seems to confirm that people associate particular facial expressions with the same emotions across cultures.

- Facial expressions and emotional states interact with each other through a variety of feedback mechanisms.
- A person's facial expression may reflect the person's emotional state.
- Facial expressions that occur as a result of an individual's emotional state may themselves feed back information that influences the person's emotions.

Answer Choices

1. Artificially producing the Duchenne smile can cause a person to have pleasant feelings.

2. Facial expressions and emotional states interact with each other through a variety of feedback mechanisms.

3. People commonly believe that they can control their facial expressions so that their true emotions remain hidden.

4. A person's facial expression may reflect the person's emotional state.

5. Ekman argued that the ability to accurately recognize the emotional content of facial expressions was valuable for human beings.

6. Facial expressions that occur as a result of an individual's emotional state may themselves feed back information that influences the person's emotions.

Correct Choices

Choice 2, "Facial expressions and emotional states interact with each other through a variety of feedback mechanisms," is correct because it is a general statement that is developed throughout the passage. Questions about the nature of this interaction and details of research on this issue are discussed in every paragraph, so it is clearly a "main idea."

Choice 4, "A person's facial expression may reflect the person's emotional state," is correct because, like choice 2, it is a major idea that the passage explores in detail. Paragraphs 3, 4, 5, and 6 are devoted to discussing attempts to understand whether and how facial expressions may reflect a person's emotional state.

Choice 6, "Facial expressions that occur as a result of an individual's emotional state may themselves feed back information that influences the person's emotions," is correct because it is the main tenet of the "facial-feedback hypothesis" that is extensively discussed in paragraphs 3, 4, 5, and 6.

Incorrect Choices

Choice 1, "Artificially producing the Duchenne smile can cause a person to have pleasant feelings," is incorrect because it is a minor, supporting detail mentioned in paragraph 5 as an example of a more general, and important, statement about the links between facial expressions and emotion (see choice 6, above).

Choice 3, "People commonly believe that they can control their facial expressions so that their true emotions remain hidden," is incorrect because while it may be true, the passage does not make this claim.

Choice 5, "Ekman argued that the ability to accurately recognize the emotional content of facial expressions was valuable for human beings," is incorrect because according to the passage, Ekman did not make this argument; Charles Darwin did. Ekman's research was directed toward determining the universality of certain facial expressions, not the "value" of people's ability to recognize those expressions.

Geology and Landscape

1. ❹ This is a Factual Information question asking for specific information that can be found in paragraph 1. The correct answer is choice 4. Sentence 1 of the paragraph explicitly states that Earth's landscape changes relatively rapidly compared with Earth's overall age. Choice 1, on the frequency of landscape changes, is contradicted by the paragraph. Choice 2, that landscape changes occur only at special times, is also contradicted by the paragraph. Choice 3, the frequency of landscape changes, is not mentioned.

2. ❷ This is a Vocabulary question. The word being tested is *relatively*, and it is highlighted in the passage. The correct answer is choice 2. The sentence in which *relatively* appears is comparing Earth's time scale with the human time scale, so "comparatively" is the correct answer.

3. ❷ This is a Sentence Simplification question. As with all of these questions, a single sentence in the passage is highlighted:

> Hills and mountains are often regarded as the epitome of permanence, successfully resisting the destructive forces of nature, but in fact they tend to be relatively short-lived in geological terms.

The correct answer is choice 2. That choice contains all of the essential information in the highlighted sentence. It omits the information in the second clause of the highlighted sentence ("successfully resisting the destructive forces of nature") because that information is not essential to the meaning.

Choices 1, 3, and 4 are all incorrect because they change the meaning of the highlighted sentence. Choice 1 adds information on the age of a mountain that is not mentioned in the highlighted sentence.

Choice 3 introduces information about how long mountains resist forces of nature in absolute terms; the highlighted sentence says that the resistance is relatively short in geological terms, which is an entirely different meaning.

Choice 4 compares mountains with other landforms. The highlighted sentence does not make any such comparison.

4. ❷ This is an Inference question asking for an inference that can be supported by paragraph 2. The correct answer is choice 2: the Himalayas are higher than the Caledonian mountains. The paragraph states that younger mountains are generally higher than older mountains. It also states that the Himalayas are much younger than the Caledonians. Since the Himalayas are the younger range and younger mountain ranges are higher than older ranges, we can infer that the younger Himalayas are higher than the older Caledonians.

Choices 1 and 4 are incorrect because they explicitly contradict the passage. The height of the Himalayas is an indication of their age, and the Himalayas are about the same height that the Caledonians were 400 million years ago.

Choice 3 is incorrect because there is nothing in the paragraph about "uniform height."

5. ❸ This is a Vocabulary question. The word being tested is *relics*, and it is highlighted in the passage. Choice 3 is the correct answer. The *relics* of the Caledonian range are what is left of them. *Remains* means "what is left of something," so it is the correct answer.

6. ❸ This is a Factual Information question asking for specific information that can be found in paragraph 3. The correct answer is choice 3: mountains are formed by crustal plates hitting each other. The paragraph states that mountains are formed in three ways: by crustal plates hitting each other, by earthquakes, and by volcanoes. Choices 1, 2, and 4 are not among these causes of mountain formation; they are therefore incorrect.

7. ❶ This is a Rhetorical Purpose question. It asks why the author mentions "Carbon dioxide" in the passage. This term is highlighted in the passage. The correct answer is choice 1: carbon dioxide is mentioned to explain the origin of a chemical that can erode rocks. The author is describing a particular cause of erosion, and the starting point of that process is carbon dioxide.

8. ❷ This is a Vocabulary question. The word being tested is *seeps*, and it is highlighted in the passage. Choice 2, "flows slowly," is the correct answer. The sentence is describing the way in which rain moves underground from Earth's surface. It cannot do this by drying (choice 1), freezing (choice 3), or warming (choice 4).

9. ❷ This is a Reference question. The word being tested is *them*, and it is highlighted in the passage. Choice 2, "masses of ice," is the correct answer. This is a simple pronoun-referent question. The word *them* refers to the glaciers that are carrying eroded rock. Notice that in this case, a whole series of words separates the pronoun from its referent.

10. ❹ This is a Factual Information question asking for specific information that can be found in paragraph 6. The correct answer is choice 4, "Sand." Sentences 3 and 4 of that paragraph describe erosion in dry areas. Sand is carried by wind and bombards rock; this bombardment breaks down the rock, and, as a result, more sand is created. Thus sand is both the cause and the result of erosion, so choice 4 is correct. Glacial activity (choice 1) and tree roots (choice 3) are both mentioned only as causes of erosion. Rock debris (choice 2) is mentioned only as a result of erosion.

11. **❶** This is an Insert Text question. You can see the four black squares in paragraph 6 that represent the possible answer choices here.

Under very cold conditions, rocks can be shattered by ice and frost. Glaciers may form in permanently cold areas, and these slowly moving masses of ice cut out valleys, carrying with them huge quantities of eroded rock debris. ■ In dry areas the wind is the principal agent of erosion. ■ It carries fine particles of sand, which bombard exposed rock surfaces, thereby wearing them into yet more sand. ■ Even living things contribute to the formation of landscapes. ■ Tree roots force their way into cracks in rocks and, in so doing, speed their splitting. In contrast, the roots of grasses and other small plants may help to hold loose soil fragments together, thereby helping to prevent erosion by the wind.

The sentence provided, "Under different climatic conditions, another type of destructive force contributes to erosion," is best inserted at square 1.

Square 1 is correct because the inserted sentence is a transitional sentence, moving the discussion away from one set of climatic conditions (cold) to another set of climatic conditions (dryness). It is at square 1 that the transition between topics takes place.

Squares 2, 3, and 4 all precede sentences that provide details of dry climatic conditions. No transition is taking place at any of those places, so the inserted sentence is not needed.

12. **❶❸❺❻❼** This is a Fill in a Table question. It is completed correctly below. The correct choices for the "Constructive Processes" column are 1, 5, and 6. Choices 3 and 7 are the correct choices for the "Destructive Processes" column. Choices 2 and 4 should not be used in either column.

Directions: Three of the answer choices below are used in the passage to illustrate constructive processes, and two are used to illustrate destructive processes. Complete the table by matching appropriate answer choices to the processes they are used to illustrate. **This question is worth 3 points.**

Constructive Processes	Destructive Processes
● Collision of Earth's crustal plates	● Wind-driven sand
● Earthquakes	● Weather processes
● Volcanic activity	

Answer Choices

1. Collision of Earth's crustal plates
2. Separation of continents
3. Wind-driven sand
4. Formation of grass roots in soil
5. Earthquakes
6. Volcanic activity
7. Weather processes

Correct Choices

Choice 1: "Collision of Earth's crustal plates" (Constructive Process) belongs in this column because it is mentioned in the passage as one of the constructive processes by which mountains are formed.

Choice 3: "Wind-driven sand" (Destructive Process) belongs in this column because it is mentioned in the passage as one of the destructive forces that wear away the land.

Choice 5: "Earthquakes" (Constructive Process) belongs in this column because it is mentioned in the passage as one of the constructive forces by which mountains are formed.

Choice 6: "Volcanic activity" (Constructive Process) belongs in this column because it is mentioned in the passage as one of the constructive forces by which mountains are formed.

Choice 7: "Weather processes" (Destructive Process) belongs in this column because it is mentioned in the passage as one of the destructive forces that wear away the land.

Incorrect Choices

Choice 2: "Separation of continents" does not belong in the table because it is not mentioned in the passage as either a constructive or destructive process.

Choice 4: "Formation of grass roots in soil" does not belong in the table because it is not mentioned in the passage as either a constructive or destructive process.

Listening

Answer Key and Self-scoring Chart

Directions: Check your answers against the answer key below. Write the number 1 on the line to the right of each question if you picked the correct answer. For questions worth more than one point, follow the directions given. Total your points at the bottom of the chart.

Question Number	Correct Answer	Your Raw Points
1.	2	_____
2.	1, 3	_____
3.	4	_____
4.	2	_____
5.	3	_____
6.	4	_____
7.	3	_____
8.	1	_____
9.	1,3	_____
10.	3	_____
11.	1	_____
12.	3	_____
13.	3,4	_____
14.	4	_____
15.	1	_____
16.	2	_____
17.	4	_____
18.	1	_____
19.	2	_____
20.	2, 3	_____

For question 21, write 2 if you placed three answer choices correctly. Write 1 if you placed two choices correctly.

21.	Yes:	2,3	
	No:	1	_____
22.		1	_____
23.		1	_____
24.		3	_____
25.		1	_____
26.		2	_____
27.		3	_____
28.		4	_____

Question Number	Correct Answer	Your Raw Points
29.	2	_____
30.	2	_____
31.	3	_____
32.	1	_____
33.	2	_____

For question 34, write 2 if you placed three answer choices correctly. Write 1 if you placed two choices correctly.

34.	Functional:	1,3	
	Project:	2	_____
	TOTAL:		_____

On the next page is a table that converts your Listening section answers into a TOEFL iBT scaled score. Take the total of raw points from your answer key and find that number in the left-hand column of the table. On the right-hand side of the table is a range of TOEFL iBT Listening scores for that number of raw points. For example, if the total points from your answer key is 27, the table says your estimated TOEFL iBT Listening section scaled score is in the range of 22 to 24. Your scaled score is given as a range instead of a single number for the following reasons:

- The estimates of scores are based on the performance of students who participated in a field study for these listening comprehension questions. Those students took the test on computer. You took your practice test by listening to audio tracks and answering questions in a book. Although the two experiences are comparable, the differences make it impossible to give an exact prediction of your score.

- The students who participated in the field study were volunteers and may have differed in average ability from the actual TOEFL test-taking population.

- The conversion of scores from the field study in which these questions were administered to the current TOEFL iBT scale involved two scale conversions. Converting from one scale to another always involves some statistical error.

- You should use your score estimate as a general guide only. Your actual score on the TOEFL iBT test may be higher or lower than your score on the practice section.

Listening

Raw Point Total	Scaled Score	Raw Point Total	Scaled Score
36	28–30	17	11–16
35	28–30	16	10–15
34	28–30	15	10–15
33	28–30	14	9–13
32	27–29	13	8–12
31	26–29	12	6–12
30	25–27	11	4–10
29	25–27	10	3–10
28	24–26	9	0–9
27	22–24	8	0–9
26	21–23	7	0–7
25	21–23	6	0–5
24	17–22	5	0–3
23	16–21	4	0–3
22	16–21	3	0–3
21	16–18	2	0–3
20	14–18	1	0–3
19	13–17	0	0–3
18	13–17		

Listening Scripts and Answer Explanations

Questions 1–5

Track 11 Listening Script

Narrator

Listen to a conversation between a student and a professor.

Professor

Hey, Ellen. How are you doing?

Student

Oh, pretty good, thanks. How are you?

Professor

OK.

Student

Did you, um, have a chance to look at my grad school application . . . you know, the statement of purpose I wrote?

Professor

Well, yeah. In fact, here it is. I just read it.

Student

Oh, great! What did you think?

Professor

Basically, it's good. What you might actually do is take some of these different points here, and actually break them out into separate paragraphs. So, um, one: your purpose for applying for graduate study—uh, why do you want to go to graduate school—and an area of specialty; and, uh, why you want to do the area you're specifying; um, and what you want to do with your degree once you get it.

Student

OK.

Professor

So those are . . . they're pretty clear on those four points they want.

Student

Right.

Professor

So you might just break them out into, uh . . . you know, separate paragraphs and expand on each point some. But really what's critical with these is that, um, you've gotta let yourself come through. See, you gotta let them see you in these statements. Expand some more on what's happened in your own life and what shows your . . . your motivation and interest in this area—in geology. Let 'em see what really, what . . . what captures your imagination about this field.

Student

OK. So make it a little more . . . personal? That's OK?

Professor

That's fine. They look for that stuff. You don't wanna go overboard . . .

Student

Right.

Professor

. . . but it's critical that . . . that somebody sees what your passion is—your personal motivation for doing this.

Student

OK.

Professor

And that's gotta come out in here. Um, and let's see, uh, you might also give a little, uh—since this is your only chance to do it, you might give a little more explanation about your unique undergraduate background. So, you know, how you went through, you know, the music program; what you got from that; why you decided to change. I mean it's kind of unusual to go from music to geology, right?

Student

Yeah. I was . . . I was afraid that, you know, maybe the personal-type stuff wouldn't be what they wanted, but . . .

Professor

No, in fact it's . . . um, give an example: I . . . I had a friend, when I was an undergrad, um, went to medical school. And he put on his med school application—and he could actually tell if somebody actually read it 'cause, um, he had asthma and the reason that he wanted to go to med school was he said he wanted to do sports medicine because he, you know, he had this real interest. He was an athlete too, and . . . and wanted to help athletes who had this physical problem. And he could always tell if somebody actually read his letter, because they would always ask him about that.

Student

. . . Mmm . . . so something unique.

Professor

Yeah. So see, you know, that's what's good and, and, I think for you probably, you know, your music background's the most unique thing that you've got in your record.

Student

Right.

Professor

. . . Mmm . . . so you see, you gotta make yourself stand out from a coupla hundred applications. Does that help any?

Student

Yeah, it does. It gives me some good ideas.

Professor

And . . . what you might also do too is, you know, uh, you might get a friend to proof it or something at some point.

Student

Oh, sure . . . sure.

Professor

Also, think about presentation—how the application looks. In a way, you're actually showing some other skills here, like organization. A lot of stuff that's . . . that they're not . . . they're not formally asking for, they're looking at. So your presentation format, your grammar, all that stuff, they're looking at in your materials at the same time.

Student

Right. OK.

Answer Explanations

1. ❷ For Listening conversations that take place during a professor's office hours, it is very likely that the first question will be a Gist-purpose question. That is the case here. This discussion is about how the woman should write her graduate school application, not about an interview or whether she had been admitted. The professor already has her application and has reviewed it, so the purpose cannot be for her to give him the application. Thus choice 2 is the correct answer: she wants advice about the application.

2. ❶❸ When you are taking the TOEFL iBT test on computer, whenever you see squares in front of the question choices instead of ovals, you should recognize that the question calls for you to select two or more answers from among the choices. In this case, the professor stresses the following two items that the woman needs to include in her application letter:

   1. How her college career has made her interested in graduate school
   2. How she stands out as an individual

   Thus the correct answers are choices 1 and 3. She does not have a background in medicine (choice 2), and the professor does not mention her teachers (choice 4).

3. ❹ This is a Detail question. The professor mentions twice that the woman's decision to go from studying music to geology is unusual.

4. ❷ This is an Understanding the Function of What Is Said question. Clearly the professor is illustrating his point that a good application should individualize the writer. His friend who went to medical school is an example.

5. ❸ This is a Making Inferences question. The last thing the professor mentions to the student is that she should think about the format of her application and the statement of purpose. He says that the format of the application can demonstrate her organizational skills and strongly implies that avoiding any writing errors shows thoroughness. By making these points, he is implying

that the readers of the application will be influenced by its appearance, even if the influence is unconscious. He says nothing about the readers' expertise (choice 1); he implies that sometimes they may not read the application carefully, but he does not imply that this is what usually happens (choice 2); and he says the opposite of choice 4. The correct answer is choice 3.

Questions 6–10

Track 12 Listening Script

Narrator

Listen to part of a conversation between two students. The woman is helping the man review for a biology examination.

Male Student

OK, so . . . what do you think we should go over next?

Female Student

How about if we go over this stuff about how bacteria become resistant to antibiotics.

Male Student

OK.

Female Student

Um, but first of all, though, how many pages do we have left? I told my roommate I'd meet her at the library at seven o'clock.

Male Student

Ummm . . . There's only a few pages left. We should be finished in a few minutes.

Female Student

OK. So, ummm . . .

Male Student

About how bacteria become resistant to antibiotics.

Female Student

Oh yeah, OK. So you know that some bacteria cells are able to resist the drugs we use against them, and that's because they have these special genes that, like, protect them from the drugs.

Male Student

Right. If I remember correctly, I think the genes, like . . . weaken the antibiotics, or, like . . . stop the antibiotics from getting into the bacteria cell, something like that?

Female Student

Exactly. So when bacteria have these genes, it's very difficult for the antibiotics to kill the bacteria.

Male Student

Right.

Female Student

So do you remember what those genes are called?

Male Student

Umm . . .

Female Student

Resistance genes.

Male Student

Resistance genes. Right. Resistance genes. OK.

Female Student

And that makes sense, right? Because they help the bacteria resist the antibiotics.

Male Student

Yeah, that makes sense. OK.

Female Student

OK. But the question is: how do bacteria get the resistance genes?

Male Student

How do they get the resistance genes? They just inherit them from the parent cell, right?

Female Student

OK, yeah, that's true. They can inherit them from the parent cell, but that's not what I'm talking about.

Male Student

OK.

Female Student

I'm talking about how they get resistance genes from other cells in their environment, you know, from the other cells around them.

Male Student

Oh, I see what you mean. Umm, is that that stuff about "hopping genes," or something like that?

Female Student

Right. Although actually they're called "jumping genes," not "hopping genes."

Male Student

Oh, OK. Jumping genes.

Female Student

Yeah, but they have another name, too, that I can't think of. Umm . . . lemme see if I can find it here in the book . . .

Male Student

I think it's probably on . . .

Female Student

Oh, OK. Here it is. Transposons. That's what they're called.

Male Student

Lemme see. OK. Trans . . . po . . . sons . . . trans . . . posons. So "transposon" is another name for a jumping gene?

Female Student

Right. And these transposons are, you know, like, little bits of DNA that are able to move from one cell to another. That's why they're called "jumping genes." They kind of, you know, "jump" from one cell to another.

Male Student

OK.

Female Student

And these transposons are how resistance genes are able to get from one bacteria cell to another bacteria cell. What happens is that a resistance gene from one cell attaches itself to a transposon and then, when the transposon jumps to another cell . . .

Male Student

The other cell gets the resistance gene and . . .

Female Student

Right.

Male Student

That's how it becomes resistant to antibiotics.

Female Student

Right.

Male Student

Wow. That's really cool. So that's how it happens.

Female Student

That's how it happens.

Answer Explanations

This question set, from an early version of the TOEFL iBT test, does not exactly fit the description of TOEFL conversations given earlier in this book. Instead of being between a student and a university employee, it is between two students who are studying for an examination. We have included it here because it is good practice and it closely resembles an office hours conversation on an academic topic. It has also been field-tested with actual test takers, providing data on the difficulty level of the questions.

6. ❹ This conversation is about academic content in the area of Life Science. The man is trying to learn something for his biology test. It makes sense, then, that the first question is a Gist-content question: "What are the students

mainly discussing?" The students discuss drugs, but they are drugs that fight bacteria, so choice 1 is eliminated. They are not discussing how antibiotics are produced, but how they are resisted, so choice 2 is eliminated. If all you understood was "jumping" and "hopping," you might think they were discussing athletics, but that is not how those words are being used, so choice 3 is eliminated. Choice 4 is the correct answer: the man is learning how some bacteria acquire genes that make them resistant to antibiotics.

7. ❸ This replay question is an Understanding the Function of What Is Said question. You are asked why the woman says the following:

Um, but first of all, though, how many pages do we have left? I told my roommate I'd meet her at the library at seven o'clock.

Her statement about meeting her roommate is part of the context in which the main discussion takes place. The man is trying to learn about bacteria, but she is saying they have only a limited amount of time to spend on the discussion. The function of her statement is to tell the man that she must keep her appointment with her roommate and therefore they must finish soon.

8. ❶ This is a Detail question. When you hear a new term defined, in either a lecture or a conversation, you should note it. Here the students spend a large part of the conversation discussing why the "transposons" are called "jumping genes." The woman says twice that the reason is that the genes can migrate, or "jump," from one cell to another. The correct answer is choice 1.

9. ❶ ❸ This is another Detail question. It asks you to identify two ways that bacteria acquire the resistance gene. Both students mention that the gene can be inherited from a parent cell. They then have a longer discussion about the "jumping gene" and how a "jumping gene" can carry the resistance gene to a new cell. Nothing is mentioned about "white blood cells," and resistance genes being "carried by antibiotics" is directly contradicted by the discussion. The correct answers are choices 1 and 3.

10. ❸ The question uses the verb *inferred*, so you know this is a Making Inferences question. The students say that some bacteria "resist the drugs we use against them." From this you can infer that an antibiotic is a medicine used against some bacteria. The students say the resistance genes "weaken the antibiotics" and "stop the antibiotics." From these clues you should infer that choice 3, the resistance genes "make the treatment of bacterial diseases more difficult," is the correct answer.

Questions 11–16

Track 14 Listening Script

Narrator

Listen to part of a talk in an environmental science class.

Professor

So I wanted to discuss a few other terms here . . . actually, some, uh, some ideas about how we manage our resources.

Let's talk about what that . . . what that means. If we take a resource like water . . . well, maybe we should get a little bit more specific here—back up from the more general case—and talk about underground water in particular.

So hydrogeologists have tried to figure out . . . how much water can you take out from underground sources? This has been an important question. Let me ask you guys: how much water, based on what you know so far, could you take out of, say, an aquifer . . . under the city?

Male Student

As . . . as much as would get recharged?

Professor

OK. So we wouldn't want to take out any more than naturally comes into it. The implication is that, uh, well, if you only take as much out as comes in, you're not gonna deplete the amount of water that's stored in there, right?

Wrong, but that's the principle. That's the idea behind how we manage our water supplies. It's called "safe yield." Basically what this method says is that you can pump as much water out of a system as naturally recharges . . . as naturally flows back in.

So this principle of safe yield—it's based on balancing what we take out with what gets recharged. But what it does is, it ignores how much water naturally comes out of the system.

In a natural system, a certain amount of recharge comes in and a certain amount of water naturally flows out through springs, streams, and lakes. And over the long term the amount that's stored in the aquifer doesn't really change much. It's balanced. Now humans come in . . . and start taking water out of the system. How have we changed the equation?

Female Student

It's not balanced anymore?

Professor

Right. We take water out, but water also naturally flows out. And the recharge rate doesn't change, so the result is we've reduced the amount of water that's stored in the underground system.

If you keep doing that long enough—if you pump as much water out as naturally comes in—gradually the underground water levels drop. And when that happens, that can affect surface water. How? Well, in underground systems there are natural discharge points—places where the water flows out of the underground systems, out to lakes and streams. Well, a drop in the water level can mean those discharge points will eventually dry up. That means water's not getting to lakes and streams that depend on it. So we've ended up reducing the surface water supply, too.

You know, in the state of Arizona we're managing some major water supplies with this principle of safe yield, under a method that will eventually dry up the natural discharge points of those aquifer systems.

Now, why is this an issue? Well, aren't some of you going to want to live in this state for a while? Want your kids to grow up here, and your kids' kids? You might be concerned with . . . does Arizona have a water supply which is sustainable—key word here? What that means . . . the general definition of *sustainable* is will there be enough to meet the needs of the present without compromising the ability of the future to have the availability . . . to have the same resources?

Now, I hope you see that these two ideas are incompatible: sustainability and safe yield. Because what sustainability means is that it's sustainable for all systems dependent on the water—for the people that use it and for . . . uh, for supplying water to the dependent lakes and streams.

So I'm gonna repeat this: so if we're using a safe-yield method, if we're only balancing what we take out with what gets recharged, but—don't forget, water's also flowing out naturally—then the amount stored underground is gonna gradually get reduced and that's gonna lead to another problem. These discharge points—where the water flows out to the lakes and streams—they're gonna dry up. OK.

Answer Explanations

11. ❶ The first question in this set is a Gist-content question, as is usually the case in a lecture set. It is important to remember that you are hearing only part of the lecture.

The beginning of this excerpt shows that the professor is talking about different ways to manage natural resources. He chooses underground water as an example of a natural resource, and then goes on to discuss one particular way of managing the underground water supply called "safe yield." His focus is on the "safe-yield" approach to managing underground water supplies. Thus the correct answer is choice 1. The other choices are aspects of underground water that an environmental scientist might discuss, but they are not the focus of this excerpt.

12. ❸ The lecture makes clear that the professor does not think the "safe-yield" approach is appropriate. He communicates this indirectly in several ways, particularly when he says, "we're managing some major water supplies with this principle of safe yield, under a method that will eventually dry up the natural discharge points of those aquifer systems." Although the term "safe yield" indicates that it is safe, the professor is saying that it is, in reality, not safe, because it does not take into account the other ways that water can leave the system besides pumping water out for people's use. The correct answer is choice 3.

13. **3** **4** This is a Detail question. All four choices are possible results of removing water from an underground system, but the professor discusses only 3 and 4.

14. **4** This is an Understanding the Function of What Is Said question. The professor asks these questions:

Now, why is this an issue? Well, aren't some of you going to want to live in this state for a while? Want your kids to grow up here, and your kids' kids?

The purpose is to point out to the students that, over time, there will be serious consequences to depleting the underground water supply. He thinks the students should consider the future of the state of Arizona. Therefore the correct answer is choice 4.

15. **1** This is a Detail question. The professor defines *sustainability* as the ability to meet present and future needs. Since his main criticism of "safe-yield" management is that it is not sustainable, knowing the meaning of *sustainable* is key to understanding the lecture. "Short-term and long-term needs" are the same as "present and future needs," so choice 1 is the correct answer.

16. **2** Because the question uses the word *imply*, we expect this to be a Making Inferences question. It is, however, a very easy inference. The professor says, "these two ideas are incompatible: sustainability and safe yield." If the "safe-yield" method is incompatible with sustainability, then water supplies managed by "safe yield" are not sustainable. The correct answer is choice 2.

Questions 17–22

Track 16 Listening Script

Narrator

Listen to part of a lecture in a philosophy class. The professor has been talking about ethics.

Professor

OK. If we're going to discuss goodness and justice—what makes an individual good or a society just or virtuous—then we need to start with the ancient Greeks. So we'll start with Plato—Plato's philosophy. Now, some of you may have studied Plato's philosophy in some other course, so this might be easy. OK. At the risk of boring you, let me give you just an overview of Plato's ethical theory. Plato says the soul has—and by "soul" he simply means that which animates the body, gives it life—anyway, he says that the soul has three separate parts . . . called, um, "faculties," which I'll come back to. He believed that goodness in an individual was to be found when the three parts of the soul worked together, when they weren't in conflict, but existed in harmony. A good or just person will have a soul in which the three faculties work well together.

So how does he arrive at that analysis? Well, he starts out in his very famous work *The Republic*, um, he starts out by saying it's very difficult to get a grasp on what the individual's soul looks like. So, to get some idea of what the individual human soul is like, he says we should study the structure of society—what kinds of people and activities every society has to have. He argues that every society has to have three groups of people: workers, soldiers, and leaders. And each has a sort of defining characteristic.

Every society has to have workers like farmers or, um, people who work in factories, producing all the things that we need for everyday life. And according to Plato, the key feature of workers is that they're focused on their own desires or appetites—interested in satisfying the needs of the body. So workers are associated with desire . . . OK?

Now, if you live in a society that has a good amount of wealth—um, good agriculture, good industry—other societies are probably going to try to take it. So you need a class of soldiers, who are supposed to protect the state from external threats. Well, these soldiers, well, they're going to be in dangerous situations quite frequently, so you need people with, um, a . . . a lot of high spirit—uh, an emotional type of individual. Emotion is what characterizes this group.

And then, Plato says, the third group you need is leaders. Their main role will be to think rationally, to use their reason or intellect to make decisions. As decision makers, leaders determine what the state is to do, how the affairs of the citizens are to be run.

Plato then asks himself: OK, assume we've got such a society with these three groups. When will this society be a good, um, a . . . a just society? Well, you can only have a good society when its three parts are working well together—each doing its proper thing. And Plato believes this can only happen if workers and soldiers learn moderation, or self-control.

But why? Why do workers and soldiers have to learn self-control? Well, how can a society flourish if the workers and soldiers don't control their desires and emotions? Plato thinks that if they aren't under control, workers will sleep too much and play too much, so they're not going to get their jobs done. And soldiers need to channel their high-spiritedness in a certain direction, precisely by being courageous.

But you're not going to get that automatically. You need to teach them this kind of moderation. So you need an educational system that first of all will train the leaders, so that they'll make good decisions, so they'll know what's wise. Then make leaders responsible—um, uh, turn over to them the education of the other two groups. And through education, build a society so that the workers and soldiers learn to use their intellect to control their desires and emotions. If you had all that, then, for Plato, you'd have a good or just society.

Now, take that picture—that social, political picture—and apply it to the individual person. You remember about the soul? That it consists of three separate parts, or faculties? Can you guess what they are? Desires, emotions, and intellect—the characteristics associated with the three groups of society. And can you guess how Plato defines a good or just person? Well, it's parallel to how he characterizes a good or just society. The three parts have to be in harmony. In each of us, our desires and emotions often get the better of us, and lead us to do foolish things. They're in conflict with the intellect. So, to get them to all work together, to coexist in harmony, every person needs to be shaped in the same way that we've shaped society—through the educational system. Individuals must be educated to use their intellect to control their emotions and desires. That's harmony in the soul.

Answer Explanations

17. ❹ This is a Gist-purpose question. Most of the excerpt that you listened to was about Plato's theory that society is made up of three groups. However, the beginning and the end of the excerpt set the context for this discussion. Plato discusses society because he thinks a society is similar to an individual person. The professor is describing Plato's ideas, and she does not say whether they are true, so neither choice 1 nor choice 2 can be correct. Again, the professor is not concerned with the real, historical societies, so choice 3 cannot be correct. Only choice 4 is possible.

18. ❶ This question asks you to listen again to this statement:

Now, some of you may have studied Plato's philosophy in some other course, so this might be easy. OK. At the risk of boring you, let me give you just an overview of Plato's ethical theory.

You are then asked a Making Inferences question. The professor is anticipating that some students may have already studied *The Republic* in another class and be familiar with the basics of Plato's theory. She says that the review may be "easy" or "boring" to students already familiar with the theory, but she is talking about her review, not the theory itself. So choices 2, 3, and 4 are not implied. Choice 1, that some students might be familiar with the theory, is implied.

19. ❷ This question asks you to listen again to this part of the lecture:

But why? Why do workers and soldiers have to learn self-control? Well, how can a society flourish if the workers and soldiers don't control their desires and emotions?

Then you are asked why the professor says this:

Well, how can a society flourish if the workers and soldiers don't control their desires and emotions?

You are asked the purpose of a question, so this is an Understanding the Function of What Is Said question. The quote is an example of a rhetorical question and is really an answer to the previous question, "Why do workers and soldiers have to learn self-control?" The question "how can a society flourish . . ." is a way of saying, "A society cannot flourish if workers and soldiers do not exercise self-control." The correct answer is choice 2.

20. ❷❸ This is a Detail question that asks you to identify two points the professor makes about Plato's view of education. Since the lecture has been about both Plato's theoretical model of society and a model of human nature, you might anticipate that one point will be about society and one about the individual. According to the professor's summary, for individuals, the intellect must be strengthened through education. For the model society, the leaders must educate the other two groups. The correct answers are choices 2 and 3.

21. This question is easy to recognize as a Connecting Content question. Based on information in the lecture, you must indicate whether or not certain statements about human emotion reflect beliefs held by Plato. The chart correctly filled out looks like this:

	YES	NO
Emotion is usually controlled by the faculty of desire.		✓
Emotion ought to be controlled by the faculty of intellect.	✓	
Emotion is what motivates soldiers.	✓	

The professor discusses emotions and desires as being controlled by the intellect, but she says nothing about their being related to one another, so statement 1 is not supported by the lecture. According to the professor, Plato does believe that for people to be happy, the intellect must control emotions, so statement 2 is supported. The professor says about Plato's soldiers, "Emotion is what characterizes this group." So statement 3 is also supported by the lecture.

22. ❶ This is a Detail question. In the last two parts of the lecture, when the professor returns to discussing individuals, she says three times that in Plato's theory the parts of the individual must be in harmony. When the lecturer repeats a point two or three times, that is a good clue that it is one of the main points of the excerpt and you should be prepared to answer a question about it. The correct answer is choice 1.

Questions 23–28

Track 19 Listening Script

Narrator

Listen to part of a talk in a botany class.

Professor

OK. So we've talked about some different types of root systems of plants, and I've shown you some pretty cool slides, but now I want to talk about the extent of the root system—the overall size of the root system . . . the depth. I want to tell you about one particular experiment. I think you're going to find this pretty amazing. OK. So there was this scientist . . . this very meticulous scientist decided that the best place to see a whole root system—to actually see how big the entire system got—the best place would be to grow it . . . where?

Female Student

Um, water?

Professor

In water. So he took rye plants—it was rye plants—and he started growing them in water. Now, you've all heard of growing stuff in water before, right?

Male Student

It's done commercially, right? Uh, like to grow vegetables and flowers?

Professor

Right. They grow all kinds of commercial crops in water. So if you're growing things in water, you can add the fertilizer. What do you need to do to that water besides put fertilizer in it? Anyone ever actually tried to grow plants in water? You must bubble water through it. Bubble gas through it. I'm sorry, you must bubble gas through it. So, gas, you have to bubble through. Think about the soil we talked about last week, about growing plants in soil. Think about some of you who have killed your favorite houseplants, 'cause you loved them too much. If you overwater, why do your favorite houseplants die?

Female Student

Oh, no oxygen.

Professor

Not enough oxygen for the roots . . . which do what twenty-four hours a day in all seasons?

Female Student

Respiration?

Professor

Respire . . . respiration . . . they breathe. So if you just stick rye plants in water, it doesn't make a difference how much fertilizer you add, you also need to bubble gas through the water, so they have access to that oxygen. If they don't have that, they're in big trouble. OK. So this guy—this scientist—grew a rye plant in water so he could see the root system, how big it got—its surface area. I read about this and the book said one thousand kilometers of roots. I kept thinking: this has to be a mistake. It just doesn't make any sense to me that . . . that . . . that could be right. But that's what all the books have, and no one's ever corrected it. So let me explain to you about this rye plant. If you take a little seed of many grasses—and remember rye is a grass; if you take a tiny little seed and you germinate it—actually, take one of my least favorite grasses that starts growing about May. What's my least favorite grass that starts growing about May?

Male Student

Crabgrass.

Professor

Crabgrass.

Remember how I showed you in the lab, one little seed starts out producing one little shoot. Then at a week or so later you've got about six shoots, and then, three weeks later you've got about fifteen shoots coming out all directions like this—all those little shoots up there? Well, that's what they did with the rye. And the little seedling started and pretty soon there were several shoots, and then more shoots. In the end, that one single seed produced eighty shoots, with an average of fifty centimeters of height . . . from one seed. Eighty shoots coming out, average fifty centimeters high. When they looked at the shoot versus the root surface, they found that the shoot surface, with all of its leaves, had a total surface area of about five square meters. Now, here's the biggie: when they looked at the root surface area, you would expect that the root and the shoot would be in balance, right? So they should be pretty close in terms of surface area, right?

Male Student

Uh-un.

Professor

What's that? Did somebody say "no"? Well, you're absolutely correct. Instead of five square meters, the root system was found to have more than two hundred square meters of surface area. Where did all of that extra surface area come from? Who did it? Who was responsible for all those extra square meters of surface area? What did roots do to increase their surface area?

Female Student

Root hairs.

Professor

Root hairs, that's exactly it. So those root hairs were responsible for an incredible chunk of surface area. They constantly have to be spread out in the water so they can absorb minerals from the fertilizer, and of course they need oxygen access as well.

Answer Explanations

23. ❶ This is a Gist-content question. This lecture is not highly organized and includes interaction from the students. However, despite the short digressions, the lecturer at the beginning and at the end repeats that the point of the talk is to explain how big root systems can be compared with the other parts of the plant. She mentions nutrients and different kinds of grasses, but they are subordinate to her main point. The correct answer is choice 1.

24. ❸ This is a Detail question. The professor says that the scientist in the experiment wanted "to actually see how big the entire system got." That "entire system" refers to the root system, so the correct answer is choice 3.

25. ❶ This is an Understanding the Function of What Is Said question. You are asked to listen to this part of the lecture again:

What do you need to do to that water besides put fertilizer in it? Anyone ever actually tried to grow plants in water? You must bubble water through it. Bubble gas through it. I'm sorry, you must bubble gas through it. So, gas, you have to bubble through.

Then you are asked specifically why the professor says, "I'm sorry, you must bubble gas through it."

In real speech, people sometimes misspeak; that is, they say a word that is different from the one they intended. This happens more often in informal speech, and this discussion is informal. As you can see from the script, in the previous sentence the professor said, "You must bubble water through it." *It* refers to water. So she has said, in effect, "You must bubble water through water," which does not make sense. The professor immediately corrects herself and repeats the correction twice, so the students know she meant to say "gas." Her purpose is to correct her previous words, so choice 1 is the correct answer.

26. **2** This is an Understanding Organization question. Although this might seem to be a digression, the professor is using an example to explain why plants that are grown in water must have gas bubbled through the water. When people give houseplants too much water, they are, in effect, "growing the plants in water" unintentionally. The plants die because the roots are deprived of oxygen. The purpose of the discussion of houseplants is to explain why, in the experiment, gas was bubbled though the water. The correct answer is choice 2.

27. **3** You are asked to listen again to this part of the lecture:

I read about this and the book said one thousand kilometers of roots. I kept thinking: this has to be a mistake. It just doesn't make any sense to me that . . . that . . . that could be right. But that's what all the books have, and no one's ever corrected it. So let me explain to you about this rye plant.

Like most replay questions, this is an Understanding the Function of What Is Said question. The lecturer says that "one thousand kilometers of roots" did not make any sense to her. She seems to be expressing doubt. But her next sentence makes clear that the "one thousand kilometers" figure is accurate. She intends to explain why such a surprising, or unbelievable, statement is true. The correct answer is choice 3.

28. **4** This is a Detail question. The professor mentions crabgrass because it is more familiar to her students than rye. She is making the point that many different kinds of grasses produce many roots from a single seed. She mentions that crabgrass begins growing in May, but that is not her point (choice 1). She does not say anything about how much water it requires (choice 2). Choice 3 is the opposite of what she says. Choice 4 is the correct answer.

Questions 29–34

Track 22 Listening Script

Narrator
Listen to part of a lecture in a business management class.

Professor
OK. Uh, let's talk about organization and structure in a company. How are companies typically structured?

Female Student
Functionally.

Professor
And . . . ?

Female Student

By projects.

Professor

Right. By function . . . and by projects. Twenty years ago companies were organized in function groups, where people with a certain expertise worked together as a unit—the, uh, architects in one unit, the finance people in another unit. Well, nowadays a lot of companies are organized around projects—like a construction company could be building an office building in one city and an apartment house somewhere else, and each project has its own architects and engineers.

Now, the good thing about project organization is that it's easier to change to adapt to the needs of the project—it's a small group, a dedicated team, not the whole company.

Now, with that in mind, here's a question for you: why do we continue to organize ourselves by function, even now, when in fact we admit that projects are the lifeblood of a lot of organizations? Why do some companies maintain a functional organization instead of organizing around projects? Yes?

Female Student

Because, um, if you don't have that functional structure within your organization, chances are you'd have a harder time meeting the goals of the projects.

Professor

Why?

Female Student

Why?

Professor

Listen, let's say we got four new cars we want to design. Why do we need a functional organization? Why not just organize the company around the four projects—these people make car number one, these other people make car number two . . .

Female Student

Yeah, but who's gonna be responsible for what? You know, the way you tell who's . . .

Professor

Well . . . well, we'll appoint a manager: new car number one manager, car number two manager—they're completely responsible. Why should we have a single engineering department that has all four cars passing through it?

Female Student

When you design a car, you need the expertise of all the engineers in the company. Each engineer needs to be in touch with the entire engineering department.

Professor

Yeah, but I keep . . . I keep asking why. I wanna know why. Yes.

Male Student

Well, to eliminate redundancy's probably one of the biggest factors in an organization. So that, uh. . . so that there's, there's . . . standards of . . . for uniformity and efficiency in the organization.

Professor

OK. And . . . and that's probably the primary reason for functional organization right there—is that we want some engineering consistency. We want the same kind of technology used in all four cars. If we disperse those four engineers into four parts of the organization and they work by themselves, there's a lot less chance that the technology's gonna be the same from car to car. So instead we maintain the functional organization—that means the engineers work together in one part of the building. And their offices are next to each other because we want them to talk to each other. When an engineer works on a project, they bring the expertise of their whole functional group with them.

But there's a downside of that, though, isn't there? I mean organizing a company into functional groups is not all positive. Where's the allegiance of those engineers? It's to their coordinator, right? It's to that chief engineer. But we really want our one engineer, the engineer that's working on car number one, we want that person's loyalty to be to that project as well as to the head of the engineering group. We . . . we really want both, don't we? We want to maintain the functional organization, so we can maintain uniformity and technology transfer, and expertise. We want the cutting-edge expertise in every group. But at the same time we also want the engineer to be totally dedicated to the needs of the project. Ideally, we have a . . . a hybrid, a combination of both functional and project organization.

But there's a problem with this kind of hybrid structure. When you have both functional and project organization, well, what does that violate in terms of basic management principles?

Female Student

Unity of command.

Professor

Unity of command. That's exactly right. So this . . . this is a vicious violation of unity of command, isn't it? It says that this engineer working on a project seems to have two bosses. We . . . we got the engineering boss, and we got the project manager boss. But the project manager is responsible for the project, and is not the official manager of the engineer who works on the project. And we try to maintain peace in the organizations, and sometimes it's disrupted and we have conflicts, don't we? The project manager for car one wants a car part to fit in a particular way, for a specific situation, a specialized case. Well, the, uh, engineering director says no, we gotta have standardization. We gotta have all the cars done this way. We can't make a special mold for that particular part for that particular car. We're not gonna do that. So we got a conflict.

Answer Explanations

29. ❷ This is a Gist-content question. Although the lecture includes exchanges between the professor and the students, it is clearly organized around a comparison of the strengths and weaknesses of two different organizational principles. It is not about the automobile industry; that is just an example (choice 1). It is not even about engineering; that is a function that is used as an example (choice 3). It does not offer a resolution of the conflict it describes (choice 4). The correct choice is 2: it is about two alternative organizational structures.

30. ❷ This is an Understanding Organization question. The professor discusses the construction company as an example of the kind of company that could be organized around project teams. Choice 2 is correct. The other choices are about functional organization, the opposite organizing principle.

31. ❸ In this replay question, you listen again to a question from the professor, an answer by a student, and another question by the professor. It is an Understanding the Function of What Is Said question. In order to understand the professor's second question, you must recognize that it is a repetition of the previous question. By repeating his question after the student's answer, the professor is signaling that it has not been satisfactorily answered. He is also signaling that the answer to his question is an important point. The correct answer is choice 3: the student's answer does not include a point the professor wants to make.

32. ❶ This is a Detail question. In this lecture, the professor does not explicitly define "unity of command." But in the last part of the talk, he gives an example of the absence of unity of command: "this engineer working on a project seems to have two bosses." Choice 1 is the correct answer.

33. ❷ To answer this question, you need to recognize the difference between the examples the professor uses in the lecture and the principle that the lecture is actually about. The question asks about a "conflict" discussed in the lecture. Choices 1, 3, and 4 are about specific conflicts that might occur in one of the organizations the professor uses as examples. Only choice 2 is about the general principle of a conflict between two equally important goals. Choice 2 is the correct answer.

34. This question is easy to recognize as a Connecting Content question. Based on information in the lecture, you must indicate whether certain statements describe functional organization or project organization. The chart correctly filled out looks like this:

	Functional Organization	Project Organization
It encourages people with similar expertise to work closely together.	✓	
It helps the company to adapt quickly and meet changing needs.		✓
It helps to achieve uniformity in projects.	✓	

Speaking

Listening Scripts, Important Points, and Sample Responses with Rater Comments

Use the sample Independent and Integrated Speaking rubrics on pages 188–191 to see how responses are scored. The raters who listen to your responses will analyze them in three general categories. These categories are Delivery, Language Use, and Topic Development. All three categories have equal importance.

This section includes important points that should be covered when answering each question. All of these points must be present in a response in order for it to receive the highest score in the Topic Development category. These important points are guides to the kind of information raters expect to hear in a high-level response.

This section also refers to example responses on the accompanying audio tracks on the CD. Some responses were scored at the highest level, while others were not. The responses are followed by comments by certified ETS raters.

Question 1

Track 24 Listening Script

Narrator

Choose a place you go to often that is important to you and explain why it is important. Please include specific details in your explanation.

> **Preparation Time: 15 Seconds**
> **Response Time: 45 Seconds**

Important Points

In this question, you are asked to talk about a place you like to go often and explain why it is important to you. People who listen to your response should be able to easily follow the progression of your ideas. Responses scored at the highest level contain ideas supported with details and elaboration that go beyond simple structures. For example, the response *"I like this place because it is nice"* does not have enough detail. Why is this place nice? Developing this idea more might look like this: *"I like this place because it is quiet and peaceful. Listening to the ocean waves on the beach relaxes me and helps me to relieve stress."*

Sample Responses

Play Track 31 on the CD to hear a high-level response for Question 1.

Rater Comments

The speaker continues speaking throughout the entire 45 seconds. She speaks clearly using a variety of vocabulary and a wide range of grammar. Her reasons are well developed. She uses specific details about why France is an important place for her. Instead of just saying, *"I'm interested in French culture because it is interesting,"* she elaborates by talking about her friend, her interest in French history and culture from a young age, and the food. There is a logical progression of ideas that makes the response easy to understand.

Play Track 32 on the CD to hear a mid-level response for Question 1.

Rater Comments

This response is sustained and the speech is generally understandable. At times, though, the speaker's pronunciation makes it difficult to understand the meaning of her ideas. She really gives only one reason why she likes shopping. This reason is used repetitively without much elaboration. Shopping is something she likes very much and makes her feel better. She could have added complexity to her ideas by saying something like *"When I go shopping, I usually go with friends, and we have a good time together without thinking about jobs or schoolwork."* She also makes some basic grammatical errors and uses a limited range of vocabulary.

Question 2

Track 25 Listening Script

Narrator

Some college students choose to take courses in a variety of subject areas in order to get a broad education. Others choose to focus on a single subject area in order to have a deeper understanding of that area. Which approach to course selection do you think is better for students and why?

> **Preparation Time: 15 Seconds**
> **Response Time: 45 Seconds**

Important Points

In this question, you are asked to make a choice between two given options. In a complete, well-developed response, you should clearly state your choice/preference. You may choose both options, but you must support both of them with reasons that are detailed. If you think taking a variety of courses is better, make sure you explain in detail what your reasons are for having that opinion. Here is an example: *"Taking a variety of courses is better because it gives you an opportunity to learn about subjects outside of your field of study. Because so many fields of study are related, you never know when knowledge from one area will be helpful in another.*" This kind of response clearly shows which option was chosen and includes a detailed reason why it was chosen.

Sample Responses

Play Track 33 on the CD to hear a high-level response for Question 2.
Rater Comments

The speaker gives a thoughtful, sustained answer with ideas and reasons that progress logically. He speaks fluently and demonstrates good control of grammar and vocabulary, with only minor errors that do not obscure the meaning of his ideas. The speaker very clearly states his opinion that the answer depends on whether you are an undergraduate or a graduate student. He continues by giving a detailed reason that supports each perspective.

Play Track 34 on the CD to hear a low-level response for Question 2.
Rater Comments

Although the speaker's pronunciation is clear, his pace is slow and irregular. The clearest parts of his speech are words that he has taken from the question. He demonstrates very limited vocabulary. His thoughts are understandable at the sentence level, but there are very few connections between sentences. Such connections would help listeners to understand what is being said or enable them to predict what will likely come next. The opinion is stated in the beginning. However, he frequently uses words from the question and repeats the same idea throughout the response.

Question 3

Track 26 Listening Script

Narrator

The university is planning to eliminate its bus service. Read the article from the university newspaper about the plan. You will have 45 seconds to read the article. Begin reading now.

Reading Time: 45 Seconds

Bus Service Elimination Planned

The university has decided to discontinue its free bus service for students. The reason given for this decision is that few students ride the buses and the buses are expensive to operate. Currently, the buses run from the center of campus past university buildings and through some of the neighborhoods surrounding the campus. The money saved by eliminating the bus service will be used to expand the overcrowded student parking lots.

Narrator

Now listen to two students discussing the article.

Man

I don't like the university's plan.

Woman

Really? I've ridden those buses, and sometimes there were only a few people on the bus. It did seem like kind of a waste.

Man

I see your point. But I think the problem is the route's out of date. It only goes through the neighborhoods that've gotten too expensive for students to live in. It's ridiculous that they haven't already changed the route—you know, so it goes where most off-campus students live now. I bet if they did that, they'd get plenty of students riding those buses.

Woman

Well, at least they're adding more parking. It's gotten really tough to find a space.

Man

That's the other part I don't like, actually. Cutting back the bus service and adding parking's just gonna encourage more students to drive on campus. And that'll just add to the noise around campus and create more traffic . . . and that'll increase the need for more parking spaces . . .

Woman

Yeah, I guess I can see your point. Maybe it would be better if more students used the buses instead of driving.

Man

Right. And the university should make it easier to do that, not harder.

Narrator

The man expresses his opinion of the university's plan to eliminate the bus service. State his opinion and explain the reasons he gives for holding that opinion.

> **Preparation Time: 30 Seconds**
> **Response Time: 60 Seconds**

Important Points

The university plans to eliminate the bus service because it is too expensive to run and too few students use it. The man disagrees with the university's plan. He believes the reason few students take the bus is that the route goes to neighborhoods where students do not live. If the routes were changed, many more students would ride the bus.

The man also disagrees with the way the university plans to use the money it saves on the bus service. Building more parking lots on campus will encourage more students to drive on campus. This would increase noise and traffic on campus.

Sample Responses

Play Track 35 on the CD to hear a high-level response for Question 3.

Rater Comments

The speaker gives a clear and coherent response that is detailed and accurate. He speaks quickly, but this does not prevent him from being understood. He very clearly states the man's opinion and summarizes the man's reasons for having that opinion. He uses complex grammatical structures and a wide variety of appropriate vocabulary. As a result, his speech seems to flow automatically.

Play Track 36 on the CD to hear a mid-level response for Question 3.

Rater Comments

The speaker's first language moderately influences her pronunciation, intonation, and pacing. This requires some listener effort. She provides content that is relevant to the task, but her limitations in language use hinder her ability to accurately convey relevant details. She fills the entire time with understandable speech. However, she incorrectly repeats throughout the response time that students cannot afford to ride the bus. She also says that few students will drive cars and overcrowd the parking lots. This creates confusion for the listener. The speaker never mentions the man's concern about increased noise and traffic on campus.

Question 4

Track 27 Listening Script

Narrator

Now read the passage about the nature of social interaction. You will have 45 seconds to read the passage. Begin reading now.

Reading Time: 45 Seconds

Social Interaction

People deal with each other every day. This interaction is at the heart of social life. The study of social interaction is concerned with the influence people have over one another's behavior. People take each other into account in their daily behavior and in fact, the very presence of others can affect behavior. For example, one principle of social interaction, audience effects, suggests that individuals' work is affected by their knowledge that they are visible to others, that the presence of others tends to alter the way people behave or perform an activity.

Narrator

Now listen to part of a talk in a sociology class. The professor is discussing audience effects.

Professor

OK, so we said that the way we interact with others has an impact on our behavior . . .

In fact, there's some interesting research to suggest that in one type of interaction—when we're being observed specifically, when we know we're being watched as we perform some activity—we tend to increase the speed at which we perform that activity.

In one study, college students were asked to each put on a pair of shoes—shoes with laces they would have to tie. Now, one group of students was told that they would be observed. The second group, however, didn't know they were being observed. The students who were aware that they were being watched actually tied their shoes much faster than the students who thought they were alone.

Other studies confirm the same is true even when we're learning new activities. Let's say someone is learning a new task—for example, learning how to type. When they're conscious of being observed, they'll likely begin typing at a much faster rate than they would if they were alone.

But, and this is interesting, the study also showed that certain common behavior—things people typically do, like . . . making mistakes when you're learning something new . . . that behavior pattern will also increase. So in other words, when we're learning to type, and we know we're being watched, we'll type faster, but we'll also make more mistakes.

Narrator

Explain how the examples of tying shoes and learning to type demonstrate the principle of audience effects.

> **Preparation Time: 30 Seconds**
> **Response Time: 60 Seconds**

Important Points

The principle of audience effects suggests that when people are aware of being observed, their behavior changes. Specifically, in the two studies described, people worked faster when they were aware of being observed. In one study, two groups were told to put on shoes that tied. One group was told it would be observed, and the other was not. The group that knew it was being observed tied shoes much faster than the other group. In learning to type, those being observed type faster, but they also make more mistakes than those not aware of being observed.

Sample Responses

Play Track 37 on the CD to hear a high-level response for Question 4.

Rater Comments

The speaker speaks clearly. She identifies the concept of audience effects and the two examples from the listening. She organizes her response in a logical way that leads the listener from one sentence to the next. She supports her response with accurate details and demonstrates a sophisticated level of both grammatical structures and vocabulary. This is evident in the way she smoothly makes the transition from one idea to the next and the efficient use of language to accurately summarize the examples from the listening. There are only very minor errors in language use, and they do not prevent her response from being understood.

Play Track 38 on the CD to hear a mid-level response for Question 4.
Rater Comments
The speaker sustains his response throughout. His pronunciation and intonation are affected by his first language. These pronunciation errors make it hard to know what he means. The speaker identifies the concept and the two examples, but with inaccuracies. Instead of summarizing each experiment, he combines the summary of both experiments. This causes him to incorrectly conclude that you make more mistakes when you are being watched while tying your shoes. Additionally, the speaker sometimes stumbles when trying to form basic words (*slowlier*), which shows a moderate control of grammar and vocabulary.

Question 5

Track 28 Listening Script

Narrator

Listen to a conversation between a student and her geology professor.

Man

Mary, I'm so glad I ran into you.

Woman

Oh, hello, Professor Jensen.

Man

Listen, I know it's short notice . . . and maybe you've already made plans for spring break . . . but . . . one of my students just dropped out of the field trip to the Smithson River Caves. You're next on the waiting list, so now there's room for you to come along.

Woman

You're kidding! *[disappointed]* I didn't think there was a chance . . . and . . . well, it's a three-day trip, right? I agreed to spend next week helping Professor Clark set up the new museum exhibition. I think she's really counting on me.

Man

Yeah, three days. But you know . . . if you'd rather come on the field trip, why not speak with her and see if she has anyone to replace you?

Woman

Yeah, I'd hate to miss out on the caves. I'll definitely ask Professor Clark if there's someone else who could help her.

Man

You know . . . we don't leave until Wednesday. If you still have to help out, any chance you could get the museum setup done before then?

Woman

Oh yeah . . . not until Wednesday . . . so then, yeah . . . maybe that's possible too.

Narrator

The speakers discuss two possible solutions to the woman's problem. Describe the problem and the two solutions. Then explain what you think the woman should do and why.

> **Preparation Time: 20 Seconds**
> **Response Time: 60 Seconds**

Important Points

The problem the student faces is a conflict between an earlier commitment to help with setting up a museum exhibition and a more recent opportunity to go on a field trip led by one of her professors. She could talk to Dr. Clark about finding a replacement to help with setting up the museum exhibition. As an alternative, since the field trip does not start until later in the week, the student could try to finish setting up the exhibit before the field trip. (Note: Normally, you are asked to talk about only the one solution you support, not both solutions, as in this example.)

After summarizing the problem and solutions, you should choose the solution you think is best and give a detailed reason. For example, you could say that you think the student should stay to set up the museum exhibit because she should honor the commitment she made to Dr. Clark.

Sample Responses

Play Track 39 on the CD to hear a high-level response for Question 5.

Rater Comments

There are minor pronunciation and intonation errors, but they do not prevent the speaker's response from being understood. She uses connecting words to mark the progression of ideas. Her control of grammar and vocabulary is evident in the way she efficiently summarizes the situation from the listening. The speaker clearly identifies the problem and both solutions. She organizes her response, so it is easy to follow her ideas from one to the next. She indicates her opinion of what the student should do. Although she runs out of time before she can explain why she holds that opinion, it is clear that she understands the task.

Play Track 40 on the CD to hear a mid-level response for Question 5.

Rater Comments

The response is generally understandable. The speaker sustains speech throughout the response time. However, the sense of hesitation in the way the response is delivered requires some listener effort. The choppy delivery sometimes makes it difficult to know when one sentence or idea ends and when others begin. The speaker makes a number of errors with simple grammatical structures (*very like to, let her to take, make somebody to replace her*). Overall meaning, though, is not greatly affected by these errors. The speaker identifies the problem and describes the two solutions. A higher-level vocabulary would have been helpful to more efficiently summarize the situation. The problem and two solutions are summarized with too much detail, which prevents the speaker from having time to state her preferred solution and give a reason for it.

Question 6

Track 29 Listening Script

Narrator

Now listen to part of a talk in an economics class.

Professor

So let's talk about money. What is money? Well, typically people think of coins and paper "bills" as money . . . but that's using a somewhat narrow definition of the term. A broad definition is this: [slowly] money is anything that people can use to make purchases with. Since many things can be used to make purchases, money can have many different forms. Certainly, coins and bills are one form of money. People exchange goods and services for coins or paper bills, and they use this money . . . these bills . . . to obtain other goods and services. For example, you might give a taxi driver five dollars to purchase a ride in his taxi. And he in turn gives the five dollars to a farmer to buy some vegetables . . .

But, as I said, coins and bills aren't the only form of money under this broad definition. Some societies make use of a barter system. Basically, in a barter system people exchange goods and services directly for other goods and services. The taxi driver, for example, might give a ride to a farmer in exchange for some vegetables. Since the vegetables are used to pay for a service, by our broad definition the vegetables are used in barter as a form of money.

Now, as I mentioned, there's also a second . . . a narrower definition of money. In the United States only coins and bills are legal tender—meaning that by law, a seller must accept them as payment. The taxi driver must accept coins or bills as payment for a taxi ride. OK? But in the U.S., the taxi driver is not required to accept vegetables in exchange for a ride. So a narrower definition of money might be whatever is legal tender in a society, whatever has to be accepted as payment.

Narrator

Using points and examples from the talk, explain the two definitions of money presented by the professor.

| Preparation Time: 20 Seconds |
| Response Time: 60 Seconds |

Important Points

Under the broad definition, money is anything that can be used as payment (as a medium of exchange); for example, coins/bills and barter. If you take a taxi ride, you could use vegetables as payment for the taxi ride. Under a narrower definition, money is anything that must be accepted as payment (legal tender). In the United States, coins and bills are legal tender. A taxi driver must accept coins and bills as payment for the taxi ride. Vegetables are not legal tender in the United States, so the taxi driver does not have to accept them as payment.

Sample Responses

Play Track 41 on the CD to hear a high-level response for Question 6.

Rater Comments

The speaker's pronunciation and intonation are highly intelligible. She speaks a little too quickly at times, but the overall meaning is not lost. Her words and ideas flow easily from one idea to the next. She uses complex grammatical structures and a wide range of vocabulary. The speaker fluently summarizes the lecture, accurately recounting the broad and narrow definition. Her response is detailed and sustained. She spends too much time summarizing the first definition and example, so she does not fully explain the second definition and example. However, it is obvious from the apparent ease with which she speaks that she understands the concept and is able to talk about it.

Play Track 42 on the CD to hear a mid-level response for Question 6.

Rater Comments

The speaker's pronunciation is generally clear. She sustains speech and continues to try to elaborate her ideas. The hesitancy and choppiness indicate a lack of control of vocabulary and grammar. This significantly affects the overall intelligibility of the response. She conveys some relevant details, including an almost accurate summary of both definitions of money. However, her response is clearly incomplete. The speaker's struggle to find the right words to convey her ideas prevents her from efficiently using her time. Neither of the examples is included in the response. Most of her ideas are underdeveloped.

Writing

Listening Script, Topic Notes, and Sample Responses with Rater Comments

Use the Integrated Writing and Independent Writing scoring rubrics on pages 200–201 and 209–210 to see how responses are scored.

Writing Based on Reading and Listening

Track 30 Listening Script

Narrator

Now listen to part of a lecture on the topic you just read about.

Professor

You know, often in science, new findings force us to re-examine earlier beliefs and assumptions. And a recent study of meerkats is having exactly this effect. The study examined the meerkat's behavior quite closely, much more closely than had ever been done before. And some interesting things were found . . . like about eating habits . . . it showed that typically meerkats eat before they stand guard—so the ones standing guard had a full stomach! And the study also found that since the sentinel is the first to see a predator coming, it's the most likely to escape . . . because it often stands guard near a burrow, so it can run immediately into the burrow after giving the alarm. The other meerkats, the ones scattered about looking for food, are actually in greater danger.

And in fact, other studies have suggested that when an animal creates an alarm, the alarm call might cause the other group members either to gather together or else to move about very quickly, behaviors that might actually draw the predator's attention away from the caller, increasing that animal's own chances of survival.

And what about people—what about some human acts that might be considered altruistic? Let's take an extreme case: uh, suppose a person donates a kidney to a relative, or even to a complete stranger. A selfless act, right? But . . . doesn't the donor receive appreciation and approval from the stranger and from society? Doesn't the donor gain an increased sense of self-worth? Couldn't such nonmaterial rewards be considered very valuable to some people?

Narrator

Summarize the points made in the lecture, being sure to explain how they oppose specific points made in the reading passage.

Topic Notes

You should understand the meaning of *altruism* and *altruistic acts*. The definitions are given in the reading passage: *altruism* describes behavior that is the opposite of selfishness; it is behavior that benefits another individual or the group with no reward. The lecturer questions whether the examples meet the definition.

A high-scoring response will include the following points made by the lecturer:

Point Made in the Reading Passage	Contrasting Point from the Lecture
Human organ donors gain nothing from their action.	The donors receive appreciation and approval from the rest of society.
Sentinel meerkats go without food to stand guard.	Sentinels actually eat before the other meerkats.
Sentinel meerkats place themselves in danger from predators.	Sentinels are actually the first to escape the predators.

Responses scoring 4 and 5 discuss altruistic/nonaltruistic aspects of the three points in the table: human organ donation, meerkat sentinel eating behavior, and meerkat sentinel ability to escape.

Sample Responses with Rater Comments

Score 5 Essay

> The lecture completely refutes the passage. It is said in the lecture that, the perceived acts of altruism are nothing more than sneaky methods of gaining advantage for one's self.Contrary to the belief in the passage that sentinels risk their lives for the cause of the whole group, the professor says that the meerkat sentinels are in fact less prone to outside threats. The alarm sentinels give off causes to group to move rashly which draws the predators attention towards them, thus drawing away the attention from the sentinels. The lecture refutes the fact that these meerkats are altruistic in the sense that they gain nothing in exchange of their services. In fact, researches have shown that they have a full stomach as they perform this "altruistic" duty and have a better chance of escaping from danger because they witness it ifrst Proffesor also offers a different underlying motivation that causes people to believe that acts such as donating an organ or sharing food with someone in need are altruistic. She says that people gain appreciation as a result of such acts, which may be deemed by some much more important than materialistic gains.

Rater Comments

This answer meets all the criteria for a level 5 response to an integrated task. The writer does a good job of selecting, framing, and interweaving points from the lecture and reading, explicitly and fluently presenting accurate connections between the relevant points. All three points made by the lecturer are included. Language is used accurately and effectively, and the overall piece is well organized.

Score 4 Essay

Baed on the lecture, meerkats actually do not sacrifice themself by becoming a sentinel. Firstly, the meerkats that become a sentinel usually eats before. Secondly, these meerkats usually standing guard near their burrows. As a result, when a predator is seen, they raise an alarm and reach a safe place before the other meerkats that hunt for food. This shows that these meerkats do not put themselves in danger. In fact, the lecturer warned that the the alarm raised by these meerkats could be harmfull for the other meerkats. One of the reason is that the responses of the other meerkats to the alarm might attract attention from the predator. Based on these reasons, meerkats can not be used as an example of a mammal that performs altruistic behavior.

The lecture also pointed out that, it is not always true that individuals performing altruistic acts gain nothings for themselves. For example, when a man give one of his/her kidney to a family member or even a stranger, his/her self-worth increase. He/she feels usefull for other people. Therefore, he/she gain something from his/her action.

In sum, altruism behavior in animal and human is questioned. It is difficult for individuals sacrificies its own interest without gain anything for themselves.

Rater Comments

This response includes all the main points of the lecture. The first paragraph begins with a clear statement that sentinel meerkats do not sacrifice themselves. There are strong concluding statements in each of the first two paragraphs that are quite explicit about the import of the sentinel behavior and the organ donation. The connections to the reading could be stronger. The writer says that the sentinel meerkat "eats before," but does not make an explicit contrast to the passage that says that sentinel meerkats go without eating. The conclusion in the final paragraph is vague ("altruism . . . is questioned"). On balance then, this response is a level 4, with minor vagueness and omission. In terms of language, there are a number of minor errors: "themself," missing verb in the sentence beginning "Secondly," "One of the reason," "a man give," "It is difficult for individuals sacrificies."

Score 3 Essay

Acording to the lecture, examinig closely to the eating habits of meerkats, these animals are not altruistic, mainly because the sentinel before standing guard eats. So that it has a full stomach. Another fact is that the sentinel, being the first that sees the predator, is able to be the first in escape. Also the other meerkats that are hunting and looking for food are the ones in danger. Considering the altruistic human acts, the donation of body organs shouldn't be considered like that, mainly because when a person donates an organ he or she receives appreciation and recognition of society.

Because of this points the lecture might make the reader doubt, mainly because the eating habits of the meerkats have been studied closely, giving arguments in order to justify that meerkats aren't doing altruistic acts.

The other argument about human and their altruistic actions sounds logical and a situiation in which a person would donate organs just to get appreciation of society couls be probable.

Because of this both, reading and lecture, are completely opposite, might make the user doubt and reflect more about altruism.

Rater Comments

This response is at level 3. On the positive side, the response includes all the facts of the sentinel meerkat from the lecture as well as organ donation. However, it is very vague in how it relates (see the Level 3 description in the Scoring Guide) the various points in the lecture to the points in the reading. There is no clear reference to the claim in the reading that the sentinel is sacrificing food or any explanation of the other meerkats as being in danger. The statement commenting on organ donation, "The other argument about human and their altruistic actions sounds logical and a situation in which a person would donate organs just to get appreciation of society couls be probable," is not very clear.

Score 2 Essay

Alturism is considered an act of selfishness. A research has been made, that shows the difference of alturism between humans and a special kind of mammal which is the meerkat. There is one of the meerkat that acts as a sentinel (having eaten before going to his sentinel place), and when it it aware that a predator is coming, he instantly gives a loud cry, and makes the others to run away to protect themselves. They do not get anything for their profit (the sentinels profit but he just stays there to protect it specie.

The other example that is given, is with humans. A clear example was given to show how selfishless works in humas beings. When a person, wants to donate an organ to somebody who is part of the family or not, may be that person expects the tfamily of the person tha has received the organ to give him or her thanks because of that favour. So, in that sense they make clear that there is a sense of selfishness in human beings, because they expect someting back. However, meerkats, do not have a sense of alturism, they just do their job without expecting anything back from their community.

Rater Comments

The best part of this response is the explanation of the lecturer's point that organ donation can be seen from a selfish point of view. However, it misrepresents the concept of altruism and is confused about the meaning of the information from the lecture about the sentinel's having eaten. The response misrepresents the point of the lecture by saying that humans are selfish but meerkats are truly altruistic. Because of the significant inaccuracies about both the lecture and the reading, this response is at level 2.

Score 1 Essay

The lecture said about altruism. It happen both animal and human. First, the meerkat is a good example of altruism for animal. They have special eatting habit. The meerkat which guard and look out predator is full stomach. After finish standing guard they eat some food while other meerkat guard from predators. When they find predators then they alarm to others to hide into the shelter. Also, human is altruistic animal. People share their food with strangers or they donate food or clothing even body organs. It stated both human and animal are altruism.

This lecture make our easy to understand and organize this lecture in mind. It shows short summary about this reading, and also give us some detail information. That is outlind of this reading. In addition, every contents is related to the reading, and also offer some more information. For this reason we can make sure about this reading.

Rater Comments

Even though this response seems to include some information from the lecture (the fact that the guard meerkat "is full stomach"), it does not show how the information undermines the notion of altruism in meerkats; if anything, it is somehow construed as supporting the concept of meerkat altruism. The second paragraph contains severe language problems and communicates nothing to fulfilling the task. For these reasons, this is a level 1 response.

Writing Based on Knowledge and Experience

Question

Some young adults want independence from their parents as soon as possible. Other young adults prefer to live with their families for a longer time. Which of these situations do you think is better? Use specific reasons and examples to support your opinion.

Topic Notes

This topic, in effect, equates independence with living apart from one's family. Both broader and narrower definitions of independence and "nonindependence" are acceptable as possible responses to the given topic, even though a majority of writers will write to the dichotomy presented by the question. Some writers take a general overview, and their choices and examples are general and "philosophical." Others use specific personal examples or personal narratives in their approach to the topic. Some writers take a specific side of the issue, and others approach the topic by discussing conditions under which it is better to move away and conditions under which a young adult might do better to stay longer with the family. All these approaches are valid, on-topic responses and are judged by the raters on their merits according to the scoring guidelines for this task type.

Sample Responses with Rater Comments

Score 5 Essay—Sample 1

Every young adults will grow and live apart from their parents to form their own families. The ages for those young adults to be independent depends on each person. Some people may have to live longer with their parents and some others may not. This essay will discuss the issue of independent life and living with their families for a longer time.

Most young adults prefer to have a seperate or independent life from their parents or families as soon as possible. This is because they have a strong urge for freedom in doing what they desire. But in fact many of them fail. This should not be surprising since often they are actually not ready mentally although they are physically ready. It is widely understood that to live independently requires a lot of energy and is not easy at all. In this twenty first century, people may need more and more preparation because competition is increasing rapidly. An observation shows that many University graduated students are unemployed. Therefore, they will not be able to support and fulfill their necessities.

So living independently at an early age is not suitable for all young adults, some young adults may need to take more time to prepare themselves before going out to struggle. Young adults need to be ready to support themselves. Taking time to get more education and living with their families for a longer time may lead them to a better independent life because they will be well prepared for the hard-life outside. Still, living with their families for *too* long will not be a good idea because they could get to used to it and tend to be less independent.

The time to live independently depends on the person himself. He or she must decide whether they are ready to leave their parents to have an independent life or not. The decision will vary from one person to another. A person should judge that he is capable of fulfilling his needs without being dependent on his parents; this indicates that he is ready for his independent life. Otherwise he might need to stay longer with his parents.

Rater Comments

This well-developed essay meets all the criteria for earning a score of 5. The writer develops the topic through a detailed discussion of independence and of the suitability of living independently. The essay is unified and coherent. Sentence structure is varied, especially in paragraphs 2 and 3. The writer does not use high-level vocabulary, but word choice is correct throughout. There are minor errors ("University graduated students," "fulfill their necessities"), but these in no way interrupt the flow or meaning of the essay.

Score 5 Essay—Sample 2

Independence! Who doesn't want independece? But the bigger question is how much of an independence is being discussed here? Generally, when teenagers grow up, their needs and habit of living change. Some would like their parents to be in control of the major decisions of their lives, while on the other hand, some would not like their parents to be involved in any sort of decision making process of their lives. In my opinion, the young adults should always consult their parents as their guides. I will try to demonstrate my point in the following paragraphs.

Let's assume a teenager grows up into a young adult. Now a major decision that he/she might have had to make was to what college/university they were going to attend. If we assume that the person seek complete independence from the early age, then they are generally going to make the decision themselves. But even if they made this desicion by themself, what is the probability that this is the best desicion. We all would agree that the best lesson learned is from a mistake, but why even let that happen? This is the most important decision they would have to make so far, and if they don't ask around, if they don't look at the wider picture, how are they supposed to end up at their very best opportunity? This, is what is known as a making/breaking point because this decision of theirs can make or break a very powerful potential future.

Now, suppose they passed the first make/break point. Then comes another one when they are going to marry. Normally, in the western culture, the man and the woman choose their marriage partners themselves, so this is not much of an important issue here. But, what about the cultures that predominantly have arranged marriages? In that case, choosing a husband or a wife could be a huge decision, because generally the marriages are not as easily broken as in the western culture. So, when it comes to this point, one would definately want to know their parents thinking and their previous experiance. This could come in very handy when one has a choice to make.

To sum it up, it is very good idea to ask for parents guides, and is never a bad a idea to give up a part of independence for a better future.

Rater Comments

This essay has a rather informal, conversational tone and an "argument" that is coherently and fully developed. Sentence structure is varied throughout, and the writer consistently demonstrates command of language and English idioms, especially by using various informal expressions ("Let's assume," "We all would agree," "can make or break," "come in very handy"). The essay meets all the criteria for a score of 5.

Score 4 Essay—Sample 1

There are different opinion regarding how long young adults should live with their parents. Some argues that the sooner a young adults become independence is the better while other think that it will be beneficial if they can live with their parents longer. In my opinion both have positive and negative sides. This essay will provide arguments for each case.

Some young adults favor for leaving their parents soon. They want to live free, independence from their parents' supervision. The good thing about being independence as soon as possible is that they can learn how to live by themselves. They must think how to support their living, otherwise they will still need the help of their parents and can not be independence. Living in their own will teach them how to be tough in facing real difficulties. But, staying away from parents soon could also lead to negative behaviour if the young adults can not control themselves. They might think that they can do whatever they want with the friends they like. If their friends give bad influence on them, no one will warn them and they can have problems. Thus, I will agree for young adults to become independence as soon as possible if they are already mature enough and able to control themselves. Parents can help to judge this before they release them.

In the case of young adult is not mature enough, I believe that staying with parents will be better. Parents can provide guidance and help when their children need it. But, if the children is become too dependent on their parents, they will have difficulties in their older lives of becoming independece as the parents will not be available for them anymore. So parents in some way should teach their children about independence, for example by giving them responsibilities that should be handled without supervision.

Based on those arguments, I would like to say that either way could be better that the other depending on the maturity of young adults themselves. If they are mature and have self-control then living independently is better, otherwise they better stay with their parents until ready.

Rater Comments

The points made in this essay are thoroughly developed and concretely supported. The essay is well organized and coherent, with a nice flow. What keeps the response from scoring a 5 is the number of noticeable errors in structure and word choice: "Some argues," "favor for leaving," "Living in their own," "become independence," "if the children is become too dependent." None of these errors interferes with meaning, but their quantity and effect earn the essay a score of 4.

Score 4 Essay—Sample 2

Independence from the family at early stages of life is a common phenomena exists in our society. moving out from the family house to live on your own in early ages of your adult life has an advantages and disadvantages. However, the disadvantages outweigh the advantages.

Independency is generally good and helpful for the individual, because it teaches individuals how to take care of different responsibilities, and how to handle things by yourself. people needs to know how to live independently of others, because eventually they will have to. So, the desire to get your independence from your family when you are young adult is good because it shows the some kind of individual maturity for being aware of the ultimate situation, when you have to move out and live on your own.

On the other hand, adults should consider moving out when they are sure that they are ready for it. Being ready includes being financially, physically, and psychologically ready. One major advantage for staying with your parents is financially advantage. Because one gets to save money between the residency and daily living issues.

Nowadays, life has become harder for the new generations to live and keep up with. And in order to do that, individualls needs to be fully equiped in terms of education, support, and maturity. And by staying with the family, one would not have to worry about alot of issues, instead, one will concerntrate more on getting equiped for the next step in his life, which is moving out and getting independent of others.

In conclusion, although moving out when you are still a young adult to live independently from the family has some good point, the disadvantages of it overcome these good points.

Rater Comments

This essay is clearly organized and unified, though it does remain on a fairly abstract level. It is also generally well developed. Sentence structure is varied, but there are noticeable errors in syntax and expression ("has an advantages," "is financially advantage," "Because one gets to save money between the residency and daily living issues," "getting independent of others"). These errors earn this essay a score of 4.

Score 3 Essay—Sample 1

Right now adults have different points of view about live. Independent from their parents as soon as possible or continue to to live with their parents. Live with your parents have many differents advantage. First, some people dont want to have resposabilities, they want their parents still take the desicion. For example, house's responsabilities or pays. Secound, When peoples live with their parents they dont expend a lot money for haouse or food. Third, they belief that their family is a great company. But in the other hand, when people live along have important advantage. For example, They live independient, they dont heve limitation in their own house. They dont need to negociate with other persons or family. Morover, they have a graet oportunity to learn about how administarte a house, amd what is the real value of the money. They can understand everytuhing about responsability in their house. Finally They have more freedom.

Both live independient and live with your parents have many different disadvantage. On the first points of view, live independient, the most important problem is money and expensive. For example, right now young adults need to find a good job for live in a good place because rents are expensive. It is the same with food and services. They need to have a excellent imcome to live in good conditions. Also, they need to work in the house along because dont have company. They need to clean, do the laundry, buy the food, and cook along. Although pepole think live independient have a huge sacrifies, also live with their parents it is difficult and have a lot of disadvantage. For example, when people live with thier parents have many different limitation with activities in the house, every time need to negociate with your family. In addition,

Rater Comments

This essay is somewhat developed and is longer than the average essay with a score of 3. It has a coherent organization based on describing the pros and cons of living apart from one's parents and living with them, with supporting points. In some cases, however, this approach leads to redundancy, especially toward the end of the essay. Additionally, even discounting typographical mistakes, the various errors clearly reveal weakness in command of language ("Live with your parents have many differents advantage," "the most important problem is . . . expensive"). Meaning is also sometimes obscured ("house's responsabilities or pays," "they need to work in the house along because dont have company").

Score 3 Essay—Sample 2

Young adults show different patterns of behavior when they have to decide whether continuing to live with their family or not. For instance, in United States young adults prefer to live separated from they parents as soon as possible. This tendency reflects wises of freedom and independence. Altough these behavior has remarkable advantages and disadvantage, the advantage can overwhelm the negative effects.

It is important to recognize that by living separated from parents or family can be more risked than living with them. many young adults are victims of group pressure and gangs because of theirs parents absence.

However, a significant advantage of living by onself is that people develop ledearship skills. Individuals that live by themselves learn to do and sustain their own decisions. On the contrary, people who live with their parents are more shy and less confident. For instance, many of the greatest world leaders are or have been people that were separated from their parents when they were kids.

Another advantage of living indepently is that peolpe can fully develop their creative potential. When people is forced to difficult situations, they can surprise us with outstanding abilities and values that otherwise remained hidden. A good example are blind people, these person show a remarkable ability for art and music. In a similar way, when parents are absent or too away for help, individuals manage to survive and be successful.

Rater Comments

Though slightly stronger than the average essay with a score of 3, this essay fails to earn a score of 4 mainly because of errors that obscure meaning ("reflects wises of freedom and independence"). Also, connections among ideas are not always completely clear. For example, the details used to support the points made in paragraphs 3 and 4 are concrete but not well connected to each other or to the generalizations made by the writer.

Score 2 Essay—Sample 1

> In my opinion,it is better when adults live with their families for a longer time. Some young adults make a big mistake going away from their families.They want independence,but sometimes it can cause a lot of problems.A lot of young adults in my country,depend of their parents.Ofcause they can do whatever they want. They can find a job,earn their own money,start a family,and so one,but they prefer to stay wiht their families and be depended.In my country parents allways care about their children.They support them by giving money,some advise.If you are young adults you can allways ask your parents about help,and they will s

Rater Comments

Limited in development and lacking any organizing principle, this essay is squarely in the 2 range. The generalizations made are only barely supported. There are errors ("prefer to stay wiht their families and be depended," "ask your parents about help"), but it is the lack of development and extremely unclear connections between ideas ("A lot of young adults in my country,depend of their parents.Ofcause they can do whatever they want") that limit this essay to a score of 2.

Score 2 Essay—Sample 2

> In my opoinion, young adults live with their families longer time is better than they become independent from their parents because they can recive living supports and advise from their parents.
>
> Some young adults want live by themselves eventhought they are not financialy independent. Therefore, their credit history is destoryed by irresponsible payments. Futhermore, when they have their own family, these credit dermages cause their worsest future.
>
> If they live with their family, they can get great advise from their family who know them very well. For example, when they are in great denger sutuation, only their family come to resucu them, so they can protect them self.
>
> For these resons, I think that young adults live with their families for long time is better than they become independent quickerly.

Rater Comments

More developed than the average essay with a score of 2, this response fails to earn a 3 because it contains so many language errors ("recive living supports," "quickerly") and sentences that obscure meaning ("these credit dermages cause their worsest future," "only their family come to resucu them, so they can protect them self"). These language weaknesses make it difficult for the reader to understand the ideas the writer tries to present.

Score 1 Essay—Sample 1

> These days most of the youngs adults wants to live independence from their parents. In my case I want to live independence only in my college years because I believ in hetrogeneous family.
>
>   Nowadays young adults want to live independence because of privacy and second reasons is if they live independence then they will also learn take care of themself.

Rater Comments

This essay essentially repeats the writing question twice and then briefly addresses the task. It is characterized by underdevelopment with very little elaboration. There are errors, but it is the lack of development that earns this essay a score of 1.

Score 1 Essay—Sample 2

> I have learnd a lot of tihng since I came to the U.S.A. It wasn't until I came here that I never seperated from my parents. In here, not only did I gain information everything, but I also felt love's value who i loved.
>
>   That's why I insiste that young adults have to live without parents.

Rater Comments

This essay fails to make any coherent points and is filled with errors of language and usage. These weaknesses earn it a score of 1.

7 Authentic TOEFL iBT Practice Test 2

In this chapter you will find the second of three authentic TOEFL iBT Practice Tests. You can take the test in two different ways:

- **In the book:** You can read through the test questions in the following pages, marking your answers in the spaces provided. To hear the listening portions of the test, follow instructions to play the numbered audio tracks on the CD-ROM that accompanies this book.

- **On the CD:** For a test-taking experience that more closely resembles the actual TOEFL iBT test, you can take this same test on your computer using the accompanying CD-ROM. Reading passages and questions will appear on-screen, and you can enter your answers by clicking on the spaces provided. Follow instructions to hear the listening portions of the test.

Following this test, you will find answer keys and scoring information. You will also find scripts for the listening portions. Complete answer explanations, as well as sample test taker spoken responses and essays, are also provided.

TOEFL iBT Practice Test 2
READING

Directions: This section measures your ability to understand academic passages in English.

The Reading section is divided into separately timed parts.

Most questions are worth 1 point, but the last question for each passage is worth more than 1 point. The directions for the last question indicate how many points you may receive.

You will now begin the Reading section. There are three passages in the section. You should allow **20 minutes** to read each passage and answer the questions about it. You should allow **60 minutes** to complete the entire section.

At the end of this Practice Test you will find an answer key, information to help you determine your score, and explanations of the answers.

FEEDING HABITS OF EAST AFRICAN HERBIVORES

Buffalo, zebras, wildebeests, topi, and Thomson's gazelles live in huge groups that together make up some 90 percent of the total weight of mammals living on the Serengeti Plain of East Africa. They are all herbivores (plant-eating animals), and they all appear to be living on the same diet of grasses, herbs, and small bushes. This appearance, however, is illusory. When biologist Richard Bell and his colleagues analyzed the stomach contents of four of the five species (they did not study buffalo), they found that each species was living on a different part of the vegetation. The different vegetational parts differ in their food qualities: lower down, there are succulent, nutritious leaves; higher up are the harder stems. There are also sparsely distributed, highly nutritious fruits, and Bell found that only the Thomson's gazelles eat much of these. The other three species differ in the proportion of lower leaves and higher stems that they eat: zebras eat the most stem matter, wildebeests eat the most leaves, and topi are intermediate.

How are we to understand their different feeding preferences? The answer lies in two associated differences among the species, in their digestive systems and body sizes. According to their digestive systems, these herbivores can be divided into two categories: the nonruminants (such as the zebra, which has a digestive system like a horse) and the ruminants (such as the wildebeest, topi, and gazelle, which are like the cow). Nonruminants cannot extract much energy from the hard parts of a plant; however, this is more than made up for by the fast speed at which food passes through their guts. Thus, when there is only a short supply of poor-quality food, the wildebeest, topi, and gazelle enjoy an advantage. They are ruminants and have a special structure (the rumen) in their stomachs, which contains microorganisms that can break down the hard parts of plants. Food passes only slowly through the ruminant's gut because ruminating—digesting the hard parts—takes time. The ruminant continually regurgitates food from its stomach back to its mouth to chew it up further (that is what a cow is doing when "chewing cud"). Only when it has been chewed up and digested almost to a liquid can the food pass through the rumen and on through the gut. Larger particles cannot pass through until they have been chewed down to size. Therefore, when food is in short supply, a ruminant can last longer than a non-ruminant because it can derive more energy out of the same food. The difference can partially explain the eating habits of the Serengeti herbivores. The zebra chooses areas where there is more low-quality food. It migrates first to unexploited areas and chomps the abundant low-quality stems before moving on. It is a fast-in/fast-out feeder, relying on a high output of incompletely digested food. By the time the wildebeests (and other ruminants) arrive, the grazing and trampling of the zebras will have worn the vegetation down. As the ruminants then set to work, they eat down to the lower, leafier parts of the vegetation. All of this fits in with the differences in stomach contents with which we began.

The other part of the explanation is body size. Larger animals require more food than smaller animals, but smaller animals have a higher metabolic rate. Smaller animals can therefore live where there is less food, provided that such food is of high energy content. That is why the smallest of the herbivores, Thomson's gazelle, lives on fruit that is very nutritious but too thin on the ground to support a larger animal. By contrast, the large zebra lives on the masses of low-quality stem material.

The differences in feeding preferences lead, in turn, to differences in migratory habits. The wildebeests follow, in their migration, the pattern of local rainfall. The other species do likewise. But when a new area is fueled by rain, the mammals migrate toward it in a set order to exploit it. The larger, less fastidious feeders, the zebras, move in first; the choosier, smaller wildebeests come later; and the smallest species of all, Thomson's gazelle, arrives last. The later species all depend on the preparations of the earlier one, for the actions of the zebra alter the vegetation to suit the stomachs of the wildebeest, topi, and gazelle.

PARAGRAPH 1

Buffalo, zebras, wildebeests, topi, and Thomson's gazelles live in huge groups that together make up some 90 percent of the total weight of mammals living on the Serengeti Plain of East Africa. They are all herbivores (plant-eating animals), and they all appear to be living on the same diet of grasses, herbs, and small bushes. This appearance, however, is illusory. When biologist Richard Bell and his colleagues analyzed the stomach contents of four of the five species (they did not study buffalo), they found that each species was living on a different part of the vegetation. The different vegetational parts differ in their food qualities: lower down, there are succulent, nutritious leaves; higher up are the harder stems. There are also sparsely distributed, highly nutritious fruits, and Bell found that only the Thomson's gazelles eat much of these. The other three species differ in the proportion of lower leaves and higher stems that they eat: zebras eat the most stem matter, wildebeests eat the most leaves, and topi are intermediate.

Directions: Mark your answer by filling in the oval next to your choice.

1. The word "illusory" in the passage is closest in meaning to
   ○ definite
   ○ illuminating
   ○ misleading
   ○ exceptional

2. The word "sparsely" in the passage is closest in meaning to
   ○ widely
   ○ thinly
   ○ clearly
   ○ freshly

3. Which of the following questions about Richard Bell's research is NOT answered in paragraph 1?
   ○ Which of the herbivores studied is the only one to eat much fruit?
   ○ Which part of the plants do wildebeests prefer to eat?
   ○ Where did the study of herbivores' eating habits take place?
   ○ Why were buffalo excluded from the research study?

GO ON TO THE NEXT PAGE ➘

How are we to understand their different feeding preferences? The answer lies in two associated differences among the species, in their digestive systems and body sizes. According to their digestive systems, these herbivores can be divided into two categories: the nonruminants (such as the zebra, which has a digestive system like a horse) and the ruminants (such as the wildebeest, topi, and gazelle, which are like the cow). Nonruminants cannot extract much energy from the hard parts of a plant; however, this is more than made up for by the fast speed at which food passes through their guts. Thus, when there is only a short supply of poor-quality food, the wildebeest, topi, and gazelle enjoy an advantage. They are ruminants and have a special structure (the rumen) in their stomachs, which contains microorganisms that can break down the hard parts of plants. Food passes only slowly through the ruminant's gut because ruminating—digesting the hard parts—takes time. The ruminant continually regurgitates food from its stomach back to its mouth to chew it up further (that is what a cow is doing when "chewing cud"). Only when it has been chewed up and digested almost to a liquid can the food pass through the rumen and on through the gut. Larger particles cannot pass through until they have been chewed down to size. Therefore, when food is in short supply, a ruminant can last longer than a nonruminant because it can derive more energy out of the same food. The difference can partially explain the eating habits of the Serengeti herbivores. The zebra chooses areas where there is more low-quality food. It migrates first to unexploited areas and chomps the abundant low-quality stems before moving on. It is a fast-in/fast-out feeder, relying on a high output of incompletely digested food. By the time the wildebeests (and other ruminants) arrive, the grazing and trampling of the zebras will have worn the vegetation down. As the ruminants then set to work, they eat down to the lower, leafier parts of the vegetation. All of this fits in with the differences in stomach contents with which we began.

4. The word "associated" in the passage is closest in meaning to

○ obvious
○ significant
○ expected
○ connected

5. The author mentions the cow and the horse in paragraph 2 in order to

○ distinguish the functioning of their digestive systems from those of East African mammals
○ emphasize that their relatively large body size leads them to have feeding practices similar to those of East African mammals
○ illustrate differences between ruminants and nonruminants through the use of animals likely to be familiar to most readers
○ emphasize similarities between the diets of cows and horses and the diets of East African mammals

6. According to paragraph 2, which of the following herbivores has to eat large quantities of plant stems because it gains relatively little energy from each given quantity of this food?

- ○ The gazelle
- ○ The wildebeest
- ○ The zebra
- ○ The topi

7. Paragraph 2 suggests that which of the following is one of the most important factors in determining differences in feeding preferences of East African herbivores?

- ○ The availability of certain foods
- ○ The differences in stomach structure
- ○ The physical nature of vegetation in the environment
- ○ The ability to migrate when food supplies are low

8. According to paragraph 2, all of the following are true of East African gazelles EXCEPT:

- ○ They digest their food very quickly.
- ○ Microorganisms help them digest their food.
- ○ They are unable to digest large food particles unless these are chewed down considerably.
- ○ They survive well even if food supplies are not abundant.

PARAGRAPH 3

The other part of the explanation is body size. Larger animals require more food than smaller animals, but smaller animals have a higher metabolic rate. Smaller animals can therefore live where there is less food, provided that such food is of high energy content. That is why the smallest of the herbivores, Thomson's gazelle, lives on fruit that is very nutritious but too thin on the ground to support a larger animal. By contrast, the large zebra lives on the masses of low-quality stem material.

9. The phrase "provided that" in the passage is closest in meaning to

- ○ as long as
- ○ unless
- ○ as if
- ○ even though

GO ON TO THE NEXT PAGE ↘

PARAGRAPH 4

The differences in feeding preferences lead, in turn, to differences in migratory habits. The wildebeests follow, in their migration, the pattern of local rainfall. The other species do likewise. But when a new area is fueled by rain, the mammals migrate toward it in a set order to exploit it. The larger, less fastidious feeders, the zebras, move in first; the choosier, smaller wildebeests come later; and the smallest species of all, Thomson's gazelle, arrives last. The later species all depend on the preparations of the earlier one, for the actions of the zebra alter the vegetation to suit the stomachs of the wildebeest, topi, and gazelle.

10. The word "fastidious" in the passage is closest in meaning to

○ rapid
○ determined
○ flexible
○ demanding

11. According to paragraph 4, which of the following mammals exhibits a feeding behavior that is beneficial to the other herbivores that share the same habitat?

○ Topi
○ Zebra
○ Wildebeest
○ Gazelle

12. According to the passage, which of the following is true of wildebeests?

○ They eat more stem matter than zebras do.
○ They are able to digest large food particles if the food is of a high quality.
○ They tend to choose feeding areas in which the vegetation has been worn down.
○ They are likely to choose low-quality food to eat in periods when the quantity of rainfall is low.

PARAGRAPH 4

The differences in feeding preferences lead, in turn, to differences in migratory habits. ■ The wildebeests follow, in their migration, the pattern of local rainfall. ■ The other species do likewise. ■ But when a new area is fueled by rain, the mammals migrate toward it in a set order to exploit it. ■ The larger, less fastidious feeders, the zebras, move in first; the choosier, smaller wildebeests come later; and the smallest species of all, Thomson's gazelle, arrives last. The later species all depend on the preparations of the earlier one, for the actions of the zebra alter the vegetation to suit the stomachs of the wildebeest, topi, and gazelle.

13. Look at the four squares [■] that indicate where the following sentence could be added to the passage.

The sequence in which they migrate correlates with their body size.

Where would the sentence best fit?

○ The differences in feeding preferences lead, in turn, to differences in migratory habits. **The sequence in which they migrate correlates with their body size.** The wildebeests follow, in their migration, the pattern of local rainfall. ■ The other species do likewise. ■ But when a new area is fueled by rain, the mammals migrate toward it in a set order to exploit it. ■ The larger, less fastidious feeders, the zebras, move in first; the choosier, smaller wildebeests come later; and the smallest species of all, Thomson's gazelle, arrives last. The later species all depend on the preparations of the earlier one, for the actions of the zebra alter the vegetation to suit the stomachs of the wildebeest, topi, and gazelle.

○ The differences in feeding preferences lead, in turn, to differences in migratory habits. ■ The wildebeests follow, in their migration, the pattern of local rainfall. **The sequence in which they migrate correlates with their body size.** The other species do likewise. ■ But when a new area is fueled by rain, the mammals migrate toward it in a set order to exploit it. ■ The larger, less fastidious feeders, the zebras, move in first; the choosier, smaller wildebeests come later; and the smallest species of all, Thomson's gazelle, arrives last. The later species all depend on the preparations of the earlier one, for the actions of the zebra alter the vegetation to suit the stomachs of the wildebeest, topi, and gazelle.

○ The differences in feeding preferences lead, in turn, to differences in migratory habits. ■ The wildebeests follow, in their migration, the pattern of local rainfall. ■ The other species do likewise. **The sequence in which they migrate correlates with their body size.** But when a new area is fueled by rain, the mammals migrate toward it in a set order to exploit it. ■ The larger, less fastidious feeders, the zebras, move in first; the choosier, smaller wildebeests come later; and the smallest species of all, Thomson's gazelle, arrives last. The later species all depend on the preparations of the earlier one, for the actions of the zebra alter the vegetation to suit the stomachs of the wildebeest, topi, and gazelle.

GO ON TO THE NEXT PAGE ↘

○ The differences in feeding preferences lead, in turn, to differences in migratory habits. ■ The wildebeests follow, in their migration, the pattern of local rainfall. ■ The other species do likewise. ■ But when a new area is fueled by rain, the mammals migrate toward it in a set order to exploit it. **The sequence in which they migrate correlates with their body size.** The larger, less fastidious feeders, the zebras, move in first; the choosier, smaller wildebeests come later; and the smallest species of all, Thomson's gazelle, arrives last. The later species all depend on the preparations of the earlier one, for the actions of the zebra alter the vegetation to suit the stomachs of the wildebeest, topi, and gazelle.

14. **Directions**: An introductory sentence for a brief summary of the passage is provided below. Complete the summary by selecting the THREE answer choices that express the most important ideas in the passage. Some sentences do not belong in the summary because they express ideas that are not presented in the passage or are minor ideas in the passage. **This question is worth 2 points.**

East African herbivores, though they all live in the same environment, have a range of feeding preferences.

-
-
-

Answer Choices

1. The survival of East African mammals depends more than anything else on the quantity of highly nutritious fruits that they are able to find.

2. An herbivore's size and metabolic rate affect the kinds of food and the quantities of food it needs to eat.

3. Zebras and wildebeests rarely compete for the same food resources in the same locations.

4. The different digestive systems of herbivores explain their feeding preferences.

5. Migratory habits are influenced by feeding preferences.

6. Patterns in the migratory habits of East African herbivores are hard to establish.

LOIE FULLER

The United States dancer Loie Fuller (1862–1928) found theatrical dance in the late nineteenth century artistically unfulfilling. She considered herself an artist rather than a mere entertainer, and she, in turn, attracted the notice of other artists.

Fuller devised a type of dance that focused on the shifting play of lights and colors on the voluminous skirts or draperies she wore, which she kept in constant motion principally through movements of her arms, sometimes extended with wands concealed under her costumes. She rejected the technical virtuosity of movement in ballet, the most prestigious form of theatrical dance at that time, perhaps because her formal dance training was minimal. Although her early theatrical career had included stints as an actress, she was not primarily interested in storytelling or expressing emotions through dance; the drama of her dancing emanated from her visual effects.

Although she discovered and introduced her art in the United States, she achieved her greatest glory in Paris, where she was engaged by the Folies Bergère in 1892 and soon became "La Loie," the darling of Parisian audiences. Many of her dances represented elements or natural objects—Fire, the Lily, the Butterfly, and so on—and thus accorded well with the fashionable Art Nouveau style, which emphasized nature imagery and fluid, sinuous lines. Her dancing also attracted the attention of French poets and painters of the period, for it appealed to their liking for mystery, their belief in art for art's sake, a nineteenth-century idea that art is valuable in itself rather than because it may have some moral or educational benefit, and their efforts to synthesize form and content.

Fuller had scientific leanings and constantly experimented with electrical lighting (which was then in its infancy), colored gels, slide projections, and other aspects of stage technology. She invented and patented special arrangements of mirrors and concocted chemical dyes for her draperies. Her interest in color and light paralleled the research of several artists of the period, notably the painter Seurat, famed for his Pointillist technique of creating a sense of shapes and light on canvas by applying extremely small dots of color rather than by painting lines. One of Fuller's major inventions was underlighting, in which she stood on a pane of frosted glass illuminated from underneath. This was particularly effective in her *Fire Dance* (1895), performed to the music of Richard Wagner's "Ride of the Valkyries." The dance caught the eye of artist Henri de Toulouse-Lautrec, who depicted it in a lithograph.

As her technological expertise grew more sophisticated, so did the other aspects of her dances. Although she gave little thought to music in her earliest dances, she later used scores by Gluck, Beethoven, Schubert, Chopin, and Wagner, eventually graduating to Stravinsky, Fauré, Debussy, and Mussorgsky, composers who were then considered progressive. She began to address more ambitious themes in her dances such as *The Sea,* in which her dancers invisibly agitated a huge expanse of silk, played upon by colored lights. Always open to scientific and technological innovations, she befriended the scientists Marie and Pierre Curie upon their discovery of radium and created a *Radium Dance,* which simulated the phosphorescence of that element. She both appeared in films—then in an early stage of development—and made them herself; the hero of her fairy-tale film *Le Lys de la Vie* (1919) was played by René Clair, later a leading French film director.

GO ON TO THE NEXT PAGE ↘

At the Paris Exposition in 1900, she had her own theater, where, in addition to her own dances, she presented pantomimes by the Japanese actress Sada Yocco. She assembled an all-female company at this time and established a school around 1908, but neither survived her. Although she is remembered today chiefly for her innovations in stage lighting, her activities also touched Isadora Duncan and Ruth St. Denis, two other United States dancers who were experimenting with new types of dance. She sponsored Duncan's first appearance in Europe. Her theater at the Paris Exposition was visited by St. Denis, who found new ideas about stagecraft in Fuller's work and fresh sources for her art in Sada Yocco's plays. In 1924 St. Denis paid tribute to Fuller with the duet *Valse à la Loie.*

PARAGRAPH 1

The United States dancer Loie Fuller (1862–1928) found theatrical dance in the late nineteenth century artistically unfulfilling. She considered herself an artist rather than a mere entertainer, and she, in turn, attracted the notice of other artists.

Directions: Mark your answer by filling in the oval next to your choice.

1. What can be inferred from paragraph 1 about theatrical dance in the late nineteenth century?

○ It influenced many artists outside of the field of dance.
○ It was very similar to theatrical dance of the early nineteenth century.
○ It was more a form of entertainment than a form of serious art.
○ It was a relatively new art form in the United States.

PARAGRAPH 2

Fuller devised a type of dance that focused on the shifting play of lights and colors on the voluminous skirts or draperies she wore, which she kept in constant motion principally through movements of her arms, sometimes extended with wands concealed under her costumes. She rejected the technical virtuosity of movement in ballet, the most prestigious form of theatrical dance at that time, perhaps because her formal dance training was minimal. Although her early theatrical career had included stints as an actress, she was not primarily interested in storytelling or expressing emotions through dance; the drama of her dancing emanated from her visual effects.

2. According to paragraph 2, all of the following are characteristic of Fuller's type of dance EXCEPT

○ experimentation using color
○ large and full costumes
○ continuous movement of her costumes
○ technical virtuosity of movement

3. The word "prestigious" in the passage is closest in meaning to

○ highly regarded
○ financially rewarding
○ demanding
○ serious

4. Which of the sentences below best expresses the essential information in the highlighted sentence in the passage? Incorrect choices change the meaning in important ways or leave out essential information.

   ○ Fuller was more interested in dance's visual impact than in its narrative or emotional possibilities.

   ○ Fuller used visual effects to dramatize the stories and emotions expressed in her work.

   ○ Fuller believed that the drama of her dancing sprang from her emotional style of storytelling.

   ○ Fuller's focus on the visual effects of dance resulted from her early theatrical training as an actress.

PARAGRAPH 3

Although she discovered and introduced her art in the United States, she achieved her greatest glory in Paris, where she was engaged by the Folies Bergère in 1892 and soon became "La Loie," the darling of Parisian audiences. Many of her dances represented elements or natural objects—Fire, the Lily, the Butterfly, and so on—and thus accorded well with the fashionable Art Nouveau style, which emphasized nature imagery and fluid, sinuous lines. Her dancing also attracted the attention of French poets and painters of the period, for it appealed to their liking for mystery, their belief in art for art's sake, a nineteenth-century idea that art is valuable in itself rather than because it may have some moral or educational benefit, and their efforts to synthesize form and content.

5. The word "engaged" in the passage is closest in meaning to

   ○ noticed
   ○ praised
   ○ hired
   ○ attracted

6. The word "synthesize" in the passage is closest in meaning to

   ○ improve
   ○ define
   ○ simplify
   ○ integrate

7. According to paragraph 3, why was Fuller's work well received in Paris?

   ○ Parisian audiences were particularly interested in artists and artistic movements from the United States.

   ○ Influential poets tried to interest dancers in Fuller's work when she arrived in Paris.

   ○ Fuller's work at this time borrowed directly from French artists working in other media.

   ○ Fuller's dances were in harmony with the artistic values already present in Paris.

GO ON TO THE NEXT PAGE ◥

Fuller had scientific leanings and constantly experimented with electrical lighting (which was then in its infancy), colored gels, slide projections, and other aspects of stage technology. She invented and patented special arrangements of mirrors and concocted chemical dyes for her draperies. Her interest in color and light paralleled the research of several artists of the period, notably the painter Seurat, famed for his Pointillist technique of creating a sense of shapes and light on canvas by applying extremely small dots of color rather than by painting lines. One of Fuller's major inventions was underlighting, in which she stood on a pane of frosted glass illuminated from underneath. This was particularly effective in her *Fire Dance* (1895), performed to the music of Richard Wagner's "Ride of the Valkyries." The dance caught the eye of artist Henri de Toulouse-Lautrec, who depicted it in a lithograph.

8. According to paragraph 4, Fuller's *Fire Dance* was notable in part for its

○ use of colored gels to illuminate glass
○ use of dyes and paints to create an image of fire
○ technique of lighting the dancer from beneath
○ draperies with small dots resembling the Pointillist technique of Seurat

As her technological expertise grew more sophisticated, so did the other aspects of her dances. Although she gave little thought to music in her earliest dances, she later used scores by Gluck, Beethoven, Schubert, Chopin, and Wagner, eventually graduating to Stravinsky, Fauré, Debussy, and Mussorgsky, composers who were then considered progressive. She began to address more ambitious themes in her dances such as *The Sea,* in which her dancers invisibly agitated a huge expanse of silk, played upon by colored lights. Always open to scientific and technological innovations, she befriended the scientists Marie and Pierre Curie upon their discovery of radium and created a *Radium Dance,* which simulated the phosphorescence of that element. She both appeared in films—then in an early stage of development—and made them herself; the hero of her fairy-tale film *Le Lys de la Vie* (1919) was played by René Clair, later a leading French film director.

9. Why does the author mention Fuller's "*The Sea*"?

○ To point out a dance of Fuller's in which music did not play an important role
○ To explain why Fuller sometimes used music by progressive composers
○ To illustrate a particular way in which Fuller developed as an artist
○ To illustrate how Fuller's interest in science was reflected in her work

10. The word "agitated" in the passage is closest in meaning to

○ emerged from beneath
○ created movement in
○ arranged themselves in
○ pretended to be

PARAGRAPH 6

At the Paris Exposition in 1900, she had her own theater, where, in addition to her own dances, she presented pantomimes by the Japanese actress Sada Yocco. She assembled an all-female company at this time and established a school around 1908, but neither survived her. Although she is remembered today chiefly for her innovations in stage lighting, her activities also touched Isadora Duncan and Ruth St. Denis, two other United States dancers who were experimenting with new types of dance. She sponsored Duncan's first appearance in Europe. Her theater at the Paris Exposition was visited by St. Denis, who found new ideas about stagecraft in Fuller's work and fresh sources for her art in Sada Yocco's plays. In 1924 St. Denis paid tribute to Fuller with the duet *Valse à la Loie*.

11. According to paragraph 6, what was true of Fuller's theater at the Paris Exposition?

○ It presented some works that were not by Fuller.
○ It featured performances by prominent male as well as female dancers.
○ It became a famous school that is still named in honor of Fuller.
○ It continued to operate as a theater after Fuller died.

12. The passage mentions which of the following as a dance of Fuller's that was set to music?

○ *Fire Dance*
○ *Radium Dance*
○ *Le Lys de la Vie*
○ *Valse à la Loie*

GO ON TO THE NEXT PAGE ⬊

PARAGRAPH 5

As her technological expertise grew more sophisticated, so did the other aspects of her dances. ■ Although she gave little thought to music in her earliest dances, she later used scores by Gluck, Beethoven, Schubert, Chopin, and Wagner, eventually graduating to Stravinsky, Fauré, Debussy, and Mussorgsky, composers who were then considered progressive. ■ She began to address more ambitious themes in her dances such as *The Sea,* in which her dancers invisibly agitated a huge expanse of silk, played upon by colored lights. ■ Always open to scientific and technological innovations, she befriended the scientists Marie and Pierre Curie upon their discovery of radium and created a *Radium Dance,* which simulated the phosphorescence of that element. ■ She both appeared in films—then in an early stage of development—and made them herself; the hero of her fairy-tale film *Le Lys de la Vie* (1919) was played by René Clair, later a leading French film director.

13. Look at the four squares [■] that indicate where the following sentence could be added to the passage.

    For all her originality in dance, her interests expanded beyond it into newly emerging artistic media.

    Where would the sentence best fit?

○ As her technological expertise grew more sophisticated, so did the other aspects of her dances. **For all her originality in dance, her interests expanded beyond it into newly emerging artistic media.** Although she gave little thought to music in her earliest dances, she later used scores by Gluck, Beethoven, Schubert, Chopin, and Wagner, eventually graduating to Stravinsky, Fauré, Debussy, and Mussorgsky, composers who were then considered progressive. ■ She began to address more ambitious themes in her dances such as *The Sea,* in which her dancers invisibly agitated a huge expanse of silk, played upon by colored lights. ■ Always open to scientific and technological innovations, she befriended the scientists Marie and Pierre Curie upon their discovery of radium and created a *Radium Dance,* which simulated the phosphorescence of that element. ■ She both appeared in films—then in an early stage of development—and made them herself; the hero of her fairy-tale film *Le Lys de la Vie* (1919) was played by René Clair, later a leading French film director.

○ As her technological expertise grew more sophisticated, so did the other aspects of her dances. ■ Although she gave little thought to music in her earliest dances, she later used scores by Gluck, Beethoven, Schubert, Chopin, and Wagner, eventually graduating to Stravinsky, Fauré, Debussy, and Mussorgsky, composers who were then considered progressive. **For all her originality in dance, her interests expanded beyond it into newly emerging artistic media.** She began to address more ambitious themes in her dances such as *The Sea,* in which her dancers invisibly agitated a huge expanse of silk, played upon by colored lights. ■ Always open to scientific and technological innovations, she befriended the scientists Marie and Pierre Curie upon their discovery of radium and created a *Radium Dance,* which simulated the phosphorescence of that element. ■ She both appeared in films—then in an early stage of development—and made them herself; the hero of her fairy-tale film *Le Lys de la Vie* (1919) was played by René Clair, later a leading French film director.

○ As her technological expertise grew more sophisticated, so did the other aspects of her dances. ■ Although she gave little thought to music in her earliest dances, she later used scores by Gluck, Beethoven, Schubert, Chopin, and Wagner, eventually graduating to Stravinsky, Fauré, Debussy, and Mussorgsky, composers who were then considered progressive. ■ She began to address more ambitious themes in her dances such as *The Sea,* in which her dancers invisibly agitated a huge expanse of silk, played upon by colored lights. **For all her originality in dance, her interests expanded beyond it into newly emerging artistic media.** Always open to scientific and technological innovations, she befriended the scientists Marie and Pierre Curie upon their discovery of radium and created a *Radium Dance*, which simulated the phosphorescence of that element. ■ She both appeared in films—then in an early stage of development—and made them herself; the hero of her fairy-tale film *Le Lys de la Vie* (1919) was played by René Clair, later a leading French film director.

○ As her technological expertise grew more sophisticated, so did the other aspects of her dances. ■ Although she gave little thought to music in her earliest dances, she later used scores by Gluck, Beethoven, Schubert, Chopin, and Wagner, eventually graduating to Stravinsky, Fauré, Debussy, and Mussorgsky, composers who were then considered progressive. ■ She began to address more ambitious themes in her dances such as *The Sea,* in which her dancers invisibly agitated a huge expanse of silk, played upon by colored lights. ■ Always open to scientific and technological innovations, she befriended the scientists Marie and Pierre Curie upon their discovery of radium and created a *Radium Dance*, which simulated the phosphorescence of that element. **For all her originality in dance, her interests expanded beyond it into newly emerging artistic media.** She both appeared in films—then in an early stage of development—and made them herself; the hero of her fairy-tale film *Le Lys de la Vie* (1919) was played by René Clair, later a leading French film director.

GO ON TO THE NEXT PAGE ↘

14. **Directions:** An introductory sentence for a brief summary of the passage is provided below. Complete the summary by selecting the THREE answer choices that express the most important ideas in the passage. Some sentences do not belong in the summary because they express ideas that are not presented in the passage or are minor ideas in the passage. **This question is worth 2 points.**

Loie Fuller was an important and innovative dancer.

-
-
-

Answer Choices

1. Fuller believed that audiences in the late nineteenth century had lost interest in most theatrical dance.

2. Fuller transformed dance in part by creating dance interpretations of works by poets and painters.

3. Fuller's work influenced a number of other dancers who were interested in experimental dance.

4. Fuller introduced many technical innovations to the staging of theatrical dance.

5. Fuller continued to develop throughout her career, creating more complex works and exploring new artistic media.

6. By the 1920s, Fuller's theater at the Paris Exposition had become the world center for innovative dance.

GREEN ICEBERGS

Icebergs are massive blocks of ice, irregular in shape; they float with only about 12 percent of their mass above the sea surface. They are formed by glaciers—large rivers of ice that begin inland in the snows of Greenland, Antarctica, and Alaska—and move slowly toward the sea. The forward movement, the melting at the base of the glacier where it meets the ocean, and waves and tidal action cause blocks of ice to break off and float out to sea.

Icebergs are ordinarily blue to white, although they sometimes appear dark or opaque because they carry gravel and bits of rock. They may change color with changing light conditions and cloud cover, glowing pink or gold in the morning or evening light, but this color change is generally related to the low angle of the Sun above the horizon. However, travelers to Antarctica have repeatedly reported seeing green icebergs in the Weddell Sea and, more commonly, close to the Amery Ice Shelf in East Antarctica.

One explanation for green icebergs attributes their color to an optical illusion when blue ice is illuminated by a near-horizon red Sun, but green icebergs stand out among white and blue icebergs under a great variety of light conditions. Another suggestion is that the color might be related to ice with high levels of metallic compounds, including copper and iron. Recent expeditions have taken ice samples from green icebergs and ice cores—vertical, cylindrical ice samples reaching down to great depths—from the glacial ice shelves along the Antarctic continent. Analyses of these cores and samples provide a different solution to the problem.

The ice shelf cores, with a total length of 215 meters (705 feet), were long enough to penetrate through glacial ice—which is formed from the compaction of snow and contains air bubbles—and to continue into the clear, bubble-free ice formed from seawater that freezes onto the bottom of the glacial ice. The properties of this clear sea ice were very similar to the ice from the green iceberg. The scientists concluded that green icebergs form when a two-layer block of shelf ice breaks away and capsizes (turns upside down), exposing the bubble-free shelf ice that was formed from seawater.

A green iceberg that stranded just west of the Amery Ice Shelf showed two distinct layers: bubbly blue-white ice and bubble-free green ice separated by a one-meter-long ice layer containing sediments. The green ice portion was textured by seawater erosion. Where cracks were present, the color was light green because of light scattering; where no cracks were present, the color was dark green. No air bubbles were present in the green ice, suggesting that the ice was not formed from the compression of snow but instead from the freezing of seawater. Large concentrations of single-celled organisms with green pigments (coloring substances) occur along the edges of the ice shelves in this region, and the seawater is rich in their decomposing organic material. The green iceberg did not contain large amounts of particles from these organisms, but the ice had accumulated dissolved organic matter from the seawater. It appears that unlike salt, dissolved organic substances are not excluded from the ice in the freezing process. Analysis shows that the dissolved organic material absorbs enough blue wavelengths from solar light to make the ice appear green.

Chemical evidence shows that platelets (minute flat portions) of ice form in the

GO ON TO THE NEXT PAGE ↘

water and then accrete and stick to the bottom of the ice shelf to form a slush (partially melted snow). The slush is compacted by an unknown mechanism, and solid, bubble-free ice is formed from water high in soluble organic substances. When an iceberg separates from the ice shelf and capsizes, the green ice is exposed.

The Amery Ice Shelf appears to be uniquely suited to the production of green icebergs. Once detached from the ice shelf, these bergs drift in the currents and wind systems surrounding Antarctica and can be found scattered among Antarctica's less colorful icebergs.

PARAGRAPH 1

Icebergs are massive blocks of ice, irregular in shape; they float with only about 12 percent of their mass above the sea surface. They are formed by glaciers—large rivers of ice that begin inland in the snows of Greenland, Antarctica, and Alaska—and move slowly toward the sea. The forward movement, the melting at the base of the glacier where it meets the ocean, and waves and tidal action cause blocks of ice to break off and float out to sea.

Directions: Mark your answer by filling in the oval next to your choice.

1. According to paragraph 1, all of the following are true of icebergs EXCEPT:

○ They do not have a regular shape.
○ They are formed where glaciers meet the ocean.
○ Most of their mass is above the sea surface.
○ Waves and tides cause them to break off glaciers.

PARAGRAPH 2

Icebergs are ordinarily blue to white, although they sometimes appear dark or opaque because they carry gravel and bits of rock. They may change color with changing light conditions and cloud cover, glowing pink or gold in the morning or evening light, but this color change is generally related to the low angle of the Sun above the horizon. However, travelers to Antarctica have repeatedly reported seeing green icebergs in the Weddell Sea and, more commonly, close to the Amery Ice Shelf in East Antarctica.

2. According to paragraph 2, what causes icebergs to sometimes appear dark or opaque?

○ A heavy cloud cover
○ The presence of gravel or bits of rock
○ The low angle of the Sun above the horizon
○ The presence of large cracks in their surface

One explanation for green icebergs attributes their color to an optical illusion when blue ice is illuminated by a near-horizon red Sun, but green icebergs stand out among white and blue icebergs under a great variety of light conditions. Another suggestion is that the color might be related to ice with high levels of metallic compounds, including copper and iron. Recent expeditions have taken ice samples from green icebergs and ice cores—vertical, cylindrical ice samples reaching down to great depths—from the glacial ice shelves along the Antarctic continent. Analyses of these cores and samples provide a different solution to the problem.

3. Which of the sentences below best expresses the essential information in the highlighted sentence in the passage? Incorrect choices change the meaning in important ways or leave out essential information.

⭘ One explanation notes that green icebergs stand out among other icebergs under a great variety of light conditions, but this is attributed to an optical illusion.

⭘ One explanation for the color of green icebergs attributes their color to an optical illusion that occurs when the light from a near-horizon red Sun shines on a blue iceberg.

⭘ One explanation for green icebergs attributes their color to a great variety of light conditions, but green icebergs stand out best among other icebergs when illuminated by a near-horizon red Sun.

⭘ One explanation attributes the color of green icebergs to an optical illusion under special light conditions, but green icebergs appear distinct from other icebergs under a great variety of light conditions.

GO ON TO THE NEXT PAGE ↘

PARAGRAPH 4

The ice shelf cores, with a total length of 215 meters (705 feet), were long enough to penetrate through glacial ice—which is formed from the compaction of snow and contains air bubbles—and to continue into the clear, bubble-free ice formed from seawater that freezes onto the bottom of the glacial ice. The properties of this clear sea ice were very similar to the ice from the green iceberg. The scientists concluded that green icebergs form when a two-layer block of shelf ice breaks away and capsizes (turns upside down), exposing the bubble-free shelf ice that was formed from seawater.

4. The word "penetrate" in the passage is closest in meaning to

○ collect
○ pierce
○ melt
○ endure

5. According to paragraph 4, how is glacial ice formed?

○ By the compaction of snow
○ By the freezing of seawater on the bottom of ice shelves
○ By breaking away from the ice shelf
○ By the capsizing of a two-layer block of shelf ice

6. According to paragraph 4, ice shelf cores helped scientists explain the formation of green icebergs by showing that

○ the ice at the bottom of green icebergs is bubble-free ice formed from frozen seawater
○ bubble-free ice is found at the top of the ice shelf
○ glacial ice is lighter and floats better than sea ice
○ the clear sea ice at the bottom of the ice shelf is similar to ice from a green iceberg

PARAGRAPH 5

A green iceberg that stranded just west of the Amery Ice Shelf showed two distinct layers: bubbly blue-white ice and bubble-free green ice separated by a one-meter-long ice layer containing sediments. The green ice portion was textured by seawater erosion. Where cracks were present, the color was light green because of light scattering; where no cracks were present, the color was dark green. No air bubbles were present in the green ice, suggesting that the ice was not formed from the compression of snow but instead from the freezing of seawater. Large concentrations of single-celled organisms with green pigments (coloring substances) occur along the edges of the ice shelves in this region, and the seawater is rich in their decomposing organic material. The green iceberg did not contain large amounts of particles from these organisms, but the ice had accumulated dissolved organic matter from the seawater. It appears that unlike salt, dissolved organic substances are not excluded from the ice in the freezing process. Analysis shows that the dissolved organic material absorbs enough blue wavelengths from solar light to make the ice appear green.

7. Why does the author mention that "The green ice portion was textured by seawater erosion"?

○ To explain why cracks in the iceberg appeared light green instead of dark green
○ To suggest that green ice is more easily eroded by seawater than white ice is
○ To support the idea that the green ice had been the bottom layer before capsizing
○ To explain how the air bubbles had been removed from the green ice

8. The word "accumulated" in the passage is closest in meaning to

○ collected
○ frozen
○ released
○ covered

9. The word "excluded" in the passage is closest in meaning to

○ kept out
○ compressed
○ damaged
○ gathered together

GO ON TO THE NEXT PAGE ◥

PARAGRAPH 6

Chemical evidence shows that platelets (minute flat portions) of ice form in the water and then accrete and stick to the bottom of the ice shelf to form a slush (partially melted snow). The slush is compacted by an unknown mechanism, and solid, bubble-free ice is formed from water high in soluble organic substances. When an iceberg separates from the ice shelf and capsizes, the green ice is exposed.

10. The word "accrete" in the passage is closest in meaning to

○ advance
○ transfer
○ flatten out
○ come together

11. Which of the following is NOT explained in the passage?

○ Why blocks of ice break off where glaciers meet the ocean
○ Why blocks of shelf ice sometimes capsize after breaking off
○ Why green icebergs are commonly produced in some parts of Antarctica
○ Why green icebergs contain large amounts of dissolved organic pigments

12. The passage supports which of the following statements about the Amery Ice Shelf?

○ The Amery Ice Shelf produces only green icebergs.
○ The Amery Ice Shelf produces green icebergs because its ice contains high levels of metallic compounds such as copper and iron.
○ The Amery Ice Shelf produces green icebergs because the seawater is rich in a particular kind of soluble organic material.
○ No green icebergs are found far from the Amery Ice Shelf.

PARAGRAPHS 2 AND 3

Icebergs are ordinarily blue to white, although they sometimes appear dark or opaque because they carry gravel and bits of rock. They may change color with changing light conditions and cloud cover, glowing pink or gold in the morning or evening light, but this color change is generally related to the low angle of the Sun above the horizon. ■ However, travelers to Antarctica have repeatedly reported seeing green icebergs in the Weddell Sea and, more commonly, close to the Amery Ice Shelf in East Antarctica.

■ One explanation for green icebergs attributes their color to an optical illusion when blue ice is illuminated by a near-horizon red Sun, but green icebergs stand out among white and blue icebergs under a great variety of light conditions. ■ Another suggestion is that the color might be related to ice with high levels of metallic compounds, including copper and iron. ■ Recent expeditions have taken ice samples from green icebergs and ice cores—vertical, cylindrical ice samples reaching down to great depths—from the glacial ice shelves along the Antarctic continent. Analyses of these cores and samples provide a different solution to the problem.

13. Look at the four squares [■] that indicate where the following sentence could be added to the passage.

    Scientists have differed as to whether icebergs appear green as a result of light conditions or because of something in the ice itself.

    Where would the sentence best fit?

○ Icebergs are ordinarily blue to white, although they sometimes appear dark or opaque because they carry gravel and bits of rock. They may change color with changing light conditions and cloud cover, glowing pink or gold in the morning or evening light, but this color change is generally related to the low angle of the Sun above the horizon. **Scientists have differed as to whether icebergs appear green as a result of light conditions or because of something in the ice itself.** However, travelers to Antarctica have repeatedly reported seeing green icebergs in the Weddell Sea and, more commonly, close to the Amery Ice Shelf in East Antarctica.

    ■ One explanation for green icebergs attributes their color to an optical illusion when blue ice is illuminated by a near-horizon red Sun, but green icebergs stand out among white and blue icebergs under a great variety of light conditions. ■ Another suggestion is that the color might be related to ice with high levels of metallic compounds, including copper and iron. ■ Recent expeditions have taken ice samples from green icebergs and ice cores—vertical, cylindrical ice samples reaching down to great depths—from the glacial ice shelves along the Antarctic continent. Analyses of these cores and samples provide a different solution to the problem.

○ Icebergs are ordinarily blue to white, although they sometimes appear dark or opaque because they carry gravel and bits of rock. They may change color with changing light conditions and cloud cover, glowing pink or gold in the morning or evening light, but this color change is generally related to the low angle of the Sun above the horizon. ■ However, travelers to Antarctica have repeatedly reported seeing green icebergs in the Weddell Sea and, more commonly, close to the Amery Ice Shelf in East Antarctica.

    Scientists have differed as to whether icebergs appear green as a result of light conditions or because of something in the ice itself. One explanation for green icebergs attributes their color to an optical illusion when blue ice is illuminated by a near-horizon red Sun, but green icebergs stand out among white and blue icebergs under a great variety of light conditions. ■ Another suggestion is that the color might be related to ice with high levels of metallic compounds, including copper and iron. ■ Recent expeditions have taken ice samples from green icebergs and ice cores—vertical, cylindrical ice samples reaching down to great depths—from the glacial ice shelves along the Antarctic continent. Analyses of these cores and samples provide a different solution to the problem.

GO ON TO THE NEXT PAGE ↘

○ Icebergs are ordinarily blue to white, although they sometimes appear dark or opaque because they carry gravel and bits of rock. They may change color with changing light conditions and cloud cover, glowing pink or gold in the morning or evening light, but this color change is generally related to the low angle of the Sun above the horizon. ■ However, travelers to Antarctica have repeatedly reported seeing green icebergs in the Weddell Sea and, more commonly, close to the Amery Ice Shelf in East Antarctica.

■ One explanation for green icebergs attributes their color to an optical illusion when blue ice is illuminated by a near-horizon red Sun, but green icebergs stand out among white and blue icebergs under a great variety of light conditions. **Scientists have differed as to whether icebergs appear green as a result of light conditions or because of something in the ice itself.** Another suggestion is that the color might be related to ice with high levels of metallic compounds, including copper and iron. ■ Recent expeditions have taken ice samples from green icebergs and ice cores—vertical, cylindrical ice samples reaching down to great depths—from the glacial ice shelves along the Antarctic continent. Analyses of these cores and samples provide a different solution to the problem.

○ Icebergs are ordinarily blue to white, although they sometimes appear dark or opaque because they carry gravel and bits of rock. They may change color with changing light conditions and cloud cover, glowing pink or gold in the morning or evening light, but this color change is generally related to the low angle of the Sun above the horizon. ■ However, travelers to Antarctica have repeatedly reported seeing green icebergs in the Weddell Sea and, more commonly, close to the Amery Ice Shelf in East Antarctica.

■ One explanation for green icebergs attributes their color to an optical illusion when blue ice is illuminated by a near-horizon red Sun, but green icebergs stand out among white and blue icebergs under a great variety of light conditions. ■ Another suggestion is that the color might be related to ice with high levels of metallic compounds, including copper and iron. **Scientists have differed as to whether icebergs appear green as a result of light conditions or because of something in the ice itself.** Recent expeditions have taken ice samples from green icebergs and ice cores—vertical, cylindrical ice samples reaching down to great depths—from the glacial ice shelves along the Antarctic continent. Analyses of these cores and samples provide a different solution to the problem.

14. **Directions:** An introductory sentence for a brief summary of the passage is provided below. Complete the summary by selecting the THREE answer choices that express the most important ideas in the passage. Some sentences do not belong in the summary because they express ideas that are not presented in the passage or are minor ideas in the passage. **This question is worth 2 points.**

Several suggestions, ranging from light conditions to the presence of metallic compounds, have been offered to explain why some icebergs appear green.

-
-
-

Answer Choices

1. Ice cores were used to determine that green icebergs were formed from the compaction of metallic compounds, including copper and iron.

2. All ice shelves can produce green icebergs, but the Amery Ice Shelf is especially well suited to do so.

3. Green icebergs form when a two-layer block of ice breaks away from a glacier and capsizes, exposing the bottom sea ice to view.

4. Ice cores and samples revealed that both ice shelves and green icebergs contain a layer of bubbly glacial ice and a layer of bubble-free sea ice.

5. Green icebergs are white until they come into contact with seawater containing platelets and soluble organic green pigments.

6. In a green iceberg, the sea ice contains large concentrations of organic matter from the seawater.

STOP. This is the end of the Reading section of TOEFL iBT Practice Test 2.

LISTENING

Directions: This section measures your ability to understand conversations and lectures in English.

You should listen to each conversation and lecture only **once**.

After each conversation or lecture, you will answer some questions about it. The questions typically ask about the main idea and supporting details. Some questions ask about the purpose of a speaker's statement or a speaker's attitude. Answer the questions based on what is stated or implied by the speakers.

You may take notes while you listen. You may use your notes to help you answer the questions. Your notes will **not** be scored.

In some questions, you will see this icon: This means that you will hear, but not see, part of the question.

Most questions are worth 1 point. If a question is worth more than 1 point, it will have special directions that indicate how many points you can receive.

It will take about **60 minutes** to listen to the conversations and lectures and to answer the questions. You will have **35 minutes** to respond to the questions. You should answer each question, even if you must guess the answer.

At the end of this Practice Test you will find an answer key, information to help you determine your score, scripts for the audio tracks, and explanations of the answers.

Listen to Track 43 on the CD.

Questions

Directions: Mark your answer by filling in the oval or square next to your choice.

1. Why does the student go to see the professor?
   ○ For suggestions on how to write interview questions
   ○ For assistance in finding a person to interview
   ○ To ask for advice on starting a business
   ○ To schedule an interview with him

2. Why does the student mention her high school newspaper?
   ○ To inform the professor that she plans to print the interview there
   ○ To explain why the assignment is difficult for her
   ○ To show that she enjoys writing for school newspapers
   ○ To indicate that she has experience with conducting interviews

3. How does the professor help the student?
   ○ He gives her a list of local business owners.
   ○ He allows her to interview business owners in her hometown.
   ○ He suggests that she read the business section of the newspaper.
   ○ He gives her more time to complete the assignment.

4. What does the professor want the students to learn from the assignment?

○ That starting a business is risky

○ Why writing articles on local businesses is important

○ How to develop a detailed business plan

○ What personality traits are typical of business owners

5. *Listen again to part of the conversation by playing Track 44.* 🎧 **Play Audio**
   Then answer the question.

What does the student imply?

○ She is surprised by the professor's reaction.

○ The professor has not quite identified her concern.

○ The professor has guessed correctly what her problem is.

○ She does not want to finish the assignment.

GO ON TO THE NEXT PAGE ↘

Listen to Track 45 on the CD. Play Audio

Questions

6. What does the professor mainly discuss?

○ Various errors in early calendars

○ Why people came to believe that Earth moves around the Sun

○ Examples of various types of calendars used in different cultures

○ The belief that the position of planets and stars can predict future events

7. The professor discusses various theories on how Stonehenge was used. What can be inferred about the professor's opinion?

○ She is sure Stonehenge was used as a calendar.

○ She believes the main use for Stonehenge was probably as a temple or a tomb.

○ She thinks that the stones were mainly used as a record of historical events.

○ She admits that the purpose for which Stonehenge was constructed may never be known.

8. According to the professor, how was the Mayan calendar mainly used?

○ To keep track of long historical cycles

○ To keep track of the lunar months

○ To predict the outcome of royal decisions

○ To allow priests to compare the orbits of Earth and Venus

9. According to the professor, what was the basis of the ancient Chinese astrological cycle?
   - ○ The cycle of night and day
   - ○ The orbit of the Moon
   - ○ The cycle of the seasons
   - ○ The orbit of the planet Jupiter

10. How did the Romans succeed in making their calendar more precise?
    - ○ By changing the number of weeks in a year
    - ○ By adding an extra day every four years
    - ○ By carefully observing the motion of the planet Jupiter
    - ○ By adopting elements of the Chinese calendar

11. How does the professor organize the lecture?
    - ○ By mentioning the problem of creating a calendar, then describing various attempts to deal with it
    - ○ By speaking of the modern calendar first, then comparing it with earlier ones
    - ○ By discussing how a prehistoric calendar was adapted by several different cultures
    - ○ By emphasizing the advantages and disadvantages of using various time cycles

GO ON TO THE NEXT PAGE

Listen to Track 46 on the CD.

Questions

12. What is the lecture mainly about?
  - ○ How dolphins produce the sounds they make
  - ○ How dolphins teach their young to identify signature whistles
  - ○ The professor's experience with dolphins on a research boat
  - ○ Various ways dolphins communicate with one another

13. According to a theory the professor mentions, why do dolphins travel side by side?
  - ○ To view each other's bubble streams
  - ○ To hear each other's signature whistles
  - ○ To avoid interfering with other dolphins' sonar clicks
  - ○ To keep mothers close to their young

14. What does the professor imply about bubble streams?
  - ○ They help protect dolphins from predators.
  - ○ Their function is similar to that of signature whistles.
  - ○ They do not appear to serve a communicative function.
  - ○ Dolphins use them to sense the movement of the water.

15. Why does the professor mention the time she spent on a boat doing research?

○ To encourage students to do fieldwork

○ To inform students about a paper she wrote

○ To show how scientists collect data on marine life

○ To illustrate that dolphins are difficult to locate

16. *Listen again to part of the lecture by playing Track 47. Then answer the question.*

What does this example illustrate?

○ The differences between land and marine mammals

○ The importance of burst pulses as a way dolphins communicate

○ One reason dolphins travel in large groups

○ One way dolphins use signature whistles

GO ON TO THE NEXT PAGE

Listen to Track 48 on the CD.

Questions

17. Why does the student go to Professor Kirk's office?

○ To find out if he needs to take a certain class to graduate

○ To respond to Professor Kirk's invitation

○ To ask Professor Kirk to be his advisor

○ To ask Professor Kirk to sign a form

18. Why is the woman surprised at the man's request?

○ He has not tried to sign up for Introduction to Biology at the registrar's office.

○ He has waited until his senior year to take Introduction to Biology.

○ A journalism student should not need a biology class.

○ Professor Kirk no longer teaches Introduction to Biology.

19. What does the man say about his advisor?

○ She encouraged the man to take a science class.

○ She encouraged the man to major in journalism.

○ She is not aware of the man's problem.

○ She thinks very highly of Professor Kirk.

20. How will the man probably try to communicate his problem to Professor Kirk?

⭕ By calling her

⭕ By sending an email to her

⭕ By leaving her a note

⭕ By visiting her during office hours

21. *Listen to Track 49 to answer the question.* 🎧 **Play Audio**

Why does the man say this to the woman?

⭕ To thank the woman for solving his problem

⭕ To politely refuse the woman's suggestion

⭕ To explain why he needs the woman's help

⭕ To show that he understands that the woman is busy

GO ON TO THE NEXT PAGE ◣

Listen to Track 50 on the CD.

Questions

22. What is the lecture mainly about?

○ Various theories explaining why Mars cannot sustain life

○ Various causes of geological changes on Mars

○ The development of views about the nature of Mars

○ Why it has been difficult to obtain information about Mars

23. According to the professor, what was concluded about Mars after the first spacecraft flew by it in 1965?

○ It had few geological features of interest.

○ It was similar to Earth but colder.

○ It had at one time supported life.

○ It had water under its surface.

24. What does the professor imply about conditions on Mars billions of years ago? *Choose 2 answers.*

☐ Mars was probably even drier than it is today.

☐ The atmospheric pressure and the temperature may have been higher than they are today.

☐ Mars was inhabited by organisms that have since become fossilized.

☐ Large floods were shaping the planet's surface.

25. What is the possible significance of the gullies found on Mars in recent years?

○ They may indicate current volcanic activity on Mars.

○ They may indicate that the surface of Mars is becoming increasingly drier.

○ They may indicate the current existence of water on Mars.

○ They may hold fossils of organisms that once existed on Mars.

26. *Listen to Track 51 to answer the question.* 🎧 Play Audio

Why does the professor say this?

○ To stress that Mars is no longer interesting to explore

○ To describe items that the spacecraft brought back from Mars

○ To share his interest in the study of fossils

○ To show how much the view of Mars changed based on new evidence

27. *Listen again to part of the lecture by playing Track 52.* 🎧 Play Audio
    Then answer the question.

Why does the student say this?

○ To ask for clarification of a previous statement

○ To convey his opinion

○ To rephrase an earlier question

○ To express his approval

GO ON TO THE NEXT PAGE ➘

 Listen to Track 53 on the CD.

Questions

28. What does the professor mainly discuss?
○ The design and creation of the Statue of Liberty
○ The creators of two colossal statues in the United States
○ The purpose and symbolism of colossal statues
○ The cost of colossal statues in ancient versus modern times

29. What evidence does the professor give that supports the idea that modern-day colossal statues are valued social and political symbols?
○ They are very costly to build.
○ They are studied in classrooms around the world.
○ They are designed to last for thousands of years.
○ They are inspired by great poetry.

30. According to the professor, what was one result of the Great Depression of the 1930s?
○ International alliances eroded.
○ Immigration to the United States increased.
○ The public experienced a loss of confidence.
○ The government could no longer provide funds for the arts.

31. According to the professor, why did the state of South Dakota originally want to create a colossal monument?

- ○ To generate income from tourism
- ○ To symbolize the unity of society
- ○ To commemorate the Great Depression
- ○ To honor United States Presidents

32. Why does the professor discuss the poem by Emma Lazarus?

- ○ To emphasize the close relationship between literature and sculpture
- ○ To illustrate how the meaning associated with a monument can change
- ○ To stress the importance of the friendship between France and the United States
- ○ To point out a difference between Mount Rushmore and the Statue of Liberty

33. *Listen again to part of the lecture by playing Track 54. Then answer the question.*

What does the professor imply about the poem by Emma Lazarus?

- ○ It is one of his favorite poems.
- ○ Few people have read the entire poem.
- ○ He does not need to recite the full text of the poem.
- ○ Lazarus was not able to complete the poem.

STOP. This is the end of the Listening section of TOEFL iBT Practice Test 2.

SPEAKING

Directions: The following Speaking section of the test will last approximately **20 minutes**. To complete it, you will need a CD player, as well as a recording device that you can play back to listen to your responses.

During the test, you will answer six speaking questions. Two of the questions ask about familiar topics. Four questions ask about short conversations, lectures, and reading passages. You may take notes as you listen to the conversations and lectures. The questions and the reading passages are printed here. The time you will have to prepare your response and to speak is printed below each question. You should answer all of the questions as completely as possible in the time allowed. The preparation time begins immediately after you hear the question. You will be told when to begin to prepare and when to begin speaking.

Play the CD tracks listed in the test instructions. Record each of your responses.

At the end of this Practice Test you will find scripts for the audio tracks, important points for each question, directions for listening to sample spoken responses, and comments on those responses by official raters.

Questions

1. You will now be asked a question about a familiar topic. After you hear the question, you will have 15 seconds to prepare your response and 45 seconds to speak.

Now play Track 55 on the CD to hear Question 1.

What kind of reading material, such as novels, magazines, or poetry, do you most like to read in your free time? Explain why you find this kind of reading material interesting.

Preparation Time: 15 Seconds
Response Time: 45 Seconds

2. You will now be asked to give your opinion about a familiar topic. After you hear the question, you will have 15 seconds to prepare your response and 45 seconds to speak.

Now play Track 56 on the CD to hear Question 2.

Some students would prefer to live with roommates. Others would prefer to live alone. Which option would you prefer and why?

Preparation Time: 15 Seconds
Response Time: 45 Seconds

3. You will now read a short passage and then listen to a conversation on the same topic. You will then be asked a question about them. After you hear the question, you will have 30 seconds to prepare your response and 60 seconds to speak.

Now play Track 57 on the CD to hear Question 3.

Reading Time: 50 Seconds

University May Build New Student Apartments Off Campus

The Department of Student Housing is considering whether to build new student housing off campus in a residential area of town. Two of the major factors influencing the decision will be parking and space. Those who support building off campus argue that building new housing on campus would further increase the number of cars on and around campus and consume space that could be better used for future projects that the entire university community could benefit from. Supporters also say that students might even have a richer college experience by being connected to the local community and patronizing stores and other businesses in town.

The woman expresses her opinion of the university's plan. State her opinion and explain the reasons she gives for holding that opinion.

Preparation Time: 30 Seconds
Response Time: 60 Seconds

GO ON TO THE NEXT PAGE ➘

4. You will now read a short passage and then listen to a talk on the same academic topic. You will then be asked a question about them. After you hear the question, you will have 30 seconds to prepare your response and 60 seconds to speak.

Now play Track 58 on the CD to hear Question 4.

Reading Time: 45 Seconds

Actor-observer

People account for their own behavior differently from how they account for the behavior of others. When observing the behavior of others, we tend to attribute their actions to their character or their personality rather than to external factors. In contrast, we tend to explain our own behavior in terms of situational factors beyond our own control rather than attributing it to our own character. One explanation for this difference is that people are aware of the situational forces affecting them but not of situational forces affecting other people. Thus, when evaluating someone else's behavior, we focus on the person rather than the situation.

Explain how the two examples discussed by the professor illustrate differences in the ways people explain behavior.

Preparation Time: 30 Seconds
Response Time: 60 Seconds

5. You will now listen to a conversation. You will then be asked a question about it. After you hear the question, you will have 20 seconds to prepare your response and 60 seconds to speak.

Now play Track 59 on the CD to hear Question 5.

The speakers discuss two possible solutions to the woman's problem. Briefly summarize the problem. Then state which solution you prefer and why.

Preparation Time: 20 Seconds
Response Time: 60 Seconds

GO ON TO THE NEXT PAGE

6. *You will now listen to part of a lecture. You will then be asked a question about it. After you hear the question, you will have 20 seconds to prepare your response and 60 seconds to speak.*

Now play Track 60 on the CD to hear Question 6.

Using points and examples from the talk, explain how learning art can impact a child's development.

Preparation Time: 20 Seconds
Response Time: 60 Seconds

STOP. This is the end of the Speaking section of TOEFL iBT Practice Test 2.

WRITING

Directions: This section measures your ability to use writing to communicate in an academic environment. There will be two writing tasks.

For the first writing task, you will read a passage and listen to a lecture and then answer a question based on what you have read and heard. For the second task, you will answer a question based on your own knowledge and experience.

At the end of this Practice Test you will find a script for the audio track, topic notes, sample test taker essays, and comments on those essays by official raters.

Turn the page to see the directions for the first writing task.

Writing Based on Reading and Listening

Directions: For this task, you will read a passage about an academic topic and you will listen to a lecture about the same topic. You may take notes while you read and listen.

Then you will write a response to a question that asks you about the relationship between the lecture you heard and the reading passage. Try to answer the question as completely as possible using information from the reading passage and the lecture. The question does not ask you to express your personal opinion. You may refer to the reading passage again when you write. You may use your notes to help you answer the question.

Typically, an effective response will be 150 to 225 words. Your response will be judged on the quality of your writing and on the completeness and accuracy of the content.

You should allow **3 minutes** to read the passage. Then listen to the lecture. Then allow **20 minutes** to plan and write your response.

Write your response in the space provided.

Professors are normally found in university classrooms, offices, and libraries doing research and lecturing to their students. More and more, however, they also appear as guests on television news programs, giving expert commentary on the latest events in the world. These television appearances are of great benefit to the professors themselves as well as to their universities and the general public.

Professors benefit from appearing on television because by doing so they acquire reputations as authorities in their academic fields among a much wider audience than they have on campus. If a professor publishes views in an academic journal, only other scholars will learn about and appreciate those views. But when a professor appears on TV, thousands of people outside the narrow academic community become aware of the professor's ideas. So when professors share their ideas with a television audience, the professors' importance as scholars is enhanced.

Universities also benefit from such appearances. The universities receive positive publicity when their professors appear on TV. When people see a knowledgeable faculty member of a university on television, they think more highly of that university. That then leads to an improved reputation for the university. And that improved reputation in turn leads to more donations for the university and more applications from potential students.

Finally, the public gains from professors' appearing on television. Most television viewers normally have no contact with university professors. When professors appear on television, viewers have a chance to learn from experts and to be exposed to views they might otherwise never hear about. Television is generally a medium for commentary that tends to be superficial, not deep or thoughtful. From professors on television, by contrast, viewers get a taste of real expertise and insight.

Now play Track 61 on the CD.

Question

Summarize the points made in the lecture, being sure to explain how they oppose specific points made in the reading passage.

You must finish your answer in 20 minutes.

_____

_____

_____

_____

_____

_____

_____

_____

_____

_____

_____

GO ON TO THE NEXT PAGE ↘

Writing Based on Knowledge and Experience

Directions: For this task, you will write an essay in response to a question that asks you to state, explain, and support your opinion on an issue.

Typically, an effective essay will contain a minimum of 300 words. Your essay will be judged on the quality of your writing. This includes the development of your ideas, the organization of your essay, and the quality and accuracy of the language you use to express your ideas.

You have **30 minutes** to plan and complete your essay.

Write your essay in the space provided.

Question

Do you agree or disagree with the following statement?

Young people enjoy life more than older people do.

Use specific reasons and examples to support your answer.

_____

_____

_____

_____

_____

_____

_____

_____

_____

_____

_____

_____

_____

_____

GO ON TO THE NEXT PAGE

STOP. This is the end of the Writing section of TOEFL iBT Practice Test 2.

Answers, Explanations, and Listening Scripts

Reading

Answer Key and Self-scoring Chart

Directions: Check your answers against the answer key below. Write the number 1 on the line to the right of each question if you picked the correct answer. (For questions worth more than one point, follow the directions given.) Total your points at the bottom of the chart.

Question Number	Correct Answer	Your Raw Points
Feeding Habits of East African Herbivores		
1.	3	_____
2.	2	_____
3.	4	_____
4.	4	_____
5.	3	_____
6.	3	_____
7.	2	_____
8.	1	_____
9.	1	_____
10.	4	_____
11.	2	_____
12.	3	_____
13.	4	_____

For question 14, write 2 if you picked all three correct answers. Write 1 if you picked two correct answers.

14.	2,4,5	_____

Question Number	Correct Answer	Your Raw Points
Loie Fuller		
1.	3	_____
2.	4	_____
3.	1	_____
4.	1	_____
5.	3	_____
6.	4	_____
7.	4	_____
8.	3	_____
9.	3	_____
10.	2	_____
11.	1	_____
12.	1	_____
13.	4	_____

For question 14, write 2 if you picked all three correct answers. Write 1 if you picked two correct answers.

14.	3,4,5	_____

Question Number	Correct Answer	Your Raw Points
Green Icebergs		
1.	3	_____
2.	2	_____
3.	4	_____
4.	2	_____
5.	1	_____
6.	4	_____
7.	3	_____
8.	1	_____
9.	1	_____
10.	4	_____
11.	2	_____
12.	3	_____
13.	2	_____

For question 14, write 2 if you picked all three correct answers. Write 1 if you picked two correct answers.

14.	3,4,6	_____
TOTAL:		_____

Below is a table that converts your Reading section answers into a TOEFL iBT Reading scaled score. Take the total of raw points from your answer key and find that number in the left-hand column of the table. The right-hand column of the table gives a TOEFL iBT Reading scaled score for each number of raw points. For example, if the total points from your answer key is 26, the table shows a scaled score of 18.

You should use your score estimate as a general guide only. Your actual score on the TOEFL iBT test may be higher or lower than your score on the practice version.

Reading Comprehension

Raw Point Total	Scaled Score	Raw Point Total	Scaled Score
45	30	22	14
44	30	21	13
43	29	20	12
42	29	19	11
41	29	18	9
40	28	17	8
39	28	16	7
38	27	15	6
37	27	14	5
36	26	13	4
35	26	12	3
34	25	11	2
33	24	10	1
32	23	9	0
31	23	8	0
30	22	7	0
29	21	6	0
28	20	5	0
27	19	4	0
26	18	3	0
25	17	2	0
24	16	1	0
23	15	0	0

Answer Explanations

Feeding Habits of East African Herbivores

1. **3** This is a Vocabulary question. The word being tested is *illusory*. It is highlighted in paragraph 1. The correct answer is choice 3, "misleading." In other words, the idea that all East African herbivores have the same diet is false, or misleading.

2. **2** This is a Vocabulary question. The word being tested is *sparsely*. It is highlighted in paragraph 1. The correct answer is choice 2, "thinly." In other words, highly nutritious fruits can be found only in small quantities and in few areas, so we say that they are thinly distributed.

3. **4** This is a Negative Factual Information question asking for specific information that can be found in paragraph 1. The correct answer is choice 4. While the text states clearly that buffalo were not studied, it never states *why* they were not studied. The text provides the answer to the question in choice 1 by stating that Thomson's gazelles eat a large amount of fruit. The text provides the answer to the question in choice 2 by stating that wildebeests prefer to eat leaves. The text provides the answer to the question in choice 3 by indicating that the study took place on the Serengeti Plain in East Africa.

4. **4** This is a Vocabulary question. The word being tested is *associated*. It is highlighted in paragraph 2. The correct answer is choice 4, "connected." In other words, the differences between the species are related, or connected.

5. **3** This is a Rhetorical Purpose question. It is asking you why the author mentions the cow and the horse in paragraph 2. The correct answer is choice 3. Cows and horses are animals that are familiar to most people, so they are a useful reference point for the reader to understand the types of animals that are ruminants and nonruminants. Choice 1 is incorrect because the author is actually trying to show that the digestive systems of cows and horses are similar to those of some East African mammals. Choice 2 is incorrect because there is no comparison made between the body size of cows and horses and that of East African mammals. The effect of body size on the feeding habits of East African mammals is discussed in paragraph 3. Choice 4 is incorrect because the diets of cows and horses are not discussed at all in the passage. Therefore a comparison to the diets of East African mammals cannot be emphasized or even made.

6. **3** This is a Factual Information question asking for specific information that can be found in paragraph 2. The correct answer is choice 3. The paragraph describes in detail the large amount of low-quality stems that zebras eat. The gazelle, wildebeest, and topi given in choices 1, 2, and 4, respectively, are all ruminants. The paragraph states specifically that ruminants are able to derive

a large amount of energy from a given quantity of food, unlike nonruminants such as zebras.

7. ❷ This is an Inference question asking for an inference that can be supported by paragraph 2. The correct answer is choice 2, "The differences in stomach structure." Paragraph 2 is devoted to discussing the differences in feeding preferences that result from the different digestive systems, and therefore different stomach structures, of ruminants and nonruminants. The factors given in choices 1, 3, and 4 are all mentioned in paragraph 2, but they are more indirectly and occasionally related to feeding preferences, whereas the differences in stomach structures are shown in the paragraph to always be the primary factor in feeding preferences.

8. ❶ This is a Negative Factual Information question asking for specific information that can be found in paragraph 2. The correct answer is choice 1. The paragraph states that gazelles are ruminants and that it "takes time" for ruminants to digest their food. Therefore it is incorrect to say that gazelles digest their food quickly. The information given in choices 2, 3, and 4 is stated in the paragraph as facts about ruminants.

9. ❶ This is a Vocabulary question. The phrase being tested is *provided that*. It is highlighted in the paragraph. The correct answer is choice 1, "as long as." In other words, small animals can live with less food as long as, or if, that food has enough energy.

10. ❹ This is a Vocabulary question. The word being tested is *fastidious*. It is highlighted in the passage. The correct answer is choice 4, "demanding." In other words, zebras are not very demanding or particular feeders.

11. ❷ This is a Factual Information question asking for specific information that can be found in paragraph 4. The correct answer is choice 2, "Zebra." The paragraph states that zebras arrive first at a given habitat and "The later species all depend on the preparations of" the zebra. According to sentences 4 and 5, the topi, wildebeest, and gazelle given in choices 1, 3, and 4, respectively, all arrive at a given habitat after the zebra and therefore benefit from the results of the zebra's actions on the vegetation of the habitat.

12. ❸ This is a Factual Information question asking for specific information that can be found in the passage. The correct answer is choice 3. Paragraph 2 states that zebras wear down the vegetation in a given habitat, and then ruminants, such as wildebeests, arrive to feed on the remaining, lower, leafier vegetation. Paragraph 1 supports this idea by stating that wildebeests prefer to eat lower leaves. Choice 1 is contradicted in several places: paragraphs 1 and 2 each state that zebras eat stems, and wildebeests eat leaves. Choice 2 is contradicted in paragraph 2, which states that large food particles simply cannot pass through the digestive system of ruminants such as wildebeests. Choice 4 is contradicted in paragraph 2, which states that ruminants such as

wildebeests do not have to resort to eating low-quality food because they can derive energy from the same quantity of food for a long time.

13. ❹ This is an Insert Text question. You can see the four black squares in paragraph 4 that represent the possible answer choices here.

> The differences in feeding preferences lead, in turn, to differences in migratory habits. ■ The wildebeests follow, in their migration, the pattern of local rainfall. ■ The other species do likewise. ■ But when a new area is fueled by rain, the mammals migrate toward it in a set order to exploit it. ■ The larger, less fastidious feeders, the zebras, move in first; the choosier, smaller wildebeests come later; and the smallest species of all, Thomson's gazelle, arrives last. The later species all depend on the preparations of the earlier one, for the actions of the zebra alter the vegetation to suit the demands of the wildebeest, topi, and gazelle.

The sentence provided, "The sequence in which they migrate correlates with their body size," is best inserted at square 4.

Square 4 is correct because the phrase "The sequence" refers to the set order in which mammals migrate, which is mentioned in the sentence preceding square 4. Furthermore, the phrase "correlates with their body size" prepares the reader for the discussion of the larger, smaller, and smallest animals mentioned in the sentence following square 4.

Squares 1, 2, and 3 are incorrect because none of the preceding or following sentences makes a clear reference to a sequence or to body size.

14. ❷❹❺ This is a Prose Summary question. It is completed correctly below. The correct choices are 2, 4, and 5. Choices 1, 3, and 6 are therefore incorrect.

Directions: An introductory sentence for a brief summary of the passage is provided below. Complete the summary by selecting the THREE answer choices that express the most important ideas in the passage. Some answer choices do not belong in the summary because they express ideas that are not presented in the passage or are minor ideas in the passage. **This question is worth 2 points.**

East African herbivores, though they all live in the same environment, have a range of feeding preferences.

- An herbivore's size and metabolic rate affect the kinds of food and the quantities of food it needs to eat.
- The different digestive systems of herbivores explain their feeding preferences.
- Migratory habits are influenced by feeding preferences.

Answer Choices

1. The survival of East African mammals depends more than anything else on the quantity of highly nutritious fruits that they are able to find.

2. An herbivore's size and metabolic rate affect the kinds of food and the quantities of food it needs to eat.

3. Zebras and wildebeests rarely compete for the same food resources in the same locations.

4. The different digestive systems of herbivores explain their feeding preferences.

5. Migratory habits are influenced by feeding preferences.

6. Patterns in the migratory habits of East African herbivores are hard to establish.

Correct Choices

Choice 2, "An herbivore's size and metabolic rate affect the kinds of food and the quantities of food it needs to eat," is correct because it is a main idea introduced in paragraph 2 and elaborated on in paragraph 3. Sentence 2 in paragraph 2 states that body size is one of two main factors that explain feeding preferences. Paragraph 3 then explains in detail why body size is a main factor.

Choice 4, "The different digestive systems of herbivores explain their feeding preferences," is correct because it is a major idea that is elaborated on at length in paragraph 2. This paragraph details the different digestive systems of ruminants and nonruminants and then describes the resulting feeding habits of those two types of mammals.

Choice 5, "Migratory habits are influenced by feeding preferences," is correct because this is a major idea that is introduced in paragraph 2 and elaborated on in paragraph 4. It is a logical follow-up to the discussion in paragraphs 1 and 2 of the reasons for different feeding preferences.

Incorrect Choices

Choice 1, "The survival of East African mammals depends more than anything else on the quantity of highly nutritious fruits that they are able to find," is incorrect according to the passage. Paragraph 1 states that only Thomson's gazelles eat fruit. Other East African mammals discussed in the passage eat only stems and leaves.

Choice 3, "Zebras and wildebeests rarely compete for the same food resources in the same locations," is incorrect because it is a minor idea in the passage. The feeding habits of zebras and wildebeests are discussed in the passage as specific examples of the larger ideas given in choices 2, 4, and 5.

Choice 6, "Patterns in the migratory habits of East African herbivores are hard to establish," is contradicted by the passage. Paragraph 4 states that species follow the pattern of local rainfall in their migrations.

Loie Fuller

1. ❸ This is an Inference question asking about an inference that can be supported by paragraph 1. The correct answer is choice 3. The phrase "mere entertainer" in sentence 2 suggests that entertainment is less serious than art. Choice 1 is incorrect because we know only that other artists were attracted to Loie Fuller as an artist; there is no information about what fields these artists were in or if their work was actually influenced by Loie Fuller. Choice 2 is incorrect because there is no information about theatrical dance in the early nineteenth century. Choice 4 is incorrect because there is no indication in the paragraph about the length of time theatrical dance had been practiced.

2. ❹ This is a Negative Factual Information question asking for specific information that can be found in paragraph 2. Choice 4 is the correct answer. Sentence 2 in the paragraph states that Loie Fuller rejected technical virtuosity, so it cannot be a characteristic of her type of dance. The information in choices 1, 2, and 3 is stated in sentence 1 as part of her type of dance.

3. ❶ This is a Vocabulary question. The word being tested is *prestigious*. It is highlighted in the passage. The correct answer is choice 1, "highly regarded." According to the paragraph, ballet was a distinguished, or highly regarded, dance form.

4. ❶ This is a Sentence Simplification question. As with all of these questions, a single sentence in the passage is highlighted:

> Although her early theatrical career had included stints as an actress, she was not primarily interested in storytelling or expressing emotions through dance; the drama of her dancing emanated from her visual effects.

The correct answer is choice 1. Choice 1 contains all of the essential information in the tested sentence. It omits the information in the first clause ("Although her early theatrical career had included stints as an actress") because this information is secondary to Loie Fuller's main interest in dance.

Choices 2, 3, and 4 are all incorrect because they change the meaning of the highlighted sentence. Choices 2 and 3 are incorrect because the highlighted sentence states that Fuller was not interested in storytelling, so to say that she dramatized stories or had a particular style of storytelling is incorrect.

Choice 4 is incorrect because the highlighted sentence indicates the opposite idea: it indicates that Fuller's early career had little effect on her style of dance.

5. ❸ This is a Vocabulary question. The word being tested is *engaged*. It is highlighted in the passage. The correct answer is choice 3, "hired." In other words, Fuller began to work for the Folies Bergère.

6. ❹ This is a Vocabulary question. The word being tested is *synthesize*. It is highlighted in the passage. The correct answer is choice 4, "integrate." According to the passage, French poets and painters wanted to blend, or integrate, form and content.

7. ❹ This is a Factual Information question asking for specific information that can be found in paragraph 3. The correct answer is choice 4. Sentence 2 in this paragraph states that Fuller's dances were in accord, or agreed, with the Art Nouveau style that was fashionable in Paris at the time. Choice 1 is incorrect because the paragraph says only that Parisian audiences liked Fuller's work; artists and artistic movements from the United States, in general, are not mentioned in this paragraph. Choice 2 is incorrect because the paragraph states that poets themselves were interested in Fuller's work. It does not state that poets tried to make other people interested in her work. Choice 3 is incorrect because the paragraph states in the first sentence that Fuller discovered and introduced her ideas herself; she did not borrow or take them from other artists.

8. ❸ This is a Factual Information question asking for specific information that can be found in paragraph 4. The correct answer is choice 3. Sentence 4 in the paragraph states that Fuller invented the technique of underlighting, or lighting the dancer from beneath. Choices 1, 2, and 4 are incorrect because they inaccurately describe how certain techniques were used by Fuller. Furthermore, none of these techniques is mentioned in connection with Fuller's *Fire Dance*.

9. ❸ This is a Rhetorical Purpose question asking why the author mentions Fuller's dance titled *The Sea*. The correct answer is choice 3. The paragraph begins by stating that aspects of Fuller's expertise with dance grew along with her technical expertise. *The Sea* is mentioned as an example of one way that Fuller's expertise grew, or one way that she developed as an artist, which, in this case, is in the scope of her themes. Choices 1 and 2 are incorrect because *The Sea* is not mentioned in connection with the use of music. Choice 4 is incorrect because *The Sea* is not mentioned in connection with science. The paragraph states that science is the theme of a different dance by Fuller, the *Radium Dance*.

10. ❷ This is a Vocabulary question. The word being tested is *agitated*. It is highlighted in the passage. The correct answer is choice 2, "created movement in." According to the paragraph, Fuller's dancers made a large piece of silk move.

11. ❶ This is a Factual Information question asking for specific information that can be found in paragraph 6. The correct answer is choice 1. Sentence 1 in this paragraph states that Fuller presented works by another artist, Sada Yocco. Choice 2 is incorrect because the paragraph states that Fuller created

an all-female dance company at the time of the Paris Exposition, but we do not know if that company, or any particular company, performed in Fuller's theater. Choice 3 is incorrect because the paragraph states only that she established a school in 1908; we do not know that the school directly resulted from the Paris Exposition. Furthermore, we do not know from the paragraph that a school exists today that is named after Fuller. Choice 4 is incorrect because the paragraph does not state that Fuller's theater continued to operate after the Paris Exposition ended.

12. ❶ This is a Factual Information question asking for specific information that can be found in the passage. The correct answer is choice 1. *Fire Dance* is discussed in paragraph 4. It was performed to the music of Richard Wagner. The works given in choices 2, 3, and 4 are all mentioned in the passage, but only choice 2, *Radium Dance*, is a work by Fuller. However, the passage does not say that it was set to music. *Le Lys de la Vie* is a film, and *Valse à la Loie* is a dance by another artist.

13. ❹ This is an Insert Text question. You can see the four black squares in paragraph 5 that represent the possible answer choices here.

As her technological expertise grew more sophisticated, so did other aspects of her dances. ■ Although she gave little thought to music in her earliest dances, she later used scores by Gluck, Beethoven, Schubert, Chopin, and Wagner, eventually graduating to Stravinsky, Fauré, Debussy, and Mussorgsky, composers who were then considered progressive. ■ She began to address more ambitious themes in her dances such as *The Sea*, in which her dancers invisibly agitated a huge expanse of silk, played upon by colored lights. ■ Always open to scientific and technological innovations, she befriended the scientists Marie and Pierre Curie upon their discovery of radium and created *Radium Dance*, which simulated the phosphorescence of that element. ■ She both appeared in films—then in an early stage of development—and made them herself; the hero of her fairy-tale film *Le Lys de la Vie* (1919) was played by René Clair, later a leading French film director.

The sentence provided, "For all of her originality in dance, her interests expanded beyond it into newly emerging artistic media," is best inserted at square 4.

The "newly emerging artistic media" are elaborated on with the information about films in the sentence following square 4.

Squares 1, 2, and 3 are incorrect because the information provided in the sentences before and after each of these squares is focused on Fuller's dance work, whereas the given sentence directs the reader away from Fuller's dance work and toward other forms of art.

14. ❸❹❺ This is a Prose Summary question. It is completed correctly below. The correct choices are 3, 4, and 5. Choices 1, 2, and 6 are therefore incorrect.

Directions: An introductory sentence for a brief summary of the passage is provided below. Complete the summary by selecting the THREE answer choices that express the most important ideas in the passage. Some answer choices do not belong in the summary because they express ideas that are not presented in the passage or are minor ideas in the passage. **This question is worth 2 points.**

Loie Fuller was an important and innovative dancer.

- Fuller's work influenced a number of other dancers who were interested in experimental dance.
- Fuller introduced many technical innovations to the staging of theatrical dance.
- Fuller continued to develop throughout her career, creating more complex works and exploring new artistic media.

Answer Choices

1. Fuller believed that audiences in the late nineteenth century had lost interest in most theatrical dance.

2. Fuller transformed dance in part by creating dance interpretations of works by poets and painters.

3. Fuller's work influenced a number of other dancers who were interested in experimental dance.

4. Fuller introduced many technical innovations to the staging of theatrical dance.

5. Fuller continued to develop throughout her career, creating more complex works and exploring new artistic media.

6. By the 1920s, Fuller's theater at the Paris Exposition had become the world center for innovative dance.

Correct Choices

Choice 3: "Fuller's work influenced a number of other dancers who were interested in experimental dance." This is a main idea, presented in paragraph 6. Fuller's influence on dancers who later became famous for their own work is discussed.

Choice 4: "Fuller introduced many technical innovations to the staging of theatrical dance." This is a main theme of the passage that is repeated in several paragraphs. Her technical innovations are detailed at length in paragraph 4 but are also mentioned in paragraphs 5 and 6.

Choice 5: "Fuller continued to develop throughout her career, creating more complex works and exploring new artistic media." This main idea is the focus of paragraph 5, which discusses her use of music, the more complex themes that she addressed in her dances, and also the films that she appeared in and directed.

Choice 1, "Fuller believed that audiences in the late nineteenth century had lost interest in most theatrical dance," is incorrect because, while it could be true, the passage never makes this claim. The passage suggests only that Fuller lost interest in theatrical dance.

Choice 2, "Fuller transformed dance in part by creating dance interpretations of works by poets and painters," is incorrect because the passage does not state that Fuller based her dances on the works of other artists. The passage states several times that Fuller's work was entirely original: she developed her own work and, in fact, invented many techniques.

Choice 6, "By the 1920s, Fuller's theater at the Paris Exposition had become the world center for innovative dance," is incorrect because Fuller's theater existed for only one year, the year of the Paris Exposition (1900). Furthermore, the passage makes no claim about any particular place as being the "center for innovative dance."

Green Icebergs

1. ❸ This is a Negative Factual Information question testing specific information in paragraph 1. The correct answer is choice 3. The information in choice 3 is contradicted in sentence 1, which states that icebergs "float with only about 12 percent of their mass above the sea surface." The information given in the other choices is stated in the paragraph.

2. ❷ This is a Factual Information question testing specific information in paragraph 2. The correct answer is choice 2. The information in choice 2 is taken directly from sentence 1 in the paragraph, which states that icebergs "sometimes appear dark or opaque because they carry gravel and bits of rock." Choice 1 is incorrect because, as sentence 2 states, cloud cover may result in "pink or gold" colors, not dark colors. Choice 3 is incorrect because "the low angle of the Sun above the horizon" is discussed as a possible cause of pink or gold colors. Choice 4 is incorrect because the issue of large cracks in icebergs is not discussed in paragraph 2.

3. ❹ This is a Sentence Simplification question. As with all of these questions, a single sentence in the passage is highlighted:

One explanation for green icebergs attributes their color to an optical illusion when blue ice is illuminated by a near-horizon red Sun, but green icebergs stand out among white and blue icebergs under a great variety of light conditions.

The correct answer is choice 4. This choice contains all of the essential information, which is that (1) one explanation for the color of green icebergs is that the green color is due to an optical illusion related to the position of the Sun, but that (2) there is reason to doubt this theory because green icebergs stand out among white and blue icebergs under a great variety of light conditions.

Choice 1 is incorrect because it confuses the evidence against the theory with the theory itself.

Choice 2 correctly explains the theory but leaves out the essential information of the evidence against the theory.

Choice 3 is incorrect because it misrepresents the theory by saying that the green color occurs in a wide variety of light conditions, whereas the highlighted sentence says that it occurs in a very specific light condition—"a near-horizon red Sun."

4. **②** This is a Vocabulary question. The word being tested is *penetrate*. It is highlighted in the passage. The correct answer is choice 2, "pierce." In other words, ice shelf cores were long enough to pierce through glacial ice.

5. **①** This is a Factual Information question testing specific information in paragraph 4. The correct answer is choice 1. Sentence 1 in the paragraph discusses "glacial ice—which is formed from the compaction of snow." Choice 2 is incorrect because the information given describes sea ice, a different type of ice. Choice 3 is incorrect because the information given describes the first step in the formation of green icebergs. Choice 4 is incorrect because the information given describes the second step in the formation of green icebergs.

6. **④** This is a Factual Information question testing specific information in paragraph 4. The correct answer is choice 4. Sentence 2 in the paragraph states that clear sea ice is "very similar" to the ice from green icebergs. Choices 1, 2, and 3 do not answer the question asked. Choice 1 is also incorrect because it mistakenly identifies green icebergs as having frozen seawater at the bottom, whereas sentence 1 in the paragraph says that frozen seawater is found on the bottom of glacial ice. Choice 2 is incorrect because the information given is the opposite of what is stated in the passage, which is that bubble-free ice is formed and found on the bottom of shelf ice. Choice 3 is incorrect because the information given is not discussed in the passage at all.

7. **③** This is a Rhetorical Purpose question. It tests why the author mentions that "The green ice portion was textured by seawater erosion." This sentence is highlighted in the passage. The correct answer is choice 3. The highlighted sentence is evidence that the green ice part of the iceberg was once under water. The fact that this green ice is no longer under water but is now exposed to air is evidence that the green icebergs are formed from pieces of the ice shelf that have broken off and turned upside down. Choice 1 is incorrect because the information given, while factual according to the passage, does not explain why the author includes the information that the green ice

portion was textured by seawater. Choice 2 is incorrect because there is no comparison made between the erosion of green ice and white ice in the paragraph. Choice 4 is incorrect because, while sentences 1 and 4 in the paragraph state that green ice has no bubbles, there is no information in the paragraph indicating that green ice initially has bubbles and that they are removed.

8. ❶ This is a Vocabulary question. The word being tested is *accumulated*. It is highlighted in the passage. The correct answer is choice 1, "collected." In other words, the ice gradually collected, or built up, dissolved organic matter.

9. ❶ This is a Vocabulary question. The word being tested is *excluded*. It is highlighted in the passage. The correct answer is choice 1, "kept out." In other words, dissolved organic substances are not kept out of the ice in the freezing process.

10. ❹ This is a Vocabulary question. The word being tested is *accrete*. It is highlighted in the passage. The correct answer is choice 4, "come together." In other words, platelets of ice gather on the bottom of the ice shelf.

11. ❷ This is a Negative Factual Information question testing specific information in the passage. The correct answer is choice 2. The last sentence of paragraph 4 states that green icebergs capsize, but it does not state why. The information in choice 1 is presented in the last sentence of paragraph 1. It states that forward movement, melting, and waves and tidal action cause blocks of ice to break off of glaciers. The information in choice 3 is presented in paragraph 7, which says that the Amery Ice Shelf in Antarctica is "uniquely suited to the production of green icebergs." The information in choice 4 is presented at the end of paragraph 5. It states that "dissolved organic substances are not excluded from the ice in the freezing process."

12. ❸ This is an Inference question asking for an inference that can be supported by the passage. The correct answer is choice 3. Sentences 5, 6, and 7 in paragraph 5 support this information by indicating that the seawater around these icebergs contains the decomposing material of green-pigmented organisms. This decomposing material dissolves in seawater, which then freezes as part of the iceberg. The information in choice 1 is incorrect because paragraph 7 says that the Amery Ice Shelf is well suited to the production of green icebergs. This does not mean that the Amery Ice Shelf produces *only* green icebergs. The information in choice 2 is incorrect because copper and iron are mentioned in paragraph 3 only as *possible* color sources in green icebergs. The last sentence in paragraph 3 states that a source other than copper and iron was found. The information in choice 4 is incorrect because the passage gives no indication of where all green icebergs are located. Paragraph

2 mentions the Weddell Sea in Antarctica, and paragraph 7 states that green icebergs "drift" around Antarctica. Therefore green icebergs can be found far from the Amery Ice Shelf.

13. ❷ This is an Insert Text question. You can see the four black squares in paragraphs 2 and 3 that represent the possible answer choices here.

Icebergs are ordinarily blue to white, although they sometimes appear dark or opaque because they carry gravel and bits of rock. They may change color with changing light conditions or cloud cover, glowing pink or gold in the morning or evening light, but this color change is generally related to the low angle of the Sun above the horizon. ■ However, travelers to Antarctica have repeatedly reported seeing green icebergs in the Weddell Sea and, more commonly, close to the Amery Ice Shelf in East Antarctica.

   ■ One explanation for green icebergs attributes their color to an optical illusion when blue ice is illuminated by a near-horizon red Sun, but green icebergs stand out among white and blue icebergs under a great variety of light conditions. ■ Another suggestion is that color might be related to ice with high levels of metallic compounds, including copper and iron. ■ Recent expeditions have taken ice samples from green icebergs and ice cores—vertical, cylindrical ice samples reaching down to great depths—from the glacial ice shelves along the Antarctic continent. Analyses of these cores and samples provide a different solution to the problem.

The sentence provided, "Scientists have differed as to whether icebergs appear green as a result of light conditions or because of something in the ice itself," is best inserted at square 2.

Square 2 is correct because the sentence provided introduces two possible explanations for the color of green icebergs. Paragraph 3 is the first place in the passage where explanations are offered for the color of green icebergs. The beginning of paragraph 3 is the only appropriate place to introduce these possible explanations.

Square 1 is incorrect because green icebergs are mentioned for the first time in the last sentence in paragraph 2. It does not make sense to insert the given sentence, which introduces explanations for the color of green icebergs, before the first mention of green icebergs.

Square 3 is incorrect because its position is *between* the detailed discussions of the two explanations introduced in the given sentence. The given sentence introduces the two explanations; therefore it must come *before* the discussions.

Square 4 is incorrect because its position is *after* the detailed discussions of the two explanations introduced in the given sentence. The given sentence introduces the two explanations; therefore it must come *before* the discussions.

14. ❸❹❻ This is a Prose Summary question. It is completed correctly below. The correct choices are 3, 4, and 6. Choices 1, 2, and 5 are therefore incorrect.

Directions: An introductory sentence for a brief summary of the passage is provided below. Complete the summary by selecting the THREE answer choices that express the most important ideas in the passage. Some answer choices do not belong in the summary because they express ideas that are not presented in the passage or are minor ideas in the passage. **This question is worth 2 points.**

Several suggestions, ranging from light conditions to the presence of metallic compounds, have been offered to explain why some icebergs appear green.

- Green icebergs form when a two-layer block of ice breaks away from a glacier and capsizes, exposing the bottom sea ice to view.
- Ice cores and samples revealed that both ice shelves and green icebergs contain a layer of bubbly glacial ice and a layer of bubble-free sea ice.
- In a green iceberg, the sea ice contains large concentrations of organic matter from the seawater.

Answer Choices

1. Ice cores were used to determine that green icebergs were formed from the compaction of metallic compounds, including copper and iron.

2. All ice shelves can produce green icebergs, but the Amery Ice Shelf is especially well suited to do so.

3. Green icebergs form when a two-layer block of ice breaks away from a glacier and capsizes, exposing the bottom sea ice to view.

4. Ice cores and samples revealed that both ice shelves and green icebergs contain a layer of bubbly glacial ice and a layer of bubble-free sea ice.

5. Green icebergs are white until they come into contact with seawater containing platelets and soluble organic green pigments.

6. In a green iceberg, the sea ice contains large concentrations of organic matter from the seawater.

Correct Choices

Choice 3, "Green icebergs form when a two-layer block of ice breaks away from a glacier and capsizes, exposing the bottom sea ice to view," is correct because it summarizes important parts of paragraphs 4 and 5. These explain that green icebergs are capsized pieces of ice that have broken off of an ice shelf.

Choice 4, "Ice cores and samples revealed that both ice shelves and green icebergs contain a layer of bubbly glacial ice and a layer of bubble-free sea ice," is correct because it summarizes the key information in paragraphs 3 and 4 that explains how scientists were able to determine how green icebergs are formed. The scientists compared ice from green icebergs to ice from ice shelves by drilling ice core samples out of ice shelves.

Choice 6, "In a green iceberg, the sea ice contains large concentrations of organic matter from the seawater," is correct because it summarizes the key information from paragraph 5 about the source of the green pigments in green icebergs.

Incorrect Choices

Choice 1, "Ice cores were used to determine that green icebergs were formed from the compaction of metallic compounds, including copper and iron," is incorrect because it is factually incorrect according to the passage. The last sentence in paragraph 3 contradicts this idea.

Choice 2, "All ice shelves can produce green icebergs, but the Amery Ice Shelf is especially well suited to do so," is incorrect because the passage does not state at any point that ice shelves other than the Amery Ice Shelf can produce green icebergs.

Choice 5, "Green icebergs are white until they come into contact with seawater containing platelets and soluble organic green pigments," is incorrect because the passage never discusses whether green icebergs are originally white, or any particular color.

Listening

Answer Key and Self-scoring Chart

Directions: Check your answers against the answer key below. Write the number 1 on the line to the right of each question if you picked the correct answer. Total your points at the bottom of the chart.

Question Number	Correct Answer	Your Raw Points
1.	2	_____
2.	4	_____
3.	3	_____
4.	4	_____
5.	2	_____
6.	3	_____
7.	1	_____
8.	1	_____
9.	4	_____
10.	2	_____
11.	1	_____
12.	4	_____
13.	3	_____
14.	2	_____
15.	1	_____
16.	4	_____
17.	4	_____
18.	2	_____
19.	1	_____
20.	3	_____
21.	2	_____
22.	3	_____
23.	1	_____

For question 24, write 1 if you picked both correct answers. Write 0 if you picked only one correct answer or no correct answers.

24.	2,4	_____
25.	3	_____
26.	4	_____
27.	2	_____
28.	3	_____
29.	1	_____
30.	3	_____
31.	1	_____
32.	2	_____
33.	3	_____
TOTAL:		_____

Below is a table that converts your Listening section answers into a TOEFL iBT Listening scaled score. Take the total of raw points from your answer key and find that number in the left-hand column of the table. The right-hand column of the table gives a TOEFL iBT Listening scaled score for each total of raw points. For example, if the total points from your answer key is 27, the table shows a scaled score of 23.

You should use your score estimate as a general guide only. Your actual score on the TOEFL iBT test may be higher or lower than your score on the practice version.

Listening

Raw Point Total	Scaled Score
33	30
32	29
31	28
30	27
29	26
28	25
27	23
26	22
25	21
24	19
23	18
22	17
21	15
20	14
19	13
18	11
17	10
16	9
15	8
14	7
13	6
12	5
11	5
10	4
9	3
8	3
7	2
6	2
5	1
4	0
3	0
2	0
1	0
0	0

Listening Scripts and Answer Explanations

Questions 1–5

Track 43 Listening Script

Narrator

Listen to a conversation between a student and a professor.

Professor

Sandy, how's class been going for you this semester?

Female Student

[genuine enthusiasm] Oh, it's great. I really like your business psychology class, but I have one major concern about the last assignment: you know—the one where we have to interview a local business owner, uh, I mean entrepreneur?

Professor

Are you having trouble coming up with interview questions?

Female Student

Well, that's just it. I mean I worked on my high school newspaper for years, so I actually have great questions to ask. The thing is . . . I'm new to the area, and I don't know people off campus . . . So I was wondering if . . . well, could you possibly give me the name of someone I could interview . . . ?

Professor

You don't know anyone who owns a business?

Female Student

Well, yeah, back home . . . my next-door neighbors—they own a shoe store, and they're really successful—but they're not local.

Professor

Well, it wouldn't be fair to the other students if I gave you the name of a contact—but I could help you figure out a way to find someone on your own. Let's see . . . Do you read the local newspaper?

Female Student

Sure, whenever I have the time.

Professor

Well, the business section in the paper often has stories about local business people who've been successful. If you find an article, you could call the person who is profiled.

Female Student

You mean, just call them up . . . out of the blue . . . and ask them if they'll talk to me?

Professor

Sure, why not?

Female Student

Well, aren't people like that awfully busy? Too busy to talk to a random college student.

Professor

Many people enjoy telling the story of how they got started. Remember, this is a business psychology class, and for this assignment, I want you to get some real insight about business owners, their personality, what drives them to become an entrepreneur.

Female Student

Like, how they think?

Professor

And what motivates them. Why did they start their business? I'm sure they'd talk to you, especially if you tell them you might start a business someday.

Female Student

I'm not sure I'd have the guts to do that. Opening a business seems so risky, so scary.

Professor

Well, you can ask them if they felt that way too. Now you just need to find someone to interview to see if your instincts are correct.

Track 44 Listening Script (Question 5)

Narrator

Listen again to part of the conversation.

Professor

Are you having trouble coming up with interview questions?

Student

Well, that's just it. I mean I worked on my high school newspaper for years, so I actually have great questions to ask.

Narrator

What does the student imply?

Answer Explanations

1. ❷ This is a Gist-purpose question. This type of question is typically asked first in listening conversations that take place in a professor's office. At the beginning of the conversation, the student explains that she does not know anyone off campus to interview for her business class assignment and asks the professor if he could recommend someone. This is why she came to his

office, so choice 2 is correct. The student mentions that she has already written her questions; therefore she does not need suggestions on how to write them (choice 1). She does not ask for advice on how she might start a business (choice 3). She does not say anything about scheduling an interview or any further meetings with the professor (choice 4).

2. ❹ This is an Understanding the Function of What Is Said question. Choice 1 is incorrect because the interview is for a class assignment, not for publication in a newspaper. The student suggests that working on her high school newspaper has made part of the assignment—coming up with questions—easy for her, not difficult (choice 2). And while it may be true that she enjoys newspaper work (choice 3), that is not why she mentions her high school paper. She mentions it to show she is an experienced interviewer; thus the correct choice is 4.

3. ❸ This is a Detail question. To help the student solve her problem, the professor does not offer a list of business owners (choice 1), nor does he offer to change the due date of the student's assignment (choice 4). The student mentions people who own a shoe store in her hometown, but she does not ask the professor to allow her to interview them (choice 2) because she realizes that the assignment is to interview owners of a *local* business. The professor helps the student by referring her to the business section of the local newspaper, which often prints stories about successful businesspeople in the local area; thus choice 3 is correct.

4. ❹ This is another Detail question. It is the student, not the professor, who says that opening a business seems risky (choice 1); the assignment does not involve writing an article (choice 2) or developing a detailed business plan (choice 3). The professor says explicitly that he wants the class to learn about the personalities of business owners and what motivates them. Therefore choice 4 is the correct answer.

5. ❷ This is a Making Inferences question. The conversation begins with the student telling the professor that she has a concern about the assignment, but she does not say at first exactly what her concern is. When the professor asks if she is having trouble coming up with interview questions, he is trying to find out what her specific concern is. When she says that she has written some great questions already, she is telling him indirectly that interview questions are not the problem. He has not quite identified her concern, so choice 2 is the correct answer, and choice 3, which states the opposite, is incorrect. Nothing in the student's words or tone of voice suggests that she does not want to finish the assignment (choice 4) or that she is surprised by what the professor has said to her (choice 1).

Questions 6–11

Track 45 Listening Script

Narrator

Listen to part of a lecture in an anthropology class.

Professor

OK, I, I want to begin today by talking about calendars. *[jokingly]* I know, some of you are thinking it's not all that fascinating, right? But listen, the next time you look at a calendar, I want you to keep something in mind. There are at least three natural ways of measuring the . . . the passage of time—by day, by month, and by year. And these are all pretty easy to see, right? I mean a day is based on one rotation of Earth. A month is how long the Moon takes to move around the Earth. And a year is the time it takes for Earth to move around the Sun, right? So they're all based on natural events. But the natural clocks of Earth, the Moon, and the Sun run on different times, and you can't divide any one of these time periods by another one without having some messy fraction left over. I mean one lunar month—that's the time it takes for the Moon to go around Earth—one month is about 29 and a half days . . . not really a nice round number. And one year is a little more than 365 days. So these are obviously numbers that don't divide into each other very neatly. And this makes it pretty difficult to create some sort of tidy calendar that really works.

Not that different cultures haven't tried. Have any of you ever been to Stonehenge? *[pause]* No . . . you know, that amazing circle of giant stones in England? Well, if you ever go, and find yourself wondering why this culture way back in prehistoric England would go to so much work to construct this monumental ring of enormous stones, . . . well, keep in mind that a lot of us think it was designed, at least partially, as a calendar—to mark when the seasons of the year begin, according to the exact day when the Sun comes up from a particular direction. I have colleagues who insist it's a temple, maybe, or a tomb . . . but they can't deny that it was also used as a calendar . . . probably to help figure out, for example, when farmers should begin their planting each year.

The Mayans, in Central America, also invented a calendar, but for a different purpose. The Mayans, especially the royalty and priests, wanted to look at long cycles of history—so the calendar they used had to be able to count far into the future as well as far into the past. And not only were the Mayans keeping track of the natural timekeepers we mentioned before—Earth, the Moon, and the Sun—but another natural timekeeper: the planet Venus.

Venus rises in the sky as the morning star every 584 days, and the Venus cycle was incorporated in the Mayan calendar. So the Mayans kept track of long periods of time, and they did it so accurately, in fact, that their calendar is considered about as complicated and sophisticated as any in the world.

Now, the ancient Chinese believed very strongly in astrology—the idea that you can predict future events based on the positions of the stars and planets like, say, Jupiter. Incidentally, the whole Chinese system of astrology was based on the fact that the planet Jupiter goes around the Sun once every 12 years, so one orbit of Jupiter lasts 12 of our Earth years. Apparently, that's why the Chinese calendar has a cycle of 12 years. You know, like, "The Year of the Dragon," "The Year of the Tiger," and so on . . . all parts of a 12-year astrological cycle, that we get from the orbit of Jupiter.

Calendars based on the orbits of other planets, though, are a lot less common than those based on the cycle of the Moon—the lunar month. I could mention any number of important cultures around the world that have depended on lunar calendars, but there really isn't time.

So let's go right to the calendar that's now used throughout most of the world—a solar calendar—based on the number of days in a year. This calendar's mainly derived from the one the ancient Romans devised a couple thousand years ago. I mean the Romans—with more than a little help from the Greeks—realized that a year actually lasts about 365 and one-quarter days. And so they decided to round off most years to 365 days but make every fourth year into a leap year. I mean, somehow, you have to account for that extra one-fourth of a day each year, so every four years, they made the calendar one day longer. By adding the leap year, the Romans were able to make a calendar that worked so well—that, with a few minor adjustments, this calendar is still widely used today.

Answer Explanations

6. ❸ This is a Gist-content question. Choice 3 is correct because the professor spends almost the entire lecture discussing four types of calendars used historically in England, Central America, China, and ancient Rome, as well as the modern calendar used throughout the world today. Errors in early calendars (choice 1) are not discussed; in fact, the professor emphasizes how surprisingly accurate and sophisticated these early calendars were. Choice 4 is incorrect because astrology—the belief that the position of stars and planets can predict events—is mentioned only in the context of the Chinese calendar. Why people came to believe that Earth moves around the Sun (choice 2) is not discussed at all.

7. ❶ This is an Understanding the Speaker's Attitude question. The professor indirectly expresses her certainty that Stonehenge served as a calendar by stating, "a lot of us think it was designed, at least partially, as a calendar." Her use of the pronoun *us* indicates that she includes herself in that group. When mentioning colleagues who think Stonehenge served another purpose, she adds that "they can't deny that it was also used as a calendar." Thus the correct answer is choice 1.

8. ❶ This is a Detail question. Choice 1 is correct because the professor states that the Mayans were interested in tracking long cycles of history. There is no mention of lunar months in the discussion of the Mayan calendar (choice 2). It was the ancient Chinese, not the Mayans, who wanted a calendar system to predict events (choice 3). The Mayan calendar was *based on* the appearance of Venus in the morning sky and on the movements of other natural timekeepers like Earth, but comparing the orbits of Earth and Venus (choice 4) was not the calendar's *purpose*.

9. ❹ This is another Detail question. Choice 4 is correct because the professor states that the ancient Chinese calendar was based on Jupiter's 12-year-long orbit around the Sun, not on night-day cycles (choice 1), the Moon (choice 2), or the seasons (choice 3).

10. ❷ This is also a Detail question. Choice 2 is correct because the professor says that the ancient Romans put an extra day into the calendar every 4 years to account for the actual length of a single Earth orbit, which is 365¼ days. According to the professor, this addition, which improved the calendar's precision, is what made the calendar work so well that it is still widely used.

11. ❶ This is an Understanding Organization question. Before discussing any specific calendars, the professor identifies a problem: that all calendars are based on natural astronomical cycles, which are not coordinated with one another mathematically. The professor then describes various historical calendars and the natural cycles on which they were based, ending with a description of the modern calendar and its solution to the coordination problem. Thus choice 1 is correct.

Questions 12–16

Track 46 Listening Script

Narrator

Listen to part of a lecture in a biology class.

Professor

We've been discussing animal communication. Um, today we're going to talk about dolphins. Now, dolphins make a wide range of communicative sounds and also display something called vocal learning, which is the ability of an animal to modify its vocalizations based on its experience with other animals.

Ah, there are many types of dolphin vocalizations. We, we still don't know their precise meanings—partly, I suppose, because we haven't really tried that hard to figure out their precise meanings—but we do know that dolphins use vocalizations as a way of communicating with one another. And we've categorized their vocalizations into three types: whistles, clicks, and burst pulses.

The dolphin whistles are very high-frequency sounds, ah, partially above the range of human hearing. What's fascinating is, each dolphin has a signature whistle, which is unique to each individual dolphin. It allows them to call to and identify each other. *[seeing hand raised]* Jennifer?

Female Student

Kind of like learning someone's name? So . . . do dolphin parents choose names for their children?

Professor

Well, again that's something we don't know, but we do know that no two signature whistles sound identical. And, members of the same family, their signature whistles have similar elements. Dolphins use them as contact calls—ah, they they call to each other while traveling and foraging. It helps keep the group together, and helps mothers and children find each other. Think of it like . . . ah, if you were traveling in the forest with one other person who was just out of sight, you'd call out, "Are you there?" and the other person would respond. But if there were several people in the forest, you would have to call that person's name to call to them.

In, in addition to whistles, dolphins produce clicks, which are actually sonar or sound waves. They use the clicks to communicate, but, more importantly, to navigate and hunt. How? Well, the sonar clicks bounce off objects, and then the dolphins convert the incoming signals into a three-dimensional picture . . . a, a mental map . . . of what's around them. The clicks are extremely sensitive and accurate. The sonar clicks are also very strong. And there's this theory that one reason dolphins swim side by side is to avoid interference from each other's sonar clicks. Interference would be confusing . . . it would prevent them from getting an accurate picture of their surroundings. Ah, and what's interesting is, dolphins will turn off their sonar when another dolphin passes in front.

Ah, the third category of dolphin vocalizations is burst pulses. These are all this other sounds the dolphin makes—squawks, squeals, barks, groans, and so on. Burst pulses are used to display aggression, show dominance, and attract a mate. But whistles, clicks, and burst pulses aren't the only ways dolphins communicate. Um, does anyone remember any other ways?

Male Student

In the book, it said that they also slap their tails against the water. Oh, and . . . the air that comes out when they breathe or whistle . . . the . . . ah . . . the bubble streams? They can control how the air bubbles come out. I thought that was really interesting.

Professor

Yes . . . the bubble streams are very interesting. Dolphins can identify and locate each other by their bubble streams, and they can imitate the bubble stream patterns of other dolphins . . . sort of like saying hello. So as you can see, dolphins use many different sounds and behaviors to convey messages to each other.

I'd like to tell you about when I was a graduate student . . . and . . . I spent one summer on a boat in the Atlantic Ocean studying marine life. One morning there were about 25 dolphins swimming with the boat. We could hear their clicks and whistles as they called to each other. Now, we were there as impartial scientists, to do research, but . . . how could we not notice the beauty as the bubble streams made patterns in the water and the dolphins appeared to dance and play? It's wonderful when you do fieldwork and actually experience something you've been studying in a classroom. So if you ever have the opportunity . . . go for it.

Track 47 Listening Script (Question 16)

Narrator

Listen again to part of the lecture. Then answer the question.

Professor

Think of it like . . . ah, if you were traveling in the forest with one other person who was just out of sight, you'd call out, "Are you there?" and the other person would respond. But if there were several people in the forest, you would have to call that person's name to call to them.

Narrator
What does this example illustrate?

Answer Explanations

12. ❹ This is a Gist-content question. Choice 4 is correct because everything the professor discusses relates to dolphin communication. In some lectures, the main topic does not become clear until the professor has been talking for a few seconds or a minute. However, in this case, the professor announces the topic almost immediately: after reminding the class that they have "been discussing animal communication," she says, "today we're going to talk about dolphins."

13. ❸ This is a Detail question. Choice 3 is correct. The professor explicitly refers to a theory that says one of the reasons dolphins swim side by side is to avoid interference from each other's sonar clicks. Dolphins do not need to swim side by side to see their bubble streams (choice 1) or to hear their signature whistles (choice 2). Choice 4 is incorrect because the professor says that mother dolphins use signature whistles, not swimming side by side, to locate their young.

14. ❷ This is a Making Inferences question that requires the integration of information from two parts of the lecture. Early in the lecture, the professor says that each dolphin has a unique signature whistle and that dolphins use these whistles to call to and identify one another. Later, she makes a similar statement about bubble streams: dolphins use bubble streams to identify and greet each other. The professor does not actually use the word *function* in describing signature whistles or bubble streams, and she does not make any *explicit* statements to compare their functions. Instead, by giving a similar description of them in different parts of the lecture, she *implies* that their functions are similar, making choice 2 the correct answer.

15. ❶ This is an Understanding the Speaker's Attitude question. At the end of the lecture, the professor speaks enthusiastically about the time she spent on a boat doing research. She says that fieldwork is a "wonderful" way to "experience something you've been studying in a classroom." By giving such a positive description of her personal experience on a research boat, she is encouraging her students to do fieldwork too, if they ever have the opportunity. Therefore choice 1 is correct.

16. ❹ This is an Understanding Organization question. Choice 4 is correct because the professor uses the example of calling another person's name in a forest as an analogy, to illustrate how dolphins call to and identify each other using signature whistles. In an analogy like this, the similarity between people

and dolphins is what is important, not their differences, so choice 1 is incorrect. Burst pulses (choice 2) are used by dolphins for displaying aggression, showing dominance, and attracting a mate; although those functions are all related to communication, they are not illustrated by the example. Choice 3 is incorrect because there is nothing about the size of groups mentioned in the lecture.

Questions 17–21

Track 48 Listening Script

Narrator

Listen to part of a conversation between a student and a university employee.

Employee

Oh, hello . . . can I help you?

Student

Um . . . yeah . . . I'm looking for Professor Kirk; is she here? I mean is this her office?

Employee

Yes, you're in the right place—Professor Kirk's office is right behind me—but no . . . she's not here right now.

Student

Um, do you know when she'll be back?

Employee

Well, she's teaching all morning. She won't be back until . . . let me check . . . hmm, she won't be back until . . . after lunch. That's when she has her office hours. Perhaps you could come back then?

Student

Oh, unfortunately no. I have class this afternoon. And I was really hoping to talk to her today. Hey, um, do you know if . . . she's accepting any more students into her Introduction to Biology class?

Employee

You wanna know if you can take the class?

Student

Yes, if she's letting any more students sign up, I'd like, I'd like to join the class.

Employee

Introduction to Biology is a very popular class, especially when she teaches it. A lot of students take it.

Student

Yeah, that's why the registrar said it was full. I've got the form the registrar gave me, um, to get her permission to take the class. It's all filled out except for her signature.

I'm hoping she'll let me in even though the class is full. You, see, I'm a senior this year, and, uh . . . this'll be my last semester, so it's my last chance . . .

Employee

Oh, wow, really. I mean most students fulfill their science requirement the first year.

Student

Well, I mean, um . . . to be honest, I kept putting it off. I'm not really a big fan of science classes in general, and with the labs and everything, I've never quite found the time.

Employee

Your advisor didn't say anything?

Student

Well, to tell you the truth, she's been after me to take a class like this for a while, but I'm double-majoring in art and journalism and so my schedule's been really tight with all the classes I gotta take, so somehow I never . . .

Employee

[politely cutting in] Well, perhaps you could leave the form with me and I'll see if she'll sign it for you.

Student

You know, I appreciate that, but maybe I should explain the problem to her in person . . . I didn't want to do it, but I guess I'll have to send her an email.

Employee

Hmm. You know, not all professors check their emails regularly—I . . . I'm not sure if Professor Kirk does it or not. Here's an idea . . . why don't you stick a note explaining your situation under her door and ask her to call you if she needs more information?

Student

Hey, that's a good idea, and then I can leave the form with you—if you still don't mind.

Track 49 Listening Script (Question 21)

Narrator

Why does the man say this to the woman:

Student

You know, I appreciate that, but maybe I should explain the problem to her in person . . .

Answer Explanations

17. ❹ This is a Gist-purpose question. The student wants Professor Kirk to give him permission to enroll in a course that is already full. In order to do this, the professor must sign a form that the student has brought with him. That is why he is there; thus choice 4 is correct. The student already knows that he

must take a science course in order to graduate (choice 1). There is no indication that Professor Kirk has invited the student to her office (choice 2), and the student already has an advisor (choice 3).

18. ❷ This is a Detail question. When the man says he will graduate soon, the woman says, "Oh, wow" and points out that most students fulfill their science requirement their first year. This indicates that she is surprised that the man has waited so long, making choice 2 the correct answer. None of the other choices is factually true, according to the information in the conversation.

19. ❶ This is another Detail question. Choice 1 is correct because it paraphrases the man's statement that his advisor has "been after me to take a class like this for a while." She wants him to take the class because she is aware of the man's situation and knows he cannot graduate without the science class. Therefore choice 3, which states that she is unaware of his problem, is incorrect. There is nothing in the conversation indicating that the advisor encouraged the man to major in journalism (choice 2). And although Professor Kirk's popularity among students is mentioned in the conversation, no reference is made to the advisor's opinion of Professor Kirk (choice 4).

20. ❸ This is a Connecting Content question. After the woman suggests that the man stick a note under Professor Kirk's door, the man says, "that's a good idea," indicating that he will follow her advice. Thus choice 3 is correct. There is some discussion about sending an email (choice 2), but that idea is rejected. There is no discussion of calling Professor Kirk (choice 1), and the man explains early in the conversation that his schedule conflicts with the professor's office hours (choice 4).

21. ❷ This is an Understanding the Function of What Is Said question. In the replayed audio, the man rejects the woman's offer to give the form to Professor Kirk. Instead of simply saying, "No," the man says he does "appreciate" her offer but thinks it would be better for him to speak with Professor Kirk directly. Choice 2 captures both the man's politeness and his intention. The man's problem is not yet solved (choice 1), and he has already explained what he needs (choice 3). Choice 4 is incorrect because the woman implied earlier that it is Professor Kirk, not she, who is busy.

Questions 22–27

Track 50 Listening Script

Narrator

Listen to part of a lecture in an astronomy class.

Professor

I'm sure y'all have been following the news about Mars. A lot of spacecraft have been visiting the planet recently—some have gone into orbit around it, while others have landed on it. And, they've sent back a . . . an abundance of data that's reshaping our knowledge . . . our vision of the planet in a lot of ways. Is there anything that you've been particularly struck by in all the news reports?

Female Student

Well, they seem to mention water a lot, which kinda surprised me, as I have this picture in my head that Mars is dry . . . sorta dry and dead.

Professor

You're not the only one. You know, for centuries, most of our knowledge of the planet came from what we saw through telescopes, so, obviously, it was pretty limited—and our views of the planet were formed as much by writers . . . as they were by serious scientists. When the first science-fiction stories came out, Mars was described as being a lot like Earth except *[pauses to let students finish his sentence]*

Male Student

I know: the planet was red and, uh, the people were green. I've seen some of those old movies. *[half laughing, half sarcastic]* What were they thinking? I mean really . . . they . . .

Professor

[interrupting] Well, it seems silly to us now, but those ideas were quite imaginative and, occasionally, scary in their time. Anyway, we began to rethink our image of Mars when the first spacecraft flew by the planet in 1965 and sent pictures back to Earth. Those pictures showed a planet that looked a lot more like our Moon than Earth—lots of craters and not much else. It was bitterly cold, it had a very thin atmosphere, and that atmosphere was mostly carbon dioxide. So the view of Mars after this first flyby mission was that dry, dead planet that Lisa mentioned.

But, then there were more visits to the planet in the 1970s—and this time the spacecraft didn't just fly by; they orbited . . . or landed. This allowed us to receive much more detailed images of the planet, and it turned out to be a pretty interesting place. Mars had . . . has a lot more than craters—it has giant volcanoes and deep canyons. It also showed signs of dried-up riverbeds and plains that had been formed by massive floods. So we concluded that there must have been water on the planet at one time—billions of years ago. Now, what does it take for water to exist?

Male Student

You need to have a warm-enough temperature so that it doesn't freeze.

Professor

That's one thing—and the other is that you need enough atmospheric pressure, thick-enough air so that the water doesn't instantly vaporize. The Mars we see today doesn't have either of those conditions—it is too cold and the air is too thin—but a long time ago, there may have been a thicker atmosphere that created a greenhouse effect that raised temperatures—and maybe that combination produced water on the surface of the planet. So maybe Mars wasn't just a dead, boring rock; maybe, it was, uh, a fascinating fossil that was once alive and dynamic—worthy of exploration. *[pause]* Now let's jump forward a few decades to the beginning of this century, and a new generation of orbiters and landers that have been sent to Mars. Of course, the scientific instruments now surveying Mars are far more sophisticated than the instruments of the '70s, so we're getting all kinds of new data for analysis. And, not surprisingly, that data is challenging our notions of what Mars is like. Lisa, you mentioned that a lot of the news reports talked about water—do you remember any of the details?

Female Student

Well, they were showing these pictures of these long, uh, cuts in the ground, which would be gullies here; I mean on Earth. They say that since, uh, gullies are usually formed by water, it seems like they might be evidence that water still exists on Mars, but I didn't get how that worked.

Professor

I'm not surprised. There're a lot of theories . . . a lot of speculation . . . and some argue the formations aren't caused by water at all. But there're some ingenious theories that assume that there's a lot of water right under the planet's surface that somehow is causing the gullies to form. If we could only get a lander there . . . but the gullies aren't in places where we can send landers yet. Anyway, if there is some kind of water activity, it may change our view of the planet once again . . . to something that's not dead, not even a fossil, but rather a planet like Earth that undergoes cycles—think of our ice ages—over long periods of time. Maybe Mars could sustain water again at some distant date.

Track 51 Listening Script (Question 26)

Narrator

Why does the professor say this:

Professor

So maybe Mars wasn't just a dead, boring rock; maybe, it was, uh, a fascinating fossil that was once alive and dynamic—worthy of exploration.

Track 52 Listening Script (Question 27)

Male Student

I know: the planet was red and, uh, the people were green. I've seen some of those old movies. *[half laughing, half sarcastic]* What were they thinking? I mean really . . .

Narrator

Why does the student say this:

Male Student

What were they thinking?

Answer Explanations

22. ❸ This is a Gist-content question. The professor begins by saying that an abundance of data is reshaping "our vision of the planet in a lot of ways." He goes on to discuss how Mars was imagined before it was visited by spacecraft,

and then how, in recent years, successive spacecraft have sent back detailed images that are providing an increasingly realistic view of the planet. Thus choice 3 is correct.

23. ❶ This is a Detail question. Choice 1 is correct because the professor says that the images obtained in 1965 made Mars appear as dry and dead as the Moon, with "lots of craters and not much else." He mentions the 1965 view that Mars was very cold, but he does not say that the images showed it to be similar to Earth (choice 2)—quite the opposite. The existence of life on Mars in the distant past is presented not as a conclusion (choice 3) but as a matter of theory and speculation coming after the 1970s orbits and the even more recent Mars landings. The theory that water exists under Mars's surface (choice 4) is also a recent development.

24. ❷❹ This is a Making Inferences question. Note that the square boxes in front of the answer choices indicate that you must select two correct answers. In the lecture, the professor contrasts the dry conditions of Mars today with the possibility that Mars had water on its surface billions of years ago. Choice 2, which says that the atmospheric pressure and the temperature may have been higher on Mars in the past than they are today, forms part of his explanation of how Mars could once have had water. Choice 4 is also correct because part of the evidence for the existence of water on Mars is the plains and the dried-up riverbeds currently visible on Mars's surface; according to the professor, they could have been created by flooding.

25. ❸ This is a Detail question. One of the students mentions that she has seen news reports that showed gullies on Mars, and she says that they seem to be evidence of water. The professor confirms that gullies may indeed be evidence of water on Mars and says that there are theories that water under the surface caused the gullies to form. Thus choice 3 is correct. The professor mentions volcanoes on Mars (choice 1) and Mars's dry climate (choice 2), but he does not associate either with gullies. References are made to fossils but not to any actual fossils (choice 4); the professor uses the word *fossil* metaphorically when he likens the entire planet to an object that may be dead but that is nevertheless worth investigating because it was once alive.

26. ❹ This is an Understanding Organization question. In this replayed statement, the professor uses imagery to describe the early conception of Mars—"a dead, boring rock"—and the modern conception formed by additional evidence—"a fascinating fossil that was once alive and dynamic." By making this contrast, the professor both sums up the lecture and emphasizes that the change in our view of Mars was a very significant one. Thus the correct answer is choice 4.

27. ❷ This is an Understanding the Function of What Is Said question. The student's comment is an indirect criticism of early filmmakers for their unrealistic portrayals of Mars. Thus choice 2 is correct. His opinion is a negative one,

so he is not expressing approval (choice 4). The student is not seeking clarification or rephrasing a previous question, so choices 1 and 3 do not accurately reflect the intention of his statement.

Questions 28–33

Track 53 Listening Script

Narrator

Listen to part of a lecture in an art history class. The professor has been talking about colossal statues.

Professor

We've been looking at colossal statues—works of exceptionally huge size—and their essentially public role, in commemorating a political or religious figure. We've seen how some of these statues date back thousands of years . . . like the statues of the pharaohs of ancient Egypt—which you can still visit today—and how others, though surviving only in legend, have fired the imagination of writers and artists right up to our own time, such as the Colossus of Rhodes, that 110-foot statue of the Greek god Helios [HEE-lee-us]. Remember, this same word, *colossus*—which means a giant or larger-than-life-size statue—is what today's term *colossal* derives from.

Now, it was one thing to build such statues, at an equally colossal cost, when the funds were being allocated by ancient kings and pharaohs. But if we're going to think about modern-day colossal statues, we need to reexamine more closely their role as social and political symbols, in order to understand why a society today—a society of free, taxpaying citizens—would agree to allocate so much of its resources to erecting them. A good example to start out with would be Mount Rushmore.

Now, many of you have probably seen pictures of Mount Rushmore; perhaps you've actually visited the place. Mount Rushmore, in South Dakota, is a colossal representation of the faces of four U.S. Presidents: George Washington, Thomas Jefferson, Theodore Roosevelt, and Abraham Lincoln, carved directly into a mountain. Imagine: each of those faces in the rock is over 60 feet high! Now, carving their faces took over six and a half years, and cost almost a million dollars. And this was in the 1930s, during the worst economic depression in U.S. history! Does that strike any of you as odd?

Well, I personally think that the Great Depression of the 1930s actually makes this more understandable, not less so. Often it's the case that, precisely at times of hardship—when the very fabric of society seems to be unraveling and confidence is eroding—uh, that people clamor for some public expression of strength and optimism, perhaps as a way of symbolizing its endurance in the face of difficulty.

So with that in mind, let's go back to Mount Rushmore. Actually, the original motivation for a colossal monument in South Dakota had very little to do with all this symbolism . . . and everything to do with money: you see, it was first conceived of basically as a tourist attraction, and it was supposed to feature the images of legendary figures of the American West, like the explorers Lewis and Clark. The government of South Dakota thought it would bring lots of money into the state.

It was only later on that the sculptor—the artist who designed and oversaw the project, a man named Gutzon Borglum—decided the project should be a monument honoring four of the most-respected Presidents in U.S. history; much more than a tourist attraction . . . its very prominence and permanence became perceived as a symbol of the endurance of U.S. ideals and the greatness of the country's early leaders. So, you see, what began as a tourist attraction became something far loftier.

Let's look at another example of this phenomenon.

The Statue of Liberty is another colossal statue—*[indicating by his tone of voice that his assumption is a near certainty]* one that I assume a number of you are familiar with. But, umm, I would guess that—like many people today—you don't realize that, when it was designed, over a century ago—by a French sculptor—it was intended to symbolize the long friendship between the people of France and the people of the United States—one which dated back to France's support of the American colonies' war for independence from the British.

But the shift in the statue's meaning started soon after it was built. Back in 1883, Emma Lazarus wrote that famous poem—you know, the one that goes: "Give me your tired, your poor. . ." *[pause]* and so on and so forth. That poem describes the Statue of Liberty as a beacon of welcome for the entire world. Well, in the early 1900s, it was put on a plaque on the pedestal that the Statue of Liberty stands on.

From that point on, the Statue of Liberty was no longer perceived as just a gift between friendly republics. It now became a tribute to the United States' history of immigration and openness.

This association was strengthened in the imagination of the general public just a few decades after the statue's completion, with the immigration waves of the early twentieth century . . . especially since the statue happened to be the first sign of America seen by those immigrants sailing into the port of New York. So, as with Mount Rushmore, the original motivation for this colossal statue was forgotten, and the statue is now valued for more important reasons.

Track 54 Listening Script (Question 32)

Professor

Back in 1883, Emma Lazarus wrote that famous poem—you know, the one that goes: "Give me your tired, your poor . . ." *[pause]* and so on and so forth.

Narrator

Why does the professor discuss the poem by Emma Lazarus?

Answer Explanations

28. ❸ This is a Gist-content question. The lecture is part of a larger art history lecture on the general topic of colossal statues. Having completed his discussion of ancient colossal statues, the professor now focuses on modern times and begins by raising this question: why would elected officials be willing to invest enormous sums of public money to create colossal statues? To understand why, he says, one needs to "reexamine more closely their role as social

and political symbols." Choice 3 best expresses that idea. Choices 1, 2, and 4 are mentioned but are not the main focus of this excerpt.

29. ❶ This is a Making Inferences question. In examining the role of modern colossal statues as social and political symbols, the professor explains that these very expensive statues are built only when free, taxpaying citizens agree to fund their construction. If these symbols are so costly to build, then the people who agree to fund their construction must place a high value on them. Therefore choice 1 is correct. While it is probably true that important colossal statues are discussed in many classrooms (choice 2), this fact is not mentioned by the professor. The fact that the statues last thousands of years is discussed with regard to ancient, not modern, statues (choice 3). A famous poem is discussed in the lecture, but this poem was inspired by the Statue of Liberty, not the other way around (choice 4).

30. ❸ This is a Detail question. In his discussion of the Great Depression, the professor says that people's confidence gets eroded in times of financial hardship, making choice 3 correct. While the other events may have resulted from the Great Depression, they are not mentioned by the professor in this regard.

31. ❶ This is a Detail question. At the opening and again at the closing of his discussion of Mount Rushmore, the professor says that the monument was originally intended as a tourist attraction to bring money to the state of South Dakota. Choice 1 is correct because it paraphrases these statements. The unity of society (choice 2) is addressed in the lecture in connection with colossal statues, and symbolizing this ideal might have been one of the sculptor's goals. Nevertheless, the professor emphasizes that neither unifying society nor the Great Depression (choice 3) was the original motivation for the state of South Dakota. Choice 4 is incorrect for the same reason: honoring United States Presidents was not the original purpose of the statue; in fact, the monument started out as a depiction of legendary figures of the American West, not United States Presidents.

32. ❷ This is an Understanding Organization question. Choice 2 is correct because the professor talks about Emma Lazarus's poem as a second example of how the meaning associated with a monument can change. Before mentioning the poem, the professor points out that the Statue of Liberty was given to the United States by France as a gift symbolizing the long friendship between the two countries. But then Lazarus wrote the poem describing the statue as a beacon of welcome for the entire world. The professor says that the poem gave a new meaning to the statue and that this meaning strengthened after the poem was placed on the statue's pedestal. The professor is not making a general observation about literature and sculpture (choice 1). He mentions the friendship between the United States and France only to set up a contrast with the newer meaning of the statue (choice 3). And he discusses the poem to show a similarity, not a difference, between Mount Rushmore

and the Statue of Liberty, that similarity being the fact that the symbolism of both monuments has shifted over time.

33. ❸ You are asked to listen again to part of the lecture and to decide what the professor is implying about the poem.

Back in 1883, Emma Lazarus wrote that famous poem—you know, the one that goes: "Give me your tired, your poor . . . " *[pause]* and so on and so forth.

This is a Making Inferences question. To arrive at the correct answer (choice 3), you must understand that the expression "so on and so forth" is typically used when a listener does not need any further information to understand what the speaker is referring to. In this case, the professor assumes that the students are very familiar with the poem, so he does not need to recite more than the first few words of it.

Speaking

Listening Scripts, Important Points, and Sample Responses with Rater Comments

Use the sample Independent and Integrated Speaking rubrics on pages 188–191 to see how responses are scored. The raters who listen to your responses will analyze them in three general categories. These categories are Delivery, Language Use, and Topic Development. All three categories have equal importance.

This section includes important points that should be covered when answering each question. All of these points must be present in a response in order for it to receive the highest score in the Topic Development category. These important points are guides to the kind of information raters expect to hear in a high-level response.

This section also refers to example responses on the accompanying audio tracks on the CD. Some responses were scored at the highest level, while others were not. The responses are followed by comments from certified ETS raters.

Question 1

Track 55 Listening Script

Narrator

What kind of reading material, such as novels, magazines, or poetry, do you most like to read in your free time? Explain why you find this kind of reading material interesting.

> **Preparation Time: 15 Seconds**
> **Response Time: 45 Seconds**

Important Points

In this question, you are asked to talk about what type of material you like to read in your free time and why you find this material interesting. People who listen to your response should clearly understand what kind of material you read and the reason or reasons it interests you. Responses scored at higher levels contain at least one clear, well-developed reason for the preferred reading material and avoid vague explanations such as *"I like to read magazines because they contain a lot of interesting information."* A more developed response might begin *"I like to read news magazines because they provide more detailed information about current events than television news shows or newspapers can,"* and then continue on to explain how the added details in news magazines are interesting or beneficial. Note that raters are only going to consider how well you explain your interest, not make judgments about what you read. It does not matter whether your favorite reading materials are physics journals or comic books!

Sample Responses

Play Track 62 on the CD to hear a high-level response for Question 1.
Rater Comments

The speaker identifies her preferred reading material—plays—and gives a very well-developed explanation for why she enjoys them. She uses plenty of supporting details and examples in her response. As her answer progresses, she identifies one author, Shakespeare, whose plays she especially enjoys reading, then further explains why his plays are meaningful to her. She uses a wide range of vocabulary and grammatical constructions with ease, and while her pronunciation is not perfect, it is easy to understand.

Play Track 63 on the CD to hear a mid-level response for Question 1.
Rater Comments

The speaker states what kind of reading material he likes, but he does not develop his answer with much detail. He could have developed his answer better if he had chosen only one type of material—books or novels. For example, he could have explained what sport he likes to read about in magazines, why he is interested in that sport, and how magazines help him maintain his interest. His speech is easy to understand, but he has minor problems with pacing, often pausing to think of the next word to say. His vocabulary range is somewhat narrow.

Question 2

Track 56 Listening Script

Narrator

Some students would prefer to live with roommates. Others would prefer to live alone. Which option would you prefer and why?

| Preparation Time: 15 Seconds |
| Response Time: 45 Seconds |

Important Points

In this question, you need to state whether you, as a student, would prefer to live with roommates or live alone, and then you need to explain your preference. You should explain your reason or reasons fully and clearly, using details and examples where you can. For instance, you could say you prefer to live with a roommate and then explain one or two reasons, such as having someone to discuss problems with, being able to share the cooking and cleaning, or avoiding loneliness. If you want to talk about the advantages or disadvantages of *both* options and say they are equally good, that is permissible. However, it might be more difficult for you to finish discussing both options in the time allowed.

Sample Responses

Play Track 64 on the CD to hear a high-level response for Question 2.

Rater Comments

This speaker's response presents a clear progression of ideas. He chooses to discuss an advantage of living with a roommate before he describes the disadvantages, which, to him, are stronger than the advantage. He gives an example of how a roommate might be a problem, then states his preference—living alone—and relates it to his personal experience. His pronunciation is easy to understand, and he speaks very fluently. A few of his word choices are not precise, but this would not prevent a listener from understanding his ideas.

Play Track 65 on the CD to hear a low-level response for Question 2.

Rater Comments

For the first part of his response, the speaker is only reading the question aloud and not actually answering it. His pronunciation is strongly affected by his first language, so the listener must make a great effort to try to understand what he is saying. His response is marked by long pauses as he tries to think of the next word to say, indicating that he possesses a very limited English vocabulary. The lowest level of the rubric describes the characteristics of this response.

Question 3

Track 57 Listening Script

Narrator

Read the article from the university newspaper about the plan to build new student housing. You will have 50 seconds to read the article. Begin reading now.

Reading Time: 50 Seconds

University May Build New Student Apartments Off Campus

The Department of Student Housing is considering whether to build new student housing off campus in a residential area of town. Two of the major factors influencing the decision will be parking and space. Those who support building off campus argue that building new housing on campus would further increase the number of cars on and around campus and consume space that could be better used for future projects that the entire university community could benefit from. Supporters also say that students might even have a richer college experience by being connected to the local community and patronizing stores and other businesses in town.

Narrator

Now listen to two students discussing the article.

Woman

I can't believe these plans. It just doesn't make sense to me.

Man

Really? Seemed OK to me, especially the argument about the cars.

Woman

Yeah, I know. But the thing is, it doesn't matter where students live 'cause they still have to get to class somehow, right? At least if they built new dorms on campus, students would use campus transportation . . .

Man

[interrupting] . . . instead of their cars. I see what you're getting at. If they live off campus, they're *still* going to have to drive and park on campus. Might even create more traffic.

Woman

Exactly.

Man

OK. Still, though . . . the point about students interacting more with people in the community: that doesn't seem to be a bad thing, does it?

Woman

But the more time spent off campus, in town, the less time spent on campus. What about all the clubs, shows, discussions, a—all the campus happenings that just kind of . . . happen? It's important to be *on* campus to really take advantage of these things. Having a different living experience shouldn't be given up at the expense of not being as much a part of the *university* community.

Narrator

The woman expresses her opinion of the university's plan. State her opinion and explain the reasons she gives for holding that opinion.

> **Preparation Time: 30 Seconds**
> **Response Time: 60 Seconds**

Important Points

The woman disagrees with the housing department's plan to build new student housing off campus. She thinks students will still have to drive to campus to get to class, so there will not be any decrease in the number of cars around campus. She also thinks students will miss opportunities to be involved in on-campus activities, which are just as important as the experience of living in town.

Sample Responses

Play Track 66 on the CD to hear a high-level response for Question 3.
Rater Comments

The speaker gives a sustained, coherent response that accurately and efficiently explains the woman's opinion of the main points of the newspaper article. He did not waste time by including unimportant details from the conversation or reading. His pacing is fluid, and he demonstrates good control of a variety of grammatical structures and vocabulary. His pronunciation is exceptionally clear.

Play Track 67 on the CD to hear a mid-level response for Question 3.
Rater Comments

This speaker covers all the important points of the woman's opinion. However, the speaker never states what the university plan is, so she does not make it entirely clear what, in general, the woman in the conversation is disagreeing with. Her response contains some minor errors in word choice, such as *assist* rather than *attend*, but overall she demonstrates good control of both vocabulary and grammar. Her pacing is usually steady, though with a number of hesitations that require listener effort at times.

Question 4

Track 58 Listening Script

Narrator

Now read the passage about a topic in psychology. You will have 45 seconds to read the passage. Begin reading now.

Reading Time: 45 Seconds

Actor-observer

People account for their own behavior differently from how they account for the behavior of others. When observing the behavior of others, we tend to attribute their actions to their character or their personality rather than to external factors. In contrast, we tend to explain our own behavior in terms of situational factors beyond our own control rather than attributing it to our own character. One explanation for this difference is that people are aware of the situational forces affecting them but not of situational forces affecting other people. Thus, when evaluating someone else's behavior, we focus on the person rather than the situation.

Narrator

Now listen to part of a lecture in a psychology class.

Professor

So we encounter this in life all the time, but many of us are unaware that we do this . . . even psychologists who study it . . . like me. For example, the other day I was at the store and I was getting in line to buy something. But just before I was actually in line, some guy comes out of nowhere and cuts right in front of me. Well, I was really annoyed and thought, "That was rude!" I assumed he was just a selfish, inconsiderate person when, in fact, I had no idea why he cut in line in front of me or whether he even realized he was doing it. Maybe he didn't think I was actually in line yet . . . But my immediate reaction was to assume he was a selfish or rude person.

OK, so a few days after that, I was at the store again. Only this time I was in a real hurry—I was late for an important meeting—and I was frustrated that everything was taking so long. And what's worse, all the checkout lines were long, and it seemed like everyone was moving so slowly. But then I saw a slightly shorter line! But some woman with a lot of stuff to buy was walking toward it, so I basically ran to get there first, before her, and, well, I did. Now, I didn't think of myself as a bad or rude person for doing this. I had an important meeting to get to—I was in a hurry, so, you know, I had done nothing wrong.

Narrator

Explain how the two examples discussed by the professor illustrate differences in the ways people explain behavior.

> **Preparation Time: 30 Seconds**
> **Response Time: 60 Seconds**

Important Points

We explain others' behavior differently from how we explain our own behavior. The professor describes how he thought that the man who cut ahead of him in line was a rude person. This example shows that we tend to explain the behavior of others by attributing it to their character or personality. Then the professor describes how he similarly cut into line but did not think of himself as rude, because he was late for a meeting. This illustrates how we explain our own behavior not in terms of our character, but by attributing it to situational factors.

Sample Responses

Play Track 68 on the CD to hear a high-level response for Question 4.

Rater Comments

This speaker clearly shows how the professor's examples illustrate the idea that we explain other people's behavior one way and our own behavior in a different way. He covers the main points efficiently in the time allotted. His response is sustained and fluid, and his pronunciation is easy to understand, with only occasional, minor difficulties. There are several minor grammatical errors that do not hinder understanding, and overall he demonstrates good control of grammatical structures.

Play Track 69 on the CD to hear a mid-level response for Question 4.

Rater Comments

The speaker is able to cover both of the professor's examples in a basic way, but he never clearly connects the second example to the concept from the reading (that people explain their own behavior based on situational factors, not character). His pronunciation is easy to understand, but his response is still difficult to follow at times because of his frequent hesitations.

Question 5

Track 59 Listening Script

Narrator

Now listen to part of a conversation between a student and her advisor.

Advisor

OK, Becky, so . . . you've chosen all your courses for next term?

Student

Well, not really, professor. Actually, I've got a problem.

Advisor

Oh?

Student

Yeah, well, I still need to take an American literature course; it's required for graduation. But I've been putting it off. But since my next term is my last . . .

Advisor

Yeah, you can't put it off any longer!

Student

Right. The thing is, though . . . it's not offered next term.

Advisor

I see. Hmm. Ah, how about . . . ah, taking the course at another university?

Student

I thought about that. It's offered at City College, but . . . that's so far away. Commuting back and forth would take me a couple of hours, you know, a big chunk of time with all my other studies and everything.

Advisor

True, but it's been done. Or . . . ah, there are a couple of graduate courses in American literature. Why not take one of those?

Student

Yeah, but . . . wouldn't that be hard, though? I mean . . . it's a graduate course; that'd be pretty intense.

Advisor

Yeah, it'd probably mean more studying than you're used to, but I'm sure it's not beyond your abilities.

Narrator

The speakers discuss two possible solutions to the woman's problem. Briefly summarize the problem. Then state which solution you prefer and why.

| Preparation Time: 20 Seconds |
| Response Time: 60 Seconds |

Important Points

The student's problem is that she must take a course to graduate, but the course is not being offered next term, and she is supposed to graduate at the end of next term.

For this task, notice that the question does *not* tell you to discuss both of the solutions. After summarizing the problem, you need to say only which *one* of the solutions from the conversation you prefer and why. If you agree with the first solution, you would say that you think she should take the course at another university. You could support your choice by saying, for example, that although she would have to commute back and forth, the course would be easier than a graduate course, and it might be a good experience for her to meet students from another university.

If you choose the second solution, you would say that you think she should take the graduate version of the course at her university. You could support your choice by saying, for example, that this way she would not have to waste time commuting, and even if the graduate-level course is more difficult, she would probably learn more, and it would look impressive in her academic record.

Sample Responses

Play Track 70 on the CD to hear a high-level response for Question 5.

Rater Comments

The speaker fulfills the task by summarizing the problem and explaining her preferred solution. She refers to relevant points from the conversation with a coherent progression of ideas. She has chosen to describe both solutions, which the question does not require, but since she is a fluent speaker, she is able to do this as well as support her recommendation within the time limit. Her pronunciation is clear, and although her pace varies at times, it does not require listener effort to follow what she is saying.

Play Track 71 on the CD to hear a mid-level response for Question 5.

Rater Comments

The speaker does not demonstrate a high level of fluency. She pauses after every two or three words, which requires the listener to make some effort to follow her ideas. She does explain the problem and gives her preferred solution, although she does not really support her preference for the second solution. Her lack of fluency prevents her from giving a full answer in the time allotted.

Question 6

Track 60 Listening Script

Narrator

Now listen to part of a lecture in a child development class.

Professor

OK. Young children and art. Research suggests that learning art skills can benefit a young child's development. Umm . . . two of the ways it can do this is by providing a platform to express complex emotions and by encouraging persistence.

Now, what do I mean when I say "a platform to express complex emotions"? Young children have limited vocabulary. So how would they communicate the feeling of pride, for example? A drawing, though, making a drawing of feeling proud . . . this is something a young child could do. So a little girl might draw herself jumping up in the air next to her bike. In the drawing, her arms are raised up in the air and she's smiling. Children can communicate their emotions, whether positive or negative, through the drawing—mm—better than they could with words.

And encouraging persistence? Art skills can help children to develop patience and concentration to persist in an activity . . . the willingness to keep trying to reach a goal. So suppose there's a little boy who wants to mold a lump of clay into the shape of a car. The first attempt doesn't look too much like a car. He's disappointed but wants to try again. The second, third, fourth try still don't look quite right, but there's improvement with every attempt. So, after some time, he gets to the point where he's satisfied with his creation. The newly shaped clay car is an instant reminder of an accomplishment—a success resulting from his persistence. The boy may be able to transfer this lesson toward other situations and activities because, well, he's had the experience of successfully accomplishing a goal through hard work.

Narrator

Using points and examples from the talk, explain how learning art can impact a child's development.

> **Preparation Time: 20 Seconds**
> **Response Time: 60 Seconds**

Important Points

Learning art skills can have an important impact on the emotional development of young children in two ways. One is by helping them to express complex emotions. Drawing can, for example, help children express emotions that they cannot express in words. The little girl expressed pride when she drew a picture of herself looking proud of learning to ride a bike.

The second way art can help young children is by teaching them persistence. After spending time perfecting an art piece—such as the little boy sculpting a car out of clay—they can see their success.

Sample Responses

Play Track 72 on the CD to hear a high-level response for Question 6.
Rater Comments

This speaker efficiently summarizes the key points from the lecture in order to explain how learning art skills can influence a child's development. His speech is highly intelligible and fluid, though there are a few minor lapses in flow. His response also demonstrates good control of both basic and more complex grammatical structures as used in spoken language.

Play Track 73 on the CD to hear a mid-level response for Question 6.
Rater Comments

The speaker makes major errors in content as he attempts to summarize the lecture. He does not mention the second point—that learning the value of persistence is one of the ways that art can help children's emotional development. Also, his summary of the first point is inaccurate; he confuses the example for the second point with the example for the first point (helping children express emotions). His pronunciation is generally clear, but his response lacks full coherence; it is not always easy to see how one idea connects to the next.

Writing

Listening Script, Topic Notes, and Sample Responses with Rater Comments

Use the Integrated Writing and Independent Writing scoring rubrics on pages 200–201 and 209–210 to see how responses are scored.

Writing Based on Reading and Listening

Track 61 Listening Script

Narrator

Now listen to part of a lecture on the topic you just read about.

Professor

Lately, we've been seeing some professors on television. Though it's sometimes claimed to be a good thing, we should question whether anybody really benefits from it. First of all, it's not good for the professors themselves—not from a professional standpoint. Rightly or wrongly, a professor who appears on TV tends to get the reputation among fellow professors of being someone who is not a serious scholar—someone who chooses to entertain rather than to educate. And for that reason, TV professors may not be invited to important conferences—important meetings to discuss their academic work. They may even have difficulty getting money to do research. So for professors, being a TV celebrity has important disadvantages.

A second point is that being on TV can take a lot of a professor's time—not just the time on TV but also time figuring out what to present and time spent rehearsing, travel time, even time getting made up to look good for the cameras. And all this time comes out of the time the professor can spend doing research, meeting with students, and attending to university business. So you can certainly see there are problems for the university and its students when professors are in the TV studio and not on campus.

So who does benefit? The public? Umm . . . that's not so clear either. Look, professors do have a lot of knowledge to offer, but TV networks don't want really serious, in-depth academic lectures for after-dinner viewing. What the networks want is the academic title, not the intellectual substance. The material that professors usually present on TV—such as background on current events, or some brief historical introduction to a new movie version of a great literary work—this material is not much different from what viewers would get from a TV reporter who had done a little homework.

Narrator

Summarize the points made in the lecture, being sure to explain how they oppose specific points made in the reading passage.

Topic Notes

You should understand the reasons presented in the lecture for why it is not necessarily good that professors appear on television. The lecturer questions each of the benefits mentioned in the reading passage: about the professor's reputation, about the professor's time, and about educating the public.

A high-scoring response will include the following points made by the lecturer that address the points made in the reading passage:

Point Made in the Reading Passage	Contrasting Point from the Lecture
TV appearances improve the professor's reputation.	1. Their reputation suffers, because they are considered entertainers by their peers and not serious scholars. 2. As a result, they may get fewer invitations to academic conferences or lose research funding.
TV appearances benefit the university and lead to more student applications and more donations.	Professors spend a lot of time preparing for the TV appearances, which takes away from their true academic work, such as teaching and doing research.
TV appearances benefit the public because the public is exposed to more in-depth knowledge about a subject.	Professors generally do not give in-depth academic lectures on TV.

Responses with scores of 4 and 5 generally clearly discuss all three of the main points in the table.

Sample Responses with Rater Comments

Score 5 Essay

The passage introduced three reasons why professors should appear on TV: gaining reputation for the professor, for the college, and to educate the general public. However, the lecture disagrees.

Professors who appear frequently on TV are not generally viewed as a serious scholar. As a result, those professors will receive less invitation to attend academic conferences or less likely to receive research grant. This seriously hinders the professor's opportunity to further grow as a researcher

Professors who frequently appear on TV also has negative effect on students and the university. Appearing on TV takes a lot of time to prepare, including preperation for the material, transportation time, and even time to dress up. This precious time can also be used to teach class, help students, or even do further research. As a result, professors who appear on TV waste a lot of time that they can contribute to teaching and research.

Professors appearing on TV doesn't usually help educating the general public. The TV network is not interested in having the professor explaining the intellectual substances of their researches. Rather, they are interested in having them explain some basic background information or history. This type of information can be easily presented by a serious reporter who has done his work properly.

Because of the above reasons, it is highly questionable whether professors appearing on TV has any advantage. In fact, it could bring negative consequence both to the professors themselves and the universities they teach.

Rater Comments

This response successfully conveys all three of the main points from the lecture. The response is well organized and developed. Explicit connection between the reading passage and the lecture is explained in the first and final paragraphs. In each body paragraph, the writer opens with a topic sentence that captures how the lecture point opposes the point made in the reading passage in general, and the writer proceeds to develop the lecturer's point using relevant details and examples. The language used by the writer is not perfect; there are minor grammatical errors in subject-verb agreement and preposition use ("Professors . . . has negative effect," "preperation for the material," "the universities they teach"). However, note that the Scoring Guide for the integrated task allows level 5 responses to contain occasional minor errors that do not result in inaccurate or imprecise presentation of content or connections. The errors in this response do not interfere with meaning or disrupt the flow of the response.

Score 4 Essay

The reading passage was talking about the advantages of being on TV as a professor. They say that apperaing on television will increase the reputation of a professor. But in the lecture the professor was talking about disadvantages on being on TV as a Professor. At first, it is not good for a professor to be on TV. Because when he apears on TV his reputation among the other Professors decrease. This is the effect of entertaining instead of making researches. Under Professors you are rated by your reasearches and speeches on events. Other professors think that a professor should make reasearches instead of being a TV celebraty.

Another reason against professors on TV is, that it takes to much time. When they are on TV, they have to prepare for the interview and they have to travel to the studio and so on. In this time they can not make researches and look after their students. It is important to any professor to look after the students. Then if a professor is always away, he will get a bad reputation among the students. And without students he will lose his job.

This stands in opposite to the reading. In the articel they wrote that it is good to be on TV, because you can reach a wider audiance. You can present academic topics to a new audience. And so you give people a chance to hear about topics they have never herad befor. But the Problem is that it is superficial. And this is the point critizised in the lecture. The TV networks do not want to educate the people. They want to entertain the people. So for a professor a TV Show is wasting time.

Rater Comments

The opening sentences of this response provide an effective introduction to a discussion of the three points. The main idea of the first point, that professors who appear on television may lose their reputation among their colleagues, is clearly stated, but the writer does not mention the consequences of a professor's lost reputation. The statement that professors are "rated by researches and speeches on events" is unclear. The second idea, that professors who appear on television do not spend enough time on research and teaching, is well developed. However, the conclusion that "without students he will lose his job" is not mentioned in the lecture and seems somewhat overstated. In the third paragraph, the point concerning possible benefits of these television appearances to the public is summarized quite well, but there are minor structural flaws. For example, the first sentence ("This stands in opposite to the reading.") suggests that the paragraph will refer back to information that was stated before, but a new topic is then introduced. Overall, the response summarizes the lecture and how it relates to the reading passage quite well. However, the fact that some details from the lecture are left out or conveyed imprecisely, along with minor problems in the connection of ideas and language errors that occasionally interfere with clarity, all contribute to the score of 4 for this response.

Score 3 Essay

The question which is asked is to know if the apparition of a professor on television is a good or a bad think? On this point, the text and the lecture completely disagree.

First, we can think that it is a good thing for the professors themselves. It seems to be something logical because today a lot of people want to be known and the television is perhaps the best thing to be known. But what the lecture say is that such a professor don't have a good reputation. People think they are not very serious when they pass on television. The effect is that they are no more invited to important conferences.

In what concerned the students and the university, the text shows the facts that some of these apparitions can bring some donation to the university, what is very good. But in the other hand according to the lecture, this professor spend a lot of time travelling and during that time, he isn't available for the students or for the researches and the university lose therefore some money.

Finally for the public himself, they could learn some interesting things and it could be a very big chance because a lot of these persons haven't had the chance going in the university. But it is true that such intervention isn't often best as something that a journalist could prepare.

Rater Comments

The writer organizes the response fairly well. After a brief introduction, each reading passage point is briefly summarized and then followed by ideas from the related point in the lecture. However, the response earns a score of 3 because the writer's summaries of the lecture suffer from several problems. There is imprecision (the idea that "people" rather than fellow academics think the professor appearing on television is not serious); there is omission (the idea that television networks are not interested in in-depth lectures is missing); and there is poor connection of ideas (the idea that a university loses "some money" is not connected to the idea that television appearances take away from professors' time at the university). Most importantly, there are lapses of clarity due to the writer's poor language control. Errors in word choice ("pass on television," "intervention isn't often best as something") obscure meaning to such an extent that the lecturer's response to the first point is conveyed only vaguely, and the response to the last point is completely unclear. Although the writer of this response may have had a good grasp of many ideas he or she wanted to write about, he or she failed to communicate those ideas clearly to the reader.

Score 2 Essay

> The lecture was about the same main point as the reading passage. But it's offer an other view point. Indeed it's realy interessante to see the two explainations.
>
> In the reading passage the TV is presented like really benefits for all the univercity. It's really good for the professor an the campus. But the professor from the lecture make advertising. she thinks that it's not really good for all. A professor spends a lot of time too make a television appereance. And may be it's not his rolle. He is payed to make cours and reasarch. the student could be the loser of this association. Nevertheless the television could have benefics. In fact when a professor is on TV, he raise the reputation of the university and he could have more sponsor for his reasarch. And the public haven't the best course.
>
> To conclude the television appearances must be take with becarefully and not too superficialy. In this way the relation beetwen the universery and the TV will be profitable.

Rater Comments

This response earns a score of 2 primarily because it summarizes only one of the main points from the lecture. The writer discusses the point that television appearances require a lot of time from professors who may then neglect their teaching and researching duties. This is developed with a fair amount of detail, although there are usage errors ("the TV is presented like really benefits for all the univercity," "the loser of this association," "the public haven't the best course") that obscure the writer's meaning to some degree. There is brief mention of benefits to the professor and the public, but these points are not developed or clear. The connection between the reading passage and the lecture is also misrepresented, and the overall topic (professors appearing on television) is not clear. A reader who is not already familiar with the reading passage and the lecture would not understand what the response is about.

Score 1 Essay

In the set of materials the reading passage provides some information regard the professors work and their experience on television appeareance. While the listening passage focus on experience of professors on tv and their benefits.

The professors appear as guest on television news programs.They do expert commentary on the last events in the world.This appearance give great benefits to professors.They acquire reputationsas authorities in their academic field.When they appears on tv many people become aware of the professors ideas.Also the university receive positive publicity when the professors speak on tv.

Another benefit is the opportunity for may people to listening andto learn from experts,In the listening passage

Rater Comments

Although the language in this response is relatively clear, the response can receive only a score of 1 because it does not present any information from the lecture. Main points are taken only from the reading passage, and the connection between the reading passage and the lecture is misrepresented.

Writing Based on Knowledge and Experience

Question

Do you agree or disagree with the following statement?

Young people enjoy life more than older people do.

Use specific reasons and examples to support your answer.

Topic Notes

This topic requires you to write about whether young people enjoy life more than older people do. If you agree with this statement, you should present examples and reasons. For example, young people may tend to go out more and participate in fun activities while older people may tend to stay at home more. Another reason that older people may enjoy life less is because they have more responsibilities and pressure from work, family, and money than young people. A third reason might be that young people are more physically fit and able to enjoy more activities than older people.

If you disagree with this statement in your response, you should present examples and reasons that older people enjoy life more. For example, older people may better know what satisfies them and makes them happy than young people do.

Some good responses explain that the group that enjoys life more depends on where they live. All of these approaches can be developed into a good response.

Sample Responses with Rater Comments

Score 5 Essay—Sample 1

People often complain about seing themselves becoming older too quickly. But does that mean that they are enjoying their lives less than they did before? Personally, I rather disagree with this statement. It would probably be more accurate to say that every time of a person's life is worth being lived and enjoyed.

There is no denying that young people have far less responsibilities with, for instance, family and work. Thus, they can spend more time on their hobbies than people who are working all day long and who have to care about their children at night when they come home. But one cannot overlook that having a family to care about can be considered as a satisfying pleasure in itself. Besides, many people find fullfillment in their work and enjoy spending most of their time on it.

Moreover, it is customary to say that older people tend to have more health problems than teenagers or students do. However, it is well worth noticing that this assertion cannot be taken as a general rule, as also many young people develop painfull illnesses. A striking example of a disease which tends to affect more and more teenagers is back ache, because they are sitting for too long periods of time and doing too little sport to compensate. Consequently, the argument supporting that good health makes life more enjoyable when you are young may be called into question.

In addition to that, one should not forget that today's teenagers are expected to take important decisions about their future at an early age, and that they have to cope with heavy responsibilities even before getting their first school degree. As it becomes more and more difficult to find a job these days, young people have to worry about what to study and they even often have to fix priorities according to what the job market offers, and not according to their personal preferences.

Last but not least, one cannot forget that after working hard for long years, people retire and are then given the chance to concentrate on their centers of interest and hobbies again. Up to a certain point, when taking into account the arguments of the previous paragraph concerning the early responsibilities teenagers have to assume, pensioners are even more free to enjoy their lives without thinking of potential problems of the future.

To put it in a nutshell, that all amounts to saying that there is no period of time in a person's life which is more prone to hapiness than the others. People only have to learn to make the best of every situation and of what they have . . . even if it is easier said than done!

Rater Comments

This well-structured essay meets all the criteria needed to earn a score of 5. It takes issue with the statement presented. It first develops its points somewhat inductively. In paragraph 2, it presents reasons why younger people may enjoy life more (fewer responsibilities) but ends by explaining why these same responsibilities can be fulfilling for older people. Paragraph 3 advances the claim that older people have more health problems and goes on to explain that young people can have health issues as well. The last point developed in paragraphs 4 and 5 discusses how younger people have to worry about their studies and their future, while older people who are retired are free to enjoy their lives—their hobbies and interests. Sentence structures are varied and complex, and the response displays good vocabulary choice; these allow the writer to convey meaning accurately. There is a minor organizational issue: the writer makes the statement in the introductory paragraph, "It would probably be more accurate to say that every time of a person's life is worth being lived and enjoyed," and also concludes with this same notion. This is a bit misleading because the focus of the body paragraphs is not on enjoyment at all stages of life—much is discussed about things that are not so pleasant at particular times of life. However, this misleading statement is not a major issue, and the bulk of the essay is a well-organized, coherent discussion of why it cannot be said that younger people enjoy life more than older people do.

Score 5 Essay—Sample 2

Personally I agree to the statement "young people enjoy life more than older people do", in that I believe the younger you are, the more possibilities you have of entertainment. The latter is a way to enjoy life, however it is not the only way. But depending on one's age, there are different ways of having fun experiences and interests.

Life can be enjoyed on an intellectual level by achieving more and more knowledge about the world, the human behaviour, past cultures and works of art. In order to learn more about the world, one must study. Studying is made easier for younger people in our society in that universities and colleges and most likely to accept a high school graduate rather than a retired man. Therefore it becomes harder for older people to have the opportunity to enjoy the privileges of studying and of acquiring knowledge. This however does not mean it cannot be done. In fact there are specific study programs designed for older people, either online or in special universities.

By certain individuals, enjoying life means to be involved in the society and to have fun. Unfortunately our society tends to alienate the old in that they are considered "less active". This is a mistake of the community. It is true that the older one gets the harder it is for him or her to be an active part in the society physically. However, the general term of "having fun" and being involved in society can be analysed at different levels and under many diverse points of views. Older people may have fun playing cards, while the younger ones finds fun in attending rave parties. Once again there are more opportunities for younger people to be involved in social events such as parties and sports related happenings. But it doesn't mean there are NO opportunities for older people.

The older population is more limited also due to a physical factor that prevents their capability of performing and resistance. Therefore a younger person may enjoy life by practicing a certain sport, while an older person may have difficulties playing a sport and being of actual competition in it. But older people can still get great joy from watching sports.

Younger people have more access, freedom and possibilities to attend social events. Furthermore they tend to have less responsabilites such as a family. A younger person may have less responsabilites in that perhaps he or she is not yet married. This becomes an advantage in "having fun", being that more time can be dedicated to theirselves rather than to their families. But for older people their fun is exactly the satifying they get from raising families so it's just a different fun again.

In conclusion, I believe that younger people are given more chances by society and their physical status to "enjoy life". They have more possibilities of attending mundane events, of studying and of playing sports. Furthermore younger people tend to have more time to dedicate to theirselves and to their enjoyment of life, and less responsabilites. However an older person may also enjoy life, in a different way as I have explained.

Rater Comments

This essay meets all the requirements for a score of 5 by using well-developed examples that are relevant to the topic and by using highly varied vocabulary. The introductory paragraph clearly states the writer's position that although younger people may have more opportunities to enjoy life, older people can enjoy it as well, but just differently. This is followed by the first point that society makes it easier for younger people to study and gain knowledge but that programs for older people also exist. The point is well developed and supports the writer's objective. In the third and fourth paragraphs, the writer discusses how society may alienate older people because of their level of physical ability but then explains that older people may enjoy less physical activities that younger people may not enjoy, such as playing card games. This writer's final point in paragraph 5, that younger people have fewer responsibilities, is also clear. All the points in the essay are developed in great detail, and the writer draws logical conclusions from each example. The advanced vocabulary used also adds to the essay's high score. The essay does present some errors in usage ("I agree to the statement," "By certain individuals"), but these errors do not interfere with the meaning and effectiveness of the writing.

Score 4 Essay—Sample 1

Yes, I agree that young people enjoy life more than older people do.

Life is full of joy and happiness when one is young and full of energy, when one does not have any care for anyone and does not have much knowledge or experience of bitterness and sorrow of life.

Young people can enjoy life because they are usually free of many diseases the older people suffer from. They can easily run, jump and do many things which is not possible for many olders. Thus physical fitness allow them to enjoy the life.

They can enjoy life because they do not need to care for earning, for rent and pay other utilities bills. Finacial difficulties does not impress their young heart as much as doest to the adults. They usually deopend on their gardians for money. Therefore, they do not need to face the stresses concerning earning and maintaining daily livelihood.

Unlike older people they are never alone. At home they are accompanied by either parents or other family members. at the streets they have their friends. If they do not have friends in a new community, they can make them very easily which could not be said about adults. In order to communicate with the other children they do not feel any barrier or complexity.

Being young they do not face many problems of life which adults do. They do not have enough knowledge about life which can make them unhappy. They seldom think about aging and death. They think that they would never grow old and die.

Therefore, there are many things in youth like young age, company, lack of care for money and lack of knowledg about the dark sides of life make them to feel happy and enjoy their life more than older people.

Rater Comments

This essay contains four points that address the topic and support the writer's opinion that younger people enjoy life more than older people do. The points are generally well developed, distinct from each other, and introduced with clear topic sentences in each body paragraph. The writer uses a nice range of vocabulary and strives to make the essay flow by using appropriate transitions and sentence structures ("Therefore, they do not need to face the stresses . . ."). Along with slightly less than full elaboration of points, errors in word choice (". . . they do not need to care for earning") and grammar ("things which is not possible for many olders," "Finacial difficulties does not . . .," "there are many things . . . make them to feel happy") do not interfere with meaning but are frequent enough to earn this essay a score of 4.

Score 4 Essay—Sample 2

Although young peolpe are more outgoing than older people, I do not agree with this statement. Older people are mostly retired and have much more time and money to go on trips and travel to other countrys. Younger people on the other hand have to learn often and do not have that much money to travel a lot. But they are more interested in discovering new countrys and make new experiences. In comparison, older people already have a lot of experience and they often, just want to visite places where they have been before rather than go on exiting trips.

However, older peole often have problems with their health and therefore they are not as flexible as young people are. Young people can do whatever they want, whithout thinking about their health. Older people therefore are more interested in their own family, which is often the most important topic in their lifes. And to my opinion it is far better to see your own grantchildren growing up than going into discos and stay up all night, what a lot of younger people do.

To sum up the main points, I do not think that younger people enjoy their life more than older people do, because there are so many things that older people can do which younger can not do. To my opinion older people enjoy their lifes different than younger people do, but there is no better way.

Rater Comments

This essay presents a fairly well-developed argument against the idea that younger people enjoy life more than older people do. The writer discusses two main points—that older people benefit more from the ability to travel and enjoy family time than younger people do—with a good amount of detail. While the overall meaning of the essay is clear, some of the ideas and connections are disjointed. In the second paragraph, for example, it is not clear how "therefore" connects the idea that older people may be more interested in family because younger people can do whatever they want without concern for their health. This minor structural flaw obscures the writer's intentions. A few errors in usage ("make new experiences," "what a lot of younger people do") that do not interfere with meaning also contribute to earning this essay a score of 4.

Score 3 Essay—Sample 1

Nowadays, young people have a lot of opportunities to enjoy life, more than older people have known when they were young. Thought, values especially in the way to bring up children have changed. I think that young people enjoy life more than older people do for that reason and for several others. Young people are usually in good health, so they have more envy to live their life, more than older people who may have health problems or do not want to have too much activities. It is obvious that young people have time to enjoy their life, they are still on studies so they can have several activities, they have the possibility to do a lot of new experiences. Older people usually have a job and a family to look after, thet cannot do what they want, they have to give stability to them and their family. Nomad people are often single, it is difficult to enjoy your life free when you have assignments.

Moreover, when you are young you are very curious, interested by all you may learn. It is the exemple of the young child who wants to discover his environment. Generally, older people have already done a lot of things in their life such as sports, travels...

Young people want to learn others things, they like to meet with friends to go to cinema or to museum. The best way to discover other cultures is obviously to travel to foreign countries and meet locals to understand their culturs without judgments. I think the best way to discover other countries is to travel to them or to study during a year in them. Study abroad is a very exciting experience during which you can learn a lot, especially on yourself. I think it makes you grow up. You have to be adaptive, to ask you questions . . .

Finally, young people are incitated to move, to enjoy their lives through media, who help them to wide their mind to discovers and to other cultures. It is fundamental to young to discover all the world and open them to others, it should be a way to give them the possibility to continue to enjoy their life when they will be older.

Rater Comments

This essay earns a score of 3 because it lacks development of its key points. The writer lists a number of reasons to support the idea that younger people enjoy life more than older people do. Some of these reasons are fairly clear, but they are not substantiated by concrete examples that can be readily understood as supporting the overall idea the writer presents in the first two sentences. It is not clear how the example of nomadic people relates to the idea that older people have more responsibilities. The most developed paragraph, about meeting friends and traveling abroad, has a number of ideas relevant to the question asked, but it is fairly difficult to understand how the ideas within the paragraph are connected. It is also difficult to see how all of the information is related to the topic or the writer's opinion overall. For example, the writer does not explain how the statements that older people may have missed opportunities when they were young ties into the writer's point. While much of the essay's meaning is clear, this response is marked by some errors in grammar and word choice ("incitated to move," "wide their mind"), and some of these are very difficult to understand ("more envy to live"). These types of errors limit the essay to a score of 3.

Score 3 Essay—Sample 2

Life is a long travel that everybody can enjoyed. As young people discover new things everydays, older can use their own experiences to get more entertainment. The way, people, young or old, live their life is something that can not be discussed untill they do not hurt anybody.

In one hand, when you are a young people, you can learn, and find new things everydays. You meet lot of people in your primary school, your High School and your College. The young part of the life is done to enjoy every moments that will be cut of the future adult life. Futhermore, the fact that you are a young people allow you to communicate easily and to gain experiences fastly from your errors. Although, you also need advices from older peolpe who have certainly lived what you have to ask.

In the other hand, older peolple have all the information that make life pleasant to live. Therefor peolple can think that, they will not enjoy life. In fact, if you already have all the advice you need to live, you can do something more exciting. Something like travel all around the world or take a new job because you have learned everything you thought you have to know. Moreover you also can interest to things that you have left behing. I mean when you were a student. It is not possible to take every courses you want to. But when you have done lot of things you can come back to the field that passionated you.

In short, I would say that if you do not enjoy your life when you are young you can not enjoy life when you are older. Therby, it is really important to take every moments as a single one and to enjoy it as if it was the only one you have.

Rater Comments

This essay cannot earn a score higher than a 3 for a number of reasons. It displays numerous errors in word choice and expression ("something that can not be discussed until they do not hurt anybody," "you also can interest to things") and grammar ("discover new things everydays," "the field that passionated you") that are either distracting to the reader or occasionally obscure meaning. The writer promises in the introductory paragraph to elaborate on two main points—that younger people can discover new things and that older people can use their experience to enjoy life. However, these ideas are at best somewhat developed in paragraphs 2 and 3, though at times, the connections within each of these two paragraphs is a little unclear. Especially in the third paragraph, it is difficult to know exactly what the point is that the writer is trying to make until the end of the paragraph. Finally, the statement "if you do not enjoy life when you are young you can not enjoy life when you are older" is used as a conclusion, but this is a new idea that is not expressed or developed earlier in the body of the essay.

Score 2 Essay—Sample 1

I'm not sure it's true that young people enjoy life more than older people. I think two categories have a different types of passions, different types of hobbies and lifestyles.

Young people, like me, love to stay with the friends, play music, dance and go around the world,

Older people are most quiet; like to stay at home with the family to watch tv or to read a book.

I think it's normal the people think the young people have more vitality than older people, it's a natural cycle of life.

When old peolpe was young, also they love to stay with friends or to go to dance, but than their life changed, they came to work and they had a family.

Rater Comments

Lack of development, primarily, earns this essay a score of 2. The writer's main point seems to be that it is not really the case that younger people enjoy life more; rather, the way younger and older people approach life is different in terms of their "passions" and "types of hobbies and lifestyles." This would be a fine approach as a response to the question, but the writer simply does not give enough examples or any explanation in support. A score of 2 is given to responses that have limited development and insufficient exemplification and details to support generalizations.

Score 2 Essay—Sample 2

What means exactly 'enjoy life'? Everyone has it's opinion about life. But it is right that we can thin that young people enjoy life more than older people do if we seeing in general.: They make often more activities and are always happy.

Firstly, as mentionned above , young people make more activities than older. The maim reaom is a physical reason. They have not the same body than older people

For example a lot of young people make physical activities. They make sport each week. They play sport in club , have a lot of friends in the club. they like going in night clubs with their friends. We can say that they enjoy life.

> Secondly, an other reason is that young people have not a private life ; a work, a household.... they have more time.
>
> They don't know that 'time is money' They dont have jobs. They have not a woman, they must not going to supermarket after the work etc. they are always happy.
>
> To sum up, young people enjoy life more than older for a certain point of view. In my opinion , it's very difficult to say that because we can says that a man who works each day , who is married and who have childrens can enjoy life more than younger people do. So, it's a query of mind. They enjoy life in a different way.

Rater Comments

Although this essay is longer than many responses with a score of 2, consistent and numerous errors in grammar ("What means exactly 'enjoy life'? Everyone has it's opinion . . . ," "they must not going to supermarket after the work") and usage ("They make sport each week," "They have not the same body . . . ," "going in night clubs," ". . . query of mind") are present throughout and limit the essay to a score of 2.

Score 1 Essay—Sample 1

> I agree with this this statement, young people enjoy life more than older people do beacause youn people are more dynamics than older peole.
>
> the young people living a different life, because the life has been changed than the previus generation.
>
> For the young people learn to use the new tecnologies are most user friendly, for older people are many difficult use the new tecnology.

Rater Comments

This essay earns a score of 1 mainly because it lacks any development of the main ideas. There are no examples or explanations to support the points that young people are happy because younger generations are different and may be able to use technology more easily. Also, the unclear usage ("young people are more dynamics") is not followed by any elaboration, so, again, no meaningful development is present.

Score 1 Essay—Sample 2

> Young people enjoy life more than older people do.
>
> First of all young people has free mind of preoccupation of life and that is a cause that enjoy life more than older people do.
>
> Young people attend with apprension a week-end when go enjoy at pub, disco where there are a party.
>
> Older people research a relax no a party and go out home only for go at work.

Rater Comments

This essay lacks any coherently developed points beyond a restatement of the question. Word choice and usage ("attend with apprension a week-end when go enjoy;" "Older people research a relax") and grammatical errors ("Older people . . . go out home only for go at work") strongly obscure meaning. This under-developed response, with no meaningful details, cannot receive anything but a score of 1.

8 Authentic TOEFL iBT Practice Test 3

n this chapter you will find the third of three authentic TOEFL iBT Practice Tests. You can take the test in two different ways:

- **In the book:** You can read through the test questions in the following pages, marking your answers in the spaces provided. To hear the listening portions of the test, follow instructions to play the numbered audio tracks on the CD-ROM that accompanies this book.

- **On the CD:** For a test-taking experience that more closely resembles the actual TOEFL iBT test, you can take this same test on your computer using the accompanying CD-ROM. Reading passages and questions will appear on-screen, and you can enter your answers by clicking on the spaces provided. Follow instructions to hear the listening portions of the test.

Following this test, you will find answer keys and scoring information. You will also find scripts for the listening portions. Complete answer explanations, as well as sample test taker spoken responses and essays, are also provided.

TOEFL iBT Practice Test 3
READING

Directions: This section measures your ability to understand academic passages in English.

The Reading section is divided into separately timed parts.

Most questions are worth 1 point, but the last question for each passage is worth more than 1 point. The directions for the last question indicate how many points you may receive.

You will now begin the Reading section. There are three passages in the section. You should allow **20 minutes** to read each passage and answer the questions about it. You should allow **60 minutes** to complete the entire section.

At the end of this Practice Test you will find an answer key, information to help you determine your score, and explanations of the answers.

ARCHITECTURE

Architecture is the art and science of designing structures that organize and enclose space for practical and symbolic purposes. Because architecture grows out of human needs and aspirations, it clearly communicates cultural values. Of all the visual arts, architecture affects our lives most directly for it determines the character of the human environment in major ways.

Architecture is a three-dimensional form. It utilizes space, mass, texture, line, light, and color. To be architecture, a building must achieve a working harmony with a variety of elements. Humans instinctively seek structures that will shelter and enhance their way of life. It is the work of architects to create buildings that are not simply constructions but also offer inspiration and delight. Buildings contribute to human life when they provide shelter, enrich space, complement their site, suit the climate, and are economically feasible. The client who pays for the building and defines its function is an important member of the architectural team. The mediocre design of many contemporary buildings can be traced to both clients and architects.

In order for the structure to achieve the size and strength necessary to meet its purpose, architecture employs methods of support that, because they are based on physical laws, have changed little since people first discovered them—even while building materials have changed dramatically. The world's architectural structures have also been devised in relation to the objective limitations of materials. Structures can be analyzed in terms of how they deal with downward forces created by gravity.

They are designed to withstand the forces of *compression* (pushing together), *tension* (pulling apart), *bending*, or a combination of these in different parts of the structure.

Every development in architecture has been the result of major technological changes. Materials and methods of construction are integral parts of the design of architectural structures. In earlier times it was necessary to design structural systems suitable for the materials that were available, such as wood, stone, or brick. Today technology has progressed to the point where it is possible to invent new building materials to suit the type of structure desired. Enormous changes in materials and techniques of construction within the last few generations have made it possible to enclose space with much greater ease and speed and with a minimum of material. Progress in this area can be measured by the difference in weight between buildings built now and those of comparable size built one hundred years ago.

Modern architectural forms generally have three separate components comparable to elements of the human body: a supporting *skeleton* or frame, an outer *skin* enclosing the interior spaces, and *equipment,* similar to the body's vital organs and systems. The equipment includes plumbing, electrical wiring, hot water, and air-conditioning. Of course in early architecture—such as igloos and adobe structures—there was no such equipment, and the skeleton and skin were often one.

Much of the world's great architecture has been constructed of stone because of its beauty, permanence, and availability. In the past, whole cities grew from the arduous task of cutting and piling stone upon stone. Some of the world's finest stone architecture can be seen in the ruins of the ancient Inca city of Machu Picchu high in the eastern Andes Mountains of Peru. The doorways and windows are made possible by placing over the open spaces thick stone beams that support the weight from above. A structural invention had to be made before the physical limitations of stone could be overcome and new architectural forms could be created. That invention was the *arch*, a curved structure originally made of separate stone or brick segments. The arch was used by the early cultures of the Mediterranean area chiefly for underground drains, but it was the Romans who first developed and used the arch extensively in aboveground structures. Roman builders perfected the semicircular arch made of separate blocks of stone. As a method of spanning space, the arch can support greater weight than a horizontal beam. It works in compression to divert the weight above it out to the sides, where the weight is borne by the vertical elements on either side of the arch. The arch is among the many important structural breakthroughs that have characterized architecture throughout the centuries.

PARAGRAPH 1

Architecture is the art and science of designing structures that organize and enclose space for practical and symbolic purposes. Because architecture grows out of human needs and aspirations, it clearly communicates cultural values. Of all the visual arts, architecture affects our lives most directly for it determines the character of the human environment in major ways.

Directions: Mark your answer by filling in the oval next to your choice.

1. According to paragraph 1, all of the following statements about architecture are true EXCEPT:

   ○ Architecture is a visual art.
   ○ Architecture reflects the cultural values of its creators.
   ○ Architecture has both artistic and scientific dimensions.
   ○ Architecture has an indirect effect on life.

PARAGRAPH 2

Architecture is a three-dimensional form. It utilizes space, mass, texture, line, light, and color. To be architecture, a building must achieve a working harmony with a variety of elements. Humans instinctively seek structures that will shelter and enhance their way of life. It is the work of architects to create buildings that are not simply constructions but also offer inspiration and delight. Buildings contribute to human life when they provide shelter, enrich space, complement their site, suit the climate, and are economically feasible. The client who pays for the building and defines its function is an important member of the architectural team. The mediocre design of many contemporary buildings can be traced to both clients and architects.

2. The word "enhance" in the passage is closest in meaning to

   ○ protect
   ○ improve
   ○ organize
   ○ match

3. The word "feasible" in the passage is closest in meaning to

   ○ in existence
   ○ without question
   ○ achievable
   ○ most likely

GO ON TO THE NEXT PAGE ↘

P A R A G R A P H 3

In order for the structure to achieve the size and strength necessary to meet its purpose, architecture employs methods of support that, because they are based on physical laws, have changed little since people first discovered them—even while building materials have changed dramatically. The world's architectural structures have also been devised in relation to the objective limitations of materials. Structures can be analyzed in terms of how they deal with downward forces created by gravity. They are designed to withstand the forces of *compression* (pushing together), *tension* (pulling apart), *bending*, or a combination of these in different parts of the structure.

4. Which of the sentences below best expresses the essential information in the highlighted sentence in the passage? Incorrect choices change the meaning in important ways or leave out essential information.

○ Unchanging physical laws have limited the size and strength of buildings that can be made with materials discovered long ago.

○ Building materials have changed in order to increase architectural size and strength, but physical laws of structure have not changed.

○ When people first started to build, the structural methods used to provide strength and size were inadequate because they were not based on physical laws.

○ Unlike building materials, the methods of support used in architecture have not changed over time because they are based on physical laws.

5. The word "devised" in the passage is closest in meaning to

○ combined
○ created
○ introduced
○ suggested

P A R A G R A P H 4

Every development in architecture has been the result of major technological changes. Materials and methods of construction are integral parts of the design of architectural structures. In earlier times it was necessary to design structural systems suitable for the materials that were available, such as wood, stone, or brick. Today technology has progressed to the point where it is possible to invent new building materials to suit the type of structure desired. Enormous changes in materials and techniques of construction within the last few generations have made it possible to enclose space with much greater ease and speed and with a minimum of material. Progress in this area can be measured by the difference in weight between buildings built now and those of comparable size built one hundred years ago.

6. The word "integral" is closest in meaning to

○ essential
○ variable
○ practical
○ independent

7. According to paragraph 4, which of the following is true about materials used in the construction of buildings?

○ Because new building materials are hard to find, construction techniques have changed very little from past generations.

○ The availability of suitable building materials no longer limits the types of structures that may be built.

○ The primary building materials that are available today are wood, stone, and brick.

○ Architects in earlier times did not have enough building materials to enclose large spaces.

8. In paragraph 4, what does the author imply about modern buildings?

○ They occupy much less space than buildings constructed one hundred years ago.

○ They are not very different from the buildings of a few generations ago.

○ They weigh less in relation to their size than buildings constructed one hundred years ago.

○ They take a long time to build as a result of their complex construction methods.

PARAGRAPH 5

Modern architectural forms generally have three separate components comparable to elements of the human body: a supporting *skeleton* or frame, an outer *skin* enclosing the interior spaces, and *equipment*, similar to the body's vital organs and systems. The equipment includes plumbing, electrical wiring, hot water, and air-conditioning. Of course in early architecture—such as igloos and adobe structures—there was no such equipment, and the skeleton and skin were often one.

9. Which of the following correctly characterizes the relationship between the human body and architecture that is described in paragraph 5?

○ Complex equipment inside buildings is the one element in modern architecture that resembles a component of the human body.

○ The components in early buildings were similar to three particular elements of the human body.

○ Modern buildings have components that are as likely to change as the human body is.

○ In general, modern buildings more closely resemble the human body than earlier buildings do.

GO ON TO THE NEXT PAGE ↘

Much of the world's great architecture has been constructed of stone because of its beauty, permanence, and availability. In the past, whole cities grew from the arduous task of cutting and piling stone upon stone. Some of the world's finest stone architecture can be seen in the ruins of the ancient Inca city of Machu Picchu high in the eastern Andes Mountains of Peru. The doorways and windows are made possible by placing over the open spaces thick stone beams that support the weight from above. A structural invention had to be made before the physical limitations of stone could be overcome and new architectural forms could be created. That invention was the *arch*, a curved structure originally made of separate stone or brick segments. The arch was used by the early cultures of the Mediterranean area chiefly for underground drains, but it was the Romans who first developed and used the arch extensively in aboveground structures. Roman builders perfected the semicircular arch made of separate blocks of stone. As a method of spanning space, the arch can support greater weight than a horizontal beam. It works in compression to divert the weight above it out to the sides, where the weight is borne by the vertical elements on either side of the arch. The arch is among the many important structural breakthroughs that have characterized architecture throughout the centuries.

10. The word "arduous" in the passage is closest in meaning to

○ difficult
○ necessary
○ skilled
○ shared

11. Why does the author include a description of how the "doorways and windows" of Machu Picchu were constructed?

○ To indicate that the combined skeletons and skins of the stone buildings of Machu Picchu were similar to igloos and adobe structures
○ To indicate the different kinds of stones that had to be cut to build Machu Picchu
○ To provide an illustration of the kind of construction that was required before arches were invented
○ To explain how ancient builders reduced the amount of time necessary to construct buildings from stone

12. According to paragraph 6, which of the following statements is true of the arch?

○ The Romans were the first people to use the stone arch.
○ The invention of the arch allowed new architectural forms to be developed.
○ The arch worked by distributing the structural load of a building toward the center of the arch.
○ The Romans followed earlier practices in their use of arches.

PARAGRAPH 5

■ Modern architectural forms generally have three separate components comparable to elements of the human body: a supporting *skeleton* or frame, an outer *skin* enclosing the interior spaces, and *equipment*, similar to the body's vital organs and systems. ■ The equipment includes plumbing, electrical wiring, hot water, and air-conditioning. ■ Of course in early architecture—such as igloos and adobe structures—there was no such equipment, and the skeleton and skin were often one. ■

13. Look at the four squares [■] where the following sentence could be added to the passage.

However, some modern architectural designs, such as those using folded plates of concrete or air-inflated structures, are again unifying skeleton and skin.

Where would the sentence best fit?

○ **However, some modern architectural designs, such as those using folded plates of concrete or air-inflated structures, are again unifying skeleton and skin.** Modern architectural forms generally have three separate components comparable to elements of the human body: a supporting *skeleton* or frame, an outer *skin* enclosing the interior spaces, and *equipment*, similar to the body's vital organs and systems. ■ The equipment includes plumbing, electrical wiring, hot water, and air-conditioning. ■ Of course in early architecture—such as igloos and adobe structures—there was no such equipment, and the skeleton and skin were often one. ■

○ ■ Modern architectural forms generally have three separate components comparable to elements of the human body: a supporting *skeleton* or frame, an outer *skin* enclosing the interior spaces, and *equipment*, similar to the body's vital organs and systems. **However, some modern architectural designs, such as those using folded plates of concrete or air-inflated structures, are again unifying skeleton and skin.** The equipment includes plumbing, electrical wiring, hot water, and air-conditioning. ■ Of course in early architecture—such as igloos and adobe structures—there was no such equipment, and the skeleton and skin were often one. ■

○ ■ Modern architectural forms generally have three separate components comparable to elements of the human body: a supporting *skeleton* or frame, an outer *skin* enclosing the interior spaces, and *equipment*, similar to the body's vital organs and systems. ■ The equipment includes plumbing, electrical wiring, hot water, and air-conditioning. **However, some modern architectural designs, such as those using folded plates of concrete or air-inflated structures, are again unifying skeleton and skin.** Of course in early architecture—such as igloos and adobe structures—there was no such equipment, and the skeleton and skin were often one. ■

GO ON TO THE NEXT PAGE ↘

○ ■ Modern architectural forms generally have three separate components comparable to elements of the human body: a supporting *skeleton* or frame, an outer *skin* enclosing the interior spaces, and *equipment*, similar to the body's vital organs and systems. ■ The equipment includes plumbing, electrical wiring, hot water, and air-conditioning. ■ Of course in early architecture—such as igloos and adobe structures—there was no such equipment, and the skeleton and skin were often one. **However, some modern architectural designs, such as those using folded plates of concrete or air-inflated structures, are again unifying skeleton and skin.**

14. **Directions:** An introductory sentence for a brief summary of the passage is provided below. Complete the summary by selecting the THREE answer choices that express the most important ideas in the passage. Some answer choices do not belong in the summary because they express ideas that are not presented in the passage or are minor ideas in the passage. **This question is worth 2 points.**

Architecture uses forms and space to express cultural values.

-
-
-

Answer Choices

1. Architects seek to create buildings that are both visually appealing and well suited for human use.

2. Both clients and architects are responsible for the mediocre designs of some modern buildings.

3. Over the course of the history of building, innovations in materials and methods of construction have given architects ever greater freedom to express themselves.

4. Modern buildings tend to lack the beauty of ancient stone buildings such as those of Machu Picchu.

5. Throughout history buildings have been constructed like human bodies, needing distinct "organ" systems in order to function.

6. The discovery and use of the arch typifies the way in which architecture advances by developing more efficient types of structures.

THE LONG-TERM STABILITY OF ECOSYSTEMS

Plant communities assemble themselves flexibly, and their particular structure depends on the specific history of the area. Ecologists use the term "succession" to refer to the changes that happen in plant communities and ecosystems over time. The first community in a succession is called a pioneer community, while the long-lived community at the end of succession is called a climax community. Pioneer and successional plant communities are said to change over periods from 1 to 500 years. These changes— in plant numbers and the mix of species—are cumulative. Climax communities themselves change but over periods of time greater than about 500 years.

An ecologist who studies a pond today may well find it relatively unchanged in a year's time. Individual fish may be replaced, but the number of fish will tend to be the same from one year to the next. We can say that the properties of an ecosystem are more stable than the individual organisms that compose the ecosystem.

At one time, ecologists believed that species diversity made ecosystems stable. They believed that the greater the diversity the more stable the ecosystem. Support for this idea came from the observation that long-lasting climax communities usually have more complex food webs and more species diversity than pioneer communities. Ecologists concluded that the apparent stability of climax ecosystems depended on their complexity. To take an extreme example, farmlands dominated by a single crop are so unstable that one year of bad weather or the invasion of a single pest can destroy the entire crop. In contrast, a complex climax community, such as a temperate forest, will tolerate considerable damage from weather or pests.

The question of ecosystem stability is complicated, however. The first problem is that ecologists do not all agree what "stability" means. Stability can be defined as simply lack of change. In that case, the climax community would be considered the most stable, since, by definition, it changes the least over time. Alternatively, stability can be defined as the speed with which an ecosystem returns to a particular form following a major disturbance, such as a fire. This kind of stability is also called *resilience*. In that case, climax communities would be the most fragile and the *least* stable, since they can require hundreds of years to return to the climax state.

Even the kind of stability defined as simple lack of change is not always associated with maximum diversity. At least in temperate zones, maximum diversity is often found in mid-successional stages, not in the climax community. Once a redwood forest matures, for example, the kinds of species and the number of individuals growing on the forest floor are reduced. In general, diversity, by itself, does not ensure stability. Mathematical models of ecosystems likewise suggest that diversity does not guarantee ecosystem stability—just the opposite, in fact. A more complicated system is, in general, more likely than a simple system to break down. (A fifteen-speed racing bicycle is more likely to break down than a child's tricycle.)

Ecologists are especially interested in knowing what factors contribute to the resilience of communities because climax communities all over the world are being severely damaged or destroyed by human activities. The destruction caused by the volcanic explosion of Mount St. Helens, in the northwestern United States, for example, pales in comparison to the destruction caused by humans. We need to know what

GO ON TO THE NEXT PAGE ↘

aspects of a community are most important to the community's resistance to destruction, as well as its recovery.

Many ecologists now think that the relative long-term stability of climax communities comes not from diversity but from the "patchiness" of the environment; an environment that varies from place to place supports more kinds of organisms than an environment that is uniform. A local population that goes extinct is quickly replaced by immigrants from an adjacent community. Even if the new population is of a different species, it can approximately fill the niche vacated by the extinct population and keep the food web intact.

PARAGRAPH 1

Plant communities assemble themselves flexibly, and their particular structure depends on the specific history of the area. Ecologists use the term "succession" to refer to the changes that happen in plant communities and ecosystems over time. The first community in a succession is called a pioneer community, while the long-lived community at the end of succession is called a climax community. Pioneer and successional plant communities are said to change over periods from 1 to 500 years. These changes—in plant numbers and the mix of species—are cumulative. Climax communities themselves change but over periods of time greater than about 500 years.

Directions: Mark your answer by filling in the oval next to your choice.

1. The word "particular" in the passage is closest in meaning to

   ○ natural
   ○ final
   ○ specific
   ○ complex

2. According to paragraph 1, which of the following is NOT true of climax communities?

   ○ They occur at the end of a succession.
   ○ They last longer than any other type of community.
   ○ The numbers of plants in them and the mix of species do not change.
   ○ They remain stable for at least 500 years at a time.

PARAGRAPH 2

An ecologist who studies a pond today may well find it relatively unchanged in a year's time. Individual fish may be replaced, but the number of fish will tend to be the same from one year to the next. We can say that the properties of an ecosystem are more stable than the individual organisms that compose the ecosystem.

3. According to paragraph 2, which of the following principles of ecosystems can be learned by studying a pond?

   ○ Ecosystem properties change more slowly than individuals in the system.
   ○ The stability of an ecosystem tends to change as individuals are replaced.
   ○ Individual organisms are stable from one year to the next.
   ○ A change in the numbers of an organism does not affect an ecosystem's properties.

PARAGRAPH 3

At one time, ecologists believed that species diversity made ecosystems stable. They believed that the greater the diversity the more stable the ecosystem. Support for this idea came from the observation that long-lasting climax communities usually have more complex food webs and more species diversity than pioneer communities. Ecologists concluded that the apparent stability of climax ecosystems depended on their complexity. To take an extreme example, farmlands dominated by a single crop are so unstable that one year of bad weather or the invasion of a single pest can destroy the entire crop. In contrast, a complex climax community, such as a temperate forest, will tolerate considerable damage from weather or pests.

4. According to paragraph 3, ecologists once believed that which of the following illustrated the most stable ecosystems?

- ○ Pioneer communities
- ○ Climax communities
- ○ Single-crop farmlands
- ○ Successional plant communities

PARAGRAPH 4

The question of ecosystem stability is complicated, however. The first problem is that ecologists do not all agree what "stability" means. Stability can be defined as simply lack of change. In that case, the climax community would be considered the most stable, since, by definition, it changes the least over time. Alternatively, stability can be defined as the speed with which an ecosystem returns to a particular form following a major disturbance, such as a fire. This kind of stability is also called *resilience*. In that case, climax communities would be the most fragile and the *least* stable, since they can require hundreds of years to return to the climax state.

5. According to paragraph 4, why is the question of ecosystem stability complicated?

- ○ The reasons for ecosystem change are not always clear.
- ○ Ecologists often confuse the word "stability" with the word "resilience."
- ○ The exact meaning of the word "stability" is debated by ecologists.
- ○ There are many different answers to ecological questions.

6. According to paragraph 4, which of the following is true of climax communities?

- ○ They are more resilient than pioneer communities.
- ○ They can be considered both the most and the least stable communities.
- ○ They are stable because they recover quickly after major disturbances.
- ○ They are the most resilient communities because they change the least over time.

GO ON TO THE NEXT PAGE ↘

Even the kind of stability defined as simple lack of change is not always associated with maximum diversity. At least in temperate zones, maximum diversity is often found in mid-successional stages, not in the climax community. Once a redwood forest matures, for example, the kinds of species and the number of individuals growing on the forest floor are reduced. In general, diversity, by itself, does not ensure stability. Mathematical models of ecosystems likewise suggest that diversity does not guarantee ecosystem stability—just the opposite, in fact. A more complicated system is, in general, more likely than a simple system to break down. (A fifteen-speed racing bicycle is more likely to break down than a child's tricycle.)

7. Which of the following can be inferred from paragraph 5 about redwood forests?

○ They become less stable as they mature.
○ They support many species when they reach climax.
○ They are found in temperate zones.
○ They have reduced diversity during mid-successional stages.

8. The word "guarantee" in the passage is closest in meaning to

○ increase
○ ensure
○ favor
○ complicate

9. In paragraph 5, why does the author provide the information that "A fifteen-speed racing bicycle is more likely to break down than a child's tricycle"?

○ To illustrate a general principle about the stability of systems by using an everyday example
○ To demonstrate that an understanding of stability in ecosystems can be applied to help understand stability in other situations
○ To make a comparison that supports the claim that, in general, stability increases with diversity
○ To provide an example that contradicts mathematical models of ecosystems

PARAGRAPH 6

Ecologists are especially interested in knowing what factors contribute to the resilience of communities because climax communities all over the world are being severely damaged or destroyed by human activities. The destruction caused by the volcanic explosion of Mount St. Helens, in the northwestern United States, for example, pales in comparison to the destruction caused by humans. We need to know what aspects of a community are most important to the community's resistance to destruction, as well as its recovery.

10. The word "pales" in the passage is closest in meaning to
   ○ increases proportionally
   ○ differs
   ○ loses significance
   ○ is common

PARAGRAPH 7

Many ecologists now think that the relative long-term stability of climax communities comes not from diversity but from the "patchiness" of the environment; an environment that varies from place to place supports more kinds of organisms than an environment that is uniform. A local population that goes extinct is quickly replaced by immigrants from an adjacent community. Even if the new population is of a different species, it can approximately fill the niche vacated by the extinct population and keep the food web intact.

11. Which of the sentences below best expresses the essential information in the highlighted sentence in the passage? Incorrect choices change the meaning in important ways or leave out essential information.
   ○ Ecologists now think that the stability of an environment is a result of diversity rather than patchiness.
   ○ Patchy environments that vary from place to place do not often have high species diversity.
   ○ Uniform environments cannot be climax communities because they do not support as many types of organisms as patchy environments.
   ○ A patchy environment is thought to increase stability because it is able to support a wide variety of organisms.

12. The word "adjacent" in the passage is closest in meaning to
   ○ foreign
   ○ stable
   ○ fluid
   ○ neighboring

GO ON TO THE NEXT PAGE ↘

PARAGRAPH 6

■ Ecologists are especially interested in knowing what factors contribute to the resilience of communities because climax communities all over the world are being severely damaged or destroyed by human activities. ■ The destruction caused by the volcanic explosion of Mount St. Helens, in the northwestern United States, for example, pales in comparison to the destruction caused by humans. ■ We need to know what aspects of a community are most important to the community's resistance to destruction, as well as its recovery. ■

13. Look at the four squares [■] that indicate where the following sentence could be added to the passage.

In fact, damage to the environment by humans is often much more severe than by natural events and processes.

Where would the sentence best fit?

○ **In fact, damage to the environment by humans is often much more severe than by natural events and processes.** Ecologists are especially interested in knowing what factors contribute to the resilience of communities because climax communities all over the world are being severely damaged or destroyed by human activities. ■ The destruction caused by the volcanic explosion of Mount St. Helens, in the northwestern United States, for example, pales in comparison to the destruction caused by humans. ■ We need to know what aspects of a community are most important to the community's resistance to destruction, as well as its recovery. ■

○ ■ Ecologists are especially interested in knowing what factors contribute to the resilience of communities because climax communities all over the world are being severely damaged or destroyed by human activities. **In fact, damage to the environment by humans is often much more severe than by natural events and processes.** The destruction caused by the volcanic explosion of Mount St. Helens, in the northwestern United States, for example, pales in comparison to the destruction caused by humans. ■ We need to know what aspects of a community are most important to the community's resistance to destruction, as well as its recovery. ■

○ ■ Ecologists are especially interested in knowing what factors contribute to the resilience of communities because climax communities all over the world are being severely damaged or destroyed by human activities. ■ The destruction caused by the volcanic explosion of Mount St. Helens, in the northwestern United States, for example, pales in comparison to the destruction caused by humans. **In fact, damage to the environment by humans is often much more severe than by natural events and processes.** We need to know what aspects of a community are most important to the community's resistance to destruction, as well as its recovery. ■

○ ■ Ecologists are especially interested in knowing what factors contribute to the resilience of communities because climax communities all over the world are being severely damaged or destroyed by human activities. ■ The destruction caused by the volcanic explosion of Mount St. Helens, in the northwestern United States, for example, pales in comparison to the destruction caused by humans. We need to know what aspects of a community are most important to the community's resistance to destruction, as well as its recovery. **In fact, damage to the environment by humans is often much more severe than by natural events and processes.**

14. **Directions:** An introductory sentence for a brief summary of the passage is provided below. Complete the summary by selecting the THREE answer choices that express the most important ideas in the passage. Some answer choices do not belong in the summary because they express ideas that are not presented in the passage or are minor ideas in the passage. **This question is worth 2 points.**

The process of succession and the stability of a climax community can change over time.

-
-
-

Answer Choices

1. The changes that occur in an ecosystem from the pioneer to the climax community can be seen in one human generation.

2. Ecologists agree that climax communities are the most stable types of ecosystems.

3. A high degree of species diversity does not always result in a stable ecosystem.

4. Disagreements over the meaning of the term "stability" make it difficult to identify the most stable ecosystems.

5. The level of resilience in a plant community contributes to its long-term stability.

6. The resilience of climax communities makes them resistant to destruction caused by humans.

DEPLETION OF THE OGALLALA AQUIFER

The vast grasslands of the High Plains in the central United States were settled by farmers and ranchers in the 1880s. This region has a semiarid climate, and for 50 years after its settlement, it supported a low-intensity agricultural economy of cattle ranching and wheat farming. In the early twentieth century, however, it was discovered that much of the High Plains was underlain by a huge aquifer (a rock layer containing large quantities of groundwater). This aquifer was named the Ogallala aquifer after the Ogallala Sioux Indians, who once inhabited the region.

The Ogallala aquifer is a sandstone formation that underlies some 583,000 square kilometers of land extending from northwestern Texas to southern South Dakota. Water from rains and melting snows has been accumulating in the Ogallala for the past 30,000 years. Estimates indicate that the aquifer contains enough water to fill Lake Huron, but unfortunately, under the semiarid climatic conditions that presently exist in the region, rates of addition to the aquifer are minimal, amounting to about half a centimeter a year.

The first wells were drilled into the Ogallala during the drought years of the early 1930s. The ensuing rapid expansion of irrigation agriculture, especially from the 1950s onward, transformed the economy of the region. More than 100,000 wells now tap the Ogallala. Modern irrigation devices, each capable of spraying 4.5 million liters of water a day, have produced a landscape dominated by geometric patterns of circular green islands of crops. Ogallala water has enabled the High Plains region to supply significant amounts of the cotton, sorghum, wheat, and corn grown in the United States. In addition, 40 percent of American grain-fed beef cattle are fattened here.

This unprecedented development of a finite groundwater resource with an almost negligible natural recharge rate—that is, virtually no natural water source to replenish the water supply—has caused water tables in the region to fall drastically. In the 1930s, wells encountered plentiful water at a depth of about 15 meters; currently, they must be dug to depths of 45 to 60 meters or more. In places, the water table is declining at a rate of a meter a year, necessitating the periodic deepening of wells and the use of ever-more-powerful pumps. It is estimated that at current withdrawal rates, much of the aquifer will run dry within 40 years. The situation is most critical in Texas, where the climate is driest, the greatest amount of water is being pumped, and the aquifer contains the least water. It is projected that the remaining Ogallala water will, by the year 2030, support only 35 to 40 percent of the irrigated acreage in Texas that it supported in 1980.

The reaction of farmers to the inevitable depletion of the Ogallala varies. Many have been attempting to conserve water by irrigating less frequently or by switching to crops that require less water. Others, however, have adopted the philosophy that it is best to use the water while it is still economically profitable to do so and to concentrate on high-value crops such as cotton. The incentive of the farmers who wish to conserve water is reduced by their knowledge that many of their neighbors are profiting by using great amounts of water, and in the process are drawing down the entire region's water supplies.

In the face of the upcoming water supply crisis, a number of grandiose schemes have been developed to transport vast quantities of water by canal or pipeline from the Mississippi, the Missouri, or the Arkansas rivers. Unfortunately, the cost of water obtained through any of these schemes would increase pumping costs at least ten-fold, making the cost of irrigated agricultural products from the region uncompetitive on the national and international markets. Somewhat more promising have been recent experiments for releasing capillary water (water in the soil) above the water table by injecting compressed air into the ground. Even if this process proves successful, however, it would almost triple water costs. Genetic engineering also may provide a partial solution, as new strains of drought-resistant crops continue to be developed. Whatever the final answer to the water crisis may be, it is evident that within the High Plains, irrigation water will never again be the abundant, inexpensive resource it was during the agricultural boom years of the mid-twentieth century.

PARAGRAPH 1

The vast grasslands of the High Plains in the central United States were settled by farmers and ranchers in the 1880s. This region has a semiarid climate, and for 50 years after its settlement, it supported a low-intensity agricultural economy of cattle ranching and wheat farming. In the early twentieth century, however, it was discovered that much of the High Plains was underlain by a huge aquifer (a rock layer containing large quantities of groundwater). This aquifer was named the Ogallala aquifer after the Ogallala Sioux Indians, who once inhabited the region.

Directions: Mark your answer by filling in the oval next to your choice.

1. According to paragraph 1, which of the following statements about the High Plains is true?

○ Until farmers and ranchers settled there in the 1880s, the High Plains had never been inhabited.

○ The climate of the High Plains is characterized by higher-than-average temperatures.

○ The large aquifer that lies underneath the High Plains was discovered by the Ogallala Sioux Indians.

○ Before the early 1900s there was only a small amount of farming and ranching in the High Plains.

GO ON TO THE NEXT PAGE ↘

The Ogallala aquifer is a sandstone formation that underlies some 583,000 square kilometers of land extending from northwestern Texas to southern South Dakota. Water from rains and melting snows has been accumulating in the Ogallala for the past 30,000 years. Estimates indicate that the aquifer contains enough water to fill Lake Huron, but unfortunately, under the semiarid climatic conditions that presently exist in the region, rates of addition to the aquifer are minimal, amounting to about half a centimeter a year.

2. According to paragraph 2, all of the following statements about the Ogallala aquifer are true EXCEPT:

○ The aquifer stretches from South Dakota to Texas.
○ The aquifer's water comes from underground springs.
○ Water has been gathering in the aquifer for 30,000 years.
○ The aquifer's water is stored in a layer of sandstone.

3. Which of the sentences below best expresses the essential information in the highlighted sentence in the passage? Incorrect choices change the meaning in important ways or leave out essential information.

○ Despite the current impressive size of the Ogallala aquifer, the region's climate keeps the rates of water addition very small.
○ Although the aquifer has been adding water at the rate of only half a centimeter a year, it will eventually accumulate enough water to fill Lake Huron.
○ Because of the region's present climatic conditions, water is being added each year to the aquifer.
○ Even when the region experiences unfortunate climatic conditions, the rates of addition of water continue to increase.

PARAGRAPH 3

The first wells were drilled into the Ogallala during the drought years of the early 1930s. The ensuing rapid expansion of irrigation agriculture, especially from the 1950s onward, transformed the economy of the region. More than 100,000 wells now tap the Ogallala. Modern irrigation devices, each capable of spraying 4.5 million liters of water a day, have produced a landscape dominated by geometric patterns of circular green islands of crops. Ogallala water has enabled the High Plains region to supply significant amounts of the cotton, sorghum, wheat, and corn grown in the United States. In addition, 40 percent of American grain-fed beef cattle are fattened here.

4. The word "ensuing" in the passage is closest in meaning to
   ◯ continuing
   ◯ surprising
   ◯ initial
   ◯ subsequent

5. In paragraph 3, why does the author provide the information that 40 percent of American cattle are fattened in the High Plains?
   ◯ To suggest that crop cultivation is not the most important part of the economy of the High Plains
   ◯ To indicate that not all economic activity in the High Plains is dependent on irrigation
   ◯ To provide another example of how water from the Ogallala has transformed the economy of the High Plains
   ◯ To contrast cattle-fattening practices in the High Plains with those used in other regions of the United States

GO ON TO THE NEXT PAGE ↘

PARAGRAPH 4

This unprecedented development of a finite groundwater resource with an almost negligible natural recharge rate—that is, virtually no natural water source to replenish the water supply—has caused water tables in the region to fall drastically. In the 1930s, wells encountered plentiful water at a depth of about 15 meters; currently, they must be dug to depths of 45 to 60 meters or more. In places, the water table is declining at a rate of a meter a year, necessitating the periodic deepening of wells and the use of ever-more-powerful pumps. It is estimated that at current withdrawal rates, much of the aquifer will run dry within 40 years. The situation is most critical in Texas, where the climate is driest, the greatest amount of water is being pumped, and the aquifer contains the least water. It is projected that the remaining Ogallala water will, by the year 2030, support only 35 to 40 percent of the irrigated acreage in Texas that it supported in 1980.

6. The word "unprecedented" in the passage is closest in meaning to
   ○ difficult to control
   ○ without any restriction
   ○ unlike anything in the past
   ○ rapidly expanding

7. The word "virtually" in the passage is closest in meaning to
   ○ clearly
   ○ perhaps
   ○ frequently
   ○ almost

8. According to paragraph 4, all of the following are consequences of the heavy use of the Ogallala aquifer for irrigation EXCEPT:
   ○ The recharge rate of the aquifer is decreasing.
   ○ Water tables in the region are becoming increasingly lower.
   ○ Wells now have to be dug to much greater depths than before.
   ○ Increasingly powerful pumps are needed to draw water from the aquifer.

9. According to paragraph 4, compared with all other states that use Ogallala water for irrigation, Texas
   ○ has the greatest amount of farmland being irrigated with Ogallala water
   ○ contains the largest amount of Ogallala water underneath the soil
   ○ is expected to face the worst water supply crisis as the Ogallala runs dry
   ○ uses the least amount of Ogallala water for its irrigation needs

The reaction of farmers to the inevitable depletion of the Ogallala varies. Many have been attempting to conserve water by irrigating less frequently or by switching to crops that require less water. Others, however, have adopted the philosophy that it is best to use the water while it is still economically profitable to do so and to concentrate on high-value crops such as cotton. The incentive of the farmers who wish to conserve water is reduced by their knowledge that many of their neighbors are profiting by using great amounts of water, and in the process are drawing down the entire region's water supplies.

10. The word "inevitable" in the passage is closest in meaning to
   ○ unfortunate
   ○ predictable
   ○ unavoidable
   ○ final

11. Paragraph 5 mentions which of the following as a source of difficulty for some farmers who try to conserve water?
   ○ Crops that do not need much water are difficult to grow in the High Plains.
   ○ Farmers who grow crops that need a lot of water make higher profits.
   ○ Irrigating less frequently often leads to crop failure.
   ○ Few farmers are convinced that the aquifer will eventually run dry.

P
A
R
A
G
R
A
P
H

6

In the face of the upcoming water supply crisis, a number of grandiose schemes have been developed to transport vast quantities of water by canal or pipeline from the Mississippi, the Missouri, or the Arkansas rivers. Unfortunately, the cost of water obtained through any of these schemes would increase pumping costs at least tenfold, making the cost of irrigated agricultural products from the region uncompetitive on the national and international markets. Somewhat more promising have been recent experiments for releasing capillary water (water in the soil) above the water table by injecting compressed air into the ground. Even if this process proves successful, however, it would almost triple water costs. Genetic engineering also may provide a partial solution, as new strains of drought-resistant crops continue to be developed. Whatever the final answer to the water crisis may be, it is evident that within the High Plains, irrigation water will never again be the abundant, inexpensive resource it was during the agricultural boom years of the mid-twentieth century.

12. According to paragraph 6, what is the main disadvantage of the proposed plans to transport river water to the High Plains?
   ○ The rivers cannot supply sufficient water for the farmers' needs.
   ○ Increased irrigation costs would make the products too expensive.
   ○ The costs of using capillary water for irrigation will increase.
   ○ Farmers will be forced to switch to genetically engineered crops.

GO ON TO THE NEXT PAGE ➤

The reaction of farmers to the inevitable depletion of the Ogallala varies. Many have been attempting to conserve water by irrigating less frequently or by switching to crops that require less water. ■ Others, however, have adopted the philosophy that it is best to use the water while it is still economically profitable to do so and to concentrate on high-value crops such as cotton. ■ The incentive of the farmers who wish to conserve water is reduced by their knowledge that many of their neighbors are profiting by using great amounts of water, and in the process are drawing down the entire region's water supplies. ■

In the face of the upcoming water supply crisis, a number of grandiose schemes have been developed to transport vast quantities of water by canal or pipeline from the Mississippi, the Missouri, or the Arkansas rivers. ■ Unfortunately, the cost of water obtained through any of these schemes would increase pumping costs at least tenfold, making the cost of irrigated agricultural products from the region uncompetitive on the national and international markets.

13. Look at the four squares [■] that indicate where the following sentence could be added to the passage.

But even if uncooperative farmers were to join in the conservation efforts, this would only delay the depletion of the aquifer.

Where would the sentence best fit?

○ The reaction of farmers to the inevitable depletion of the Ogallala varies. Many have been attempting to conserve water by irrigating less frequently or by switching to crops that require less water. **But even if uncooperative farmers were to join in the conservation efforts, this would only delay the depletion of the aquifer.** Others, however, have adopted the philosophy that it is best to use the water while it is still economically profitable to do so and to concentrate on high-value crops such as cotton. ■ The incentive of the farmers who wish to conserve water is reduced by their knowledge that many of their neighbors are profiting by using great amounts of water, and in the process are drawing down the entire region's water supplies. ■

In the face of the upcoming water supply crisis, a number of grandiose schemes have been developed to transport vast quantities of water by canal or pipeline from the Mississippi, the Missouri, or the Arkansas rivers. ■ Unfortunately, the cost of water obtained through any of these schemes would increase pumping costs at least tenfold, making the cost of irrigated agricultural products from the region uncompetitive on the national and international markets.

○ The reaction of farmers to the inevitable depletion of the Ogallala varies. Many have been attempting to conserve water by irrigating less frequently or by switching to crops that require less water. ■ Others, however, have adopted the philosophy that it is best to use the water while it is still economically profitable to do so and to concentrate on high-value crops such as cotton. **But even if uncooperative farmers were to join in the conservation efforts, this would only delay the depletion of the aquifer.** The incentive of the farmers who wish to conserve water is reduced by their knowledge that many of their neighbors are profiting by using great amounts of water, and in the process are drawing down the entire region's water supplies. ■

In the face of the upcoming water supply crisis, a number of grandiose schemes have been developed to transport vast quantities of water by canal or pipeline from the Mississippi, the Missouri, or the Arkansas rivers. ■ Unfortunately, the cost of water obtained through any of these schemes would increase pumping costs at least tenfold, making the cost of irrigated agricultural products from the region uncompetitive on the national and international markets.

○ The reaction of farmers to the inevitable depletion of the Ogallala varies. Many have been attempting to conserve water by irrigating less frequently or by switching to crops that require less water. ■ Others, however, have adopted the philosophy that it is best to use the water while it is still economically profitable to do so and to concentrate on high-value crops such as cotton. ■ The incentive of the farmers who wish to conserve water is reduced by their knowledge that many of their neighbors are profiting by using great amounts of water, and in the process are drawing down the entire region's water supplies. **But even if uncooperative farmers were to join in the conservation efforts, this would only delay the depletion of the aquifer.**

In the face of the upcoming water supply crisis, a number of grandiose schemes have been developed to transport vast quantities of water by canal or pipeline from the Mississippi, the Missouri, or the Arkansas rivers. ■ Unfortunately, the cost of water obtained through any of these schemes would increase pumping costs at least tenfold, making the cost of irrigated agricultural products from the region uncompetitive on the national and international markets.

○ The reaction of farmers to the inevitable depletion of the Ogallala varies. Many have been attempting to conserve water by irrigating less frequently or by switching to crops that require less water. ■ Others, however, have adopted the philosophy that it is best to use the water while it is still economically profitable to do so and to concentrate on high-value crops such as cotton. ■ The incentive of the farmers who wish to conserve water is reduced by their knowledge that many of their neighbors are profiting by using great amounts of water, and in the process are drawing down the entire region's water supplies. ■

In the face of the upcoming water supply crisis, a number of grandiose schemes have been developed to transport vast quantities of water by canal or pipeline from the Mississippi, the Missouri, or the Arkansas rivers. **But even if uncooperative farmers were to join in the conservation efforts, this would only delay the depletion of the aquifer.** Unfortunately, the cost of water obtained through any of these schemes would increase pumping costs at least tenfold, making the cost of irrigated agricultural products from the region uncompetitive on the national and international markets.

GO ON TO THE NEXT PAGE ↘

14. **Directions:** An introductory sentence for a brief summary of the passage is provided below. Complete the summary by selecting the THREE answer choices that express the most important ideas in the passage. Some answer choices do not belong in the summary because they express ideas that are not presented in the passage or are minor ideas in the passage. **This question is worth 2 points.**

The Ogallala aquifer is a large underground source of water in the High Plains region of the United States.

-
-
-

Answer Choices

1. The use of the Ogallala for irrigation has allowed the High Plains to become one of the most productive agricultural regions in the United States.

2. The periodic deepening of wells and the use of more-powerful pumps would help increase the natural recharge rate of the Ogallala.

3. Given the aquifer's low recharge rate, its use for irrigation is causing water tables to drop and will eventually lead to its depletion.

4. In Texas, a great deal of attention is being paid to genetic engineering because it is there that the most critical situation exists.

5. Releasing capillary water and introducing drought-resistant crops are less promising solutions to the water supply crisis than bringing in river water.

6. Several solutions to the upcoming water supply crisis have been proposed, but none of them promises to keep the costs of irrigation low.

STOP. This is the end of the Reading section of TOEFL iBT Practice Test 3.

LISTENING

Directions: This section measures your ability to understand conversations and lectures in English.

You should listen to each conversation and lecture only **once**.

After each conversation or lecture, you will answer some questions about it. The questions typically ask about the main idea and supporting details. Some questions ask about the purpose of a speaker's statements or a speaker's attitude. Answer the questions based on what is stated or implied by the speakers.

You may take notes while you listen. You may use your notes to help you answer the questions. Your notes will **not** be scored.

In some questions, you will see this icon: This means that you will hear, but not see, part of the question.

Most questions are worth 1 point. If a question is worth more than 1 point, it will have special directions that indicate how many points you can receive.

It will take about **60 minutes** to listen to the conversations and lectures and to answer the questions. You will have **35 minutes** to respond to the questions. You should answer each question, even if you must guess the answer.

At the end of this Practice Test you will find an answer key, information to help you determine your score, scripts for the audio tracks, and explanations of the answers.

Turn the page to begin the Listening section.

Listen to Track 74 on the CD. Play Audio

Questions

Directions: Mark your answer by filling in the oval or square next to your choice.

1. Why does the woman come to the office?
   ○ To notify the university of her change of address
   ○ To find out where her physics class is being held
   ○ To get directions to the science building
   ○ To complain about her physics class's being canceled

2. What happened to the letter the university sent to the woman?
   ○ She threw it away by mistake.
   ○ Her roommate forgot to give it to her.
   ○ It was sent to her old mailing address.
   ○ It was sent to another student by mistake.

3. Why was the woman's physics class canceled?
   ○ Not enough students signed up to take the class.
   ○ No professors were available to teach the class.
   ○ The university changed its requirements for physics students.
   ○ There were no classrooms available in the science building at that hour.

4. What does the man suggest the woman do before the beginning of next semester?

○ Consult with her advisor about her class schedule

○ Check with the registrar's office about the location of the class

○ Register for her classes early

○ Call the physics department

5. *Listen again to part of the conversation by playing Track 75. Then answer the question.*

What does the man imply when he says this?

○ He knows the physics class has been canceled.

○ He is not sure where the science building is.

○ Many of the room assignments have been changed.

○ The woman can check for herself where her class is.

GO ON TO THE NEXT PAGE ➘

 Listen to Track 76 on the CD. Play Audio

Questions

6. What does the professor mainly discuss?
○ Major changes in the migratory patterns of hummingbirds
○ The adaptation of hummingbirds to urban environments
○ Concern about the reduction of hummingbird habitat
○ The impact of ecotourism on hummingbird populations

7. What does the professor imply might cause a decrease in the hummingbird population?
○ An increase in the ecotourism industry
○ An increase in the use of land to raise crops and cattle
○ A decrease in banding studies
○ A decrease in the distance traveled during migration

8. What does the professor say people have done to help hummingbirds survive?
○ They have built a series of hummingbird feeding stations.
○ They have supported new laws that punish polluters of wildlife habitats.
○ They have replanted native flowers in once polluted areas.
○ They have learned to identify various hummingbird species.

9. What way of collecting information about migrating hummingbirds does the professor mention?

- ⃝ Receiving radio signals from electronic tracking devices
- ⃝ Being contacted by people who recapture banded birds
- ⃝ Counting the birds that return to the same region every year
- ⃝ Comparing old and young birds' migration routes

10. What does the professor imply researchers have learned while studying hummingbird migration?

- ⃝ Hummingbirds have totally disappeared from some countries due to recent habitat destruction.
- ⃝ Programs to replant flowers native to hummingbird habitats are not succeeding.
- ⃝ Some groups of hummingbirds have changed their migration patterns.
- ⃝ Some plant species pollinated by hummingbirds have become extinct.

11. *Listen again to part of the lecture by playing Track 77.* [Play Audio] *Then answer the question.*

What does the professor imply when she says this?

- ⃝ There is disagreement about the idea she has presented.
- ⃝ She does not plan to discuss all the details.
- ⃝ Her next point may seem to contradict what she has just said.
- ⃝ The point she will make next should be obvious to the students.

GO ON TO THE NEXT PAGE ↘

Listen to Track 78 on the CD.

Questions

12. What is the main purpose of the lecture?

○ To discuss the style of an early filmmaker

○ To describe different types of filmmaking in the 1930s

○ To discuss the emergence of the documentary film

○ To describe Painlevé's influence on today's science-fiction films

13. Why are Painlevé's films typical of the films of the 1920s and 1930s?

○ They do not have sound.

○ They are filmed underwater.

○ They are easy to understand.

○ They are difficult to categorize.

14. According to the professor, how did Painlevé's films confuse the audience?

○ They show animals out of their natural habitat.

○ They depict animals as having both human and animal characteristics.

○ The narration is scientific and difficult to understand.

○ The audiences of the 1920s and 1930s were not used to films shot underwater.

15. Why does the professor mention sea horses?

  ◯ To explain that they were difficult to film in the 1930s

  ◯ To point out that Cousteau made documentaries about them

  ◯ To illustrate Painlevé's fascination with unusual animals

  ◯ To explain why Painlevé's underwater films were not successful

16. Why does the professor compare the film styles of Jacques Cousteau and Jean Painlevé?

  ◯ To explain how Painlevé influenced Cousteau

  ◯ To emphasize the uniqueness of Painlevé's filming style

  ◯ To emphasize the artistic value of Cousteau's documentary films

  ◯ To demonstrate the superiority of Painlevé's filmmaking equipment

17. *Listen to Track 79 to answer the question.*

What does the student imply when he says this?

  ◯ He does not like Jean Painlevé's films.

  ◯ He thinks that the professor should spend more time discussing Jacques Cousteau's films.

  ◯ He believes that high-quality filmmakers are usually well known.

  ◯ He believes that Jean Painlevé's films have been unfairly overlooked.

GO ON TO THE NEXT PAGE ↘

Listen to Track 80 on the CD.

Questions

18. Why does the student go to see the professor?
   ○ To ask about a class assignment
   ○ To find out about a mid-semester project
   ○ To get information about summer jobs
   ○ To discuss ways to improve his grade

19. What was originally located on the site of the lecture hall?
   ○ A farmhouse
   ○ A pottery factory
   ○ A clothing store
   ○ A bottle-manufacturing plant

20. What is mentioned as an advantage of working on this project?
   ○ Off-campus travel is paid for.
   ○ Students can leave class early.
   ○ The location is convenient.
   ○ It fulfills a graduation requirement.

21. What is the professor considering doing to get more volunteers?

○ Offering extra class credit

○ Paying the students for their time

○ Asking for student volunteers from outside her class

○ Providing flexible work schedules

22. What information does the student still need to get from the professor?

○ The name of the senior researcher

○ What book he needs to read before the next lecture

○ When the training session will be scheduled

○ Where the project is located

GO ON TO THE NEXT PAGE ↘

Listen to Track 81 on the CD.

Questions

23. What does the professor mainly discuss?
○ The oldest known cave art
○ How ancient cave art is dated
○ The homes of Paleolithic humans
○ How Paleolithic humans thought about animals

24. Why does the professor mention his daughter?
○ To describe her reaction to seeing the paintings
○ To explain the universal appeal of the Chauvet paintings
○ To demonstrate the size of most Paleolithic cave art
○ To emphasize his point about the age of the Chauvet paintings

25. What is the professor's opinion about the art at the Chauvet cave?
○ It is extremely well done.
○ It probably reflected the artists' religious beliefs.
○ It is less sophisticated than the art at Lascaux and Altamira.
○ It is probably not much older than the art at Lascaux and Altamira.

26. According to the professor, what is the significance of charcoal marks on the walls of the Chauvet cave?

○ They suggest that Paleolithic people cooked their food in the cave.

○ They prove that people came to the cave long after the paintings were made.

○ They show how much light the Paleolithic artists needed for their work.

○ They were used in recent times to date the paintings.

27. Compared with other Paleolithic art, what is unusual about the animals painted at Chauvet?

○ Most of them are horses.

○ Many of them are dangerous.

○ Many of them are shown alongside humans.

○ All of them are species that are still found in France.

28. What are two questions about the Chauvet cave artists that the professor raises but cannot answer?
    Choose 2 answers.

☐ How they lighted their work area

☐ How they obtained pigments for their paints

☐ Why they chose to paint certain animals and not others

☐ Why they placed their art in dark, uninhabited places

GO ON TO THE NEXT PAGE ◥

Listen to Track 82 on the CD.

Questions

29. What is the lecture mainly about?

○ Different ways of magnifying the spectrum of a star

○ How a chemical element was first discovered on the Sun

○ How astronomers identify the chemical elements in a star

○ Why the spectra of different stars are composed of different colors

30. What does the professor explain to one of the students about the term "radiation"?

○ It is defined incorrectly in the textbook.

○ It was first used in the nineteenth century.

○ It is rarely used by astronomers.

○ It does not refer only to harmful energy.

31. What can be inferred about two stars if their spectra have similar spectral line patterns?

○ The stars are approximately the same distance from the Earth.

○ The stars probably have some chemical elements in common.

○ The stars have nearly the same brightness.

○ The stars are probably of the same size.

32. According to the professor, what is the purpose of heating an element in a spectroscopic flame test?

○ To cause an element to emit light

○ To study an element in combination with other elements

○ To remove impurities from the element

○ To measure an element's resistance to heat

33. *Listen to Track 83 to answer the question.* 🎧 Play Audio

Why does the professor say this?

○ He is about to provide some background information.

○ He is about to repeat what he just said.

○ He intends to focus on the history of astronomy.

○ He intends to explain two different points of view.

34. *Listen to Track 84 to answer the question.* 🎧 Play Audio

Why does the professor ask this?

○ To check the students' understanding of their reading assignment

○ To give the students a hint to the answer to his previous question

○ To emphasize how important it is for astronomers to study Greek

○ To remind the students about the historical background of astronomy

STOP. This is the end of the Listening section of TOEFL iBT Practice Test 3.

SPEAKING

Directions: The following Speaking section of the test will last approximately **20 minutes**. To complete it, you will need a CD player, as well as a recording device that you can play back to listen to your response.

During the test, you will answer six speaking questions. Two of the questions ask about familiar topics. Four questions ask about short conversations, lectures, and reading passages. You may take notes as you listen to the conversations and lectures. The questions and the reading passages are printed here. The time you will have to prepare your response and to speak is printed below each question. You should answer all of the questions as completely as possible in the time allowed. The preparation time begins immediately after you hear the question. On the actual test, you will be told when to begin to prepare and when to begin speaking.

Play the CD tracks listed in the test instructions. Record each of your responses.

At the end of this Practice Test you will find scripts for the audio tracks, important points for each question, directions for listening to sample spoken responses, and comments on those responses by official raters.

Questions

1. You will now be asked a question about a familiar topic. After you hear the question, you will have 15 seconds to prepare your response and 45 seconds to speak.

Now play Track 85 on the CD to hear Question 1.

What characteristics do you think make someone a good parent? Explain why these characteristics are important to you.

> **Preparation Time: 15 Seconds**
> **Response Time: 45 Seconds**

2. You will now be asked to give your opinion about a familiar topic. After you hear the question, you will have 15 seconds to prepare your response and 45 seconds to speak.

Now play Track 86 on the CD to hear Question 2.

Some students prefer to work on class assignments by themselves. Others believe it is better to work in a group. Which do you prefer? Explain why.

> **Preparation Time: 15 Seconds**
> **Response Time: 45 Seconds**

3. You will now read a short passage and then listen to a conversation on the same topic. You will then be asked a question about them. After you hear the question, you will have 30 seconds to prepare your response and 60 seconds to speak.

Now play Track 87 on the CD to hear Question 3.

Reading Time: 45 Seconds

Hot Breakfasts Eliminated

Beginning next month, Dining Services will no longer serve hot breakfast foods at university dining halls. Instead, students will be offered a wide assortment of cold breakfast items in the morning. These cold breakfast foods, such as breads, fruit, and yogurt, are healthier than many of the hot breakfast items that we will stop serving, so health-conscious students should welcome this change. Students will benefit in another way as well, because limiting the breakfast selection to cold food items will save money and allow us to keep our meal plans affordable.

The woman expresses her opinion of the change that has been announced. State her opinion and explain her reasons for holding that opinion.

Preparation Time: 30 Seconds
Response Time: 60 Seconds

GO ON TO THE NEXT PAGE ↘

4. You will now read a short passage and then listen to a talk on the same academic topic. You will then be asked a question about them. After you hear the question, you will have 30 seconds to prepare your response and 60 seconds to speak.

Now play Track 88 on the CD to hear Question 4.

Reading Time: 50 Seconds

Cognitive Dissonance

Individuals sometimes experience a contradiction between their actions and their beliefs—between what they are doing and what they believe they should be doing. These contradictions can cause a kind of mental discomfort known as *cognitive dissonance*. People experiencing cognitive dissonance often do not want to change the way they are acting, so they resolve the contradictory situation in another way: they change their interpretation of the situation in a way that minimizes the contradiction between what they are doing and what they believe they should be doing.

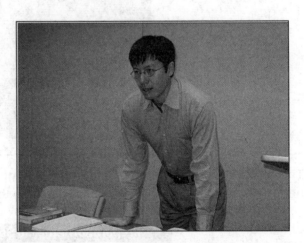

Using the example discussed by the professor, explain what cognitive dissonance is and how people often deal with it.

Preparation Time: 30 Seconds
Response Time: 60 Seconds

5. You will now listen to a conversation. You will then be asked a question about it. After you hear the question, you will have 20 seconds to prepare your response and 60 seconds to speak.

Now play Track 89 on the CD to hear Question 5.

The speakers discuss two possible solutions to the woman's problem. Briefly summarize the problem. Then state which of the solutions you recommend and explain why.

Preparation Time: 20 Seconds
Response Time: 60 Seconds

GO ON TO THE NEXT PAGE ➘

6. You will now listen to part of a lecture. You will then be asked a question about it. After you hear the question, you will have 20 seconds to prepare your response and 60 seconds to speak.

Now play Track 90 on the CD to hear Question 6.

Using the examples from the talk, explain how persuasive strategies are used in advertising.

| Preparation Time: 20 Seconds |
| Response Time: 60 Seconds |

STOP. This is the end of the Speaking section of TOEFL iBT Practice Test 3.

WRITING

Directions: This section measures your ability to use writing to communicate in an academic environment. There will be two writing tasks.

For the first writing task, you will read a passage and listen to a lecture and then answer a question based on what you have read and heard. For the second task, you will answer a question based on your own knowledge and experience.

At the end of this Practice Test you will find a script for the audio track, topic notes, sample test taker essays, and comments on those essays by official raters.

Turn the page to see the directions for the first writing task.

Writing Based on Reading and Listening

Directions: For this task, you will read a passage about an academic topic and you will listen to a lecture about the same topic. You may take notes while you read and listen.

Then you will write a response to a question that asks you about the relationship between the lecture you heard and the reading passage. Try to answer the question as completely as possible using information from the reading passage and the lecture. The question does not ask you to express your personal opinion. You may refer to the reading passage when you write. You may use your notes to help you answer the question.

Typically, an effective response will be 150 to 225 words. Your response will be judged on the quality of your writing and on the completeness and accuracy of the content.

You should allow **3 minutes** to read the passage. Then listen to the lecture. Then allow **20 minutes** to plan and write your response.

Write your response in the space provided.

Rembrandt is the most famous of the seventeenth-century Dutch painters. However, there are doubts whether some paintings attributed to Rembrandt were actually painted by him. One such painting is known as *Portrait of an Elderly Woman in a White Bonnet*. The painting was attributed to Rembrandt because of its style, and indeed the representation of the woman's face is very much like that of portraits known to be by Rembrandt. But there are problems with the painting that suggest it could not be a work by Rembrandt.

First, there is something inconsistent about the way the woman in the portrait is dressed. She is wearing a white linen cap of a kind that only servants would wear—yet the coat she is wearing has a luxurious fur collar that no servant could afford. Rembrandt, who was known for his attention to the details of his subjects' clothing, would not have been guilty of such an inconsistency.

Second, Rembrandt was a master of painting light and shadow, but in this painting these elements do not fit together. The face appears to be illuminated by light reflected onto it from below. But below the face is the dark fur collar, which would absorb light rather than reflect it. So the face should appear partially in shadow—which is not how it appears. Rembrandt would never have made such an error.

Finally, examination of the back of the painting reveals that it was painted on a panel made of several pieces of wood glued together. Although Rembrandt often painted on wood panels, no painting known to be by Rembrandt uses a panel glued together in this way from several pieces of wood.

For these reasons the painting was removed from the official catalog of Rembrandt's paintings in the 1930s.

Now play Track 91 on the CD. Play Audio

Question

Summarize the points made in the lecture, being sure to explain how they answer the specific problems presented in the reading passage.

You must finish your answer in 20 minutes.

_____

_____

_____

_____

_____

_____

_____

_____

_____

_____

_____

GO ON TO THE NEXT PAGE ▶

Writing Based on Knowledge and Experience

Directions: For this task, you will write an essay in response to a question that asks you to state, explain, and support your opinion on an issue.

Typically, an effective essay will contain a minimum of 300 words. Your essay will be judged on the quality of your writing. This includes the development of your ideas, the organization of your essay, and the quality and accuracy of the language you use to express your ideas.

You have 30 minutes to plan and complete your essay.

Write your essay in the space provided.

Question

Do you agree or disagree with the following statement?

It is more important to keep your old friends than it is to make new friends.

Use specific reasons and examples to support your answer.

_____

_____

_____

_____

_____

_____

_____

_____

_____

_____

_____

_____

_____

_____

GO ON TO THE NEXT PAGE ↘

_____

_____

_____

_____

_____

_____

_____

_____

_____

_____

_____

_____

_____

_____

_____

_____

_____

_____

_____

_____

_____

STOP. This is the end of the Writing section of TOEFL iBT Practice Test 3.

Answers, Explanations, and Listening Scripts

Reading

Answer Key and Self-scoring Chart

Directions: Check your answers against the answer key below. Write the number 1 on the line to the right of each question if you picked the correct answer. For questions worth more than one point, follow the directions given. Total your points at the bottom of the chart.

Question Number	Correct Answer	Your Raw Points
Architecture		
1.	4	_____
2.	2	_____
3.	3	_____
4.	4	_____
5.	2	_____
6.	1	_____
7.	2	_____
8.	3	_____
9.	4	_____
10.	1	_____
11.	3	_____
12.	2	_____
13.	4	_____

For question 14, write 2 if you picked all three correct answers. Write 1 if you picked two correct answers.

14.	1,3,6	_____

Question Number	Correct Answer	Your Raw Points
The Long-term Stability of Ecosystems		
1.	3	_____
2.	3	_____
3.	1	_____
4.	2	_____
5.	3	_____
6.	2	_____
7.	3	_____
8.	2	_____
9.	1	_____
10.	3	_____
11.	4	_____
12.	4	_____
13.	2	_____

For question 14, write 2 if you picked all three correct answers. Write 1 if you picked two correct answers.

14.	3,4,5	_____

Question Number	Correct Answer	Your Raw Points
Depletion of the Ogallala Aquifer		
1.	4	_____
2.	2	_____
3.	1	_____
4.	4	_____
5.	3	_____
6.	3	_____
7.	4	_____
8.	1	_____
9.	3	_____
10.	3	_____
11.	2	_____
12.	2	_____
13.	3	_____

For question 14, write 2 if you picked all three correct answers. Write 1 if you picked two correct answers.

14.	1,3,6	_____
TOTAL:		_____

Below is a table that converts your Reading section answers into a TOEFL iBT Reading scaled score. Take the total of raw points from your answer key and find that number in the left-hand column of the table. The right-hand column of the table gives a TOEFL iBT Reading scaled score for each number of raw points. For example, if the total points from your answer key is 26, the table shows a scaled score of 17.

You should use your score estimate as a general guide only. Your actual score on the TOEFL iBT test may be higher or lower than your score on the practice version.

Reading Comprehension

Raw Point Total	Scaled Score	Raw Point Total	Scaled Score
45	30	22	13
44	29	21	11
43	29	20	10
42	29	19	9
41	29	18	8
40	28	17	7
39	28	16	5
38	27	15	4
37	27	14	3
36	26	13	2
35	25	12	2
34	25	11	1
33	24	10	1
32	23	9	0
31	22	8	0
30	21	7	0
29	20	6	0
28	19	5	0
27	18	4	0
26	17	3	0
25	16	2	0
24	15	1	0
23	14	0	0

Answer Explanations

Architecture

1. ④ This is a Negative Factual Information question asking for specific information that can be found in paragraph 1. The correct answer is choice 4. Sentence 3 in the paragraph states that "architecture affects our lives most directly," which makes the information in choice 4 incorrect. The information in choices 1 to 3 is stated in sentences 1 and 2 in the paragraph.

2. ② This is a Vocabulary question. The word being tested is *enhance*. It is highlighted in the passage. The correct answer is choice 2, "improve." In other words, humans seek structures that will improve, or better, their lives.

3. ③ This is a Vocabulary question. The word being tested is *feasible*. It is highlighted in the passage. The correct answer is choice 3, "achievable." In other words, buildings contribute to human life when they are economically achievable, or possible.

4. ④ This is a Sentence Simplification question. As with all of these questions, a single sentence in the passage is highlighted:

> In order for the structure to achieve the size and strength necessary to meet its purpose, architecture employs methods of support that, because they are based on physical laws, have changed little since people first discovered them—even while building materials have changed dramatically.

The correct answer is choice 4. Choice 4 contains all of the essential information in the highlighted sentence. It omits the information from the introductory phrase about the size and strength of a structure because the information is not essential to the meaning of the sentence.

Choices 1, 2, and 3 are all incorrect because they change the meaning of the highlighted sentence. Choice 1 is incorrect because it inaccurately states that physical laws have limited the size and strength of buildings, whereas the highlighted sentence does not indicate this.

Choice 2 is incorrect because it wrongly makes a connection between building materials and building strength and size, whereas the highlighted sentence does not make such a connection.

Choice 3 is incorrect because it wrongly states that the structural methods initially used by people were not based on physical laws, whereas the highlighted sentence states that structural methods that are based on physical laws have been in use since their discovery.

5. ❷ This is a Vocabulary question. The word being tested is *devised*. It is highlighted in the passage. The correct answer is choice 2, "created." In other words, the world's architectural structures have also been created, or made, in relation to the objective limitations of materials.

6. ❶ This is a Vocabulary question. The word being tested is *integral*. It is highlighted in the passage. The correct answer is choice 1, "essential." In other words, materials and methods of construction are essential, or vital, parts of the design of architectural structures.

7. ❷ This is a Factual Information question asking for specific information that can be found in paragraph 4. The correct answer is choice 2. Sentence 3 in the paragraph indicates that in the past, structures were built using the available materials. However, sentence 4 in the paragraph indicates that today new materials can be created as needed depending on the design of the structure. Choice 1 is incorrect because sentence 5 in the paragraph indicates that there have been substantial changes in materials and designs in the recent past. Choice 3 is incorrect because sentence 4 in the paragraph indicates that there are many types of materials available today. Choice 4 is incorrect because sentence 5 in the paragraph indicates that it is possible to enclose space more quickly and easily than in the past. It does not indicate that architects were not able to enclose space.

8. ❸ This is an Inference question asking for an inference that can be supported by paragraph 4. The correct answer is choice 3. Sentence 5 in the paragraph states that structures are now created with a minimum of material, and sentence 6 indicates that there is a difference in weight between buildings being built now and those that were built one hundred years ago. The combined information from these two sentences suggests that modern buildings weigh less than buildings constructed one hundred years ago. Choice 1 is incorrect because there is no discussion of the amount of space that buildings constructed in the past or those built now occupy. Choice 2 is incorrect because sentence 5 in the paragraph states that substantial changes have been made to modern buildings compared with buildings constructed one hundred years ago. Choice 4 is incorrect because sentence 5 in the paragraph indicates that modern buildings can be built more quickly than those built one hundred years ago.

9. ❹ This is an Inference question asking for an inference that can be supported by paragraph 5. The correct answer is choice 4. The reader is required to connect the information in sentences 1 and 3 in the paragraph. Sentence 1 indicates that modern architecture has several components comparable to the human body, whereas sentence 3 indicates that early architecture had few such components. The information in these two sentences suggests that modern buildings more closely resemble the human body than earlier buildings do. Choice 1 is incorrect because sentence 1 in the paragraph indicates that there are three components of modern architecture (skeleton, skin,

equipment) that resemble the human body, not just one. Choice 2 is incorrect because sentence 3 in the paragraph states that early architecture did not have interior equipment, which is one of the three particular elements discussed in the paragraph as being comparable to the human body. Choice 3 is incorrect because there is no discussion or implication of how modern buildings or the human body may change.

10. ❶ This is a Vocabulary question. The word being tested is *arduous*. It is highlighted in the passage. The correct answer is choice 1, "difficult." In other words, cutting and piling stone upon stone was a difficult, or demanding, task.

11. ❸ This is a Rhetorical Purpose question. It is asking why the author includes the description of how the "doorways and windows" of Machu Picchu were constructed. The phrase being tested is highlighted in the passage. The correct answer is choice 3. The author discusses the stone structures used to support doorways and windows in order to provide an example of how the physical limitations of stone were overcome before the invention of the arch. Choice 1 is incorrect because there is no comparison made in the passage between the buildings of Machu Picchu and igloos and adobe structures. Choice 2 is incorrect because, while the passage does state that stone was used in the buildings of Machu Picchu, it never discusses the kind of stone used. Choice 4 is incorrect because there is no discussion of the time needed to construct buildings from stone.

12. ❷ This is a Factual Information question asking for specific information that can be found in paragraph 6. The correct answer is choice 2. Sentences 5 and 6 in the paragraph indicate that the arch allowed new architectural forms to be created. The remainder of the paragraph elaborates on structures created as a result of the arch. Choice 1 is incorrect because sentence 7 in the paragraph indicates that early Mediterranean cultures were the first to use the arch, not the Romans. Choice 3 is incorrect because sentence 10 in the paragraph indicates that the weight of a structure is distributed to the sides of the arch. Choice 4 is incorrect because sentence 7 indicates that the Romans created new uses for the arch, namely in aboveground structures.

13. ❹ This is an Insert Text question. You can see the four black squares in paragraph 5 that represent the possible answer choices here.

■ Modern architectural forms generally have three separate components comparable to elements of the human body: a supporting *skeleton* or frame, an outer *skin* enclosing the interior spaces, and *equipment*, similar to the body's vital organs and systems. ■ The equipment includes plumbing, electrical wiring, hot water, and air-conditioning. ■ Of course in early architecture—such as igloos and adobe structures—there was no such equipment, and the skeleton and skin were often one. ■

The sentence provided, "However, some modern architectural designs, such as those using folded plates of concrete or air-inflated structures, are again unifying skeleton and skin," is best inserted at square 4.

Square 4 is correct because it is the only place that supports both a contrasting idea and a repeated reference to the unification of skeleton and skin. The inserted sentence represents a contrast to the main idea of the paragraph. The inserted sentence also contains the phrase "again unifying skeleton and skin," indicating that there must be a previous discussion related to unifying the skeleton and skin of a structure. Square 4 is the only place in this paragraph that follows such a discussion.

None of the other answer choices follows a discussion of the unifying of a structure's skeleton and skin, nor do the other answer choices provide a suitable point of contrast for the insert sentence.

14. **❶❸❻** This is a Prose Summary question. It is completed correctly below. The correct choices are 1, 3, and 6. Choices 2, 4, and 5 are therefore incorrect.

Directions: An introductory sentence for a brief summary of the passage is provided below. Complete the summary by selecting the THREE answer choices that express the most important ideas in the passage. Some answer choices do not belong in the summary because they express ideas that are not presented in the passage or are minor ideas in the passage. **This question is worth 2 points.**

Architecture uses forms and space to express cultural values.

- Architects seek to create buildings that are both visually appealing and well suited for human use.
- Over the course of the history of building, innovations in materials and methods of construction have given architects ever greater freedom to express themselves.
- The discovery and use of the arch typifies the way in which architecture advances by developing more efficient types of structures.

Answer Choices

1. Architects seek to create buildings that are both visually appealing and well suited for human use.

2. Both clients and architects are responsible for the mediocre designs of some modern buildings.

3. Over the course of the history of building, innovations in materials and methods of construction have given architects ever greater freedom to express themselves.

4. Modern buildings tend to lack the beauty of ancient stone buildings such as those of Machu Picchu.

5. Throughout history buildings have been constructed like human bodies, needing distinct "organ" systems in order to function.

6. The discovery and use of the arch typifies the way in which architecture advances by developing more efficient types of structures.

Correct Choices

Choice 1, "Architects seek to create buildings that are both visually appealing and well suited for human use," is correct because it is a broad statement that is developed in the first two paragraphs. The first two paragraphs discuss in detail how architecture can affect and possibly improve people's lives.

Choice 3, "Over the course of the history of building, innovations in materials and methods of construction have given architects ever greater freedom to express themselves," is correct because it is a general statement that is developed in paragraphs 3 and 4. These paragraphs discuss in detail how materials and methods have changed and improved over the history of building, continually providing architects the chance to create new designs.

Choice 6, "The discovery and use of the arch typifies the way in which architecture advances by developing more efficient types of structures," is correct because it captures the main idea of paragraph 6, which provides a lengthy discussion of the ways that the arch has allowed new architectural forms to be created.

Incorrect Choices

Choice 2, "Both clients and architects are responsible for the mediocre designs of some modern buildings," is incorrect because it is only a minor, supporting detail, which is mentioned in the last sentence of paragraph 2. It supports the larger idea in the paragraph that the quality of an architectural design depends on a variety of factors.

Choice 4, "Modern buildings tend to lack the beauty of ancient stone buildings such as those of Machu Picchu," is incorrect because there is no discussion in the passage of the level of attractiveness of modern buildings.

Choice 5, "Throughout history buildings have been constructed like human bodies, needing distinct 'organ' systems in order to function," is incorrect because paragraph 5 states that early architecture did not have equipment, such as plumbing and wiring, that is comparable to vital organs in the human body.

The Long-term Stability of Ecosystems

1. ❸ This is a Vocabulary question. The word being tested is *particular*. It is highlighted in the passage. The correct answer is choice 3, "specific." In other words, the specific structure of plant communities depends on the history of the area.

2. ❸ This is a Negative Factual Information question asking for specific information that can be found in paragraph 1. The correct answer is choice 3. The last sentence of the paragraph indicates that the plants and species of climax communities change. Choice 1 is true according to the information in sentence 3 in the paragraph, which states that the community that follows

succession is a climax community. Choice 2 is true according to sentences 4 to 6 in the paragraph, which indicate that pioneer and succession communities last as long as 500 years, while climax communities last more than 500 years. Choice 4 is true according to the last sentence of the paragraph, which indicates that climax communities exist for periods longer than 500 years.

3. ❶ This is a Factual Information question asking for specific information that can be found in paragraph 2. The correct answer is choice 1. Sentence 3 in the paragraph states that "the properties of an ecosystem are more stable," or change more slowly, than individuals within the system. Choice 2 is contradicted by sentences 1 and 3 in the paragraph, which indicate that ecosystems remain unchanged as individuals are replaced. Choice 3 is contradicted by sentence 2 in the paragraph, which indicates that individual organisms change from year to year. Choice 4 is incorrect because there is no information in the paragraph about a change in the number of an organism and how that will affect an ecosystem. Furthermore, sentence 2 in the paragraph states that the number of fish, for example, will usually stay the same.

4. ❷ This is a Factual Information question asking for specific information that can be found in paragraph 3. The correct answer is choice 2. Sentence 3 in the paragraph indicates that climax communities have more stable ecosystems than pioneer communities. Choice 1 is incorrect because sentence 3 in the paragraph states that pioneer communities are less stable than climax communities. Choice 3 is incorrect because sentence 5 in the paragraph indicates that single-crop farmlands are unstable. Choice 4 is incorrect because successional plant communities are not discussed in the paragraph.

5. ❸ This is a Factual Information question asking for specific information that can be found in paragraph 4. The correct answer is choice 3. The first two sentences of the paragraph indicate that ecosystem stability is complicated because ecologists do not agree on the meaning of the word *stability*. Choice 1 is incorrect because it is not discussed in the paragraph. Furthermore, the idea stated in choice 1 is contradicted in sentence 5 of the paragraph, which states that disturbances such as fires can change an ecosystem. Choice 2 is incorrect because there is no discussion of confusion on the part of ecologists about the concept of resilience. Resilience is simply defined in the paragraph. Choice 4 is incorrect because the main idea of the paragraph is to show that the questions of different ecologists are the cause of complications. Furthermore, sentences 4 and 7 in the paragraph provide clear answers to the questions posed by ecologists.

6. ❷ This is a Factual Information question asking for specific information provided in paragraph 4. The correct answer is choice 2. Sentences 4 and 7 in the paragraph indicate different perspectives on climax communities: they can be viewed as the most or least stable communities. Choice 1 is incorrect because, according to the resilience theory of ecosystem stability, it is contra-

dicted by sentence 7, which indicates that climax communities are the least resilient. Choice 3 is also contradicted by sentence 7, which indicates that climax communities take a long time to recover after a major disturbance. Choice 4 is incorrect because it is a misunderstanding of the concept of resilience. According to sentence 5 in the paragraph, a resilient community will revert back to a particular form after a major disturbance.

7. **❸** This is an Inference question asking for an inference that can be supported by paragraph 5. The correct answer is choice 3. Sentence 2 introduces the discussion of diversity in successional communities in temperate zones, and sentence 3 presents redwood forests as an example of such a community. Choice 1 is incorrect because we can infer the opposite, according to the paragraph. Sentence 3 indicates that the diversity in a redwood forest decreases as the forest matures, and sentence 5 indicates that increased diversity can lead to instability. Choice 2 is incorrect because sentences 2 and 3 indicate that the number of species declines in a redwood forest at the climax stage. Choice 4 is incorrect because sentences 2 and 3 indicate the opposite, namely that redwood forests have maximum diversity in successional stages.

8. **❷** This is a Vocabulary question. The word being tested is *guarantee*. It is highlighted in the passage. The correct answer is choice 2, "ensure." In other words, diversity does not ensure ecosystem stability.

9. **❶** This is a Rhetorical Purpose question. It is testing why the author provides the information that "A fifteen-speed racing bicycle is more likely to break down than a child's tricycle." The sentence being tested is highlighted in the passage. The correct answer is choice 1. Sentence 6 in the paragraph asserts the general principle that a complicated system is more likely to break down than a simple one. Sentence 7, the highlighted sentence, provides an example about bicycles that the average reader can relate to. Choice 2 is incorrect because it emphasizes stability, whereas the highlighted information provides an example of the issues related to the complexity of a particular system. Choice 3 is incorrect because sentence 5 in the paragraph indicates the opposite, specifically that stability does not necessarily increase with diversity. Therefore the highlighted sentence cannot be compared to the incorrect information given in Choice 3. Choice 4 is incorrect because the example provided in the highlighted sentence actually supports the mathematical models mentioned in sentence 5.

10. **❸** This is a Vocabulary question. The word being tested is *pales*. It is highlighted in the passage. The correct answer is choice 3, "loses significance." In other words, the destruction caused by the explosion of Mount St. Helens loses significance when compared with the destruction caused by humans.

11. ❹ This is a Sentence Simplification question. As with all of these questions, a single sentence in the passage is highlighted:

> Many ecologists now think that the relative long-term stability of climax communities comes not from diversity but from the "patchiness" of the environment; an environment that varies from place to place supports more kinds of organisms than an environment that is uniform.

The correct answer is choice 4. That choice takes all of the essential information in the two clauses of the highlighted sentence and simplifies it into one concise sentence. It omits information from the second clause that is repetitive and therefore not essential to the meaning.

Choice 1 is incorrect because its meaning is the opposite of that of the highlighted sentence. Choice 1 states that diversity is the key to stability, whereas the highlighted sentence indicates that stability does not come from diversity but rather comes from patchiness.

Choice 2 incorrectly indicates a causal relationship between patchy environments and diversity.

Choice 3 is incorrect because there is no indication in the highlighted sentence that uniform environments cannot be climax communities.

12. ❹ This is a Vocabulary question. The word being tested is *adjacent*. It is highlighted in the passage. The correct answer is choice 4, "neighboring." In other words, a local population that goes extinct is quickly replaced by organisms from a neighboring, or nearby, community.

13. ❷ This is an Insert Text question. You can see the four black squares that represent the answer choices here.

> ■ Ecologists are especially interested in knowing what factors contribute to the resilience of communities because climax conditions all over the world are being severely damaged or destroyed by human activities. ■ The destruction caused by the volcanic explosion of Mount St. Helens, in the northwestern United States, for example, pales in comparison to the destruction caused by humans. ■ We need to know what aspects of a community are most important to the community's resistance to destruction, as well as its recovery. ■

The sentence provided, "In fact, damage to the environment by humans is often much more severe than by natural events and processes," is best inserted at square 2.

Square 2 is correct because it is the best place in the paragraph to elaborate on the idea, introduced in sentence 1, that humans contribute to damage done to the environment. The phrase "In fact" is used to indicate elaboration. Also, the phrase "natural events and processes" in the given sentence provides a logical connection to the example in sentence 2 about the volcanic explosion of Mount St. Helens.

Square 1 is incorrect because it does not make sense to begin the paragraph with a sentence that elaborates on the idea of human damage to the environment before the idea has been introduced.

Square 3 is incorrect because it does not make sense to follow the specific example about the damage caused by the explosion of Mount St. Helens in sentence 2 with a more general statement about damage done by "natural events and processes."

Square 4 is incorrect because the sentence preceding this square discusses a community's resistance to destruction. This square is not a logical place to insert a sentence that specifically elaborates on a different idea.

14. **❸❹❺** This is a Prose Summary question. It is completed correctly below. The correct choices are 3, 4, and 5. Choices 1, 2, and 6 are therefore incorrect.

Directions: An introductory sentence for a brief summary of the passage is provided below. Complete the summary by selecting the THREE answer choices that express the most important ideas in the passage. Some answer choices do not belong in the summary because they express ideas that are not presented in the passage or are minor ideas in the passage. **This question is worth 2 points.**

The process of succession and the stability of a climax community can change over time.

- A high degree of species diversity does not always result in a stable ecosystem.
- Disagreements over the meaning of the term "stability" make it difficult to identify the most stable ecosystems.
- The level of resilience in a plant community contributes to its long-term stability.

Answer Choices

1. The changes that occur in an ecosystem from the pioneer to the climax community can be seen in one human generation.

2. Ecologists agree that climax communities are the most stable types of ecosystems.

3. A high degree of species diversity does not always result in a stable ecosystem.

4. Disagreements over the meaning of the term "stability" make it difficult to identify the most stable ecosystems.

5. The level of resilience in a plant community contributes to its long-term stability.

6. The resilience of climax communities makes them resistant to destruction caused by humans.

Correct Choices

Choice 3, "A high degree of species diversity does not always result in a stable ecosystem," is correct because it is a main idea that is developed throughout most of the passage. The first three paragraphs introduce and develop the idea that diversity may result in a stable ecosystem. But paragraphs 4, 5, and 7 introduce arguments to support the idea that diversity does not always result in a stable ecosystem.

Choice 4, "Disagreements over the meaning of the term "stability" make it difficult to identify the most stable ecosystems," is correct because the key idea that ecosystem stability is difficult to quantify is introduced in paragraph 4 and developed throughout the rest of the passage.

Choice 5, "The level of resilience in a plant community contributes to its long-term stability," is correct because it mentions one important form of stability that is introduced in paragraph 4 and further developed in paragraph 6 in the discussion of environmental damage caused by humans.

Incorrect Choices

Choice 1, "The changes that occur in an ecosystem from the pioneer to the climax community can be seen in one human generation," is incorrect because paragraph 1 states that a pioneer community alone can change over a period as long as 500 years. Furthermore, a climax community typically changes over a period longer than 500 years.

Choice 2, "Ecologists agree that climax communities are the most stable types of ecosystems," is incorrect because climax communities are described as unstable at several points in the passage, beginning in paragraph 3. The last sentence of paragraph 4 states that climax communities could be the least stable communities, while sentence 2 in paragraph 5 suggests that successional communities may be more stable than climax communities.

Choice 6, "The resilience of climax communities makes them resistant to destruction caused by humans," is incorrect because it is a misreading of sentence 1 in paragraph 6. The sentence indicates that ecologists would like to know if resilience could make climax communities resistant to destruction. Climax communities are currently being damaged or destroyed by humans and are not therefore resistant to such destruction.

Depletion of the Ogallala Aquifer

1. **4** This is a Factual Information question asking for specific information that can be found in paragraph 1. The correct answer is choice 4. Sentence 2 in the paragraph indicates that there was "low-intensity" farming and ranching in the High Plains region for a short period after it was settled in the 1880s. Choice 1 is incorrect because there is no information in the paragraph that indicates the High Plains had no inhabitants before the 1880s. The paragraph only indicates that the region had not been permanently settled by a particular group—farmers and ranchers. Choice 2 is incorrect because there is no mention of temperatures in the paragraph. The paragraph states that the region had a semiarid climate, but that alone does not give an indication of the temperature. Choice 3 is incorrect because the paragraph does not state who actually discovered the aquifer. The paragraph only indicates that the aquifer is named after the Ogallala Indians because they once lived in the region.

2. **2** This is a Negative Factual Information question asking for specific information that can be found in paragraph 2. The correct answer is choice 2. The information in choice 2 is incorrect according to the paragraph, which states that the water comes "from rains and melting snows." There is no mention of underground springs in the paragraph. The information in choice 1 about location is stated in sentence 1 of the paragraph. The information in choice 3 about time is stated in sentence 2 of the paragraph. The information in choice 4 about sandstone is stated in sentence 1 of the paragraph.

3. **1** This is a Sentence Simplification question. As with all of these questions, a single sentence in the passage is highlighted:

> Estimates indicate that the aquifer contains enough water to fill Lake Huron, but unfortunately, under the semiarid climatic conditions that presently exist in the region, rates of addition to the aquifer are minimal, amounting to about half a centimeter a year.

The correct answer is choice 1. The essential information about the size of the aquifer and the rate of addition is expressed in simplified, concise language, but the extra details used to help the reader visualize the information have been removed.

Choice 2 incorrectly indicates that the aquifer does not currently have the large amount of water that could fill Lake Huron, whereas the highlighted sentence states that the aquifer does have this large amount of water.

Choice 3 incorrectly implies that the region's present climatic conditions positively affect the aquifer by adding water. However, the highlighted sentence states that the region's dry weather negatively affects the aquifer because it prevents substantial amounts of water from being added.

Choice 4 incorrectly states that the rates of addition of water are increasing; the highlighted sentence indicates that the rate is steady at half a centimeter a year.

4. ❹ This is a Vocabulary question. The word being tested is *ensuing*. The word is highlighted in the passage. The correct answer is choice 4, "subsequent." In other words, the subsequent rapid expansion of irrigation culture transformed the economy of the region.

5. ❸ This is a Rhetorical Purpose question. It is testing why the author provides the information that 40 percent of American cattle are fattened in the High Plains. The correct answer is choice 3. Sentence 2 of the paragraph provides the general statement that irrigation agriculture "transformed the economy of the region," and the remainder of the paragraph provides 3 examples of this transformation. The information about cattle is the last of these examples in the paragraph. Choice 1 incorrectly implies that crop cultivation was less important than other factors in the economy of the region. However, the paragraph only provides examples of factors that contributed to the transformation of the region's economy; it does not indicate whether one factor was more or less important than another. Choice 2 incorrectly indicates that economic activity was not dependent on irrigation. However, sentence 2 in the paragraph states explicitly that the economic transformation was a result of irrigation agriculture. Choice 4 is incorrect because there is no comparison in the paragraph between cattle-fattening practices in the High Plains and those in other places. The last sentence in the paragraph states only that 40 percent of certain cattle are fattened in this region; there is no discussion of the practices themselves.

6. ❸ This is a Vocabulary question. The word being tested is *unprecedented*. The word is highlighted in the passage. The correct answer is choice 3, "unlike anything in the past." In other words, a finite groundwater resource with a low natural recharge rate is unlike anything that existed in the past.

7. ❹ This is a Vocabulary question. The word being tested is *virtually*. The word is highlighted in the passage. The correct answer is choice 4, "almost." In other words, there is almost no natural water source to replenish the water supply in the aquifer.

8. ❶ This is a Negative Factual Information question asking for specific information that can be found in paragraph 4. The correct answer is choice 1. Sentence 1 in the paragraph indicates that the aquifer has a low recharge

rate, but there is no indication that this recharge rate is a result of irrigation. Furthermore, sentence 1 implies that the recharge rate is steady, not decreasing. The information in choice 2 about water tables is provided in sentence 1 in the paragraph. The information in choice 3 about the depth of wells is provided in sentence 2 in the paragraph. The information in choice 4 about water pumps is provided in sentence 3 in the paragraph.

9. ❸ This is a Factual Information question asking for specific information that can be found in paragraph 4. The correct answer is choice 3. Sentences 4 and 5 in the paragraph indicate that much of the aquifer will dry out and specify "The situation is most critical in Texas." Choice 1 is incorrect because there is no indication in the paragraph as to which area has the greatest amount of farmland being irrigated. Choice 2 is incorrect because there is no indication in the paragraph as to which area has the largest amount of Ogallala water beneath its soil. Choice 4 incorrectly states that Texas uses the least amount of Ogallala water, whereas sentence 5 states that in Texas "the greatest amount of water is being pumped."

10. ❸ This is a Vocabulary question. The word being tested is *inevitable*. The word is highlighted in the paragraph. The correct answer is choice 3, "unavoidable." In other words, the reaction of farmers to the unavoidable depletion of the Ogallala varies.

11. ❷ This is a Factual Information question asking for specific information that can be found in paragraph 5. The correct answer is choice 2. Sentence 4 in the paragraph indicates that some farmers are less motivated to conserve water because other farmers make money by using large amounts of water. Choice 1 is incorrect because it attributes some farmers' difficulties to the difficulty of growing certain crops. However, sentence 2 in the paragraph states only that some farmers have switched to crops that use less water; this is not presented as a difficulty. Choice 3 incorrectly states that irrigating less frequently leads to crop failure, whereas sentence 2 in the paragraph mentions less frequent irrigation only as a method of conserving water. Choice 4 incorrectly implies that there are many farmers who do not believe that the aquifer will run dry. However, the paragraph does not explicitly state what farmers believe or do not believe. Only the reactions of farmers to the depletion of the aquifer are discussed. We can infer from these reactions that many farmers do believe the aquifer will run dry.

12. ❷ This is a Factual Information question asking for specific information that can be found in paragraph 6. The correct answer is choice 2. Sentence 2 in the paragraph states that the cost of agricultural products irrigated with transported river water would become too high and therefore uncompetitive. Choice 1 is incorrect because it states that there is not sufficient river water to meet farmers' needs, but sentence 1 in the paragraph implies that there

are "vast quantities" of river water that could be used for irrigation purposes. Choice 3 is incorrect because the paragraph does not indicate that the cost of using capillary water will increase, but instead, sentence 4 in the paragraph indicates that using capillary water will cause the cost of water to increase. Choice 4 incorrectly states that farmers will be forced to switch to genetically engineered crops; the paragraph indicates that there are multiple possible solutions to the water supply crisis that farmers may choose from.

13. ❸ This is an Insert Text question. You can see the four black squares that represent the answer choices here.

The reaction of farmers to the inevitable depletion of the Ogallala varies. Many have been attempting to conserve water by irrigating less frequently or by switching to crops that require less water. ■ Others, however, have adopted the philosophy that it is best to use the water while it is still economically profitable to do so and to concentrate on high-value crops such as cotton. ■ The incentive of the farmers who wish to conserve water is reduced by their knowledge that many of their neighbors are profiting by using great amounts of water, and in the process are drawing down the entire region's water supplies. ■

In the face of the upcoming water supply crisis, a number of grandiose schemes have been developed to transport vast quantities of water by canal or pipeline from the Mississippi, the Missouri, or the Arkansas rivers. ■ Unfortunately, the cost of water obtained through any of these schemes would increase pumping costs at least tenfold, making the cost of irrigated agricultural products from the region uncompetitive on the national and international markets.

The sentence provided, "But even if uncooperative farmers were to join in the conservation efforts, this would only delay the depletion of the aquifer," is best inserted at square 3. The preceding sentence refers to farmers who use great amounts of water, or uncooperative farmers, and the following sentence at the beginning of the next paragraph refers to the water supply crisis, or the depletion of the aquifer. Square 3 is the only place that provides logical connections to both the preceding and following sentences.

Square 1 is incorrect because the preceding sentence refers to cooperative farmers who have attempted to conserve water, and the following sentence already provides a contrast to these cooperative farmers with the words "Others, however." Therefore the sentence provided would be repetitive.

Square 2 is incorrect because the following sentence continues to discuss farmers, whereas the sentence provided leads the reader to expect a further discussion of the depletion of the aquifer.

Square 4 is incorrect because the topic of the preceding and following sentences is potential solutions to the water crisis. There is no connection to be made with the actions of uncooperative farmers.

14. ❶❸❻ This is a Prose Summary question. It is completed correctly below. The correct choices are 1, 3, and 6. Choices 2, 4, and 5 are therefore incorrect.

Directions: An introductory sentence for a brief summary of the passage is provided below. Complete the summary by selecting the THREE answer choices that express the most important ideas in the passage. Some answer choices do not belong in the summary because they express ideas that are not presented in the passage or are minor ideas in the passage. **This question is worth 2 points.**

The Ogallala aquifer is a large underground source of water in the High Plains region of the United States.

- The use of the Ogallala for irrigation has allowed the High Plains to become one of the most productive agricultural regions in the United States.
- Given the aquifer's low recharge rate, its use for irrigation is causing water tables to drop and will eventually lead to its depletion.
- Several solutions to the upcoming water supply crisis have been proposed, but none of them promises to keep the costs of irrigation low.

Answer Choices

1. The use of the Ogallala for irrigation has allowed the High Plains to become one of the most productive agricultural regions in the United States.

2. The periodic deepening of wells and the use of more-powerful pumps would help increase the natural recharge rate of the Ogallala.

3. Given the aquifer's low recharge rate, its use for irrigation is causing water tables to drop and will eventually lead to its depletion.

4. In Texas, a great deal of attention is being paid to genetic engineering because it is there that the most critical situation exists.

5. Releasing capillary water and introducing drought-resistant crops are less promising solutions to the water supply crisis than bringing in river water.

6. Several solutions to the upcoming water supply crisis have been proposed, but none of them promises to keep the costs of irrigation low.

Correct Choices

Choice 1, "The use of the Ogallala for irrigation has allowed the High Plains to become one of the most productive agricultural regions in the United States," is correct because it is the main idea of paragraph 3. This choice summarizes the background information needed to understand the later discussion of the depletion of the aquifer.

Choice 3, "Given the aquifer's low recharge rate, its use for irrigation is causing water tables to drop and will eventually lead to its depletion," is correct because it is a main idea that is developed throughout paragraphs 3 to 5.

The information in this choice concisely captures the cause of the aquifer's depletion.

Choice 6, "Several solutions to the upcoming water supply crisis have been proposed, but none of them promises to keep the costs of irrigation low," is correct because this is the main idea of the final paragraph of the passage. The information in this choice concisely captures the likely results of the aquifer's depletion.

Incorrect Choices

Choice 2, "The periodic deepening of wells and the use of more-powerful pumps would help increase the natural recharge rate of the Ogallala," is incorrect because it is a misreading of the information given in paragraph 4 about wells and pumps. Paragraph 4 states different information, which is that the low recharge rate of the aquifer has resulted in the need to deepen wells and use more-powerful pumps.

Choice 4, "In Texas, a great deal of attention is being paid to genetic engineering because it is there that the most critical situation exists," is incorrect because paragraph 6 states that genetic engineering is being considered as one of several solutions to the water supply crisis, but it is never stated who, exactly, is considering this solution. Furthermore, while it is true according to paragraph 4 that Texas has the most critical situation, there is no mention in the passage of what solutions Texas, in particular, is considering.

Choice 5, "Releasing capillary water and introducing drought-resistant crops are less promising solutions to the water supply crisis than bringing in river water," is incorrect because the passage never indicates that one of these solutions is more or less promising than the others. The passage indicates in the last sentence only that all potential solutions will lead to more expensive irrigation water.

Listening

Answer Key and Self-scoring Chart

Directions: Check your answers against the answer key below. Write the number 1 on the line to the right of each question if you picked the correct answer. Total your points at the bottom of the chart.

Question Number	Correct Answer	Your Raw Points
1.	2	_____
2.	3	_____
3.	1	_____
4.	4	_____
5.	4	_____
6.	3	_____
7.	2	_____
8.	3	_____
9.	2	_____
10.	3	_____
11.	4	_____
12.	1	_____
13.	4	_____
14.	2	_____
15.	3	_____
16.	2	_____
17.	3	_____
18.	2	_____
19.	1	_____
20.	3	_____
21.	1	_____
22.	3	_____
23.	1	_____
24.	4	_____
25.	1	_____
26.	2	_____
27.	2	_____

For question 28, write 1 if you picked both correct answers. Write 0 if you picked only one correct answer or no correct answers.

28.	3,4	_____
29.	3	_____
30.	4	_____
31.	2	_____
32.	1	_____
33.	1	_____
34.	2	_____
TOTAL:		_____

Below is a table that converts your Listening section answers into a TOEFL iBT Listening scaled score. Take the total of raw points from your answer key and find that number in the left-hand column of the table. The right-hand column of the table gives a TOEFL iBT Listening scaled score for each number of raw points. For example, if the total points from your answer key is 27, the table shows a scaled score of 20.

You should use your score estimate as a general guide only. Your actual score on the TOEFL iBT test may be higher or lower than your score on the practice version.

Listening

Raw Point Total	Scaled Score
34	30
33	28
32	26
31	25
30	24
29	23
28	22
27	20
26	19
25	18
24	17
23	16
22	15
21	14
20	13
19	12
18	10
17	9
16	8
15	7
14	6
13	5
12	4
11	3
10	2
9	1
8	0
7	0
6	0
5	0
4	0
3	0
2	0
1	0
0	0

Listening Scripts and Answer Explanations

Questions 1–5

Track 74 Listening Script

Narrator

Listen to a conversation between a student and a receptionist at the registrar's office on the first day of the semester.

Female Student

Excuse me, uh, I'm supposed to be having my physics class in the science building, but no one's in the classroom . . . Could you tell me where the class is? Physics 403? Has it been moved?

Receptionist

Well, there's a room assignment sheet on the bulletin board outside this office . . .

Female Student

Yeah, I know, but my class isn't listed there. There must be some kinda mistake or something. Could you look it up, please?

Receptionist

Mm, okay, let me check on the computer. It's physics, right? Wait, did you say Physics 403?

Female Student

Yeah.

Receptionist

Well, I'm sorry, but . . . it says here that it was canceled . . . You should've gotten a letter from the registrar's office about this . . .

Female Student

What? I never got it.

Receptionist

Are you sure? 'Cause it says on the computer that the letter was sent out to students a week ago.

Female Student

Really? I shoulda gotten it by now . . . I wonder if I threw it away with all the junk mail by mistake . . .

Receptionist

Well, it does happen . . . Um, let me check something. What's your name?

Female Student

Woodhouse. Laura Woodhouse.

Receptionist

OK, ummm, Woodhouse . . . let me see . . . ah, it says here we sent it to your apartment on . . . uh . . . Center Street.

Female Student

Oh, that's my old apartment . . . I moved out of there a little while ago . . .

Receptionist

Well . . . and I suppose you haven't changed your mailing address at the administration office. Well, that would explain it.

Female Student

Yeah, I guess that's it. But, how can they cancel a class after offering it? If I'd known this was gonna happen, I'd've taken it last semester.

Receptionist

I know, it's really inconvenient for you; I understand that, but, um . . . if we don't have enough students signed up for the course, the college can't offer it. You know, it's, um, a practical issue, like, we can't have an instructor when there're only a few students in the class. You see what I mean?

Female Student

I guess, but now I don't know what course I should take instead.

Receptionist

Okay, let's see . . . do you have any courses you were gonna take next semester? If you do, you might wanna take 'em now and sign up for Physics 403 next semester.

Female Student

Yeah, I guess I could do that. I just hope it won't be canceled again. Do you know how many people have to be enrolled in order to keep a class from being canceled?

Receptionist

Well, it depends on the class, but for that class, you have to have . . . um . . . let's see . . . usually it'd be at least 10 people, but since it was canceled this semester, they might even do it with less. But you know what you should do? Give the physics department a call a coupla weeks before the semester starts. They'll be able to tell you if they're planning to go through with it . . . It's their decision, actually.

Female Student

Oh, OK, I'll do that. Thanks for the info.

Receptionist

No problem. Sorry about the class . . . Oh, why don't you go change your mailing address now; it'll only take a minute.

Female Student

Oh, oh, sure, I'll do that right away.

Answer Explanations

1. ❷ This is a Gist-purpose question. Before coming to the registrar's office, the woman had been to where her physics class was supposed to meet. Finding the room empty, she assumes that the class must be meeting elsewhere and goes to the registrar's office to find out the new location. Choice 2 therefore is the correct answer. She and the man discuss her change of address (choice 1) only after she learns that the class had been canceled. She does not need to know where the science building is (choice 3) because she has already been there. She does complain about the course's being canceled (choice 4), but only after the man informs her about it.

2. ❸ This is a Connecting Content question. Identifying the correct answer, choice 3, requires integrating information that the man and the woman exchange—his telling her that the college sent the cancellation notice to the woman's apartment on Center Street, and her replying that she had moved away from that address. The woman initially speculates that she might have thrown away the letter (choice 1), but she did not. Nothing about a roommate (choice 2) or about the notice's having been sent to the wrong student (choice 4) is mentioned or implied by either speaker.

3. ❶ This is a Detail question. The correct answer, choice 1, paraphrases the man's explanation that the college cannot offer a course if too few students sign up to take it. This point is reinforced later when the man says that, generally, at least 10 students must sign up for a course or it will be canceled.

4. ❹ This is also a Detail question. Toward the end of the conversation, the man advises the woman to call the physics department before the next semester begins to find out if enough people had signed up for Physics 403. Thus choice 4 is correct.

5. ❹ You are asked to listen again to this part of the conversation:

Female Student

Excuse me, uh, I'm supposed to be having my physics class in the science building, but no one's in the classroom . . . Could you tell me where the class is? Physics 403? Has it been moved?

Receptionist

Well, there's a room assignment sheet on the bulletin board outside this office . . .

Then you are asked what the man implies when he says this:

Well, there's a room assignment sheet on the bulletin board outside this office . . .

Like most replay questions, this is an Understanding the Function of What Is Said question. In responding to the woman's question by pointing out that class locations are on display nearby, the receptionist implies that the woman can get that information without his help. Thus choice 4 is correct. At this point in the conversation, the receptionist has not yet checked the computer, which is how he discovers the cancellation (choice 1). It is possible that the receptionist does not know where the science building is (choice 2) and that many room assignments have been changed (choice 3), but the conversation does not touch on either of these possibilities.

Questions 6–11

Track 76 Listening Script

Narrator
Listen to part of a lecture in an environmental science class.

Professor
Now, we've been talking about the loss of animal habitat from housing developments, um, growing cities . . . small habitat losses. But today I want to begin talking about what happens when habitat is reduced across a large area. There are, of course, animal species that require large areas of habitat . . . and, um, some migrate over very long distances. So what's the impact of habitat loss on those animals? Animals that need large areas of habitat?

Well, I'll use the hummingbirds as an example. Now, you know a hummingbird is amazingly small. But even though it's really tiny, it migrates over very long distances . . . travels up and down the Western Hemisphere . . . the Americas . . . back and forth between where it breeds in the summer and the warmer climates where it spends the winter. So we would say that this whole area over which it migrates is its habitat, because on this long-distance journey, it needs to come down to feed and sleep every so often, right?

Well, the hummingbird beats its wings—get this—about 3,000 times per minute. So you think, wow, it must need a lot of energy, a lot of food, right? Well, it does—it drinks a lot of nectar from flowers and feeds on some insects—but it's energy-efficient, too. You can't say it isn't. I mean as it flies all the way across the Gulf of Mexico, it uses up almost none of its body fat. But that doesn't mean it doesn't need to eat! So hummingbirds have to rely on plants in their natural habitat. And it goes without saying, but . . . well, the opposite is true as well. Plants depend on hummingbirds too. There are some flowers that can only be pollinated by the hummingbird. Without it stopping to feed and spreading pollen from flower to flower, these plants would cease to exist!

But the problem, well . . . as natural habitat along these migration routes is developed by humans for housing or agriculture, or, um, cleared for raising cattle, for instance . . . there's less food available for migrating hummingbirds. Their nesting sites are affected, too . . . the same . . . by the same sorts of human activities. And all of these activities pose a real threat to the hummingbird population.

So, to help them survive, we need to preserve their habitats . . . And one of the concrete ways people have been doing this is by cleaning up polluted habitat areas . . . and then replanting flowers, uh, replanting native flowers that hummingbirds feed on.

Promoting ecological tourism is another way to help save their habitat. As the number of visitors—ecotourists who come to hummingbird habitats to watch the birds—the more the number of visitors grows, the more local businesses profit. So ecological tourism can bring financial rewards. All the more reason to value these beautiful little creatures and their habitat, right?

But to understand more about how to protect and support hummingbirds the best we can, we've gotta learn more about their breeding . . . nesting . . . sites and, uh, migration routes—and also about the natural habitats we find there. That should help us determine how to prevent further decline in the population.

A good research method . . . a good way to learn more . . . is by, um, running a banding study. Banding the birds allows us to track them over their lifetime. It's a practice that's been used by researchers for years. In fact, most of what we know about hummingbirds comes from banding studies . . . where we, uh, capture a hummingbird and make sure all the information about it—like . . . its weight and, um, age and length—are all recorded . . . put into international . . . an international information database. And, then we place an extremely lightweight band around one of its legs . . . well, what looks like a leg—although, technically it's considered part of the bird's foot. Anyway, these bands are perfectly safe. And some hummingbirds have worn them for years with no evidence of any problems. The band is labeled with a tracking number . . . oh, and there's a phone number on the band for people to call, for free, to report a banded bird they've found or recaptured.

So when a banded bird is recaptured and reported, we learn about its migration route, its growth . . . and how long it's been alive . . . its life span. One recaptured bird had been banded almost 12 years earlier! She's one of the oldest hummingbirds on record.

Another interesting thing we've learned is . . . that some hummingbirds, uh, they no longer use a certain route; they travel by a different route to reach their destination. And findings like these have been of interest to biologists and environmental scientists in a number of countries, who are trying to understand the complexities of how changes in a habitat . . . affect the species in it—species like the hummingbirds.

Answer Explanations

6. ❸ This is a Gist-content question. After the professor establishes loss of wildlife habitat as the general topic, she turns to the hummingbird's migratory routes as an extended example of the potential impact of losing large habitats and efforts being made to reverse this trend. Thus choice 3 is the correct answer. Changes in the migratory patterns of hummingbirds (choice 1) are discussed only briefly at the end of the lecture as an interesting finding. The adaptation of hummingbirds to urban environments (choice 2) is not mentioned at all. Ecotourism (choice 4) is mentioned only in passing, as one of a number of ways to preserve habitats.

7. ❷ This is a Making Inferences question. Choice 2 is the correct answer. The professor explains how land along hummingbird migration routes is being used in farming and cattle raising, among other things. She points out that

these activities reduce food availability for hummingbirds and affect their nesting sites. In saying that these human activities all "pose a real threat to the hummingbird population," she implies a potential decrease in the population if more land is used this way.

8. ❸ This is a Detail question. The professor explicitly states that people have been trying to preserve hummingbird habitats by cleaning up polluted areas and then planting native flowers for the birds to feed on. Thus choice 3 is the corect answer. Building feeding stations (choice 1), punishing polluters (choice 2), and identifying various species (choice 4) are also things that people could conceivably do to help hummingbirds survive, but the professor does not mention any of them.

9. ❷ This is another Detail question. Choice 2 is correct. The professor describes a research study designed to collect information about hummingbird migration. This research involves placing lightweight bands on hummingbirds. Information is collected when people who find or recapture the hummingbirds use the phone number on the band to contact the researchers. The study does not involve radio tracking devices (choice 1), counting yearly returns by birds to the same region (choice 3), or comparing the migration routes of old and young birds (choice 4).

10. ❸ This is a Connecting Content question. A research finding mentioned at the end of the lecture is that some hummingbirds have stopped using certain routes "to reach their destination." Since the destinations the professor is referring to are migration destinations, she is implying that for some hummingbirds, a change in migration patterns has occurred. Choice 3 is therefore the correct answer. The other answer choices consist of specific statements concerning habitats (choice 1), preservation efforts (choice 2), and food sources (choice 4); nothing the professor says in the lecture supports these specific statements.

11. ❹ You are asked to listen again to this part of the lecture:

So hummingbirds have to rely on plants in their natural habitat. And it goes without saying, but . . . well, the opposite is true as well. Plants depend on hummingbirds too.

You are then asked what the professor implies when she says this:

And it goes without saying . . .

This is an Understanding the Function of What Is Said question. Choice 4 is the correct answer. "It goes without saying" is a common phrase used by speakers to signal that they are about to say (or have just said) something that probably does not need to be said because it is very obvious. The other answer choices are all potential misunderstandings of this phrase.

Questions 12–17

Track 78 Listening Script

Narrator

Listen to part of a lecture in a film history class.

Professor

Okay, we've been discussing film in the 1920s and '30s, and, ah, how back then, film categories as we know them today had not yet been established. We, ah, said that, by today's standards, many of the films of the '20s and '30s would be considered "hybrids"; that is, a mixture of styles that wouldn't exactly fit into any of today's categories. And in that context, today we're going to talk about a, a filmmaker who began making very unique films in the late 1920s. He was French, and his name was Jean Painlevé.

Jean Painlevé was born in 1902. He made his first film in 1928. Now, in a way, Painlevé's films conform to norms of the '20s and '30s; that is, they don't fit very neatly into the categories we use to classify films today. That said, even by the standards of the '20s and '30s, Painlevé's films were a unique hybrid of styles. He had a special way of fusing—or, or some people might say confusing—science and fiction; his films begin with facts, but then they become more and more fictional—they gradually add more and more fictional elements. In fact, Painlevé was known for saying that "science is fiction."

Painlevé was a, a pioneer in underwater filmmaking, and a lot of his short films focus on the aquatic animal world. He liked to show small underwater creatures displaying what seemed like familiar human characteristics—what we think of as unique to humans. He might take a, a clip of a mollusk going up and down in the water and set it to music—you know, to make it look as if the mollusk were dancing to the music like a human being. That sort of thing. But then he'd suddenly change the image or narration to remind us how different the animals are, how unlike humans. He confused his audience in the way he portrayed the animals he filmed, mixing up our notions of the categories "human" and "animal." The films make us a little uncomfortable at times because we're uncertain about what we're seeing. It gives his films an uncanny feature . . . the familiar made unfamiliar, the normal made suspicious. He liked twists; he liked the unusual. In fact, one of his favorite sea animals was the sea horse because with sea horses, it's the male that gets pregnant, it's the male that carries the babies. And he thought that was great. His first and most celebrated underwater film is about the sea horse.

Susan? You have a question?

Female Student

But underwater filmmaking wasn't that unusual, was it? I mean weren't there other people making movies underwater?

Professor

Well, actually it was pretty rare at that time. I mean we're talking the early 1930s here.

Female Student

But what about Jacques Cousteau? Wasn't he, like, an innovator, you know, with underwater photography, too?

Professor

Ah, Jacques Cousteau. Well, Painlevé and Cousteau did both film underwater, and they were both innovators, so you're right in that sense, but that's pretty much where the similarities end. First of all, Painlevé was about 20 years ahead of Cousteau . . . Um, and Cousteau's adventures were high-tech, with lots of fancy equipment, whereas Painlevé kind of patched equipment together as he needed it . . . Uh, Cousteau usually filmed large animals, usually in the open sea, whereas Painlevé generally filmed smaller animals, and, and he liked to film in shallow water . . . Uh, what else? Well, the main difference was that Cousteau simply investigated and presented the facts; he, he didn't mix in fiction. He was a strict documentarist; he set the standard, really, for the nature documentary. Painlevé, on the other hand, as we said before, mixed in elements of fiction, and his films are much more artistic, incorporating music as an important element.

John, you have a question?

Male Student

Well, maybe I shouldn't be asking this . . . Uh, but if Painlevé's films are so special, so good, why haven't we ever heard of them? I mean everyone's heard of Jacques Cousteau . . .

Professor

Well, that's a fair question. Uh, the short answer is that Painlevé's style just never caught on with the general public. I mean it probably goes back, at least in part, to what we mentioned earlier, that, that people didn't know what to make of his films, that they were confused by them. Whereas Cousteau's documentaries were very straightforward, uh, met people's expectations more than Painlevé's films did. But your true film-history buffs know about him, and Painlevé's still highly respected in many circles.

Answer Explanations

12. ❶ This is a Gist-purpose question. The correct answer is choice 1. The professor begins the lecture by briefly reviewing a previous discussion about films of the 1920s and 1930s and their hybrid style. Then he turns to a discussion of the style of one particular filmmaker, Jean Painlevé, and spends the rest of the lecture talking about him and his films.

13. ❹ This is a Connecting Content question. Choice 4 is the correct answer. Identifying it requires integrating two important pieces of information. The first is the professor's statement at the beginning of the lecture that films from the 1920s and '30s do not fit neatly into today's film categories. The second piece of information comes right afterward, when the professor says that "Painlevé's films conform to norms of the '20s and '30s," meaning that his films, too, are difficult to categorize.

14. ❷ This is a Detail question. The professor discusses the confusing aspects of Painlevé's films at considerable length and focuses, in particular, on the way Painlevé mixes up the audience's notions of human and animal characteristics. Thus the correct answer is choice 2.

15. ❸ This is an Understanding Organization question. The reason that the professor discusses sea horses is to illustrate the unusualness of Painlevé's subject matter. Painlevé's first film was about sea horses, which are unusual because the males carry the babies. Choice 3 is therefore the correct answer.

16. ❷ This is another Connecting Content question. The professor compares the film styles of Jacques Cousteau and Painlevé in response to an objection raised by the female student. She questions the professor's characterization of Painlevé's films as special and points out that other filmmakers, like Cousteau, also made underwater films. The professor emphasizes the uniqueness of Painlevé's films by explaining that Cousteau's films were straightforward, fact-based documentaries that met people's expectations, unlike Painlevé's films, which mixed fact with fiction in a way that was both unique and confusing. Thus choice 2 is the correct answer.

17. ❸ You are asked to decide what the student is implying when he says this:

> Well, maybe I shouldn't be asking this . . . Uh, but if Painlevé's films are so special, so good, why haven't we ever heard of them? I mean everyone's heard of Jacques Cousteau . . .

This is an Understanding the Function of What Is Said question. After listening to what the professor has been saying about Painlevé's films, the student cannot understand why they are not more popular or better known. The student's replayed statement suggests that he believes that Painlevé's films deserve the same level of recognition that Cousteau's films have received. Thus choice 3 is the correct answer.

Questions 18–22

Track 80 Listening Script

Narrator

Listen to a conversation between a student and a professor.

Male Student

Hi, Professor Archer. You know how in class last week you said that you were looking for students who were interested in volunteering for your archaeology project?

Professor

Of course. Are you volunteering?

Male Student

Yes, I am. It sounds really interesting. But, ummm, do I need to have any experience with these kinds of projects?

Professor

No, not really. I assume that most students taking the introductory-level class will have little or no experience with archaeological research, but that's OK.

Male Student

Oh, good—that's a relief. Actually, that's why I'm volunteering for the project—to get experience. What kind of work is it?

Professor

Well, as you know, we're studying the history of the campus this semester. This used to be an agricultural area, and we already know that where the main lecture hall now stands there once were a farmhouse and barn that were erected in the late 1700s. We're excavating near the lecture hall to see what types of artifacts we find—you know, things people used in the past that got buried when the campus was constructed. We've already begun to find some very interesting items like, um, old bottles, buttons, pieces of clay pottery . . .

Male Student

Buttons and clay pottery? Did the old owners leave in such a hurry that they left their clothes and dishes behind?

Professor

That's just one of the questions we hope to answer with this project.

Male Student

Wow—and it's all right here on campus . . .

Professor

That's right, no traveling involved. I wouldn't expect volunteers to travel to a site, especially in the middle of the semester. We expect to find many more things, but we do need more people to help.

Male Student

So . . . how many student volunteers are you looking for?

Professor

I'm hoping to get five or six. I've asked for volunteers in all the classes I teach, but no one's responded. You're the first person to express interest.

Male Student

Uh . . . sounds like it could be a lot of work. Is there . . . umm . . . is there any way I can use the experience to get some extra credit in class? I mean can I write a paper about it?

Professor

I think it'll depend on what type of work you do in the excavation, but I imagine we can arrange something. Well, actually, I've been considering offering extra credit for class because I've been having a tough time getting volunteers . . . Extra credit is always a good incentive for students.

Male Student

And . . . how often would you want the volunteers to work?

Professor

We're asking for three or four hours per week, depending on your schedule. A senior researcher—I think you know John Franklin, my assistant—is on-site every day.

Male Student

Sure, I know John. By the way, will there be some sort of training?

Professor

Yes, uh, I wanna wait till Friday to see how many students volunteer. And then I'll schedule a training class next week at a time that's convenient for everyone.

Male Student

OK, I'll wait to hear from you. Thanks a lot for accepting me!

Answer Explanations

18. ❷ This is a Gist-purpose question. The correct answer is choice 2. The student opens the conversation by asking the professor about her request for volunteers for an archaeology project. The project's timing—the middle of the semester—is mentioned later, when the professor says that she would not expect students to travel to a site in the middle of the semester. Choosing the correct answer thus requires the integration of these two pieces of information from different parts of the conversation. Choice 1 is incorrect because the project is voluntary, not an assignment. It takes place during the semester, not during the summer (choice 3). Although the student asks about extra credit, presumably to improve his grade (choice 4), he brings this up as an afterthought, when he hears how much work is involved.

19. ❶ This is a Detail question. The professor states that the lecture hall was built where a farmhouse and barn from the 1700s once stood. Thus choice 1 is correct. Pottery (choice 2), clothes (choice 3), and bottles (choice 4) are mentioned in the context of artifacts—items that may have belonged to the farm's owners.

20. ❸ This is a Detail question. The on-campus location of the project is mentioned several times during the conversation, and both speakers cite this as an advantage: volunteers will not need to travel. Thus choice 3 is correct.

21. ❶ This is another Detail question. Choice 1 is correct. When the student asks if he could earn extra credit for volunteering, the professor responds by pointing out that she is considering offering extra credit as an incentive for more students to volunteer. The other three choices could be plausible incentives as well, but the professor does not mention any of them as a way to get more volunteers.

22. ❸ This is a Connecting Content question. When the student asks about training, the professor notes that she has not scheduled a specific time for it, and he responds that he will wait to hear from her. Choice 3 is therefore the correct answer. The professor already provided the name of the senior researcher (choice 1), so this is not information the student still needs. Books (choice 2) are not mentioned at all in the conversation. As for the project's location (choice 4), this is information the student was given early on.

Questions 23–28

Track 81 Listening Script

Narrator

Listen to part of a lecture in an art history class. The professor has been discussing the origins of art.

Professor

Some of the world's oldest preserved art is the cave art of Europe, most of it in Spain and France. And, uh, the earliest cave paintings found to date are those of the Chauvet cave in France, discovered in 1994.

And, you know, I remember when I heard about the results of the dating of the Chauvet paintings. I said to my wife, "Can you believe these paintings are over 30,000 years old?" and my three-year-old daughter piped up and said, "Is that older than my great-grandmother?" That was the oldest age she knew. And, you know, come to think of it, it's pretty hard for me to really understand how long 30,000 years is too. I mean, we tend to think the people who lived at that time must have been pretty primitive . . . but I'm gonna show you some slides in a few minutes, and I think you'll agree with me that this art is anything but primitive—they're masterpieces. And they look so real, so alive, that it's very hard to imagine that they're so very old.

Now, not everyone agrees on exactly how old. A number of the Chauvet paintings have been dated—by a lab—to 30,000 or more years ago. That would make them not just older than any other cave art, but about twice as old as the art in the caves at Altamira or Lascaux, which you may have heard of.

Some people find it hard to believe Chauvet is so much older than Altamira and Lascaux, and they noted that only one lab did the dating for Chauvet, without independent confirmation from any other lab.

But be that as it may, whatever the exact date, whether it's 15,000, 20,000, or 30,000 years ago, the Chauvet paintings are from the dawn of art, so they're a good place to start our discussion of cave painting.

Now, one thing you've gotta remember is the context of these paintings. Paleolithic humans—that's the period we're talking about here, the Paleolithic, the early Stone Age, not too long after humans first arrived in Europe. The climate was significantly colder then, and so rock shelters—shallow caves—were valued as homes protected from the wind and rain. And in some cases at least, artists drew on the walls of their homes. But many of the truly great cave art sites—like Chauvet—were never inhabited. These paintings were made deep inside a dark cave, where no natural light can penetrate. There's no evidence of people ever living here—cave bears, yes, but not humans.

You would have had to make a special trip into the cave to make the paintings, and a special trip to go see it, and each time you'd have to bring along torches to light your way. And people did go see the art—there's charcoal marks from their torches on the cave walls, clearly dating from thousands of years after the paintings were made—so we can tell people went there. They came, but they didn't stay. Deep inside a cave like that is not really a place you'd want to stay, so, uh, why? What inspired the Paleolithic artists to make such beautiful art in such inaccessible places? We'll never really know, of course, though it's interesting to speculate.

But, uh . . . getting to the paintings themselves. Virtually all Paleolithic cave art represents animals, and Chauvet is no exception. The artists were highly skilled at using—or even enhancing—the natural shape of the cave walls to give depth and perspective to their drawings. The sense of motion and vitality in these animals—well, wait till I show you the slides. Anyway, most Paleolithic cave art depicts large herbivores. Horses are most common overall, with deer and bison pretty common too. Probably animals they hunted. But earlier, at Chauvet, there's a significant interest in large, dangerous animals. Lots of rhinoceroses, lions, mammoths, bears . . . remember that the ranges of many animal species were different back then, so all these animals actually lived in the region at that time—but, uh, the Chauvet artists didn't paint people. There's a half-man, half-bison creature, and there's outlines of human hands, but no depiction of a full human.

So why these precise animals? Why not birds . . . fish . . . snakes? Was it for their religion? Magic? Or sheer beauty? We don't know, but whatever it was, it was worth it to them to spend hours deep inside a cave, with just a torch between them and utter darkness. So, on that note, let's dim the lights so we can see these slides and actually look at the techniques they used.

Answer Explanations

23. ❶ This is a Gist-content question. The professor begins by pointing out that Europe is the home of the oldest examples of preserved cave art. He then identifies the Chauvet cave in France as the site of the earliest cave paintings, dating from "the dawn of art." The rest of the lecture focuses on various aspects of the paintings in the Chauvet cave. Thus choice 1 is the correct

answer. The other choices contain words or ideas that the professor refers to, but they are not the main topic of the lecture.

24. ❹ This is an Understanding Organization question. The professor mentions his young daughter's effort to grasp a very long time line through her most familiar frame of reference: her great-grandmother. He mentions his daughter to reinforce the difficulty that he personally has grasping the notion of 30,000 years—the age of the cave drawings he is talking about. Choice 4 is therefore the correct answer.

25. ❶ This is an Understanding the Speaker's Attitude question. You are asked to identify an opinion that is expressed by the professor. Choice 1 is correct because it paraphrases the professor's description of the Chauvet drawings as "masterpieces." The professor only speculates about the *possible* religious significance of the drawings, which is different from saying that the drawings *probably* reflected the artists' religious beliefs (choice 2). He mentions Lascaux and Altamira not to compare the sophistication of drawings in those caves with the Chauvet drawings (choice 3), but to compare them in terms of age. Choice 4 misstates the age comparison: the professor believes that the Chauvet drawings are considerably older.

26. ❷ This is a Making Inferences question. The professor says that the charcoal marks on the walls of the Chauvet cave came from torches of people who went to see the paintings. He also says that the marks date from thousands of years after the paintings were made. Since the date of the marks can be established relative to when the paintings were made, the relative date of the visits can be established as well—thousands of years after the paintings were made. Thus choice 2 is the correct answer.

27. ❷ This is a Detail question. Choice 2 is correct. The professor first notes that the animals represented in most Paleolithic art were large herbivores—plant-eating animals that were probably hunted. He then contrasts these animals with the large, dangerous animals depicted at Chauvet, including rhinoceroses, lions, mammoths, and bears.

28. ❸❹ This is another Detail question. The two correct answers come from different parts of the lecture. In the middle of the lecture, the professor discusses a curious aspect of the Chauvet paintings—their location deep inside an inaccessible cave where sunlight cannot reach. He says, "We'll never really know" what led artists to create beautiful art in such a remote place (choice 4). Later in the lecture, he wonders aloud why the cave artists drew rhinoceroses, lions, mammoths, and bears instead of other animals, like birds, fish, or snakes. Here, too, he says, we do not know the reason. Thus choice 3 is also correct.

Questions 29–34

Track 82 Listening Script

Narrator

Listen to part of a lecture in an astronomy class.

Professor

Now, astronomy didn't really, uh, balloon into the science it is today until the development of spectroscopy. Spectroscopy is basically the study of spectra and spectral lines of light, and specifically for us, the light from stars. It makes it possible to analyze the light emitted from stars. When you analyze this light, you can figure out their distance from the Earth and identify what they're made of—determine their chemical composition.

Before we get into that, though, it's probably a good thing to back up a bit. You all know how when you take a crystal prism and pass a beam of sunlight through it, you get a spectrum which looks like a continuous band of rainbow colors. The light that we see with our human eyes as a band of rainbow color falls in the range of what's called visible light. And visible light spectroscopy is probably the most important kind of spectroscopy.

Anyone wanna take a stab at the scientific term for visible light? . . . And I'm sure all of you know this because you all did the reading for today . . .

Female Student

Optical radiation. But I thought being exposed to radiation's dangerous.

Professor

Yes and no. If you're talking about radiation like in the element uranium, yeah, that's dangerous, but radiation as a general term actually refers to anything that spreads away from its source, so optical radiation is just visible light energy spreading out.

OK, so we've got a spectrum of a beam of sunlight and it looks like the colors bleed into each other; uh, there're no interruptions, just a band flowing from violet to green to yellow to . . . you get the idea. Well, what happens if the sunlight spectrum is magnified? Maybe you all didn't do the reading. Well, here's what you'd see:

a spectral line

I want you to notice that this spectrum is interrupted by dark lines, called spectral lines. If you really magnified the spectrum of the sunlight, you could identify more than a hundred thousand of 'em. They may look kinda randomly placed, but they actually form many distinct patterns. And if you were looking at the spectrum of some other star, the colors would be the same, but the spectral lines would break it up at different places, making different patterns. Each pattern stands for a distinct chemical element, and so different sets or patterns of spectral lines mean that the star has a different chemical composition.

Female Student

So how do we know which spectral patterns match up with which elements?

Professor

Well, a kind of spectroscopic library of elements was compiled using flame tests. A known element—uh, say a piece of iron, for example—is heated in a pure gas flame. The iron eventually heats to the point that it radiates light. This light is passed through a prism, which breaks it up into a spectrum, and a unique pattern, kind of like a chemical fingerprint, of spectral lines for that element appears. This process was repeated over and over again for many different elements. So we can figure out the chemical makeup of another star by comparing the spectral pattern it has to the pattern of the elements in the library.

Oh! An interesting story about how one of the elements was discovered through spectroscopy. There was a pretty extensive library of spectral line patterns of elements even by the 1860s. A British astronomer was analyzing a spectrograph of sunlight and he noticed a particular pattern of spectral lines that didn't match anything in the library. So he put two and two together and decided there was an element in the Sun that hadn't been discovered here on the Earth yet. Any guesses about what that element is? It's actually turned out to be pretty common, and I'm sure all of you know it. OK. Let's try something else. Any of you happen to be familiar with the Greek word for *Sun*, by chance?

Male Student

Something like *helios* or something like that? . . . Oh! It must be *helium*. So you're sayin' that helium was discovered on the Sun first?

Professor

Yes. And this is a good example of how important spectroscopy is in astronomy.

Answer Explanations

29. ❸ This is a Gist-content question. At the beginning of the lecture, the professor defines spectroscopy and notes its importance to astronomy as a method that allows astronomers to determine the chemical composition of stars. The rest of the lecture is intended to help students understand the technique and how it can be used in this way. Thus choice 3 is the correct answer. Choice 1 is incorrect because the professor merely describes what a magnified spectrum looks like and how it can be used; he does not actually explain how this magnification is achieved technically. Choices 2 and 4 are incorrect because they each represent only a small part of the lecture, not the main topic.

30. ❹ This is a Detail question. The student expresses a mistaken view about radiation—she thinks that all radiation is harmful. The professor corrects this misimpression first by acknowledging that some forms of radiation, like radiation from the element uranium, are indeed harmful to living organisms. He then gives a general definition of radiation as *anything* that spreads out from its source. Finally, he points out that some forms of radiation, like visible light energy, are not harmful. Thus choice 4 is correct.

31. ❷ This is a Making Inferences question. The correct answer is choice 2, and it can be inferred from the professor's account of the relationship between spectral line patterns and chemical elements. Every chemical element, he explains, has a unique spectral line pattern that corresponds to it, and these spectral line patterns make it possible to identify what the elements are in a star. If two stars are similar in terms of their spectral line patterns, it is reasonable to infer that they are similar in terms of the elements they contain.

32. ❶ This is a Detail question. The professor explains that spectroscopic flame tests were used to create a library of the visible light spectra produced by various elements that exist in stars. In order to get an element to emit light, the element must be heated. Therefore choice 1 is correct. The other choices describe other reasons a scientist might possibly heat a chemical element in a flame, but the professor does not mention any of them.

33. ❶ You are asked why the professor says this:

Before we get into that, though, it's probably a good thing to back up a bit.

This is an Understanding the Function of What Is Said question. The sentence signals that the professor is about to interrupt the flow of his lecture to provide some information that might help the students better understand the main topic. The correct answer therefore is choice 1. Recalling the context of this statement—what the professor said immediately before and immediately after the replay—is important. Before the replay, the professor introduces some abstract and possibly unfamiliar concepts. After the replayed statement, he provides a familiar, concrete analogy that may make the concepts more accessible: a prism breaking visible light into a rainbow of colors. Referring to your notes could therefore be helpful in getting this answer right.

34. ❷ You are asked why the professor asks this:

Any of you happen to be familiar with the Greek word for *Sun*, by chance?

This is another Understanding the Function of What Is Said question. The professor makes two attempts to help students guess that the element in the Sun discovered by a British astronomer in the 1860s was helium. The first hint the professor gives is that the element is common on Earth. When no one is able to identify the element, the professor provides a second hint, which is contained in the replayed statement. The correct answer therefore is choice 2.

Speaking

Listening Scripts, Important Points, and Sample Responses with Rater Comments

Use the sample Independent and Integrated Speaking rubrics on pages 188–191 to see how responses are scored. The raters who listen to your responses will analyze them in three general categories. These categories are Delivery, Language Use, and Topic Development. All three categories have equal importance.

This section includes important points that should be covered when answering each question. All of these points must be present in a response in order for it to receive the highest score in the Topic Development category. These important points are guides to the kind of information raters expect to hear in a high-level response.

This section also refers to example responses on the accompanying audio tracks on the CD. Some responses were scored at the highest level, while others were not. The responses are followed by explanations of their scores.

Question 1

Track 85 Listening Script

Narrator

What characteristics do you think make someone a good parent? Explain why these characteristics are important to you.

> **Preparation Time: 15 Seconds**
> **Response Time: 45 Seconds**

Important Points

In this question, you should talk about a characteristic or quality of a good parent. You should select one or two characteristics (such as being patient, being kind, being strict) and explain why you think the characteristic is important for a parent to have. For example, if you say being patient helps make someone a good parent, you could explain why by adding *"Children make a lot of mistakes as they learn and grow, and parents who are patient don't make their children nervous or fearful about making mistakes from time to time . . . and that helps them grow into more confident adults."*

You should be careful to avoid vague responses such as *"Parents should be patient because this is good for children."* Such statements do not make it clear why it is important for parents to be patient.

Sample Responses

Play Track 92 on the CD to hear a high-level response for Question 1.

Rater Comments

The speaker's pronunciation is clear and her delivery is fluent. She chooses two characteristics—being strict and being loving—and supports each one, though she develops the first one in more detail. She uses a variety of appropriate vocabulary and phrases, such as *follow the parents' lead* and *to look up to*. She is also able to use appropriate word forms, such as *strict* and *strictness*, correctly and without hesitation.

Play Track 93 on the CD to hear a mid-level response for Question 1.

Rater Comments

This speaker talks about three things good parents do: trust their children, listen to their children, and communicate with their children. However, the support for her ideas is vague and unclear; for example, she only says trust is very important but does not explain why. While her pronunciation is easy to understand, she pauses frequently in order to choose the next word, which makes her answer somewhat difficult to follow. Her basic grammar is adequate, but she is unable to use very advanced grammatical constructions; for example, she says *children may be better understand*, rather than *better understood*, by the parents.

Question 2

Track 86 Listening Script

Narrator

Some students prefer to work on class assignments by themselves. Others believe it is better to work in a group. Which do you prefer? Explain why.

| Preparation Time: 15 Seconds |
| Response Time: 45 Seconds |

Important Points

In this question, you need to say whether you prefer to work alone or in groups to complete class assignments, and then explain the reason for your preference. You should not simply give a list of reasons, such as *"I prefer to work in groups because it is more interesting plus many people help and also you can learn from other people . . ."* It is better if you develop one or two reasons fully. For example, if you prefer to work in groups, you could say, *"I prefer working in groups because usually in group work, different people know different things about the topic, and because of that, you get a deeper understanding of the assignment. For example, there was a student from Venezuela in a group assignment I had, and we were supposed to describe how crude oil prices are set. She helped us understand problems in oil production in a much deeper way because her parents worked in oil production . . ."*

Sample Responses

Play Track 94 on the CD to hear a high-level response for Question 2.

Rater Comments

This is a fully developed response to the question. She gives two reasons for preferring to work by herself—having strong opinions and managing time well—and gives a clear explanation of why each is more suitable for working alone. Her speech is fluent, and she uses appropriate intonation and stress on certain words (such as "*I*" in *the way **I** see them*) to convey meaning. She uses advanced-level vocabulary, such as *a structured approach,* and high-level grammatical constructions with ease.

Play Track 95 on the CD to hear a low-level response for Question 2.

Rater Comments

While her pronunciation is clear, this speaker struggles and often fails to come up with words to express her meaning, such as using *good things* rather than the more appropriate and specific *advantages* or *benefits*. Since she spends time trying to describe benefits of both group work and working alone, she ran out of time before she could support her true preference for working alone, other than saying it allows more independence. Her answer is very choppy and vague. She does not demonstrate that she has command of grammar beyond a very basic level.

Question 3

Track 87 Listening Script

Narrator

The university's Dining Services Department has announced a change. Read an announcement about this change. You will have 45 seconds to read the announcement. Begin reading now.

Reading Time: 45 Seconds

Hot Breakfasts Eliminated

Beginning next month, Dining Services will no longer serve hot breakfast foods at university dining halls. Instead, students will be offered a wide assortment of cold breakfast items in the morning. These cold breakfast foods, such as breads, fruit, and yogurt, are healthier than many of the hot breakfast items that we will stop serving, so health-conscious students should welcome this change. Students will benefit in another way as well, because limiting the breakfast selection to cold food items will save money and allow us to keep our meal plans affordable.

Narrator

Now listen to two students discussing the announcement.

Woman

Do you believe any of this? It's ridiculous.

Man

What do you mean? It is important to eat healthy foods . . .

Woman

Sure it is, but they're saying yogurt's better for you than an omelet . . . or than hot cereal? I mean whether something's hot or cold, that shouldn't be the issue. Except maybe on a really cold morning, but in that case, which is going to be better for you—a bowl of cold cereal or a nice warm omelet? It's obvious; there's no question.

Man

I'm not going to argue with you there.

Woman

And this whole thing about saving money . . .

Man

What about it?

Woman

Well, they're actually going to make things worse for us, not better. 'Cause if they start cutting back and we can't get what we want right here, on campus, well, we're going to be going off campus and pay off-campus prices, and you know what? That will be expensive. Even if it's only two or three mornings a week, it can add up.

Narrator

The woman expresses her opinion of the change that has been announced. State her opinion and explain her reasons for holding that opinion.

Preparation Time: 30 Seconds
Response Time: 60 Seconds

Important Points

The woman does not think that Dining Services should stop providing hot breakfast foods. She says that for health, the temperature of the food is not the issue (except on cold days, when warm food is better). She also says that the change will not make breakfasts more affordable, but rather will make them more expensive, since students will have to go off campus (where the prices are higher) to buy the food they want.

Sample Responses

Play Track 96 on the CD to hear a high-level response for Question 3.

Rater Comments

This response covers all the key points of the article and conversation with great clarity and supporting details. The speaker's pronunciation is very clear, and he uses good rhythm and intonation. He uses a good variety of vocabulary and idiomatic expressions that help him express his meaning clearly.

Play Track 97 on the CD to hear a mid-level response for Question 3.

Rater Comments

This speaker does a fairly good job of explaining the woman's disagreement with the proposal in the article, but her speech is very choppy (not fluent). She has to pause often to think of the correct word or phrase to say. Sometimes her limited vocabulary prevents her from clearly expressing what she means (for example, the meaning of *the offer is their last offer for choosing* is unclear). Her pronunciation is generally easy to understand but occasionally requires listener effort.

Question 4

Track 88 Listening Script

Narrator

Read the passage from a sociology textbook. You have 50 seconds to read the passage. Begin reading now.

> **Reading Time: 50 Seconds**

Cognitive Dissonance

Individuals sometimes experience a contradiction between their actions and their beliefs—between what they are doing and what they believe they should be doing. These contradictions can cause a kind of mental discomfort known as *cognitive dissonance*. People experiencing cognitive dissonance often do not want to change the way they are acting, so they resolve the contradictory situation in another way: they change their interpretation of the situation in a way that minimizes the contradiction between what they are doing and what they believe they should be doing.

Narrator

Now listen to part of a lecture about this topic in a sociology class.

Professor

This is a true story—from my own life. In my first year in high school, I was addicted to video games. I played them all the time, and I wasn't studying enough—I was failing chemistry; that was my hardest class. So this was a conflict for me because I wanted a good job when I grew up, and I believed—I knew—that if you want a good career, you gotta do well in school. But . . . I just couldn't give up video games.

I was completely torn. And my solution was to . . . to change my perspective. See, the only class I was doing really badly in was chemistry. In the others I was, I was okay. So I asked myself if I wanted to be a chemist when I grew up, and the fact is I didn't. I was pretty sure I wanted to be a sociologist. So . . . I told myself my chemistry class didn't matter because sociologists don't really need to know chemistry. In other words, I changed my understanding of what it meant to do well in school. I reinterpreted my situation: I used to think that doing well in school meant doing well in all my classes, but now I decided that succeeding in school meant only doing well in the classes that related directly to my future career.

I eliminated the conflict, at least in my mind.

Narrator

Using the example discussed by the professor, explain what cognitive dissonance is and how people often deal with it.

> **Preparation Time: 30 Seconds**
> **Response Time: 60 Seconds**

Important Points

Cognitive dissonance occurs when people's beliefs and actions are in conflict with each other. People deal with cognitive dissonance by changing their interpretation of the situation. For example, the professor could not stop playing video games even though he believed it was causing him to fail chemistry. He then told himself that since he wanted to be a sociologist, he did not need to do well in chemistry.

Sample Responses

Play Track 98 on the CD to hear a high-level response for Question 4.

Rater Comments

This speaker efficiently and accurately explains the concept of cognitive dissonance and how people deal with it, as in the professor's example. Her speech is fluid, and she uses intonation and stress effectively to convey emphasis and meaning—for example, by stressing the words *actions* and *interpretation* as a contrast to demonstrate how people deal with cognitive dissonance (by changing their interpretation of a situation rather than their actions). She uses advanced-level vocabulary with accuracy and ease.

Play Track 99 on the CD to hear a mid-level response for Question 4.

Rater Comments

In this response, the speaker conveys the relevant information in the task, but not always with precision. For instance, when describing the professor's example, instead of saying the professor changed his *interpretation* of the situation, she says he began to *make up his own opinion*. Her pronunciation is clear, but her speech is marked by many pauses and hesitations.

Question 5

Track 89 Listening Script

Narrator

Listen to a conversation between two students.

Man

Hey, Marnie. What's wrong?

Woman

Oh . . . I'm just struggling about what to do . . . I won an award from the Creative Writing Institute for a story I wrote, and . . .

Man

[questioning] That doesn't sound like anything's wrong!

Woman

Well, it's a huge honor to win, and there's an award ceremony they've invited me to attend—which I'm so excited about—but—and here's what's frustrating—I've got a biology exam that's scheduled for the same time.

Man

Uh-oh. Well, have you talked to your professor about this?

Woman

Yeah . . . she said I could write a five-page paper instead, and I have lots of ideas and know I could do a good job, but . . .

Man

But what?

Woman

Well, writing a paper would take up so much time . . . a lot more time than studying for and taking the exam. I have lots of other schoolwork to deal with.

Man

[negative tone] Oh. *[pause]* Or you could have someone else receive the award for you . . . I mean go in your place and accept it on your behalf?

Woman

Maybe. I'd still get the award and the money that way . . .

Man

Ooh—you won money too?

Woman

Yeah, pretty cool, huh? But anyways, my parents were really looking forward to coming and seeing me onstage shaking hands with the Institute's president and all. I'd hate to disappoint them.

Man

True. I'm sure they're really proud.

Woman

Like I said, I'm still struggling about what to do.

Narrator

The speakers discuss two possible solutions to the woman's problem. Briefly summarize the problem. Then state which of the solutions you recommend and explain why.

Preparation Time: 20 Seconds
Response Time: 60 Seconds

Important Points

The woman won an award, but the ceremony to accept the award is at the same time as her biology exam.

For this task, notice that the question does *not* tell you to discuss both of the solutions. After summarizing the problem, you need to say only which *one* of the solutions from the conversation you prefer and why. If you agree with the first solution, you would say that you think she should write a paper instead of taking the exam. You could support your choice by saying, for example, that even though this would take a lot of time, it would allow her to attend the ceremony, which is important because her parents would like to watch her get the award.

If you choose the second solution, you would say that you think she should have someone else go to the ceremony and accept the award in her place. You could support your choice by saying, for example, that writing the paper would take too much time from studying for her other classes, which are important for her success as a student, and that her parents would surely understand and support that decision.

Sample Responses

Play Track 100 on the CD to hear a high-level response for Question 5.
Rater Comments

This speaker is very fluent and conveys a great deal of information in the time allotted. Although she needed to state and support only the solution she is recommending, she chose to describe both solutions in her answer before recommending one. Because she is so fluent, describing both did not cause her to run out of time before she finished her response. She fully supported her recommendation. Her speech is easy to understand and well paced. She also demonstrates good control of both basic and more advanced grammar and vocabulary.

Play Track 101 on the CD to hear a mid-level response for Question 5.

Rater Comments

The speaker runs out of time before she can fully support the solution she is recommending, which is to write the five-page paper. She also does not explain the problem very clearly at the beginning, never saying that the exam and award ceremony are at the same time. Her pronunciation is quite clear, and her pacing is good at the beginning but then becomes slower and choppy by the end of her response.

Question 6

Track 90 Listening Script

Narrator

Now listen to part of a lecture in a psychology class. The professor is discussing advertising strategies.

Professor

In advertising, various strategies are used to persuade people to buy products. In order to sell more products, advertisers will often try to make us believe that a product will meet our needs or desires perfectly . . . even if it's not true. The strategies they use can be subtle, uh, "friendly" forms of persuasion that are sometimes hard to recognize.

In a lot of ads, repetition is a key strategy. Research shows that repeated exposure to a message, even something meaningless or untrue, is enough to make people accept it or see it in a positive light. You've all seen the car commercials on TV . . . like . . . uh, the one that refers to its "roomy" cars . . . over and over again. You know which one I mean . . . this guy is driving around and he keeps stopping to pick up different people—he picks up 3 or 4 people. And each time, the narrator says, "Plenty of room for friends, plenty of room for family, plenty of room for everybody." The same message is repeated several times in the course of the commercial. Now, the car, uh, the car actually looks kind of small . . . it's not a very big car at all, but you get the sense that it's pretty spacious. You'd think that the viewer would reach the logical conclusion that the slogan, uh, misrepresents the product. Instead, what usually happens is that when the statement "plenty of room" is repeated often enough, people are actually convinced it's true.

Um, another strategy they use is to get a celebrity to advertise a product. It turns out that we're more likely to accept an advertising claim made by somebody famous—a person we admire and find appealing. We tend to think they're trustworthy. So . . . um, you might have a car commercial that features a well-known race car driver. Now, it may not be a very fast car—uh, it could even be an inexpensive vehicle with a low performance rating. But if a popular race car driver is shown driving it, and saying, "I like my cars fast!" then people will believe the car is impressive for its speed.

Narrator

Using the examples from the talk, explain how persuasive strategies are used in advertising.

Preparation Time: 20 Seconds
Response Time: 60 Seconds

Important Points

Advertisers persuade people to buy their products by using persuasive strategies. One strategy is repetition of information (which may not be true information), such as when an advertisement for a small car keeps repeating that it has plenty of room. Another strategy is to use celebrities, because people trust them. For example, a famous race car driver might be used in an advertisement for a car (to give the impression the car is fast, even if it is not).

Sample Responses

Play Track 102 on the CD to hear a high-level response for Question 6.

Rater Comments

The speaker conveys all of the main and supporting points from the lecture. His speech is clear and fluid, and although he does not pronounce *subtle* correctly, this is a minor error that does not interfere with overall understanding of his speech. His pacing slows down at times as he attempts to recall information, but it is still easy to follow what he is saying. He also uses a variety of advanced-level vocabulary and grammatical constructions with good control.

Play Track 103 on the CD to hear a mid-level response for Question 6.

Rater Comments

This speaker discusses both advertising strategies described in the lecture, but in a vague way that is sometimes difficult to understand. For instance, he never mentions that the first example refers to a car advertisement, so it is unclear what he means when he says the message that *lots of your friends have space in it* is repeated. His pronunciation is easy to understand, but he pauses frequently throughout his response and demonstrates only a limited vocabulary range and control of grammar.

Writing

Listening Script, Topic Notes, and Sample Responses with Rater Comments

Use the Integrated Writing and Independent Writing scoring rubrics on pages 200–201 and 209–210 to see how responses are scored.

Writing Based on Reading and Listening

Track 91 Listening Script

Narrator

Now listen to part of a lecture on the topic you just read about.

Professor

Everything you just read about *Portrait of an Elderly Woman in a White Bonnet* is true, and yet, after a thorough reexamination of the painting, a panel of experts has recently concluded that it's indeed a work by Rembrandt. And here's why.

First, the fur collar. X-rays and analysis of the pigments in the paint have shown that the fur collar wasn't part of the original painting. The fur collar was painted over the top of the original painting about a hundred years after the painting was made. Why? Someone probably wanted to increase the value of the painting by making it look like a formal portrait of an aristocratic lady.

Second, the supposed error with light and shadow. Once the paint of the added fur collar was removed, the original painting could be seen. In the original painting the woman is wearing a simple collar of light-colored cloth. The light-colored cloth of this collar reflects light that illuminates part of the woman's face. That's why the face is not in partial shadow. So in the original painting, light and shadow are very realistic and just what we would expect from Rembrandt.

Finally, the wood panel. It turns out that when the fur collar was added, the wood panel was also enlarged with extra wood pieces glued to the sides and the top to make the painting more grand—and more valuable. So the original painting is actually painted on a single piece of wood—as would be expected from a Rembrandt painting. And in fact, researchers have found that the piece of wood in the original form of *Portrait of an Elderly Woman in a White Bonnet* is from the very same tree as the wood panel used for another painting by Rembrandt, his *Self-Portrait with a Hat*.

Narrator

Summarize the points made in the lecture, being sure to explain how they answer the specific problems presented in the reading passage.

Topic Notes

You should understand the reasons presented in the lecture that address the concerns in the reading passage. While the reading passage explains why people do not think the painting *Portrait of an Elderly Woman* was created by Rembrandt, the lecture presents new evidence showing that the painting was indeed created by Rembrandt.

A high-scoring essay will include the following points made by the lecturer and will explain how they address the points made in the reading passage:

Point Made in the Reading Passage	Contrasting Point from the Lecture
The fur collar in the painting does not match clothing typical of a servant woman, a detail that Rembrandt would not have overlooked.	The fur collar was added later in an attempt to increase the painting's value.
The light and shadow appear incorrectly in the painting, but Rembrandt was a master of painting light and shadow.	The light and shadow appeared incorrectly because of the fur collar that was added later. Once the fur collar was removed, revealing the original white collar, the light and shadow appeared correctly.
The portrait was painted on multiple wood panels, which was not typical of Rembrandt's works.	The original was painted on a single wood panel. Additional wood panels were added to the painting later in an attempt to increase its value.

Responses with scores of 4 and 5 generally clearly discuss all three main points in the table.

Sample Responses with Rater Comments

Score 5 Essay

Both texts deal with the question wheather or not the painting "Portrait of an Elderly Woman in a White Bonnet" was painted by the most famous Dutch painter Rembrandt. The text clearly states, that many facts prove that it wasn't painted by Rembrandt himself, but just attributed to him because of its style. In the lecture however the professor gives proof why it is in fact a work of the famous Dutch painter.

The first contradicting fact are the clothes of the woman in the portrait. She is wearing a white linen cap which gives her the appearance of a simple servant, whereas the luxurious fur collar she also wears doesn't fit. In the lecture is said, that after a thorough research people found out that the fur collar was added to the painting about 100 years later in order to increase the value of the workpiece, because now it illustrated an aristocratic lady instead of a servant.

Another problem with the painting was the display of light and shadow. Rembandt was known as a master of painting light and shadow, yet contradictionally the elements in the work don't fit together. But this problem could also be explained by now. By removing the additional fur collar one could see that the lady is wearing a simple light colored cloth, which reflects light into her face.

The third aspect which let people wonder about the origins of the painting was the fact, that the panel was made of several pieces of wood glued together instead of just one panel which was usual for works of Rembrandt. But the additional panels were also added later to enlarge the paiting. by doing this the painting seemed to be more valuable.

Another interesting fact is, that the main panel is made from the same tree like another painting of Rembrandt, 'Selfportrait with a hat'.

In the end it is clear that this painting is indeed a work of the Dutch painter and it should be reintegrated in the catalog of Rembrandt's paintings.

Rater Comments

This essay earns a score of 5 because it successfully explains the opposing relationship between the reading and the lecture and goes on to identify all the important points and details. The response is appropriately organized, with the topic stated in the first and final paragraphs and each main point discussed in separate body paragraphs. Each main point is discussed clearly and with a good amount of detail. The writer, for example, correctly represents in the second paragraph the idea that the fur collar was added to the painting at a later date to make it appear more valuable. In the third paragraph, the light-and-shadow inconsistency is not described in concrete terms, but the writer does indicate it in general terms and explains its cause. Connectors and connecting phrases ("Another problem," "By removing the additional fur collar," "In the end") help make the writing cohesive and easy to read. The language is generally accurate, and minor errors ("In the lecture is said," "after a thorough research," "contradictionally") do not interfere with meaning.

Score 4 Essay

The author of the text points out several facts that do not fit in the image that Rembrandt painted the painting himself.

The woman portraited wears a linen cap and is therefore recognizable as a servant. Although, she also wears a valuable collar which a servent could never had afforded at the time the painting was done. Rembrandt, who cared a lot about the clothing of the people he painted, would not have made such a mistake.

The professor gives an explanation for this inconsistency using facts which were propably not known to the author. The collar was added about 100 years after the painting was originally done, perhaps to make it more valuable portraiing a aristocratic person instead of a simple servant.

A second error in the painting which is mentioned in the text can also be explained by the later added collar. In the original painting the white linnen reflected the light, enlightening the face of the model from below. When adding the collar the artist did not fit this enlightment to the new clothing.

The text also mentions that the painting is done on glued together wood panels, which is untypical for Rembrandt. The professor explains that the painting was enlarged by gluing woods to the sides, long after Rembrandt painted it.

In that way the addition of the collar and wood let the original Rem

Rater Comments

This essay effectively addresses the topic by summarizing most of the important information in the reading and lecture. The first point, discussed in paragraph 2—concerning the servant woman's clothing—is the best-developed idea. The fourth paragraph correctly identifies the addition of the fur collar as a source of another problem, but it does not clearly explain what the problem is and how it arose. Although the writer correctly indicates that the original white collar in the painting reflects light onto the woman's face, it is not clear what the "second error in the painting which is mentioned in the text" is. A clearer response would have explained that the apparent errors of light and shadow in the painting could be explained by the fur collar that was added to the painting later. The third point, in the fifth paragraph—concerning the wood panel—is discussed in a fair amount of detail, although the writer leaves out the reason for adding the side panels. Language errors in the response are minor, but they sometimes interfere with meaning. In the second paragraph, for example, "Although" is not a well-chosen connector, and the phrase "Rembrandt, who cared a lot about the clothing" is a bit imprecise. In the fourth paragraph, the clause "the artist did not fit this enlightment to the new clothing" also creates a minor lapse in clarity. Overall, the response earns a score of 4 due to minor omissions and minor lapses of clarity.

Score 3 Essay

There are doubts whether Rembramdt painted Portrait of an Elderly Woman in a White Bonnet. The reading says that the painting wasn't paint by Rembrandt because of the leck of consistency observed. On the other hand the lecture says that Rembrandt is the real painter. The opinion expressed in the lecture is based on a third examination of the painting when the experts decided that Rembrandt is the real painter because of the examination of the fur colar, the light and shadow that were realistic and finally the elements of the wood panel.

Examining the fur colar from the painting, the experts noticed that the actual colar was painted over the top of the original painting over 100 years later. The reason of doing this was to increase the value of the painting.

Further on the light and color were very realistic, says the lecture. This opinion is formulated in opossition to the one from the reading that says that in this painting this elements do not fit together.

Finally the last reason why the lecture affirms that the painting belongs to Rebmrandt is based on the examination of the wood panel. Even though the wood panel was enlarged it was used the same tree that Rembrandt used in Self Portrait with a Hat.

In conclusion it seems that the argument given by the lecture overpower the reading part.

Rater Comments

Although this response clearly describes the relationship between the reading and the lecture in the first paragraph, it earns a score of 3 because it lacks some important details related to the three main points that follow. In the second paragraph, the writer does explain that the fur collar was added to the painting 100 years after it was created to increase its value, but the writer does not explain the initial problem mentioned in the reading (that the fur collar was not consistent with a servant woman's apparel). This makes it difficult for a reader who is not familiar with the passage and the lecture to see how the information about the collar is relevant to the topic. The third paragraph, in contrast, does indicate that the information from the reading and the information from the lecture regarding light and shadow differ, but this section lacks most of the important details. The third point, in paragraph 4, is not expressed precisely. The writer indicates that the fact that the wood came from the same tree as the wood for another Rembrandt painting is proof of its authenticity, yet it is not clear whether the writer is referring to the original panel or to the added panels. The writer also does not explain why the original panel was enlarged. Overall, the essay responds to the task and touches on all three main ideas, but these ideas are either vaguely or imprecisely conveyed. The language is generally clear, with only a few minor errors ("the painting wasn't paint by Rembrandt," "this elements do not fit together") that do not interfere with meaning.

Score 2 Essay

The reading explains why the painting can't be attribuited to Rembrant but in the listenig resolvs many mistakes. Is very important to know that the portrait was paint over the original by another painter abotut a hundred years later its realzation. That explains why some caracteristics of Rembrant paintigs don't appear on the portrait.

In the painting there is an error in how the light is reflected on the face of the woman, but the listenig say that a part of waer was originally white and not black so the light effect aws correct.

The second painter made many errors but no errors had painted by Rembrant.

Another mistake is the material used for paint. Rembrant used only one pieace of wood but the portrait is composed by many pieces and glow, that because the peainting was enlarged

Rater Comments

This response earns a score of 2 because it offers limited details related to the main points and contains multiple language errors that either are distracting or interfere with meaning ("a hundred years later its realzation," "a part of waer was originally white," "composed by many pieces and glow"). Structurally, the essay is difficult to follow because the issues raised in the reading are not effectively connected to the related information from the lecture. The first point, that the painting was altered by another painter, lacks important information about the fur collar and the discrepancy between the collar and the servant woman's customary clothing. In the second paragraph, the writer explains why light did not reflect correctly in the painting, but since the explanation is not connected to the addition of the fur collar, it remains somewhat unclear. The final point is not expressed clearly and lacks many important details.

Score 1 Essay

There is a problem with one of the picture of Rembrant becouse it isn't probably of Rembrant: .

Study say that becouse there are some problems with the painting.

The first is that there is someting inconsistent about the way the woman in the portrait is dressed. Rembrant who was known for his attention to the details couldn't wear the lady with a white linear cap and at the same time is wearing a luxurious fur collar.

The second thing is that Rembrant was very able to paint light and shadow, but in this painting the face appears to be illuminated by lights and the the the dark fur collar, which would absorb light, so the faca should appear partially in shadow.

The 3rd problem is about the panel of the painting. The panel of the paintig was made of several pieces of wood glued together but Rembrant didn't use a pannel glued together but only wood pannels.

Rater Comments

This essay earns a score of 1 because it presents information from the reading passage only. The writer copies many phrases from the reading passage, and when the writer tries to paraphrase the passage content, errors often interfere with meaning. A response that leaves out all or most of the information from the lecture cannot receive a score higher than 1.

Writing Based on Knowledge and Experience

Question

Do you agree or disagree with the following statement?

It is more important to keep your old friends than it is to make new friends.

Use specific reasons and examples to support your answer.

Topic Notes

This topic asks you to write about whether keeping old friends is more important than making new friends. Successful responses can agree with the statement, disagree with the statement, or discuss why old and new friends are equally important. No matter which position you take, it is important to support your opinion with details and examples.

If you agree with the statement, you should present and develop reasons that old friends are better than new friends. Some reasons for preferring old friends may include their ability to understand you, their willingness to help you in difficult situations, and interests and experiences they share with you. As part of supporting this approach, you could also mention that new friends do not have these attributes.

If you disagree with the statement, you should present and develop reasons that new friends are better than old friends. Some reasons for preferring new friends may include the opportunity to learn about different opinions and cultures, the chance to have new experiences, and the benefit of being around friends who understand changes in your life.

If you believe that old and new friends are equally important, you should present a balanced argument that explains the benefits of both types of friends. This can include points mentioned above, but many reasons not mentioned here can also be used in an effective essay.

Sample Responses with Rater Comments

Score 5 Essay—Sample 1

In a lifetime, we are bound to meet many people, we get on well with some of them and they become our friends. As we grow up we meet new people and make new friends but it does not imply that they will replace our old ones. That is why I disagree with people who think that keeping old friends is more important than making new friends.

I think that there is no matter of more importance. Since old friends and new friends do not bring us the same things, we can not compare them. Indeed old friends are the ones we can count on; we trust them, they know us well, we have complicity and real friendship is just wondrful. When I feel sad or when I need to talk to someone about a serious problem, I go to see my old friends because they are reliable and I know that they will understand me more than anyone else. My old friends are very important to me and I agree with the fact that it is important to keep them and make efforts to keep contact.

However, I must admit that we are bound to lose some of our old friends sometimes. For example, I had a very good friend a few years ago but we do not see each other anymore since I moved in an other town. I guess that we also grew up and took a different way and there is no use to keep old friends when you realize that you have nothing left in common.

Therefore, it is also very important to make new friends. That is a way to learn, to change and they bring us different things. Making new friends makes us more open-minded, and in this way we can discover new personalities. For my part I enjoy making new friends, at school, at work, on holidays. I am conscious not to have close relationships with them at first but I need to be with other people and have fun. Sometimes they just remain acquaintances but they can also become good friends who could become old friends one day. For instance, I met a german girl on holiday two years ago and we got on very well, so we kept in touch and I went to visit her in Germany twice. She belongs to this kind of people who you know that they will be important in your life, and who you know you can have a long and strong friendship with.

As a conclusion I would say that everybody need to have a a at least few real and strong friendship.

Rater Comments

This level 5 essay effectively responds to the question by arguing the importance of having both old and new friends. The essay is organized logically, beginning with an introductory paragraph that states a clear thesis and continuing with three body paragraphs that develop distinct reasons that support the thesis. Each of the writer's points is well developed with appropriate details and examples. The first point, that old friends are reliable and understanding, is supported by the idea that old friends can help with serious problems. This is followed in the third paragraph by the idea that it is sometimes possible to lose old friendships. Here, the writer gives the example of losing a friend because of a move and no longer having anything in common. This third paragraph provides a nice connection between the ideas of wanting to keep old friends in the second paragraph and needing to make new friends in the fourth paragraph. This cohesion is also accomplished by using effective transitions ("However, I must admit," "Therefore, it is also very important to make new friends."). The final point, that it is important to make new friends, is also well supported by details about learning new things. The essay is rounded out by a personal example that shows that new friends can become old friends. Overall, this essay has nice progression and displays consistently strong language. The few language errors ("moved in an other town," "She belongs to this kind of people who you know") that do exist do not interfere with meaning and are not prevalent enough to lower the essay's score.

Score 5 Essay—Sample 2

In the following essay I would like to express my opinion in regard to the thesis "It is more important to keep your old friends than it is to make new friends".

On the one hand, you could always say that making new friends is a lot more entertaining than keeping in touch with the old ones. There are new topics to talk about, new activities to do together, new personality traits to discover... Additionally, you also get to meet the persons who are close to your new friends. And maybe you will even receive a whole group of new friends by making one new friend.

However, you could also say that it makes much more sense to keep in touch with your old friends since they are your true friends. Firstly, you already know how they react to certain situations and therefore you know how to treat them to get along well. Secondly, I am of the conviction that it is certain that in a bit more peculiar and maybe a bit unpleasant situations it is a lot more likely that your old friends will help you out than that someone you have met barely a week ago would do the same.

I have to admit that I personally came to the conclusion that I need my old friends as well as my new friends. For me they are both equally important. I adore keeping in touch with my old friends and knowing how they will react in most situations. Of course, over the years some sort of bond and a special kind of trust has developed with my long-time friends.

However, I immensely enjoy making new friends as well. I enjoy trying out new activities and making new friends there. Furthermore, I like making friends from all kinds of different cultures and countries. And I am certain that this kind of attitude makes life much more interesting. Plus, I believe that new friends will also broaden your horizon because their beliefs may differ from your own.

Personally, I am convinced that nobody has to decide between old friends and new friends since the possibily of keeping the old friends and making new ones always exists. Therefore as a final statement I would like to say "Cherish you old friends and enjoy making new ones as well".

Rater Comments

This essay effectively addresses the topic with clear language and appropriate details, earning it a score of 5. The writer gradually develops the idea that it is not necessary to choose between having old or new friends. Initially, the writer examines both sides of the issue: the benefits of making new friends in paragraph 2 and of keeping old friends in paragraph 3. These are treated with equal value and logically lead to the author's opinion in paragraph 4 that both old and new friends are equally important. This is well supported by details such as the importance of trust in old friendships and the excitement of new experiences in new friendships. This leads to an effective concluding paragraph that states the thesis and makes the writer's overall intent clear. The language throughout the essay is strong, with only minor weaknesses or possibly just slipups in typing ("than that someone you have met barely a week ago would do the same") that do not detract from the quality of the writing. The use of transitions throughout the response generally helps the essay to progress and adds to the effectiveness of the writing.

Score 4 Essay—Sample 1

My personal experience showed me that both keeping old friends and making new ones is important: it depends on the different needs of life.

When I left my country to move in France for studing I tried to keep in contact with all my Italian friends in order to feel less far from home and to keep in mind where I am from, expecially in some moments of lonelyness. After several mounths nearly all the persons I considered as "friends" kept less and less in contact with me, making me understand that we were experiencing different stages of our life and therefore it was difficult to keep the same relationship we had before because everyone was growing in a different way.

In the meanwhile I found new friends at university and I started to discover new kinds of relationships, sometimes very different from the ones I was habitued to. For exemple at the beginning I found very strange the fact that French young people use to see each others in the "cafe`" and spend their time and their money there smooking, chatting and drinking. With my Italian friends we use to see each other outside, near the seaside for a volleyball match indeed or at someones`s home in the evening to make a pizza party togheter, without spending too much money.

These different habits make me think about how different could be one culture compare to another and how difficult would have been for me to keep the same relationship with both types of friends.

On one side I prefered the way I behaved with my old friends and I missed them, but on the other side, I realized the necessity of seeking for new friends, so I tried to agree to their habits and I experienced something else.

Today I can say that this kind of experience has been very usefull for me. Last summer, coming back home for holidays I organized a party to my house nearbye the mountains and I invited both French new friends and my Italians old ones. The result was that with the new ones I experienced something they have never done before, and this strenthned our friendship, wherease with the old ones I felt home like everytime, as I had never left, as our friendship had never been changed.

To conclude, I think both old and new friends are very importants, because trough them we can learn about our self and our changes in anytime; sometimes they are the mirror of what we were and what we become.

Rater Comments

The writer of this level 4 essay addresses the topic well and fully develops his or her point of view through sharing personal experiences. The essay begins with a clear statement of the thesis, that "keeping old friends and making new ones is important," depending on a person's needs. The writer then uses the experience of moving to another country to appropriately explain how old friends helped him or her to feel less lonely and to retain a sense of his or her native culture, and how new friends helped him or her adjust to a new culture. This example effectively leads to the conclusion that both old and new friends are helpful through life's changes. While the points in this response are well developed and organized, the essay cannot earn a score of 5 because of multiple language errors that occur throughout. Errors in both grammar ("keeped less and less in contact," "how different could be one culture") and word choice ("I was habitued") often do not obscure meaning but are frequent enough to lower the essay's score to 4.

Score 4 Essay—Sample 2

In today's society, life is becoming more impersonal and invidualist. That's why having friends, it's for me very important. But, I have a mix view when it comes to friends because it's not so easy. I don't think that one of the statement is more important than another one. I need both.

First, keeping old friends is for me the most important. If you have a friend for a long time, that's mean that he knows you very well and he can help you when you need it. For instance, if you have a problem or a decision to make, an old friend will be able to help you and give you good advices. On the contrary a new friend may not do it very well.

Second, with old friends you can share everything. You will not feel any shame because you know that he has already saw you in ridiculous situations for example.

Lastly, when you have a huge problem, it is common to say that best friends are always with you. They never let you alone and they don't care in what people think.

Although I really believe that it is very important to keep your old friends, I also think that it's necessary to make new friends. In your daily life, you're always evolving and changing; that's why sometimes you can't share everything with old friends because they just can't understand exactly your new way of thinking. With a new friend, it could be easiest to evolve ant see the things differently.

It's also important to have a large relationship with different people. Like that you will be open-minded. In this way, new friends can make you discover new things such as a new place to visit or a new sport activity. For example, I lived in Barcelone for two years and I made new friends, actually, spanih friends. It was very interesting for me to meet new people. I was alone, without my old friends, and my new friends made me feel good. I could enjoy visiting the country and going out. I also changed my mind being with them. They helped me to think in another way, because they made me share a new culture, their culture.

For all these reasons, I think that both are important. You need to keep your old friends, they will be there for everything but you also need new friends to evolve.

Rater Comments

While this essay responds to the question appropriately, it earns a score of 4 because of minor language errors and underdevelopment of the main points presented. Although the language used is generally clear and easy to understand, minor errors ("that's mean that," "he has already saw you") occur more frequently than they would in a level 5 essay. The introduction to the essay is weak. The thesis statement ("I don't think that one of the statement is more important than another one. I need both.") does not sufficiently introduce the topic, and a reader not already familiar with the topic may struggle to identify the purpose of the essay. Despite this, the essay is generally well organized. The writer makes three points to support the need for old friends and two points to support the need for new friends. Each point is clearly stated in a distinct paragraph. Some of these points (that old friends can help in times of need in the second paragraph and that new friends can help people to be open-minded in the sixth paragraph) are very well developed with details and personal examples. Other points (that you can share everything with old friends in the third paragraph and that old friends never leave you alone in the fourth paragraph) are merely stated without any supporting details. These issues lower an otherwise clear response to a score of 4.

Score 3 Essay—Sample 1

> One of the most important thing in life is to spend time with the person you consider to be your best friend, in my opinion.
>
> Firstable, nobody cannot know you better than an old friend does.
>
> Your old friend can really guess you before you begin to speak. You do not have to explain all of your feelings he knows you too much for that. This feeling of understanding is incredibly good. It is like you are not alone anymore.
>
> Secondly, keeping your old friends is the best way to have a link between your past and your life. It is a excellent pattern to know if you have changed well or not. It helps to keep your personnality and your personnal interests throught your life.
>
> In addition, Old friends continue to be friends because they helps each other with the life difficulties.
>
> The kind of helps creates a really deep love and friendship and it is why we say friends forever. It is too deep to give up. Consequently, friends become part of the family after many years. For example, I have had the same best friend since 1990. I know her and she knows me perfectly. I am closer to her than my own sister. We have share everything and we could be separate more than one month. I like her advices and our complementarity.
>
> To clarify my opinion, I would say that for me it is also good to make new friends and to change your routine. Everybody needs that to progress and to fell good. But when I am thinking about the most importamt thing my choice is clear I really need more my old friend that the new I have met.
>
> To conclude, Keep your old friends cloth to you and enj

Rater Comments

While this essay generally addresses the topic clearly, it earns a score of 3 because it features flaws in the development of some of its ideas and in overall structure. The writer lists three points to support the idea that old friends are important. The first two points, that old friends understand each other's feelings and that they provide a link to a person's past, are clearly expressed but only somewhat developed with vague explanations. The third point, that old friends can help each other through difficult times, is entirely unsupported. In addition, some elements in the response interrupt the progression of the essay. It is not clear how the sixth paragraph, which discusses the writer's best friend, supports any of the three points mentioned earlier in the essay. The first sentence in the seventh paragraph ("To clarify my opinion, I would say that for me it is also good to make new friends and to change your routine.") is also out of place and suggests that a new topic will be discussed, although the focus of the essay remains on the importance of old friends. These flaws, along with minor language errors ("they helps each other with the life difficulties," "I really need more my old friends that the new I have met."), earn this essay a score of 3.

Score 3 Essay—Sample 2

Both old friends and new friends are important for a person's social life. Old friends give you security but new friends give you the bigger advantage: to make new experiences.

For my own, I keep my new friends as more important as my old friends. That has many reasons. A person changes in the course of time in his behaviour and in his way of thinking. So, it is normal if you also change the persons which are arround of you and can talk to about your problems. It is true that an old friend know you much better and so he can maybe handle better with you when you need help but it is also true that an old friend know you too good so his advices are maybe not useful anymore for you. An old friend has often the same point of view as you, a normal consequence of a long friendship. So a new friend might it make possible to have access to new points of view and can help you more. He does not have yet a fixed opinion about you not knowing so much about your family backround, for example. An old friend which knows you since your childhood and knows your whole family is not yet in a neutral position. That makes it difficult to give you neutral advices, especially if the problems you have concerns your familiy. But not only when you have problems, a friend is useful but also in other situation in which I prefer again new friends. I know new people and with them new life styles. So I can learn a lot for my own life. As a conclusion, new friends show you new prospectives of life and help you to konw the world better.

Rater Comments

This essay earns a score of 3 primarily because of lack of organization and development of its main ideas. The writer takes the position that new friends are more important than old friends. The reasons supporting this idea, however, are not as easy to distinguish as they might have been if developed in separate paragraphs. Instead, multiple ideas are briefly mentioned in the second paragraph (that new friends accommodate changes in life, that they can offer neutral advice, and that they help build new ideas), making it a little difficult for a reader to follow the writer's logic. The writer does, however, offer some good support for the idea that new friends can offer neutral advice because they are not familiar with the friend's past and family. The response might also have been scored higher had it further developed the topic introduced at the end about new friends showing new perspectives and helping you know the world better. If these ideas had been developed with a few details or examples, this response would have been more highly rated. Most of the language used is also clear, although many minor language errors ("For my own," "neutral advices") that generally do not affect meaning do exist.

Score 2 Essay—Sample 1

This is a very interesting argument, because for me the friends are all. The old friends or the new friends are much important, but sincerally, I think that the old friends are more important than new friends. The old friend known you very well, they helped you in many occasions and they shared with you many experience.

This is true only if a friend is a real friend, like a brother. In my opinion to make new friends is important too; you can to know new persons, to meet new persons.

The importance of to keep my old friends is that they are and they will be a fixed point in my life and without them I feel lost.

For to keep my old friends I work hard...infact if one of them calls me for a help, I go to him immediatily...and I hope that He goes too.

Finally, my personal opinion on this argument is clare: "The new friends are a good thing, but you should to keep the old friends with all your heart". I don't say if in English this is a correct affermation, but in Italian is a very good thing.

I share all with my old friends, my personal items too, but a new friend is not knowed and only with the years a new friend enters in the category of the lod friends, and this is a VIP category for me.

Rater Comments

Although this response is clearly geared toward the topic, underdevelopment of the writer's main ideas and a limited command of the language earn this essay a score of 2. The writer seems to believe that it is good to have both old friends and new friends. This opinion, however, is not entirely obvious because the essay lacks a clear thesis, and the ideas presented throughout the essay seem to waver between both sides of the argument. The ideas that are included in the response are typically stated in a single sentence, without supporting details or examples. Many distracting language errors ("The old friends or the new friends are much important, but sincerally," "you can to know new persons," "I go to him immediatily...and I hope that He goes too") that occasionally interfere with meaning can also be seen throughout the response.

Score 2 Essay—Sample 2

I think that both two statement have the same importance.

About keep your old friends I can say that is important because they know your personality, your problem, or what you like. Besides this your behavior can say them if you are happy or hungry and so if you need for help. For instace if yuo are hunappy because you have recived a low graduation at school, easily they know what could say or do for make you happy. There is more compriension!

However there is several things that make important to make new friends. The major reason is that you may learn much from several personality increasing on your good behavior. Your ralationships will go to be beter than earlier. For eample if you meet a person who live much far away you can learn about several cultures or foreing language.

In conclusion is important as to keep old friends as to make new friends.

Rater Comments

This level 2 essay addresses the topic and develops two main ideas that support the opinion that both old and new friends are important. These two ideas are supported with a limited amount of detail. In the second paragraph, the point that old friends are important is supported by the example that old friends know how to make a person happy when something bad happens, such as receiving a low grade in school. In the third paragraph, the point that new friends are important is supported by the idea that new friends can offer new experiences, such as learning from different personalities or being exposed to different cultures. Overall, however, it is very difficult to extract these ideas from the language that this writer uses. The weak use of language throughout the essay and the limited development of ideas are both reasons this essay earns no higher than a score of 2.

Score 1 Essay—Sample 1

> For me is more important keep my old friends because they rispect me and i rispect there and also i know they and for this i make what we want.
>
> For me whit new friends we don't make what we can do because they konw a little and for this there are possible conflict in a new group or with a new freind.
> In conclusion i think that is important have old friends becaue i konk they and they konw me and for this the friendly going to hamony.

Rater Comments

This essay earns a score of 1 because it lacks any development of its main points and contains many language errors that obscure meaning. The writer seems to present only one idea to support the opinion that old friends are important. Because of language errors that interfere with the writer's purpose, the limited idea that is offered is almost incomprehensible.

Score 1 Essay—Sample 2

> This is a very important problematic.
>
> The old friends is the old friends, he is next the most time ant togheter we have want of all color.
>
> Old friends is important keep him by you. Came from you because to take you a handle, for cosolation, and cherful for you.
>
> I agree or diasgrre with you, but is they are the very friends at the fine to thanck them.
>
> The knew or to make the new friends is a incognit, fall of in the new problem or find special people.
>
> I bilive to find friends with behaves of respect for me, and the my rispect will be for them.
>
> The rispect is the first important a lot.

Of consequence for them i can leaves for the travell, exit to night, drinking all other, eat togheter, and i wish new experienc for live.

Like this I am happy end friendly.

If oll day are for myself always different, are day very well for life with my friend, and not important whether nmy friend is my friends is new oppure is old friends. This important, there's a party this night!

But new friends not imossible do forbid the old friends.

they think who compely at every moment the tollerance , and seldom using the handle.

I can and I must hold the old friends. but i can cope of know the new friends.

Is very good knew the new fiends and hold old friends, like this not my only, and always togheter

Rater Comments

Although substantially longer than the average essay with a score of 1, this response earns the low score because it contains consistent language errors that make the overall essay difficult, if not impossible, to comprehend.

9 Writer's Handbook for English Language Learners

Use this *Writer's Handbook* as a guide to help you write better essays in English. It covers the following topics:

- **Grammar:** explains key grammar rules and gives examples.
- **Usage:** explains important usage rules and gives examples.
- **Mechanics:** describes the basic mechanics rules and gives examples. Mechanics includes spelling and punctuation.
- **Style:** discusses key aspects of effective style.
- **Organization and Development:** gives advice about the writing process and the development of all parts of an essay.
- **Advice to Writers:** discusses different types of essays.
- **Revising, Editing, and Proofreading:** explains what to do in each stage of improving your essay.
- **Glossary:** presents definitions for terms.

Grammar

This section provides information on the following grammatical errors:

- Sentence Errors
- Word Errors
- Other Errors

Sentence Errors

Fragments

A fragment is an incomplete sentence. It does not express a complete thought, even though it starts with a capital letter and ends with a punctuation mark. It is missing either a subject or a verb or both.

Here are three examples of fragments:

Fragment: *Where there were mice and cockroaches.*

Fragment: *A movie that inspires deep emotions.*

Fragment: *Analyzing the characters' motives.*

These three groups of words cannot stand alone as complete sentences. They can be corrected in two ways. One way is to attach the fragment to a complete sentence.

> Corrected sentence: _Peter left the apartment_ _where there were mice and cockroaches._
>
> Corrected sentence: _I went to see "The Silver Star,"_ _a movie that inspires deep emotions._
>
> Corrected sentence: _Analyzing the characters' motives_ _is central to understanding a novel._

Another way to correct fragments is to add a complete subject, a complete verb, or other words that express a complete thought.

> Corrected sentence: _This is_ _where there were mice and cockroaches._
>
> Corrected sentence: _A movie that inspires deep emotions_ _is rare._
>
> Corrected sentence: _Analyzing the characters' motives_ _is important._

Summary: Sentence fragments are incomplete sentences. Sometimes readers can figure out the meaning of a fragment by rereading the sentences that come before and after it. However, turning fragments into complete sentences will improve the connections between ideas.

Run-on Sentences

Run-on sentences happen when we join sentences together without a conjunction or the correct punctuation. Run-on sentences can be very confusing to read. Here is an example: _My sister loves to dance she is very good at it._

There are several ways to correct run-on sentences:

1. Divide the run-on sentence into two separate sentences.

> Run-on sentence: _My sister loves to dance she is very good at it._
>
> Corrected sentence: _My sister loves to dance. She is very good at it._
>
> Run-on sentence: _Jim showed us his ticket someone gave it to him._
>
> Corrected sentence: _Jim showed us his ticket. Someone gave it to him._

2. Connect the parts of the run-on sentence with a coordinating conjunction and a comma. These are the most common coordinating conjunctions: _and, but, for, nor, or, so, yet._

> Run-on sentence: _My sister loves to dance she is very good at it._
>
> Corrected sentence: _My sister loves to dance,_ _and_ _she is very good at it._
>
> Run-on sentence: _She agreed to chair the meeting she didn't come._
>
> Corrected sentence: _She agreed to chair the meeting,_ _but_ _she didn't come._

3. Connect the parts of the run-on sentence with a subordinating conjunction. These are the most common subordinating conjunctions: *after, although, as, because, before, if, since, unless, until, when, whereas, while.*

> Run-on sentence: *My sister loves to dance she is very good at it.*
>
> Corrected sentence: *My sister loves to dance <u>because</u> she is very good at it.*

> Run-on sentence: *Maria and John like skiing Karen does not.*
>
> Corrected sentence: *<u>Although</u> Maria and John like skiing, Karen does not.*

4. Connect the parts of the run-on sentence with a semicolon.

> Run-on sentence: *Gordon laughed at Sandy's joke it was funny.*
>
> Corrected sentence: *Gordon laughed at Sandy's joke<u>;</u> it was funny.*

> Run-on sentence: *I thought he was here I was wrong.*
>
> Corrected sentence: *I thought he was here<u>;</u> I was wrong.*

Summary: Run-on sentences are two or more sentences that have been joined together without a conjunction or the correct punctuation. You can usually correct them by using punctuation or conjunctions.

Word Errors

Noun Forms

A noun is usually defined as a *person, place,* or *thing.*

> Person: *man, woman, waiter, John, book*
>
> Place: *home, office, town, station, Hong Kong*
>
> Thing: *table, car, apple, money, music, love, dog, monkey*

Learning a few basic rules will help you to use nouns effectively:

1. In English, some nouns are countable. That is, they are things that we can count. For example: *house.* We can count *houses.* We can have one, two, three, or more *houses.* Here are more examples of countable nouns:

> *dog, cat, animal, man, person, bottle, box, pound, coin, dollar, bowl, plate, fork, table, chair, suitcase, bag*

Countable nouns can be singular or plural.

> Singular: *I have <u>a friend</u>.*
>
> Plural: *I have <u>two friends</u>.*

2. Usually, to make nouns plural, add -*s*, as in the preceding examples (*friend, friends*). However, there are special cases where you do not add -*s*.

- When a word ends in -*ch*, -*s*, -*sh*, -*ss*, or –*x*, the plural is formed by adding -*es*. (*benches, gases, dishes, dresses, taxes*)
- When a word ends in -*y preceded by a consonant*, the plural form is -*ies*. (*parties, bodies, policies*)
- When a word ends in -*y preceded by a vowel*, the plural is formed by adding -*s*. (*trays, joys, keys*)
- When a word ends in -*o*, the more common plural ending is -*oes*. (*tomatoes, potatoes, heroes*)
- When the final -*o* is preceded by a vowel, the plural ending is -*os*. (*videos, studios*)
- When a word ends in -*f*, the plural is formed in one of two ways:
  - either by adding -*s* (*beliefs, puffs*)
  - or by changing the -*f* to -*v* and adding -*es* (*wife, wives; leaf, leaves; loaf, loaves*).
- When a word ends in -*ex* or -*ix*, the plural ending is usually -*es*. (*appendixes, indexes*)
- In certain cases, the plural form of a word is the same as the singular. (*deer, sheep, fish, series*)

3. Some nouns are uncountable. They represent things that cannot be counted. For example, we cannot count *coffee*. We can count "cups of *coffee*" or "pounds of *coffee*," but we cannot count *coffee* itself. Here are more examples of uncountable nouns:

   music, art, love, happiness, advice, information, news, furniture, luggage, rice, sugar, butter, water, electricity, gas, money

   We usually treat uncountable nouns as singular.

   Incorrect: *These furnitures are beautiful.*

   Correct: *This furniture is beautiful.*

4. Some uncountable nouns refer to abstract ideas or emotions. Abstract ideas may refer to qualities that we cannot physically touch. For example: *health, justice.*

   We cannot count abstract nouns, so they are always singular.

   Incorrect: *Healths are more important than wealths.*

   Correct: *Health is more important than wealth.*

   Incorrect: *Have funs at the reunion.*

   Correct: *Have fun at the reunion.*

5. Some nouns can be countable *and* uncountable. For example: *paper, room, hair, noise, time.* With these nouns, the singular and plural forms often have different meanings.

> Countable: *The Christmas lights make the mall very pretty.*
>
> Uncountable: *This room does not get enough light.*

> Countable: Othello *is one of Shakespeare's most famous works.*
>
> Uncountable: *I have a lot of work to do tonight.*

6. Singular nouns that are countable usually come after an article or other determiner (*a, an, the, this, my, such*).

> Incorrect: *His mother is doctor.*
>
> Incorrect: *Boy standing over there is brother.*
>
> Incorrect: *We saw child in playground.*
>
> Correct: *His mother is a doctor.*
>
> Correct: *The boy standing over there is my brother.*
>
> Correct: *We saw a child in the playground.*

Summary: Nouns are important words in a sentence because they form the subjects or objects. Some nouns can be counted and some cannot. Learning a few rules will help you to use nouns effectively.

Verb Forms

Verbs are parts of speech that express action (*jump, show*) or a state of being (*are, was*). Here are a few tips that may help you to use verbs effectively:

1. Helping verbs (also called *auxiliary verbs*) precede the main verb. All of the following verbs may be helping verbs:

> *be, am, is, are, was, were, being, been, has, have, had, do, does, did, can, will, shall, should, could, would, may, might, must*

Here are examples of sentences with helping verbs:

> *Many people don't know what they are going to do after college.*
>
> *I am going to give you step-by-step instructions.*

2. Words such as *might, must, can, would,* and *should* are also called modals. They express a wide range of meanings (ability, permission, possibility, necessity, etc.).

The following examples show one use of modals:

> *Tom might have gone to the party if he had been invited.*
>
> *If I had a million dollars, I would buy a house for my parents.*

This use of modals is called the conditional use. One event relies on another or it cannot take place. In the first example, Tom cannot go to the party without being invited. In the second example, I could buy a house for my parents only if I had a million dollars.

3. The infinitive form of the verb is formed by using the word *to* plus the simple form of the verb.

> *He is too tired to go to the barbecue.*
>
> *The manager wants to hire a new secretary.*

The infinitive can also be used as the subject or object of a sentence.

> *To invest now seems risky.*
>
> *The teacher told him to leave.*

In the first example, *To invest* is the subject of the sentence, while, in the second example, *to leave* is the object.

We can use the infinitive to show an action that is occurring at the same time as, or later than, the action of the main verb.

> *We like to play video games.*
>
> *My best friend wants to shop at that mall.*

In the first example, the *liking* is happening at the same time as the *playing*. In the second example, the *shopping* is going to happen at a later time than the *wanting*.

4. Do not use *of* after a helping verb. In some verb phrases, there are two or more verbs being used (*should have happened, might be eaten, could have decided*). Here are examples in which the word *of* is used incorrectly:

> Incorrect: *They would of stayed one more month if possible.*
>
> Incorrect: *In that time, he could of finished the project.*
>
> Correct: *They would have stayed one more month if possible.*
>
> Correct: *In that time, he could have finished the project.*

Of is a preposition, not a verb, and in each of these sentences, *of* should be replaced with the helping verb *have*.

Summary: Verbs are very important parts of a sentence. There are a few rules that you can learn to make your use of verbs more effective.

Subject-verb Agreement

In English, the subject and verb must always agree in number. Here are a few rules that will help you:

1. A singular subject takes a singular verb.

> *The teacher was happy with my answer.*
>
> *My cell phone is not working.*

In the first example, the singular subject *teacher* agrees with the singular verb *was*. In the second example, the singular subject *cell phone* agrees with the singular verb *is*.

2. A plural subject takes a plural verb.

> *My parents were happy with my grades.*
>
> *Many television stations have reported that story.*

In the first example, the plural subject *parents* matches the plural verb *were*, and in the second example, the plural subject *television stations* matches the plural verb *have*.

You should never have a plural subject with a singular verb.

> Incorrect: *Many students thinks tomorrow is a holiday.*

This sentence can be edited to make the subject and verb agree.

> Correct: *Many students think tomorrow is a holiday.*

Similarly, you should never have a singular subject with a plural verb.

> Incorrect: *The student think tomorrow is a holiday.*

This sentence can be edited to make the subject and verb agree.

> Correct: *The student thinks tomorrow is a holiday.*

3. Sometimes subjects and verbs are separated by a word or a phrase. When that happens, students sometimes forget to make them agree in number.

> Incorrect: *Your suggestions about the show was excellent.*
>
> Incorrect: *The use of cell phones during concerts are not allowed.*

> Correct: *Your suggestions about the show were excellent.*
>
> Correct: *The use of cell phones during concerts is not allowed.*

In the first example, since the subject of the sentence is *suggestions*, which is plural, the plural verb *were* is used. In the second example, the singular subject *use* needs the singular verb *is*.

4. A compound subject needs a plural verb.

When you proofread your work, correctly identify the subject in your sentences. For example, the following sentences have more than one subject:

> *The camcorder and the tripod were returned yesterday.*
>
> *Both Chantel and Rochelle are nice names.*

In the first example, the complete subject is compound (*camcorder* and *tripod*), and so the verb must be plural (*were*). In the second example, the compound subject is *Chantel and Rochelle* and needs the plural verb *are*.

5. A collective noun must have a verb that agrees with it. Collective nouns are nouns that name a group (*committee, herd, board of directors*). In American English, collective nouns are usually singular.

> Correct: *The committee is made up of twelve people.*

> Correct: *The jury has not arrived at a verdict.*

When you use a collective noun to refer to a group acting as an individual unit, you should make the verb singular. In the first example, the subject (*committee*) is singular, so it takes the singular verb *is*. In the second example, the singular subject (*jury*) takes the singular verb *has*.

However, sometimes you might want to emphasize that the group acted as individuals, each for himself or herself. Then you could write the following:

> Awkward: *The committee were divided in their opinions.*

> Awkward: *The jury have been listening to the tapes for two days.*

In these examples, the individuals in the groups are emphasized, so the plural verbs are used. However, while correct, these sentences sound awkward. You might want to change the word *committee* to *committee members* in the first example, and the word *jury* to *jury members* in the second example.

Summary: A verb should always agree with its subject. A singular subject takes a singular verb, and a plural subject takes a plural verb. Sometimes a phrase separates the subject and the verb, making it hard to find the real subject.

Pronouns

A pronoun is a word that takes the place of one or more nouns. Pronouns are words such as *he, his, she, her, hers, it, they, their, them, these, that, this, those, who, whom, which, what,* and *whose.*

If we did not have pronouns, we would have to repeat a lot of nouns. We would have to say things like:

> *Do you like the new manager? I don't like the new manager. The new manager is too unfriendly.*

With pronouns, we can say the following:

> *Do you like the new manager? I don't like him. He is too unfriendly.*

Learning a few rules will help you to use pronouns correctly and effectively:

1. Pronouns must agree with the nouns they refer to. If your pronoun refers to a girl or woman, you use a feminine pronoun (*she, her, hers*). If your pronoun refers to a boy or man, you use a masculine pronoun (*he, his, him*).

Any pronoun you use must also agree in number with the noun it refers to. If you are using a pronoun to refer to a singular noun, you must use a singular pronoun; if you are using a pronoun to replace a plural noun, you use a plural pronoun.

> *Julia reminded us that <u>she</u> would not stay late.*

> *Bob bought two computers and had <u>them</u> delivered to his office.*

In the first example, the singular pronoun *she* is used to stand for *Julia*, a female person. In the second example, the plural pronoun *them* is used to refer to the plural noun *computers*.

2. Some indefinite pronouns are always singular. Indefinite pronouns such as *each, one, every, everyone, everybody, anyone, anybody, anything, someone, somebody, either, neither, nothing, nobody, none,* and *no one* are always singular, so other pronouns that refer to them must also be singular, as in these examples:

> *<u>Neither</u> of the boys sent in his report.*

> *<u>Everyone</u> must buy her own ticket.*

Note the construction of the second sentence, in which the writer decided to use the pronoun *her*. Some people would prefer the pronoun to be *his or her* to indicate explicitly that each person, regardless of gender, is purchasing a ticket. Some instructors consider *his or her* constructions awkward and allow *everyone* to be treated as plural (*Everyone must buy their own ticket.*). Other instructors consider the plural construction not acceptable in good writing.

3. Some indefinite pronouns are always plural. These include *both* and *many*. Other pronouns that refer to *them* must also be plural.

> *<u>Both</u> of <u>them</u> are here tonight.*

> *<u>Many</u> of the managers have moved into <u>their</u> new offices.*

In the first example, *both* is plural, and so the plural pronoun *them* is used. In the second example, the plural pronoun *their* is used because *many* is plural.

4. Some indefinite pronouns can be singular or plural. Indefinite pronouns such as *all, any, more, most, none,* and *some* can be singular or plural, depending on their meaning in a context.

> *<u>Most</u> of my time <u>is</u> spent reviewing for the test.*

> *<u>Most</u> of the students <u>have</u> turned in <u>their</u> reports.*

In the first example, *most* refers to *time*, a singular noun. It thus takes the singular verb *is*. In the second example, *most* refers to the plural noun *students*. This is why it takes the plural verb *have* and is referred to by the plural pronoun *their*.

5. Overusing pronouns can cause confusion.

> Confusing: *The President informed the Vice President that all of his supporters should be meeting with him.*

Whose supporters, the President's or the Vice President's? Whom are they meeting with? This sentence needs to be revised to fix the confusion caused by the use of *him* and *his*. This can be accomplished by replacing the pronouns with the appropriate nouns.

> Clear: *The President informed the Vice President that all of the President's supporters should be meeting with the President.*

Excessive use of *it* weakens writing, especially when *it* is used to introduce a sentence, as in this example:

> Confusing: *We were visiting the museum. I saw it. It was interesting and unusual. I was amazed by it.*

You can improve *it* by explaining what the first *it* refers to.

> Clear: *We were visiting the museum. I saw the space exhibit. It was interesting and unusual. I was amazed by it.*

In this example, can you figure out what *it* stands for?

> *Although the car hit the tree, it was not damaged.*

Does *it* refer to the car or the tree? You can make the sentence clear by rewriting it.

> *The car was not damaged, although it hit the tree.*

6. When you have nouns joined by a conjunction (*and, or,* or *nor*), do not forget to make a pronoun that refers to them agree in number, as in these examples:

> *If Bob and Rick want to go, they will need to take the bus, because I don't have room in my car.*
>
> *Whether I buy a dishwasher or dryer, it will have to go in the kitchen.*

In the first example, there is a compound noun, as *Bob* and *Rick* are joined by the conjunction *and*. So the plural pronoun *they* must be used. In the second example, the noun is singular (*dishwasher* or *dryer*). Thus the singular pronoun *it* is used.

7. You should know when to use *who, whom, which,* or *that. Who* and *whom* refer to people. *Which* refers to things, and *that* can refer to either people or things.

> *The committee interviewed all the candidates who applied.*
>
> *Do you still have the magazine that I lent you last week?*
>
> *Which courses should I take in the fall?*

In the first example, *who* refers to a group of people (*candidates*). In the second example, *that* refers to a thing (*magazine*). In the third example, *which* refers to things (*courses*).

Summary: A pronoun is a word used to take the place of one or more nouns. Singular pronouns must be used to refer to singular nouns, and plural pronouns must be used to refer to plural nouns. Some indefinite pronouns can be singular or plural, according to their meaning in the sentence.

Possessive Pronouns

Possessive pronouns are used to show possession or ownership. Here are a few rules that will help you to use possessive pronouns effectively:

1. When you are using possessive pronouns such as *his*, *hers*, *mine*, *theirs*, *yours*, or *ours*, make sure that the possessive pronoun agrees in number with the noun to which it refers.

   Incorrect: *I have my car, and my husband has <u>theirs</u>.*
   Incorrect: *This is the children's room. All those toys are <u>hers</u>.*

   Correct: *I have my car, and my husband has <u>his</u>.*
   Correct: *This is the children's room. All those toys are <u>theirs</u>.*

   In the first sentence, the singular pronoun *his* should be used to show that the car belongs to the singular noun *husband*. In the second sentence, *theirs* should be used to show that the toys belong to the plural noun *children*.

2. Possessive pronouns do not take an apostrophe. *His, hers, its, ours, yours, theirs,* and *whose* are pronouns that already convey possession, so do not add an apostrophe to them.

   Incorrect: *Each art room has <u>it's</u> own sink.*
   Incorrect: *<u>His'</u> office is on the third floor.*

   Correct: *Each art room has <u>its</u> own sink.*
   Correct: *<u>His</u> office is on the third floor.*

   In the first sentence, a possessive pronoun is needed (*its*) not *it's*, which means "it is." In the second sentence, the possessive pronoun *his* is needed; *his'* is never used.

Other Ways to Show Possession

Besides possessive pronouns, there are other ways to show possession, such as using an apostrophe and an *-s* (-*'s*).

   My neighbor<u>'s</u> house is bigger than mine.

   Henry<u>'s</u> cat likes to play with our baby.

Below are some rules for indicating possession:

1. When a noun ends in *-s* and the addition of *-'s* makes the word sound odd, some writers add only an apostrophe, as in these examples:

> *I like James' company.*
>
> *This is Harris' wife, Anna.*

2. Make sure you put the apostrophe in the right place. Put the apostrophe *before* the *-s* if the word is singular.

> *The teacher's desk is right in front.* (one teacher)
>
> *My sister's haircut cost $70.* (one sister)

You will put the apostrophe *after* the *-s* only if it is a plural word.

> *We borrowed our parents' car.* (more than one parent)
>
> *I went to a party at my friends' house.* (more than one friend)

3. When two or more people share ownership, you use an apostrophe and *-s* on the last noun. When each person has separate ownership, you need to indicate that, as in these examples:

> *John and Jack's room is very messy.* (John and Jack share one room.)
>
> *Ian's and George's dreams are very different, even though the two boys come from the same family.* (Ian and George have different dreams.)

4. Do not use an apostrophe when you want to make a noun plural. An apostrophe shows possession, not the plural of a noun. These sentences are wrong: they should not have apostrophes:

> *The new student's look confused.*
>
> *There are too many car's on our street's.*

Summary: Possessive pronouns are used to show possession, or ownership. There are a few rules that can help you to use them correctly.

Prepositions

A preposition is a word that is used before a noun (or noun phrase) to give more information in a sentence. Prepositions are usually used to show where something is located or when something happened. Examples of prepositions include *in, among, between, across, at, with, beside, behind, in, into, from, during, before,* and *after.*

Prepositions are used to show place, time, and action or movement.

● Place:

> *The main office is in New York.*
>
> *I'm meeting my colleagues at the coffee shop.*

● Time:

> *Let's try to get there by 3:30.*
>
> *Please do not talk during the show.*

● Action or movement:

> *He jumped into the river.*
>
> *We flew from Los Angeles to Toronto.*

Some verbs and adjectives are usually followed by certain prepositions.

> *They always argue about money.*
>
> *I borrowed a book from the library.*

Here are more examples of words and prepositions that usually go together:

> *familiar with, afraid of, far from, close to, believe in, borrow from, lend to, absent from, nice to, argue with, made of, take off, turn on, happy with, sad about, famous for*

The following sentences contain *incorrect* use of prepositions:

> Incorrect: *I am afraid at losing my textbooks.*
>
> Incorrect: *The student argued at the teacher.*

> Correct: *I am afraid of losing my textbooks.*
>
> Correct: *The student argued with the teacher.*

The first sentence can be corrected by changing *at* to *of*. In the second sentence, the preposition that should go with *argued* is *with*.

Summary: Prepositions are used to show relationships between a noun and other parts of a sentence. There are a few rules that can help you to use prepositions correctly.

Other Errors

Wrong or Missing Word

When writing or typing quickly, people often use the wrong word or misspell words. When you begin to revise, edit, and proofread, read carefully for wrong words or words that you have left out.

One of the most frequent problems is the use of *the* instead of *they*.

> Incorrect: *The went to the store each Monday.*

The writer most likely intended the following:

> Correct: *They went to the store each Monday.*

Another common error is a missing noun after the word *the*.

Incorrect: *The go to the store each Monday.*

Correct: *The brothers go to the store each Monday.*

Summary: Wrong or missing words commonly occur but are easy to correct. Proof-read your sentences carefully.

Keyboard Errors or Typos

Sometimes while writing the first drafts of an essay, you might leave out words or make keyboard errors. They might be grammatical, usage, or mechanics errors, or they could be omitted words or typos. Proofread carefully to correct these errors when you edit and revise your writing.

Usage

This section provides information on the following usage errors:

● Article Errors

● Confused Words

● Wrong Form of Word

● Faulty Comparison

Article Errors/Determiner Errors

This section features rules and explanations for using articles and examples of how articles are used correctly when you are writing in English.

What Are Articles?

A, an, and *the* are called *articles.* These are words that come before a noun or its modifier. (A *modifier* is a word that makes a noun clearer or more specific. Modifiers tell how many or which one.)

a thinker	*an* apple	*the* house
a car	*an* old house	*the* newspapers

There are two types of articles in English. *A* and *an* are called indefinite articles. *The* is called a definite article.

When to Use *a* or *an*

A or *an* is used before a *singular* noun when the noun refers to *any* member of a group.

> James must write *an essay* for his writing class today.

> *A newspaper* is a good source of information on current events.

If the noun or the modifier that follows the article begins with a consonant sound, you should use the article *a*.

> *a* basketball   *a* new automobile

On the other hand, if the noun or its modifier begins with a vowel sound—a, e, i, o, u—you should use the article *an*.

> *an* elephant   *an* old truck

A/an is used before a noun if the noun can be counted. For example:

> I received *a letter* from my sister.

> Sending *an email* is a fast way to communicate with classmates.

Sometimes a noun or a modifier can begin with a vowel *letter* but not a vowel *sound*. For example, here the vowel *o* in the word *one* sounds like the consonant *w* in *won*:

> This will be *a* one-time charge to your account.

When to Use *the*

The is used before singular and plural nouns when the noun is a particular or specific noun. Use the article *the* if you can answer the question "Which one?" or "What?"

> *The art class* that I want to take is taught by a famous painter.

> *The students* in Mrs. Jones's class do not want to participate in *the debate*.

In addition, *the* is used in the following ways:

- To refer to things known to everyone (*the* sky, *the* stars)
- To refer to things that are unique (*the* White House)
- To refer to time (*the* past, *the* present, *the* future)

When Not to Use an Article

A/an is not used before a noun if the noun cannot be counted.

> I like to drink milk. (*Milk* is not counted.)

If a quantity of milk is specified, then the article would be used.

> I like to drink *a glass of milk* before I go to bed.

Sometimes nouns used to represent abstract general concepts (such as anger, beauty, love, or employment) do not take *a* or *an* before them.

Love is a difficult emotion to describe in words.

Money alone cannot buy happiness.

The is not used when a plural noun is used in a general sense.

Computers are helpful tools for student writers. (*Computers* refers to the general concept of computers, not to specific computers.)

The computers in that classroom are used for writing class. (*The computers* refers to a specific set of computers.)

Other Determiner Errors

The adjectives *this, that, these,* and *those* modify nouns that follow them by telling "which one." These adjectives must agree in number with the nouns they modify. *This* and *that* are used to describe a singular noun. *These* and *those* are used to describe plural nouns.

Incorrect: *I would buy these house for those reason.*

Incorrect: *This kinds of technologies will affect people's behavior.*

Correct: *I would buy this house for that reason.*

Correct: *These kinds of technologies will affect people's behavior.*

Homonyms

Certain words are known as *homonyms*. These are words that sound the same but differ in meaning, spelling, or usage. Homonyms can be of two types: words that are spelled alike and words that sound alike. Words that are spelled alike but differ in meaning are called *homographs*. An example of a homograph is the word *bear*, which can mean a type of animal or the verb *bear*, which means "to carry." Words that sound alike but differ in meaning and spelling are called *homophones*. The words *whole* and *hole* are homophones. *Whole* is an adjective meaning "complete," and *hole* is a noun meaning "an empty place." What follows are examples of some common homonyms. Always check your writing to make sure you are using the appropriate words.

here *adverb* meaning "in this place"

*We have been waiting **here** for an hour.*

hear *verb* meaning "to listen"

*Do you **hear** the birds singing?*

hole *noun* meaning "an empty place"

The children dug a big **hole** in their sandbox.

whole *adjective* meaning "with no part removed or left out; complete"

Our **whole** project will involve cooperation from everyone.

its *pronoun* possessive form of *it*

The kitten hurt **its** paw.

it's contraction of *it is*

It's not fair to leave her behind.

know *verb* meaning "to feel certain, or to recognize"

Do you **know** how to get to the subway?

no *adverb* used as a denial or refusal

The employee said **no** to the job offer.

knew *verb* past tense of the verb *to know*

The boy **knew** how to count to ten.

new *adjective* meaning "not old"

At the start of the school year, the students bought **new** books.

desert *noun* meaning "a dry and sandy place"

It rarely rains in the **desert**.

desert *verb* meaning "to abandon"

The officer commanded the troops to not **desert** their posts.

dessert *noun* meaning "the final course of a meal"

After a big meal, I enjoy a simple **dessert** of vanilla ice cream.

to *preposition* meaning "toward"

The man pointed **to** the sky.

two *adjective* or *pronoun* meaning "the number 2"

Five is **two** more than three.

too *adverb* meaning "also"

Tom and Eleanor wanted to go with them **too**.

they're *contraction* meaning "they are"

They're both coming to the party.

their *possessive pronoun* meaning "belonging to them"

*That is **their** blue house on the corner.*

there *adverb* meaning "at that place"

*Did you see anyone you knew **there**?*

through *adverb* meaning "completed, or finished"

*When she was **through** eating, she put her plate in the sink.*

threw *past tense* of the verb *throw*, meaning "tossed"

*The boy **threw** the ball to his sister.*

Other Confused Words

Besides homonyms, other words are confused in English because they are similar in spelling, sound, or meaning. Examples of some commonly confused words include *accept/except*, *advice/advise*, *affect/effect*, and *loose/lose*. Computer spell-checkers will not catch these words if you have misused them. When you review your work, proofread to see whether you have used the correct word. Even native speakers of English often make mistakes with confused words when they are writing, especially when they are in a hurry. Review the meanings of some commonly confused words.

accept *verb* meaning "to receive; to agree, or to take what is offered"

*I **accept** your kind invitation.*

except *preposition* meaning "other than, or leaving out; excluding"

*Everyone **except** Phil can attend the conference.*

advice *noun* meaning "an opinion given about what to do or how to behave"

*He has always given me valuable **advice** regarding my future plans.*

advise *verb* meaning "to recommend or counsel"

*I **advise** you to stay in school and study hard.*

affect *verb* meaning "to influence, or to produce an effect on"

*The weather can **affect** a person's mood.*

effect *noun* meaning "result"

*When students study for tests, they see a positive **effect** on their test results.*

effect *verb* meaning "to bring about"

*The governor can **effect** change in state education policies.*

loose *adjective* meaning "detached, not rigidly fixed; not tight"

*She lost her bracelet because it was too **loose** on her wrist.*

lose *verb* meaning "to be deprived, or to no longer have; to not win"

*If you don't pay attention to the signs, you might **lose** your way.*

quiet *adjective* meaning "not loud or noisy"

*Please be **quiet** when other people are speaking.*

quit *verb* meaning "to give up or abandon; to stop"

*The boys will **quit** their jobs the week before school starts.*

quite *adverb* meaning "to some extent"

*Moving to a new city will be **quite** a change for my family.*

sense *noun* meaning "consciousness, awareness, or rationality; the faculty of perceiving by means of sense organs"

*My brother had the good **sense** to keep out of trouble.*

*The doctor explained that my **sense** of smell is not functioning well.*

since *adverb* meaning "from a definite past time until now"; *conjunction* meaning "later than"

*Ginny has lived in the same house ever **since** she moved to town.*

*Karl has worked as an accountant **since** graduating from college.*

than *conjunction* used when comparing two elements

*Her puppy is smaller **than** mine.*

then *adverb* meaning "at that time, or next"

*First I will stop at the store, and **then** I will go home.*

These are just a few examples of words that are often confused in English. When you are unsure of the proper usage of a word, consult an English dictionary.

Wrong Form of Word

When you write quickly, sometimes you use a word form that is different from the one that you intended to use. One reason why this error occurs is that a word can be used in different ways in a sentence depending on its purpose.

When you revise, read your writing very carefully to find these errors. You can also get someone else to read your work and to help you see where you are not clear. Here are examples of wrong word forms that can occur:

Incorrect: *But certain types of businesses will continue to grow to <u>an extend</u>, he thinks.*

Extend is a verb, and this writer meant to use the noun *extent*.

Correct: *But certain types of businesses will continue to grow to <u>an extent</u>, he thinks.*

Here is another example of a wrong word form in a sentence:

Incorrect: *I want to work with <u>disable</u> children.*

This writer should revise *disable* to *disabled*.

Correct: *I want to work with <u>disabled</u> children.*

Learning the parts of speech can teach you how each functions in a sentence. Proofreading your own work can help you correct these errors as well.

Faulty Comparison

A faulty comparison error occurs when the word *more* is used within a comparison with a word that ends in *-er,* or when the word *most* is used within a comparison with a word that ends in *-est.*

Incorrect: *The boy with the red hair is <u>more taller than</u> the girl with the black hair.*

Incorrect: *James thinks that Mary is the <u>most prettiest</u> girl in school.*

To avoid making these kinds of errors in your writing, you should review the following rules:

When comparing one thing with another, add the ending *-er* to short words (usually of one syllable).

Correct: *The boy with the red hair is <u>taller</u> than the girl with the black hair.*

Correct: *Today it is hot, but yesterday it was even <u>hotter</u>.*

When comparing three or more things, add the ending *-est* to short words (usually of one syllable).

Correct: *The girl in the back of the room is the <u>tallest</u> girl in her entire class.*

Correct: *Yesterday was the <u>hottest</u> day ever recorded by the National Weather Service.*

In many cases, with words of two or more syllables, you do not add *-er* or *-est* to the word; instead, use the word *more* before the word when comparing two things, and use the word *most* when comparing three or more things.

Correct: *The judges must decide which of the two remaining singers is <u>more talented</u>.*

Correct: *Of the three new students, John is the <u>most intelligent</u>.*

Comparisons that are negative use *less* for comparisons of two things and *least* for comparisons of three or more things.

Correct: *The third-floor apartment is <u>less costly</u> than the first-floor apartment.*

Correct: *Of the three colleges that I've visited, this one is the <u>least expensive</u>.*

Nonstandard Verb or Word Form

The words you use in everyday conversation are often different from the words you use in standard written English. While a reader might understand these informal words—*gotta, gonna, wanna, kinda*—you should not write them in an essay. Here are two examples of nonwords used in sentences:

> Nonstandard: *I told her I gotta go to school now.*
>
> Correct: *I told her I have got to go to school now.*

> Nonstandard: *Do you wanna go to college?*
>
> Correct: *Do you want to go to college?*

Even though you can understand what the writer means, the words *gotta* and *wanna* do not exist in standard written English.

Mechanics

This section provides information on the following types of mechanics errors:

- Capitalization
- Spelling
- Punctuation
- Other Errors

Capitalization

To *capitalize* means to use capital letters. Below are some guidelines for capitalization:

1. Capitalize the first word of every sentence.

   He is the most famous director in Hollywood right now. No doubt about it.

   Give it to me. It looks like mine.

2. Capitalize all proper nouns; for example, names of individuals, objects, titles, and places.

   Francis Lloyd Mantel lives on Moore Street.

   The class is reading Adventures of Huckleberry Finn.

In the first example, "Francis Lloyd Mantel" is the name of an individual, so it is capitalized. "Moore Street" is the name of a place, so it is also a proper noun. The second example contains the title of a book, so it is capitalized.

All names are proper nouns and must be capitalized. Other examples:

- Names of institutions, places, and geographical areas

  She is a new faculty member at Stanford University.

  Their main office is in New Delhi, India.

- Names of historical events, days, months, and holidays

  Martin Luther King Day is a school holiday.

  Classes don't meet until October.

- Names of languages and proper adjectives

  He speaks Spanish and Italian fluently.

  They teach Korean dances at the academy.

3. The first-person pronoun *I* is always capitalized, even when it is in the middle of a sentence.

   It is I who sent you that letter.

   They told me that I should call for an appointment.

4. Capitalize words such as *father*, *mother*, *aunt*, and *uncle* when used with proper names or when addressing a particular person.

   Aunt Bessie and Uncle Jesse just bought a country house.

   Yes, Mom, I'm going after dinner.

   However, when these words are used with possessive pronouns, they are not proper names and therefore are not capitalized.

   My father is not at home.

   Their mother is my aunt.

   In the above examples, *father*, *mother*, and *aunt* are not capitalized because they are used with the possessives *my* and *their*.

Summary: In English, the first letter of the first word in a sentence is always capitalized. You must also capitalize all proper nouns. Proper nouns include all names and titles. The first-person pronoun *I* is always capitalized too.

Spelling

English spelling rules are complex. Here are a few rules that may help you:

1. Write *i* before *e* (*fiery, friend, dried*), except

   - after *c* (*receive*)

   - with syllables sounding like *a* as in *neighbor* (*weigh, heir, foreign*)

Note these examples:

All applicants will receive a response within three weeks.

The breakfast special is fried eggs and sausage.

Adding Endings to Words

2. If a word ends with a silent -*e*, drop the -*e* when adding a suffix that begins with a vowel (for example, the -*ing* suffix). However, do *not* drop the -*e* when the suffix begins with a consonant (for example, the -*ful* suffix).

    I like to skate. I enjoy skating.

    I could use a dictionary. A dictionary is very useful.

    In the first example (*skate–skating*), the -*e* is dropped because the -*ing* suffix begins with the vowel *i*. In the second example, the -*e* is not dropped, because the -*ful* suffix begins with the consonant *f*.

3. When -*y* is the last letter in a word and the letter before -*y* is a consonant, drop -*y* and add -*i* before adding a suffix.

    The beaches in Thailand are extremely beautiful.

    They hurried to the gate because they were so late.

    In both examples, the -*y* is replaced with -*i* (*beauty–beautiful*; *hurry–hurried*).

4. When forming the plural of a word that ends with a -*y* preceded by a vowel, just add -*s*. But if the letter before -*y* is a consonant, drop -*y* and add -*i* before adding the suffix.

    FAO Schwartz is a famous toy store. It sells all kinds of toys.

    Ladies and gentlemen, please be seated.

    In the first example, the letter *o* (a vowel) comes before -*y*. So you need to add only -*s* to form the plural noun. But in the second example, in the word *lady*, the letter *d* (a consonant) comes before -*y*. You have to drop -*y* and add -*i* to make the word plural.

5. When a word ends in a consonant preceded by one vowel, double the final consonant before adding a suffix that begins with a vowel.

    The children swim at the community pool. They love swimming.

    You should begin at the beginning. Start by writing the title.

    In the first example, the word *swim* ends with the letter *m*. In the second example, the word *begin* ends with the letter *n*. Both *m* and *n* are consonants. When adding -*ing*, a suffix starting with a vowel, you just need to double the final consonant.

Remember: when the ending begins with a vowel and the word ends in an *-e,* do not double the consonant. Instead, drop the *-e* and add the ending.

Incorrect: *The children go <u>skatting</u> in the winter.*

Correct: *The children go <u>skating</u> in the winter.*

The following examples contain *incorrect* spelling:

Incorrect: *We visited the monkey house at the zoo. There were <u>monkies</u> from all over the world.*

Incorrect: *My <u>neice</u> is a student in your class.*

In the first sentence, the plural form of *monkey* is *monkeys.* This is because when forming the plural of a word that ends with a *-y* preceded by a vowel, you should just add *-s.* In the second sentence, *niece* is the correct spelling. Remember, "*i* before *e* except after *c*" is a very useful rule!

Correct: *We visited the monkey house at the zoo. There were <u>monkeys</u> from all over the world.*

Correct: *My <u>niece</u> is a student in your class.*

These are all useful rules for learning English spelling. However, there are also some exceptions that are not covered by these rules, so it is a good idea to learn a few strategies for spelling as well.

For example, there are times when we make mistakes because we type too fast. It is easy to make the following errors on the computer:

Incorrect: *A letter <u>frrom</u> her former neighbor came in the mail today.*

Incorrect: *<u>Becuase</u> I lost my homework, I had to do it again.*

Both sentences contain typos, or mistakes we make when we type. One strategy for dealing with typos is to use the spell-check function on the computer.

However, there are mistakes that will not be caught by the spell-checker. For example:

Incorrect: *Would you know <u>weather</u> he is at work today?*

Incorrect: *Are <u>their</u> any good Indian restaurants in this area?*

In these examples, though the underlined word is spelled correctly, the use of the word in the sentence is incorrect. The spell-checker will not be able to find such errors, so after spell-checking, you should check for these errors as you read each sentence for meaning.

Another strategy is to keep a list of words that you often misspell. Memorize as many as you can. Check your writing specifically for these words.

You could also use a dictionary while you write to check the spelling of words that you are unsure of.

Summary: English spelling is complex and may sometimes seem strange. There are rules that can be memorized and learned, and there are strategies that can help you to spell better. For example, use a dictionary and the spell-check function on your computer.

Punctuation

Punctuation refers to the use of punctuation marks. Some punctuation marks, such as the *apostrophe*, are used with individual words. Some, such as *commas*, are used either to separate parts of sentences or to separate digits in numbers. Others, such as *periods, question marks*, and *exclamation points*, are used to separate sentences. They help us to make the meaning of our sentences clear.

Apostrophe

Use an apostrophe when you write a contraction. A contraction is the joining of two words by eliminating some letters and adding an apostrophe. It is a kind of short form. For example, *can't* is the contraction of *cannot, shouldn't* is the contraction of *should not*, and *let's* is the contraction of *let us*. Other contractions are *won't, it's, wouldn't,* and *couldn't*.

> They <u>won't</u> be able to enter without their tickets.

> We could hear them, but we <u>couldn't</u> see them.

In the first example, *won't* is the contraction of *will not*, and in the second sentence, *couldn't* is the contraction of *could not*.

Some people write contractions without the apostrophe. They are incorrect. The following sentence shows an incorrect use of a contraction:

> Incorrect: <u>Lets</u> go to the park tomorrow.

> Correct: <u>Let's</u> go to the park tomorrow.

Let's is the contraction of *let us*. Without the apostrophe, the word means "allow," as in this sentence:

> Correct: She <u>lets</u> us use the computer when she's not using it.

In order to be used correctly, the apostrophe must be in the proper position. Below are examples of misplaced apostrophes:

> Incorrect: We <u>could'nt</u> understand the lecture.

> Incorrect: Students <u>were'nt</u> in school in the summer.

> Correct: We <u>couldn't</u> understand the lecture.

> Correct: Students <u>weren't</u> in school in the summer.

Note that the apostrophe should replace the vowel that is being deleted.

Summary: The apostrophe is used to show contraction and possession. For other uses of the apostrophe, refer bck to the section "Possessive Pronouns."

Comma

The comma is the most common form of punctuation within a sentence. It is a signal for the reader to pause. In fact, if you read the examples below carefully, you will notice a natural pause where the commas are situated.

Learning a few basic rules will help you to use the comma effectively:

1. Use a comma and conjunction (such as *and* or *but*) to join two clauses in a compound sentence.

    The causes of the civil war were many, <u>and</u> the effects of the war were numerous.

    The experiment was incomplete, <u>but</u> the lessons learned were important.

    In the above examples, because the two clauses are independent clauses (or complete sentences) joined together by a conjunction, they need a comma between them.

2. Use a comma to connect words to the beginning or end of your sentence. We often add information to our sentences by attaching one or more words to the beginning or end. When you do that, you can use a comma to help your reader find your main message.

    Last night, my friend and I celebrated his 58th birthday.

    Many years ago, I studied French and German.

    Each of these sentences begins with a phrase that indicates time. This information is separated from the main sentence by a comma.

3. Use a comma between each item of a list when you are listing three or more items in a sentence.

    The flag was red, white, and blue.

    I bought milk, bread, cheese, and butter.

    The commas in the above examples clearly mark where one item on the list ends and the next one begins.

4. Use a comma between adjectives. If you have two adjectives together before the noun they describe, they must be separated by a comma.

    The <u>cold, wintry</u> wind chilled me to my bones.

    The <u>complex, diverse</u> cultures in the city add to its excitement.

    In the above examples, the adjectives describing *wind* and *cultures* are placed before the noun, separated by commas.

5. Use commas to set off additional information in the middle of a sentence. Some information, often telling details about the subject of the sentence, needs to be distinguished from the main part of the sentence (the verb and object). We place commas before and after these groups of words.

Ms. Johnson, <u>the company president</u>, will announce the winner.

My brother, <u>who loves to read</u>, uses the library every day.

In the above examples, if you take away the parts that are set off by commas, you still have a complete sentence.

6. Use commas to separate quoted matter from the rest of the sentence.

> *"Take a break," said the instructor.*
>
> *Nancy announces, "I'm getting married tomorrow."*

In each example, the quotation is set apart from the rest of the sentence by a comma.

7. Use commas to set off the name of a state or country when it follows a city, county, or equivalent.

> *The newspaper is based in Chicago, Illinois.*
>
> *Her flight to Beijing, China, took twelve hours.*

In the above examples, the comma is used to set off the name of a state or country from a city within it.

8. In written American English, use commas to set off numbers in groups of four or more digits and between the words for the day, month, and year of a date.

> *He won $1,000,000 in the lottery.*
>
> *The date is March 15, 2003.*

In the first example, commas are used because of the numbers (of four or more digits). In the second example, it is used in a date.

The following sentences are missing commas:

> Incorrect: *Conrad Redding the father of the bride cried at the wedding.*
>
> Incorrect: *In conclusion I believe that technology will be the main factor affecting life in the 21st century.*

In the first sentence, "the father of the bride" should be set off by a pair of commas. In the second sentence, there should be a comma after "In conclusion."

> Correct: *Conrad Redding, the father of the bride, cried at the wedding.*
>
> Correct: *In conclusion, I believe that technology will be the main factor affecting life in the 21st century.*

Summary: Commas are used to separate parts of sentences and make meaning clearer. There are rules that can help you to use commas more effectively.

Hyphen

The hyphen is the punctuation mark used to join two words together to form a compound word. The most common uses of hyphens are as part of an adjective phrase, in numbers that are spelled out, and as prefixes.

1. Hyphens with compound adjectives. Use a hyphen to join two or more words serving as a single adjective *before* a noun. For example:

   His uncle is a <u>well-known</u> author.

   However, when compound adjectives come *after* a noun, they are not hyphenated. For example:

   The author is <u>well known</u> for his mystery stories.

2. Hyphens with compound numbers. A hyphen should be used in fractions and in the numbers twenty-one and above.

   The cup is <u>three-quarters</u> full.

   Our teacher is <u>sixty-three</u> years old.

   In the above examples, the compound numbers are joined with hyphens.

3. Hyphens with prefixes. A *prefix* is a syllable or word added to the beginning of another word to change its meaning. The prefixes *self-*, *ex-*, and *great-* always require a hyphen when they are added to words.

   The instructions are <u>self-explanatory</u>.

   The children are with their <u>great-grandparents</u>.

   However, for prefixes such as *dis-*, *pre-*, *re-*, and *un-*, a hyphen is normally not used.

   My aunt <u>dislikes</u> loud music.

   The answer to that question is <u>unknown</u>.

Summary: We use hyphens to link some compound words, but not all compound words are hyphenated. In fact, American English is tending toward using fewer and fewer hyphens. Always check a recent dictionary to be sure you are hyphenating correctly.

Final Punctuation

There are a few punctuation marks that help us to end our sentences. These are the question mark, the period, and the exclamation point.

Question Mark

Use a question mark at the end of a direct question.

When did World War II <u>begin?</u>

What were the key stages in the Romantic Art <u>movement?</u>

Period

Periods are used to mark the end of a sentence that is a not a question. A period is also used at the end of an indirect question.

I just completed the project.

Cindy asked me who would be taking notes at the meeting.

Exclamation Point

Use an exclamation point after a sentence that expresses strong feeling or requires emphasis. An exclamation point also serves to make a sentence stand out.

Correct: *That was utter nonsense!*

Correct: *What absolutely gorgeous flowers! Thank you!*

The following examples contain *incorrect* use of final punctuation:

Incorrect: *Have you called Mrs. Han yet.*

Incorrect: *Oh, that's an amazing story?*

The first example is a question and needs a question mark. The second example should have either an exclamation point or a period, not a question mark.

Correct: *Have you called Mrs. Han yet?*

Correct: *Oh, that's an amazing story!*

Summary: Question marks, periods, and exclamation points are used to end sentences. Use question marks to end direct questions, periods to end other sentences, and exclamation points when you want to express strong emotions or emphasis. Do not use too many exclamation points in your writing, or you may sound as if you are shouting!

Other Errors

Compound Words

A *compound word* is a word that has two or more parts. For example, the word *everywhere* is made up of two distinct words: *every* and *where*. But as a compound word, *everywhere* has a new meaning that is different from the meanings of *every* and *where*. Although there are times when experts cannot agree if a word should be a compound, in most cases there are clear rules. In the following sentences, you can see where student writers make mistakes when using compound words:

Incorrect: *I work to support my self and my family.*

Incorrect: *You can learn from every thing happening today.*

In each of these sentences, compound words have been written incorrectly as two separate words. The underlined words in each sentence should be written as one compound word.

Correct: *I work to support <u>myself</u> and my family.*

Correct: *You can learn from <u>everything</u> happening today.*

Summary: In English, words, especially adjectives and nouns, are sometimes combined into compound words in a variety of ways. Compound words have a meaning that is different from the meanings of the two words that form them. Not all words can be joined this way. When you are not sure whether a word is a compound, check your dictionary.

Fused Words

Sometimes writers fuse two words together to form an incorrect compound word. The sentences below show examples of fused words:

Incorrect: *Some people say that <u>highschool</u> is the best time of your life.*

Incorrect: *I like to play soccer <u>alot</u>.*

Each of the underlined fused words should be two separate words.

Correct: *Some people say that <u>high school</u> is the best time of your life.*

Correct: *I like to play soccer <u>a lot</u>.*

Summary: When you join words together incorrectly, you get fused words. When you are not sure whether two words should be compounded, check your dictionary.

Duplicate Words

When writing a first draft, you might make errors simply because you are thinking faster than you can write or type. As a result, you might write the same word twice. Sometimes you might write two words in a row that, though different, function in the same way. It is very common for writers to type two verbs, pronouns, or articles in a row in early drafts.

Incorrect: *Sally's older sister <u>can may</u> help her pay for college.*

Incorrect: *He was as silly as <u>a the</u> clown.*

In each sentence, one of the underlined words should be deleted.

Correct: *Sally's older sister <u>can</u> help her pay for college.* (meaning that the sister is able to help Sally)

Correct: *Sally's older sister <u>may</u> help her pay for college.* (meaning that the sister might decide to help Sally)

Correct: *He was as silly as <u>a</u> clown.* (meaning that he generally acts clownish)

Correct: *He was as silly as <u>the</u> clown.* (meaning that he acts like a specific clown)

Summary: You "duplicate" when you write the same word twice or when you use two different words that serve the same function. A real duplicate is easy to correct, as the spell-checker will usually identify it. But if you have typed two words that serve the same function and are not sure which to keep, check a dictionary to help you choose the word with the most appropriate meaning.

Style

This section provides information on how you can address the following kinds of problems in writing:

- Word Repetition
- Inappropriate Words or Phrases
- Too Many Passive Sentences
- Too Many Long Sentences
- Too Many Short Sentences
- Sentences Beginning with Coordinating Conjunctions

Word Repetition

Repeating some words to emphasize your key points is a good writing technique. However, repeating the same words or sets of words too often gives your writing an immature style. It can also make your essay seem boring.

To write more effectively, try using a variety of vocabulary. Here are a few ideas that can help you:

1. Use synonyms (words that have similar meanings) to replace repeated words. For example, instead of repeating a common verb such as *make*, where appropriate, use synonyms like these:

   > *create, produce, perform, do, execute, bring about, cause, form, manufacture, construct, build, put up, set up, put together, compose*

   You can find synonyms in a thesaurus.

   In the following paragraph, the noun *student* is repeated too many times:

   > *Think about this situation. A <u>student</u> interviewed many <u>students</u> about what it is like to be an only child. If the teachers in charge of the school paper did not edit names of <u>students</u> from the paper or facts that would give that particular <u>student</u> away to other <u>students</u>, then serious problems could be caused for the <u>students</u> who gave their information.*

   We can improve this paragraph by using a variety of other words to refer to *student*. For example:

Think about this situation. A reporter interviewed many students about what it is like to be an only child. If the teachers in charge of the school paper did not edit the individuals' names from the paper or facts that would give each person away to the readers, then serious problems could be caused for the students who gave their information.

2. Use phrases such as *the former, the latter, the first one,* and *the other* to avoid repeating the same nouns. In the following paragraph, the same names are repeated several times:

    Of the two sisters, Grace is confident and at ease with everyone. Lily is shy and cautious. Grace always gets what she wants. Lily waits patiently for whatever comes her way. Grace never misses a chance to show off her many talents. Lily never says boo unless someone asks her a question.

    This paragraph can be improved by using a variety of phrases:

    Of the two sisters, Grace is confident and at ease with everyone. Lily is shy and cautious. The former always gets what she wants. The latter waits patiently for whatever comes her way. Grace never misses a chance to show off her many talents. Her sister never says boo unless someone asks her a question.

Summary: When you look over your writing, think about how you can replace overused words and phrases. You can use a thesaurus to help you add variety to your writing.

Inappropriate Words or Phrases

Language that is too informal, such as slang, is not appropriate for academic writing. It is not always easy to tell when an expression is too informal. Some expressions are used so often in spoken English that we may think it is all right to use them in academic writing too.

Too informal: *No way would I ever vote.*

Much better: *There is no way I would vote.*

Too informal: *People just need to get it all together and participate in democracy.*

Much better: *People need to consider their beliefs and opinions and participate in democracy.*

Summary: Written language is usually more formal than spoken language. Try to avoid expressions that are too informal when writing academic essays.

Too Many Passive Sentences

A sentence is active when the subject is the *doer* of the action. It is passive when the subject is the *receiver* of the action.

> Active sentence: *Two hundred million people saw the movie.*
>
> Passive sentence: *The movie was seen by 200 million people.*

In the above examples, the action is *seeing*. In the active sentence, the subject (*two hundred million people*) is the doer of the action. In the passive sentence, the subject (*the movie*) is the receiver of the action.

Because passive sentences are usually longer and harder to read, using too many passive sentences can make your writing slow and uninteresting. Many experts think that passive sentences should make up only about 5 percent of your writing.

Active sentences, on the other hand, generally are clearer, are more direct, and seem stronger. However, this does not mean that you should stop using passive sentences. Appropriate use of passive sentences can make your writing more powerful.

Here are a few suggestions about when to use passive sentences:

1. When the *action* is more important than the doer

    > *The theater was opened last month.*
    >
    > *New students are invited to meet the dean in Room 226.*

    In these sentences, the theater being opened and the new students being invited are more important than the "doers" (the people who opened the theater or invited the new students). In fact, the "doers" are not important enough to mention.

2. When the *receiver* of the action is more important than the doer

    > *Everyone was given a key to the gym.*
    >
    > *The letters were faxed this morning.*

    In the first sentence, we care more about the people who were given a key than the people who were doing the giving. In the second sentence, the letters that were faxed are more important than the person who did the faxing.

3. When the *result* of the action is more important than the doer

    > *Our advice was followed by our clients.*
    >
    > *The new computers were installed by the systems staff.*

    In the first sentence, the advice being followed is more important than the people giving the advice. In the second sentence, the installation of the computers is more important than the people who installed them.

4. When you do not know who did an action, do not care, or do not want your reader to know

> Passive: *A mistake was made, and all the scholarship application files were lost.*

> Passive: *This report was written at the last minute.*

The active forms of these examples would be as follows:

> Active: *I made a mistake and lost all the scholarship application files.*

> Active: *I wrote this report at the last minute.*

If you were the person who made the mistake in the first sentence, or the person who wrote the report in the second, would you choose the active or passive voice?

5. When you want to sound objective

Using passive sentences is a common practice in scientific and technical writing. When you are reporting the results of an experiment or describing a study, it helps to sound objective and fair. Thus reports are filled with sentences like these:

> *The pigeons were observed over a period of three weeks.*

> *The subjects were divided into three groups.*

The use of the passive voice in lab reports also keeps the reader focused on the experiment itself, rather than on the researchers.

Summary: When you look over your writing, think about whether you have used too many passive sentences. Passive sentences are longer and more difficult to read and understand, so use them only when they help you to emphasize something important.

Too Many Long Sentences

Experts believe that the average sentence length should be between 15 and 20 words. This length allows your reader to absorb your ideas more easily. For example, the following sentence may be confusing to read because of its length:

> *My favorite place to visit is my grandparents' house near the lake where we love to fish and swim, and we often take the boat out on the lake.*

Breaking the sentence into two (or more) can make your writing clearer and more interesting.

> *My favorite place to visit is my grandparents' house near the lake. We love to fish and swim there, and we often take the boat out on the lake.*

Good writers usually mix longer sentences with shorter ones to make their writing more effective. You may even want to try a short sentence (or a single-word sentence) after a few long ones to help you to emphasize what you are saying.

> *Benjamin Franklin, who was one of America's "founding fathers," helped write the Declaration of Independence. He also invented many things such as bifocals and the Franklin stove, and he discovered electricity. Think about that discovery. Where would we be without electricity?*

In the example above, the paragraph starts with long sentences and ends with short ones. This combination makes the paragraph more lively and effective. Compare it with the paragraph below, which is made up of only long sentences:

> *Benjamin Franklin, who was one of America's "founding fathers," helped write the Declaration of Independence. He also invented many things such as bifocals and the Franklin stove, and he discovered electricity, which became very important to modern life.*

Which paragraph do you prefer?

Summary: It is a good idea to mix long sentences with short ones. A good combination of long and short sentences makes writing lively.

Too Many Short Sentences

You may have too many short sentences in your writing. Good writing usually contains a variety of sentence lengths to make the writing more interesting. Too many short sentences often make the writing sound choppy. You should combine some of your short sentences to make the writing smoother. Here is an example of a paragraph with too many short sentences:

> *I knew my friends would throw me a party. It was for my birthday. There was something in the air. I felt it for a whole week before that. I was nervous. I was also very excited. I got home that night. My friends didn't disappoint me. I walked in my house. All my friends yelled, "Surprise!"*

The paragraph can be improved by joining some of the short sentences using sentence connectors:

> *<u>Because</u> it was my birthday, I knew my friends would throw me a party. There was something in the air <u>for a</u> whole week before that. I was nervous <u>but</u> excited <u>when</u> I got home that night. I wasn't disappointed. <u>When</u> I walked in my house, all my friends yelled, "Surprise!"*

Summary: Good writing usually contains a variety of long and short sentences. A good mix of sentence lengths makes the writing more interesting. Too many short sentences often make the writing sound choppy.

Sentences Beginning with Coordinating Conjunctions

Coordinating conjunctions are words such as *and, but, as, or, yet, for,* and *nor.* They link or join thoughts together in the middle of a sentence. For example:

> *I love pizza, <u>so</u> I eat it for breakfast.*
>
> *Mother drove to town to buy groceries, <u>but</u> she came home with a present for me.*

Coordinating conjunctions can also be used to begin sentences, as in these examples:

> *<u>And</u> I didn't like parties.*
>
> *<u>So</u> I did not do well on that test.*

When you have too many sentences beginning with coordinating conjunctions, your writing becomes choppy. To make your writing smoother, use coordinating conjunctions only when joining ideas within sentences.

In the paragraph below, the writer uses a lot of coordinating conjunctions to begin sentences:

> *Baseball is the great American sport. <u>And</u>, it is thought of as a summer pastime. <u>So</u> as soon as the weather turns warm, all the neighborhood kids find a field to toss a ball around. <u>And</u> soon they form teams and play each other. <u>But</u> all summer, they always find time to listen to pro games on the radio. <u>And</u> they watch them on TV.*

The paragraph can be improved by getting rid of beginning coordinating conjunctions:

> *Baseball, the great American sport, is thought of as a summer pastime. As soon as the weather turns warm, the neighborhood kids find a field to toss a ball around. Soon, they form teams to play each other, but all summer, they always find time to listen to pro games on the radio and to watch them on TV.*

Summary: Coordinating conjunctions are very useful for joining thoughts together in the middle of a sentence. However, try to avoid using them to begin sentences in academic writing.

Organization and Development

The purpose of this section is to explain how a strong essay is typically organized and how to develop your ideas in an essay. It will provide answers to the following questions:

Introduction

- What is an introduction?
- How do I write an introduction?

Thesis

- What is a thesis?
- How do I make sure that my reader understands my thesis?
- Do I have enough main ideas to support my thesis?

Main Ideas

- Does each of my main ideas begin with a topic sentence?
- Have I discussed each main idea completely?
- Have I arranged my ideas in an orderly manner?

Supporting Ideas

- Have I done my best to support and develop my ideas?
- Do I include enough details in each paragraph so that the main idea and topic sentence are explained fully?

Transitional Words and Phrases

- Do I use words and phrases that help the reader think about relationships between different ideas in the essay?

Conclusion

- Do I restate the importance of my ideas based on what I have written in my essay?

Introduction

What Is an Introduction?

An introduction is the first paragraph or two of an essay. It tells the reader what the essay is about and provides background for the thesis (main idea).

A good introductory paragraph does several things:

- It makes the reader want to read the essay.
- It tells the reader the overall topic of the essay.
- It tells the reader the main idea (thesis) of the essay.

How Do I Write an Introduction?

Introductions can be written in many different ways. Here are some ideas you can use to write a good introduction:

- Background about the topic
- Narrative

- Quotation
- Dramatic statistics/facts
- Shocking statement
- Questions that lead to the thesis

The following are examples of these ideas. The essay's thesis sentence is highlighted in bold.

Background About the Topic

Since the beginning of time, there have been teachers. The "classroom" teacher has many important tasks to do. A teacher has to teach information while keeping things interesting. She also sometimes has to be a referee, a coach, and a secretary. At times, a teacher has to be a nurse or just a good listener. **This career demands a lot, but it's a career I most want to have.**

Narrative

My fourth-grade teacher, Miss Vela, was not a big woman. She was about five feet tall and was no longer young. Even though she did not look very strong, she never had trouble controlling all her students. She could quiet us down with just a stare. We always wanted to make her happy because we knew how much Miss Vela cared about us. She expected us to do the best we could, and we all tried our hardest. **Miss Vela was the kind of teacher who made me know that I wanted to be a teacher.**

Quotation

"Teaching is better than tossing a pebble into a pond of water and watching those ripples move out from the middle. With teaching, you never know where those ripples will end." I remember those words of my fourth-grade teacher. Miss Vela once told me that years after they left her class, her students would come back to tell how much she helped them. Miss Vela's students said that it was because of her that they learned to work hard and to feel proud of what they did. **I would like to teach because I would like to make that kind of difference.**

Dramatic Statistics/Facts

Three out of four people said that they thought it didn't matter how many students were taught in one class. However, our class researched this and found that the opposite is true. Studies completed at a university show that having small class sizes, especially in the primary grades, makes a big difference in how much students learn. **Before we decide how many students to assign to a primary school teacher, we need to think more carefully about how important smaller class size is.**

Shocking Statement

Some teenagers today say that they think that wives should earn money and that husbands should help with child care and other household tasks. Recent studies indicate that 13 percent of teenage boys would prefer a wife to stay at home, while 96 percent of the teenage girls surveyed wanted to work outside of the home. **However, couples who marry today may have grown up in very traditional households and therefore may find it difficult to accept wives of equal, not to mention greater, job status.**

Questions That Lead to the Thesis

What exactly is "voice"? Is it a speaking voice or a singing voice? When people say that they have a voice in their head but no way to get it out, what does that mean? **"Voice" has less to do with throats and mouths than it has to do with being human, being alive.**

Thesis

What Is a Thesis?

The thesis statement tells the main idea—or most important idea—of the essay. It emphasizes the writer's idea of the topic and often answers the question, "What important or interesting things do I have to say?" Thinking about the thesis statement can help you decide what other information needs to be presented or omitted in the rest of the essay.

A good thesis statement

- gives the reader some hint about what you will say about the topic
- presents your opinion about the topic and is not just a fact or an observation
- is written as a complete statement
- does not formally "announce" your opinion about the topic

A good thesis statement gives the reader some hint about what you will say about the topic.

> Weak thesis: *Mahatma Gandhi was an interesting man.*
>
> Good thesis: *Mahatma Gandhi was a person of contradictions.*

> Weak thesis: *Television is a total waste of time.*
>
> Good thesis: *Parents should carefully choose appropriate, educational television shows for their children to watch.*

A good thesis statement presents your opinion about the topic and is not just a fact or an observation.

> Weak thesis: *London is the capital of England.*
>
> Good thesis: *For tourists interested in British history, London is an ideal travel destination.*

Weak thesis: *Many movies today are violent.*

Good thesis: *The violence in movies today makes children less sensitive to other people's suffering.*

A good thesis statement is written as a complete statement.

Weak thesis: *Should something be done about bad drivers?*

Good thesis: *Bad drivers should have to take a driving course before being allowed to drive again.*

Weak thesis: *There is a problem with the information on the Internet.*

Good thesis: *To make sure information found on the Internet is valid, Internet users must make sure the sources of the information are credible.*

A good thesis statement does not formally "announce" your opinion about the topic.

Weak thesis: *In my paper, I will write about whether schools should require uniforms.*

Good thesis: *Public schools should not require uniforms.*

Weak thesis: *The subject of this essay is drug testing.*

Good thesis: *Drug testing is needed for all professional athletes.*

How Do I Make Sure That My Reader Understands My Thesis?

Sometimes you might use a word in your introduction or thesis that you should define or explain. For example, if you are writing about "Who is a hero?" you should first explain what you think the word *hero* means. Is a hero a person who risks his or her life to save others? Is a hero a person whom you admire for any reason? People might have their own ways of thinking about a certain word. When you define the word, you help your reader better understand what you mean.

Do I Have Enough Main Ideas to Support My Thesis?

A main idea is a point that you feel strongly about. It is important to you, and you want the reader to understand this idea. Some writers like to give the reader three main ideas. However, the number of main ideas will vary among good essays. The important thing to remember is that your main ideas need to support your thesis adequately.

If you do not have enough main ideas, you may want to do some rethinking. Here are five suggestions for how to think of more ideas about your subject.

Ask yourself these questions to get you started again:

- **Who?**

  Who in my life has influenced me to consider becoming a teacher?

- **What?**

  What do teachers do?

- ### When?

    When did I start thinking about becoming a teacher?

- ### Where?

    Where are teachers needed the most?

- ### Why?

    Why would a person want to become a teacher? Why do I want to become a teacher?

- ### How? How much?

    How does a teacher learn how to teach?

    How has my idea of becoming a teacher changed over the years?

    How much does a teacher influence his or her students?

    How much time does a teacher have to work outside of school?

- ### What if? Why not?

    What if teachers do not have all of the materials they need?

    Why teach in the classroom and not just over the Internet?

Talk to others about your topic.

Lots of people are happy to share what they know. Take good notes, because you may want to quote them in your essay.

- Other students in your school probably have opinions.
- A teacher who knows about the issue or subject could give you some opinions.
- Other people who are experts may have valuable information or opinions.
- Research your subject on the Internet or in a library.
- Send an email to someone who may be an expert.

Think about the kind of writing you are doing.

Consider the questions below to help you figure out which ideas you need to add or how you should arrange those ideas.

- Are you explaining how things are alike (comparison) and different (contrast)? You can use this purpose when you are describing something *(such as how to teach primary school students compared with how to teach high school students)* or when you are analyzing different viewpoints *(such as whether children should go to school year-round).*
- Are you putting your ideas in categories? You might be able to describe something in general and then describe its particular qualities. *For example, you might want to talk about what it takes to be a good teacher and then talk about the unique qualities of a particular teacher you have had.*

- Are you giving reasons to show how a problem developed and what the effects of the problem are? *For example, if you were discussing how students' attitudes are affected by their environment, you might want first to describe what has caused a particular attitude to develop. Then you might want to discuss the effects of that attitude.*

- Are you trying to persuade someone to think like you or to do something that will improve a situation in the way that you want it to be improved? *For example, if you are trying to persuade a friend to think about an issue the way you think about it, you might want to start by saying what the issue is and why your ideas are the best.*

Start all over and see where you go this time with your writing.

Do not be afraid to start over. Lots of writers get new and better ideas when they write about something more than once.

Reread your draft.

Look at your previous draft and start where the writing is the most interesting or at the point that you think is your best statement.

- Try to write three more sentences to explain your best sentence.
- Review the three new sentences, pick the best one, and write three more sentences that explain the most important idea in that best sentence.

Main Ideas

Does Each of My Main Ideas Begin with a Topic Sentence?

Each main idea needs to be discussed fully. The main idea is part of a sentence that explains the idea. This sentence is called the topic sentence, and its goal is to help the reader think of questions about the topic.

Pretend that you are the reader of this topic sentence:

> *Not passing a test in fourth grade in Miss Vela's class made me think about what a teacher is.*

What questions do you have?

Do you want to know more about what happened to this writer in fourth grade?

Do you think that you will learn what the writer thought or meant by the words "what a teacher is"?

Use your topic sentence to prepare the reader for understanding what is written in the essay.

You can review your sentences to see which words are the influential words. They are the words that seem more important in your sentence.

In this topic sentence, which words or phrases are important?

> *Teachers don't get paid for every hour that they work.*

Would you say that "every hour that they work" are the important words?

Here are the other sentences in this paragraph:

Teachers sometimes do work even when they are not in the classroom. Sometimes my mother grades papers and projects all day on Sunday. Even though she does not get paid, she says that that is the only time she can grade all of her students' work. My neighbor spends three weeks of his summer vacation on a ship that does scientific experiments. He doesn't get paid for any of that work, but he says the things that he learns help him be a better teacher.

Use topic sentences to connect two paragraphs or two main ideas.

Here is a sample paragraph that begins with a topic sentence:

Teachers get many benefits in their careers. My neighbor has children and likes having the summer off when his children are home. Some teachers say their work is very enjoyable. At least that's what my mom says when she mixes up her magic bubble formula for science class. My mom also says that one of the benefits of teaching is that she is using her college education every day. She also gets paid to take refresher courses. But she works hard.

Can you see how the next topic sentence connects to another thought?

In fact, teachers don't get paid for every hour that they work, but the teachers that I know say that they love their work.

What do you expect the writer to tell you about in this paragraph?

Have I Discussed Each Main Idea Completely?

In good writing, you (the writer) and the reader feel as if all of your questions/concerns have been discussed. Remember that your reader needs to understand what you are writing, so discuss each idea completely.

Give each main idea its own paragraph.

Each main idea should be treated as a unit. However, if a main idea is very broad, it will need more than one paragraph, because it is too complicated to be discussed in a single paragraph.

Have I Arranged My Ideas in an Orderly Manner?

You can arrange your ideas in many different ways. You can organize your ideas in chronological order, which means the order in time in which they occurred. You can begin with the oldest point first and then use paragraphs to discuss what happened next or later.

Here are two main ideas that will be developed into paragraphs:

Idea 1

I have wanted to be a teacher ever since I failed a test in Miss Vela's class in fourth grade.

Idea 2

Then in eighth grade I had an assignment to teach a science lesson to a class in my former primary school, and that experience showed me how good I felt when the students didn't want the class to be over.

You can organize your ideas by importance, either most important to least important or the other way around.

Tip

If your writing assignment has to be completed in a short time, as in an essay test, you probably want to begin with the most important parts or reasons first.

Here are what two different writers think is their most important idea:

Writer 1

The most important reason to be a science teacher is to help the next generation learn about the Earth.

Writer 2

Getting to do fun activities is the reason why I want to be a science teacher.

Supporting Ideas

What Are Some Ways to Develop Supporting Ideas?

Supporting ideas help to convince your reader that your main idea is a good one. Here are some things that professional writers do:

- Tell a story that clarifies the main idea.
- Give examples of the main idea to explain what the paragraph is about.
- Give reasons that support the thesis. These can be facts, logical arguments, or the opinion of experts.
- Use details that are very specific so the reader can understand how this idea is different from others.
- Tell what can be seen, heard, smelled, touched, felt, or experienced.
- Try to see the idea from many different angles.
- Tell how other events, people, or things might have an influence on the main idea.
- Use metaphors or analogies to help the reader understand an idea by comparing it to something else.

Have I Done My Best to Support and Develop My Ideas?

Think of your reader as a curious person. Assume that your reader wants to know everything that you can say about this subject.

Here are some specific questions that are appropriate for certain types of writing:

- **If you are describing a problem or issue, you might want to consider the following:**

  What type of problem or issue is it?

  What are the signs that a problem or issue exists?

  Who or what is affected by the problem or issue?

  What is the history of the problem or issue—what or who caused it or contributed to it, and what is the state of the problem now?

  Why is the issue or problem significant? What makes this issue or problem important or less important?

- **If you are arguing or trying to persuade your reader to agree with your opinion, consider the following:**

  What facts or statistics could you mention as support?

  What ideas could you discuss to prove your points?

  What comparison could you make that would help the reader understand the issue?

  What expert opinion would make your opinion more valid?

  Could you support your point with some examples?

  Could you describe the views of someone holding a different opinion?

Tip

Strong arguments are often made by discussing what is good in the opponent's view. You can use expressions such as although that is a point well taken, granted, while it is true that, *or* I agree that *to discuss an opposite view.*

- **If you are analyzing literature or writing a review of a story or movie, consider these questions:**

  Can you summarize the story so that your reader knows what happens?

  Can you give the details about the place or time so that your reader has a context for understanding the story?

  What can you say about the main characters so that the reader can understand what makes them special or interesting?

  Can you describe the point where the main character(s) is (are) in a crisis and must make an interesting choice?

  Can you quote what characters say about each other or about what they are experiencing?

  Does the story have a deeper theme that you could discuss?

  Can you describe the style in which the story is told or the camera angles of the movie?

  Are there interesting images or symbols?

- **If you are describing something or providing a definition, consider the following:**

  Can you tell what the thing looks like or what its parts are?

  Can you say what it does or means?

  If what it does or means has changed over time, can you describe what it used to mean or used to do and what it now means or does?

  If what you are describing has a different name or meaning, can you tell the reader the different name or meaning?

- **If you are telling how to do or make something, consider these points:**

  Have you started at the right place—the first step—and proceeded logically?

  Have you defined any terms that might be unfamiliar to your reader?

  Have you given an example that might help your reader understand what you mean?

  Have you tried to explain your instructions clearly? Have you numbered these instructions so that the reader knows the order in which it is best to do them?

Tip

You may want to think of a way to arrange your material so that your reader can understand it better. For example, in a recipe the ingredients are listed at the top and the instructions are in short paragraphs or are numbered as steps.

Conclusion

What Is a Conclusion?

The concluding paragraph is separate from the other paragraphs and brings closure to the essay.

- It discusses the importance of your ideas.
- It restates the thesis with fresh wording.
- It sums up the main ideas of the paper.
- It can also include an anecdote, a quotation, statistics, or a suggestion.

Concluding Approaches

You might consider some of the following approaches to writing concluding paragraphs:

- Summarize main points.
- Provide a summarizing story.

- Include a provocative or memorable quotation.
- Make a prediction or suggestion.
- Leave the reader with something to think about.

Here are two different concluding paragraphs:

Good teaching requires flexibility, compassion, organization, knowledge, energy, and enthusiasm. A good teacher must decide when a student needs to be prodded and when that student needs mercy. Good teaching requires knowing when to listen and reflect and when to advise or correct. It requires a delicate balance of many skills, and often a different mix of approaches for different students and different situations. Is this profession demanding? Yes! Boring? Never! Exciting? Absolutely!

When I become a teacher, I want fourth graders like Miss Vela's. We adored her and wanted to please her. But more important, I want to be a Miss Vela for my students. I want to challenge my students to become good citizens. When the river in our town flooded its banks and some classmates had to be evacuated, Miss Vela asked us to think about what we could do. We came up with three decisions. We packed lunches for our classmates, we shared our books and pencils in class, and we gave them clothing. Later when we studied civics, we realized that we were taking care of our classmates the way the local or federal government does in a disaster. Miss Vela was helping her fourth graders become more civic minded. I'm hoping to help my students think like that when I'm a teacher.

Transitional Words and Phrases

Do I Use Transitional Words and Phrases to Take the Reader from One Idea to the Next?

Transitional words and phrases connect what a reader has already read to what the reader is going to read. They give the reader an idea of the relationships between the various ideas and supporting points. They also help to show the relationship between sentences.

You can guide the reader as he or she reads an essay by using transitional words or phrases in paragraphs and sentences.

These words can help you talk about time and the relationship between events:
today, tomorrow, next week, yesterday, meanwhile, about, before, during, at, after, soon, immediately, afterward, later, finally, then, when, next, simultaneously, as a result

These words can help you show the order of ideas:
first, second, third, finally, lastly, most important, of least importance

These words can help you show location:

above, over, below, beneath, behind, in front of, in back of, on top of, inside, outside, near, between, beside, among, around, against, throughout, off, onto, into, beyond

These words can help you compare or demonstrate similarity:

also, as, similarly, in the same way, likewise, like

These words can help you contrast or demonstrate difference:

in contrast, however, although, still, even though, on the other hand, but

These words can help you add information:

in addition, for instance, for example, moreover, next, likewise, besides, another, additionally, again, also, in fact

These words can help you clarify a point:

in other words, for instance, that is, just to reiterate, in summary

These words can help you add emphasis to a point that you are making:

truly, in fact, for this reason, again, just to reiterate

These words can help you conclude or summarize:

all in all, lastly, as a result, in summary, therefore, finally

Does Each of My Paragraphs Support and Develop/Explain the Main Idea/Topic Sentence?

Paragraphs are a group of sentences about a thought or discussion. Each paragraph is about a main topic.

Some paragraphs are long and some are short. Some paragraphs are just one sentence, which can be a very interesting way to present information.

Some contain an interesting story that can take several sentences to tell.

Some paragraphs answer all of the topic issues. Others are more like transitions between two main ideas.

Here are some questions to help you evaluate your paragraphs:

- **Have you said enough so that each paragraph is complete?**

Tip

Try giving each paragraph a title and see if, read by itself, it could be something meaningful. If the reader asked you a specific question, would this paragraph be the answer? If some of the sentences do not fit as an answer, then you should probably delete them.

- **Have you used words that need to be explained or defined?** If you are trying to sound important and do not explain what you mean, your reader might feel frustrated. Try using more than one sentence to define or explain something. Three sentences might really explain your idea!

- **Have you provided evidence (proof)? Would an example show what you mean?** Use a good example to show that what you say is true. This is important.

- **Is there a personal experience or quotation from another source that would validate what you are trying to say?**

Tip

Personal experiences are appropriate in some essays but not in others. Make sure you understand the type of information that is expected in each essay you write.

Tip

If you are quoting from another source, make certain that you are quoting (reproducing the words) accurately. Also be sure that you are using quotation marks correctly.

- **Have you used clear transitions that establish connections between sentences and ideas?** You might think of your paragraph as a train and the sentences as cars (and the topic sentence as an engine). Do all the parts of the paragraph link or fit together?

Advice to Writers

This section provides information about the different kinds of essays you may be asked to write.

- Persuasion
- Informative Writing
- Comparison/contrast
- Description
- Narration
- Cause and Effect
- Problem and Solution
- Description of a Process
- Writing as Part of an Assessment
- Response to Literature
- Writing in the Workplace

Persuasion

When you write a persuasive essay, you are trying to make the reader agree with you. You thus have to offer good reasons to support your opinion, deal with opposing views, and perhaps offer a solution.

Here is how to start:

- List specific arguments for and against your opinion (the pros and cons).

- Decide whether you need to find more information (for example, *statistics* that support your argument, *direct quotes* from experts, *examples* that make your ideas concrete, *personal experience*, *facts*).

- Think of good arguments from someone who holds the opposite view. How could you respond to that person?

Tip

In this kind of writing, you might want to keep your best argument for last.

Summary: When you write a persuasive essay, you have to be clear and convincing. Any kind of writing improves with practice. Try to practice writing and revising, and expose yourself to as many good models of persuasive essays as you can.

Informative Writing

This kind of writing presents information that helps your reader understand a subject (for example, global warming, jazz music, pollution). Informative writing can be based on formal research (reading, interviews, Internet browsing). Sometimes you may also be asked to write about a personal experience or observation.

Here is how to start:

- Find a specific focus (for example, not *recycling in general* but *the recycling of paper*).

- Choose several important points to discuss (*how paper is recycled, what recycled paper is used for*).

- Think about the supporting details for each point. These details can be facts, observations, descriptions, and/or examples (*items that use recycled paper are paper towels, greeting cards*).

Comparison/contrast

Writing a comparison/contrast paper involves comparing and contrasting two subjects. A comparison shows how two things are alike. A contrast shows how two things are different.

You can use comparison and contrast to describe, define, analyze, or make an argument—for, in fact, almost any kind of writing.

Here is how to start:

● Select two subjects that have some basic similarities or differences.

● Look for how these subjects are similar and different.

● Decide how you want to present your information. Choose one way and stick with it throughout your essay.
  - Do you want to discuss a point for one subject and then the same point for the second subject?
  - Do you want to show all the important points of one subject and then all the important points of the second subject?
  - Do you want to discuss how your two subjects are the same and then how they are different from each other?

● Remember to make clear to your reader when you are switching from one point of comparison or contrast to another. Use clear transitions. Some transition words that you may find useful are as follows:

> For similarities: *similarly, likewise, furthermore, besides*
>
> For differences: *in contrast, in comparison, on the other hand, although, however, nevertheless, on the other hand, whereas, yet*

Description

In descriptive writing, you write about people, places, things, moments, and theories with enough detail to help the reader create a mental picture of what is being described. You can do this by using a wide range of vocabulary, imaginative language, interesting comparisons, and images that appeal to the senses.

Here is how to start:

● Let the reader see, smell, hear, taste, and feel what you are writing about. Use your five senses in the description (for example, *The ancient driver nervously steered the old car down the red mud road, with me bouncing along on the backseat*.).

● Be specific (not *this dessert is good* but *the fudge brownie is moist, chewy, and very tasty*).

● Show the reader where things are located from your perspective (for example, *As I passed through the wooden gates, I heard a cough. A tiny woman came out from behind the trees*.).

● Decide whether you want to give a personal view (subjective) or a neutral viewpoint (objective).

What seems unusual or contradictory can make your subject more interesting (for example, Martin Luther King probably contributed more than anyone else to changes in civil rights, but he hardly earned any money for his speeches and work.*).*

Narration

This kind of essay offers you a chance to think and write a story about yourself, an incident, memories, and experiences. Narratives or stories usually include a plot, a setting (where something happened), characters, a climax, and an ending. Narratives are generally written in the first person, using *I*. However, as the storyteller, you can choose to "speak" like different people to make the story more interesting.

Here is how to start:

- If you are writing about a quarrel with a friend:
  - Think of what caused the quarrel.
  - Think of who is involved and how.
  - Think of how the quarrel developed, how it was settled, or whether you and your friend are talking now.
- Remember the details that make the event real to you (for example, what your friend said to you and the tone of voice your friend used).
- Try to answer the question, "What did this event mean to me?"
- Choose a way to begin; for example:
  - Build your story in scenes (the way you see in movies).
  - Summarize what happened and tell only the most important scene.
  - Begin at the ending and tell why this was such an important event.

Cause and Effect

Cause-and-effect essays are concerned with why things happen (causes) and what happens as a result (effects). In the cause-and-effect essay, it is very important that your tone be reasonable and that your presentation look factual and believable.

Here is how to start:

- Think about the event or issue you want to write about.
- Brainstorm ideas.
- Introduce your main idea.
- Find relevant and appropriate supporting details to back up your main idea. You can organize these details in the following ways:
  - *Chronological,* the order in which things/events happen
  - *Order of importance,* from least to most important or vice versa
  - *Categorical,* by dividing the topic into parts or categories

- Use appropriate transition words and phrases, such as the following:

  because, thus, therefore, due to, one cause is, another is, since, for, first, second, consequently, as a result, resulted in, one result is, another is

Problem and Solution

A problem-solution essay starts by identifying a problem (or problems) and then proposes one or more solutions. It is usually based on topics that both the writer and the reader care about (such as the quality of cafeteria food).

Here is how to start:

- Think of all the reasons that the problem exists.
  - Why did it happen?
  - How did it begin?
  - Why does it exist now?
- List possible solutions to the problem.
- Evaluate your solutions—which ones will most likely work?
- Write the pros and cons of one or more good solutions, but give the most space in your essay to the best solution.
- Explain why the best solution is the one to choose.

Description of a Process ("How-to")

This kind of essay explains how to do something (for example, *how to bake your favorite cake*) or how something occurs (for example, *how movies are made*).

For how to do something, here is how to start, along with the pertinent questions

- Think about all the equipment, skills, or materials needed.
- How many steps are there in the process? Put the steps in the right order. Why is each step important?
- What difficulties are involved in each step?
- How long does the process take?

Tip

Give any signs or any advice that can help the reader accomplish the step with success!

For how something occurs, here is how to start:

- Give any background that can help your reader understand the process.
- Tell what happens in the order that it happens.

Tip

Do not forget to explain any terms that your reader might not understand!

Process essays are usually organized according to time: they begin with the first step in the process and continue until the last step. To indicate that one step has been completed and a new one will begin, we use transitions. Some common transition words and phrases used in process essays are as follows:

first of all, first, second, third, next, soon after, after a few hours, afterward, initially, at the same time, in the meantime, before, before this, immediately before, in the meanwhile, currently, during, meanwhile, later, then, previously, at last, eventually, finally, last, last but not least, lastly

Writing as Part of an Assessment

This kind of writing may be more difficult, because you are trying to write your best in a certain place and a limited amount of time. There are a few tricks, however.

Here is how to start:

- Take a few moments to understand the question and to note down some ideas that come to mind.

- Before beginning to write, take a few moments to plan. How are you going to organize your main ideas and supporting details? Some students find making an outline to be a helpful strategy.

- During your writing, if other ideas come to mind and they feel right, use them.

- Keep track of your time, but do not panic.

- Revise. Look at the paper from the reader's point of view; reorganize and add explanations if necessary.

- Proofread if you have time.

Tip

As with any other kind of writing, writing on a test improves with practice. You can practice this skill by writing and revising essays while working within a set time limit.

Response to Literature

When you write about literature, you are telling why that work of literature (story, movie, poem, or play) is interesting and what makes it effective (for example, why it makes you laugh, why you care about the characters).

You can write about why the literary work seems true, you can analyze the characters or actions, or you can analyze how the literary work accomplishes its effect.

There are many ways to respond to literature, but here are a few ways to start, along with pertinent questions:

- Write for a while about your personal feelings about the literature. Are you most interested in the setting, the situation, the characters, or the atmosphere that the work creates? These are clues to what you can write about.

- What is the situation or the mood?

- What clues does the author give you about the true meaning of this story, poem, or movie? (For example, the many "Cinderella" stories in the world have the same meaning: kindness is rewarded no matter how poor you are.)

- Organize your thoughts and support them with examples from the literary work. Do not assume that your reader knows the story or movie that you are writing about!

Writing in the Workplace

Letters, memos, and reports are the kinds of writing that are most often done when we do business with each other. In this kind of writing, you want to make your points as quickly and clearly as possible. So try to be brief and direct.

Here is how to start:

- Organize your thoughts. Most business letters should take one page.

- Think about whether there is a special format you should follow.

- Decide if you want the reader to take action (persuasive), to understand a problem (informative), or to fix something (problem-solution). (*Refer to the relevant sections under this "Advice to Writers" heading.*)

- Write clearly and courteously.

- Include relevant quotations.

- Leave the reader with something to think about (for example, make a prediction or suggestion).

Revising, Editing, and Proofreading

The Writing Process

The writing process has several stages: planning, drafting, writing, revising, editing, and proofreading. Many writers and instructors maintain that improving your essay has three distinct stages: revising, editing, and proofreading. Review each column of the following chart to understand each stage completely.

As you write, you may wish to revise and edit your essay several times as you clarify and develop your ideas. The *Writer's Handbook* sections on Style, Organization and Development, and Advice to Writers can be very helpful as you revise and edit your essay. When you have a final version of your essay, be sure to proofread it carefully.

	Revising	Editing	Proofreading
Purpose	See the complete concept. Decide if your essay says what you want it to say. Add ideas.	Correct grammar and usage. Make changes in word choice, style, and the way you explain your ideas.	Correct typos, as well as spelling, punctuation, and formatting errors.
When	After you have written your first draft, do not do anything with it; then begin revising.	Begin when you have a complete draft of your essay.	Make this the final stage before you submit your essay.
What	Read your entire essay from beginning to end.	As you read each sentence, revise that sentence before you do the next sentence.	Read word by word and line by line to make corrections.
Strategies	Identify each part of the essay: introduction, thesis, main ideas, supporting ideas, and conclusion. Review carefully how the ideas are connected and the order of paragraphs. Do not be afraid to cut and paste, delete, or add new ideas. Ask a peer reviewer to say what is good and what could be better in your essay.	Ask your teacher, a peer editor, or a friend to give you ideas and advice. List the kinds of grammar and usage errors you make and look at those errors first. If a sentence seems right, do not revise it. Think about just the parts that seem to have problems. Use a handbook to help you correct errors and rewrite sentences.	Print a copy of your essay and make the changes on the paper copy. Read your essay aloud to your teacher or to someone who is more English proficient than you and circle identified errors. Have a peer reviewer who is more proficient in English read your essay backward. Start with the last sentence, then the second to the last, and so on. Use a dictionary, handbook, and spell-checker to help you correct errors.

Step 1: Organization and Development

Think about your topic and, if necessary, change the way your essay is organized and developed.

Step 2: Style

Read each sentence to see if your ideas are easy to understand.

Step 3: Grammar, Usage, Mechanics

Check each word and sentence for errors.

Step 4: Proofreading

Check spelling and typing as you read your final draft.

Using a Computer to Write

Computers make the writing process much easier than handwriting. Computers let you do all of the following:

- Write faster than you can with a pen
- Save or delete ideas and drafts
- Move words, paragraphs, and sentences
- Try out new ways of expressing yourself
- Locate and correct mistakes

Always remember that the computer is a tool that lets you think about how to write. You will still have to make decisions about how to draft and revise your essays and other writing.

Glossary

active voice—English sentences can be written in either the active or passive voice. In the active voice, the subject is the doer of an action. For example, in *Sam kicked the ball*, the action is *kicked*, and the doer is *Sam*. An active sentence emphasizes the doer of an action.

adjective—Adjectives give more information about nouns. In English, they usually come before nouns. For example: *a red umbrella, a rainy day, a beautiful woman*.

adverb—Adverbs are words such as *quickly, happily*, or *carefully*. They can tell more about an adjective (for example, *very big*), another adverb (for example, *very quietly*), or a verb (for example, *walk slowly*).

antecedent—A noun to which a pronoun refers is the antecedent. In the following sentence, *John* is the antecedent of the pronoun *he*: *John was late for school because he missed the bus*.

apostrophe—This punctuation mark (') shows the omission of letters in contractions (*cannot–can't*), or possession (the *girl's* dress, the *animals'* cages).

article—Articles are *a, an*, and *the*, the little words in English that come before nouns. English has two types of articles. The definite article (*the*) is used to refer to one or more specific things, animals, or people (for example, *the house on the hill*). The indefinite articles (*a, an*) are used to refer to a thing, animal, or person in a nonspecific or general way (for example, *a house, an elephant*).

clause—A clause is a group of related words that contains a subject and a verb. There are two kinds of clauses: independent and dependent. An independent clause expresses a complete thought and can be seen as a sentence (for example, *She saw Jim.*). A dependent clause is a part of a sentence and cannot stand on its own. (*When she saw Jim* is a dependent clause.) To make a complete sentence, you need to add an independent clause (for example, *When she saw Jim, she smiled.*).

collective noun—A collective noun refers to a *group* of people or animals: *population, family, troop, committee*.

comma—This punctuation mark (,) is used to separate words (*She bought apples, oranges, and grapes.*) or parts of a sentence (*He was here, but he left.*).

compound subject—This is a plural subject, a subject that consists of more than one part: *Lions, tigers, and bears are kept in the zoo.*

compound verb—This type of verb consists of more than one part: *The baby started crying.*

compound words—These are words that are made up of two words: *everywhere, boyfriend, himself, weekend*.

conclusion—This is the last paragraph of an essay, the paragraph that closes the essay. In a conclusion, you can restate the thesis or sum up the main ideas of the essay.

conjunction—A conjunction is a word that connects words, phrases, or sentences. It also shows relationships between words or clauses. There are two kinds of conjunctions: coordinating and subordinating. Coordinating conjunctions such as *and, but, or, nor,* and *for* connect parts that are equal: In the sentence *She bought a desk and a chair,* both *desk* and *chair* are nouns. Subordinating conjunctions such as *although, because, if, since,* and *when* connect parts that are not equal: In the sentence *Because he missed the train, he was late for work,* the clause *Because he missed the train* is a dependent clause, and *he was late for work* is an independent clause.

contraction—Contractions are short forms. You make a contraction when you combine two words, shorten one of them, and add an apostrophe: *cannot–can't; does not–doesn't; should not–shouldn't; it is–it's.*

dependent clause—A dependent clause is a part of a sentence and cannot stand on its own. For example, *When she saw Jim* is a dependent clause. To make a complete sentence, you need to add an independent clause: *When she saw Jim, she smiled.*

exclamation point—This mark of punctuation (!) at the end of a sentence is used to show surprise or strong emotion.

fragment—A fragment is a group of words that is not a complete sentence, even though it sometimes starts with a capital letter or ends with a punctuation mark and often contains a subject and verb.

helping verb—This type of verb is also called an auxiliary verb. Helping verbs are used with main verbs in a verb phrase: *is going; were singing; can talk; may leave; must tell; will see.*

hyphen—This mark (-) is used to separate the different parts of a compound word: *mother-in-law, self-motivated student.*

independent clause—An independent clause has a subject and a verb, expresses a complete thought, and can be seen as a sentence (for example, *She saw him.*). It can also be combined with another independent clause to make a compound sentence (*She saw him, so she called him over.*). It can also take a dependent clause to make a complex sentence (*She saw him, even though it was dark.*).

infinitive verb—An infinitive consists of the word *to* plus a *verb* (for example, *to go, to swim, to wish*). It can function as a noun, adjective, or adverb. For example: *To swim the English Channel is my friend's strongest dream.* Here, the infinitive *to swim* acts as a noun. It is the subject of the sentence.

intransitive verb—This type of verb does not need an object to complete its meaning. For example: *John ran. Bob left. Jane slept.*

introduction—An introduction is the first paragraph of an essay. Effective introductions do two basic things: grab the reader's interest and let the reader know what the whole essay is about. This is why most introductions include a thesis statement that clearly states the writer's topic and main argument.

main idea—Main ideas are the important points of an essay. They state what will be discussed in each paragraph (or set of paragraphs for longer essays). Main ideas develop the thesis statement of an essay and are in turn developed by supporting details.

modal verb—A modal verb is a kind of helping verb. Modal verbs help to express meanings such as permission (*may*), obligation (*must*), prediction (*will*, *shall*), or ability (*can*).

noun phrase—This type of phrase consists of several words that together function as the noun of a sentence. For example: *Talking to my mother made me feel better.* Here, *Talking to my mother* is a noun phrase that is acting as the subject of this sentence.

paragraph—An essay is made up of smaller sections called paragraphs. Each paragraph should focus on one main idea; you tell your reader what this idea is by using a topic sentence. A good paragraph is one in which every sentence supports the topic sentence.

passive voice—English sentences can be written in either the active or passive voice. In a passive sentence, the verb *to be* is combined with the past participle form of a verb (for example, *John was kicked*.) A passive sentence emphasizes the receiver or the results of an action.

period—In English grammar, this punctuation mark (.) is used to signal the end of a declarative sentence. (A declarative sentence is one that is not a question or an exclamation.) It is also used to indicate abbreviations (for example, *Mr., St., Ave.*).

phrase—A phrase is a group of related words with a single grammatical function (for example, a noun phrase, a verb phrase). The noun phrase acts as a noun or subject in this sentence: *The girl in the corner is Mary*.

plural—*Plural* means "more than one." In English grammar, nouns, pronouns, and verbs can take plural forms. For example, *cars* is a plural noun, *they* is a plural pronoun, and *climb* is a plural verb.

possessive pronoun—These are pronouns that show possession or ownership (for example, *my, our, his, her, their, whose*). Some possessive pronouns can function as nouns: *Is this yours? That book is mine.*

prefix—A prefix is a word part, such as *co-* in *costar*, attached to the front of a word to make a new word. For another example, the prefix *re-* can be added to the word *sell* to make the word *resell*, which means "to sell again".

preposition—Prepositions are words such as *in, of, by*, and *from*. They describe the relationship between words in a sentence. In the sentence *The professor sat on the desk*, the preposition *on* shows the location of the professor in relation to the desk.

pronoun—A pronoun can replace a noun or another pronoun. You can use pronouns such as *she, it, which*, and *they* to make your writing less repetitive.

question mark—This is the punctuation mark (?) used at the end of a direct question. For example: *Is David coming to the party?*

sentence combining—Sometimes writers combine two or more short sentences to make a longer one. The reason for doing this is that too many short sentences often make the writing sound choppy. Using sentence-combining techniques in the revising process can improve the style of your essay.

singular—*Singular* means "single," or "one." In English grammar, nouns, pronouns, and verbs can take singular forms. For example, *car* is a singular noun, *he* or *she* is a singular pronoun, and *climbs* is a singular verb in the present tense.

subject—The subject of a sentence tells who or what a sentence is about. For example, in the sentence *Stephen ran into the parking lot*, *Stephen* is the subject of the sentence.

supporting idea—Supporting ideas are the details that develop the main idea of a paragraph. They can be definitions, explanations, illustrations, opinions, evidence, and examples. They usually come after the topic sentence and make up the body of a paragraph.

tense—Tenses indicate time. Sometimes tenses are formed by changes in the verb, as in *He sings* (present tense) and *He sang* (past tense). At other times, tenses are formed by adding modals, or helping verbs. For example: *He will give me fifty dollars* (future tense); *He has given me fifty dollars* (perfect tense).

thesis—The thesis or thesis statement of an essay states what will be discussed in the whole essay. It offers your reader a quick and easy summary of the essay. A thesis statement usually consists of two parts: your topic and what you are going to say about the topic. Thesis statements are supported by main ideas.

topic sentence—The topic sentence states the main idea of a paragraph. It tells your reader what the paragraph is about. An easy way to make sure your reader understands the topic of a paragraph is to put your topic sentence near the beginning of the paragraph. (This is a good general rule for less experienced writers, although it is not the only way to do it.)

transition word or phrase—Transition words and phrases are used to connect ideas and signal relationships between them. For example, *First* can be used to signal the first of several points; *Thus* can be used to show a result.

transitive verb—Transitive verbs require an object. For example, in the sentence *He mailed the letter*, *mailed* is a transitive verb, and *letter* is its object.

verb—A verb is an "action" word (for example, *climb, jump, run, eat*). English verbs also express time. (For example, past tense verbs such as *climbed, jumped, ran,* and *ate* show that the action happened in the past.) Verbs also show states of being—"to be" words—mentioned earlier in the chapter.

verb phrase—A verb phrase is a phrase (or a group of words) that consists of a main verb (for example, *climb, jump, run, eat*) plus one or more helping verbs (for example, *may, can, has, is, are*). Examples of verb phrases are *She may go,* and *The students will receive certificates.*

Performance Feedback
for Test Takers

The scores you receive on the TOEFL iBT test indicate your performance level in each of the four skill areas: reading, listening, speaking, and writing. This Appendix provides descriptions of what test takers can typically do at each score level, as well as advice about how test takers at each level can improve their skills.

Only the "Your Performance" descriptions appear on test taker score reports. The "Advice for Improvement" is only a sample of the advice available. More extensive advice is available on the TOEFL website, www.ets.org/toefl.

Reading Skills

Level: HIGH (22–30)

Test takers who receive a score at the **HIGH** level, as you did, typically understand academic texts in English that require a wide range of reading abilities regardless of the difficulty of the texts.

YOUR PERFORMANCE

Test takers who score at the HIGH level typically:

- have a very good command of academic vocabulary and grammatical structure;
- can understand and connect information, make appropriate inferences, and synthesize ideas, even when the text is conceptually dense and the language is complex;
- can recognize the expository organization of a text and the role that specific information serves within the larger text, even when the text is conceptually dense; and
- can abstract major ideas from a text, even when the text is conceptually dense and contains complex language.

ADVICE FOR IMPROVEMENT

Read as much and as often as possible. Make sure to include academic texts on a variety of topics written in different genres and with different degrees of conceptual density as part of your reading.

- Read major newspapers, such as the *New York Times* or *Science Times*, and websites (National Public Radio [NPR] or the BBC).
- Write summaries of texts, making sure they incorporate the organizational pattern of the originals. Continually expand your vocabulary.

Practice using new words you encounter in your reading. This will help you remember both the meaning and correct usage of the new words.

Level: INTERMEDIATE (15–21)

Test takers who receive a score at the **INTERMEDIATE** level, as you did, typically understand academic texts in English that require a wide range of reading abilities, although their understanding of certain parts of the texts is limited.

YOUR PERFORMANCE

Test takers who receive a score at the INTERMEDIATE level typically:

- have a good command of common academic vocabulary, but still have some difficulty with high-level vocabulary;
- have a very good understanding of grammatical structure;
- can understand and connect information, make appropriate inferences, and synthesize information in a range of texts, but have more difficulty when the vocabulary is high level and the text is conceptually dense;
- can recognize the expository organization of a text and the role that specific information serves within a larger text, but have some difficulty when these are not explicit or easy to infer from the text; and
- can abstract major ideas from a text, but have more difficulty doing so when the text is conceptually dense.

ADVICE FOR IMPROVEMENT

Read as much and as often as possible. Study the organization of academic texts and overall structure of reading passages. Read an entire passage from beginning to end.

- Pay attention to the relationship between the **main ideas** and the **supporting details**.
- Outline the text to test your understanding of the structure of the reading passage.
- Write a summary of the entire passage.
- If the text is a comparison, be sure that your summary reflects that. If the text argues two points of view, be sure both points of view are reflected in your summary. Continually expand your vocabulary by developing a system for recording unfamiliar words.
- Group words according to topic or meaning and study the words as a list of related words.

- Study **roots**, **prefixes**, and **suffixes**; study word families.
- Use available vocabulary resources, such as a good thesaurus or a dictionary of collocations (words commonly used together).

Level: LOW (0–14)

Test takers who receive a score at the **LOW** level, as you did, typically understand some of the information presented in academic texts in English that require a wide range of reading abilities, but their understanding is limited.

YOUR PERFORMANCE

Test takers who receive a score at the LOW level typically:

- have a command of basic academic vocabulary, but their understanding of less common vocabulary is inconsistent;
- have limited ability to understand and connect information, have difficulty recognizing paraphrases of text information, and often rely on particular words and phrases rather than a complete understanding of the text;
- have difficulty identifying the author's purpose, except when that purpose is explicitly stated in the text or easy to infer from the text; and
- can sometimes recognize major ideas from a text when the information is clearly presented, memorable, or illustrated by examples, but have difficulty doing so when the text is more demanding.

ADVICE FOR IMPROVEMENT

Read as much and as often as possible. Develop a system for recording unfamiliar words.

- Group words into lists according to topic or meaning and review and study the words on a regular basis so that you remember them.
- Increase your vocabulary by analyzing word parts; study **roots**, **prefixes**, and **suffixes**; study **word families**. Study the organization of academic texts and overall structure of a reading passage. Read an entire passage from beginning to end.
- Look at connections between sentences; look at how the end of one sentence relates to the beginning of the next sentence.
- Look for the **main ideas** and **supporting details** and pay attention to the relationship between them.
- Outline a text to test your understanding of the structure of a reading passage.
- Begin by grouping paragraphs that address the same concept.
- Write one sentence summarizing the paragraphs that discuss the same idea.
- Write a summary of the entire passage.

Listening Skills

Level: HIGH (22–30)

Test takers who receive a score at the **HIGH** level, as you did, typically understand conversations and lectures in English that present a wide range of listening demands. These demands can include difficult vocabulary (uncommon terms or colloquial or figurative language), complex grammatical structures, abstract or complex ideas, and/or making sense of unexpected or seemingly contradictory information.

YOUR PERFORMANCE

When listening to lectures and conversations like these, test takers at the HIGH level typically can:

- understand main ideas and important details, whether they are stated or implied;
- distinguish more important ideas from less important ones;
- understand how information is being used (for example, to provide evidence for a claim or describe a step in a complex process);
- recognize how pieces of information are connected (for example, in a cause-and-effect relationship);
- understand many different ways that speakers use language for purposes other than to give information (for example, to emphasize a point, express agreement or disagreement, or convey intentions indirectly); and
- synthesize information, even when it is not presented in sequence, and make correct inferences on the basis of that information.

ADVICE FOR IMPROVEMENT

Further develop your listening ability with daily practice in listening in English and by challenging yourself with increasingly lengthy listening selections and more complex listening material.

- Listen to different kinds of materials on a variety of topics:
  - Focus on topics that are new to you.
  - Listen to academic lectures and public talks.
  - Listen to audio and video material on TV, radio, and the Internet.
  - Listen to programs with academic content, such as NOVA, BBC, and NPR broadcasts.
  - Listen to conversations, phone calls, and phone recordings.
  - Take live and audio-recorded tours (for example, of museums).
- Listen actively:
  - Take notes as you listen for main ideas and important details.
  - Make predictions about what you will hear next.
  - Summarize.
  - Write down new words and expressions.

- For the more difficult material you have chosen to listen to, listen several times:
  1. First listen for the main ideas and key details;
  2. Then listen again to fill in gaps in your understanding; to understand the connections between ideas, the structure of the talk, and the speaker's attitude; and to distinguish fact from opinion.

Level: INTERMEDIATE (14–21)

Test takers who receive a score at the **INTERMEDIATE** level, as you did, typically understand conversations and lectures in English that present a wide range of listening demands. These demands can include difficult vocabulary (uncommon terms or colloquial or figurative language), complex grammatical structures, and/or abstract or complex ideas. However, lectures and conversations that require the listener to make sense of unexpected or seemingly contradictory information may present some difficulty.

YOUR PERFORMANCE

When listening to conversations and lectures like these, test takers at the INTER-MEDIATE level typically can:

- understand explicitly stated main ideas and important details, especially if they are reinforced, but may have difficulty understanding main ideas that must be inferred or important details that are not reinforced;
- understand how information is being used (for example, to provide support or describe a step in a complex process);
- recognize how pieces of information are connected (for example, in a cause-and-effect relationship);
- understand, though perhaps not consistently, ways that speakers use language for purposes other than to give information (for example, to emphasize a point, express agreement or disagreement, or convey intentions indirectly); and
- synthesize information from adjacent parts of a lecture or conversation and make correct inferences on the basis of that information, but may have difficulty synthesizing information from separate parts of a lecture or conversation.

ADVICE FOR IMPROVEMENT

Practice listening in English daily. Gradually increase the amount of time that you spend listening, the length of the listening selections, and the difficulty of the material.

- Listen to different kinds of materials on a variety of topics:
  - Start with familiar topics; then move to topics that are new to you.
  - Listen to audio and video material on tape/DVD or recorded from TV, radio, and the Internet.

     ○ Listen to programs with academic content, such as NOVA, BBC, and NPR broadcasts.

     ○ Listen to conversations and phone recordings.

- Listen actively:
  - ○ Take notes as you listen for main ideas and important details.
  - ○ Ask yourself about basic information (Who? What? When? Where? Why? How?).
  - ○ Make predictions about what you will hear next.
  - ○ Summarize.
  - ○ Write down new words and expressions.

- For more difficult material, listen several times:
  1. First listen with English subtitles, if they are available;
  2. Then, without subtitles, listen for the main ideas and key details;
  3. Then listen again to fill in gaps in your basic understanding and to understand the connections between ideas.

Level: LOW (0–13)

YOUR PERFORMANCE

Test takers who receive a score at the **LOW** level, as you did, typically understand the main idea and some important details of conversations. However, test takers at the low level may have difficulty understanding lectures and conversations in English that involve abstract or complex ideas and recognizing the relationship between those ideas. Test takers at this level also may not understand sections of lectures and conversations that contain difficult vocabulary or complex grammatical structures.

ADVICE FOR IMPROVEMENT

Test takers at the LOW level typically can:

- understand main ideas when they are stated explicitly or marked as important, but may have difficulty understanding main ideas if they are not stated explicitly;
- understand important details when they are stated explicitly or marked as important, but may have difficulty understanding details if they are not repeated or clearly marked as important, or if they are conveyed over several exchanges among different speakers;
- understand ways that speakers use language to emphasize a point or to indicate agreement or disagreement, but generally only when the information is related to a central theme or is clearly marked as important; and
- make connections between the key ideas in a conversation, particularly if the ideas are related to a central theme or are repeated.

ADVICE FOR IMPROVEMENT

Practice listening in English daily. Gradually increase the amount of time that you spend listening, as well as the length of the individual listening selections.

- Listen to different kinds of materials on a variety of topics:
  - recordings on topics that are familiar to you
  - recordings of English lessons
  - audio and video material on tape/DVD or recorded from TV
  - short programs with some academic content
  - conversations

- Listen actively:
  - Take notes as you listen for main ideas and important details.
  - Ask yourself about basic information (Who? What? When? Where? Why? How?).
  - Make predictions about what you will hear next.
  - Summarize.
  - Write down new words and expressions.

- Listen several times to each recording:
  1. First listen with English subtitles, if they are available;
  2. Then, without subtitles, listen for the main ideas and key details;
  3. Then listen again to fill in gaps in your basic understanding and to understand the connections between ideas.

Speaking Skills: Speaking About Familiar Topics

Level: GOOD (3.5–4.0)

YOUR PERFORMANCE

Your responses indicate an ability to communicate your personal experiences and opinions effectively in English. Overall, your speech is clear and fluent. Your use of vocabulary and grammar is effective with only minor errors. Your ideas are generally well developed and expressed coherently.

ADVICE FOR IMPROVEMENT

Look for opportunities to speak to native speakers of English. Interaction with others will improve your speaking ability.

- Ask a native speaker to provide feedback on your pronunciation problems (if any).
- Join an Internet voice chat.

Level: FAIR (2.5–3.0)

YOUR PERFORMANCE

Your responses indicate you are able to speak in English about your personal experiences and opinions in a mostly clear and coherent manner. Your speech is mostly clear with only occasional errors. Grammar and vocabulary are somewhat limited and include some errors. At times, the limitations prevent you from elaborating fully on your ideas, but they do not seriously interfere with overall communication.

ADVICE FOR IMPROVEMENT

Think about topics related to student life (what type of classes you enjoy taking, what is the best place to study, where you would prefer to live [on or off campus]).

- Write down two reasons to explain your preference; practice speaking for one minute about each topic, using connecting words or phrases to help explain your opinion ("the reason I prefer," "this is important to me because").
- Practice speaking for a limited time on different topics without a lot of preparation. Make a list of some general speaking topics (people you admire, places you enjoy visiting, things you enjoy doing).
- Then think of a specific example for each topic (a parent, the market, reading books).
- Talk about each one for 1 minute, explaining what you admire or enjoy about each.
- Repeat your responses to each topic two or three times to build up fluency.

Level: LIMITED (1.5–2.0)

YOUR PERFORMANCE

Your responses indicate some difficulty speaking in English about everyday experiences and opinions. Listeners sometimes have trouble understanding you because of noticeable problems with pronunciation, grammar, and vocabulary. While you are able to respond partially to the questions, you are not able to fully develop your ideas, possibly due to limited vocabulary and grammar.

ADVICE FOR IMPROVEMENT

Give yourself about 20 seconds to think about what you did yesterday. After 20 seconds, begin to recount what you did. Try to talk for 1 minute.

- Pay attention to your use of the past tense.
- Try to use connecting words and phrases, such as "first," "then," and "while I was."

Give yourself about 20 seconds to think about what you will probably do tomorrow. Try to talk for 1 minute. After 20 seconds, begin to talk about what you are planning to do.

Level: WEAK (0–1.0)

YOUR PERFORMANCE

Your responses are incomplete. They contain little or no content and are difficult for listeners to understand.

ADVICE FOR IMPROVEMENT

Practice speaking about different topics without a lot of preparation. Write down several questions about various topics (your family, your hobbies, your friends, your school). Select a question and answer it aloud. Think of a story that you are familiar with. Tell the story to several people individually. Try to tell the story faster each time.

Speaking Skills: Speaking About Campus Situations

Level: GOOD (3.5–4.0)

YOUR PERFORMANCE

Your responses indicate an ability to speak effectively in English about reading material and conversations typically encountered by university students. Overall, your responses are clear and coherent, with only occasional errors of pronunciation, grammar, or vocabulary.

ADVICE FOR IMPROVEMENT

Look for opportunities to build your fluency in English.

- Take risks and engage others in conversation in English whenever possible.
- Join an Internet chat room.

Level: FAIR (2.5–3.0)

YOUR PERFORMANCE

Your responses demonstrate an ability to speak in English about reading material and experiences typically encountered by university students. You are able to convey relevant information about conversations, newspaper articles, and campus bulletins; however, some details are missing or inaccurate. Limitations of grammar, vocabulary, and pronunciation at times cause difficulty for the listener. However, they do not seriously interfere with overall communication.

ADVICE FOR IMPROVEMENT

Practice speaking in English about everyday topics that are important to students' lives. This will develop your fluency and confidence.

- Find a speaking partner. Set aside time each week to practice speaking with your partner in English.
- If you cannot find a native English speaker, find a friend who wants to practice speaking English and promise to speak only English for a certain period.
- Read articles from campus newspapers that can be found on the Internet. Discuss the articles with a speaking partner or friend. Practice summarizing the articles and expressing your opinions about the articles.

Level: LIMITED (1.5–2.0)

YOUR PERFORMANCE

Your responses indicate that you have some difficulty speaking in English about information from conversations, newspaper articles, university publications, and so on. While you are able to talk about some of the key information from these sources, limited grammar and vocabulary may prevent you from fully expressing your ideas. Problems with pronunciation make it difficult for listeners to understand you at times.

ADVICE FOR IMPROVEMENT

Develop friendships with people who want to speak English with you. Interaction with others will improve your speaking ability. If you cannot find a native speaker, find a friend who wants to practice speaking English and promise to speak only English for a certain period.

Level: WEAK (0–1.0)

YOUR PERFORMANCE

Your responses are incomplete. They include little or no information about the topic. Your speech is often difficult for listeners to understand, and the meaning is unclear.

ADVICE FOR IMPROVEMENT

Take a conversation class. This will help improve your fluency and pronunciation in English.

Speaking Skills: Speaking About Academic Course Content

Level: GOOD (3.5–4.0)

YOUR PERFORMANCE

Your responses demonstrate an ability to communicate effectively in English about academic topics typical of first-year university studies. Your speech is mostly clear and fluent. You are able to use appropriate vocabulary and grammar to explain concepts and ideas from reading or lecture material. You are able to talk about key information and relevant details with only minor inaccuracies.

ADVICE FOR IMPROVEMENT

Record yourself and then listen and transcribe what you said.

- Read a short article from a newspaper or textbook. Record yourself summarizing the article.
- Transcribe the recording and review the transcription. Think about other ways to say the same thing.

Level: FAIR (2.5–3.0)

YOUR PERFORMANCE

Your responses demonstrate that you are able to speak in English about academic reading and lecture material, with only minor communication problems. For the most part, your speech is clear and easy to understand. However, some problems with pronunciation and intonation may occasionally cause difficulty for the listener. Your use of grammar and vocabulary is adequate to talk about the topics, but some ideas are not fully developed or are inaccurate.

ADVICE FOR IMPROVEMENT

Practice speaking for a limited time on different academic topics.

- Read a short article from a newspaper or a textbook. Write down key content words from the article.
- Write down two or three questions about the article that include the content words.
- Practice answering the questions aloud. Try to include the content words in your response.
- After practicing, record your answers to the questions.

Level: LIMITED (1.5–2.0)

YOUR PERFORMANCE

In your responses, you are able to use English to talk about the basic ideas from academic reading or lecture materials, but, in general, you include few relevant or accurate details. It is sometimes difficult for listeners to understand your responses because of problems with grammar, vocabulary, and pronunciation. Overall, you are able to respond in a general way to the questions, but the amount of information in your responses is limited and the expression of ideas is often vague and unclear.

ADVICE FOR IMPROVEMENT

Practice speaking about current events.

- Read newspaper articles, editorials, and information about cultural events in English. Share the information that you read with a friend in English.
- Visit a university class and take notes in the class. Then use your notes to tell a friend about some of the information you heard in English.
- Develop your academic vocabulary. Write down important new words that you come across while reading or listening and practice pronouncing them.
- Listen to a weather report and take notes on what you heard. Then give the weather report to a friend in English.

Level: WEAK (0–1.0)

YOUR PERFORMANCE

Your responses are incomplete. They include little or no information about the topic. Your speech is often difficult for listeners to understand, and the meaning is unclear.

ADVICE FOR IMPROVEMENT

Increase your vocabulary and improve your grammar in your speech.

- Study basic grammar rules so that your speech is grammatically correct.
- As you learn new words and expressions, practice pronouncing them clearly. Record yourself as you practice.

Writing Skills: Writing Based on Reading and Listening

Level: GOOD (4.0–5.0)

YOUR PERFORMANCE

You responded well to the task, relating the lecture to the reading passage. Weaknesses, if you have any, might have to do with:

- slight imprecision in your summary of some of the main points, and/or
- use of English that is occasionally grammatically incorrect or unclear.

ADVICE FOR IMPROVEMENT

Continue to improve your ability to relate and convey information from two or more sources. For example, practice analyzing reading passages in English.

- Read two articles or chapters on the same topic or issue, write a summary of each, and then explain the ways they are similar and the ways they are different.
- Practice combining listening and reading by searching for readings related to talks and lectures with a teacher or a friend.

Level: FAIR (2.5–3.5)

YOUR PERFORMANCE

You responded to the task, relating the lecture to the reading passage, but your response indicates weaknesses, such as:

- an important idea or ideas may be missing, unclear, or inaccurate;
- it may not be clear how the lecture and the reading passage are related; and/or
- grammatical errors or vague/incorrect uses of words may make the writing difficult to understand.

ADVICE FOR IMPROVEMENT

Practice finding main points.

- Record news and informational programs in English from the television or radio, or download talks or lectures from the Internet.
- Listen and take notes. Stop the recording about every 30 seconds to write out a short summary of what you heard.
- Replay the recording to check your summary. Mark places where you are not sure if you have understood what was said or where you are not sure if you have expressed yourself well.

Level: LIMITED (1.0–2.0)

YOUR PERFORMANCE

Your response was judged as limited due to:

- failure to understand the lecture or reading passage;
- deficiencies in relating the lecture to the reading passage; and/or
- many grammatical errors and/or very unclear expressions and sentence structures.

ADVICE FOR IMPROVEMENT

Read and listen to academic articles and other material in your own language. Take notes about what you read and hear.

- Begin by taking notes in your own language and then take notes in English.
- Summarize the points in complete English sentences.
- Ask your teacher to review your writing and help you correct your errors.
- Gradually decrease the time it takes you to read the material and write the summaries.
- Practice typing on a standard English (QWERTY) keyboard.

Writing Skills: Writing Based on Knowledge and Experience

Level: GOOD (4.0–5.0)

YOUR PERFORMANCE

You responded with a well-organized and developed essay. Weaknesses, if you have any, might have to do with:

- use of English that is occasionally grammatically incorrect, unclear, or unidiomatic, and/or
- elaboration of ideas or connection of ideas that could have been stronger.

ADVICE FOR IMPROVEMENT

Continue to improve your ability to express opinions by studying the ways that published writers express their opinions.

- Read articles and essays written by professional writers that express opinions about an issue (for example, a social, environmental, or educational issue).
- Identify the writer's opinion or opinions.
- Notice how the writer addresses possible objections to the opinions, if the writer discusses these.

Level: FAIR (2.5–3.5)

YOUR PERFORMANCE

You expressed ideas with reasons, examples, and details, but your response indicated weaknesses, such as:

- you may not provide enough specific support and development for your main points;
- your ideas may be difficult to follow because of how you organize your essay or because of the language you use to connect your ideas; and/or
- grammatical errors or vague/incorrect uses of words may make the writing difficult to understand.

ADVICE FOR IMPROVEMENT

Write a response to an article or essay in English, taking the opposite viewpoint.

- Outline your response.
- Note the methods you use to support your ideas. Reread what you have written.
- Make sure your supporting ideas are clearly related to your main point.
- Note what method you use to develop each of your supporting points.
- Make sure you have developed each of your points in detail. Is there anything more you could have said to strengthen your points?

Level: LIMITED (1.0–2.0)

YOUR PERFORMANCE

You attempted to express your opinion, but your response indicates notable deficiencies, such as:

- your response contains insufficient detail;
- your ideas and your connections of ideas are difficult to understand; because of many grammatical errors and/or very unclear expressions and sentence structure; and/or
- your response is only marginally related to the question that was asked.

ADVICE FOR IMPROVEMENT

Study the organization of good paragraphs and essays. A good paragraph discusses *one* main idea. This idea is usually written in the first sentence, which is called the topic sentence. In essay writing, each paragraph should discuss one aspect of the main idea of an essay.

- Write paragraphs in English that focus on one main idea and contain several complete sentences that explain or support that idea.
- Ask your teacher to review your paragraphs for correctness.